Springer Series in Statistics

Advisors:
D. Brillinger, S. Fienberg, J. Gani, J. Hartigan
J. Kiefer, K. Krickeberg

James O. Berger

Statistical Decision Theory
Foundations, Concepts, and Methods

Springer-Verlag
New York Heidelberg Berlin

James O. Berger
Department of Statistics
Purdue University
West Lafayette, Indiana 47907
USA

AMS Classification: 60CXX

With 20 Figures.

Library of Congress Cataloging in Publication Data

Berger, James.
  Statistical decision theory, foundations, concepts, and methods.

  (Springer series in statistics)
  Bibliography: p.
  Includes index.
  1. Statistical decision. 2. Bayesian
statistical decision theory. I. Title. II. Series.
QA279.4.B47   1980   519.5'42   79-27052

© 1980 by Springer-Verlag New York Inc.

Printed in the United States of America.

9 8 7 6 5 4 3 2 1

ISBN 0-387-90471-9 Springer-Verlag New York
ISBN 3-540-90471-9 Springer-Verlag Berlin Heidelberg

To Ann, Jill, and Julie

Preface

Decision theory is generally taught in one of two very different ways. When taught by theoretical statisticians, it tends to be presented as a set of optimality principles, together with a collection of mathematical techniques useful in establishing the optimality of various statistical procedures. When taught by applied decision theorists, it is usually a course in Bayesian analysis, showing how this one decision principle can be applied in various practical situations. The original goal I had in writing this book was to find some middle ground. I wanted a book which discussed the more theoretical ideas and techniques of decision theory, but in a manner that was constantly oriented towards solving statistical problems. In particular, it seemed crucial to include a discussion of when and why the various decision principles should be used, and indeed why decision theory is needed at all.

This original goal seemed indicated by my philosophical position at the time, which can best be described as basically neutral. I felt that no one approach to decision theory (or statistics) was clearly superior to the others, and so planned a rather low key and impartial presentation of the competing ideas. In the course of writing the book, however, I turned into a rabid Bayesian. There was no single cause for this conversion; just a gradual realization that things seemed to ultimately make sense only when looked at from the Bayesian viewpoint. Specific considerations that I found particularly compelling were: (i) The Bayesian measures of accuracy of a conclusion seem more realistic than the classical measures (the final precision versus initial precision argument). (ii) In most circumstances any reasonable statistical procedure corresponds to a Bayes procedure with respect to some prior distribution, and if this prior distribution is quite unrealistic, then use of the statistical procedure seems suspect. (iii) Principles of rational behavior seem to imply that one must act as if he had a prior distribution.

My original reservations about Bayesian analysis included the concerns that the analysis can give very bad results if an incorrect prior distribution is chosen, and that Bayesian conclusions lack objectivity. The first of these concerns I still have, but the second has been replaced by the belief that only through the Bayesian viewpoint can objectivity, if desired, be achieved. The justification for this belief is again the second point mentioned earlier, that virtually any reasonable procedure will be a Bayes procedure with respect to some prior distribution (or at least some positive measure). When this is the case, it seems unreasonable to claim that a proposed procedure is objective unless it corresponds to some "objective prior distribution."

These remarks are by no means meant to be conclusive (or even understandable) arguments in themselves. Instead they are meant to convey something of the basic philosophy of the book. The first four chapters of the book describe this basic philosophy, and present the Bayesian approach to statistics. Included are often neglected subjects of importance in the implementation of the Bayesian approach, such as the construction of loss functions and the quantification of prior information. This material is a blend of arguments justifying the Bayesian viewpoint (including criticisms of classical statistical methods), presentations of actual Bayesian techniques (including the oft-maligned but usually quite reasonable use of noninformative prior distributions), and discussions of the dangers in using the Bayesian approach. In particular, a "robust" Bayesian approach is advocated, in which one attempts to protect against misspecification of the prior distribution.

The remaining four chapters of the book turn to other aspects of decision theory. Chapters 5 and 6 present the minimax and invariance approaches to decision theory. These approaches are not only interesting theoretically, but can also be of considerable aid in the analysis of decision problems, particularly when there is no, or only very vague, prior information. It is shown, however, that use of these methods with no regard for Bayesian considerations can be very bad. Chapter 7 discusses (from a decision-theoretic viewpoint) the important topic of sequential analysis. Chapter 8 introduces the more theoretical side of decision theory, with a discussion of complete class theorems.

The book is meant to be an applied book on decision theory. Theoretical results are, for the most part, presented only to the extent that they can be usefully applied to real statistical problems, and pains are taken to show how to apply any such theoretical techniques. For this reason, the mathematical and statistical level of the book is kept as low as possible. It is assumed that the reader knows calculus and some probability (at least, say, what expectations and conditional probability distributions are), and is familiar with certain basic statistical concepts such as estimation, testing, and (to a degree) sufficiency. From time to time we will pay lip service to things like measurability, and (especially in later chapters) may employ some higher mathematical facts. Knowledge of such things is not needed, however, to follow and understand the basic material.

To avoid mathematical complications, the proofs of some theorems are not given, and indeed some theorems are not even stated completely rigorously. (Such theorems are usually called "Results.") It is perhaps advisable for the reader with no or little previous exposure to decision theory to omit some of the more delicate philosophical issues and examples on a first reading, and return to them after obtaining a fairly firm grasp of the essentials.

In terms of teaching, the book is designed to be usable as a text at two different graduate levels. First, it can be used for applied statistical students (say applied masters students) as a basic introduction into the use and methodology of decision theory. As such, its purpose is also to describe the inadequacies of certain classical statistical procedures, and to instill a concern for correct formulation of a statistical problem.

At the second level, the book is intended to provide a combined applied and theoretical introduction to decision theory for doctoral students. Such students may need not only the basic methodology, but also the ability to investigate the decision-theoretic optimality properties of statistical procedures.

The book is organized so as to be easy to use at either of the above levels. Listed below are various suggested programs at each level. The indicated numbers are chapter or section numbers.

Level 1 (Applied)

1 Quarter: 1 (except 1.4, 1.7, 1.8), 2, 3 (except 3.2.3, 3.2.4, 3.2.5), 4 (except 4.4.5, 4.5, 4.6.2, 4.6.5), selected parts of 7.

1 Semester: 1 (except 1.4, 1.7, 1.8), 2, 3 (except 3.2.3), 4, 7 (except 7.4.9, 7.4.10, 7.5.4, 7.5.5, 7.6).

1 Semester (including minimax): 1 (except 1.7, 1.8), 2, 3 (except 3.2.3, 3.2.4, 3.2.5), 4 (except 4.4.5, 4.5, 4.6.2, 4.6.5), 5 (except 5.2.3, 5.2.4, 5.2.5, 5.2.6, 5.3.3), 7 (except 7.2, 7.4.7, 7.4.8, 7.4.9, 7.4.10, 7.5.4, 7.5.5, 7.6).

2 Quarters: 1 (except 1.7, 1.8), 2, 3, 4, 5 (except 5.2.5, 5.2.6), 7 (except 7.4.9, 7.4.10).

Level 2 (More Theoretical)

1 Quarter: 1, 2 (except 2.3), 3 (except 3.2.3, 3.2.4, 3.2.5), 4 (except 4.4.5, 4.6.2, 4.6.4, 4.6.5), 5 (except 5.2.3, 5.4.5), selected parts of 7.

1 Semester: 1, 2, 3 (except 3.2.3, 3.2.4, 3.2.5), 4 (except 4.4.5, 4.6.4), 5 (except 5.2.3, 5.4.5), 7 (except 7.4.9, 7.4.10), selected parts of 6 and 8.

2 Quarters: 1, 2, 3 (except 3.2.3, 3.2.4, 3.2.5), 4 (except 4.6.4), 5 (except 5.2.3), 6 (except 6.6), 7 (except 7.4.9, 7.4.10), selected parts of 8.

3 Quarters or 2 Semesters: Entire book.

When writing a book containing many intuitive ideas about statistics, there is always a problem in acknowledging the originators of the ideas. Many ideas become part of the folklore or have been independently rediscovered by a number of people. An attempt was made to acknowledge the originator of an idea or technique whenever the originator was known to me. I apologize for the undoubtedly numerous omissions. Particularly galling will no doubt be those ideas I seem to implicitly claim to have originated, which in reality were developed years ago by a score of people. Besides my apologies, all I can say is you should have written a book.

I am very grateful to a number of people who contributed in one way or another to the existence of this book. Lawrence Brown, Roger Farrell, Leon Gleser, Jack Kiefer, Herman Rubin, and William Studden were particularly helpful. Larry Brown, with penetrating insight, pointed out some logical inconsistencies in an earlier version of the book. Roger Farrell and Leon Gleser shared their thoughts in many interesting discussions. Jack Kiefer was kind enough to read and comment upon certain portions of the manuscript. Bill Studden provided very helpful critical comments for the first five chapters, and discovered a major blunder. Finally, Herman Rubin served as a constant source of aid and inspiration throughout the writing of the book. He helped me over many rough spots and tried his best to keep me from saying foolish things. Of course, none of the above people necessarily agree with what is presented in the book. (Indeed only Herman Rubin claims to be a Bayesian.) I feel that our common ground is substantial, however.

I would also like to thank Lou Anne Scott, Norma Lucas, Kathy Woods and Carolyn Knutsen for their excellent typing of the manuscript. Several graduate students, particularly T. C. Kao and Don Wallace, were also very helpful, pointing out many errors and checking a large portion of the exercises. Finally, I would like to express my appreciation to the John Simon Guggenheim Memorial Foundation and the Alfred P. Sloan Foundation. Much of the book was written during the tenure of a Guggenheim Fellowship, and parts during the tenure of a Sloan Fellowship.

West Lafayette, Indiana   JAMES BERGER
March 1980

Contents

CHAPTER 1

Basic Concepts

1.1 Introduction

Decision theory, as the name implies, is concerned with the problem of making decisions. Statistical decision theory is concerned with the making of decisions in the presence of statistical knowledge which sheds light on some of the uncertainties involved in the decision problem. We will, for the most part, assume that these uncertainties can be considered to be unknown numerical quantities, and will represent them by θ (possibly a vector or matrix).

As an example, consider the situation of a drug company deciding whether or not to market a new pain reliever. Two of the many factors affecting its decision are the proportion of people for which the drug will prove effective (θ_1), and the proportion of the market the drug will capture (θ_2). Both θ_1 and θ_2 will be generally unknown, though typically experiments can be conducted to obtain statistical information about them. This problem is one of decision theory in that the ultimate purpose is to decide whether or not to market the drug, how much to market, what price to charge, etc.

Classical statistics is directed towards the use of sample information (the data arising from the statistical investigation) in making inferences about θ. These classical inferences are, for the most part, made without regard to the use to which they are to be put. In decision theory, on the other hand, an attempt is made to combine the sample information with other relevant aspects of the problem in order to make the best decision.

In addition to the sample information, two other types of information are typically relevant. The first is a knowledge of the possible consequences of the decisions. Often this knowledge can be quantified by determining the loss that would be incurred for each possible decision and for the various possible values of θ. (Statisticians seem to be pessimistic creatures who think in terms of losses. Decision theorists in economics and business talk instead in terms of gains (utility). As our orientation will be mainly statistical, we will use the loss function terminology. Note that a gain is just a negative loss, so there is no real difference between the two approaches.)

The incorporation of a loss function into statistical analysis was first studied extensively by Abraham Wald. Indeed he can be considered to be the founder of statistical decision theory.

In the drug example, the losses involved in deciding whether or not to market the drug will be complicated functions of θ_1, θ_2, and many other factors. A somewhat simpler situation to consider is that of estimating θ_1, for use, say, in an advertising campaign. The loss in underestimating θ_1 arises from making the product appear worse than it really is (adversely affecting sales), while the loss in overestimating θ_1 would be based on the risks of possible penalties for misleading advertising.

The second source of nonsample information that is useful to consider is called prior information. This is information about θ arising from sources other than the statistical investigation. Generally, prior information comes from past experience about similar situations involving similar θ. In the drug example, for instance, there is probably a great deal of information available about θ_1 and θ_2 from different but similar pain relievers.

A compelling example of the possible importance of prior information was given by L. J. Savage (1961). He considered the following three statistical experiments:

1. A lady, who adds milk to her tea, claims to be able to tell whether the tea or the milk was poured into the cup first. In all of ten trials conducted to test this, she correctly determines which was poured first.
2. A music expert claims to be able to distinguish a page of Haydn score from a page of Mozart score. In ten trials conducted to test this, he makes a correct determination each time.
3. A drunken friend says he can predict the outcome of a flip of a fair coin. In ten trials conducted to test this, he is correct each time.

In all three situations, the unknown quantity θ is the probability of the person answering correctly. A classical significance test of the various claims would consider the null hypothesis (H_0) that $\theta = 0.5$ (i.e., the person is guessing). In all three situations this hypothesis would be rejected with a (one-tailed) significance level of 2^{-10}. Thus the above experiments give strong evidence that the various claims are valid.

In situation 2 we would have no reason to doubt this conclusion. (The outcome is quite plausible with respect to our prior beliefs.) In situation 3, however, our prior opinion that this prediction is impossible (barring a belief in extrasensory perception) would tend to cause us to ignore the experimental evidence as being a lucky streak. In situation 1 it is not quite clear what to think, and different people will draw different conclusions according to their prior beliefs of the plausibility of the claim. In these three identical statistical situations, prior information clearly cannot be ignored.

1.2 Basic Elements

The unknown quantity θ which affects the decision process is commonly called the *state of nature*. In making decisions it is clearly important to consider what the possible states of nature are. The symbol Θ will be used to denote the set of all possible states of nature. Typically, when experiments are performed to obtain information about θ, the experiments are designed so that the observations are distributed according to some probability distribution which has θ as an unknown parameter. In such situations θ will be called the *parameter* and Θ the *parameter space*.

Decisions are more commonly called *actions* in the literature. Particular actions will be denoted by a, while the set of all possible actions under consideration will be denoted $\mathscr{A}$.

As mentioned in the introduction, a key element of decision theory is the loss function. If a particular action a_1 is taken and θ_1 turns out to be the true state of nature, then a loss $L(\theta_1, a_1)$ will be incurred. Thus we will assume a *loss function* $L(\theta, a)$ is defined for all $(\theta, a) \in \Theta \times \mathscr{A}$. For technical convenience, only loss functions satisfying $L(\theta, a) \geq -K > -\infty$ will be considered. This condition is satisfied by all loss functions of interest. Chapter 2 will be concerned with showing why a loss function will typically exist in a decision problem, and with indicating how a loss function can be determined.

When a statistical investigation is performed to obtain information about θ, the outcome (a random variable) will be denoted X. Often X will be a vector, as when $X = (X_1, X_2, \ldots, X_n)$, the X_i being independent observations from a common distribution. (From now on vectors will appear in boldface type; thus $\mathbf{X}$.) A particular realization of X will be denoted x. The set of possible outcomes is the *sample space*, and will be denoted $\mathscr{X}$. (Usually $\mathscr{X}$ will be a subset of R^n, n-dimensional Euclidean space.)

The probability distribution of X will, of course, depend upon the unknown state of nature θ. Let $P_\theta(A)$ or $P_\theta(X \in A)$ denote the probability of the event A $(A \subset \mathscr{X})$, when θ is the true state of nature. For simplicity, X will be assumed to be either a continuous or a discrete random variable, with density $f(x|\theta)$. Thus if X is continuous (i.e., has a density with respect to Lebesgue measure), then

$$P_\theta(A) = \int_A f(x|\theta)dx,$$

while if X is discrete, then

$$P_\theta(A) = \sum_{x \in A} f(x|\theta).$$

Certain common probability densities and their relevant properties are given in Appendix 1.

It will frequently be necessary to consider expectations over random variables. The expectation (over X) of a function $h(x)$, for a given value of θ, is defined to be

$$E_\theta[h(X)] = \begin{cases} \int_{\mathscr{X}} h(x)f(x|\theta)dx & \text{(continuous case)}, \\ \sum_{x \in \mathscr{X}} h(x)f(x|\theta) & \text{(discrete case)}. \end{cases}$$

It would be cumbersome to have to deal separately with these two different expressions for $E_\theta[h(X)]$. Therefore, as a convenience, we will define

$$E_\theta[h(X)] = \int_{\mathscr{X}} h(x)dF^X(x|\theta),$$

where the right-hand side is to be interpreted as in the earlier expression for $E_\theta[h(X)]$. (This integral can, of course, be considered a Riemann–Stieltjes integral, where $F^X(x|\theta)$ is the cumulative distribution function of X. Readers not familiar with such terms can just treat the integral as a notational device.) Note that, in the same way, we can write

$$P_\theta(A) = \int_A dF^X(x|\theta).$$

Frequently, it will be necessary to clarify the random variables over which an expectation or probability is being taken. Superscripts on E or P will serve this role. (A superscript could be the random variable, its density, its distribution function, or its probability measure, whichever is more convenient.) Subscripts on E will denote parameter values at which the expectation is to be taken. When obvious, subscripts or superscripts will be omitted.

The third type of information discussed in the introduction was prior information concerning θ. A useful way of talking about prior information is in terms of a probability distribution on Θ. (Prior information about θ is seldom very precise. Therefore, it is rather natural to state prior beliefs in terms of probabilities of various possible values of θ being true.) The symbol $\pi(\theta)$ will be used to represent a prior density of θ (again for either the continuous or discrete case). Thus if $A \subset \Theta$,

$$P(\theta \in A) = \int_A dF^\pi(\theta) = \begin{cases} \int_A \pi(\theta)d\theta & \text{(continuous case)}, \\ \sum_{\theta \in A} \pi(\theta) & \text{(discrete case)}. \end{cases}$$

Chapter 3 discusses the construction of prior probability distributions, and also indicates what is meant by probabilities concerning θ. (After all, in most situations there is nothing "random" about θ. A typical example is when θ is an unknown but fixed physical constant (say the speed of light) which is to be determined. The basic idea is that probability statements concerning θ are then to be interpreted as "personal probabilities" reflecting the degree of personal belief in the likelihood of the given statement.)

Three examples of use of the above terminology follow.

EXAMPLE 1. In the drug example of the introduction, assume it is desired to estimate θ_2. Since θ_2 is a proportion, it is clear that $\Theta = \{\theta_2 : 0 \leq \theta_2 \leq 1\} = [0, 1]$. Since the goal is to estimate θ_2, the action taken will simply be the choice of a number as an estimate for θ_2. Hence $\mathcal{A} = [0, 1]$. (Usually $\mathcal{A} = \Theta$ for estimation problems.) The company might determine the loss function to be

$$L(\theta_2, a) = \begin{cases} \theta_2 - a & \text{if } \theta_2 - a \geq 0, \\ 2(a - \theta_2) & \text{if } \theta_2 - a \leq 0. \end{cases}$$

(The loss is in units of "utility," a concept that will be discussed in Chapter 2.) Note that an overestimate of demand (and hence overproduction of the drug) is considered twice as costly as an underestimate of demand, and that otherwise the loss is linear in the error.

A reasonable experiment which could be performed to obtain sample information about θ_2 would be to conduct a sample survey. For example, assume n people are interviewed, and the number X who would buy the drug is observed. It might be reasonable to assume that X is $\mathcal{B}(n, \theta_2)$ (see Appendix 1), in which case the sample density is

$$f(x|\theta_2) = \binom{n}{x} \theta_2^x (1 - \theta_2)^{n-x}.$$

There could well be considerable prior information about θ_2, arising from previous introductions of new similar drugs into the market. Let's say that, in the past, new drugs tended to capture between $\frac{1}{10}$ and $\frac{1}{5}$ of the market, with all values between $\frac{1}{10}$ and $\frac{1}{5}$ being equally likely. This prior information could be modeled by giving θ_2 a $\mathcal{U}(0.1, 0.2)$ prior density, i.e., letting

$$\pi(\theta_2) = 10 I_{(0.1, 0.2)}(\theta_2).$$

The above development of L, f, and π is quite crude, and usually much more detailed constructions are required to obtain satisfactory results. The techniques for doing this will be developed as we proceed.

EXAMPLE 2. A shipment of transistors is received by a radio company. It is too expensive to check the performance of each transistor separately, so a sampling plan is used to check the shipment as a whole. A random sample of n transistors is chosen from the shipment and tested. Based upon X, the number of defective transistors in the sample, the shipment will be accepted or rejected. Thus there are two possible actions: a_1—accept the shipment, and

a_2—reject the shipment. If n is small compared to the shipment size, X can be assumed to have a $\mathscr{B}(n, \theta)$ distribution, where θ is the proportion of defective transistors in the shipment.

The company determines that their loss function is $L(\theta, a_1) = 100$, $L(\theta, a_2) = 1$. (When a_2 is decided (i.e., the lot is rejected), the loss is the constant value 1, which reflects costs due to inconvenience, delay, and testing of a replacement shipment. When a_1 is decided (i.e., the lot is accepted), the loss is deemed proportional to θ, since θ will also reflect the proportion of defective radios produced. The factor 10 indicates the relative costs involved in the two kinds of errors.)

The radio company has in the past received numerous other transistor shipments from the same supplying company. Hence they have a large store of data concerning the value of θ on past shipments. Indeed a statistical investigation of the past data reveals that θ was distributed according to a $\mathscr{B}e\,(0.05, 1)$ distribution. Hence

$$\pi(\theta) = (0.05)\theta^{-0.95}I_{[0,\,1]}(\theta).$$

EXAMPLE 3. An investor must decide whether or not to buy rather risky ZZZ bonds. If the investor buys the bonds, they can be redeemed at maturity for a net gain of \$500. There could, however, be a default on the bonds, in which case the original \$1000 investment would be lost. If the investor instead puts his money in a "safe" investment, he will be guaranteed a net gain of \$300 over the same time period. The investor estimates the probability of a default to be 0.1.

Here $\mathscr{A} = \{a_1, a_2\}$, where a_1 stands for buying the bonds and a_2 for not buying. Likewise $\Theta = \{\theta_1, \theta_2\}$, where θ_1 denotes the state of nature "no default occurs" and θ_2 the state "a default occurs." Recalling that a gain is represented by a negative loss, the loss function is given by the following table.

	a_1	a_2
θ_1	-500	-300
θ_2	1000	-300

(When both Θ and $\mathscr{A}$ are finite, the loss function is most easily represented by such a table, and is called a *loss matrix*. Actions are typically placed along the top of the table, and θ values along the side.) The prior information can be written as $\pi(\theta_1) = 0.9$ and $\pi(\theta_2) = 0.1$.

Note that in this example there is no sample information from an associated statistical experiment. Such a problem is called a *no-data* problem.

It should not be construed from the above examples that every problem will have a well-defined loss function and explicit prior information. In many problems these quantities may be deemed too vague or inappropriate for use. The most important examples of this are problems of statistical inference. In statistical inference the goal is not to make a decision, but to use statistical data to improve understanding of the phenomenon of interest. Research scientists, for instance, are, in general, interested only in the construction of the best possible theory or model for the phenomenon they are investigating. They are not usually involved with using their conclusions in real life situations. As an example, a physicist trying to measure the speed of light cannot reasonably be concerned with a loss function for errors in estimation.

A scientist is usually drawing conclusions which will, hopefully, be used by a wide variety of people in different circumstances. These users may well have their own individually determined loss functions and priors, which they may wish to use in conjunction with the scientist's inferences to make decisions. The pure scientist should not in general try to impose his choices upon the user. Of course, when the scientist, through his experience, has significant prior information about the situation, he should probably report this information along with the statistical inferences obtained from the sample data. His reporting should be done in such a way, however, that it is clear what his prior opinions are and also what the data says. (More will be said about this later.)

Because of the above interpretation of the goal of inference, many statisticians exclude inference problems from the domain of decision theory. This is a mistake, in that many decision theoretic techniques shed considerable light on the problems involved in making pure inferences.

1.3 Decision Rules and Risk

While the loss function and prior information for a particular user will be fixed in a specific problem, the sample information X is a random variable. It is often important to consider "averages" of losses involving actions taken under the various possible values of X. As a first step we define

Definition 1. A (nonrandomized) *decision rule* $\delta(x)$ is a function from $\mathscr{X}$ into $\mathscr{A}$. (We will always assume that functions introduced are appropriately "measureable.") If $X = x$ is the observed value of the sample information, then $\delta(x)$ is the action which will be taken. (For a no-data problem, a decision rule is simply an action.) Two decision rules δ_1 and δ_2 are considered equivalent if $P_\theta(\delta_1(X) = \delta_2(X)) = 1$ for all θ.

EXAMPLE 1 (continued). For the situation of Example 1, $\delta(x) = x/n$ is the standard decision rule for estimating θ_2. (In estimation problems a decision rule will be called an estimator.) This estimator does not make use of the loss function or prior information given in Example 1. It will be seen later how to develop estimators which do so.

EXAMPLE 2 (continued). The decision rule

$$\delta(x) = \begin{cases} a_1 & \text{if } \dfrac{x}{n} \le 0.05, \\[2mm] a_2 & \text{if } \dfrac{x}{n} > 0.05, \end{cases}$$

is a standard type of rule for this problem.

The natural "average loss over values of X" to consider is the expected loss.

Definition 2. The *risk function* of a decision rule $\delta(x)$ is defined by

$$R(\theta, \delta) = E_\theta^X[L(\theta, \delta(X))].$$

For each θ, $R(\theta, \delta)$ is thus the expected loss (over X) incurred in using $\delta(x)$. (For a no-data problem, $R(\theta, \delta)$ is simply defined to be $L(\theta, \delta)$.)

Decision rules can be compared on the basis of risks, small values of $R(\theta, \delta)$ being desirable. Using expected loss to investigate the performance of a decision rule seems on the one hand reasonable, but on the other hand appears to be rather arbitrary. More will be said of this in Section 1.6 and in Chapter 2.

The following partial ordering of decision rules can be made on the basis of risk functions.

Definition 3. A decision rule δ_1 is *R-better* than a decision rule δ_2 if $R(\theta, \delta_1) \le R(\theta, \delta_2)$ for all $\theta \in \Theta$, with strict inequality for some θ. A rule δ_1 is *R-equivalent* to δ_2 if $R(\theta, \delta_1) = R(\theta, \delta_2)$ for all θ.

Definition 4. A decision rule δ is *admissible* if there exists no R-better decision rule. A decision rule δ is *inadmissible* if there does exist an R-better decision rule.

It is fairly clear that an inadmissible decision rule should not be used, since a decision rule with smaller risk can be found. (One might take exception to this statement if the inadmissible decision rule is simple and easy to use, while the improved rule is very complicated and offers only a slight improvement. Another more philosophical objection to this exclusion of inadmissible rules will be presented in Section 4.5.) Unfortunately, there is usually a large class of admissible decision rules for a particular problem.

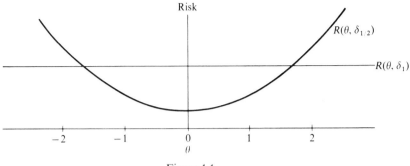

Figure 1.1

These rules will have risk functions which cross, i.e., which are better in different places. An example of these ideas is given below.

EXAMPLE 4. Assume X is $\mathcal{N}(\theta, 1)$, and that it is desired to estimate θ under loss $L(\theta, a) = (\theta - a)^2$. (This loss is called *squared-error* loss.) Consider the decision rules $\delta_c(x) = cx$. Clearly

$$
\begin{aligned}
R(\theta, \delta_c) &= E_\theta^X L(\theta, \delta_c(X)) = E_\theta^X(\theta - cX)^2 \\
&= E_\theta^X(c[\theta - X] + [1 - c]\theta)^2 \\
&= c^2 E_\theta^X[\theta - X]^2 + 2c(1 - c)\theta E_\theta^X[\theta - X] + (1 - c)^2\theta^2 \\
&= c^2 + (1 - c)^2\theta^2.
\end{aligned}
$$

Since for $c > 1$,

$$
R(\theta, \delta_1) = 1 < c^2 + (1 - c)^2\theta^2 = R(\theta, \delta_c),
$$

δ_1 is R-better than δ_c for $c > 1$. Hence the rules δ_c are inadmissible for $c > 1$. On the other hand, for $0 \leq c \leq 1$ the rules are noncomparable. For example, the risk functions of the rules δ_1 and $\delta_{1/2}$ are graphed in Figure 1.1. The risk functions clearly cross. Indeed it will be seen later that for $0 \leq c \leq 1$, δ_c is admissible. Thus the "standard" estimator δ_1 is admissible. So, however, is the rather silly estimator δ_0, which estimates θ to be zero no matter what x is observed. (This indicates that while admissibility may be a desirable property for a decision rule, it gives no assurance that the decision rule is reasonable.)

EXAMPLE 5. The following is the loss matrix of a particular no-data problem.

	a_1	a_2	a_3
θ_1	1	3	4
θ_2	-1	5	5
θ_3	0	-1	-1

The rule (action) a_2 is R-better than a_3 since $L(\theta_i, a_2) \leq L(\theta_i, a_3)$ for all θ_i, with strict inequality for θ_1. (Recall that in a no-data problem the risk is simply the loss.) Hence a_3 is inadmissible. The actions a_1 and a_2 are noncomparable, in that $L(\theta_i, a_1) < L(\theta_i, a_2)$ for θ_1 and θ_2, while the reverse inequality holds for θ_3. Thus a_1 and a_2 are admissible.

In this book we will only consider decision rules with finite risk. More formally, we will assume that the only (nonrandomized) decision rules under consideration are those in the following class.

Definition 5. Let $\mathscr{D}$ denote the class of all decision rules δ for which $R(\theta, \delta)$ $< \infty$ for all θ.

1.4 Randomized Decision Rules

In some decision situations it is necessary to take actions in a random manner. Such situations most commonly arise when an intelligent adversary is involved. As an example, consider the following game called "matching pennies."

EXAMPLE 6 (Matching Pennies). You and your opponent are to simultaneously uncover a penny. If the two coins match (i.e., are both heads or both tails) you win \$1 from your opponent. If the coins don't match, your opponent wins \$1 from you. The actions which are available to you are a_1—choose heads, or a_2—choose tails. The possible states of nature are θ_1—the opponent's coin is a head, and θ_2—the opponent's coin is a tail. The loss matrix in this game is

	a_1	a_2
θ_1	-1	1
θ_2	1	-1

Both a_1 and a_2 are admissible actions. However, if the game is to be played a number of times, then it would clearly be a very poor idea to decide to use a_1 exclusively or a_2 exclusively. Your opponent would very quickly realize your strategy, and simply choose his action to guarantee victory. Likewise, any patterned choice of a_1 and a_2 could be discerned by an intelligent opponent, who could then develop a winning strategy. The only certain way of preventing ultimate defeat, therefore, is to choose a_1 and a_2 by some random mechanism. A natural way to do this is simply to choose a_1 and a_2 with probabilities p and $1 - p$ respectively. The formal definition of such a randomized decision rule follows.

Definition 6. A *randomized decision rule* $\delta^*(x, \cdot)$ is, for each x, a probability distribution on $\mathscr{A}$, with the interpretation that if x is observed, $\delta^*(x, A)$ is the probability that an action in A (a subset of $\mathscr{A}$) will be chosen. In no-data problems a randomized decision rule, also called a *randomized action*, will simply be noted $\delta^*(\cdot)$, and is again a probability distribution on $\mathscr{A}$. Nonrandomized decision rules will be considered a special case of randomized rules, in that they correspond to the randomized rules which, for each x, choose a specific action with probability one. Indeed if $\delta(x)$ is a nonrandomized decision rule, let $\langle \delta \rangle$ denote the equivalent randomized rule given by

$$\langle \delta \rangle (x, A) = I_A(\delta(x)) = \begin{cases} 1 & \text{if } \delta(x) \in A, \\ 0 & \text{if } \delta(x) \notin A. \end{cases}$$

EXAMPLE 6 (continued). The randomized action discussed in this example is defined by $\delta^*(a_1) = p$ and $\delta^*(a_2) = 1 - p$. A convenient way to express this, using the notation of the preceding definition, is

$$\delta^* = p\langle a_1 \rangle + (1 - p)\langle a_2 \rangle.$$

EXAMPLE 7. Assume that a $\mathscr{B}(n, \theta)$ random variable X is observed, and that it is desired to test $H_0 : \theta = \theta_0$ versus $H_1 : \theta = \theta_1$ (where $\theta_0 > \theta_1$). The nonrandomized "most powerful" tests (see Chapter 8) have rejection regions of the form $C = \{x \in \mathscr{X} : x \le j\}$ $(j = 0, 1, 2, \ldots, n)$. Since $\mathscr{X}$ is discrete and finite, the size of these tests (namely $\alpha = P_{\theta_0}(C)$) can attain only a finite number of values. If other values of α are desired, randomized rules must be used. It suffices to consider the randomized rules given by

$$\delta_j^*(x, a_1) = \begin{cases} 1 & \text{if } x < j, \\ p & \text{if } x = j, \\ 0 & \text{if } x > j, \end{cases}$$

and $\delta_j^*(x, a_0) = 1 - \delta_j^*(x, a_1)$, where a_i denotes accepting H_i. (Thus if $x < j$ is observed, H_0 will be rejected with probability one. If $x > j$ is observed, H_0 will never be rejected (i.e., will always be accepted). If $x = j$ is observed, a randomization will be performed, rejecting H_0 with probability p and accepting with probability $1 - p$. Through proper choice of j and p, a most powerful test of the above form can be found for any given size α.)

The natural way to define the loss function and the risk function of a randomized decision rule is in terms of expected loss. (This will be justified in Chapter 2.)

Definition 7. The loss function $L(\theta, \delta^*(x, \cdot))$ of the randomized rule δ^* is defined to be

$$L(\theta, \delta^*(x, \cdot)) = E^{\delta^*(x, \cdot)}[L(\theta, a)],$$

where the expectation is taken over a (which by an abuse of notation will denote a random variable with distribution $\delta^*(x, \cdot)$). The risk function of δ^* will then be defined to be

$$R(\theta, \delta^*) = E_\theta^X[L(\theta, \delta^*(X, \cdot))].$$

EXAMPLE 6 (continued). As this is a no-data problem, the risk is just the loss. Clearly

$$\begin{aligned}
L(\theta, \delta^*) &= E^{\delta^*}[L(\theta, a)] = \delta^*(a_1)L(\theta, a_1) + \delta^*(a_2)L(\theta, a_2) \\
&= pL(\theta, a_1) + (1 - p)L(\theta, a_2) \\
&= \begin{cases} -p + (1 - p) = 1 - 2p & \text{if } \theta = \theta_1, \\ p - (1 - p) = 2p - 1 & \text{if } \theta = \theta_2. \end{cases}
\end{aligned}$$

Note that if $p = \frac{1}{2}$ is chosen, the loss is zero no matter what the opponent does. The randomized rule δ^* with $p = \frac{1}{2}$ thus guarantees an expected loss of zero.

EXAMPLE 7 (continued). Assume that the loss is zero if a correct decision is made and one if an incorrect decision is made. Thus

$$L(\theta_i, a_j) = \begin{cases} 0 & \text{if } i = j, \\ 1 & \text{if } i \neq j. \end{cases}$$

The loss of the randomized rule δ_j^* when $\theta = \theta_0$ is then given by

$$\begin{aligned}
L(\theta_0, \delta_j^*(x, \cdot)) &= E^{\delta_j^*(x, \cdot)}[L(\theta_0, a)] \\
&= \delta_j^*(x, a_0)L(\theta_0, a_0) + \delta_j^*(x, a_1)L(\theta_0, a_1) \\
&= \delta_j^*(x, a_1).
\end{aligned}$$

Hence

$$\begin{aligned}
R(\theta_0, \delta_j^*) &= E^X[L(\theta_0, \delta_j^*(X, \cdot))] = E^X[\delta_j^*(X, a_1)] \\
&= P_{\theta_0}(X < j) + pP_{\theta_0}(X = j).
\end{aligned}$$

Similarly, it can be shown that

$$R(\theta_1, \delta_j^*) = P_{\theta_1}(X > j) + (1 - p)P_{\theta_1}(X = j).$$

As with nonrandomized rules, we will restrict attention to randomized rules with finite risk.

Definition 8. Let $\mathscr{D}^*$ be the set of all randomized decision rules δ^* for which $R(\theta, \delta^*) < \infty$ for all θ. The concepts introduced in Definitions 3 and 4 will henceforth be considered to apply to all randomized rules in $\mathscr{D}^*$. For example, a decision rule will be said to be admissible if there exists no R-better randomized decision rule in $\mathscr{D}^*$.

Before proceeding, some discussion is in order concerning the use of randomized decision rules. Consider first the following humorous account (given in Williams (1954)) of the use of randomization. The situation is the "Colonel Blotto Problem," which involves a military battle. The exact problem need not concern us, but of interest is the response to Colonel Blotto given by the military aide (knowledgable in statistics) when asked his opinion as to what action to take. He said,

> "...keep your eye on that ant—the one on your map case. When it reaches the grease spot, look at the second hand on your watch. If it points to 6 seconds or less, you should divide your force equally between the threatened points. If it reads between 6 and 30 seconds, give the entire reserve to Dana; if between 30 and 54 seconds, give it to Harry; if between 54 and 60, pick out a new ant."

This example makes randomization look rather silly. For the given situation, however, it might be very reasonable. The military opponent of Colonel Blotto is probably an intelligent adversary, and as in Example 6 it might then be best to randomly choose an action. (This will be discussed further in Chapter 5.) The suggested randomization mechanism is a sensible technique for "on the spot" randomization.

It is relatively rare for an actual decision problem to involve an intelligent adversary. In trying to decide which of two drugs is best, for example, no intelligent opponent is involved. In such situations there seems to be no good reason to randomize, and indeed intuition argues against it. The decision maker should be able to evaluate the relative merits of each possible action, and find the best action. If there is only one best action, there can be nothing gained by randomizing (assuming there is no need to keep an opponent guessing). If there are two or more best actions, one could randomly choose among them if desired, but there seems to be no particular point in doing so. Basically, leaving the final choice of an action up to some chance mechanism just seems ridiculous. This criticism will be seen in Chapter 4 to be valid on a rather fundamental level. Therefore, we will rarely recommend the actual use of a randomized rule.

There are reasons for studying randomized rules other than their usefulness in situations involving intelligent opponents. One such reason has already been indicated in Example 7. If it is desired to use a classical procedure with certain fixed error probabilities (say to fulfill contractual obligations), randomized rules may be necessary. A more important reason for considering randomized rules is that in Chapter 5 they will be seen to be necessary for a proper understanding of minimax theory (a type of decision-theoretic analysis). Nevertheless, randomized rules will rarely be recommended for actual use. Note that the use of randomized rules should not be confused with the use of randomization in experimental design (as in the random assignment of subjects to different treatments), which is almost indisputably a valuable statistical tool.

1.5 Decision Principles

So far we have not discussed methods of actually making a decision or choosing a decision rule. The concept of inadmissibility, introduced in Section 1.3, can be used to eliminate certain obviously bad rules. As was seen, however, there are typically a large number of admissible rules to then decide among. An additional principle must be introduced in order to select a specific rule for use. In classical statistics there are a number of such principles: the maximum likelihood, unbiasedness, minimum variance, and least-squares principles to name a few. In decision theory there are also several possible principles to go by; the three most important being the Bayes principle, the minimax principle, and the invariance principle. In this section the basic goal of each of these three principles is stated. In later chapters the methods of implementation of these principles will be discussed.

I. *The Bayes Principle*

In the Bayesian approach, the goal is to make proper use of prior information ($\pi(\theta)$) about θ. There are two different versions of the approach, one designed for making inferences with no formal loss function considered, and the other designed for situations in which a loss function is involved. Both will be discussed in Chapter 4, but for now we restrict ourselves to the true decision problem in which a loss is involved.

We have already stated that decision rules will be evaluated in terms of their risk functions $R(\theta, \delta)$. (It will be seen in Chapter 4 that only nonrandomized rules need be considered in the Bayesian approach.) The problem, as pointed out earlier, is that different admissible decision rules will have risks which are better for different θ's. To the rescue comes the prior $\pi(\theta)$, which supposedly reflects which θ's are the "likely" ones to occur. It seems very reasonable to "weight" $R(\theta, \delta)$ by $\pi(\theta)$ and average. More rigorously, if we have indeed decided to evaluate procedures by their expected loss, then expectations over θ should also be included. The resulting principle is

The Bayes Principle. *A decision rule δ_1 is preferred to a rule δ_2 if*

$$E^\pi[R(\theta, \delta_1)] < E^\pi[R(\theta, \delta_2)].$$

Thus a best decision rule according to the Bayes principle is one which minimizes (over all $\delta \in \mathcal{D}$)

$$r(\pi, \delta) = E^\pi[R(\theta, \delta)].$$

Definition 9. The quantity $r(\pi, \delta)$ is called the *Bayes risk of δ* (with respect to π). If a decision rule δ^π exists which minimizes $r(\pi, \delta)$ (over all $\delta \in \mathcal{D}$), then

δ^{π} is called the *Bayes rule*. The quantity $r(\pi) = r(\pi, \delta^{\pi})$ is then called the *Bayes risk of* π.

EXAMPLE 4 (continued). The decision rules δ_c have Bayes risks

$$r(\pi, \delta_c) = E^{\pi}[R(\theta, \delta_c)] = E^{\pi}[c^2 + (1 - c)^2\theta^2]$$
$$= c^2 + (1 - c)^2 E^{\pi}[\theta^2].$$

If $\pi(\theta)$ is a $\mathcal{N}(0, \tau^2)$ density, then $r(\pi, \delta_c) = c^2 + (1 - c)^2\tau^2$. Minimizing with respect to c (by differentiating and setting equal to zero) shows that $c_0 = \tau^2/(1 + \tau^2)$ is the best value. Thus δ_{c_0} has the smallest Bayes risk among all estimators of the form δ_c. It will be shown in Chapter 4 that δ_{c_0} actually has the smallest Bayes risk among *all* estimators (for the given π). Hence δ_{c_0} is the Bayes rule (or Bayes estimator), and

$$r(\pi) = r(\pi, \delta_{c_0}) = c_0^2 + (1 - c_0)^2\tau^2$$

$$= \left(\frac{\tau^2}{1 + \tau^2}\right)^2 + \left(\frac{1}{1 + \tau^2}\right)^2 \tau^2 = \frac{\tau^2}{1 + \tau^2}$$

is the Bayes risk of π.

EXAMPLE 3 (continued). Since this is a no-data problem, decision rules are simply actions, and the risk function is simply the loss function. Hence

$$r(\pi, a_1) = E^{\pi}[L(\theta, a_1)] = \pi(\theta_1)L(\theta_1, a_1) + \pi(\theta_2)L(\theta_2, a_1)$$
$$= (0.9)(-500) + (0.1)(1000) = -350,$$

$$r(\pi, a_2) = E^{\pi}[L(\theta, a_2)] = \pi(\theta_1)L(\theta_1, a_2) + \pi(\theta_2)L(\theta_2, a_2)$$
$$= (0.9)(-300) + (0.1)(-300) = -300.$$

Clearly a_1 has smaller Bayes risk than a_2, and is hence the Bayes decision rule (or Bayes action). The Bayes risk of π is -350. The above analysis shows that the risky bonds should be purchased (according to the Bayes principle).

For no-data problems such as that above, finding the Bayes action is easy. Simply calculate $r(\pi, a)$ for each $a \in \mathscr{A}$ and choose the best action. Chapter 4 will discuss methods of obtaining the Bayes rule in more general problems.

II. *The Minimax Principle*

Complete analysis of problems using the minimax principle generally calls for consideration of randomized decision rules. Thus let $\delta^* \in \mathscr{D}^*$ be a randomized rule, and consider the quantity

$$\sup_{\theta \in \Theta} R(\theta, \delta^*).$$

This represents the worst that can happen if the rule δ^* is used. If it is desired to protect against the worst possible state of nature, one is led to using

The Minimax Principle. *A decision rule δ_1^* is preferred to a rule δ_2^* if*

$$\sup_\theta R(\theta, \delta_1^*) < \sup_\theta R(\theta, \delta_2^*).$$

Definition 10. A rule δ^{*M} is a *minimax decision rule* if it minimizes $\sup_\theta R(\theta, \delta^*)$ among all randomized rules in $\mathcal{D}^*$, i.e., if

$$\sup_{\theta \in \Theta} R(\theta, \delta^{*M}) = \inf_{\delta^* \in \mathcal{D}^*} \sup_{\theta \in \Theta} R(\theta, \delta^*).$$

The quantity on the right-hand side of the above expression is called the *minimax value* of the problem. (Replacing "inf" by "min" and "sup" by "max" shows the origin of the name "minimax.") For no-data problems, the minimax decision rule will be called simply the *minimax action*.

Sometimes it is of interest to determine the best nonrandomized rule according to the minimax principle. If such a best rule exists, it will be called the *minimax nonrandomized rule* (or *minimax nonrandomized action* in no-data problems).

EXAMPLE 4 (continued). For the decision rules δ_c,

$$\sup_\theta R(\theta, \delta_c) = \sup_\theta [c^2 + (1 - c)^2 \theta^2] = \begin{cases} 1 & \text{if } c = 1, \\ \infty & \text{if } c \neq 1. \end{cases}$$

Hence δ_1 is best among the rules δ_c, according to the minimax principle. Indeed it will be shown in Chapter 5 that δ_1 is a minimax rule and that 1 is the minimax value for the problem. By using the rule $\delta_1(x) = x$, one can thus ensure that the risk is no worse than 1 (and actually equal to 1 for all θ). Note that the minimax rule and the Bayes rule found earlier are different.

EXAMPLE 3 (continued). Clearly

$$\sup_\theta L(\theta, a_1) = \max\{-500, 1000\} = 1000,$$

$$\sup_\theta L(\theta, a_2) = \max\{-300, -300\} = -300.$$

Thus a_2 is the minimax nonrandomized action.

EXAMPLE 6 (continued). The randomized rules can be written

$$\delta_p^* = p\langle a_1 \rangle + (1 - p)\langle a_2 \rangle,$$

which recall means that a_1 is to be selected with probability p, and a_2 is to be chosen with probability $1 - p$. The loss (and hence risk) of such a rule was shown to be

$$R(\theta, \delta_p^*) = L(\theta, \delta_p^*) = pL(\theta, a_1) + (1 - p)L(\theta, a_2)$$
$$= \begin{cases} 1 - 2p & \text{if } \theta = \theta_1, \\ 2p - 1 & \text{if } \theta = \theta_2. \end{cases}$$

Hence

$$\sup_\theta R(\theta, \delta_p^*) = \max\{1 - 2p, 2p - 1\}.$$

Graphing the functions $1 - 2p$ and $2p - 1$ (for $0 \le p \le 1$) and noting that the maximum is always the higher of the two lines, it becomes clear that the minimum value of $\max\{1 - 2p, 2p - 1\}$ is 0, occurring at $p = \frac{1}{2}$. Thus $\delta_{1/2}^*$ is the minimax action and 0 is the minimax value for the problem.

The above example describes a useful technique for solving two action no-data problems. In such situations, the randomized rules are always of the form δ_p^*, and $R(\theta, \delta_p^*)$ can be graphed as a function of p (for $0 \le p \le 1$). If Θ is finite, one need only graph the lines $R(\theta, \delta_p^*)$ for each θ, and note that the highest line segments of the graph form $\sup_\theta R(\theta, \delta_p^*)$. The minimizing value of p can then be seen directly. Techniques for finding minimax rules in more difficult situations will be presented in Chapter 5.

III. *The Invariance Principle*

The invariance principle basically states that if two problems have identical formal structures (i.e., have the same sample space, parameter space, densities, and loss function), then the same decision rule should be used in each problem. This principle is employed, for a given problem, by considering transformations of the problem (say, changes of scale in the unit of measurement) which result in transformed problems of identical structure. The proscription that the decision rules in the original and transformed problem be the same leads to a restriction to so-called "invariant" decision rules. This class of rules will often be small enough so that a "best invariant" decision rule will exist. Chapter 6 will be devoted to the discussion and application of this principle.

1.6 Foundations

Before discussing methods of implementing the various decision principles, it is worthwhile to pause and reflect on certain fundamental issues upon which statistical analysis is based. In so doing a certain "philosophical" approach to decision theory will be advocated. Since classical statistical analysis is by far the most dominant approach in statistics today, it is helpful to begin with a discussion of its inadequacies.

1.6.1 Criticisms of Classical Statistics

Classical statistics encompasses a huge range of subjects and methodologies. By "classical statistics" we will essentially mean the collection of statistical techniques which do not involve formal consideration of prior information or loss, and which evaluate the accuracy of a technique in terms of its long term repetitive accuracy. Significance tests, size α tests, confidence intervals, and unbiased estimators are all familiar examples of such classical procedures. (There are, of course, classical techniques such as maximum likelihood estimation which do not formally involve the idea of repetitive accuracy. Such techniques tend to be evaluated in terms of long term repetitive accuracy, however.) Our criticism of classical statistics will be confined to three main points: (I) prior information and loss, (II) initial and final precision, and (III) formulational inadequacy.

I. *Prior Information and Loss*

The need to consider prior information and loss in decision problems has already been discussed. The failure of classical statistical analysis to take these into account is a serious criticism. Perhaps the most misused classical technique is the size α hypothesis test. When trying to make a *decision* between two hypotheses, standard $\alpha = 0.1, 0.05$, or 0.01 level tests are frequently used without regard to the losses of incorrect decisions or to prior information. This can lead to seriously inferior decisions. Problems can also arise in estimation, particularly when overestimation and underestimation have different consequences. Classical estimators can then be quite poor.

It is actually somewhat unfair to criticize classical statistics for failure to take into account prior information and loss, since it was never designed to do so. Classical statistics was mainly designed for inference problems, as was discussed earlier. What is really being criticized, therefore, is the widespread *misuse* of classical statistics to solve decision problems for which it was never intended.

II. *Initial and Final Precision*

Classical criteria for evaluating decision rules tend to measure how well the rules would perform in a long series of identical experiments. For example, a hypothesis test of size $\alpha = 0.05$ has the interpretation that, in a long series of identical tests, the null hypothesis will be incorrectly rejected only 5% of the time. A 95% confidence interval is an interval which would contain the unknown parameter in 95% of a long series of identical experiments. This type of accuracy we call *initial precision*. Before the experiment is even run, we can specify the initial precision the decision rule will have. (The terms initial and final precision were first used by Savage (1962).)

The use of initial precision in evaluating decision rules is clearly reasonable when considering a situation in which a certain statistical procedure will be routinely used over and over again in the same setting. Sampling products coming off a production line is one such situation. When dealing with a one time situation, however, it is not clear what the relevance of initial precision is. Indeed, it is then final precision which is probably of interest. By *final precision* is meant the accuracy with which it is felt the conclusion holds *after* the data or sample information has been observed. (Several measures of final precision will be given in Chapter 4.) In evaluating a one time 95% confidence interval for example, it is of little comfort to know that in 95% of a long series of such experiments the interval would contain θ. What is desired is a feeling as to how likely it is that θ is contained in the particular interval being considered. The difference is forcefully exhibited in the following well-known example.

EXAMPLE 8. Let $\mathbf{X} = (X_1, X_2, \ldots, X_n)$ be an independent sample from the $\mathcal{U}(\theta - \frac{1}{2}, \theta + \frac{1}{2})$ distribution. It is desired to give a confidence interval for θ. The classical 95% confidence interval for θ, when $n = 25$, is $(\hat{\theta} - 0.056,$ $\hat{\theta} + 0.056)$, where $\hat{\theta} = \frac{1}{2}(\min\{X_i\} + \max\{X_i\})$ is the sample midrange. Now suppose that when the experiment is conducted, the outcome x is such that $\min\{x_i\} = 3.1$ and $\max\{x_i\} = 3.2$. All that is really now known about θ is that it lies somewhere between $[\max\{x_i\} - \frac{1}{2}] = 2.7$ and $[\min\{x_i\} + \frac{1}{2}]$ $= 3.6$, with nothing in the sample giving information as to which of these possible values might be more "likely" than others. Thus to state that the classical confidence interval (3.094, 3.206) has a precision of 95% is very misleading, in that if you had to state a true feeling of the "chance" that the interval contained θ you would probably say it was something like (3.206 $- 3.094)/(3.6 - 2.7) = 0.124$. This "final precision" of 12.4% is vastly different from the initial precision of 95%. Of course, it was unlucky to obtain such an uninformative sample x, but if we do it seems silly to use initial precision as a measure of accuracy.

A similar problem can occur with a "too accurate" sample. If, for instance, $\min\{x_i\} = 3.0$ and $\max\{x_i\} = 3.96$, we know for sure (i.e., with 100% precision) that $3.46 < \theta < 3.5$. The classical procedure states that $3.424 < \theta < 3.536$ with "confidence" 95%. This conclusion also seems ridiculous, in light of our certain knowledge that θ is in the smaller interval.

The classical statistician will argue that initial precision, as a measure of accuracy, can only be interpreted through the long range viewpoint. Unfortunately it is again a case of widespread misuse, in that to nonspecialists a statement of initial precision is frequently taken as a statement concerning the precision or accuracy of the conclusion in that given instance.

A second interesting illustration of the difference between initial and final precision occurs in an example due to Cox (1958).

EXAMPLE 9. Assume an observation X which is $\mathcal{N}(\theta, \sigma^2)$ is to be observed, and that it is desired to test $H_0: \theta = 0$ versus $H_1: \theta = 10$. The experimenter will be supplied with one of two possible measuring instruments to obtain the observation X. The first has $\sigma = 1$ (a new accurate instrument), while the second has $\sigma = 10$ (an old inaccurate instrument). The experimenter will receive the first instrument with probability p and the second with probability $(1 - p)$, and will know which instrument he has received. Two possible size α tests of H_0 versus H_1 are

Test 1: Reject H_0 if $x > K_1\sigma$, where K_1 is chosen to give the desired size

$$\alpha = P_{\theta=0}(X > K_1\sigma).$$

Note that, since the test done with each instrument separately is of size α, the size of the combined experiment (i.e., the overall probability of rejecting when $\theta = 0$) is also α.

Test 2: Choose K_2 so that

$$\alpha = (1 - p) + pP_{\theta=0, \sigma=1}(X > K_2).$$

(Assume $\alpha > (1 - p)$.) Reject H_0 if $x > K_2$ for the first instrument, and *always* reject with the second instrument. From the definition of K_2, it is clear that the size of the combined test is again α.

It can be shown (see for example Cornfield (1969)) that, for many values of α and p, Test 2 is *more powerful* than Test 1 (i.e., the probability of Test 2 incorrectly accepting H_0 is less than the probability of Test 1 incorrectly accepting H_0). Hence a classical statistician concerned only with initial precision would recommend Test 2. One can imagine the reaction of the experimenter, who happens to get stuck with using the second instrument, when he is told by the statistician to ignore the experimental result and reject. If the experimenter is doing a long series of similar experiments (being assigned a different instrument each day) it might be possible to convince him to use Test 2, but if he is involved in a one-time experiment he will be considerably less than enthusiastic about the advice. The experimenter in the latter case is interested only in final precision (which is the precision he can obtain using the measuring instrument he is given). The problem of what to do in this example can most reasonably be resolved using the Bayes principle. See Cornfield (1969) for discussion of this.

Luckily (for classical statistics) it is relatively rare for the use of initial precision to cause serious problems. This is because, by coincidence, final precision and initial precision tend to coincide for many standard distributions (such as the normal distribution). This will be indicated in Chapter 4, and discussed extensively in Chapter 6.

Kiefer (1977) has overcome, in a classical fashion, some of the problems encountered through the use of standard measures of initial precision, by defining a more delicate conditional measure of initial precision. (The relevant probabilities are calculated conditionally with respect to certain parts of the sample space.) It will be indicated in Subsection 1.6.2, however, that no measure of initial precision can avoid certain fundamental difficulties. It is thus important to be able to evaluate procedures in terms of final precision.

III. Formulational Inadequacy

Many standard classical formulations of problems are too limited to allow meaningful conclusions to be reached in the majority of problems to which they are applied. The most obviously inadequate such formulation is that of a hypothesis test (or significance test) of a point null hypothesis. The following example indicates the problem.

EXAMPLE 10. A sample $X_1, \ldots, X_n$ is to be taken from a $\mathcal{N}(\theta, 1)$ distribution. It is desired to conduct a size $\alpha = 0.05$ test of $H_0: \theta = 0$ versus $H_1: \theta \neq 0$. The usual test is to reject H_0 if $\sqrt{n}|\bar{x}| > 1.96$, where $\bar{x}$ is the sample mean.

Now it is unlikely that the null hypothesis is ever exactly true. Suppose, for instance, that $\theta = 10^{-10}$, which while nonzero is probably a meaningless difference from zero in most practical contexts. If now a very large sample, say $n = 10^{24}$, is taken, then with extremely high probability $\bar{X}$ will be within 10^{-11} of the true mean $\theta = 10^{-10}$. (The standard deviation of $\bar{X}$ is only 10^{-12}.) But, for $\bar{x}$ in this region, it is clear that $10^{12}|\bar{x}| > 1.96$. Hence the classical test is virtually certain to reject H_0, even though the true mean is negligibly different from zero. This same phenomenon exists no matter what size $\alpha > 0$ is chosen and no matter how small the difference, $\varepsilon > 0$, is between zero and the true mean. For a large enough sample size, the classical test will be virtually certain to reject.

The point of the above example is that it is meaningless to state only that a point null hypothesis is rejected by a size α test (or is rejected at significance level α). We *know* from the beginning that the point null hypothesis is almost certainly not exactly true, and that this will always be confirmed by a large enough sample. What we are really interested in determining is whether or not the null hypothesis is approximately true. In Example 10, for instance, we might really be interested in detecting a difference of at least 10^{-3} from zero, in which case a better null hypothesis would be $H_0: |\theta| \leq 10^{-3}$. (There are certain situations in which it is reasonable to formulate the problem as a test of a point null hypothesis, but even then serious questions arise concerning the final precision of the classical test. This issue will be discussed in Example 10 of Chapter 4.)

As another example of this basic problem, consider standard "tests of fit," in which it is desired to see if the data fits the assumed model. (A typical example is a test for normality.) Again it is virtually certain that the model is not exactly correct, so a large enough sample will almost always reject the model. The problem here is considerably harder to correct than in Example 10, because it is much harder to specify what an "approximately correct" model is.

A historically interesting example of this phenomenon (told to me by Herman Rubin) involves Kepler's laws of planetary motion. Of interest is his first law, which states that planetary orbits are ellipses. For the observational accuracy of Kepler's time, this model fit the data well. For todays data, however, (or even for the data just 100 years after Kepler) the null hypothesis that orbits are ellipses would be rejected by a statistical significance test, due to perturbations in the orbits caused by planetary interactions. The elliptical orbit model is, of course, essentially correct, the error caused by perturbations being minor. The concern here is that an essentially correct model can be rejected by too accurate data if statistical significance tests are blindly applied without regard to the actual size of the discrepencies.

The above discussion shows that a "statistically significant" difference between the true parameter (or true model) and the null hypothesis can be an unimportant difference practically. Likewise a difference that is not significant statistically can nevertheless be very important practically. Consider the following example.

EXAMPLE 11. The effectiveness of a drug is measured by $X \sim \mathcal{N}(\theta, 9)$. The null hypothesis is that $\theta = 0$. A sample of 9 observations results in $\bar{x} = 1$. This is not significant (for a one-tailed test) at, say, the $\alpha = 0.05$ significance level. It is significant at the $\alpha = 0.16$ significance level, however, which is moderately convincing. If 1 were a practically important difference from zero, we would certainly be very interested in the drug. Indeed if we had to make a decision solely on the basis of the given data, we would probably decide that the drug was effective.

The above problems are, of course, well recognized by classical statisticians, who, while using the framework of testing point null hypotheses, do concern themselves with the real import of the results. It seems somewhat nonsensical, however, to deliberately formulate a problem wrong, and then in an adhoc fashion explain the final results in more reasonable terms. Also, there are unfortunately many users of statistics who do not understand the pitfalls of the incorrect classical formulations.

One of the main benefits of decision theory is that it forces one to think about the correct formulation of a problem. A number of decision-theoretic alternatives to classical significance tests will be introduced as we proceed, although no systematic study of such alternatives will be undertaken.

Correction of deficiencies (I) and (III) of classical statistics is the avowed goal of decision theory. Criticism (II), however, is a more fundamental problem, causing difficulties in decision theory as well as in classical statistics. The next subsection deals with the philosophical issues encountered in the study of this problem.

1.6.2 The Likelihood Principle

There is considerable controversy among statisticians concerning the establishment of a logical foundation for statistical analysis. Usually this controversy is centered around the issue of whether the classical approach, the Bayesian approach, the minimax approach, or whatever, is best for solving a statistical problem. We will certainly be very concerned with this issue as we proceed, but it is helpful to first discuss a somewhat simpler foundational issue: the likelihood principle.

The likelihood principle received its initial expression and support from R. A. Fisher and G. A. Barnard in numerous writings. Birnbaum (1962) gave compelling theoretical arguments for its justification. Before presenting these arguments, we will discuss the likelihood principle from an intuitive viewpoint.

The likelihood principle states that the actual observation, x, is the only element of the sample space $\mathscr{X}$ which is relevant to problems of decision or inference concerning θ. Opponents of the likelihood principle maintain that in evaluating the information conveyed by x, it is necessary to consider what other observations might have occurred, i.e., other points in $\mathscr{X}$. This difference in attitude is clearly illustrated by the following well-known example discussed in Lindley (1976).

EXAMPLE 12. We are given a coin and are interested in the probability, θ, of having it come up heads when flipped. It is desired to test $H_0: \theta = \frac{1}{2}$ versus $H_1: \theta > \frac{1}{2}$. An experiment is conducted by flipping the coin (independently) several times. The result of the experiment is that 9 heads and 3 tails are observed.

To a believer in the likelihood principle, the above information is all the sample information that is required to conduct a statistical analysis. Disbelievers, however, maintain that it is necessary to know $\mathscr{X}$. For example, they point out that in conducting a significance test of the above hypotheses, the significance level α depends on $\mathscr{X}$. If the experiment had been conducted by flipping the coin 12 times (so $X = [\# \text{ heads}]$ would be $\mathscr{B}(12, \theta)$), the significance level of the observation $x = 9$ would be (for $\theta = \frac{1}{2}$)

$$\alpha = P(X \geq 9) = P(\{9H, 3T\}) + P(\{10H, 2T\})$$
$$+ P(\{11H, 1T\}) + P(\{12H, 0T\})$$
$$= 0.075.$$

On the other hand, if the experiment had been conducted by flipping the coin until 3 tails were observed (so $X = [\# \text{ heads}]$ would be $\mathcal{NB}(3, \theta)$), the significance level of the observation $x = 9$ would be (for $\theta = \frac{1}{2}$)

$$\alpha = P(\{9H, 3T\}) + P(\{10H, 3T\}) + \cdots$$
$$= 0.0325.$$

If significance at the 5 % level was desired, the binomial model would not give significance, while the negative binomial model would. A disbeliever in the likelihood principle thus argues that knowledge of $\mathcal{X}$ is crucial in conducting a statistical analysis of the problem.

A proponent of the likelihood principle would deal with the above example by saying that an inadequacy of significance tests has been pointed out. The significance level α is really a measure of initial precision, and hence its use in decisions or inferences concerning θ is suspect. Put another way, how can points in $\mathcal{X}$ which have not occurred have any bearing on θ. This is amusingly phrased by Jeffreys (1961):

> "... a hypothesis which may be true may be rejected because it has not pre-dicted observable results which have not occurred."

The key point to understand here is that while the sample space $\mathcal{X}$ is crucial for an evaluation of classical measures of initial precision, the relevance of these measures to decision making is often doubtful.

A more effective argument criticizing the likelihood principle can be phrased in terms of stopping rules. The argument essentially says that if an experimenter continues sampling until he has obtained a "favorable" sample, he can obtain "biased" results. Since the choice of a sampling method can be considered equivalent to a choice of $\mathcal{X}$, the likelihood principle states that knowledge of such a sampling method is irrelevant for decisions about the underlying θ. This argument will be presented in more detail, and answered, in Chapter 7.

As the reader may have by now surmised, the author is a believer in the likelihood principle. It was essentially a long examination of Example 12 that developed this belief. The following example, due to Pratt, is perhaps even more intuitively convincing.

EXAMPLE 13 (Pratt (1962)). "An engineer draws a random sample of electron tubes and measures the plate voltages under certain conditions with a very accurate voltmeter, accurate enough so that measurement error is negligible compared with the variability of the tubes. A statistician examines the measurements, which look normally distributed and vary from 75 to 99 volts with a mean of 87 and a standard deviation of 4. He makes the ordinary normal analysis, giving a confidence interval for the true mean. Later he visits the engineer's laboratory, and notices that the voltmeter used reads only as far as 100, so the population appears to be 'censored'. This necessitates a new analysis, if the statistician is orthodox. However, the engineer says he has another meter, equally accurate and reading to 1000 volts, which he would have used if any voltage had been over 100. This is a relief to the orthodox statistician, because it means the population was effectively uncensored after all. But the next day the engineer telephones and says, 'I just discovered my high-range voltmeter was not working the day I did the experiment you analyzed for me.' The statistician ascertains that the engineer would not have held up the experiment until the meter was fixed, and informs him that a new analysis will be required. The engineer is astounded. He says, 'But the experiment turned out just the same as if the high-range meter had been working. I obtained the precise voltages of my sample anyway, so I learned exactly what I would have learned if the high-range meter had been available. Next you'll be asking about my oscilloscope.'"

In this example, two different sample spaces are being discussed. If the high-range voltmeter had been working, the sample space would have effectively been that of a usual normal distribution. Since the high-range voltmeter was broken, however, the sample space was truncated at 100, and the probability distribution of the observations would have a point mass at 100. Classical analyses (such as the obtaining of confidence intervals) would be considerably affected by this difference. The likelihood principle, on the other hand, states that this difference should have no effect on the analysis, since values of x which did not occur (here $x \geq 100$) have no bearing on inferences or decisions concerning the true mean. In this example, the likelihood principle certainly seems correct.

For later use, it is helpful to have a more formal statement of the likelihood principle. The needed concept is that of the likelihood function.

Definition 11. If the sample x has been observed, the function $l(\theta) = f(x|\theta)$, considered as a function of θ, is called the *likelihood function*.

The intuitive reason for the name "likelihood function" is that a θ for which $f(x|\theta)$ is large is more "likely" to be the true θ than a θ for which $f(x|\theta)$ is small, in that x would be a more plausible occurrence if $f(x|\theta)$ is large.

The Likelihood Principle. *In making inferences or decisions about θ after x is observed, all relevant sample information is contained in the likelihood function. Two likelihood functions are equivalent (i.e., the corresponding samples contain the same information about θ) if they are proportional to each other for the given x.*

EXAMPLE 12 (continued). If the binomial model is assumed, the likelihood function for $x = 9$ is

$$l_1(\theta) = f(x|\theta) = \binom{n}{x}\theta^x(1 - \theta)^{n-x} = 220\theta^9(1 - \theta)^3.$$

If the negative binomial model is assumed, the likelihood function for $x = 9$ is

$$l_2(\theta) = f(x|\theta) = \binom{n + x - 1}{x}\theta^x(1 - \theta)^n = 55\theta^9(1 - \theta)^3.$$

Since these two likelihood functions are proportional to each other, the likelihood principle states that the two experiments contain identical sample information about θ. Since all other possible inputs (such as the loss function and prior information) will be the same under either experiment, it can be concluded that inferences or decisions about θ should be the same for both models. This conclusion is in contrast to the conclusion under classical statistical analysis.

Some proponents of the likelihood principle endorse a stronger form of the principle than that given above. In particular, some say that if two problems have the same likelihood function, then the same inference should be made in each problem, and furthermore that this inference should be based only on the likelihood function. Both claims seems excessive. The likelihood principle, as stated here, applies only when the two likelihood functions are for the same parameter θ. It is easy to construct examples in which different parameters have the same likelihood function, and yet quite dissimilar inferences are called for. Also, we claim here only that all sample information concerning θ is summarized in the likelihood function. Prior and loss information will usually be relevant too.

The theoretical argument of Birnbaum which supports the likelihood principle is essentially a proof of the equivalence of the likelihood principle and two more intuitively natural principles. The first of these natural principles is that of sufficiency, a principle accepted by almost all statisticians. A discussion of sufficiency is given in Section 1.7. The second natural principle is usually called the conditionality principle, and can be stated as follows.

The Conditionality Principle. *Assume an experiment E is a random mixture of other experiments $\{E_n\}$, by which it is meant that only one of the E_n will actually be performed, the selected E_n being chosen by a random mechanism which is independent of the state of nature θ. Then the decision or conclusion obtained from E should be the same as the decision or conclusion obtained from the E_n that actually occurs.*

An example of the above situation is Example 9. The overall experiment is a random mixture of the two experiments which use the accurate and inaccurate measuring instruments respectively. The conditionality principle states that one should proceed by first observing which instrument is obtained, and then doing an optimal analysis using that instrument. This has a great deal of intuitive appeal, but does contradict the classical notions of initial precision based on overall pre-experimental evaluations.

For a proof that the principles of sufficiency and conditionality imply the likelihood principle (and vice versa) see Birnbaum (1962). It should be emphasized that this correspondence applies not only to decisions involving θ, but also to inferences and measures of "evidence" concerning θ that can be obtained from the experiment.

The likelihood principle does have several serious limitations. The first limitation is that it applies only to drawing conclusions about θ from the experiment, and not to planning or conducting the experiment, or to predicting future values of the random variable. In designing an experiment, the statistician tries to plan the experiment so as to obtain an optimal amount of information, and in so doing must definitely consider the types of information that can occur (i.e., the sample space $\mathscr{X}$). Likewise, in sequential analysis the statistician must decide at each stage whether or not to take more observations, which clearly involves consideration of $\mathscr{X}$. Finally, in prediction problems it is desired to predict a future value of the random variable X (or some function thereof) in which case $\mathscr{X}$ is again relevant. The likelihood principle does not apply in any of these situations. It is only applicable when the sole concern is making a decision or inference about the unknown state of nature θ, after the observation x has been taken.

The second limitation of the likelihood principle is that it applies only when the assumed model (or at least the assumed likelihood function) is correct. Consider Example 8, for instance. Here, if when $n = 25$ we observe $\min\{x_i\} = 3.1$ and $\max\{x_i\} = 3.2$, it will frequently be sensible to conclude that the model (a $\mathscr{U}(\theta - \frac{1}{2}, \theta + \frac{1}{2})$ distribution) is incorrect. If this is the case, the likelihood principle has nothing to say. Part of the attractiveness of many classical procedures is that they are not overly sensitive to errors in the assumed model. It can, therefore, be argued that unless use of the likelihood principle results in a similar insensitivity, the classical procedures are to be preferred. No global results concerning this issue are known, and it appears that the problem will have to be investigated on a case by case basis. Note, at least, that analysis via the likelihood principle is in one sense less sensitive to the model, in that only the likelihood function, and not the actual sample space, matters.

The final, yet most glaring, limitation of the likelihood principle is that it does not indicate how the likelihood function is to be used in making decisions or inferences about θ. One proposal has been to simply report the entire likelihood function, and to educate people in its interpretation. This is perhaps reasonable, but is by no means the complete solution. First of all, it is frequently also necessary to consider the prior information and loss, and the interaction of these quantities with the likelihood function. Secondly, it is not at all clear that the likelihood function, by itself, has any particular meaning. It is natural to attempt to interpret the likelihood function as some kind of probability density for θ. The ambiguity arises in the need to then specify the "measure" with respect to which it is a density. There are often many plausible choices for this measure, and the choice can have a considerable effect on the conclusion reached. This problem is basically that of choosing a "noninformative" prior distribution, and will be discussed in Chapter 3.

Of the other methods that have been proposed for using the likelihood function to draw conclusions about θ, only the Bayesian approach seems generally appropriate. This will be indicated in the next section, and in Chapter 4. (Example 27 of Chapter 4, in particular, shows the difficulties that can arise in trying to use the likelihood principle outside of Bayesian analysis.) It will also be argued, however, that a good Bayesian analysis sometimes requires a slight violation of the likelihood principle, in attempting to protect against the uncertainties in the specification of the prior distribution. The conclusion that will be reached is that analysis compatible with the likelihood principle is an ideal towards which we should strive, but an ideal which is seldom completely obtainable.

In the remainder of the book, the likelihood principle will rarely be used to actually do anything. The purpose in having such a lengthy discussion of the principle was to encourage the "post-experimental" way of thinking. Classical statistics teaches one to think in terms of "pre-experimental" measures of initial precision. The likelihood principle states that this is an error; that one should reason only in terms of the actual sample and likelihood function obtained. Approaching a statistical analysis with this viewpoint in mind is a radical departure from traditional statistical reasoning; perhaps the most radical change to be advocated in this book.

The book itself will seem to oscillate on the subject of "pre-experimental" or "post-experimental" reasoning. Indeed most of the book deals with analyzing decision rules δ, which are clearly pre-experimental in nature (being functions on $\mathcal{X}$). A (nonrandomized) decision rule can, however, be viewed as simply a collection of post-experimental actions, one for each possible observation x. In other words, we can arrive at a decision rule by finding the optimal post-experimental action for each possible observation. Thus nothing is lost by talking in terms of decision rules, and indeed considerable generality is gained; generality needed to deal with such things as experimental design and sequential analysis.

1.6.3 Choosing the Decision Principle

In deciding upon a decision principle to use, it seems desirable to seek one which is consistent with the likelihood principle. Classical statistical analysis, with its initial precision involving averages over $\mathcal{X}$, clearly violates this principle. By the same reasoning, so does evaluation of rules in terms of

$R(\theta, \delta)$! The risk $R(\theta, \delta)$ is, after all, the expected loss, the expectation being taken over the sample space $\mathscr{X}$. This risk may thus be a bad measure of the final precision of a conclusion. An explanation of our use of $R(\theta, \delta)$ thus seems in order.

It is indeed true that use of the minimax and invariance principles will violate the likelihood principle. It will be shown in Chapter 4, however, that the Bayes principle can be phrased in such a way as to be based on the likelihood principle. It will furthermore be shown that in making a decision "rationally" one acts as if he were behaving according to the Bayes principle. For these two reasons, our philosophical preference will always be for analysis according to the Bayes principle.

Unfortunately, in practice things are not so clear cut. The key to the Bayesian approach lies in the specification of the prior information $\pi(\theta)$, and it is here that difficulties can arise. The prior $\pi(\theta)$ can seldom be specified accurately (if at all) and errors in the specification of π can have a large adverse effect on the correctness of the final decision. To conduct a careful Bayesian analysis, therefore, it is necessary to investigate the effects of inaccurate specification of the prior. It will be seen that the best way to do this is often through examination of the risk function $R(\theta, \delta^\pi)$ of the Bayes rule, or alternatively through consideration of certain classical properties of the Bayes rule. To put this another way, in choosing a satisfactory prior distribution, $\pi(\theta)$, it is often helpful to consider the risk function and other measures of initial precision. While we do not, therefore, claim that the risk function is a good measure of the final precision of a conclusion, we do assert that it is a useful tool to consider.

Although convincing arguments in favor of the above approach to choosing a decision rule will be given, the reasoning is somewhat unappealing philosophically. We started out by stating a desire to act in accordance with the likelihood principle, a desire which could be "rationally" satisfied by the Bayesian approach. But then, as an aid in choosing π, it is suggested that the risk function be considered. Since the use of $R(\theta, \delta)$ violates the likelihood principle, the overall analysis thus violates the likelihood principle.

The difficulty here is in some ways one of time. If an infinite amount of time were available to contemplate the problem, it would be possible to determine $\pi(\theta)$ exactly and use a pure Bayesian analysis satisfying the likelihood principle. With only a finite amount of time, however, it is necessary to approximate prior beliefs. The best methods of investigating the appropriateness of a given approximation involve using the risk function. Hence we are forced, by our presumably finite lives as statisticians, to violate the likelihood principle. This is an instance of what Good calls type II rationality (see Good (1973b) for example), in that when the "loss" in time to the statistician is taken into account, it may be optimal to settle for using a rough and ready approximation to the theoretically optimal statistical rule.

There are also a large number of statistical problems in which prior information is either unavailable or too vague for use. In such problems there is no logically compelling principle by which to proceed. The classical measures of initial precision, and the related $R(\theta, \delta)$, are then very useful quantities to consider in the development of good decision rules. Another useful technique (which incidentally satisfies the likelihood principle) is a modification of the Bayesian technique involving "noninformative" priors. (This will be discussed in Chapter 4.) Unfortunately, none of these methods is foolproof. Examples will be given in which they lead to the construction of bad decision rules. In the absence of prior information, therefore, it is good to be able to develop decision rules by several different methods, and then compare them in an attempt to detect unappealing features. In a similar vein, if one is looking for simple statistical procedures which can be used by people relatively uneducated in statistics, then minimax rules, invariant rules, noninformative prior Bayes rules, and classical procedures based on initial precision are usually quite safe and sound (though probably not optimal).

It should also be emphasized that, in some situations, the use of $R(\theta, \delta)$ as a measure of performance is logically sound. When dealing with a repetitive situation such as lot inspection sampling, for instance, overall average loss is the proper thing to consider. In questions of experimental design, $R(\theta, \delta)$ is also important. When deciding on the sample size, for example, it is necessary to compare the cost of sampling with the expected loss in making an inaccurate decision. This naturally involves $R(\theta, \delta)$, since before experimentation it is not known which x will be observed.

Many of the arguments and ideas that have been presented in this section will be illustrated and expanded as we proceed through the book. It is probably a good idea to periodically reread this section, in that many inadequately explained points will be clear in the light of later knowledge.

1.7 Sufficient Statistics

The concept of a sufficient statistic is of great importance in simplifying statistical problems. Intuitively, a sufficient statistic is a function of the data which summarizes all the available sample information concerning θ. For example, if an independent sample $X_1, \ldots, X_n$ for a $\mathcal{N}(\mu, \sigma^2)$ distribution is to be taken, it is well known that $T = (\bar{X}, S^2)$ is a sufficient statistic for $\theta = (\mu, \sigma^2)$. (Here $S^2 = \sum (X_i - \bar{X})^2/(n - 1)$.)

It is assumed that the reader is familiar with the concept of sufficiency and with the methods of finding sufficient statistics. We will content ourselves here with a rather brief discussion of sufficiency, including a presentation of the major decision-theoretic result concerning sufficiency. The following formal definition of sufficiency uses the concept of a conditional distribution, with which the reader is also assumed familiar.

Definition 12. Let X be a random variable whose distribution depends on the unknown parameter θ, but is otherwise known. A function T of X is said to be a *sufficient statistic* for θ if the conditional distribution of X, given $T(X) = t$, is independent of θ (with probability one).

For understanding the nature of a sufficient statistic and for the development of the decision-theoretic result concerning sufficiency, the concept of a partition of the sample space must be introduced.

Definition 13. If $T(X)$ is a statistic with range $\mathscr{I}$ (i.e., $\mathscr{I} = \{T(x): x \in \mathscr{X}\}$), the *partition of $\mathscr{X}$ induced by T* is the collection of all sets of the form

$$\mathscr{X}_t = \{x \in \mathscr{X}: T(x) = t\}$$

for $t \in \mathscr{I}$.

Note that if $t_1 \neq t_2$, then $\mathscr{X}_{t_1} \cap \mathscr{X}_{t_2} = \varnothing$, and also observe that $\bigcup_{t \in \mathscr{I}} \mathscr{X}_t = \mathscr{X}$. Thus $\mathscr{X}$ is divided up (or partitioned) into the disjoint sets $\mathscr{X}_t$.

Definition 14. A *sufficient partition* of $\mathscr{X}$ is a partition induced by a sufficient statistic T.

Consider now the formal definition of sufficiency given in Definition 12. The conditional distribution of X, given $T(X) = t$, is clearly a distribution giving probability one to the set $\mathscr{X}_t$. Indeed the distribution can usually be represented by a density, to be denoted $f_t(x)$, on $\mathscr{X}_t$. The density does not depend upon θ, since by Definition 12 the conditional distribution is independent of θ. This implies, in particular, that the densities $f_t(x)$ are known, being explicitly calculable from $f(x|\theta)$.

The intuitive reason that a sufficient statistic is said to contain all the sample information concerning θ can be seen from the above considerations. Basically, the random variable X can be thought of as arising first from the random generation of T, followed by the random choice of x from $\mathscr{X}_t$ (t being the observed value of T) according to the density $f_t(x)$. This second stage involves a randomization not involving θ, and hence can carry no information about θ. Indeed, from a given t, we could artificially carry out this randomization, reconstructing a sample with the same original distribution as X.

In developing the decision-theoretic result concerning sufficiency, the concept of a conditional expectation will be needed. The conditional expectation of a function $h(x)$, given $T = t$, will be denoted $E^{X|t}[h(X)]$, and, providing the conditional density f_t exists, is given by

$$E^{X|t}[h(X)] = \begin{cases} \int_{\mathscr{X}_t} h(x) f_t(x) dx & \text{continuous case,} \\ \sum_{x \in \mathscr{X}_t} h(x) f_t(x) & \text{discrete case.} \end{cases}$$

We will also need the standard probabilistic result that

$$E^X[h(X)] = E^T E^{X|T}[h(X)].$$

Finally, for any statistic $T(X)$, we will define randomized decision rules $\delta^*(t, \cdot)$, based on T, to be the usual randomized decision rules with $\mathscr{I}$ being considered the sample space. The risk function of such a rule is clearly

$$R(\theta, \delta^*) = E^T[L(\theta, \delta^*(T, \cdot))].$$

Theorem 1. *Assume that T is a sufficient statistic for θ, and let $\delta_0^*(x, \cdot)$ be any randomized rule in $\mathscr{D}^*$. Then (subject to measurability conditions) there exists a randomized rule $\delta_1^*(t, \cdot)$, depending only on $T(x)$, which is R-equivalent to δ_0^*.*

PROOF. For $A \subset \mathscr{A}$ and $t \in \mathscr{I}$ define

$$\delta_1^*(t, A) = E^{X|t}[\delta_0^*(X, A)].$$

Thus $\delta_1^*(t, \cdot)$ is formed by averaging δ_0^* over $\mathscr{X}_t$, with respect to the conditional distribution of X given $T = t$. It is easy to check that, for each t, $\delta_1^*(t, \cdot)$ is a probability distribution on $\mathscr{A}$. Assuming it is also appropriately measurable, it follows that δ_1^* is a randomized decision rule based on $T(x)$. Note that the sufficiency of T is needed to ensure that δ_1^* does not depend on θ.

Observe next that

$$L(\theta, \delta_1^*(t, \cdot)) = E^{\delta_1^*(t, \cdot)}[L(\theta, a)] = E^{X|t}E^{\delta_0^*(X, \cdot)}[L(\theta, a)].$$

It follows that

$$\begin{aligned}
R(\theta, \delta_1^*) &= E^T[L(\theta, \delta_1^*(T, \cdot))] \\
&= E^T E^{X|T} E^{\delta_0^*(X, \cdot)}[L(\theta, a)] \\
&= E^X E^{\delta_0^*(X, \cdot)}[L(\theta, a)] \\
&= E^X[L(\theta, \delta_0^*(X, \cdot))] = R(\theta, \delta_0^*). \qquad \square
\end{aligned}$$

The above theorem applies also to a nonrandomized rule δ_0, through the identification of δ_0 and $\langle \delta_0 \rangle$ discussed in Section 1.4. Note, however, that even though δ_0 is nonrandomized, the equivalent δ_1^* may be randomized. Indeed it is clear that

$$\begin{aligned}
\delta_1^*(t, A) &= E^{X|t}[\langle \delta_0 \rangle(X, A)] \\
&= E^{X|t}[I_A(\delta_0(X))] \\
&= P^{X|t}(\delta_0(X) \in A).
\end{aligned}$$

When evaluating decision rules through risk functions, Theorem 1 implies that it is only necessary to consider rules based on a sufficient statistic. If a rule is not a function of the sufficient statistic, another rule can be found that is a function of the sufficient statistic and has the same risk function.

From a "post-experimental" viewpoint, it is even easier to argue that all sample information concerning θ is contained in a sufficient statistic. Indeed if T is sufficient for θ, the factorization theorem for sufficient statistics states that (under suitable conditions) the likelihood function can be written as

$$l(\theta) = f(x|\theta) = h(x)g(T(x)|\theta),$$

where h does not depend on θ. Hence the likelihood function is proportional to $g(T(x)|\theta)$, and the likelihood principle implies that all decisions and inferences concerning θ can be made through T.

1.8 Convexity

In several places throughout the book, the concepts of convexity and concavity will be used. The needed definitions and properties of convexity are summarized in this section. Some immediate applications concerning sufficiency and randomized rules are also given.

As mentioned earlier, boldface letters explicitly indicate vectors or matrices. Here we will be concerned with vectors $\mathbf{x} \in R^m$, so that $\mathbf{x} = (x_1, x_2, \ldots, x_m)^t$.

Definition 15. A set $\Omega \subset R^m$ is *convex* if for any two points $\mathbf{x}$ and $\mathbf{y}$ in Ω, the point $[\alpha \mathbf{x} + (1 - \alpha)\mathbf{y}]$ is in Ω for $0 \le \alpha \le 1$. (Note that $\{[\alpha \mathbf{x} + (1 - \alpha)\mathbf{y}]: 0 \le \alpha \le 1\}$ is the line segment joining $\mathbf{x}$ and $\mathbf{y}$. Hence Ω is convex if the line segment between any two points in Ω is a subset of Ω.)

Definition 16. If $\{\mathbf{x}^1, \mathbf{x}^2, \ldots\}$ is a sequence of points in R^m, and $0 \le \alpha_i \le 1$ are numbers such that $\sum_{i=1}^{\infty} \alpha_i = 1$, then $\sum_{i=1}^{\infty} \alpha_i \mathbf{x}^i$ (providing it is finite) is called a *convex combination* of the $\{\mathbf{x}^i\}$. The *convex hull* of a set Ω is the set of all points which are convex combinations of points in Ω.

Intuitively, the convex hull of a set is formed by connecting all points of the set by lines, and then filling in the interiors of the surfaces and solids so formed. It is easy to check that the convex hull of a set Ω is itself convex, and (somewhat more difficult) that it is the smallest convex set containing Ω.

Examples of convex sets are ellipses and regular polygons in R^2 (the interiors being considered part of the sets); and solid pyramids, cubes, and balls in R^3. In Figure 1.2, the set Ω_1 is convex, while Ω_2 is not.

If Ω_1 is a finite set of points in R^m, the convex hull of Ω_1 is the polygonal solid formed by joining the points and filling in the interiors. An example in R^2 is shown in Figure 1.3.

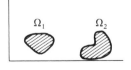

Figure 1.2

Figure 1.3

Definition 17. A real-valued function $g(\mathbf{x})$ defined on a convex set Ω is *convex* if

$$g(\alpha\mathbf{x} + (1 - \alpha)\mathbf{y}) \leq \alpha g(\mathbf{x}) + (1 - \alpha)g(\mathbf{y})$$

for all $\mathbf{x} \in \Omega$, $\mathbf{y} \in \Omega$, and $0 < \alpha < 1$. If the inequality is strict for $\mathbf{x} \neq \mathbf{y}$, then g is *strictly convex*. If

$$g(\alpha\mathbf{x} + (1 - \alpha)\mathbf{y}) \geq \alpha g(\mathbf{x}) + (1 - \alpha)g(\mathbf{y}),$$

then g is *concave*. If the inequality is strict for $\mathbf{x} \neq \mathbf{y}$, then g is *strictly concave*.

Intuitively, convex functions are bowl shaped, while concave functions are upside-down bowl shaped. The name "convex function" arises from the fact that the set of points lying above the graph of a convex function forms a convex set. Examples of convex functions on R^1 are x^2, $|x|$, and e^x. Indeed x^2 and e^x are strictly convex. Examples of concave functions are $-x^2$ (on R^1) and $\log x$ (on $(0, \infty)$).

Verifying convexity or concavity directly from the definitions above is difficult. The following lemma provides an easy calculational tool for verifying convexity or concavity.

Lemma 1. *Let $g(\mathbf{x})$ be a function defined on an open convex subset Ω of R^m for which all second-order partial derivatives*

$$g^{(i, j)}(\mathbf{x}) = \frac{\partial^2}{\partial x_i \, \partial x_j} g(\mathbf{x})$$

exist and are finite. Then g is convex if and only if the matrix G of second-order partial derivatives (i.e., the $(m \times m)$ matrix with elements $g^{(i, j)}(\mathbf{x})$) is non-negative definite for all $\mathbf{x} \in \Omega$ (i.e., $\mathbf{z}^t G \mathbf{z} \geq 0$ for all $\mathbf{z} \in R^m$ and $\mathbf{x} \in \Omega$). Likewise, g is concave if $-G$ is nonnegative definite. If G is positive (negative) definite, then g is strictly convex (strictly concave).

The proof of this lemma is a standard mathematical result and will be omitted. Note that for $m = 1$, the lemma says that g is convex (concave) if $g''(x) \geq 0$ ($g''(x) \leq 0$), where g'' is the second derivative of g.

EXAMPLE 14. For $g(x) = x^2$ and $g(x) = e^x$, it is clear that $g''(x) > 0$, so that these functions are strictly convex on R^1. In R^2, the function $g(x_1, x_2) =$

$x_1^2 + x_1 x_2 + x_2^2$ is strictly convex, since its matrix of second-order partial derivatives is

$$\begin{pmatrix} 2 & 1 \\ 1 & 2 \end{pmatrix},$$

which is positive definite.

Several very useful results concerning convex functions can be established from a theorem known as Jensen's inequality. Before giving the theorem, we state a needed lemma. The proofs of the lemma and of Jensen's inequality will be given in Subsection 5.2.5 (Chapter 5).

Lemma 2. *Let* $\mathbf{X}$ *be an m-variate random vector such that* $E[|\mathbf{X}|] < \infty$ *and* $P(\mathbf{X} \in \Omega) = 1$, *where* Ω *is a convex subset of* R^m. *Then* $E[\mathbf{X}] \in \Omega$.

Theorem 2 (Jensen's Inequality). *Let* $g(\mathbf{x})$ *be a convex real-valued function defined on a convex subset* Ω *of* R^m, *and let* $\mathbf{X}$ *be an m-variate random vector for which* $E[|\mathbf{X}|] < \infty$. *Suppose also that* $P(\mathbf{X} \in \Omega) = 1$. *Then*

$$g(E[\mathbf{X}]) \leq E[g(\mathbf{X})],$$

with strict inequality if g *is strictly convex and* $\mathbf{X}$ *is not concentrated at a point.* (*Note from Lemma 2 that* $E[\mathbf{X}] \in \Omega$, *so that* $g(E[\mathbf{X}])$ *is defined.*)

EXAMPLE 15. Since $g(x) = x^2$ is strictly convex on R^1, it follows from Jensen's inequality that if X has finite mean and is not concentrated at a point, then

$$(E[X])^2 = g(E[X]) < E[g(X)] = E[X^2],$$

a well-known probabilistic result.

Our first use of Jensen's inequality will be to show that when the loss function is convex, only nonrandomized decision rules need be considered.

Theorem 3. *Assume that* $\mathscr{A}$ *is a convex subset of* R^m, *and that for each* $\theta \in \Theta$ *the loss function* $L(\theta, \mathbf{a})$ *is a convex function of* $\mathbf{a}$. *Let* δ^* *be a randomized decision rule in* $\mathscr{D}^*$ *for which* $E^{\delta^*(x,\,\cdot)}[|\mathbf{a}|] < \infty$ *for all* $x \in \mathscr{X}$. *Then* (*subject to measurability conditions*) *the nonrandomized rule*

$$\delta(x) = E^{\delta^*(x,\,\cdot)}[\mathbf{a}]$$

has $L(\theta, \delta(x)) \leq L(\theta, \delta^*(x, \cdot))$ *for all* x *and* θ.

PROOF. From Lemma 2 it is clear that $\delta(x) \in \mathscr{A}$. Jensen's inequality then gives that

$$L(\theta, \delta(x)) = L(\theta, E^{\delta^*(x,\,\cdot)}[\mathbf{a}]) \leq E^{\delta^*(x,\,\cdot)}[L(\theta, \mathbf{a})] = L(\theta, \delta^*(x, \cdot)). \qquad \square$$

EXAMPLE 16. Let $\Theta = \mathscr{A} = R^1$ and $L(\theta, a) = (\theta - a)^2$. (The decision problem is thus to estimate θ under squared-error loss.) Clearly randomized rules $\delta^*(x, \cdot)$ must have $E^{\delta^*(x, \cdot)}[|a|] < \infty$ in order to have finite loss, so that, by the above theorem, $\delta(x) = E^{\delta^*(x, \cdot)}[a]$ has loss less than or equal to that of $\delta^*(x, \cdot)$ for all x and θ. Indeed since L is strictly convex, it can be shown that $\delta(x)$ has smaller loss than $\delta^*(x, \cdot)$ for all x for which $\delta^*(x, \cdot)$ is nondegenerate.

A second well-known consequence of Jensen's inequality is the Rao–Blackwell theorem.

Theorem 4 (Rao–Blackwell). *Assume that $\mathscr{A}$ is a convex subset of R^m and that $L(\theta, \mathbf{a})$ is a convex function of $\mathbf{a}$ for all $\theta \in \Theta$. Suppose also that T is a sufficient statistic for θ, and that $\delta^0(x)$ is a nonrandomized decision rule in $\mathscr{D}$. Then the decision rule, based on $T(x) = t$, defined by*

$$\delta^1(t) = E^{X|t}[\delta^0(X)],$$

is R-equivalent to or R-better than δ^0, provided the expectation exists.

PROOF. By the definition of a sufficient statistic, the expectation above does not depend on θ, so that δ^1 is an obtainable decision rule. By Jensen's inequality

$$L(\theta, \delta^1(t)) = L(\theta, E^{X|t}[\delta^0(X)]) \leq E^{X|t}[L(\theta, \delta^0(X))].$$

Hence

$$\begin{aligned}
R(\theta, \delta^1) &= E_\theta^T[L(\theta, \delta^1(T))] \\
&\leq E_\theta^T[E^{X|T}\{L(\theta, \delta^0(X))\}] \\
&= E_\theta^X[L(\theta, \delta^0(X))] \\
&= R(\theta, \delta^0).
\end{aligned} \qquad \square$$

Observe that the Rao–Blackwell theorem could have been obtained directly from Theorems 1 and 3. Theorem 1 and the ensuing discussion show that the rule defined by

$$\delta_1^*(t, A) = E^{X|t}[I_A(\delta^0(X))]$$

is equivalent to δ^0. Letting $\mu_X(A) = I_A(\delta^0(X))$, Theorem 3 then implies that

$$\delta^1(t) = E^{\delta_1^*(t, \cdot)}[\mathbf{a}] = E^{X|t}E^{\mu_X}[\mathbf{a}] = E^{X|t}[\delta^0(X)]$$

is R-equivalent to or R-better than δ^0.

When the loss is convex and there is a sufficient statistic T for θ, Theorems 1 and 3 can be combined to show that (from the viewpoint of risk) only nonrandomized rules based on T need be considered. This results in a great simplification of the problem.

Exercises

Sections 1.3 and 1.5

1. Let X have a $\mathcal{P}(\theta)$ distribution, $\Theta = (0, \infty)$ and $\mathcal{A} = [0, \infty)$. The loss function is
   $L(\theta, a) = (\theta - a)^2$. Consider decision rules of the form $\delta_c(x) = cx$. Assume $\pi(\theta) = e^{-\theta}$
   is the prior density.
   (a) Find $R(\theta, \delta_c)$.
   (b) Show that δ_c is inadmissible if $c > 1$.
   (c) Find $r(\pi, \delta_c)$.
   (d) Find the value of c which minimizes $r(\pi, \delta_c)$.
   (e) Find the best rule of the form δ_c in terms of the minimax principle.

2. An insurance company is faced with taking one of the following 3 actions: a_1: increase
   sales force by 10%; a_2: maintain present sales force; a_3: decrease sales force by 10%.
   Depending upon whether or not the economy is good (θ_1), mediocre (θ_2), or bad (θ_3),
   the company would expect to lose the following amounts of money in each case:

		Action Taken		
		a_1	a_2	a_3
State of Economy	θ_1	-10	-5	-3
	θ_2	-5	-5	-2
	θ_3	1	0	-1

   (a) Determine if each action is admissible or inadmissible.
   (b) The company believes that θ has the probability distribution $\pi(\theta_1) = 0.2$,
   $\pi(\theta_2) = 0.3$, $\pi(\theta_3) = 0.5$. Order the actions according to their Bayes risks and
   state the Bayes action.
   (c) Order the actions according to the minimax principle and find the minimax
   nonrandomized action.

3. A company has to decide whether to accept or reject a lot of incoming parts. (Label
   these actions a_1 and a_2 respectively.) The lots are of three types: θ_1 (very good), θ_2
   (acceptable), and θ_3 (bad). The loss $L(\theta_i, a_j)$ incurred in making the decision is given
   in the following table.

	a_1	a_2
θ_1	0	3
θ_2	1	2
θ_3	3	0

   The prior belief is that $\pi(\theta_1) = \pi(\theta_2) = \pi(\theta_3) = \frac{1}{3}$.
   (a) What is the Bayes action?
   (b) What is the minimax nonrandomized action?

4. A professional baseball team is concerned about attendance for the upcoming year. They must decide whether or not to implement a half-million dollar promotional campaign. If the team is a contender, they feel that $4 million in attendance revenues will be earned (regardless of whether or not the promotional campaign is implemented). Letting θ denote the team's proportion of wins, they feel the team will be a contender if $\theta \geq 0.6$. If $\theta < 0.6$, they feel their attendance revenues will be $1 + 5\theta$ million dollars without the promotional campaign, and $2 + \frac{10}{3}\theta$ million dollars with the promotional campaign. It is felt that θ has a $\mathscr{U}(0, 1)$ distribution.
   (a) Describe $\mathscr{A}$, Θ, and $L(\theta, a)$.
   (b) What is the Bayes action?
   (c) What is the minimax nonrandomized action?

5. A farmer has to decide whether or not to plant his crop early. If he plants early and no late frost occurs, he will gain $5000 in extra harvest. If he plants early and a late frost does occur, he will lose $2000 as the cost of reseeding. If he doesn't plant early his gain will be $0. Consulting the weather service, he finds that the chance of a late frost is about 0.6.
   (a) Describe $\mathscr{A}$, Θ, the loss matrix, and the prior distribution.
   (b) What is the Bayes action?
   (c) What is the minimax nonrandomized action?

6. The owner of a ski shop must order skis for the upcoming season. Orders must be placed in quantities of 25 pairs of skis. The cost *per pair* of skis is $50 if 25 are ordered, $45 if 50 are ordered, and $40 if 75 are ordered. The skis will be sold at $75 per pair. Any skis left over at the end of the year can be sold (for sure) at $25 a pair. If the owner runs out of skis during the season, he will suffer a loss of "goodwill" among unsatisfied customers. He rates this loss at $5 per unsatisfied customer. For simplicity, the owner feels that demand for the skis will be 30, 40, 50, or 60 pair of skis, with probabilities 0.2, 0.4, 0.2, and 0.2 respectively.
   (a) Describe $\mathscr{A}$, Θ, the loss matrix, and the prior distribution.
   (b) Which actions are admissible?
   (c) What is the Bayes action?
   (d) What is the minimax nonrandomized action?

7. Find the minimax (randomized) action in
   (a) Exercise 3.
   (b) Exercise 4.
   (c) Exercise 5.

8. In Example 2, what would be the Bayes action and what would be the minimax action if no sample information X was obtained?

Section 1.4

9. Assume that $n = 10$ and $\theta_0 = \frac{2}{3}$ in Example 7 (Section 1.4). Find the most powerful randomized test of size $\alpha = 0.05$.

Section 1.6

10. A coin has probability θ of turning up heads when flipped. It is known that $\theta = \frac{1}{3}$ or $\theta = \frac{2}{3}$, and it is desired to test $H_0 : \theta = \frac{1}{3}$ versus $H_1 : \theta = \frac{2}{3}$. The coin will be flipped 100 times, and the number of heads, x, observed. If $x < 50$, then H_0 will be accepted;

if $x > 50$, then H_1 will be accepted; and if $x = 50$, then H_0 and H_1 will each be accepted with probability $\frac{1}{2}$.
   (a) Before x is observed, calculate the probability that the above decision rule will result in an incorrect decision. (This is the initial precision.)
   (b) Assume $x = 50$ is observed. What (intuitively) is the probability of now making an incorrect decision? (This is the final precision.)

11. Show by a formal application of the likelihood principle (as in Example 12 (continued)) that the condition of the high-range voltmeter should have no effect on the statistical analysis in Example 13.

Sections 1.7 and 1.8

12. Assume a random variable $X \sim \mathscr{B}(n, \theta)$ is observed. It is desired to estimate θ under squared-error loss. Find a nonrandomized decision rule δ which is R-better than the randomized decision rule

$$\delta^* = \tfrac{1}{2}\langle \delta_1 \rangle + \tfrac{1}{2}\langle \delta_2 \rangle,$$

where $\delta_1(x) = x/n$ and $\delta_2(x) = \frac{1}{2}$. Also, calculate $R(\theta, \delta_1)$, $R(\theta, \delta_2)$, and $R(\theta, \delta^*)$.

13. Assume $X = (X_1, X_2, \ldots, X_n)$ is observed, where the X_i are (independently) $\mathcal{N}(\theta, 1)$. It is desired to estimate θ under a loss $L(\theta, a)$. Let $\tilde{X}$ denote the median of the observations, and note that the mean $\bar{X}$ is sufficient for θ.
   (a) Find the conditional density (on $\mathscr{X}_t$) of $(X_1, X_2, \ldots, X_{n-1})$ given $\bar{X}$.
   (b) Find a randomized rule, based on $\bar{X}$, which is R-equivalent to $\delta(\mathbf{x}) = \tilde{x}$. (The integration need not be performed.)
   (c) If the loss is convex in a, show that $\delta'(\mathbf{x}) = \bar{x}$ is R-better than or R-equivalent to $\delta(\mathbf{x}) = \tilde{x}$. (Hint: Show that $E^{X|\bar{X}=t}[\tilde{X}] = t$. Use a symmetry argument based on Part (a), noting that the $Z_i = X_i - \bar{X}$ ($i = 1, \ldots, n$) have the same distribution as the $-Z_i$ ($i = 1, \ldots, n$).)

14. Let $X = (X_1, X_2, \ldots, X_n)$ be a sample from the $\mathcal{U}(\alpha, \beta)$ distribution. It is desired to estimate the mean $\theta = (\alpha + \beta)/2$ under squared-error loss.
   (a) Show that $T = (\min\{X_i\}, \max\{X_i\})$ is a sufficient statistic for θ. (You may use the factorization theorem.)
   (b) Show that the estimator given by

$$E^{X|T}[\bar{X}] = \tfrac{1}{2}(\max\{X_i\} + \min\{X_i\})$$

is R-better than or R-equivalent to the sample mean $\bar{X}$.

15. Prove that the following functions are convex:
   (a) e^{cx}, for $-\infty < x < \infty$.
   (b) $x^c (c \geq 1)$, for $0 < x < \infty$.
   (c) $\sum_{i=1}^{m} c_i x_i$, for $\mathbf{x} = (x_1, \ldots, x_m)^t \in R^m$.

16. Prove that the following functions are concave:
   (a) $\log x$, for $0 < x < \infty$.
   (b) $(1 - e^{-cx})$, for $-\infty < x < \infty$.
   (c) $-\exp\{\sum_{i=1}^{m} c_i x_i\}$, for $\mathbf{x} = (x_1, \ldots, x_m)^t \in R^m$.

17. Which of the functions in Exercises 15 and 16 are strictly convex or strictly concave.

18. If $y_i \geq 0$, $i = 1, \ldots, m$, and $\alpha_i \geq 0$, $i = 1, \ldots, m$, with $\sum_{i=1}^{m} \alpha_i = 1$, then prove that $\prod_{i=1}^{m} y_i^{\alpha_i} \leq \sum_{i=1}^{m} \alpha_i y_i$. (Hint: Let $x_i = \log y_i$ and use Jensen's inequality.)

CHAPTER 2

Utility and Loss

2.1 Introduction

In evaluating the consequences of possible actions, two major problems are encountered. The first is that the values of the consequences may not have any obvious scale of measurement. For example, prestige, customer goodwill, and reputation are important to many businesses, but it is not clear how to evaluate their importance in a concrete way. A typical problem of this nature arises when a relatively exclusive company is considering marketing its "name" product in discount stores. The immediate profit which would accrue from increased sales is relatively easy to estimate, but the longterm effect of a decrease in prestige is much harder to deal with.

Even when there is a clear scale (usually monetary) by which consequences can be evaluated, the scale may not reflect true "value" to the decision maker. As an example, consider the value to you of money. Assume you have the opportunity to do a rather unpleasant task for $100. At your present income level, you might well value the $100 dollars enough to do the task. If, on the other hand, you first received a million dollars, the value to you of an additional $100 would be much less, and you would probably choose not to do the task. In other words, the value of $1,000,100 is probably not the same as the value of $1,000,000 plus the value of $100. As another example, suppose you are offered a choice between receiving a gift of $10,000 or participating (for free) in a gamble wherein you have a 50–50 chance of winning $0 or $25,000. Most of us would probably choose the sure $10,000. If this is the case, then the expected "value" of the gamble is less than $10,000. In the ensuing sections, a method of determining true value will be discussed. This will then be related to the development of the loss function.

40

2.2 Utility Theory

To work mathematically with ideas of "value," it will be necessary to assign numbers indicating how much something is valued. Such numbers are called *utilities*, and *utility theory* deals with the development of such numbers.

To begin, it is necessary to clearly delineate the possible consequences which are being considered. The set of all consequences of interest will be called the set of *rewards*, and will be denoted by $\mathcal{R}$. Quite frequently $\mathcal{R}$ will be the real line (such as when the consequences can be given in monetary terms), but often the elements of $\mathcal{R}$ will consist of nonnumerical quantities such as mentioned in the introduction.

Often there is uncertainty as to which of the possible consequences will actually occur. Thus the results of actions are frequently probability distributions on $\mathcal{R}$. Let $\mathcal{P}$ denote the set of all such probability distributions. It is usually necessary to work with values and preferences concerning probability distributions in $\mathcal{P}$. This would be easy to do if a real-valued function $U(r)$ could be constructed such that the "value" of a probability distribution $P \in \mathcal{P}$ would be given by the expected utility $E^P[U(r)]$. If such a function exists, it is called a *utility function*.

A precise formulation of the problem begins with the assumption that it is possible to state preferences among elements of $\mathcal{P}$. (If one cannot decide the relative worth of various consequences, there is no hope in trying to construct measures of their value.) The following notation will be used to indicate preferences.

Definition 1. If P_1 and P_2 are in $\mathcal{P}$, then $P_1 \prec P_2$ means that P_2 is preferred to P_1; $P_1 \approx P_2$ means that P_1 is equivalent to P_2; and $P_1 \preccurlyeq P_2$ means that P_1 is not preferred to P_2.

A reward $r \in \mathcal{R}$ will be identified with the probability distribution in $\mathcal{P}$ which gives probability one to the point r. This probability distribution will be denoted $\langle r \rangle$. (See Section 1.4 for a similar use of this notational device.) Hence the above definition applies also to rewards.

The goal is to find a function $U(r)$ which represents (through expected value) the true preference pattern on $\mathcal{P}$ of the decision maker. In other words, a function U is sought such that if P_1 and P_2 are in $\mathcal{P}$, then P_2 is preferred to P_1 if and only if

$$E^{P_1}[U(r)] < E^{P_2}[U(r)].$$

The function U is then the desired quantification of the decision maker's preferrence or value pattern, and can be called a utility function.

It is by no means clear that a utility function need exist. We will shortly give a brief discussion of certain conditions which guarantee the existence of a utility function. First, however, a useful method for constructing a utility function (assuming one exists) is given. In the construction, we will be concerned with mixtures of probability distributions of the form $P = \alpha P_1 + (1 - \alpha)P_2$, where $0 \leq \alpha \leq 1$. This, of course, is the probability distribution for which $P(A) = \alpha P_1(A) + (1 - \alpha)P_2(A)$, $A \subset \mathcal{R}$. Note, in particular, that $P = \alpha\langle r_1 \rangle + (1 - \alpha)\langle r_2 \rangle$ is the probability distribution giving probability α to r_1 and probability $1 - \alpha$ to r_2.

Construction of U

Step 1: To begin the construction of U, choose two rewards, r_1 and r_2, which are not equivalent. Assume they are labeled so that $r_1 \prec r_2$. Let $U(r_1) = 0$ and $U(r_2) = 1$.

Any choice of r_1 and r_2 is acceptable, but it is best to choose them in a convenient fashion. If there is a worst reward and a best reward, it is often convenient to choose r_1 and r_2 as these. For monetary rewards, choosing $r_1 = 0$ is usually helpful. The choice of r_1 and r_2 really serves only to set the scale for U. However, values of $U(r)$ for other r will be established by comparison with r_1 and r_2. Hence r_1 and r_2 should be chosen to make comparisons as easy as possible.

There are a variety of ways to proceed with the construction of U. One can simply compare each $r \in \mathcal{R}$ with r_1 and r_2, assigning a value, $U(r)$, to r which seems reasonable in comparison with $U(r_1) = 0$ and $U(r_2) = 1$. This is usually a difficult process, however, and it is often useful to consider "betting" situations as an aid to judgement. This is done as follows.

Step 2: For a reward r_3 such that $r_1 \prec r_3 \prec r_2$, find the α $(0 < \alpha < 1)$ such that

$$r_3 \approx P = \alpha\langle r_1 \rangle + (1 - \alpha)\langle r_2 \rangle.$$

Define

$$U(r_3) = E^P[U(r)] = \alpha U(r_1) + (1 - \alpha)U(r_2) = 1 - \alpha.$$

Determining α is the difficult part of the procedure. The idea is that since r_3 is preferred to r_1, while r_2 is preferred to r_3, there should be a "gamble," in which you get r_1 with probability α and r_2 with probability $(1 - \alpha)$, which is of the same value as r_3. Another way of stating this is to say that, if you were given reward r_3, you would be willing to "pay" it (but nothing better) in order to play the gamble $\alpha\langle r_1 \rangle + (1 - \alpha)\langle r_2 \rangle$. Such an α will virtually always exist and be unique. It takes practice at introspection to find it, however.

Step 3: For a reward r_3 such that $r_3 \prec r_1$, find the α $(0 < \alpha < 1)$ such that

$$r_1 \approx P = \alpha\langle r_3 \rangle + (1 - \alpha)\langle r_2 \rangle.$$

Then to have

$$0 = U(r_1) = E^P[U(r)] = \alpha U(r_3) + (1 - \alpha)U(r_2) = \alpha U(r_3) + (1 - \alpha),$$

we must define

$$U(r_3) = \frac{-(1 - \alpha)}{\alpha}.$$

Step 4: For a reward r_3 such that $r_2 \prec r_3$, find the α $(0 < \alpha < 1)$ such that

$$r_2 \approx P = \alpha\langle r_1 \rangle + (1 - \alpha)\langle r_3 \rangle.$$

Then to have

$$1 = U(r_2) = E^P[U(r)] = \alpha U(r_1) + (1 - \alpha)U(r_3) = (1 - \alpha)U(r_3),$$

we must define

$$U(r_3) = \frac{1}{1 - \alpha}.$$

Step 5: Periodically check the construction process for consistency by comparing new combinations of rewards. For example, assume the utilities of
r_3, r_4, and r_5 have been found by the preceding technique, and that $r_3 \prec r_4$
$\prec r_5$. Then find the α $(0 < \alpha < 1)$ such that

$$r_4 \approx P = \alpha\langle r_3 \rangle + (1 - \alpha)\langle r_5 \rangle.$$

It should then be true that

$$U(r_4) = \alpha U(r_3) + (1 - \alpha)U(r_5).$$

If this relationship is not (approximately) satisfied by the previously determined utilities, then an error has been made and the utilities must be altered
to attain consistency. This process of comparing and recomparing is often
how the best judgements can be made.

Recall that, for U to be a utility function, the expected utilities of the $P \in \mathscr{P}$
must be ordered in the same way as the true preferences concerning the P.
For this to be the case (and indeed for the above construction to be possible),
the preferences among elements of $\mathscr{P}$ must in some sense be rational. We list
here a set of "rationality axioms" which guarantee that the preference pattern
is suitable.

Axiom 1. If P_1 and P_2 are in $\mathscr{P}$, then either $P_1 \prec P_2$, $P_1 \approx P_2$, or $P_2 \prec P_1$.

Axiom 2. If $P_1 \preccurlyeq P_2$ and $P_2 \preccurlyeq P_3$, then $P_1 \preccurlyeq P_3$.

Axiom 3. If $P_1 \prec P_2$, then $\alpha P_1 + (1 - \alpha)P_3 \prec \alpha P_2 + (1 - \alpha)P_3$ for any
$0 < \alpha < 1$ and P_3 in $\mathscr{P}$.

Axiom 4. If $P_1 \prec P_2 \prec P_3$, there are numbers $0 < \alpha < 1$ and $0 < \beta < 1$ such that

$$\alpha P_1 + (1 - \alpha)P_3 \prec P_2 \quad \text{and} \quad P_2 \prec \beta P_1 + (1 - \beta)P_3.$$

Axiom 1 simply formalizes the requirement that one must be able to state preferences among the elements of $\mathscr{P}$. Axiom 2 requires a natural transitivity in the preference pattern. Axiom 3 is related to the conditionality principle discussed in Section 1.6, and also seems quite natural. It simply states that if P_2 is preferred to P_1, then, in a choice between two random situations which are identical except that P_2 will occur with probability α in one and P_1 with probability α in the other, the situation involving P_2 will be preferred. Axiom 4 says, in a loose sense, that there is no infinitely desirable or infinitely bad reward (no heaven or hell). If, for example, P_1 was considered to be infinitely bad, then presumably there would be no $\beta > 0$ for which one would risk having P_1 occur (with probability β) in an attempt to achieve P_3 instead of P_2 (i.e., for which $P_2 \prec \beta P_1 + (1 - \beta)P_3$). This axiom might be objected to, on the basis that a "reward" such as death is infinitely bad. If death was really felt to be infinitely bad compared to other consequences, however, one would never risk the additional chance of dying incurred by, say, crossing a street or driving a car.

For a proof that these axioms imply the existence of a utility function, see DeGroot (1970). (Some additional rather technical assumptions are needed to verify that the above construction results in a utility function.) The existence of a utility function is actually assured under even weaker axioms than those above. (See Rubin (1974).) Thus the preference pattern of any "rational" person can be described by a utility function.

It should be mentioned that utility functions are unique only for a particular scaling, i.e., a particular choice of the initial r_1 and r_2. Indeed if $U(r)$ is a utility function, then $bU(r) + c$ ($b > 0$) is also a utility function, since it leads to the same preferences among elements of $\mathscr{P}$. (If $E^{P_1}[U(r)] < E^{P_2}[U(r)]$, then $E^{P_1}[bU(r) + c] < E^{P_2}[bU(r) + c]$ and vice versa.) It is also of interest to note that Axiom 4 requires the utility function to be bounded. To see this, observe that if there exists a sequence of rewards $r_1, r_2, \ldots$ such that $U(r_n) \to \infty$, then a probability distribution $P = p_1\langle r_1 \rangle + p_2\langle r_2 \rangle + \cdots$ can always be found such that $E^P[U(r)] = \infty$. This will clearly lead to a violation of Axiom 4. (Choose P_3 in the statement of the axiom to be the above P.) A similar argument holds if $U(r_n) \to -\infty$. Although it is very reasonable to have a bounded utility function, a weaker set of axioms can be constructed under which unbounded utility functions are allowed.

EXAMPLE 1. You face the decision of what to do on a Saturday afternoon for recreation. There are two choices available: a_1—see a football game, and a_2—go to a movie. You would really rather see the football game, but there is a 40% chance of rain, which would ruin the afternoon. Let θ_1 denote the state of nature "it rains" and θ_2 denote "no rain." Clearly $\pi(\theta_1) = 0.4 =$

$1 - \pi(\theta_2)$. To carry out a Bayesian analysis as in Chapter 1, it is necessary to determine the loss matrix. Instead, let us consider the "utility matrix" (since loss will just be negative utility).

The four consequences or rewards of interest are $r_1 = (a_1, \theta_1)$, $r_2 = (a_1, \theta_2)$, $r_3 = (a_2, \theta_1)$, and $r_4 = (a_2, \theta_2)$. (Here (a_i, θ_j) denotes action a_i being taken and θ_j being the state of nature that occurs.) Clearly the preference ordering is

$$r_1 \prec r_4 \prec r_3 \prec r_2.$$

The reasoning is that r_1 is a ruined afternoon; r_4 is okay, but you will regret somewhat not having gone to the game since it didn't rain; r_3 is an enjoyable afternoon, and you congratulate yourself on making a good decision about the weather; and r_2 is the best afternoon.

To construct U it is natural to use the worst and best rewards, r_1 and r_2, as the initial points. Hence let $U(r_1) = 0$ and $U(r_2) = 1$. To determine $U(r_4)$, compare r_4 with the gamble $\alpha\langle r_1 \rangle + (1 - \alpha)\langle r_2 \rangle$. After some soul searching, assume it is concluded that r_4 is equivalent to $0.4\langle r_1 \rangle + 0.6\langle r_2 \rangle$. In other words, you would just as soon see the movie and have no rain occur, as you would play the gamble of having a ruined afternoon with probability 0.4 or the best afternoon with probability 0.6. Thus $U(r_4) = (1 - \alpha) = 0.6$. (It should be noted that there is nothing sacred about thinking in terms of gambles. If you decide r_4 rates as about a 0.6 on a scale from 0 to 1 (r_1 being 0 and r_2 being 1), that is fine. For many people, however, the gambling mechanism proves useful.) Likewise, let us say it is determined that

$$r_3 \approx 0.3\langle r_1 \rangle + 0.7\langle r_2 \rangle.$$

Then $U(r_3) = 1 - \alpha = 0.7$.

It is, at this point, a good idea to check the construction of U by comparing a different combination of rewards, say r_2, r_3, and r_4. Find an α such that

$$r_3 \approx \alpha\langle r_4 \rangle + (1 - \alpha)\langle r_2 \rangle.$$

Let's say $\alpha = 0.6$ is felt to be correct. But if the utility function is accurate, we know that

$$0.7 = U(r_3) = \alpha U(r_4) + (1 - \alpha)U(r_2) = 0.6\alpha + (1 - \alpha),$$

or $\alpha = 0.75$. This does not agree with the value of 0.6 that was obtained from direct comparison. Hence there is an inconsistency. It is thus necessary to go back and reexamine all the comparisons made, until a consistent set of utilities is obtained. Let us assume that the end result of this process is that $U(r_4) = 0.6$ and $U(r_3) = 0.75$ are decided upon.

Having the utility function, we can proceed directly to find the optimal action in terms of expected utility. (Recall that expected utility is, by construction, the proper way to evaluate uncertain rewards.) Clearly, the expected utility of action a_1 is

$$E^\pi[U(r)] = \pi(\theta_1)U(r_1) + \pi(\theta_2)U(r_2)$$
$$= (0.4)(0) + (0.6)(1) = 0.6,$$

while the expected utility of action a_2 is

$$E^\pi[U(r)] = \pi(\theta_1)U(r_3) + \pi(\theta_2)U(r_4)$$
$$= (0.4)(0.75) + (0.6)(0.6) = 0.66.$$

Thus the optimal action is to go to the movie.

When the set $\mathcal{R}$ is large, the construction of U becomes much more difficult. The formal construction procedure is time-consuming and can, hence, only be done at a few points of $\mathcal{R}$. Often, however, $U(r)$ at other points can be estimated from the values of U at these few points. A common situation in which this can be done is when $\mathcal{R}$ is an interval of the real line. $U(r)$ will then typically be a smooth function of r which can be graphed from knowledge at a few points. The most important example of this is when the rewards are monetary, so that U is a utility function for money. (This case will be treated separately in the next section.) Other situations in which $\mathcal{R}$ is an interval can arise, however. The following is an example.

EXAMPLE 2. A doctor must control the blood sugar count of a patient. The "reward" for a treatment he administers is the blood sugar count of the patient. The set of all rewards $\mathcal{R}$ can be taken to be the set of all reasonable blood sugar counts, and can be approximated by an interval $(B_{\min}, B_{\max})$. A reasonable utility function for this situation is given in Figure 2.1. B_N is the normal level, and has the highest utility. As the blood sugar count gets higher or lower, the utility drops. $U(r)$ could be reasonably sketched from values at a few points.

To determine a utility function that you know will behave as in Figure 2.1, it is useful to do the construction by segments. In this example, first construct $U(r)$ from $B_{\min}$ to B_N. Next find $U(B_{\max})$ by comparison of $B_{\max}$ to $B_{\min}$ and B_N. Then construct $U(r)$ from B_N to $B_{\max}$, using B_N and $B_{\max}$ as the reference

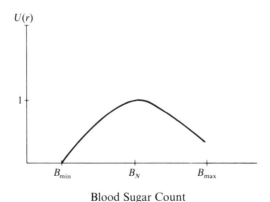

Blood Sugar Count

Figure 2.1

points in the construction. The needed changes in the formulas for $U(r)$ should be clear.

In many problems, the rewards are actually vectors $r = (r_1, r_2, \ldots, r_m)$. In medical situations, for example, a treatment could have several side effects upon the patient, besides the intended effect upon the illness. The resulting $\mathscr{R}$ would be a rectangle in R^m, and the construction of $U(r)$ on this set would be very difficult. It is often assumed in such situations that

$$U(r) = \sum_{i=1}^{m} K_i U_i(r_i). \tag{2.1}$$

The problem then simplifies to finding each of the one-dimensional utility functions $U_i(r_i)$, and then determining the *scaling constants* K_i. (These can be found by the same kind of comparison technique that is used in the construction of a utility function.) The simplifying assumption (2.1) need not always be reasonable, of course, especially when there is considerable "interaction" between coordinates of r. (Two side effects of a drug might be acceptable separately, but very dangerous if they occur together.) A more complicated model, such as

$$U(r) = \sum_{i=1}^{m} K_i U_i(r_i) + \sum_{i=1}^{m} \sum_{j=1}^{m} K_{ij} U_i(r_i) U_j(r_j),$$

might then prove satisfactory. Keeney and Raiffa (1976) deal with this problem in depth.

2.3 The Utility of Money

As indicated in the introduction, the marginal value of money for most people is decreasing. This means, for instance, that the difference in value between $\$(z + 100)$ and $\$z$ is decreasing as z increases. An additional $\$100$ is quite valuable when $z = 0$, but of little importance when $z = 1,000,000$. A typical utility function $U(r)$, for positive amounts of money r, is shown in Figure 2.2. Indeed the function typically levels off, i.e., is bounded. (I doubt if anyone would give much value to additional money beyond $\$10^{100}$.)

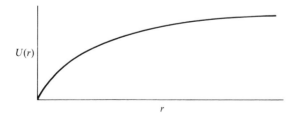

Figure 2.2

To get a better feeling for such a utility function, let's consider the construction of a personal utility function for money. In dealing with such a situation, there is a "backwards" method of construction (discussed in Becker, DeGroot, and Marschak (1964)) that is very useful. Begin, as before, by choosing $r_1 < r_2$ and setting $U(r_1) = 0$, $U(r_2) = 1$. (It is assumed that if $r_1 < r_2$ then $r_1 \prec r_2$.) The following steps will lead to a graph of $U(r)$ for $r_1 < r < r_2$.

Step 1. Find r_3 so that $U(r_3) = \frac{1}{2}$. Since, for $P = \frac{1}{2}\langle r_1 \rangle + \frac{1}{2}\langle r_2 \rangle$,

$$\tfrac{1}{2} = \tfrac{1}{2}U(r_1) + \tfrac{1}{2}U(r_2) = E^P[U(r)],$$

this is equivalent to finding the reward r_3 which is valued as highly as the gamble $\frac{1}{2}\langle r_1 \rangle + \frac{1}{2}\langle r_2 \rangle$. This type of 50–50 gamble is easy to think of, making the determination of r_3 relatively easy.

Step 2. Find r_4 and r_5 such that $U(r_4) = \frac{1}{4}$ and $U(r_5) = \frac{3}{4}$. Since

$$\tfrac{1}{4} = \tfrac{1}{2}U(r_1) + \tfrac{1}{2}U(r_3) \quad \text{and} \quad \tfrac{3}{4} = \tfrac{1}{2}U(r_3) + \tfrac{1}{2}U(r_2),$$

r_4 is obviously the point equivalent to the gamble $\frac{1}{2}\langle r_1 \rangle + \frac{1}{2}\langle r_3 \rangle$, and r_5 is the point equivalent to $\frac{1}{2}\langle r_3 \rangle + \frac{1}{2}\langle r_2 \rangle$.

Step 3. Since

$$U(r_3) = \tfrac{1}{2} = \tfrac{1}{2}U(r_4) + \tfrac{1}{2}U(r_5),$$

r_3 must be equivalent to the gamble $\frac{1}{2}\langle r_4 \rangle + \frac{1}{2}\langle r_5 \rangle$. This provides a very valuable check on the determinations made so far. If the two are not felt to be equivalent, it is necessary to reevaluate in Steps 1 and 2.

Step 4. Continue the above process of finding the points with utilities $i/2^n$ and checking for consistency, until a sufficient number of points have been found to enable a graph of $U(r)$ to be made.

The advantages of this second method of finding $U(r)$ are that only simple gambles of the form $\frac{1}{2}\langle r_i \rangle + \frac{1}{2}\langle r_j \rangle$ need be considered, and also that there is an easy check for consistency.

It is informative to construct a typical utility function for money using this approach. Consider a person, Mr. Jones, who earns \$10,000 per year and has \$500 in the bank. Let us construct a reasonable utility function for him on $\mathscr{R} = (-1000, 1000)$. This will be a utility function for the value of *additional* money which Mr. Jones might receive (or lose). A utility function could be constructed for the value Mr. Jones places on his total "fortune." It tends to be somewhat easier, however, to think in terms of the value of changes from the status quo. (Actually, if $U(r)$ is a utility function for total fortune (which happens to be r_0 at the moment), then the utility function for additional money, m, should be

$$U^*(m) = U(m + r_0) - U(r_0).$$

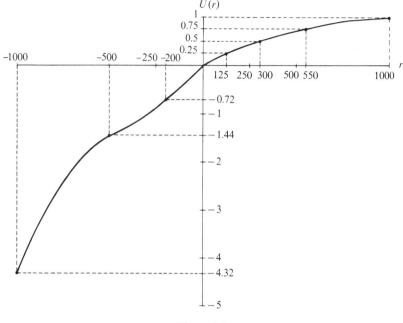

Figure 2.3

Generally, however, the utility function of a person will change with time, so that, if feasible, it is probably best to develop directly the utility function for additional money in each new situation.)

It is easiest to do the construction in three segments: $(-1000, -500)$, $(-500, 0)$, and $(0, 1000)$. Starting with $(0, 1000)$, set $U(0) = 0$, $U(1000) = 1$. Next, determine r so that $r \approx \frac{1}{2}\langle 0 \rangle + \frac{1}{2}\langle 1000 \rangle$. (Recall that this signifies that the rewards zero and 1000 each have probability $\frac{1}{2}$ of occurring.) Mr. Jones might reasonably decide that a sure reward of $r = 300$ is as good as a 50–50 chance at 0 or 1000. Hence $U(300) = \frac{1}{2}$. Let us say he next decides that $100 \approx \frac{1}{2}\langle 0 \rangle + \frac{1}{2}\langle 300 \rangle$ and $500 \approx \frac{1}{2}\langle 300 \rangle + \frac{1}{2}\langle 1000 \rangle$. Then $U(100) = \frac{1}{4}$ and $U(500) = \frac{3}{4}$. To check for consistency, he determines an r such that $r \approx \frac{1}{2}\langle 100 \rangle + \frac{1}{2}\langle 500 \rangle$. He deems $r = 250$ to be appropriate. Unfortunately this is inconsistent, in that the answer should have been $r = 300$. Through reexamination, Mr. Jones arrives at the consistent choices $U(125) = \frac{1}{4}$, $U(300) = \frac{1}{2}$, $U(550) = \frac{3}{4}$. Using these, he sketches $U(r)$ as indicated in Figure 2.3.

Turning next to the interval $(-500, 0)$, the first step is to determine $U(-500)$. Mr. Jones decides he can best compare -500, 0, and 500. Indeed he feels

$$0 \approx \tfrac{1}{3}\langle -500 \rangle + \tfrac{2}{3}\langle 500 \rangle.$$

Noting from Figure 2.3 that $U(500) \cong 0.72$, it follows that

$$0 = U(0) = \tfrac{1}{3}U(-500) + \tfrac{2}{3}(0.72),$$

or $U(-500) = -1.44$. It is next determined that $-200 \approx \frac{1}{2}\langle 500 \rangle + \frac{1}{2}\langle 0 \rangle$, so that $U(-200) = \frac{1}{2}U(-500) + \frac{1}{2}U(0) = -0.72$. Two more halfway points are determined, and the curve between -500 and 0 sketched.

Finally, the interval $(-1000, -500)$ must be dealt with. In comparing -1000 to -500 and 0, it is determined that $-500 \approx \frac{1}{3}\langle -1000 \rangle + \frac{2}{3}\langle 0 \rangle$. (Mr. Jones is very averse to losing more money than he has.) Hence

$$-1.44 = U(-500) = \tfrac{1}{3}U(-1000) + \tfrac{2}{3}U(0),$$

or $U(-1000) = -4.32$. It would be a good idea to check this for consistency by comparison of, say, 0 with -1000 and 1000. Other halfway points are found, and the sketch of $U(r)$ completed.

Note that $U(r)$ is concave, except for the segment from -500 to 0. In this segment, Mr. Jones is apparently willing to engage in slightly unfavorable gambles to possibly avoid a sure loss of money. For example, since $U(0) = 0$, $U(-500) = -1.44$, and $U(-210) \cong -0.75$, it is clear that $\frac{1}{2}\langle -500 \rangle + \frac{1}{2}\langle 0 \rangle$ is preferred to -210. ($U(-210) = -0.75 < -0.72 = \frac{1}{2}U(-500) + \frac{1}{2}U(0)$.) Mr. Jones would rather take a 50–50 chance at losing all or nothing than lose a sure \$210.

Several features of utility functions such as that above are of interest.

(i) $U(r)$ is approximately linear for small values of r. I, personally, would be quite willing to take a 50–50 gamble on winning or losing 25¢. Hence I am sure that my utility function is linear up to 25¢. Professional gamblers would probably feel the same way about amounts up to several hundred or thousand dollars. General Motors probably feels the same way about amounts into the hundreds of thousands or millions of dollars. In other words, General Motors would not be averse to, say, participating in a speculative project where \$500,000 could be lost, as long as the expected outcome was reasonably high. (They would want some expected profit of course.) Thus as a general rule, when r is small compared to, say, the income of the person or business involved, $U(r)$ can be treated as linear.

(ii) $U(r)$ is usually concave (at least for $r > 0$). This is due to the fact that the marginal utility of money is typically decreasing. The marginal utility of money can be thought of as $U'(r) = dU(r)/dr$. If $U'(r)$ is decreasing, then $dU'(r)/dr = U''(r) < 0$, which implies that U is concave.

(iii) $U(r)$ is often quite different for $r \geq 0$ and $r < 0$ (different in shape, not just sign). It is, therefore, generally desirable to construct $U(r)$ separately for $r \geq 0$ and $r < 0$.

(iv) $U(r)$ is typically bounded. (Thus there usually exists a $B < \infty$ such that $|U(r)| \leq B$ for all $r \in \mathcal{R}$.) As an example, few people would feel that additional money beyond $\$10^{100}$ is of much utility, so $U(10^{100})$ is pretty close to an upper bound on U.

This last property of U provides an interesting resolution to the so called St. Petersburg paradox. This paradox arises from consideration of the following gambling game. A fair coin will be flipped until a tail first appears. The reward will be 2^n, where n is the number of flips it takes until a tail appears. The expected value of the game is

$$\sum_{n=1}^{\infty} 2^n P(n \text{ flips}) = \sum_{n=1}^{\infty} 2^n \cdot \frac{1}{2^n} = \infty.$$

In spite of this, few people are willing to pay very much money to play the game, since the probability of winning much money is small. (For example, the probability of winning 16 or more dollars is only $\frac{1}{8}$.) Utility theory resolves the paradox by showing that, if it costs c dollars to play the game, then the true value of playing is

$$\sum_{n=1}^{\infty} U(2^n - c) \cdot 2^{-n},$$

where U is the utility function for a change in fortune (with, say, $U(0) = 0$). One should or should not play the game, depending upon whether this quantity is positive or negative. It will be left as an exercise to show that, for typical utility functions, this quantity is negative when c is large.

A parametric utility theory for money has been suggested. The motivation for such a theory arises from the observation that many real life utility functions can be matched quite well to curves of certain functional forms. The most commonly suggested functional form is

$$U(r) = b \log(cr + 1). \tag{2.2}$$

(Throughout the book, "log" will denote logarithm to the base e.) The constant c is generally chosen to be quite small, so that $U(r) \cong bcr$ for small or moderate $|r|$. Also, $U(r)$ is concave, and, while not bounded, is fairly level. Hence the usual properties of a utility function for money are satisfied by this function. The parametric approach suggests that, rather than going through the difficult procedure of constructing U, one should just choose b and c in (2.2) until $U(r)$ seems reasonable. This can be easily done by obtaining $U(r)$ at two points (other than $r = 0$) by the usual method, and then solving for b and c. Keeney and Raiffa (1976) discuss this and other parametric models.

2.4 The Loss Function

As in Example 1, analysis of a decision problem can be done in terms of a utility function. Each pair (θ, a) (θ the state of nature and a the action) determines some reward r, which has utility $U(r)$. This can, for convenience, be denoted $U(\theta, a)$, and represents the true gain to the statistician when action a is taken and θ turns out to be the true state of nature.

A slight confusion can arise when θ is a statistical parameter. The problem is that then θ and a will seldom directly determine the reward. A typical example is when a business does a marketing survey concerning a new product. From the survey, they hope to obtain an estimate of θ, the proportion of the population that would be interested in buying the product. What they are really interested in, of course, is their ultimate profit, which depends upon how many people actually buy the product. This will depend upon a number of extraneous factors, the state of the economy being one. These factors are typically random themselves. Thus the ultimate reward for taking action a when θ is the true state of nature is a random variable, say Z, which has a distribution depending upon θ and a. In such a situation, it is of course proper to define

$$U(\theta, a) = E_{\theta, a}[U(Z)].$$

It would have been logically correct to define θ at the beginning as the overall state of nature, i.e., θ would not only have a component representing the proportion of interested buyers, but would also have components reflecting all the other uncertain factors. In practice, however, it is intuitively easier to separate the components about which statistical information will be obtained, from the components for which only guesses can be made. This is in part because the statistical analysis tends to be more complicated, and in part because the nonstatistical randomness is usually easier to think about when isolated. Thus, in the previous marketing example, it seems best to proceed by (i) determining $U(r)$, where r here stands for profits, (ii) determining the distribution of the random variable Z (which is again profits) for given θ and a, and (iii) calculating $U(\theta, a) = E_{\theta, a}[U(Z)]$. Chapter 3 will present some useful techniques for carrying out step (ii).

In situations such as discussed above, one must be careful to define Z as the *overall* outcome of the random situation. The following example indicates the reason for caution.

EXAMPLE 3. Consider the following game. A coin is to be flipped n times. Each toss is independent of the others, and on any given toss the coin has probability 0.6 of coming up heads. For every toss on which the coin comes up heads, $1000 is won, while for every tail $1000 is lost. Let Z_i denote the amount won (1000 or -1000) on the ith flip of the coin. Assume that the utility function for a change, r, in monetary fortune is

$$U(r) = \begin{cases} r^{1/3} & \text{if } r \geq 0, \\ 2r^{1/3} & \text{if } r < 0. \end{cases}$$

For $n = 1$, the outcome of the game is Z_1, and the expected utility of the outcome is

$$E[U(Z_1)] = (0.6)U(1000) + (0.4)U(-1000)$$
$$= (0.6)(10) + (0.4)(-20) = -2.$$

Since this is negative, it would not be desirable to play the game with only one flip.

For $n > 1$, it would be wrong to say that the expected utility is $\sum_{i=1}^{n} E[U(Z_i)] = -2n$. The true outcome is $Z = \sum_{i=1}^{n} Z_i$, and the correct expected utility is $E[U(Z)]$. For large enough n, this will be positive, in which case it would be desirable to play the game. (It will be left as an exercise to determine how large n needs to be.)

The idea in the above example is rather obvious, but it has some disturbing implications. Consider, for instance, a business which is trying to decide whether or not to market a new product, and also whether or not to buy a new computer. If the financial results of given actions in the two decision problems are outcomes Z_1 and Z_2 (possibly random) which will both occur in the same time period of interest, then decisions should be based on overall expected utility, namely $E[U(Z_1 + Z_2)]$. This means that problems for a decision maker cannot be considered in isolation, but must be combined together in one grand mélange. In a sense, this is natural. A business, for instance, must consider the overall financial picture in deciding on specific issues. Nevertheless, this need to combine problems can impose a considerable hardship on the decision maker trying to construct a loss function.

The above difficulty does not arise when the utility function is linear. This is because a linear utility function satisfies $U(\sum Z_i) = \sum U(Z_i)$. Hence for linear utility, decision problems can be considered separately.

Once $U(\theta, a)$ has been obtained, the loss function can simply be defined as

$$L(\theta, a) = -U(\theta, a). \tag{2.3}$$

The desire to maximize utility then becomes the desire to minimize loss. By developing L through the utility theory construction, we also have the important fact that expected loss is the proper measure of loss in random situations. This justifies the use of expected loss as a decision criterion when talking about randomized rules, risks, and Bayes risks.

Note that any linear function of L, such as $bL(\theta, a) + c$ $(b > 0)$, could serve as the loss function as well as $L(\theta, a)$. This is because an optimal action or decision rule, obtained from any reasonable decision principle, is the same for all such linearly transformed losses. For example, the Bayes principle chooses δ to minimize

$$E^{\pi}[R(\theta, \delta)] = E^{\pi}E^{X}_{\theta}L(\theta, \delta(X)).$$

The δ which minimizes this will clearly also minimize

$$b(E^{\pi}E^{X}_{\theta}[L(\theta, \delta(X))]) + c = E^{\pi}E^{X}_{\theta}[bL(\theta, \delta(X)) + c],$$

which is the Bayes risk for the linearly transformed loss.

Loss functions are usually bounded from below, i.e.,

$$\inf_{\theta} \inf_{a} L(\theta, a) = B > -\infty.$$

In such situations, the transformed loss function

$$L^*(\theta, a) = L(\theta, a) - B$$

will always be nonnegative. It is convenient to talk in terms of nonnegative losses, so it will often be assumed that the above transformation has been made. Note also that, when derived from a utility function, the loss L^* can be written as

$$L^*(\theta, a) = \sup_\theta \sup_a U(\theta, a) - U(\theta, a).$$

This actually seems somewhat more sensible as a measure of loss than does the earlier definition in (2.3), in that $L^*(\theta, a)$ measures the true amount "lost" by not having the most favorable possibility occur. The analysis with L^* will not differ from the analysis with L, however. (It could be argued that the true amount "lost" is $\bar{L}(\theta, a) = \sup_a U(\theta, a) - U(\theta, a)$, since one has no control over which θ occurs. This loss is called *regret loss*, and will be discussed in Subsection 5.4.5. Interestingly enough, $\bar{L}$ is equivalent to L and L^* for Bayesian analysis, but can lead to different, and generally more reasonable, results for other decision principles.)

In making a decision or evaluating a decision rule, the loss function should, ideally, be developed as above. Often, however, analyses of decision rules are carried out for certain "standard" losses. Three of these will be briefly discussed.

I. *Squared-Error Loss*

The loss function $L(\theta, a) = (\theta - a)^2$ is called *squared-error loss*. There are a number of reasons why it is often considered in evaluating decision rules. It was originally used in estimation problems when unbiased estimators of θ were being considered, since $R(\theta, \delta) = E_\theta L(\theta, \delta(X)) = E_\theta[\theta - \delta(X)]^2$ would then be the variance of the estimator. A second reason for the popularity of squared-error loss is due to its relationship to classical least-squares theory. The similarity between the two makes squared-error loss seem familiar to statisticians. Finally, for most decision analyses, the use of squared-error loss makes the calculations relatively straightforward and simple.

The above justifications for squared-error loss really have very little merit. The question is—does squared-error loss typically reflect the true loss function in a given situation? The initial reaction is, probably, no. As in the discussion of utility theory, one can reason that the loss function should usually be bounded and (at least for large errors) concave. Squared-error loss is neither of these. The convexity of squared-error loss is particularly disturbing. (Large errors are penalized, perhaps, much too severely.)

There are a number of situations, however, in which squared-error loss may be appropriate. For example, in many statistical problems for which a loss symmetric in $(\theta - a)$ is suitable, the exact functional form of the loss is not crucial to the conclusion. Squared-error loss may then be a useful approximation to the true loss. Several problems of this nature will be encountered in later chapters.

Another situation in which squared-error loss can arise is when

$$L(\theta, a) = -U(\theta, a) = -E_{\theta, a}[U(Z)], \qquad (2.4)$$

as mentioned earlier. Exercise 14 deals with such a situation, and shows how a loss similar to squared-error loss can occur naturally.

If, more generally, the sample information is quite accurate in a problem with a loss as in (2.4), then $L(\theta, a)$ can frequently be approximated by squared-error loss. For example, assume $Z = h(\theta - a, Y)$, where the distribution of Y does not depend on θ or a. (The reward is thus a function of the accuracy of estimating θ (as measured by $\theta - a$) and some random variable Y which does not depend on θ or a. For example, Y could be a random variable reflecting the future state of the economy.) For convenience, define $g(\theta - a, Y) = U(h(\theta - a, Y))$. Since the sample information about θ is quite accurate, $\theta - a$ will be small. Thus $g(\theta - a, Y)$ can be expanded in a Taylor series about 0, giving

$$g(\theta - a, Y) \cong g(0, Y) + (\theta - a)g'(0, Y) + \tfrac{1}{2}(\theta - a)^2 g''(0, Y).$$

(The derivatives are, of course, with respect to the first argument of g. Higher-order terms will tend to be negligible because they involve higher powers of the small $(\theta - a)$.) Letting

$$K_1 = -E^Y[g(0, Y)], \qquad K_2 = -E[g'(0, Y)], \quad \text{and} \quad K_3 = -\tfrac{1}{2}E[g''(0, Y)],$$

it follows that

$$L(\theta, a) = -E[U(Z)] \cong K_1 + K_2(\theta - a) + K_3(\theta - a)^2.$$

Completing squares gives

$$L(\theta, a) \cong K_3\left(\theta - a + \frac{K_2}{2K_3}\right)^2 + \left(K_1 - \frac{K_2^2}{4K_3}\right).$$

Providing K_3 is a positive constant, this loss is equivalent (for decision making) to the transformed loss

$$L(\theta, a) = \left(\theta - a + \frac{K_2}{2K_3}\right)^2.$$

This would be squared-error loss if it weren't for the constant $K_2/2K_3$. When $K_2 = 0$ (which would occur if $g(0, y)$ was a symmetric function of y, and Y had a symmetric distribution), there is no problem. Otherwise, however, the constant represents the fact that either overestimation or underestimation (depending on the sign of K_2) is desired.

To analyze a decision problem with

$$L(\theta, a) = (\theta - a + c)^2,$$

merely consider the new action space

$$\mathcal{A}^* = \{a - c : a \in \mathcal{A}\}.$$

For $a^* \in \mathcal{A}^*$, the loss corresponding to L is $L^*(\theta, a^*) = (\theta - a^*)^2$. The analysis in this transformed problem is thus done with squared-error loss. If δ^* is an optimal decision rule in the transformed problem, then $\delta = \delta^* + c$ will be optimal in the original problem.

A generalization of squared-error loss, which is of interest, is

$$L(\theta, a) = w(\theta)(\theta - a)^2.$$

This loss is called *weighted squared-error loss*, and has the attractive feature of allowing the squared error, $(\theta - a)^2$, to be weighted by a function of θ. This will reflect the fact that a given error in estimation often varies in harm according to what θ happens to be.

The final variant of squared-error loss which will be considered is quadratic loss. If $\boldsymbol{\theta} = (\theta_1, \ldots, \theta_p)^t$ is a vector to be estimated by $\mathbf{a} = (a_1, \ldots, a_p)^t$, and $\mathbf{Q}$ is a $p \times p$ positive definite matrix, then

$$L(\boldsymbol{\theta}, \mathbf{a}) = (\boldsymbol{\theta} - \mathbf{a})^t \mathbf{Q} (\boldsymbol{\theta} - \mathbf{a})$$

is called *quadratic loss*. When $\mathbf{Q}$ is diagonal, this reduces to

$$L(\boldsymbol{\theta}, \mathbf{a}) = \sum_{i=1}^{p} q_i (\theta_i - a_i)^2,$$

and is a natural extension of squared-error loss to the multivariate situation.

II. *Linear Loss*

When the utility function is approximately linear (as is often the case over a reasonable segment of the reward space), the loss function will tend to be linear. Thus of interest is the *linear loss*

$$L(\theta, a) = \begin{cases} K_0(\theta - a) & \text{if } \theta - a \geq 0, \\ K_1(a - \theta) & \text{if } \theta - a < 0. \end{cases}$$

The constants K_0 and K_1 can be chosen to reflect the relative importance of underestimation and overestimation. These constants will usually be different. When they are equal, the loss is equivalent to

$$L(\theta, a) = |\theta - a|,$$

which is called *absolute error loss*. If K_0 and K_1 are functions of θ, the loss will be called *weighted linear loss*. Linear loss (or weighted linear loss) is quite often a useful approximation to the true loss.

III. *"0–1" Loss*

In the two-action decision problem (of which hypothesis testing is an example) it is typically the case that a_0 is "correct" if $\theta \in \Theta_0$, and a_1 is correct if $\theta \in \Theta_1$. (This could correspond to testing $H_0 : \theta \in \Theta_0$ versus $H_1 : \theta \in \Theta_1$.) The loss

$$L(\theta, a_i) = \begin{cases} 0 & \text{if } \theta \in \Theta_i, \\ 1 & \text{if } \theta \in \Theta_j \, (j \neq i), \end{cases}$$

is called "0–1" *loss*. In words, this loss is zero if a correct decision is made, and 1 if an incorrect decision is made. The interest in this loss arises from the fact that, in a testing situation, the risk function of a decision rule (or test) $\delta(x)$ is simply

$$R(\theta, \delta) = E_\theta[L(\theta, \delta(X))] = P_\theta(\delta(X) \text{ is the incorrect decision}).$$

This is either a probability of type I or type II error, depending on whether $\theta \in \Theta_0$ or $\theta \in \Theta_1$.

In practice, "0–1" loss will rarely be a good approximation to the true loss. More realistic losses are

$$L(\theta, a_i) = \begin{cases} 0 & \text{if } \theta \in \Theta_i, \\ K_i & \text{if } \theta \in \Theta_j \, (i \neq j), \end{cases}$$

and

$$L(\theta, a_i) = \begin{cases} 0 & \text{if } \theta \in \Theta_i, \\ K_i(\theta) & \text{if } \theta \in \Theta_j \, (i \neq j). \end{cases}$$

Actually, even when a "correct" decision is made, $L(\theta, a)$ may very well be nonzero, so that the full generality of the loss may be needed. Note, however, that only two functions, $L(\theta, a_0)$ and $L(\theta, a_1)$, must be determined.

For the most part, examples in the book will use the above three losses or variants of them. This is done mainly to make the calculations relatively easy. It should be emphasized that these losses need not necessarily be suitable for a given problem. Indeed, about the only way to decide if they are suitable is to do a utility analysis. When the standard losses are not felt to be reasonable, an analysis with an appropriate utility loss should be carried out. Typically, such an analysis will require a calculator or computer to carry out the calculations, but that is no great hardship in these days of computerized statistics.

2.5 Criticisms

The classical statistician will attack the use of loss functions as (i) nonobjective, (ii) difficult, and (iii) inaccurate. The first criticism refers once again to the difference between decision problems and inference problems. When trying to advance the general state of knowledge, objectivity is a desirable trait—i.e., personal prejudices should intrude as little as possible. (It can happen, however, that, even in inference, the consideration of loss functions is unavoidable.) When trying to make a decision, on the other hand, asking for objectivity is obviously silly. We should use all the information at our disposal to make the best decision, even if the information is very personal, as are utilities.

The second criticism is justified. The construction of an accurate loss function and the subsequent analysis can be time consuming. Unfortunately, there is no good alternative. The amount of time that one is willing to spend must of course depend on the importance of the problem. For a problem of little value, only crude estimates of loss need be obtained. At the other extreme, problems of great importance may deserve exhaustive utility analyses. It may be hard, but it's the only game in town besides inspired guesswork.

The third criticism is also valid. It is hard to accurately determine the loss, and inaccuracies may lead to bad decisions. The real point here is that the mathematical development may lead one blindly to a conclusion which is bad. This will be seen to be a real danger when trying to use prior information, and can also arise through consideration of the loss.

A method of investigating this problem is through a study of robustness. By *robustness* is meant the sensitivity of the performance of a decision rule to assumptions in the model about which one feels uncertain (to paraphrase Herman Rubin). Here, for example, it is useful to study the robustness of a decision rule with respect to the loss function. When the loss function is changed in a plausible manner, is the decision rule still pretty much the same or has it changed drastically? In the former case, the rule is robust and can be used with confidence. In the latter case, great care must be taken. In business and economics, an investigation as to robustness is called *sensitivity analysis*.

Much of the criticism of decision theory is aimed at the use of "convenience losses," such as those discussed in the preceding section. It is always tempting to take the easy path and use a simple "standard loss," with possibly bad results. This criticism is directed at the misuse of decision theory, however, rather than at decision theory proper. Nevertheless, exceptional concern with the misuse of decision theory is justified, because of the fact that, through an improper choice of the prior and loss, a statistician can reach any conclusion he desires! (Just make the other conclusions too costly or too "improbable" according to prior information.) Hence a special guard must be mounted against misuse of decision theory.

Exercises

1. Determine your utilities for the grade you will receive in this course. (A, B, C, D, and F are the possibilities.) Include at least one check for consistency.

2. Let $\mathscr{R}$ consist of three elements, r_1, r_2, and r_3. Assume that $r_3 \prec r_2 \prec r_1$. The utility function is $U(r_3) = 0$, $U(r_2) = u$, and $U(r_1) = 1$, where $0 < u < 1$.

(a) If $P = (p_1, p_2, p_3)$ and $Q = (q_1, q_2, q_3)$ are two elements of $\mathscr{P}$ (i.e., probability distributions on $\mathscr{R}$), state a numerical condition (in terms of the p_i, q_j, and u) under which $P \prec Q$.

(b) Assume $(0.3, 0.3, 0.4) \prec (0.5, 0, 0.5)$. What can you say about the relationship between $(0.2, 0.5, 0.3)$ and $(0.4, 0.2, 0.4)$? What can you say about u?

3. Sketch your personal utility function for changes in monetary fortune over the interval from $\$-1,000$ to $\$1,000$.

4. Without referring to your utility function as sketched in Exercise 3, decide which gamble you prefer in each of the following pairs:
(a) $\frac{1}{4}\langle 250 \rangle + \frac{3}{4}\langle 0 \rangle$ or $\frac{1}{2}\langle 40 \rangle + \frac{1}{2}\langle 70 \rangle$;
(b) $\frac{1}{2}\langle 400 \rangle + \frac{1}{2}\langle -100 \rangle$ or $\frac{2}{3}\langle 150 \rangle + \frac{1}{3}\langle 0 \rangle$;
(c) $\frac{1}{2}\langle 1000 \rangle + \frac{1}{2}\langle -1000 \rangle$ or $\frac{1}{2}\langle 50 \rangle + \frac{1}{2}\langle -50 \rangle$.
Now find which gamble would be preferred in Parts (a) to (c), as determined by your utility function constructed in Exericse 3. If there is a discrepancy, revise your sketch.

5. Try to find constants b and c so that, for $0 \le r \le 1000$,

$$U(r) = b \log(cr + 1)$$

matches the utility function you constructed in Exercise 3.

6. Mr. Rubin has determined that his utility function for a change in fortune on the interval $-100 \le r \le 500$ is

$$U(r) = (0.62)\log[(0.004)r + 1].$$

(a) He is offered a choice between $\$100$ and the chance to participate in a gamble wherein he wins $\$0$ with probability $\frac{2}{3}$ and $\$500$ with probability $\frac{1}{3}$. Which should he choose?

(b) Suppose he is offered instead a chance to *pay* $\$100$ to participate in the gamble. Should he do it?

7. A person is given a stake of $m > 0$ dollars, which he can allocate between an event A of fixed probability α $(0 < \alpha < 1)$ and its complement A^c. Let x $(0 \le x \le m)$ be the amount he allocates to A, so that $(m - x)$ is the amount allocated to A^c. The person's reward is the amount he has allocated to either A or A^c, which ever actually occurs. Thus he can choose among all gambles of the form $[\alpha\langle x \rangle + (1 - \alpha)\langle m - x \rangle]$. Being careful to consider every possible pair of values of α and m, find the optimal allocation of the m dollars when the person's utility function U is defined on the interval $[0, m]$ of monetary gains as follows:
(a) $U(r) = r^\beta$, where $\beta > 1$.
(b) $U(r) = r$.
(c) $U(r) = r^\beta$, where $0 < \beta < 1$.
(d) $U(r) = \log(r + 1)$.

8. Which of the utility functions in Exercise 7 are concave and which are convex?

9. (DeGroot (1970)) Assume that Mr. A and Mr. B have the same utility function for a change, x, in their fortune, given by $U(x) = x^{1/3}$. Suppose now that one of the two men receives, as a gift, a lottery ticket which yields either a reward of r dollars $(r > 0)$ or a reward of 0 dollars, with probability $\frac{1}{2}$ each. Show that there exists a number $b > 0$ having the following property: Regardless of which man receives the

lottery ticket, he can sell it to the other man for b dollars and the sale will be advantageous to both men.

10. An investor has $1000 to invest in speculative stocks. He is considering investing m dollars in stock A and $(1000 - m)$ dollars in stock B. An investment in stock A has a 0.6 chance of doubling in value, and a 0.4 chance of being lost. An investment in stock B has a 0.7 chance of doubling in value, and a 0.3 chance of being lost. The investor's utility function for a change in fortune, x, is $U(x) = \log(0.0007x + 1)$ for $-1000 \le x \le 1000$.
    (a) What is $\mathscr{R}$ (for a fixed m)? (It consists of four elements.)
    (b) What is the optimal value of m in terms of expected utility?
    (*Note*: This perhaps indicates why most investors opt for a diversified portfolio of stocks.)

11. Consider the gambling game described in the St. Petersburg paradox, and assume that the utility function for a change in fortune, x, is given by

$$U(x) = \begin{cases} 100 & \text{if } x > 100, \\ x & \text{if } |x| \le 100, \\ -100 & \text{if } x < -100. \end{cases}$$

Find the largest amount c that one should be willing to pay to play the game.

12. Consider the gambling game described in the St. Petersburg paradox, and assume that the utility function, $U(x)$, for a change in fortune, x, is bounded, monotonically increasing on R^1, and satisfies $U(0) = 0$. Show that the utility of playing the game is negative for a large enough cost c.

13. For which n in Example 3 is the expected utility positive?

14. An automobile company is about to introduce a new type of car into the market. It must decide how many of these new cars to produce. Let a denote the number of cars decided upon. A market survey will be conducted, with information obtained pertaining to θ, the proportion of the population which plans on buying a car and would tend to favor the new model. The company has determined that the major outside factor affecting the purchase of automobiles is the state of the economy. Indeed, letting Y denote an appropriate measure of the state of the economy, it is felt that $Z = (1 + Y)(10^7)\theta$ cars could be sold. Y is unknown, but is thought to have a $\mathscr{U}(0, 1)$ distribution.
    Each car produced will be sold at a profit of $500, unless the supply (a) exceeds the demand (Z). If $a > Z$, the extra $a - Z$ cars can be sold at a loss of $300 each. The company's utility function for money is linear (say $U(m) = m$) over the range involved. Determine $L(\theta, a)$. (The answer is

$$L(\theta, a) = \begin{cases} -500a & \text{if } \dfrac{a}{10^7} \le \theta, \\[2mm] \dfrac{(4225)(10^7)}{40}\left[\dfrac{8}{13(10^7)}a - \theta\right]^2 - \dfrac{(2625)(10^7)\theta}{4} & \text{if } \theta \le \dfrac{a}{10^7} \le 2\theta, \\[2mm] 300a - (1200)(10^7)\theta & \text{if } \dfrac{a}{10^7} \ge 2\theta. \end{cases}$$

Note that in the middle region above, the loss is really a weighted squared-error loss, plus a term involving only θ.)

CHAPTER 3

Prior Information and Subjective Probability

As mentioned in Chapter 1, an important element of many decision problems is the prior information concerning θ. It was stated that a convenient way to quantify such information is in terms of a probability distribution on Θ. In this chapter, methods and problems involved in the construction of such probability distributions will be discussed.

3.1 Subjective Probability

The first point that must be discussed is the meaning of probabilities concerning events (subsets) in Θ. The classical concept of probability involves a long sequence of repetitions of a given situation. For example, saying that a fair coin has probability $\frac{1}{2}$ of coming up heads, when flipped, means that, in a long series of independent flips of the coin, heads will occur about $\frac{1}{2}$ of the time. Unfortunately, this frequency concept won't suffice when dealing with probabilities about θ. For example, consider the problem of trying to determine θ, the proportion of smokers in the United States. What meaning does the statement $P(0.3 < \theta < 0.35) = 0.5$ have? Here θ is simply some number we happen not to know. Clearly it is either in the interval $(0.3, 0.35)$ or it is not. There is nothing random about it. As a second example, let θ denote the unemployment rate for next year. It is somewhat easier here to think of θ as random, since the future is uncertain, but how can $P(3\% < \theta < 4\%)$ be interpreted in terms of a sequence of identical situations? The unemployment situation next year will be a unique, one-time event.

The theory of subjective probability has been created to enable one to talk about probabilities when the frequency viewpoint does not apply. The main idea is to let the probability of an event reflect the personal belief in the "chance" of the occurrence of the event. For example, you may have a personal feeling as to the chance that θ (in the unemployment example) will be between 3% and 4%, even though no frequency probability can be assigned to the event. There is, of course, nothing terribly surprising about this. It is common to think in terms of personal probabilities all the time; when betting on the outcome of a football game, when evaluating the chance of rain tomorrow, and in many other situations.

The calculation of a frequency probability is theoretically straightforward. One simply determines the relative frequency of the event of interest. A subjective probability, however, can only be determined by introspection. It is worthwhile to briefly discuss techniques for doing this.

The simplest way of determining subjective probabilities is to compare events, determining relative likelihoods. Say, for example, that it is desired to find $P(E)$. Simply compare E with, say, E^c (the complement of E). If E is felt to be twice as likely to occur as E^c, then clearly $P(E) = \frac{2}{3}$ and $P(E^c) = \frac{1}{3}$.

Betting situations are also useful to consider, if only because they tend to make the mind evaluate more carefully. To determine $P(E)$ by this mechanism, imagine a situation in which you will receive z if E occurs and $(1 - z)$ if E^c occurs, where $0 \leq z \leq 1$. The idea is then to choose z until you are indifferent between the two possibilities, in which case, by utility theory, it should be true that

$$U(z)P(E) = U(1 - z)(1 - P(E)).$$

It follows that $P(E) = U(1 - z)/[U(z) + U(1 - z)]$. If z involves a small unit of money, U is probably approximately linear, so that $P(E) = 1 - z$.

Theoretically, the above betting mechanism seems somewhat circular. We tended to construct utility functions by considering probabilistic bets, and now we try to construct probabilities from knowledge of the utility function. The dilemma can be resolved by noting that, in the construction of the utility function, *any* probability mechanism can be used, in particular, frequency probabilities from a convenient source.

As with utility theory, a set of axioms of rational behavior can be constructed, under which subjective probabilities can be considered to exist and behave in the fashion of usual probabilities. The axioms are essentially obvious things like transitivity (i.e., if A is thought more likely to occur than B, and B is thought more likely to occur than C, then A should be thought more likely to occur than C). See DeGroot (1970) for details.

A word of caution should be inserted concerning the problems in eliciting subjective probabilities from nonstatisticians. Care must be taken to ensure that they act rationally. It would not be unusual to have a nonstatistician conclude that $P(A) = \frac{1}{3}$, $P(B) = \frac{1}{3}$, and P (either A or B occurring) $= \frac{3}{4}$, an irrational statement to someone trained in probability. Studies (see Hogarth (1975)) have also indicated that novices have great trouble in accurately specifying large or small probabilities.

3.2 Prior Information

In some situations, θ can actually be considered to be a random variable. An example of this, mentioned earlier, is lot inspection, wherein a shipment of items is received periodically and inspected to determine θ, the proportion of defectives. Assuming the shipments are supposedly identical (from the same company each time, etc.), they can be considered to be a sequence of identical trials, and θ can be thought of as a random variable in the frequency sense. More commonly, however, θ has no such random interpretation, and the ideas of subjective probability must be used to interpret probabilities involving θ. In later chapters we will tend to talk as if θ really is a random variable. This is mainly a matter of convenience, and it should be remembered that this will usually mean random in a subjective sense only.

   As stated in the introduction, it is convenient to quantify prior information in terms of a probability density $\pi(\theta)$ on Θ. We now discuss methods of determining such a prior density.

3.2.1 Subjective Determination of the Prior Density

Let us first consider the situation in which $\pi(\theta)$ is to be determined wholly subjectively. If Θ is discrete, the problem is simply one of determining the subjective probability of each element of Θ. The techniques in the preceding section should prove adequate for this. When Θ is continuous, the problem of constructing $\pi(\theta)$ is considerably more difficult. Several useful techniques will be discussed.

I. *The Histogram Approach*

When Θ is an interval of the real line, the most obvious approach to use is the histogram approach. Divide Θ into intervals, determine the subjective probability of each interval, and then plot a probability histogram. From this histogram, a smooth density $\pi(\theta)$ can be sketched.

   There is no clearcut rule which establishes how many intervals, what size intervals, etc., should be used in the histogram approach. For some problems, only very crude histograms and priors will be needed, while for others, highly detailed versions will be required. The exact needs will be determined by robustness considerations which will be discussed later. Two other difficulties with the histogram approach are that the prior density so obtained is somewhat difficult to work with, and that the prior density has no tails (i.e., gives probability one to a bounded set). The problems caused by this lack of a tail will be indicated later.

II. *The Relative Likelihood Approach*

This approach is also of most use when Θ is a subset of the real line. It consists simply of comparing the intuitive "likelihoods" of various points in Θ, and directly sketching a prior density from these determinations. Again, it may be useful to consider betting situations in determining these relative likelihoods.

EXAMPLE 1. Assume $\Theta = [0, 1]$. It is usually a good idea to begin by determining the relative likelihoods of the "most likely" and "least likely" parameter points. Suppose that the parameter point $\theta = \frac{3}{4}$ is felt to be the most likely, while $\theta = 0$ is the least likely. Also, $\frac{3}{4}$ is estimated to be three times as likely to be the true value of θ as is 0. It is deemed sufficient (for an accurate sketch) to determine the relative likelihoods of three other points, $\frac{1}{4}, \frac{1}{2}$, and 1. For simplicity, all points are compared with $\theta = 0$. It is decided that $\theta = \frac{1}{2}$ and $\theta = 1$ are twice as likely as $\theta = 0$, while $\theta = \frac{1}{4}$ is 1.5 times as likely as $\theta = 0$. Assign the base point $\theta = 0$ the prior density value 1. Figure 3.1 shows the resulting (unnormalized) prior density. More points could, of course, be included if a more accurate sketch were desired. Note that, as always in such determinations, it is a good idea to check for consistency by comparing other pairs of points. For example, do $\theta = \frac{1}{2}$ and $\theta = 1$ really have the same (subjective) likelihood?

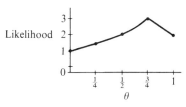

Figure 3.1

The prior density found in the previous example is not proper, in the sense that it does not integrate to one. A constant c could be found for which $c\pi(\theta)$ is a proper density, but fortunately there is no need to do so. The reason is that the Bayes rule is the same whether $\pi(\theta)$ or $c\pi(\theta)$ is used as the prior density. (This is clear since

$$r(c\pi, \delta) = \int_\Theta R(\theta, \delta)c\pi(\theta)d\theta = cr(\pi, \delta),$$

so that a δ minimizing $r(c\pi, \delta)$ will also minimize $r(\pi, \delta)$.)

A difficulty is encountered when the relative likelihood approach is used with unbounded Θ. Then, since the relative likelihood determinations can only be done in a finite region, one must decide what to do outside this region. Two particular problems arise. The first is that of determining the shape of the density outside the finite region. (For example, should it be decreasing like θ^{-2} or like $e^{-\theta}$?) Some observations concerning this problem will be presented in the section on Bayesian robustness. The second problem concerns the need to now normalize the density. In particular, it is important that the carefully determined central part of the density have integrated mass correctly proportional to the outside tail of the density. This can be done by simply determining the prior probabilities of the central region and the outer region subjectively, and then making sure that the estimated prior density gives corresponding mass to the two regions.

III. *Matching a Given Functional Form*

This approach is the most used (and misused) approach to determining a prior density. The idea is to simply assume that $\pi(\theta)$ is of a given functional form, and to then choose the density of this given form which most closely matches prior beliefs. In Example 1, for instance, one might assume that $\pi(\theta)$ is a $\mathscr{B}e(\alpha, \beta)$ density. It is then only necessary to choose α and β. Several ways of choosing such parameters will now be considered.

The easiest way of subjectively determining prior parameters is to calculate them from estimated prior moments. For example, if the prior is assumed to have a $\mathscr{N}(\mu, \sigma^2)$ functional form, one need only decide upon a prior mean and a prior variance to specify the density. Likewise for a $\mathscr{B}e(\alpha, \beta)$ functional form, one can estimate the prior mean, μ, and variance, σ^2, and use the relationships $\mu = \alpha/(\alpha + \beta), \sigma^2 = \alpha\beta/[(\alpha + \beta)^2(\alpha + \beta + 1)]$ to determine α and β.

Unfortunately, the estimation of prior moments is often an extremely uncertain undertaking. The difficulty lies in the fact that the tails of a density can have a drastic effect on its moments. For example, if the tail of a density on $(0, \infty)$ behaves like $K\theta^{-2}$, the density has no moments whatsoever (since for any $b > 0$, $\int_b^\infty \theta(K\theta^{-2})d\theta = K \int_b^\infty \theta^{-1} d\theta = \infty$). But if K is small, this tail will have almost insignificant probability. Since it is probabilities that can be most reasonably specified subjectively, a tail of small probability cannot realistically be known. Nevertheless its influence on the moments can be great, at least when dealing with unbounded (or very large) parameter spaces. This "simple" method of subjectively determining parameters is thus suspect. (For bounded parameter spaces, such as $\Theta = [0, 1]$, the subjective determination of prior moments is more reasonable, since the tail will then have much less of an effect on the moments.)

A better method of determining prior parameters is to subjectively estimate several fractiles of the prior distribution, and then choose the parameters of the given functional form to obtain a density matching these fractiles as closely as possible. (An α-fractile of a continuous distribution is a point $z(\alpha)$ such that a random variable with this distribution has probability α of being less than or equal to $z(\alpha)$.) Since it is precisely the estimation of probabilities of regions (or equivalently the determination of fractiles) that is easiest to do subjectively, this approach is considerably more attractive than the moment approach. There are available many tables of fractiles of standard densities which facilitate the application of this approach.

EXAMPLE 2. Assume $\Theta = (-\infty, \infty)$ and that the prior is thought to be from the normal family. It is subjectively determined that the median of the prior is 0, and the quartiles (i.e., $\frac{1}{4}$-fractile and $\frac{3}{4}$-fractile) are -1 and 1. Since, for a normal distribution, the mean and median are equal, it is clear that the desired normal mean is $\mu = 0$. Using tables of normal probabilities, it is also clear that the variance of the normal prior must be $\sigma^2 = 2.19$ (since $P(Z < -1/(2.19)^{1/2}) = \frac{1}{4}$, when Z is $\mathcal{N}(0, 1)$). Hence π will be chosen to be a $\mathcal{N}(0, 2.19)$ density.

If, alternatively, it is assumed that the prior is Cauchy, one finds that the $\mathscr{C}(0, 1)$ density is the appropriate choice. (The median is zero, and it can be checked that $\int_{-\infty}^{-1} (1/\pi[1 + \theta^2])d\theta = \frac{1}{4}$.)

From the above example, two interesting observations can be made. First, for a given assumed functional form, only a small number of fractiles need typically be found to determine the specific choice of the prior. Although this makes the analysis quite simple, it is troublesome, since what should be done if other fractiles don't agree with the implied choice? The answer is obvious—if there is unavoidable significant disagreement between the densities of a certain functional form and subjectively chosen fractiles of the prior, that functional form should be discarded as an appropriate model for the prior. Often, this can best be seen by sketching (subjectively) the prior density using methods I or II, and then seeing if a reasonable graphical match can be obtained using the density of the given functional form. (The question unanswered here is what constitutes a "reasonable match" or "significant disagreement." More will be said about this later, but the unfortunate fact is that there is no definitive answer. Basically a "reasonable match" is one in which the differences between the two densities have little effect on the final Bayes rule obtained. Whether or not this is true for a given problem can often be determined only by specific calculation of each of the implied Bayes rules.)

The second observation that can be made from Example 2 is that considerably different functional forms can often be chosen for the prior density. The obvious question is whether or not the choice of functional form is important. It will be seen that the answer is often yes, and certain functional forms will be advocated as generally superior.

One other technique for determining the parameters of a given functional form deserves mention. This technique goes by several names, among them the "technique of equivalent sample size" and the "device of imaginary results." (See Good (1950).) The technique is best understood through an example.

EXAMPLE 3. Assume a sample $X_1, \ldots, X_n$ from a $\mathcal{N}(\theta, 1)$ distribution is observed. The sample mean, $\overline{X}$, has a $\mathcal{N}(\theta, 1/n)$ distribution. Suppose it is felt that a normal prior density is appropriate. It is quite easy to guess the mean μ of a normal prior, but determination of the prior variance, σ^2, can be difficult. In the next chapter it will be seen that the Bayesian approach results in the combining of the sample information and prior information into what is called the "posterior distribution" for θ. In the situation of this example, the mean of the posterior distribution (and, in a sense, the best "guess" for θ) is

$$\bar{x}\left(\frac{\sigma^2}{\sigma^2 + 1/n}\right) + \mu\left(\frac{1/n}{\sigma^2 + 1/n}\right).$$

This suggests that the prior variance, σ^2, plays the same role as $1/n$ in the determination of θ. Hence the idea of equivalent sample size is to determine an n^* such that a sample of that size would make $\bar{x}$ as convincing an estimate of θ as the subjective guess μ. Then $\sigma^2 = 1/n^*$ would be an appropriate prior variance.

This approach, though interesting conceptually, has two major drawbacks. First, it is useful only when certain specific (and often unsuitable) functional forms of the prior are assumed. Second, people who are not extremely well trained statistically do not have good judgement concerning the evidence conveyed by a sample of size n. Indeed people tend to considerably underestimate the amount of information carried by a sample of size n. (See Hogarth (1975) for indications of this.)

IV. *CDF Determination*

Another technique for determining the prior is through subjective construction of the CDF (cumulative distribution function). This can be done by subjectively determining several α-fractiles, $z(\alpha)$, plotting the points $(z(\alpha), \alpha)$, and sketching a smooth curve joining them. This can be a reasonably accurate technique, but will not be considered further since, for the most part, we will be working with prior densities.

Of the four approaches discussed above for subjectively determining a prior distribution, approaches I and II should be the most useful. Personally, the author prefers the relative likelihood approach, but some may have a better feeling for the histogram approach.

Approach III is useful in two situations. The first such situation is when a density of a standard functional form can be found which gives a good match to the prior density obtained by approaches I or II. The use of this standard density can then considerably simplify the ensuing work. The second situation is when only very vague prior information is available. One might just as well then use a standard functional form for the prior density, providing the vague prior information can be incorporated into the standard functional form, *and providing the resulting procedure is robust*. (More will be said of this later.)

The discussion has so far been limited to the univariate situation, in which Θ is a subset of R^1. The problems in trying to determine a multivariate prior density can be considerable. The easiest approach is again the use of a given functional form, since then only a few parameters need be determined subjectively. Also easy is the case in which the coordinates, θ_i, of $\boldsymbol{\theta}$ are thought to be independent. The prior $\pi(\boldsymbol{\theta})$ is then just the product of the univariate prior densities of the θ_i, which can be determined as above. When neither of these simplifying assumptions is thought to be realistic, the best way to proceed is by determining conditional and marginal prior densities. For example, if $\pi(\theta_1, \theta_2)$ is sought, determine by the usual univariate techniques $\pi(\theta_2|\theta_1)$ (the conditional density of θ_2 given θ_1) for various values of θ_1, and also determine $\pi_1(\theta_1)$ (the marginal density of θ_1). Since $\pi(\theta_1, \theta_2) = \pi_1(\theta_1)\pi(\theta_2|\theta_1)$, the joint prior density can thus be approximated.

3.2.2 Noninformative Priors

One attractive feature of the Bayesian approach to statistics is its deterministic simplicity. Once a loss and prior have been chosen (the hard part), the calculation of the Bayes rule will be seen to be straightforward. This simplicity makes appealing attempts to use the Bayesian approach even when no, or limited, prior information is available. What is needed in such situations is a *noninformative prior*, by which is meant a prior which contains no information about θ (or more crudely which "favors" no possible values of θ over others). For example, in testing between two simple hypotheses, the prior which gives probability $\frac{1}{2}$ to each of the hypotheses is clearly noninformative. The following is a more complex example.

EXAMPLE 4. Suppose the parameter of interest is a normal mean θ, so that the parameter space is $\Theta = (-\infty, \infty)$. If a noninformative prior density is desired, it seems reasonable to give equal weight to all possible values of θ. Unfortunately, if $\pi(\theta) = c > 0$ is chosen, then π has infinite mass (i.e., $\int \pi(\theta)d\theta = \infty$) and is not a proper density. Nevertheless, such π can be successfully worked with. The choice of c is unimportant, so that typically the noninformative prior density for this problem is chosen to be $\pi(\theta) = 1$. This is often called the *uniform density on R^1*, and was introduced and used by Laplace.

As in the above example, it will frequently happen that the natural noninformative prior is an *improper prior*, namely one which has infinite mass. We will now turn to the problem of determining noninformative priors.

The simplest situation to consider is when Θ is a finite set, consisting of say n elements. The obvious noninformative prior is to then give each element of Θ probability $1/n$. When Θ is infinite, however, no such obvious solution is obtainable, and we must turn to intuitive arguments.

Perhaps the most useful method of determining a noninformative prior is through consideration of the structure of the problem. In particular, it is helpful to consider transformations or reformulations of the problem which intuitively should not affect the noninformative prior. The following discussion and examples show how this can lead to the development of reasonable noninformative priors. (This approach had its beginnings with Jeffreys (see, for example, Jeffreys (1961)) and has been used in Jaynes (1968), Villegas (1977) and elsewhere. For many situations, this approach corresponds to the more formal mathematical approach of finding invariant priors. This will be discussed further in Chapter 6.)

EXAMPLE 5 (Location Parameters). Suppose that $\mathscr{X}$ and Θ are subsets of R^p, and that the density of X is of the form $f(x - \theta)$ (i.e., depends only on $(x - \theta)$). The density is then said to be a *location density*, and θ is called a *location parameter* (or sometimes a *location vector* when $p \geq 2$). The $\mathscr{N}(\theta, \sigma^2)$ (σ^2 fixed), $\mathscr{T}(\alpha, \mu, \sigma^2)$ (α and σ^2 fixed), $\mathscr{C}(\alpha, \beta)$ (β fixed), and $\mathscr{N}_p(\theta, \Sigma)$ (Σ fixed) densities are all examples of location densities. Also, a sample of independent identically distributed random variables is said to be from a location density if their common density is a location density.

To derive a noninformative prior for this situation, imagine that, instead of observing X, we observe the random variable $Y = X + c$ ($c \in R^p$). Defining $\eta = \theta + c$, it is clear that Y has density $f(y - \eta)$. If now $\mathscr{X} = \Theta = R^p$, then the sample space and parameter space for the (Y, η) problem are also R^p. The (X, θ) and (Y, η) problems are thus identical in structure, and it seems reasonable to insist that they have the same noninformative prior. (Another way of thinking of this is to note that observing Y really amounts to observing X with a different unit of measurement, one in which the "origin" is c and not zero. Since the choice of an origin for a unit of measurement is quite arbitrary, the noninformative prior should perhaps be independent of this choice.)

Letting π and π^* denote the noninformative priors in the (X, θ) and (Y, η) problems respectively, the above argument implies that π and π^* should be equal, i.e., that

$$P^\pi(\theta \in A) = P^{\pi^*}(\eta \in A) \tag{3.1}$$

for any set A in R^p. Since $\eta = \theta + c$, it should also be true (by a simple change of variables) that

$$P^{\pi^*}(\eta \in A) = P^\pi(\theta + c \in A) = P^\pi(\theta \in A - c), \tag{3.2}$$

where $A - c = \{z - c : z \in A\}$. Combining (3.1) and (3.2) shows that π should satisfy

$$P^\pi(\theta \in A) = P^\pi(\theta \in A - c). \tag{3.3}$$

Furthermore, this argument applies no matter which $\mathbf{c} \in R^p$ is chosen, so that (3.3) should hold for all $\mathbf{c} \in R^p$. Any π satisfying this relationship is said to be a *location invariant* prior.

Assuming that the prior has a density, we can write (3.3) as

$$\int_A \pi(\boldsymbol{\theta})d\boldsymbol{\theta} = \int_{A-\mathbf{c}} \pi(\boldsymbol{\theta})d\boldsymbol{\theta} = \int_A \pi(\boldsymbol{\theta} - \mathbf{c})d\boldsymbol{\theta}.$$

If this is to hold for all sets A, it can be shown that it must be true that

$$\pi(\boldsymbol{\theta}) = \pi(\boldsymbol{\theta} - \mathbf{c})$$

for all $\boldsymbol{\theta}$. Setting $\boldsymbol{\theta} = \mathbf{c}$ thus gives

$$\pi(\mathbf{c}) = \pi(\mathbf{0}).$$

Recall, however, that this should hold for all $\mathbf{c} \in R^p$. The conclusion is that π must be a constant function. It is convenient to choose the constant to be 1, so the *noninformative prior density for a location parameter* is $\pi(\boldsymbol{\theta}) = 1$. (This conclusion can be shown to follow from (3.3), even without the assumption that the prior has a density.)

EXAMPLE 6 (Scale Parameters). A (one-dimensional) *scale density* is a density of the form

$$\sigma^{-1}f\left(\frac{x}{\sigma}\right),$$

where $\sigma > 0$. The parameter σ is called a *scale parameter*. The $\mathcal{N}(0, \sigma^2)$, $\mathcal{T}(\alpha, 0, \sigma^2)$ (α fixed), and $\mathcal{G}(\alpha, \beta)$ (α fixed) densities are all examples of scale densities. Also, a sample of independent identically distributed random variables is said to be from a scale density if their common density is a scale density.

To derive a noninformative prior for this situation, imagine that, instead of observing X, we observe the random variable $Y = cX$ ($c > 0$). Defining $\eta = c\sigma$, an easy calculation shows that the density of Y is $\eta^{-1}f(y/\eta)$. If now $\mathcal{X} = R^1$ or $\mathcal{X} = (0, \infty)$, then the sample and parameter spaces for the (X, σ) problem are the same as those for the (Y, η) problem. The two problems are thus identical in structure, which again indicates that they should have the same noninformative prior. (Here the transformation can be thought of as simply a change in the scale of measurement, from say inches to feet.) Letting π and π^* denote the priors in the (X, σ) and (Y, η) problems, respectively, this means that the equality

$$P^\pi(\sigma \in A) = P^{\pi^*}(\eta \in A)$$

should hold for all $A \subset (0, \infty)$. Since $\eta = c\sigma$, it should also be true that

$$P^{\pi^*}(\eta \in A) = P^\pi(\sigma \in c^{-1}A),$$

where $c^{-1}A = \{c^{-1}z: z \in A\}$. Putting these together, it follows that π should satisfy

$$P^\pi(\sigma \in A) = P^\pi(\sigma \in c^{-1}A). \tag{3.4}$$

This should hold for all $c > 0$, and any distribution π for which this is true is called *scale invariant*.

The mathematical analysis of (3.4) proceeds as in the preceding example. Write (3.4) (assuming densities) as

$$\int_A \pi(\sigma)d\sigma = \int_{c^{-1}A} \pi(\sigma)d\sigma = \int_A \pi(c^{-1}\sigma)c^{-1}\,d\sigma,$$

and conclude that, for this to hold for all A, it must be true that

$$\pi(\sigma) = c^{-1}\pi(c^{-1}\sigma)$$

for all σ. Choosing $\sigma = c$, it follows that

$$\pi(c) = c^{-1}\pi(1).$$

Setting $\pi(1) = 1$ for convenience, and noting that the above equality must hold for all $c > 0$, it follows that a reasonable *noninformative prior for a scale parameter* is $\pi(\sigma) = \sigma^{-1}$. Observe that this is also an improper prior, since $\int_0^\infty \sigma^{-1}\,d\sigma = \infty$.

An interesting natural application of this noninformative prior is to the "table entry" problem. This problem arose from the study of positive entries in various "natural" numerical tables, such as tables of positive physical constants, tables of population sizes of cities, etc. The problem is to determine the relative frequencies of the integers 1 through 9 in the *first* significant digit of the table entries. Intuitively, one might expect each digit to occur $\frac{1}{9}$ of the time. Instead, it has been found that i ($i = 1, \ldots, 9$) occurs with a relative frequency of about $\log(1 + i^{-1})/\log 10$.

Numerous explanations of this phenomenon have been proposed. The explanation of interest to us is that, since the scale of measurement of these positive entries is quite arbitrary, one might expect the distribution of table entries to be scale invariant. This suggests using $\pi(\sigma) = \sigma^{-1}$ to describe the distribution of table entries σ. Since this is not a proper density, it cannot be formally considered the distribution of σ. Nevertheless, one can use it (properly normalized) to represent the actual distribution of σ on any interval (a, b) where $0 < a < b < \infty$. For example, consider the interval $(1, 10)$. Then the properly normalized version of π is $\pi(\sigma) = \sigma^{-1}/\log 10$. In this region, σ will have first digit i when it lies in the interval $[i, i + 1)$. The probability of this is

$$p_i = \int_i^{i+1} [\sigma \log 10]^{-1}\,d\sigma = \frac{\log(i + 1) - \log i}{\log 10} = \frac{\log(1 + i^{-1})}{\log 10},$$

which is precisely the relative frequency that is observed in reality. One might object to the rather arbitrary choice of the interval (1, 10), but the following compelling result can be obtained: if the p_i are calculated for an arbitrary interval (a, b), then as $a \to 0$ or $b \to \infty$ or both, the p_i will converge to the values $\log(1 + i^{-1})/\log 10$. This apparent natural occurrence of the non-informative prior may be mere coincidence, but it is intriguing.

One problem that frequently arises when dealing with noninformative priors is the need to consider truncated parameter spaces. For example, θ could be a location parameter, but it might be known that $\theta > 0$. With a restricted parameter space such as this, the transformations given in Example 5 no longer result in structurally identical problems. The intuitive derivation of the natural noninformative prior then seems inappropriate.

On the other hand, it does seem rather natural for a restricted parameter space to just inherit the noninformative prior from the full parameter space. The fact that θ cannot be negative, above, should not influence our feelings concerning the relative likelihoods of positive θ (assuming we have no further information). Thus for a location parameter with θ known to be positive, it is still reasonable to use $\pi(\theta) = 1$ (for $0 < \theta < \infty$) as the noninformative prior. (Note that it is not merely the form of Θ that determines the noninformative prior. In the above situation, Θ is $(0, \infty)$, exactly as in the usual situation for a scale parameter. Nevertheless, the reasonable noninformative prior is $\pi(\theta) = 1$, not $\pi(\theta) = \theta^{-1}$ as in the scale parameter case.)

The derivations of the noninformative priors in the two previous examples should not be considered completely compelling. There is indeed a logical flaw in the analyses, caused by the fact that the final priors are improper. The difficulty arises in the argument that if two problems have identical structure, they should have the same noninformative prior. The problem here is that, when improper, noninformative priors are not unique. Multiplying an improper prior π by a constant K results in an equivalent prior, in the sense that all decisions and inferences in Bayesian analysis will be identical for the priors π and $K\pi$. Thus there is no reason to insist that π^* and π, in Examples 5 and 6, must be identical. They need only be constant multiples of each other. In Example 5, for instance, this milder restriction will give, in place of (3.1), the relationship

$$P^\pi(A) = h(\mathbf{c})P^{\pi^*}(A), \tag{3.5}$$

where $h(\mathbf{c})$ is some positive function and P is to be interpreted more liberally as a "measure." The analogue of Equation (3.2), namely

$$P^{\pi^*}(A) = P^\pi(A - \mathbf{c}), \tag{3.6}$$

should remain valid, being as it merely specifies that a change of variables should not affect the measure. Combining (3.5) and (3.6) gives, in place of (3.3), the relationship

$$P^\pi(A) = h(\mathbf{c})P^\pi(A - \mathbf{c}). \tag{3.7}$$

In integral form this becomes

$$\int_A \pi(\boldsymbol{\theta})d\boldsymbol{\theta} = h(\mathbf{c}) \int_{A-\mathbf{c}} \pi(\boldsymbol{\theta})d\boldsymbol{\theta} = h(\mathbf{c}) \int_A \pi(\boldsymbol{\theta} - \mathbf{c})d\boldsymbol{\theta}.$$

For this to hold for all A, it must be true that

$$\pi(\boldsymbol{\theta}) = h(\mathbf{c})\pi(\boldsymbol{\theta} - \mathbf{c}).$$

Setting $\boldsymbol{\theta} = \mathbf{c}$, it follows that $h(\mathbf{c}) = \pi(\mathbf{c})/\pi(\mathbf{0})$. The conclusion is that π need only satisfy the functional equation

$$\pi(\boldsymbol{\theta} - \mathbf{c}) := \frac{\pi(\mathbf{0})\pi(\boldsymbol{\theta})}{\pi(\mathbf{c})}. \tag{3.8}$$

There are many improper priors, besides the uniform, which satisfy this relationship. An example is $\pi(\boldsymbol{\theta}) = \exp\{\boldsymbol{\theta}^t\mathbf{z}\}$, where $\mathbf{z}$ is any fixed vector. A prior satisfying (3.8) is called *relatively location invariant*.

The above problem will be encountered in virtually any situation for which improper noninformative priors must be considered. There will be a wide class of "logically possible" noninformative priors. (See Hartigan (1964) and Stein (1965) for general results of this nature.) Selecting from among this class can be difficult. For certain statistical problems, a natural choice does exist, namely the right invariant Haar measure. A general discussion of this concept requires group theory, and will be delayed until Chapter 6. It is a fact, however, that the noninformative priors given in Examples 5 and 6 are the right invariant Haar measures. The following example presents an important situation in which the straightforward invariance argument of Examples 5 and 6 does not lead to the right invariant Haar measure.

EXAMPLE 7 (Location-Scale Parameters). A *location-scale* density is a density of the form $\sigma^{-1}f((x - \theta)/\sigma)$, where $\theta \in R^1$ and $\sigma > 0$ are the unknown parameters. The $\mathcal{N}(\theta, \sigma^2)$ density is the crucial example of a location-scale density. A sample of independent identically distributed random variables is said to be from a location-scale density if their common density is a location-scale density.

To determine a noninformative prior, the natural transformations to consider are $Y = cX + b$, $\eta = c\theta + b$, and $\xi = c\sigma$, where $b \in R^1$ and $c > 0$. (This transformation would correspond to, say, changing the unit of measurement from degrees centigrade to degrees Fahrenheit.) A direct invariance argument, as in Examples 5 and 6, then shows that the noninformative prior should be $\pi(\theta, \sigma) = \sigma^{-2}$. It will be seen in Chapter 6, however, that the right-invariant Haar density for this problem is $\pi(\theta, \sigma) = \sigma^{-1}$. (This prior would also arise if θ and σ were considered to be independent, and the noninformative priors for each, separately, were multiplied together.) We will thus, for the most part, consider $\pi(\theta, \sigma) = \sigma^{-1}$ to be the noninformative prior for a location-scale parameter.

The above example indicates that the naive invariance or reformulation method of finding a noninformative prior distribution is not foolproof. Indeed it is but one of a number of techniques that have been proposed for finding a noninformative prior. The chief competitor to the method is a technique of Box and Tiao, which seeks a transformation of the problem in which the transformed density is approximately a location density. The transformed parameter is then given the uniform density, which determines (via the inverse transformation) the noninformative prior in the original problem. (For a good discussion of this technique, see Box and Tiao (1973).) This is a very reasonable approach, but can be difficult to implement. Also, it will often give an answer that differs from the answer obtained by the invariance or reformulation approach. In dealing with a Poisson parameter θ, for instance, the Box and Tiao approach leads to $\pi(\theta) = \theta^{-1/2}$ for the noninformative prior, while the reformulation approach will be seen in the Exercises to give $\pi(\theta) = \theta^{-1}$. There is no clearcut way of saying which is correct. (A right-invariant Haar measure does not exist for this situation.) Indeed the main problem in dealing with noninformative priors is that there is often no such thing as a "correct" noninformative prior. One can only try to make a reasonable choice. This can sometimes be very difficult, as the following example shows.

EXAMPLE 8. Assume θ is a binomial parameter. The parameter space is thus $\Theta = [0, 1]$. Three plausible noninformative prior densities are $\pi_1(\theta) = 1$, $\pi_2(\theta) = \theta^{-1}(1 - \theta)^{-1}$, and $\pi_3(\theta) = [\theta(1 - \theta)]^{-1/2}$. The first is the "natural" uniform density, the second can be derived by a complicated reformulation argument (see Villegas (1977), who in fact shows that if $\boldsymbol{\theta} = (\theta_1, \ldots, \theta_k)^t$ is the parameter of a multinomial distribution, then $\pi(\boldsymbol{\theta}) = \prod_{i=1}^{k} \theta_i^{-1}$ is the correct noninformative prior by the reformulation principle), and the third arises from the approach of Box and Tiao. All three possibilities are reasonable.

In situations such as the above example, it will often make little difference (in terms of the resulting Bayes rule) which noninformative prior is used. If the choice does make a significant difference, however, then one cannot avoid a more careful consideration of prior information. Indeed a proper subjective Bayesian approach is then probably called for. (See, for instance, Example 27 in Chapter 4.)

As a final note of caution, it will be seen in Chapter 4 that even "unanimously acclaimed" noninformative priors (such as those for location parameters or scale parameters) can lead to inferior decision rules. Thus while Bayesian analysis with noninformative priors can be a very useful tool, as with most general statistical techniques it cannot always be implemented and can sometimes give less than satisfactory results.

3.2.3 Maximum Entropy Priors

A situation which lies between those of the two previous subsections often prevails. Frequently partial prior information is available, outside of which it is desired to use a prior that is as noninformative as possible. For example, suppose the prior mean is specified, and among prior distributions with this mean the most noninformative distribution is sought.

A useful method of dealing with this problem (developed by Jaynes (1968)) is through the concept of entropy. Entropy is most easily understood for discrete distributions, with which we, therefore, begin.

Definition 1. Assume Θ is discrete, and let π be a probability density on Θ. The *entropy* of π, to be denoted $\mathscr{E}n(\pi)$, is defined as

$$\mathscr{E}n(\pi) = -\sum_{\Theta} \pi(\theta_i)\log \pi(\theta_i).$$

(If $\pi(\theta_i) = 0$, the quantity $\pi(\theta_i)\log \pi(\theta_i)$ is defined to be zero.)

Entropy has a direct relationship to information theory, and in a sense measures the amount of uncertainty inherent in the probability distribution. (See Rosenkranz (1977) for an interesting discussion of this.)

EXAMPLE 9. Assume $\Theta = \{\theta_1, \theta_2, \ldots, \theta_n\}$. If $\pi(\theta_k) = 1$, while $\pi(\theta_i) = 0$ for $i \neq k$, then clearly the probability distribution describes exactly which parameter point will occur. The "uncertainty" is zero. Correspondingly,

$$\mathscr{E}n(\pi) = -\sum_{i=1}^{n} \pi(\theta_i)\log \pi(\theta_i) = 0.$$

At the other extreme, the "most uncertain" or *maximum entropy* probability distribution is that with $\pi(\theta_i) = 1/n$ for all i. For this π,

$$\mathscr{E}n(\pi) = -\sum_{i=1}^{n} \frac{1}{n}\log\left(\frac{1}{n}\right) = \log n.$$

(It can be shown that $\mathscr{E}n(\pi) \leq \log n$ for all proper π.) Note that this maximum entropy distribution is the same as the noninformative prior distribution for a discrete Θ.

Assume now that partial prior information concerning θ is available. It is convenient to consider information in the form of restrictions on the $\pi(\theta_i)$. Indeed assume that

$$E^{\pi}[g_k(\theta)] = \sum_{i} \pi(\theta_i)g_k(\theta_i) = \mu_k, \qquad k = 1, \ldots, m. \tag{3.9}$$

Two examples should indicate the scope of this type of restriction.

EXAMPLE 10. Assume $\Theta \subset R^1$, $g_1(\theta) = \theta$, and $g_k(\theta) = (\theta - \mu_1)^k$ for $2 \leq k \leq m$. Then (3.9) corresponds to the specification of the first m central moments, μ_i, of π.

EXAMPLE 11. Assume $\Theta \subset R^1$, and

$$g_k(\theta) = I_{(-\infty, z_k]}(\theta).$$

Clearly

$$E^\pi[g_k(\theta)] = P^\pi(\theta \leq z_k),$$

so, by (3.9), z_k is the μ_k-fractile of π. Hence this choice of the g_k corresponds to the specification of m fractiles of π.

It seems reasonable to seek the prior distribution which maximizes entropy among all those distributions which satisfy the given set of restrictions (i.e., given prior information). Intuitively this should result in a prior which incorporates the available prior information, but otherwise is as noninformative as possible. The solution to the maximization of $\mathscr{E}n(\pi)$ subject to (3.9) (and, of course, to $\sum \pi(\theta_i) = 1$) is well known, but the derivation is beyond the scope of this book. The solution is given (provided the density defined is proper) by

$$\bar{\pi}(\theta_i) = \frac{\exp\{\sum_{k=1}^m \lambda_k g_k(\theta_i)\}}{\sum_i \exp\{\sum_{k=1}^m \lambda_k g_k(\theta_i)\}},$$

where the λ_k are constants to be determined from the constraints in (3.9). (The proof of this can be found in many books on the calculus of variations. See, for example, Ewing (1969).)

EXAMPLE 12. Assume $\Theta = \{0, 1, 2, \ldots\}$, and it is thought that $E^\pi[\theta] = 5$. This restriction is of the form (3.9) with $g_1(\theta) = \theta$ and $\mu_1 = 5$. The restricted maximum entropy prior is, therefore,

$$\bar{\pi}(\theta) = \frac{e^{\lambda_1 \theta}}{\sum_{\theta=0}^\infty e^{\lambda_1 \theta}} = (1 - e^{\lambda_1})(e^{\lambda_1})^\theta.$$

This is clearly a $\mathscr{G}e(e^{\lambda_1})$ density, the mean of which (from Appendix 1) is $(1 - e^{\lambda_1})/e^{\lambda_1}$. Setting this equal to $\mu_1 = 5$, and solving, gives $e^{\lambda_1} = \frac{1}{6}$. Hence $\bar{\pi}$ is $\mathscr{G}e(\frac{1}{6})$.

If Θ is continuous, the use of maximum entropy becomes more complicated. The first difficulty is that there is no longer a completely natural definition of entropy. Jaynes (1968) makes a strong case for defining entropy as

$$\mathscr{E}n(\pi) = -E^\pi\left[\log \frac{\pi(\theta)}{\pi_0(\theta)}\right] = -\int \pi(\theta)\log\left(\frac{\pi(\theta)}{\pi_0(\theta)}\right)d\theta,$$

where $\pi_0(\theta)$ is the natural "invariant" noninformative prior for the problem. (See Subsection 3.2.2.) Unfortunately, the difficulties and uncertainties in determining a noninformative prior make this definition somewhat ambiguous. It can still be useful, however.

In the presence of partial prior information of the form

$$E^\pi[g_k(\theta)] = \int_\Theta g_k(\theta)\pi(\theta)d\theta = \mu_k, \qquad k = 1, \ldots, m, \tag{3.10}$$

the (proper) prior density (satisfying these restrictions) which maximizes $\mathscr{E}n(\pi)$ is given (provided it exists) by

$$\bar{\pi}(\theta) = \frac{\pi_0(\theta)\exp[\sum_{k=1}^m \lambda_k g_k(\theta)]}{\int_\Theta \pi_0(\theta)\exp[\sum_{k=1}^m \lambda_k g_k(\theta)]d\theta},$$

where the λ_k are constants to be determined from the constraints in (3.10). This is exactly analogous to the discrete case, and can also be derived from arguments involving the calculus of variations.

EXAMPLE 13. Assume $\Theta = R^1$, and that θ is a location parameter. The natural noninformative prior is then $\pi_0(\theta) = 1$. It is believed that the true prior mean is μ and the true prior variance is σ^2. These restrictions are of the form (3.10) with $g_1(\theta) = \theta$, $\mu_1 = \mu$, $g_2(\theta) = (\theta - \mu)^2$, and $\mu_2 = \sigma^2$. The maximum entropy prior, subject to these restrictions, is thus

$$\bar{\pi}(\theta) = \frac{\exp[\lambda_1\theta + \lambda_2(\theta - \mu)^2]}{\int_\Theta \exp[\lambda_1\theta + \lambda_2(\theta - \mu)^2]d\theta},$$

where λ_1 and λ_2 are to be chosen so that (3.10) is satisfied. Clearly

$$\lambda_1\theta + \lambda_2(\theta - \mu)^2 = \lambda_2\theta^2 + (\lambda_1 - 2\mu\lambda_2)\theta + \lambda_2\mu^2$$

$$= \lambda_2\left[\theta - \left(\mu - \frac{\lambda_1}{2\lambda_2}\right)\right]^2 + \left[\lambda_1\mu - \frac{\lambda_1^2}{4\lambda_2}\right].$$

Hence

$$\bar{\pi}(\theta) = \frac{\exp\{\lambda_2[\theta - (\mu - \lambda_1/2\lambda_2)]^2\}}{\int_{-\infty}^\infty \exp\{\lambda_2[\theta - (\mu - \lambda_1/2\lambda_2)]^2\}d\theta}.$$

The denominator is a constant, so $\bar{\pi}(\theta)$ is recognizable as a normal density with mean $\mu - \lambda_1/2\lambda_2$ and variance $-1/2\lambda_2$. Choosing $\lambda_1 = 0$ and $\lambda_2 = -1/2\sigma^2$ satisfies (3.10). Thus $\bar{\pi}(\theta)$ is a $\mathcal{N}(\mu, \sigma^2)$ density.

Several difficulties arise in trying to use the maximum entropy approach to determine a prior. The first difficulty has already been mentioned, namely the need (in the continuous case) to use a noninformative prior in the derivation of $\bar{\pi}$. This problem is not too serious, however, as any reasonable noninformative prior will usually give satisfactory results.

A more serious problem is that often $\bar{\pi}$ will not exist. The following example demonstrates this.

EXAMPLE 14. In the situation of Example 13, assume that the only restriction given is $E^{\pi}[\theta] = \mu$. The solution $\bar{\pi}$ must then be of the form

$$\bar{\pi}(\theta) = \frac{\exp\{\lambda_1\theta\}}{\int_{-\infty}^{\infty} \exp\{\lambda_1\theta\}d\theta}.$$

It is clear, however, that $\bar{\pi}$ cannot be a proper density for any λ_1. Hence there is no solution.

The same problem would be encountered if the restrictions consisted of the specification of several fractiles of the prior. Again no $\bar{\pi}$ of the required form could possibly be a proper density.

A plausible method of overcoming the above difficulty is to use a truncated parameter space whenever $\bar{\pi}$ does not exist for the original parameter space. In Example 14, for instance, it is probably safe to say that $-10^{80} < \theta < 10^{80}$ (with probability one). Using this as a parameter space is thus very reasonable, and $\bar{\pi}$ will then exist.

The final difficulty in the use of maximum entropy lies in the choice of the restrictions. Choosing moment restrictions is easiest analytically, but is generally inferior to the use of fractile restrictions from the viewpoint of robustness. In other words, a $\bar{\pi}$ derived from fractile restrictions will be much safer to use than a $\bar{\pi}$ derived from moment considerations. (It is relatively safe to use the first moment as a restriction. It is mainly the use of higher moments that is bad.) Again, discussion of this must be delayed until Chapter 4. Note also, that (as mentioned earlier) it is generally much easier to subjectively specify prior fractiles than to specify prior moments.

3.2.4 Determination of the Prior from Past Data

When θ is truly a random variable, there will often be data available on past determinations of θ (as in the lot inspection example). This past data can be used to estimate the prior distribution, π. The techniques of so determining π are part of the "empirical Bayes" field of statistics, an area of study originating with H. Robbins (1955).

If values $\theta_1, \theta_2, \ldots, \theta_n$ of θ from past similar situations are available, it is clear that they should be used in the construction of π. If they are the sole input, the problem is simply the standard statistical problem of determining a density from a series of observations from the density. There is a large statistical literature on this subject. Here, we will merely mention three possible simple techniques: (1) Construct a histogram and sketch a reasonable prior density; (2) Assume a plausible functional form for the prior and estimate the parameters of this functional form from the θ_i (see Subsection

3.2.1); (3) Use the discrete density estimate $\hat{\pi}_0$ which gives probability $1/n$ to each of the points θ_i. (The estimate $\hat{\pi}_0$ can be written

$$\hat{\pi}_0(\theta) = \frac{1}{n} [\text{the number of } \theta_i \text{ equal to } \theta],$$

this to be understood as a point mass when positive.) Numerous continuous density estimates are also given in the literature.

Unfortunately, only rarely will the past θ's themselves be known. More common is knowledge just of the data, x_i, arising from the past θ_i. (Actually, the data need not be "past" data. Often one is simultaneously making inferences or decisions about several similar parameters $\theta_1, \ldots, \theta_n$, which can be considered to have a common prior distribution. Data arising from this situation (often called the compound decision problem) can be used in the same way as past data.) The recovery of prior information from the x_i can be difficult, due to the fact that the X_i are (unconditionally) distributed according to the marginal density

$$m(x) = \int_\Theta f(x|\theta) dF^\pi(\theta) = \begin{cases} \int_\Theta f(x|\theta)\pi(\theta) d\theta & \text{(continuous case)}, \\ \sum_\Theta f(x|\theta)\pi(\theta) & \text{(discrete case)}. \end{cases}$$

(The joint density of X and θ is $h(x, \theta) = f(x|\theta)\pi(\theta)$.) The marginal density can easily be estimated from the x_i, but estimating π is a much harder problem.

In some situations, it may suffice to use an estimate of the marginal density m as the estimate of π. This is reasonable when $f(x|\theta)$ is thought to be quite concentrated compared to π. The rationale for then using an estimate of m is that the variation in the X_i is due to two sources: the variation in the θ_i (described by π), and the variation of X_i for fixed θ_i (described by $f(x_i|\theta_i)$). If the variation due to f is much smaller than that due to π, then the X_i will essentially vary as the θ_i vary, making an estimate of m reasonable as an estimate of π. In deciding whether or not this approximation is reasonable, it is useful to compare the conditional variance of X_i (for a fixed θ_i) to the estimated unconditional variance of X_i (say estimated by $s^2 = (1/n)\sum_{i=1}^n (x_i - \bar{x})^2$). For example if the variance of f is 1, while $s^2 = 25$, it seems likely that most of the variability of the X_i is due to π.

To apply the above method of estimating π, it is necessary to estimate $m(x)$ from the x_i. This is again just the problem of density estimation as discussed earlier. The simplest estimate is $\hat{m}_0$, the discrete density which gives probability $1/n$ to each of the points x_i.

If the variability of the X_i is not felt to be due mainly to the variability of the θ_i, or if the amount of past data is very large (giving hope of accurate estimation of π), then the above approach to estimating π is inadequate. Two other approaches are available, however: the use of a given functional form, and the distance method.

I. *Use of a Given Functional Form*

If π is assumed to be of a particular functional form, it is necessary only to estimate the parameters of the functional form. The easiest way to do this is to estimate (using the x_i) the required number of moments of $m(x)$, and to use these to estimate the parameters of π. The relationships needed to do this (when at most two parameters must be determined) are given in the following lemma.

Lemma 1. *Let $\mu_f(\theta)$ and $\sigma_f^2(\theta)$ denote the conditional mean and variance of the X_i (i.e., the mean and variance with respect to the density $f(x|\theta)$). Let μ_m and σ_m^2 denote the marginal mean and variance of the X_i (with respect to $m(x)$). Assuming these quantities exist, then*

$$\mu_m = E^\pi[\mu_f(\theta)],$$
$$\sigma_m^2 = E^\pi[\sigma_f^2(\theta)] + E^\pi[(\mu_f(\theta) - \mu_m)^2].$$

PROOF. For ease in understanding, the proof will only be done when $\pi(\theta)$ is continuous. The proof for the discrete case is similar. Clearly

$$\mu_m = E^m[X_i] = \int_{\mathscr{X}} x_i m(x_i) dx_i$$

$$= \int_{\mathscr{X}} x_i \int_{\Theta} f(x_i|\theta)\pi(\theta)d\theta \, dx_i$$

$$= \int_{\Theta} \pi(\theta) \int_{\mathscr{X}} x_i f(x_i|\theta)dx_i \, d\theta$$

$$= \int_{\Theta} \pi(\theta)\mu_f(\theta)d\theta = E^\pi[\mu_f(\theta)].$$

Likewise,

$$\sigma_m^2 = E^m[(X_i - \mu_m)^2] = \int_{\mathscr{X}} (x_i - \mu_m)^2 \int_{\Theta} f(x_i|\theta)\pi(\theta)d\theta \, dx_i$$

$$= \int_{\Theta} \pi(\theta) \int_{\mathscr{X}} (x_i - \mu_m)^2 f(x_i|\theta)dx_i \, d\theta$$

$$= E^\pi(E_\theta^f[X_i - \mu_m]^2)$$

$$= E^\pi(E_\theta^f[(X_i - \mu_f(\theta)) + (\mu_f(\theta) - \mu_m)]^2)$$

$$= E^\pi(E_\theta^f[(X_i - \mu_f(\theta))^2 + 2(X_i - \mu_f(\theta))(\mu_f(\theta) - \mu_m) + (\mu_f(\theta) - \mu_m)^2]).$$

Since $E_\theta^f(X_i - \mu_f(\theta))^2 = \sigma_f^2(\theta)$ and

$$E_\theta^f[2(X_i - \mu_f(\theta))(\mu_f(\theta) - \mu_m)] = 2(E_\theta^f[X_i] - \mu_f(\theta))(\mu_f(\theta) - \mu_m) = 0,$$

it is clear that

$$\sigma_m^2 = E^\pi[\sigma_f^2(\theta)] + E^\pi[(\mu_f(\theta) - \mu_m)^2]. \qquad \square$$

Corollary 1

(i) *If $\mu_f(\theta) = \theta$, then $\mu_m = \mu_\pi$, where $\mu_\pi = E^\pi[\theta]$ is the prior mean.*
(ii) *If, in addition, $\sigma_f^2(\theta) = \sigma_f^2$ (a constant independent of θ), then $\sigma_m^2 = \sigma_f^2 + \sigma_\pi^2$, where σ_π^2 is the prior variance.*

PROOF. The result is obvious from Lemma 1. $\square$

   The quantities $E^\pi[\mu_f(\theta)]$, $E^\pi[\sigma_f^2(\theta)]$, and $E^\pi[\mu_f(\theta) - \mu_m]^2$ can usually be easily expressed in terms of the parameters of the prior. Since μ_m and σ_m^2 are the (marginal) mean and variance of the X_i's, they can be estimated from the data. The equations in Lemma 1 and Corollary 1 can thus be used to estimate the parameters of the prior.

EXAMPLE 15. Let $X_i \sim \mathcal{N}(\theta_i, 1)$, $i = 1, \ldots, n$, be past independent observations. Suppose it is thought that the θ_i are normally distributed, with unknown mean μ_π and variance σ_π^2. From Corollary 1, it is clear that $\mu_\pi = \mu_m$ and $\sigma_\pi^2 = \sigma_m^2 - 1$. The obvious estimates for μ_m and σ_m^2 are

$$\bar{x} = \frac{1}{n} \sum_{i=1}^n x_i \quad \text{and} \quad s^2 = \frac{1}{n-1} \sum_{i=1}^n (x_i - \bar{x})^2,$$

respectively. Reasonable estimates of μ_π and σ_π^2 are thus $\bar{x}$ and $s^2 - 1$. Actually, since $s^2 - 1$ can be negative, it would be more reasonable to estimate σ_π^2 by

$$(s^2 - 1)^+ = \begin{cases} s^2 - 1 & \text{if } s^2 - 1 \geq 0, \\ 0 & \text{if } s^2 - 1 < 0. \end{cases}$$

The estimated prior is thus a $\mathcal{N}(\bar{x}, (s^2 - 1)^+)$ distribution.

   In situations such as that above, the ultimate goal will be to make decisions concerning a *current* value of θ, based on a current X. A natural idea is to include this current X in the estimation of the prior parameters. This is generally a very good idea, leading to a desirable robustness, as we shall see later. (In a sense, including the current X provides protection against having assumed a wrong functional form for the prior.) The combination of relative ease of application and considerable safety in use makes this approach to the determination of π (from past data) quite attractive.

II. *Determination of π by the Distance Method*

If a large number of past observations x_i are available, one might hope to approximate $m(x)$ directly, and then somehow use the integral relationship

$$m(x) = \int_\Theta f(x|\theta) dF^\pi(\theta)$$

to accurately determine π. The difficulty arises from the fact that only an estimate $\hat{m}$ of m is obtainable, and for such an estimate the equation

$$\hat{m}(x) = \int_{\Theta} f(x|\theta)dF^{\pi}(\theta)$$

need have no solution, π. Hence all we can seek is an estimate of π, say $\hat{\pi}$, for which

$$m_{\hat{\pi}}(x) = \int_{\Theta} f(x|\theta)dF^{\hat{\pi}}(\theta)$$

is close (in some sense) to $\hat{m}(x)$. A reasonable measure of "distance" between two such densities is

$$d(\hat{m}, m_{\hat{\pi}}) = E^{\hat{m}}\left[\log\frac{\hat{m}(X)}{m_{\hat{\pi}}(X)}\right] = \begin{cases} \int_{\mathscr{X}} \hat{m}(x)\log\left[\frac{\hat{m}(x)}{m_{\hat{\pi}}(x)}\right]dx & \text{(continuous case)}, \\ \sum_{\mathscr{X}} \hat{m}(x)\log\left[\frac{\hat{m}(x)}{m_{\hat{\pi}}(x)}\right] & \text{(discrete case)}. \end{cases}$$

This measure of distance is related to the concept of entropy discussed in the previous subsection. Indeed, letting π_0 denote a noninformative prior, it is clear from Subsection 3.2.3 that the entropy of a prior π in the continuous case is simply $-d(\pi, \pi_0)$. For the finite discrete case with n possible parameter points, so that the noninformative prior is $\pi_0(\theta) = 1/n$, the entropy of π is $n - d(\pi, \pi_0)$. Thus the entropy of a prior is directly related to how "close" the prior is to a noninformative prior (which recall is supposed to represent a complete lack of knowledge about θ).

Using the above measure of distance, the goal is to seek the $\hat{\pi}$ which minimizes $d(\hat{m}, m_{\hat{\pi}})$. Note that

$$d(\hat{m}, m_{\hat{\pi}}) = E^{\hat{m}}\left[\log\frac{\hat{m}(X)}{m_{\hat{\pi}}(X)}\right] = E^{\hat{m}}[\log \hat{m}(X)] - E^{\hat{m}}[\log m_{\hat{\pi}}(X)].$$

Since only the last term of this expression depends on $\hat{\pi}$, it is clear that minimizing $d(\hat{m}, m_{\hat{\pi}})$ (over $\hat{\pi}$) is equivalent to maximizing

$$E^{\hat{m}}[\log m_{\hat{\pi}}(X)]. \tag{3.11}$$

Finding the $\hat{\pi}$ which maximizes (3.11) is a difficult problem. One situation which is relatively easy to deal with is the situation in which Θ is finite, say $\Theta = \{\theta_1, \ldots, \theta_k\}$. Letting $p_i = \hat{\pi}(\theta_i)$, it is clear that, for this situation,

$$m_{\hat{\pi}}(x) = \sum_{i=1}^{k} f(x|\theta_i)p_i.$$

Hence, finding the optimal $\hat{\pi}$ reduces to the problem of maximizing

$$E^{\hat{m}}\left[\log\left(\sum_{i=1}^{k} f(X|\theta_i)p_i\right)\right]$$

over all p_i such that $0 \leq p_i \leq 1$ and $\sum_{i=1}^{k} p_i = 1$. Recall that $\hat{m}$ is the estimate of $m(x)$ obtained from the past observations $x_1, \ldots, x_n$. The simplest such estimate $\hat{m}_0$ (as discussed earlier) is simply the discrete density which gives probability $1/n$ to each of the x_i. For this choice of $\hat{m}$,

$$E^{\hat{m}_0}\left[\log\left(\sum_{i=1}^{k} f(X|\theta_i)p_i\right)\right] = \sum_{j=1}^{n} \frac{1}{n} \log\left(\sum_{i=1}^{k} f(x_j|\theta_i)p_i\right).$$

The maximization of this last quantity over the p_i is a straightforward linear programming problem.

For continuous θ, little is known about the problem of maximizing (3.11). A very reasonable approach, given in Maritz (1970) (see also Lord and Cressie (1975)), is to only consider $\hat{\pi}$ which are step functions of say N steps (i.e., $\hat{\pi}(\theta) = c_i$ for $a_i \leq \theta < a_{i+1}$, where $a_0 < a_1 < \cdots < a_N$, $c_i \geq 0$, and $\sum_{i=0}^{(N-1)}$ $(a_{i+1} - a_i)c_i = 1$). One can then seek to maximize (3.11) over the constants a_i and c_i. This can be done on a computer.

3.2.5 Combining Past Data and Subjective Information

When past data exists concerning θ, there is often considerable subjective information also available. If this subjective information is based on impressions gained from the past data, then there is a duplication in knowledge, and one should simply proceed with either a subjective or "past data" determination of π. When, however, the subjective information arises from another source (for example prior beliefs held without having seen the past data) then it is clearly desirable to try to combine the subjective and past data information.

Unfortunately, there is no established method of doing this. (A recent method proposed by Antoniak (1974), based on the Dirichlet process of Ferguson (1973), has hope of proving successful, but a considerable amount of research needs to be done to establish its effectiveness.) One reasonable adhoc way to proceed is as follows. Determine the subjective prior $\pi_S(\theta)$ (ignoring the past data) and the past data prior $\pi_D(\theta)$ (ignoring the subjective information), as in Subsections 3.2.1 and 3.2.4. Then decide upon an N for which the degree of confidence in π_S would be equivalent to the degree of confidence in a past data prior based on N past observations. (See the discussion of "equivalent sample size" in Subsection 3.2.1 for a related concept.) If n is the actual number of past observations used in constructing π_D, a natural choice for the combined prior π is then

$$\pi(\theta) = \frac{N}{n + N} \pi_S(\theta) + \frac{n}{n + N} \pi_D(\theta).$$

A second possible adhoc procedure for determining π is to assume a given functional form for the prior, and then to combine the past data with the subjective beliefs in estimating the parameters of the functional form.

Weighted averages (as above) of the past data parameter estimates and subjective parameter estimates should prove suitable as overall parameter estimates.

3.3 Criticisms

Few statisticians would object to a Bayesian analysis when dealing with a repetitive situation in which θ is random and for which there is a considerable amount of past data from which to construct the prior. Criticism is mainly directed at the use of subjective priors when θ is not random. Part of this criticism is philosophical in nature, objecting to subjective probabilities concerning θ. No particularly convincing arguments in support of such an objection have been raised, however, and we have seen ample evidence to the contrary.

Two serious criticisms which can be raised against the use of prior information is that priors are difficult to construct and are nonobjective. Little can be said about the first criticism. Priors are hard to construct. If they are needed for a sound analysis of the problem, however, this is merely an unfortunate fact of life.

The criticism of nonobjectivity is directed mainly at the use of subjective proper prior distributions. A Bayesian would respond to this criticism in two ways. First, he would argue that if prior information does exist, it would be foolish to ignore it just for the sake of objectivity. Second, he (or at least some Bayesians) would argue that if objectivity were truly desired, then only the Bayesian approach could guarantee it. The rationale for such a statement lies in the fact that virtually any reasonable decision rule will be Bayes with respect to some (possibly improper) prior. (This will be indicated, for certain situations, in Chapter 8.) It then seems reasonable to argue that a rule is "objective" only if it corresponds to an objective prior distribution. The natural choice for an objective prior is a noninformative prior, so the argument essentially concludes that the only way to be objective is to perform a Bayesian analysis with a noninformative prior. This argument seems very strong. The difficulties involved in defining and using noninformative priors (partially discussed in Subsection 3.2.2) prevent this argument from being totally compelling, however.

A more significant criticism of the use of prior information is that the potential for misuse is considerable. Consider the situation of a person trying to decide whether $\theta \in (0, 1)$ or $\theta \in [1, 5)$. From the very statement of the problem, it is likely that θ is thought to be somewhere around 1, but a person not well versed in Bayesian analysis might choose to use the prior $\pi(\theta) = \frac{1}{5}$ (on $\Theta = (0, 5)$), reasoning that, to be fair, all θ should be given equal weight. The resulting Bayes decision will probably be that $\theta \in [1, 5)$ (regardless of what any experimental data says) because the prior gives this conclusion 4 times the probability of the conclusion that $\theta \in (0, 1)$. The potential for misuse by careless or unscrupulous people is obvious. Perhaps the best reply to this criticism is to point out that the best way to prevent misuse is by proper education concerning prior information. Also, in reporting conclusions from Bayesian analyses, the prior (and data and loss) should be reported separately, in order to allow others to evaluate the reasonableness of the subjective inputs.

The most serious question which can be raised concerning prior information is that of robustness. Do slight changes in the prior cause significant changes in the decision procedure? The unfortunate answer is—sometimes yes. The following example demonstrates this.

EXAMPLE 2 (continued). The normal and Cauchy densities in Example 2 were both matches to the given prior information. Assume it is desired to find the Bayes procedure for estimating θ under squared-error loss, based on the observation $X \sim \mathcal{N}(\theta, 1)$. If the prior is assumed to be the $\mathcal{N}(0, 2.19)$ density, the Bayes estimator is

$$\delta_1(x) = x - \frac{x}{3.19}.$$

(This will be shown in Chapter 4.) If the prior is instead $\mathscr{C}(0, 1)$, the Bayes estimator *for large x* (say $|x| \geq 4$) is approximately

$$\delta_2(x) \cong x - \frac{2x}{2 + x^2}.$$

(See Berger and Srinivasan (1978).) For large $|x|$, δ_1 and δ_2 are quite different. If $x = 10$, for instance, $\delta_1(x) = 6.87$ and $\delta_2(x) = 9.80$. Thus the usual estimator $\delta_0(x) = 10$ is changed 3.13 standard deviations by δ_1, but only 0.20 standard deviations by δ_2. The change for δ_1 is substantial, while the change for δ_2 is not. Which is better? Well if $x = 10$ is observed, it seems quite likely that the prior information is wrong. (The observation x should be within, say, ± 3 of θ, and θ should not be out near 7.) Since the prior seems quite wrong, making the substantial correction called for by δ_1 seems inappropriate. The estimator δ_2 is more attractive in that it reverts (with high probability) to the usual estimator, δ_0, when θ is far from where the prior says it should be.

In the above example, note that the difference between the two priors is mainly in the functional form. This causes concern in that it is precisely the functional form of a prior that is difficult to determine. Fractiles or parameters of the prior can readily be determined, but the correct shape is very elusive. Further discussion of this robustness problem will be delayed until Chapter 4.

3.4 The Statistician's Role

For the most part, this book is written as though the statistician is the decision maker in a problem of direct concern to him. Far more frequently, however, the statistician will be acting as a technical consultant to a client who has a statistical decision problem to deal with. A common problem faced by statisticians, in such a situation, is that of eliciting from the client the necessary information to perform the analysis. Besides the classical concerns of modeling and design, the decision theorist must also worry about obtaining accurate loss functions and priors. This can be difficult if the client has little or no statistical training. For example, the concept of probability is of obvious importance in constructing $\pi(\theta)$, yet many clients may not have a good understanding of it. The statistician will, therefore, often find himself partly in the role of a teacher, explaining certain aspects of utility theory and probability to a client, in an attempt to obtain from him the loss function and the prior. The statistician must be wary in such situations of the tendency to take the easy way out and decide, himself, upon a loss function and a prior. An excellent discussion of this problem, along with an example in which nonstatisticians were guided in constructing their priors, is given in Winkler (1967b).

There are, of course, situations in which only limited prior information and loss information is needed to conduct a decision analysis. The simple no-data Bayesian decision problems solved in Chapter 1 are of this type. Other more complicated examples will be seen later. The information needed from clients in such problems is usually very easy to obtain.

Exercises

Section 3.1

1. Automobiles are classified as economy size (small), midsize (medium), or full size (large). Decide subjectively what proportion of each type of car occurs in your area.

Subsection 3.2.1

2. Let θ denote the highest temperature that will occur outdoors tomorrow, near your place of residence. Using the histogram approach, find your subjective prior density for θ.

3. Using the relative likelihood approach, determine your prior density for θ in the situation of Exercise 2.

4. Consider the situation of Exercise 2.
   (a) Determine the $\frac{1}{4}$ and $\frac{1}{2}$ fractiles of your prior density for θ.
   (b) Find the normal density matching these fractiles.
   (c) Find, subjectively, the $\frac{1}{10}$ and $\frac{2}{3}$ fractiles of your prior distribution for θ. (Do not use the normal distribution from (b) to obtain these.) Are these consistent with

the normal distribution in (b)? Is the normal density a good fit for your prior density of θ?

5. Repeat Exercise 4 (b) and (c), but with "normal distribution" replaced by "Cauchy distribution." Note: If $X \sim \mathscr{C}(0, \beta)$, then

$$P(0 < X < s) = \pi^{-1} \tan^{-1}(s/\beta).$$

6. Let θ denote the unemployment rate next year. Determine your subjective probability density for θ. Can it be matched with a $\mathscr{B}e(\alpha, \beta)$ density?

Subsection 3.2.2

7. For each of the following densities, state whether the density is a location, scale, or location-scale density, and give the natural noninformative prior for the unknown parameters:
   (a) $\mathscr{U}(\theta - 1, \theta + 1)$,
   (b) $\mathscr{C}(0, \beta)$,
   (c) $\mathscr{T}(\alpha, \mu, \sigma^2)$ (α fixed),
   (d) $\mathscr{P}a(x_0, \alpha)$ (α fixed).

8. By an "invariance under reformulation" argument, show that a reasonable non-informative prior for a Poisson parameter θ is $\pi(\theta) = \theta^{-1}$. (*Hint*: A Poisson random variable X usually arises as the number of occurrences of a (rare) event in a time interval T. The parameter θ is the average number of occurrences in time T. Since the specification of T is rather arbitrary, consider the experiment which would result if the time interval used was cT ($c > 0$). This idea was due to Jaynes (1968).)

9. In the "table entry" problem of Example 6, verify the following statement: As $a \to 0$ or $b \to \infty$ or both, the p_i will converge to the values $[\log(1 + i^{-1})/\log 10]$.

10. In Example 7, complete the transformation argument which suggests that the non-informative prior should be $\pi(\theta, \sigma) = \sigma^{-2}$.

Subsection 3.2.3

11. Assume $X \sim \mathscr{N}(\theta, 1)$ is to be observed, but that it is known that $\theta > 0$. It is further believed that θ has a prior distribution with mean μ. Show that the prior density of θ which maximizes entropy, subject to these constraints, is the $\mathscr{E}(\mu)$ density.

12. Assume a scale parameter θ is to be estimated (so that the natural noninformative prior is θ^{-1}). It is believed that $a < \theta < b$, and that the median ($\frac{1}{2}$-fractile) of the prior density is z. Show that the prior density which maximizes entropy, subject to these constraints, is

$$\pi(\theta) = \begin{cases} \theta^{-1}\left[2\log\left(\dfrac{z}{a}\right)\right]^{-1} & \text{if } a < \theta < z, \\[2ex] \theta^{-1}\left[2\log\left(\dfrac{b}{z}\right)\right]^{-1} & \text{if } z < \theta < b. \end{cases}$$

13. Assume θ is from a location density. It is believed that $-K < \theta < K$, and that θ has prior mean $\mu \neq 0$. Show that the prior distribution which maximizes entropy, subject to these constraints, is given by

$$\pi(\theta) = \frac{ze^{z\theta/K}}{2K \sinh(z)} I_{(-K, K)}(\theta),$$

where z is the solution to the equation

$$(K^{-1}\mu z + 1)\tanh(z) - z = 0.$$

(Sinh and tanh stand for hyperbolic sine and hyperbolic tangent, respectively.)

Subsection 3.2.4

14. If $f(x|\theta)$ is a $\mathcal{B}(n, \theta)$ density and $\pi(\theta)$ is a $\mathcal{U}(0, 1)$ density, find the marginal density, $m(x)$, of X.

15. Suppose a Poisson parameter, θ, is thought to have a $\mathcal{G}(\alpha, \beta)$ prior distribution. There are available n independent past observations $x_1, \ldots, x_n$. Each X_i was $\mathcal{P}(\theta_i)$. Using the "given functional form" approach, show that a reasonable guess for the prior density is $\mathcal{G}(\hat{\alpha}, \hat{\beta})$, where (assuming $0 < \bar{x} < s^2$)

$$\hat{\alpha} = \frac{\bar{x}^2}{s^2 - \bar{x}}, \qquad \hat{\beta} = \frac{s^2 - \bar{x}}{\bar{x}}.$$

Subsection 3.2.5

16. In terms of the distance measure $d(f, g)$ given in Subsection 3.2.4, which of the two densities (on R^1),

$$g_1(x) = (6\pi)^{-1/2}e^{-x^2/6} \quad \text{or} \quad g_2(x) = 0.5e^{-|x|},$$

is closer to $f(x) = (2\pi)^{-1/2}e^{-x^2/2}$.

17. A test of $H_0: \theta = 1$ versus $H_1: \theta = 2$ is to be conducted, where θ is the parameter of a $\mathcal{U}(0, \theta)$ distribution. (Assume θ can only be 1 or 2.) It is desired to estimate the prior probability that $\theta = 1$, i.e., $\pi(1) = 1 - \pi(2)$. There are available n independent past observations $x_1, \ldots, x_n$, each of which had a $\mathcal{U}(0, \theta_i)$ distribution (with the θ_i having been a random sample from the prior distribution).
   (a) Show that, according to the "minimum distance" method, the optimal estimate of $\pi(1)$ is

$$\hat{\pi}(1) = [P^{\hat{m}}(0 < X < 1) - P^{\hat{m}}(1 < X < 2)]^+,$$

   where $\hat{m}$ is the estimated marginal distribution of the X_i.
   (b) If the simple estimate $\hat{m}_0$ is used (see Subsection 3.2.4), show that

$$P^{\hat{m}_0}(1 < X < 2) = \frac{1}{n} [\text{the number of } x_i \text{ between 1 and 2}],$$

$$P^{\hat{m}_0}(0 < X < 1) = \frac{1}{n} [\text{the number of } x_i \text{ between 0 and 1}].$$

CHAPTER 4

Bayesian Analysis

4.1 Introduction

This chapter is devoted to the implementation and evaluation of decision-theoretic analysis based on the Bayes principle introduced in Section 1.5. Bayesian analysis has many vocal supporters. This is largely due to the fact that there are compelling "rationality" arguments which support the use of the Bayesian approach. It is enlightening to begin with a discussion of these arguments.

The first justification of the Bayesian approach is quite direct, but presupposes the existence of a (possibly subjective) prior probability distribution π, and of a loss function L developed through utility considerations. Given these two quantities, one is forced, by the nature of utility theory, to use overall expected loss, namely $r(\pi, \delta) = E^{\pi}[R(\theta, \delta)]$, in evaluating decision rules.

The above argument has the obvious fault of presupposing the existence of a prior and a loss. If one is not willing to assume the existence of these quantities, it seems that a different decision principle should be used. Unfortunately, it turns out that, in some sense, there are no rational methods of statistical analysis other than the Bayesian approach. To show this, it is necessary to introduce axioms of rational behavior as in Chapter 2. Indeed one begins by assuming that a preference ordering exists among decision rules $\delta^* \in \mathscr{D}^*$. (This preference ordering is simply that determined by the decision method.) As in Section 2.1, rationality axioms for this preference ordering can be given, and it can be concluded that the preference ordering must admit a utility function $U(\delta^*)$. To be consistent, we will talk in terms of the "risk" function $r(\delta^*) = -U(\delta^*)$, rather than the utility function.

The next step of the argument is to consider the decision problem of choosing $\delta^* \in \mathscr{D}^*$ when θ is assumed known. It is reasonable to assume that this can be done (it should be easier than choosing δ^* when θ is unknown), and that the decision method corresponds to a rational preference pattern. As before, it can be concluded that for each θ, the preference pattern admits a "risk" function (negative utility) $R_\theta(\delta^*)$.

The relationship between $r(\delta^*)$ and $R_\theta(\delta^*)$ is given by what is called the fundamental theorem of Bayesian analysis. The fundamental theorem states that $r(\delta^*)$ must be a "positive linear functional" of $R_\theta(\delta^*)$, which under reasonable regularity conditions implies (by the Riesz representation theorem) that

$$r(\delta^*) = E^\pi[R_\theta(\delta^*)]$$

for some measure π on Θ. This last quantity looks very much like Bayes risk, and can indeed be so interpreted.

It is enlightening to consider the situation in which a loss function $L(\theta, a)$ has been developed through utility considerations. (The rewards are considered to be all pairs (θ, a), and a utility function for such rewards is constructed. For this to be possible, of course, it is necessary to assume a rational preference pattern among such rewards. This certainly seems reasonable, however.) In such a situation, it must be true that $R_\theta(\delta^*)$ is the expected loss of δ^*, i.e.,

$$R_\theta(\delta^*) = R(\theta, \delta^*) = E^X[L(\theta, \delta^*(X))].$$

It follows from the fundamental theorem that

$$r(\delta^*) = E^\pi[R(\theta, \delta^*)],$$

and it can further be shown that π is a finite measure (and hence without loss of generality a probability measure). There is a mathematical quirk of the fundamental theorem, by which π need only be a "finitely additive" measure, but in practice, this is just a minor technicality. The overall conclusion of the fundamental theorem is thus that any rational method of choosing among decision rules corresponds to the ordering induced by $r(\pi, \delta^*)$ for some prior π.

The proof of the fundamental theorem is beyond the scope of this book. It rests heavily on the conditionality principle discussed in Subsection 1.6.2. The interested reader can find proofs in Savage (1962), Ferguson (1967) (a simple and easily understandable case), and Rubin (1974) (the most general known result).

It should be noted that the fundamental theorem applies also to choosing decision rules in inference problems, providing there is assumed to be only one preference pattern among decision rules. Frequently in inference problems, procedures are desired which will be adequate for a wide range of preference patterns, the idea being that the inference should be useful to a wide range of users. Even in such situations, however, the statistician can imagine trying to act in some "average" optimal fashion, giving validity to the fundamental theorem. Of course the quantification of this "average" loss might be extremely difficult.

The fundamental theorem can be criticized for taking a "pre-experimental" viewpoint instead of a "post-experimental" viewpoint, in that it considers preferences among the δ^* rather than preferences among the actions after experimentation. This criticism can be answered, as in Subsection 1.6.2, by pointing out that no generality is lost in considering decision rules. A decision rule can just be considered to be a collection of post-experimental actions, and there is nothing inherently wrong in deciding, before the experiment, which action will be taken if the observation is x. The use of δ^* and $R(\theta, \delta^*)$ can just be thought of as a "thought experiment," helpful in clarifying attitudes concerning preferences among decisions. It will indeed be seen in Section 4.4 that Bayesian analysis leads to the same conclusion whether pre-experimental or post-experimental reasoning is used.

Bayesians often quote the fundamental theorem as saying that if a person desires to be rational, he must act in a Bayesian fashion (i.e., choose a prior and a loss and find the Bayes rule). This is a misinterpretation of the fundamental theorem. The theorem says that a rational person acts as if he had a prior and a loss, but does not state that he must choose a prior and a loss and use the Bayes principle. Conceivably, one could somehow determine $r(\delta^*)$ directly, or equivalently find a direct "rational" decision mechanism which avoids consideration of π. No such alternate rational decision mechanism has ever been found, however, and in practice it is hard to imagine how $r(\delta^*)$ could ever be found except through determination of π and L. In a somewhat unscientific sense, the fundamental theorem indicates that any rational preference pattern among the δ^* is composed of a loss component and a component that can be interpreted as prior information. It seems unreasonable to imagine that the more complicated $r(\delta^*)$ could somehow be directly found for a situation in which its simpler components could not be determined.

For those who look askance at rationality axioms, it is worthwhile to observe that a similar conclusion can be reached with considerably less formalism. It is a fact (to be partially demonstrated in this chapter and extensively discussed in Chapter 8) that most reasonable statistical rules are Bayes rules with respect to some (possibly improper) prior. Whether or not one believes in actually constructing priors, this correspondence cannot be ignored. It seems quite unreasonable to use a decision rule which corresponds to a prior which does not reflect true prior beliefs.

It should not be concluded from the above arguments that we are endorsing a simple Bayesian approach, in which one simply writes down guesses for the prior and the loss and performs a Bayesian analysis. This may be no more "rational" than any other decision method, in that the chosen π and L can never be more than approximations to the true π and L. What we are really saying is that it is irrational to refuse to consider prior information and loss. We actually will advocate a Bayesian approach, but only a cautious one in which the choice of π is affected not only by subjective inputs, but also by consideration of non-Bayesian quantities such as $R(\theta, \delta)$. Some discussion of this has already been given in Subsection 1.6.3 and Chapter 3, and the subject will receive considerable attention in this chapter, particularly Section 6.

In Sections 4.2 and 4.3 the purely Bayesian (as opposed to Bayesian decision-theoretic) approach will be discussed. This type of analysis attempts to make use of $\pi(\theta)$, but not of a loss function L. As such, it is basically designed to deal with inference problems, and can be very useful in this regard. Section 4.4 returns to the basic problem of Bayesian decision making in the presence of a loss function. Section 4.5 discusses certain results concerning admissibility and inadmissibility of Bayes rules.

4.2 The Posterior Distribution

Bayesian analysis is performed by combining the prior information $(\pi(\theta))$ and the sample information (x) into what is called the posterior distribution of θ given x, from which all decisions and inferences are made. This section discusses the meaning and calculation of this distribution.

4.2.1 Definition and Determination

The *posterior distribution of θ given x* (or *posterior* for short) will be denoted $\pi(\theta|x)$, and, as the notation indicates, is defined to be the conditional distribution of θ given the sample observation x. Noting that θ and X have joint (subjective) density

$$h(x, \theta) = \pi(\theta)f(x|\theta),$$

and (as in Subsection 3.2.4) that X has marginal (unconditional) density

$$m(x) = \int_\Theta f(x|\theta)dF^\pi(\theta).$$

it is clear that (providing $m(x) \neq 0$)

$$\pi(\theta|x) = \frac{h(x, \theta)}{m(x)}.$$

The name "posterior distribution" is indicative of the role of $\pi(\theta|x)$. Just as the prior distribution reflects beliefs about θ *prior* to experimentation, so $\pi(\theta|x)$ reflects the updated beliefs about θ after (*posterior* to) observing the sample x. In other words, the posterior distribution combines the prior beliefs about θ with the information about θ contained in the sample, x, to give a composite picture of the final beliefs about θ. Note that the likelihood principle is implicitly assumed in the above statement, in that there is felt to be no sample information about θ other than that contained in $f(x|\theta)$ (for the given x).

In calculating the posterior distribution, it is often helpful to use the concept of sufficiency. Indeed if T is a sufficient statistic for θ with density $g(t|\theta)$, the following result can be established. (The proof is left as an exercise.)

Lemma 1. *Assume $m(t)$ (the marginal density of t) is greater than zero, and that the factorization theorem holds. Then, if $T(x) = t$,*

$$\pi(\theta|x) = \pi(\theta|t) = \frac{\pi(\theta)g(t|\theta)}{m(t)}.$$

The reason for determining $\pi(\theta|x)$ from a sufficient statistic T (if possible) is that $g(t|\theta)$ and $m(t)$ are usually much easier to handle than $f(x|\theta)$ and $m(x)$.

EXAMPLE 1. Assume $X \sim \mathcal{N}(\theta, \sigma^2)$, where θ is unknown but σ^2 is known. Let $\pi(\theta)$ be a $\mathcal{N}(\mu, \tau^2)$ density, where μ and τ^2 are known. Then

$$h(x, \theta) = \pi(\theta)f(x|\theta) = (2\pi\sigma\tau)^{-1} \exp\left\{-\frac{1}{2}\left[\frac{(\theta-\mu)^2}{\tau^2} + \frac{(x-\theta)^2}{\sigma^2}\right]\right\}.$$

To find $m(x)$, note that defining

$$\rho = \tau^{-2} + \sigma^{-2} = \frac{\tau^2 + \sigma^2}{\tau^2\sigma^2}$$

and completing squares gives

$$\frac{1}{2}\left[\frac{(\theta-\mu)^2}{\tau^2} + \frac{(x-\theta)^2}{\sigma^2}\right] = \frac{1}{2}\left[\left(\frac{1}{\tau^2} + \frac{1}{\sigma^2}\right)\theta^2 - 2\left(\frac{\mu}{\tau^2} + \frac{x}{\sigma^2}\right)\theta + \left(\frac{\mu^2}{\tau^2} + \frac{x^2}{\sigma^2}\right)\right]$$

$$= \frac{1}{2}\rho\left[\theta^2 - \frac{2}{\rho}\left(\frac{\mu}{\tau^2} + \frac{x}{\sigma^2}\right)\theta\right] + \frac{1}{2}\left(\frac{\mu^2}{\tau^2} + \frac{x^2}{\sigma^2}\right)$$

$$= \frac{1}{2}\rho\left[\theta - \frac{1}{\rho}\left(\frac{\mu}{\tau^2} + \frac{x}{\sigma^2}\right)\right]^2 - \frac{1}{2\rho}\left(\frac{\mu}{\tau^2} + \frac{x}{\sigma^2}\right)^2$$

$$+ \frac{1}{2}\left(\frac{\mu^2}{\tau^2} + \frac{x^2}{\sigma^2}\right)$$

$$= \frac{1}{2}\rho\left[\theta - \frac{1}{\rho}\left(\frac{\mu}{\tau^2} + \frac{x}{\sigma^2}\right)\right]^2 + \frac{(\mu-x)^2}{2(\sigma^2 + \tau^2)}.$$

Hence

$$h(x, \theta) = (2\pi\sigma\tau)^{-1} \exp\left\{-\frac{1}{2}\rho\left[\theta - \frac{1}{\rho}\left(\frac{\mu}{\tau^2} + \frac{x}{\sigma^2}\right)\right]^2\right\}\exp\left\{-\frac{(\mu-x)^2}{2(\sigma^2 + \tau^2)}\right\}$$

and

$$m(x) = \int_{-\infty}^{\infty} h(x, \theta)d\theta = (2\pi\rho)^{-1/2}(\sigma\tau)^{-1} \exp\left\{-\frac{(\mu - x)^2}{2(\sigma^2 + \tau^2)}\right\}$$

It follows that

$$\pi(\theta|x) = \frac{h(x, \theta)}{m(x)} = \left(\frac{\rho}{2\pi}\right)^{1/2} \exp\left\{-\frac{1}{2}\rho\left[\theta - \frac{1}{\rho}\left(\frac{\mu}{\tau^2} + \frac{x}{\sigma^2}\right)\right]^2\right\}.$$

Note, from the above equations, that the marginal distribution of X is $\mathcal{N}(\mu, (\sigma^2 + \tau^2))$ and the posterior distribution of θ given x is $\mathcal{N}(\mu(x), \rho^{-1})$, where

$$\mu(x) = \frac{1}{\rho}\left(\frac{\mu}{\tau^2} + \frac{x}{\sigma^2}\right) = \frac{\sigma^2}{\sigma^2 + \tau^2}\mu + \frac{\tau^2}{\sigma^2 + \tau^2}x = x - \frac{\sigma^2}{\sigma^2 + \tau^2}(x - \mu).$$

As a concrete example, consider the situation wherein a child is given an intelligence test. Assume that the test result X is $\mathcal{N}(\theta, 100)$, where θ is the true IQ (intelligence) level of the child, as measured by the test. (In other words, if the child were to take a large number of independent similar tests, his average score would be about θ.) Assume also that, in the population as a whole, θ is distributed according to a $\mathcal{N}(100, 225)$ distribution. Using the above equations, it follows that, unconditionally, X is $\mathcal{N}(100, 325)$, while the posterior distribution of θ given x is normal with mean

$$\mu(x) = \frac{(100)(100) + x(225)}{(100 + 225)} = \frac{400 + 9x}{13}$$

and variance

$$\rho^{-1} = \frac{(100)(225)}{(100 + 225)} = \frac{900}{13} = 69.23.$$

Thus, if a child scores 115 on the test, his true IQ θ has a $\mathcal{N}(110.39, 69.23)$ posterior distribution.

EXAMPLE 2. Assume a sample $\mathbf{X} = (X_1, \ldots, X_n)$ from a $\mathcal{N}(\theta, \sigma^2)$ distribution is to be taken (σ^2 known), and that θ has a $\mathcal{N}(\mu, \tau^2)$ density. Since $\bar{X}$ is sufficient for θ, it follows from Lemma 1 that $\pi(\theta|x) = \pi(\theta|\bar{x})$. Noting that $\bar{X} \sim \mathcal{N}(\theta, \sigma^2/n)$, it can be concluded from Example 1 that the posterior distribution of θ given $\mathbf{x} = (x_1, \ldots, x_n)$ is $\mathcal{N}(\mu(\mathbf{x}), \rho^{-1})$, where

$$\mu(\mathbf{x}) = \frac{\sigma^2/n}{(\tau^2 + \sigma^2/n)}\mu + \frac{\tau^2}{(\tau^2 + \sigma^2/n)}\bar{x}$$

and $\rho = (n\tau^2 + \sigma^2)/\tau^2\sigma^2$.

EXAMPLE 3. A blood test is to be conducted to help indicate whether or not a person has a particular disease. The result of the test is either positive (denoted $x = 1$) or negative (denoted $x = 0$). Letting θ_1 denote the state of nature "the disease is present" and θ_2 denote the state of nature "no disease is present," assume it is known that $f(1|\theta_1) = 0.8$, $f(0|\theta_1) = 0.2$, $f(1|\theta_2) = 0.3$, and $f(0|\theta_2) = 0.7$. According to prior information, $\pi(\theta_1) = 0.05$ and $\pi(\theta_2) = 0.95$. Then

$$m(1) = f(1|\theta_1)\pi(\theta_1) + f(1|\theta_2)\pi(\theta_2) = 0.04 + 0.285 = 0.325,$$

$$m(0) = f(0|\theta_1)\pi(\theta_1) + f(0|\theta_2)\pi(\theta_2) = 0.01 + 0.665 = 0.675,$$

$$\pi(\theta|x = 1) = \frac{f(1|\theta)\pi(\theta)}{m(1)} = \begin{cases} \dfrac{0.04}{0.325} = 0.123 & \text{if } \theta = \theta_1, \\[2mm] \dfrac{0.285}{0.325} = 0.877 & \text{if } \theta = \theta_2, \end{cases}$$

and

$$\pi(\theta|x = 0) = \frac{f(0|\theta)\pi(\theta)}{m(0)} = \begin{cases} \dfrac{0.01}{0.675} = 0.0148 & \text{if } \theta = \theta_1, \\[2mm] \dfrac{0.665}{0.675} = 0.9852 & \text{if } \theta = \theta_2. \end{cases}$$

It is interesting to note that, even if the blood test is positive, there is still only a 12.3% chance of the disease being present.

In discrete situations, such as Example 3, the formula for $\pi(\theta|x)$ is commonly known as Bayes's theorem, and was discovered by Bayes (1763). The typical phrasing of Bayes's theorem is in terms of disjoint events $A_1, A_2, \ldots,$ A_n, whose union has probability one (i.e., one of the A_i is certain to occur). Prior probabilities $P(A_i)$, for the events, are assumed known. An event B occurs, for which $P(B|A_i)$ (the conditional probability of B given A_i) is known for each A_i. Bayes's theorem then states that

$$P(A_i|B) = \frac{P(B|A_i)P(A_i)}{\sum_{j=1}^{n} P(B|A_j)P(A_j)}.$$

These probabilities reflect our revised opinions about the A_i, in light of the knowledge that B has occurred. Replacing A_i by θ_i and B by x, shows the equivalence of this to the formula for the posterior distribution.

EXAMPLE 4. In airplanes there is a warning light that goes on if the landing gear fails to fully extend. Sometimes the warning light goes on even when the landing gear has extended. Let A_1 denote the event "the landing gear extends" and A_2 denote the event "the landing gear fails to extend." (Note that A_1 and A_2 are disjoint and one of the two must occur.) Let B be the event that the warning light goes on. It is known that the light will go on with probability 0.999 if A_2 occurs (i.e., $P(B|A_2) = 0.999$), while $P(B|A_1) = 0.005$. Records show that $P(A_1) = 0.997$ and $P(A_2) = 0.003$. It is desired to determine the probability that the landing gear has extended, even though the warning light has gone on. This is simply $P(A_1|B)$, and from Bayes's theorem is given by

$$P(A_1|B) = \frac{(0.005)(0.997)}{(0.005)(0.997) + (0.999)(0.003)} = 0.62.$$

4.2.2 Conjugate Families

In general, $m(x)$ and $\pi(\theta|x)$ are not easily calculable. If, for example, X is $\mathcal{N}(\theta, \sigma^2)$ and θ is $\mathcal{C}(\mu, \beta)$, then $\pi(\theta|x)$ can only be evaluated numerically. A large part of the Bayesian literature is devoted to finding prior distributions for which $\pi(\theta|x)$ can be easily calculated. These are the so called *conjugate priors*.

Definition 1. Let $\mathcal{F}$ denote the class of density functions $f(x|\theta)$ (indexed by θ). A class $\mathcal{P}$ of prior distributions is said to be a *conjugate family* for $\mathcal{F}$ if $\pi(\theta|x)$ is in the class $\mathcal{P}$ for all $f \in \mathcal{F}$ and $\pi \in \mathcal{P}$.

Example 1 shows that the class of normal priors is a conjugate family for the class of normal (sample) densities. (If X has a normal density and θ has a normal prior, then the posterior density of θ given x is also normal).

For a given class of densities $\mathcal{F}$, a conjugate family can frequently be determined by examining the likelihood functions $l_x(\theta) = f(x|\theta)$, and choosing, as a conjugate family, the class of distributions with the same functional form as these likelihood functions.

When dealing with conjugate priors, there is generally no need to explicitly calculate $m(x)$. The reason is that, since $\pi(\theta|x) = h(x, \theta)/m(x)$, the factors involving θ in $\pi(\theta|x)$ must be the same as the factors involving θ in $h(x, \theta)$. Hence it is only necessary to look at the factors involving θ in $h(x, \theta)$, and see if these can be recognized as belonging to a particular distribution. If so, $\pi(\theta|x)$ is that distribution. The marginal density $m(x)$ can then be determined, if desired, by dividing $h(x, \theta)$ by $\pi(\theta|x)$. An example of the above ideas follows.

EXAMPLE 5. Assume $\mathbf{X} = (X_1, \ldots, X_n)$ is a sample from a Poisson distribution. Thus $X_i \sim \mathcal{P}(\theta)$, $i = 1, \ldots, n$, and

$$f(\mathbf{x}|\theta) = \prod_{i=1}^{n} \left[\frac{\theta^{x_i} e^{-\theta}}{x_i!} \right] = \frac{\theta^{n\bar{x}} e^{-n\theta}}{\prod_{i=1}^{n} [x_i!]}.$$

Here, $\mathcal{F}$ is the class of all such densities. Observing that the likelihood function for such densities resembles a gamma density, a plausible guess for a conjugate family of prior distributions is the class of gamma distributions. Thus assume $\theta \sim \mathscr{G}(\alpha, \beta)$, and observe that

$$h(\mathbf{x}, \theta) = f(\mathbf{x}|\theta)\pi(\theta) = \frac{e^{-n\theta}\theta^{n\bar{x}}}{\prod_{i=1}^{n} [x_i!]} \cdot \frac{\theta^{\alpha-1}e^{-\theta/\beta}I_{(0,\infty)}(\theta)}{\Gamma(\alpha)\beta^\alpha}$$

$$= \frac{e^{-\theta(n+1/\beta)}\theta^{(n\bar{x}+\alpha-1)}I_{(0,\infty)}(\theta)}{\Gamma(\alpha)\beta^\alpha \prod_{i=1}^{n} [x_i!]}.$$

The factors involving θ in this last expression are clearly recognizable as belonging to a $\mathscr{G}(n\bar{x} + \alpha, [n + 1/\beta]^{-1})$ distribution. This must then be $\pi(\theta|\mathbf{x})$. Since this posterior is a gamma distribution, it follows that the class of gamma distributions is indeed a conjugate family for $\mathscr{F}$.

In this example, $m(\mathbf{x})$ can be determined by dividing $h(\mathbf{x}, \theta)$ by $\pi(\theta|\mathbf{x})$ and cancelling factors involving θ. The result is

$$m(\mathbf{x}) = \frac{h(\mathbf{x}, \theta)}{\pi(\theta|\mathbf{x})} = \frac{(\Gamma(\alpha)\beta^\alpha \prod_{i=1}^{n} [x_i!])^{-1}}{\{\Gamma(\alpha + n\bar{x})[n + 1/\beta]^{-(\alpha+n\bar{x})}\}^{-1}}.$$

Besides providing for easy calculation of $\pi(\theta|x)$, conjugate priors have the intuitively appealing feature of allowing one to begin with a certain functional form for the prior and end up with a posterior of the same functional form, but with parameters updated by the sample information. In Example 1, for instance, the prior mean μ gets updated by x to become the posterior mean

$$\mu(x) = \frac{\tau^2}{\sigma^2 + \tau^2}x + \frac{\sigma^2}{\sigma^2 + \tau^2}\mu.$$

The prior variance τ^2 is combined with the sample variance σ^2 to give the posterior variance

$$\rho^{-1} = \left(\frac{1}{\sigma^2} + \frac{1}{\tau^2}\right)^{-1}.$$

This updating of parameters provides an easy way of seeing the effect of prior and sample information. It also makes useful the concept of equivalent sample size discussed in Chapter 3.

These attractive properties of conjugate priors are, however, only of secondary importance compared to the basic question of whether or not a conjugate prior can be chosen which gives a reasonable approximation to the true prior. Many Bayesians say this can be done, arguing for example that, in dealing with a normal mean, the class of $\mathscr{N}(\mu, \tau^2)$ priors is rich enough to include approximations to most reasonable priors. Unfortunately, in Section 3.3 we saw cause to doubt this belief, observing that using a normal prior can result in unappealing conclusions. (Section 4.6 will deal more extensively with this problem.) Hence the use of conjugate priors, while simple, must be looked at with suspicion. (Most of the examples and problems in this chapter will make use of conjugate priors, due to the resulting ease in calculation. Be wary of the use of conjugate priors in real problems, however.)

4.2.3 The Predictive Distribution

In the previous subsections, $m(x)$ (the marginal distribution of X) was used only in the construction of the posterior distribution. It is worthwhile to note that $m(x)$ is sometimes of interest in its own right, since it (supposedly) gives the distribution of the sample that will actually occur. Indeed, $m(x)$ is some-times called the *predictive distribution*, due to this property of describing the expected behavior of the sample. In Example 1, for instance, the actual distribution of IQ test scores will be $\mathcal{N}(100, 325)$. In Example 3, the predictive distribution is simply $m(1)$ and $m(0)$, the overall probabilities of positive and negative blood tests respectively. These probabilities might be of interest if, say, all positive tests were to be followed up by a more complicated chemical analysis. The probability $m(1)$ gives the proportion of the blood tests that will need this more complicated analysis, allowing plans to be made for the logistics of the testing.

4.2.4 Improper Priors

The analysis leading to the posterior distribution can formally be carried out even if $\pi(\theta)$ is an improper prior. For example, if $X \sim \mathcal{N}(\theta, \sigma^2)$ (σ^2 known) and the noninformative prior $\pi(\theta) = 1$ is used, then

$$h(x, \theta) = f(x|\theta)\pi(\theta) = f(x|\theta),$$

$$m(x) = \int_{-\infty}^{\infty} f(x|\theta)d\theta = (2\pi)^{-1/2}\sigma^{-1} \int_{-\infty}^{\infty} \exp\left\{\frac{-(x-\theta)^2}{2\sigma^2}\right\}d\theta = 1,$$

and

$$\pi(\theta|x) = \frac{h(x, \theta)}{m(x)} = (2\pi)^{-1/2}\sigma^{-1} \exp\left\{\frac{-(\theta-x)^2}{2\sigma^2}\right\}.$$

Hence the posterior distribution of θ given x is $\mathcal{N}(x, \sigma^2)$. Of course, this posterior distribution cannot rigorously be considered to be the conditional distribution of θ given x, but various heuristic arguments can be given to support such an interpretation. For example, taking a suitable sequence of finite priors $\pi_n(\theta)$, which converge to $\pi(\theta)$ as $n \to \infty$, it can be shown that the corresponding posteriors, $\pi_n(\theta|x)$, converge to $\pi(\theta|x)$. Other arguments using finitely-additive probability measures can be given to support the informal interpretation of $\pi(\theta|x)$ as the conditional density of θ given x.

4.3 Bayesian Inference

As mentioned previously, inference problems about θ can be dealt with using Bayesian analysis. The idea is that since the posterior distribution supposedly contains all the available information about θ (both sample and prior information) any inferences concerning θ should be made solely through this distribution. This intuitive idea tends to be viewed as an obvious truth by its proponents, while its opponents look upon it as illfounded and oversimplified. The main bone of contention is, of course, the use of the prior $\pi(\theta)$. Statistical inference problems usually occur from investigations in which it is desired to be objective. The use of prior information in the inference is criticized for an obvious lack of objectivity.

This criticism can be answered in two ways. First, if significant prior information does exist, then ignoring it for the sake of objectivity seems ill advised. Nevertheless, the difficulties in accurately specifying prior information (and convincing others that this prior information is reasonable) suggest that it is probably wise to use prior information sparingly in inference problems.

The second and more convincing answer to the criticism of a lack of objectivity, is that the analysis can be done using noninformative priors. Such priors supposedly reflect a complete lack of information about θ, and can hence be considered objective. Indeed this approach to Bayesian inference has been embraced heartily by some statisticians (Jaynes (1968) and Box and Tiao (1973) for example) as the *only* objective method of inference. Their argument is that other methods could contain hidden "favoritism" for certain θ, and that the only way to ensure this doesn't happen is through the use of a noninformative prior. (Box and Tiao (1973) actually recommend only "locally noninformative" priors, i.e., priors which behave like noninformative priors locally and then tail off to zero. The rules they recommend are the same as the rules calculated from noninformative priors, however, so the difference seems solely cosmetic.) This is reminiscent of the discussion in Section 4.1 concerning the argument that any rational method of choosing a procedure corresponds to a choice of a prior distribution for θ. If objectivity is desired, this implied prior should be an objective prior.

Though appealing, this argument for Bayesian inference with noninformative priors is not totally compelling. The two holes in the argument are that (i) there is usually no such thing as a clearcut noninformative prior (see Subsection 3.2.2); and (ii) noninformative priors are usually improper, making the interpretation of the posterior distribution unclear. Indeed examples will be seen in which inference through noninformative priors is not optimal.

It is a sign of the considerable prejudice against Bayesian analysis that the above two objections to inference with noninformative priors are considered damning by many statisticians. To this author, all they indicate is that the approach is not the magic solution to all inference problems (as claimed by some) but rather an approach which, as with most others, must be used carefully and with a healthy amount of skepticism. On the whole, however, it can be argued that Bayesian inference with noninformative priors is the most attractive approach to inference; due to its simplicity (which will be seen in this section), its efforts at achieving objectivity, and (most importantly) that it seems to work. Incidences in which it gives unsatisfactory answers are extremely rare, more so than for any other method of inference.

Statistical inference is not the main subject of this book, so we will do no more than indicate the basic elements of the Bayesian approach to inference. For a thorough treatment of many standard statistical problems using this approach, see the excellent book of Box and Tiao (1973).

In this section we look at some standard ways of using the posterior distribution to make inferences about θ. Box and Tiao (1973) maintain that the best way of conveying the necessary information is to simply give the posterior density. This has considerable merit. One can often best get a feeling for θ through, say, a visual inspection of the graph of its believed (posterior) density. More standard uses of the posterior are still helpful, however, and will be presented in the remainder of the section. Several of these uses lead to measures of final precision. Indeed any measure of accuracy based on the posterior distribution is a measure of final precision, since it depends only on the observed sample x.

4.3.1 Estimation

To estimate θ, a number of classical techniques can be applied to the posterior distribution. The most common classical technique is maximum likelihood estimation, which chooses, as the estimate of θ, the value $\hat{\theta}$ which maximizes the likelihood function $l(\theta) = f(x|\theta)$. The analogous Bayesian estimate is defined as follows.

Definition 2. The *generalized maximum likelihood* estimate of θ is the largest mode, $\hat{\theta}$, of $\pi(\theta|x)$ (i.e., the value $\hat{\theta}$ which maximizes $\pi(\theta|x)$, considered as a function of θ).

Obviously $\hat{\theta}$ has the interpretation of being the "most likely" value of θ, given the prior and the sample x.

EXAMPLE 1 (continued). When f and π are normal densities, the posterior density was seen to be $\mathcal{N}(\mu(x), \rho^{-1})$. A normal density achieves its maximum value at the mean, so the generalized maximum likelihood estimate of θ in this situation is

$$\hat{\theta} = \mu(x) = \frac{\sigma^2\mu}{\sigma^2 + \tau^2} + \frac{\tau^2 x}{\sigma^2 + \tau^2}.$$

EXAMPLE 6. Assume

$$f(x|\theta) = e^{-(x-\theta)}I_{(\theta,\,\infty)}(x),$$

and $\pi(\theta) = [\pi(1 + \theta^2)]^{-1}$. Then

$$\pi(\theta|x) = \frac{e^{-(x-\theta)}I_{(\theta,\,\infty)}(x)}{m(x)(1 + \theta^2)\pi}.$$

To find the $\hat\theta$ maximizing this quantity, note first that only $\theta \le x$ need be considered. (If $\theta > x$, then $I_{(\theta,\,\infty)}(x) = 0$ and $\pi(\theta|x) = 0$.) For such θ,

$$\frac{d}{d\theta}\pi(\theta|x) = \frac{e^{-x}}{m(x)\pi}\left[\frac{e^\theta}{1 + \theta^2} - \frac{2\theta e^\theta}{(1 + \theta^2)^2}\right]$$

$$= \frac{e^{-x}}{m(x)\pi}\frac{e^\theta(\theta - 1)^2}{(1 + \theta^2)^2}.$$

Since this derivative is always positive, $\pi(\theta|x)$ is increasing for $\theta \le x$. It follows that $\pi(\theta|x)$ is maximized at $\hat\theta = x$, which is thus the generalized maximum likelihood estimate of θ.

Other common Bayesian estimates of θ include the mean and the median of $\pi(\theta|x)$. In Example 1 these clearly coincide with $\mu(x)$, the mode. In Example 6, however, the mean and median will differ from the mode, and must be calculated numerically.

The mean and median (and mode) are relatively easy to find when the prior, and hence posterior, are from a conjugate family of distributions. In Example 5, for instance, $\pi(\theta|x)$ is $\mathcal{G}(\alpha + n\bar{x}, [n + 1/\beta]^{-1})$, which has mean $[\alpha + n\bar{x}]/[n + 1/\beta]$. The median can be found using tables of the gamma distribution.

The mean and median of the posterior are frequently better estimates of θ than the mode. It is probably worthwhile to calculate and compare all three in a Bayesian study, especially with regard to their robustness to changes in the prior.

As mentioned at the beginning of this section, Bayesian inference using a noninformative prior is often an easy and reasonable method of analysis. The following example gives a simple demonstration of this in an estimation problem.

EXAMPLE 7. A not uncommon situation is to observe $X \sim \mathcal{N}(\theta, \sigma^2)$ (for simplicity assume σ^2 is known), where θ is a measure of some clearly positive quantity. The classical estimate of θ is x, which is clearly unsuitable when x turns out to be negative. A reasonable way of developing an alternative estimate (assuming no specific prior knowledge is available) is to use the noninformative prior $\pi(\theta) = I_{(0,\,\infty)}(\theta)$ (since θ is a location parameter). The resulting posterior is

$$\pi(\theta|x) = \frac{e^{-(\theta-x)^2/2\sigma^2}I_{(0,\,\infty)}(\theta)}{\int_0^\infty e^{-(\theta-x)^2/2\sigma^2}\,d\theta}.$$

Making the change of variables $\eta = (\theta - x)/\sigma$, the mean of the posterior can be seen to be

$$E^{\pi(\theta|x)}[\theta] = \frac{\int_0^\infty \theta \exp\{-(\theta - x)^2/2\sigma^2\}d\theta}{\int_0^\infty \exp\{-(\theta - x)^2/2\sigma^2\}d\theta}$$

$$= \frac{\int_{-(x/\sigma)}^\infty (\sigma\eta + x)\exp\{-\eta^2/2\}\sigma \, d\eta}{\int_{-(x/\sigma)}^\infty \exp\{-\eta^2/2\}\sigma \, d\eta}$$

$$= x + \frac{(2\pi)^{-1/2}\sigma \int_{-(x/\sigma)}^\infty \eta \exp\{-\eta^2/2\}d\eta}{P(Z > -(x/\sigma))} \qquad (Z \text{ is } \mathcal{N}(0, 1))$$

$$= x + \frac{(2\pi)^{-1/2}\sigma e^{-x^2/2\sigma^2}}{P(Z > -(x/\sigma))}.$$

This estimate of θ is quite reasonable and is easy to use.

4.3.2 Credible Regions

Along with an estimate of θ, it is customary in statistics to give an associated confidence region. In Bayesian terminology, a confidence region is called a credible region.

Definition 3. A $100(1 - \alpha)\%$ *credible region* for θ is a subset C of Θ such that

$$1 - \alpha \leq P(C|x) = \int_C dF^{\pi(\theta|x)}(\theta) = \begin{cases} \int_C \pi(\theta|x)d\theta & \text{(continuous case),} \\ \sum_{\theta \in C} \pi(\theta|x) & \text{(discrete case).} \end{cases}$$

Since the posterior distribution is an actual probability distribution on Θ, one can speak meaningfully (though usually subjectively) of the probability that θ is in C. This is in contrast to classical confidence regions, which can only be interpreted in terms of probability of coverage (the probability that the sample will be such that the resulting confidence region contains θ). Note that the classical probability of coverage is a measure of initial precision, while the Bayesian coverage probability is a measure of final precision. (*After* observing x, the Bayesian feels θ has probability at least $1 - \alpha$ of being in C.)

In choosing a credible region for θ, it is usually desirable to try to minimize its size. It can easily be seen that to do this, one should include in the region only those points with the highest posterior density (the "most likely" values of θ). (Actually, this minimizes specifically the volume of the credible region. It may be desirable to minimize other types of size. See Subsection 6.6.3 for a discussion of this.)

Definition 4. The $100(1 - \alpha)\%$ HPD *credible region* for θ (HPD stands for highest posterior density), is the subset C of Θ of the form

$$C = \{\theta \in \Theta : \pi(\theta|x) \geq k(\alpha)\},$$

where $k(\alpha)$ is the largest constant such that

$$P(C|x) \geq 1 - \alpha.$$

EXAMPLE 1 (continued). Since the posterior density of θ given x is $\mathcal{N}(\mu(x), \rho^{-1})$, which is unimodal and symmetric about $\mu(x)$, it is clear that the $100(1 - \alpha)\%$ HPD credible region is given by

$$C = \left(\mu(x) + z\left(\frac{\alpha}{2}\right)\rho^{-1/2}, \mu(x) - z\left(\frac{\alpha}{2}\right)\rho^{-1/2}\right),$$

where $z(\alpha)$ is the α-fractile of a $\mathcal{N}(0, 1)$ distribution.

In the IQ example, where the child who scores 115 on the intelligence test has a $\mathcal{N}(110.39, 69.23)$ posterior distribution for θ, it follows that a 95% HPD credible region for θ is

$$(110.39 + (-1.96)(69.23)^{1/2}, 110.39 + (1.96)(69.23)^{1/2}) = (94.08, 126.70).$$

Note that since, conditionally, a test score X is $\mathcal{N}(\theta, 100)$, the classical 95% confidence interval for θ is

$$(115 - (1.96)(10), 115 + (1.96)(10)) = (95.4, 134.6).$$

EXAMPLE 8. In Subsection 4.2.4 it was shown that if $X \sim \mathcal{N}(\theta, \sigma^2)$ (σ^2 known) and the noninformative prior $\pi(\theta) = 1$ is used, then the posterior distribution of θ given x is $\mathcal{N}(x, \sigma^2)$. It follows that the $100(1 - \alpha)\%$ HPD credible region for θ is

$$C = \left(x + z\left(\frac{\alpha}{2}\right)\sigma, x - z\left(\frac{\alpha}{2}\right)\sigma\right).$$

This is exactly the same as the classical confidence region for θ. Note, however, that C would be interpreted differently by Bayesian and classical statisticians. To a Bayesian, the probability that θ is in C is actually $1 - \alpha$, while, to the classical statistician, θ would be contained in C in $100(1 - \alpha)\%$ of identical experiments.

In the above example, it is interesting that the classical procedure and confidence level coincide with the noninformative Bayesian procedure and credible level. Some Bayesians maintain (and not without justification) that the only reason classical confidence procedures have survived for so long is that, for the all-important normal distribution, the initial precision of the classical procedure coincides (by luck) with the true final precision. This is by no means the case for all distributions, however. In the situation of Example 8 of Chapter 1, for instance, it can be shown (the calculation is left as an exercise) that the Bayesian $100(1 - \alpha)\%$ HPD credible region for θ (using the noninformative prior) can be considerably different and *vastly more sensible* then the classical confidence region.

Bayesian credible regions based on noninformative priors can also be much easier to calculate than their classical counterparts, particularly in situations where simple sufficient statistics do not exist. The following example illustrates this.

EXAMPLE 9. Assume $\mathbf{X} = (X_1, \ldots, X_n)$ is a sample from a $\mathscr{C}(\theta, 1)$ distribution. Since θ is a location parameter, the noninformative prior $\pi(\theta) = 1$ is appropriate. The posterior distribution of θ given $\mathbf{x} = (x_1, \ldots, x_n)$ is then given by

$$\pi(\theta | \mathbf{x}) = \frac{\prod_{i=1}^{n} [1 + (x_i - \theta)^2]^{-1}}{\int_{-\infty}^{\infty} \prod_{i=1}^{n} [1 + (x_i - \theta)^2]^{-1} \, d\theta}.$$

While this is not an overly attractive posterior to work with, finding a $100(1 - \alpha)\%$ HPD credible region on a computer is a relatively simple undertaking. The answer obtained would be "objective," and $1 - \alpha$ would be a good measure of final precision. Contrast this attractive analysis with the classical approach. It is not at all clear what to choose as a classical confidence region, and, if one was obtained, it would be difficult to develop any feeling for its final precision.

HPD credible regions can have undesirable features. For example, if f is normal and π is Cauchy, then $\pi(\theta | x)$ can be bimodal, leading to an HPD credible region which consists of two disjoint intervals. In such a situation it would probably be better to use the smallest *interval* which has probability $1 - \alpha$, than to use the HPD credible region (unless of course it is plausible to have two disjoint intervals).

4.3.3 Hypothesis Testing

In classical hypothesis testing, a null hypothesis $H_0 : \theta \in \Theta_0$ and an alternative hypothesis $H_1 : \theta \in \Theta_1$ are specified. A test procedure is evaluated in terms of the probabilities of Type I and Type II error. These probabilities of error represent the chance that a sample is observed for which the test procedure will result in the wrong hypothesis being accepted. This again is a measure of initial precision.

In Bayesian analysis, the task of deciding between H_0 and H_1 is conceptually more straightforward. One merely calculates the posterior probabilities $\alpha_0 = P(\Theta_0 | x)$ and $\alpha_1 = P(\Theta_1 | x)$, and decides between H_0 and H_1 accordingly. Since α_0 and α_1 are actually the (subjective) probabilities of H_0 and H_1 being true, they are measures of final precision.

The ratio α_0/α_1 is often called the *posterior odds ratio*, and indicates the relative plausibility of the two alternatives. Note that this ratio can be written

$$\frac{\alpha_0}{\alpha_1} = \frac{\int_{\Theta_0} dF^{\pi(\theta|x)}(\theta)}{\int_{\Theta_1} dF^{\pi(\theta|x)}(\theta)} = \frac{\int_{\Theta_0} f(x|\theta)dF^{\pi}(\theta)}{\int_{\Theta_1} f(x|\theta)dF^{\pi}(\theta)},$$

so that $m(x)$ need not be calculated to determine the ratio.

The above ideas can clearly be extended to the multiple decision problem, in which there are more than two hypotheses to be considered. An example follows.

EXAMPLE 1 (continued). The child taking the IQ test is to be classified as having below average IQ (less than 90), average IQ (90 to 110), or above average IQ (over 110). Calling these three regions Θ_1, Θ_2, and Θ_3 respectively, and recalling that the posterior is $\mathcal{N}(110.39, 69.23)$, a table of normal probabilities can be used to show that $P(\Theta_1|x = 115) = 0.007$, $P(\Theta_2|x = 115) = 0.473$, and $P(\Theta_3|x = 115) = 0.520$.

A difficulty arises if one attempts to deal in a Bayesian fashion with a classical two-sided hypothesis test of the form $H_0: \theta = \theta_0$ versus $H_1: \theta \neq \theta_0$. When θ is a continuous parameter, the single point θ_0 will usually have prior (and hence posterior) probability zero. In such a situation, H_0 can never be accepted by a Bayesian test. Of course, a similar problem exists with a classical test, in that for a large enough sample the test is virtually certain to reject H_0. (See Example 10 of Chapter 1.)

The problem here is mainly one of formulation. It is not really seriously proposed that $\theta = \theta_0$ *exactly*. What is usually desired is to find out if θ is "close" to θ_0 or not. A far more reasonable formulation, therefore, is to specify a null hypothesis of the form $H_0: \theta \in (\theta_0 - b, \theta_0 + b)$, where b is chosen to reflect what "close to θ_0" means. In the IQ example, for instance, a classical test of the hypothesis that a child has average IQ versus the alternative that his IQ is not average would be stated as $H_0: \theta = 100$ versus $H_1: \theta \neq 100$. A better formulation would be $H_0: \theta \in (90,110)$ versus $H_1: \theta \notin (90, 110)$, for which a Bayesian analysis could certainly be performed.

There do exist some continuous situations in which a Bayesian test of a point null hypothesis is a reasonable approximation to reality. Consider, for example, an attempt to analyze a chemical by observing the strength, θ, of its reaction with a known chemical. If it is desired to test whether or not the unknown chemical is a specific compound with an *accurately* known reaction strength θ_0, it is reasonable to test $H_0: \theta = \theta_0$ versus $H_1: \theta \neq \theta_0$. Actually, a more exact null hypothesis would be $H_0: \theta \in (\theta_0 - \varepsilon, \theta_0 + \varepsilon)$, where ε is the accuracy to which θ_0 is known, but if ε is very small compared to the experimental sampling error, the point null hypothesis is a very reasonable approximation. Another situation, in which a point null hypothesis is quite reasonable, is in an experiment concerning extrasensory perception. If, for example, a subject is trying to guess which of five possible symbols is on a hidden card, it would be correct to test $H_0: \theta = \frac{1}{5}$ versus $H_1: \theta \neq \frac{1}{5}$, where θ is the probability of the subject guessing correctly. Other examples, from genetics and forensic science, in which point null hypotheses are reasonable, can be found in Lindley (1957) and Lindley (1977).

In conducting a Bayesian analysis of a situation such as above, it is appropriate to give θ_0 a prior probability $\pi_0 > 0$, while spreading the remaining probability, $1 - \pi_0$, among the values $\theta \neq \theta_0$.

EXAMPLE 10. Assume $X \sim \mathcal{N}(\theta, \sigma^2)$ (σ^2 known) is observed, on the basis of which it is desired to test $H_0: \theta = \theta_0$ versus $H_1: \theta \neq \theta_0$. The prior probability of θ_0 is π_0, while, for $\theta \neq \theta_0$, the prior has density equal to $(1 - \pi_0)\pi_1(\theta)$, $\pi_1(\theta)$ being a $\mathcal{N}(\mu, \tau^2)$ density. Letting $f(x|\theta)$ denote the $\mathcal{N}(\theta, \sigma^2)$ density, it is clear that

$$h(x, \theta) = \begin{cases} f(x|\theta_0)\pi_0 & \text{if } \theta = \theta_0, \\ f(x|\theta)(1 - \pi_0)\pi_1(\theta) & \text{if } \theta \neq \theta_0, \end{cases}$$

and that

$$m(x) = f(x|\theta_0)\pi_0 + (1 - \pi_0) \int_{\{\theta \neq \theta_0\}} f(x|\theta)\pi_1(\theta)d\theta.$$

The integration above is not affected by the exclusion of θ_0, and can be performed, as in Example 1, to yield

$$m(x) = f(x|\theta_0)\pi_0 + (1 - \pi_0)g(x),$$

where $g(x)$ is the density from a $\mathcal{N}(\mu, \sigma^2 + \tau^2)$ distribution. The posterior density is then given by

$$\pi(\theta|x) = \begin{cases} \dfrac{h(x, \theta_0)}{m(x)} = \dfrac{f(x|\theta_0)\pi_0}{f(x|\theta_0)\pi_0 + (1 - \pi_0)g(x)} & \text{if } \theta = \theta_0, \\[3mm] \dfrac{h(x, \theta)}{m(x)} = \dfrac{f(x|\theta)(1 - \pi_0)\pi_1(\theta)}{f(x|\theta_0)\pi_0 + (1 - \pi_0)g(x)} & \text{if } \theta \neq \theta_0. \end{cases}$$

Defining $\Theta_0 = \{\theta_0\}$ and $\Theta_1 = \{\theta: \theta \neq \theta_0\}$, it is clear that $P(\Theta_0|x) = \pi(\theta_0|x)$, and $P(\Theta_1|x) = 1 - \pi(\theta_0|x)$. The posterior odds ratio is thus

$$\frac{P(\Theta_0|x)}{P(\Theta_1|x)} = \frac{\pi(\theta_0|x)}{1 - \pi(\theta_0|x)}$$

$$= \frac{f(x|\theta_0)\pi_0}{(1 - \pi_0)g(x)}$$

$$= \frac{\pi_0 \sigma^{-1} \exp\{-(x - \theta_0)^2/2\sigma^2\}}{(1 - \pi_0)(\sigma^2 + \tau^2)^{-1/2} \exp\{-(x - \mu)^2/2[\sigma^2 + \tau^2]\}}.$$

Combining the exponentials and completing squares gives

$$\frac{P(\Theta_0|x)}{P(\Theta_1|x)} = \frac{\pi_0}{1-\pi_0}\left(1+\frac{\tau^2}{\sigma^2}\right)^{1/2}\exp\left\{-\frac{(x-[\theta_0+(\theta_0-\mu)\sigma^2/\tau^2])^2}{2\sigma^2(1+\sigma^2/\tau^2)}\right\}$$

$$\times\exp\left\{\frac{(\theta_0-\mu)^2}{2\tau^2}\right\}.$$

An easy calculation shows that $P(\Theta_0|x) > P(\Theta_1|x)$ (i.e., $P(\Theta_0|x) > \frac{1}{2}$) if and only if

$$\left|\frac{(x-\theta_0)}{\sigma}+\frac{(\mu-\theta_0)\sigma}{\tau^2}\right|$$

$$< \left(1+\frac{\sigma^2}{\tau^2}\right)^{1/2}\left\{\log\left[\left(\frac{\pi_0}{1-\pi_0}\right)^2\left(1+\frac{\tau^2}{\sigma^2}\right)\right]+\frac{(\theta_0-\mu)^2}{\tau^2}\right\}^{1/2}.$$

Note that as $\sigma \to 0$, this region becomes approximately the region in which

$$|x-\theta_0| < \sigma[\log\sigma^{-2}]^{1/2}.$$

It is interesting to compare the Bayesian reasoning in this example with that from a classical analysis. For simplicity, assume that $\pi_0 = \frac{1}{2}$, $\tau = 1$, $\mu = \theta_0$, and $\sigma^2 = \exp(-25)$ (which would arise if X was the sample mean from a sample of size approximately $\exp(25)$ from a $\mathcal{N}(\theta, 1)$ distribution). Then, by the above calculation, it is clear that the posterior probability of θ_0 exceeds $\frac{1}{2}$ if

$$\left|\frac{(x-\theta_0)}{\sigma}\right| < (1+e^{-25})^{1/2}(\log[1+e^{25}])^{1/2} \cong 5.$$

In other words, the null hypothesis is quite believable from the Bayesian viewpoint, even if x is five standard deviations away. This, of course, is in direct conflict with classical reasoning, which will reject H_0 at significance level $\alpha = 5.1 \times 10^{-7}$ (for a two-sided significance test) when the observation is five standard deviations from θ_0. This substantial disagreement has come to be called Lindley's paradox, and was discussed in Lindley (1957).

The difficulty in this situation is caused by the occurrence of an implausible event, and the need to find an explanation for it. Basically, the observation x should not be five standard deviations from θ_0. It is very unlikely that an extreme sample like this would occur if θ_0 was true, but it is also enormously unlikely that the true θ would be within 5σ of θ_0 (according to the prior beliefs). Statistical analysis is always suspect in such situations, the possibility of an error in the model looming large. The prior assumptions should, in particular, be scrutinized very carefully, since they are having such a strong effect on the conclusion. If, as an example, the null hypothesis arose from theoretical considerations, then one might suspect that the theoretical calculations (or model) were slightly wrong. In terms of the prior, this would mean that values of θ close to θ_0 are considerably more likely than other values of θ, perhaps invalidating the Bayesian analysis. If after careful consideration, however, one remains convinced of the validity of all assumptions, including the prior beliefs, then the Bayesian conclusion seems correct. For an interesting discussion of this, focusing in particular on the question of sensitivity to the prior, see Shafer (1979).

4.4 Bayesian Decision Theory

In this section the influence of the loss function will be considered as well as that of the prior information. Thus we will again be dealing with true decision problems. Unless otherwise stated, it will also be assumed that the prior is a proper prior and that the problem has a finite Bayes risk.

4.4.1 Normal and Extensive Forms of Analysis

The *normal form* of Bayesian analysis consists of choosing a decision rule to minimize $r(\pi, \delta)$ directly, as discussed in Section 1.5. This approach was used in the examples and exercises of Chapter 1. In general, however, it is difficult to approach the problem from this direction. An alternative method is suggested by noting that

$$
\begin{aligned}
r(\pi, \delta) &= \int_\Theta R(\theta, \delta) dF^\pi(\theta) \\[2mm]
&= \int_\Theta \int_{\mathcal{X}} L(\theta, \delta(x)) dF^{X|\theta}(x) dF^\pi(\theta) \\[2mm]
&= \begin{cases}
\displaystyle \int_{\mathcal{X}} \left[\int_\Theta L(\theta, \delta(x)) f(x|\theta) dF^\pi(\theta) \right] dx & \text{(continuous case),} \\[4mm]
\displaystyle \sum_{x \in \mathcal{X}} \left[\int_\Theta L(\theta, \delta(x)) f(x|\theta) dF^\pi(\theta) \right] & \text{(discrete case).}
\end{cases}
\end{aligned}
\tag{4.1}
$$

(The interchange in order of integration above is valid by Fubini's theorem, since $L(\theta, a) \geq -K > -\infty$, and the measures are finite.) It is clear that to minimize the last expressions in (4.1), $\delta(x)$ should be chosen to minimize

$$
\int_\Theta L(\theta, \delta(x)) f(x|\theta) dF^\pi(\theta)
$$

for each $x \in \mathcal{X}$. This can be understood intuitively by noting that if a minimizes

$$
\int_\Theta L(\theta, a) f(x|\theta) dF^\pi(\theta),
$$

then a minimizes

$$[m(x)]^{-1} \int_\Theta L(\theta, a) f(x|\theta) dF^\pi(\theta) = \int_\Theta L(\theta, a) dF^{\pi(\theta|x)}(\theta).$$

This last quantity is called the *posterior expected loss* of the action a, and is simply the expected loss with respect to $\pi(\theta|x)$, the posterior distribution of θ given x. This can be summarized as

Result 1. *A Bayes rule can be found by choosing, for each x, an action which minimizes the posterior expected loss, or, equivalently, which minimizes*

$$\int_\Theta L(\theta, a) f(x|\theta) dF^\pi(\theta). \tag{4.2}$$

(Note that the posterior expected loss might have more than one minimizing action, so there might be more than one Bayes rule.)

The method given in Result 1 for determining a Bayes rule is called the *extensive form* of Bayesian analysis. (The names "normal form" and "extensive form" were first used by Raiffa and Schlaifer (1961).) It is intuitively easier to understand when thought of in terms of minimizing the posterior expected loss, but it is often easier to implement by minimizing (4.2), since $m(x)$ need not then be determined. (This is especially true when a computer or calculator is used to carry out the minimization.) The extensive form of Bayesian analysis is usually much simpler than the normal form, and should generally be the method used to find a Bayes rule. Indeed, many Bayesians recognize *only* the extensive form of analysis for finding Bayes rules, arguing directly that $\pi(\theta|x)$ describes the post-experimental (possibly subjective) beliefs about θ, and that, providing the loss has been developed through utility theory, posterior expected loss must be used in evaluating an action. This argument asserts that the only reasonable measure of the final precision of an action is its posterior expected loss, and that, while helpful for other purposes, $r(\pi, \delta)$ is a measure of initial precision and is not necessarily relevant to the choice of an action. As discussed previously, this argument is essentially correct. Luckily, the result of Bayesian analysis is the same whether the pre-experimental or post-experimental viewpoint is taken, so we can use whichever viewpoint is most convenient.

The above discussion also indicates a plausible method of dealing with problems in which $r(\pi, \delta^*)$ is infinite for all δ^*. The normal form of Bayesian analysis is then meaningless, but the extensive form can usually be implemented. (The posterior expected loss will usually be finite.) Thus if the Bayes risk is infinite, we will *define* the Bayes rule as that given by Result 1. To indicate the difference, however, we will refer to such a rule as a *formal Bayes rule*.

It is of interest to note, from Result 1, that Bayesian analysis does satisfy the likelihood principle. This is clear, since in minimizing (over a)

$$\int L(\theta, a) f(x|\theta) dF^\pi(\theta),$$

the only sample information used is the likelihood function for the observed x.

As a final comment, note that Result 1 has been shown to hold only among the class of nonrandomized rules. It is easy to show, however, (the proof is left as an exercise) that the same result holds among the class of randomized decision rules. In other words, any rule which minimizes the posterior expected loss (for all x) is Bayes among the class $\mathscr{D}^*$ of all randomized rules. It also follows that a nonrandomized Bayes rule can always be found. (If there is more than one action minimizing the posterior expected loss, simply choose the Bayes rule to be one of these actions. One can randomly choose among these actions if desired, but there is no need to do so.)

4.4.2 Estimation

In Bayesian estimation of a real-valued parameter θ, the loss which is easiest to deal with is squared-error loss $(L(\theta, a) = (\theta - a)^2)$. The posterior expected loss is then

$$\int_\Theta (\theta - a)^2 \, dF^{\pi(\theta|x)}(\theta).$$

The value of a which minimizes this can be found by expanding the quadratic expression, differentiating with respect to a, and setting equal to zero. The result (assuming all integrals are finite) is

$$0 = \frac{d}{da}\left[\int_\Theta \theta^2 \, dF^{\pi(\theta|x)}(\theta) - 2a \int_\Theta \theta \, dF^{\pi(\theta|x)}(\theta) + a^2 \int_\Theta dF^{\pi(\theta|x)}(\theta)\right]$$

$$= -2E^{\pi(\theta|x)}[\theta] + 2a.$$

Solving for a gives the following result.

Result 2. If $L(\theta, a) = (\theta - a)^2$, the Bayes rule is

$$\delta^\pi(x) = E^{\pi(\theta|x)}[\theta],$$

which is the mean of the posterior distribution of θ given x.

EXAMPLE 1 (continued). If f and π are normal, the posterior is $\mathcal{N}(\mu(x), \rho^{-1})$. This has mean $\mu(x)$, so the Bayes rule for squared-error loss is

$$\delta^\pi(x) = \mu(x) = \frac{\sigma^2 \mu}{\sigma^2 + \tau^2} + \frac{\tau^2 x}{\sigma^2 + \tau^2}.$$

For weighted squared-error loss the following result holds. (The proof will be left as an exercise.)

Result 3. *If* $L(\theta, a) = w(\theta)(\theta - a)^2$, *the Bayes rule is*

$$\delta^\pi(x) = \frac{E^{\pi(\theta|x)}[\theta w(\theta)]}{E^{\pi(\theta|x)}[w(\theta)]}$$

$$= \frac{\int \theta w(\theta) f(x|\theta) dF^\pi(\theta)}{\int w(\theta) f(x|\theta) dF^\pi(\theta)}.$$

From the last expression in Result 3, it is interesting to note that the weight function, $w(\theta)$, plays a role analogous to that of the prior $\pi(\theta)$. This is important to note, in that robustness concerns involving $w(\theta)$ are thus the same as robustness concerns involving the prior.

For the quadratic loss $L(\boldsymbol{\theta}, \mathbf{a}) = (\boldsymbol{\theta} - \mathbf{a})'\mathbf{Q}(\boldsymbol{\theta} - \mathbf{a})$ ($\boldsymbol{\theta}$ and $\mathbf{a}$ are now vectors and $\mathbf{Q}$ is a positive definite matrix), it can be shown that the Bayes estimator is still the posterior mean. (Interestingly, $\mathbf{Q}$ has no effect.)

For absolute error loss, the following result holds. Recall that a median is a $\frac{1}{2}$-fractile of a distribution. (In general, a point $z(\alpha)$ is an α-fractile of the distribution of a random variable X if $P(X \leq z(\alpha)) \geq \alpha$ and $P(X < z(\alpha)) \leq \alpha$.)

Result 4. *If* $L(\theta, a) = |\theta - a|$, *any median of* $\pi(\theta|x)$ *is a Bayes estimator of* θ.

PROOF. Let m denote a median of $\pi(\theta|x)$, and let $a > m$ be another action. Note that

$$L(\theta, m) - L(\theta, a) = \begin{cases} m - a & \text{if } \theta \leq m, \\ 2\theta - (m + a) & \text{if } m < \theta < a, \\ a - m & \text{if } \theta \geq a, \end{cases}$$

from which it follows that

$$L(\theta, m) - L(\theta, a) \leq (m - a)I_{(-\infty, m]}(\theta) + (a - m)I_{(m, \infty)}(\theta).$$

Since $P(\theta \leq m|x) \geq \frac{1}{2}$, so that $P(\theta > m|x) \leq \frac{1}{2}$, it can be concluded that

$$E^{\pi(\theta|x)}[L(\theta, m) - L(\theta, a)] \leq (m - a)P(\theta \leq m|x) + (a - m)P(\theta > m|x)$$
$$\leq (m - a)\tfrac{1}{2} + (a - m)\tfrac{1}{2} = 0,$$

establishing that m has posterior expected loss at least as small as a. A similar argument holds for $a < m$, completing the proof. $\square$

In the IQ example, the posterior was normal with mean $\mu(x)$, which, for a normal distribution, is also the median. Hence the Bayes estimator is the same in this example, whether squared error or absolute error loss is used. Indeed, when the posterior is unimodal and symmetric, it can be shown that, for any loss of the form $L(|\theta - a|)$ which is increasing in $|\theta - a|$, the Bayes estimator is the median of the posterior. This partially indicates that, when underestimation and overestimation are of equal concern (merely a verbal statement of the condition that L be a function of $|\theta - a|$), the exact function of $|\theta - a|$ which is used as the loss is not too crucial (i.e., the Bayes rule is robust with respect to this part of the loss). Recall, however, that any weight function, $w(\theta)$, in the loss can have a significant effect.

Perhaps the most useful standard loss is linear loss. The proof of the following result will be left as an exercise.

Result 5. *If*

$$L(\theta, a) = \begin{cases} K_0(\theta - a) & \text{if } \theta - a \geq 0, \\ K_1(a - \theta) & \text{if } \theta - a < 0, \end{cases}$$

any $(K_0/(K_0 + K_1))$-fractile of $\pi(\theta|x)$ is a Bayes estimate of θ.

EXAMPLE 1 (continued). In estimating the child's IQ, it is deemed to be twice as harmful to underestimate as to overestimate. A linear loss is felt to be appropriate, so the loss in Result 5 is used with $K_0 = 2$ and $K_1 = 1$. The $\frac{2}{3}$-fractile of a $\mathcal{N}(0, 1)$ distribution is about 0.43, so the $\frac{2}{3}$-fractile of a $\mathcal{N}(110.39, 61.23)$ distribution (which is $\pi(\theta|x)$) is

$$110.39 + (0.43)(61.23)^{1/2} = 113.97.$$

This is the Bayes estimate of θ.

It should again be emphasized that, while easy to work with, none of the above standard losses need be suitable for a given real problem. If this is the case, it will usually be necessary to calculate and minimize the posterior expected loss numerically. This can be done with a computer or, in many cases, with a programmable hand calculator.

4.4.3 Finite Action Problems and Hypothesis Testing

In estimation there are generally an infinite number of actions to choose from. Many interesting statistical problems involve only a finite number of actions, however. The most important finite action problem is, of course, hypothesis testing.

The finite action Bayesian decision problem is easily solved when considered in extensive form. If $\{a_1, \ldots, a_k\}$ are the available actions and $L(\theta, a_i)$ the corresponding losses, the Bayes action is simply that for which the posterior expected loss $E^{\pi(\theta|x)}[L(\theta, a_i)]$ is the smallest. Several specific finite action problems will now be considered.

In testing $H_0 : \theta \in \Theta_0$ versus $H_1 : \theta \in \Theta_1$, the actions of interest are a_0 and a_1, where a_i denotes acceptance of H_i. Actually, this is to a degree putting the cart before the horse, since in true decision problems the hypotheses are usually determined by the available actions. In other words, the decision maker is often faced with two possible courses of action, a_0 and a_1. He determines that, if $\theta \in \Theta_0$, then action a_0 is appropriate, while if $\theta \in \Theta_1$, then a_1 is best. While the distinction as to whether the hypotheses or actions come first is important in discussing reasonable formulations of hypothesis testing problems, it makes no difference in the formal analysis of a given problem.

When the loss is "0–1" loss $(L(\theta, a_i) = 0$ if $\theta \in \Theta_i$ and $L(\theta, a_i) = 1$ if $\theta \in \Theta_j, j \neq i)$, then

$$E^{\pi(\theta|x)}[L(\theta, a_1)] = \int L(\theta, a_1) dF^{\pi(\theta|x)}(\theta) = \int_{\Theta_0} dF^{\pi(\theta|x)}(\theta) = P(\Theta_0|x),$$

and

$$E^{\pi(\theta|x)}[L(\theta, a_0)] = P(\Theta_1|x).$$

Hence the Bayes decision is simply the hypothesis with the larger posterior probability.

For the more realistic "$0-K_i$" loss,

$$L(\theta, a_i) = \begin{cases} 0 & \text{if } \theta \in \Theta_i, \\ K_i & \text{if } \theta \in \Theta_j \, (j \neq i), \end{cases}$$

the posterior expected losses of a_0 and a_1 are $K_0 P(\Theta_1|x)$ and $K_1 P(\Theta_0|x)$ respectively. The Bayes decision is again that corresponding to the smallest posterior expected loss.

It is useful to observe the relationship of these Bayesian tests with classical hypothesis tests. In the Bayesian test, the null hypothesis is rejected (i.e., action a_1 is taken) when

$$\frac{K_0}{K_1} > \frac{P(\Theta_0|x)}{P(\Theta_1|x)}. \tag{4.3}$$

Usually $\Theta_0 \cup \Theta_1 = \Theta$, in which case

$$P(\Theta_0|x) = 1 - P(\Theta_1|x).$$

Inequality (4.3) can then be rewritten

$$\frac{K_0}{K_1} > \frac{1 - P(\Theta_1|x)}{P(\Theta_1|x)} = \frac{1}{P(\Theta_1|x)} - 1,$$

or

$$P(\Theta_1|x) > \frac{K_1}{K_0 + K_1}.$$

Thus in classical terminology, the rejection region of the Bayesian test is

$$C = \left\{ x : P(\Theta_1|x) > \frac{K_1}{K_0 + K_1} \right\}.$$

Typically, C is of exactly the same form as the rejection region of a classical (say likelihood ratio) test. An example of this follows.

EXAMPLE 1 (continued). Assume f and π are normal and that it is desired to test $H_0: \theta \geq \theta_0$ versus $H_1: \theta < \theta_0$ under "0-K_i" loss. Noting that $\pi(\theta|x)$ is a $\mathcal{N}(\mu(x), \rho^{-1})$ density, the Bayes test rejects H_0 if

$$\frac{K_1}{K_0 + K_1} < P(\Theta_1|x) = \left(\frac{\rho}{2\pi}\right)^{1/2} \int_{-\infty}^{\theta_0} \exp\left\{\frac{-\rho(\theta - \mu(x))^2}{2}\right\} d\theta$$

$$= (2\pi)^{-1/2} \int_{-\infty}^{\rho^{1/2}(\theta_0 - \mu(x))} \exp\left\{\frac{-\eta^2}{2}\right\} d\eta$$

(making the change of variables $\eta = \rho^{1/2}(\theta - \mu(x))$). Letting $z(\alpha)$ denote the α-fractile of a $\mathcal{N}(0, 1)$ distribution, it follows that the Bayes test rejects H_0 if

$$\rho^{1/2}(\theta_0 - \mu(x)) > z\left(\frac{K_1}{K_0 + K_1}\right).$$

Recalling that

$$\mu(x) = \frac{\tau^2}{\sigma^2 + \tau^2} x + \frac{\sigma^2}{\sigma^2 + \tau^2} \mu$$

and rearranging terms, gives the equivalent condition

$$x < \theta_0 + \frac{\sigma^2}{\tau^2}(\theta_0 - \mu) - \sigma^2 \rho^{1/2} z\left(\frac{K_1}{K_0 + K_1}\right).$$

The classical uniformly most powerful size α tests are of the same form, rejecting H_0 when

$$x < \theta_0 + \sigma z(\alpha).$$

In classical testing, the "critical value" of the rejection region is determined by α, while in the Bayesian test it is determined by the loss and prior information.

In situations such as that above, the Bayesian method can be thought of as providing a rational way of choosing the size of the test. Classical statistics provides no such guidelines, with the result being that certain "standard" sizes (0.1, 0.05, 0.01) have come to be most frequently used. Such an adhoc choice is clearly suspect in a true decision problem. Indeed even classical statisticians will tend to say that, in a true decision problem, the size should be chosen according to "subjective" factors. This is, of course, precisely what the Bayesian approach does.

There are many decision problems with more than two possible actions. For instance, a frequently faced situation in hypothesis testing is the existence of an indifference region. The idea here is that, besides the actions a_0 and a_1, which will be taken if $\theta \in \Theta_0$ or $\theta \in \Theta_1$, a third action a_2 representing indifference will be taken if $\theta \in \Theta_2$. For example, assume it is desired to test which of two drugs is the most effective. Letting θ_1 and θ_2 denote the probabilities of cures using the two drugs, a reasonable way to formulate the problem is as a test of the three hypotheses $H_0: \theta_1 - \theta_2 < -\varepsilon$, $H_1: \theta_1 - \theta_2 > \varepsilon$, and $H_2: |\theta_1 - \theta_2| \leq \varepsilon$, where $\varepsilon > 0$ is chosen so that when $|\theta_1 - \theta_2| \leq \varepsilon$ the two drugs are considered equivalent.

Even in classical hypothesis testing there are usually three actions taken: a_0—accept H_0, a_1—accept H_1, and a_2—conclude there is not significant evidence for accepting either H_0 or H_1. The choice among these actions is classically made through an informal choice of desired error probabilities. Attacking the problem from a Bayesian decision-theoretic viewpoint (including the specification of $L(\theta, a_2)$) seems more appealing.

Another type of common finite action problem is the classification problem, in which it is desired to classify an observation as belonging to one of several possible categories. An example follows.

EXAMPLE 1 (continued). For the IQ example in which it is desired to classify the child as a_1—below average $(\theta < 90)$, a_2—average $(90 \leq \theta \leq 110)$, or a_3—above average $(\theta > 110)$, the following losses are deemed appropriate:

$$L(\theta, a_1) = \begin{cases} 0 & \text{if } \theta < 90, \\ \theta - 90 & \text{if } 90 \leq \theta \leq 110, \\ 2(\theta - 90) & \text{if } \theta > 110, \end{cases}$$

$$L(\theta, a_2) = \begin{cases} 90 - \theta & \text{if } \theta < 90, \\ 0 & \text{if } 90 \leq \theta \leq 110, \\ \theta - 110 & \text{if } \theta > 110, \end{cases}$$

$$L(\theta, a_3) = \begin{cases} 2(110 - \theta) & \text{if } \theta < 90, \\ 110 - \theta & \text{if } 90 \leq \theta \leq 110, \\ 0 & \text{if } \theta > 110. \end{cases}$$

(These could arise, for example, if children are put into one of three reading groups (slow, average, and fast) depending on their IQ classification.) Since $\pi(\theta|x)$ is $\mathcal{N}(110.39, 69.23)$, the posterior expected losses are

$$E^{\pi(\theta|x)}[L(\theta, a_1)] = \int_{90}^{110} (\theta - 90)\pi(\theta|x)d\theta + \int_{110}^{\infty} 2(\theta - 90)\pi(\theta|x)d\theta$$

$$= 6.49 + 27.83 = 34.32,$$

$$E^{\pi(\theta|x)}[L(\theta, a_2)] = \int_{-\infty}^{90} (90 - \theta)\pi(\theta|x)d\theta + \int_{110}^{\infty} (\theta - 110)\pi(\theta|x)d\theta$$

$$= 0.02 + 3.53 = 3.55,$$

$$E^{\pi(\theta|x)}[L(\theta, a_3)] = \int_{-\infty}^{90} 2(110 - \theta)\pi(\theta|x)d\theta + \int_{90}^{110} (110 - \theta)\pi(\theta|x)d\theta$$

$$= 0.32 + 2.95 = 3.27.$$

(The preceding integrals are calculated by first transforming to a $\mathcal{N}(0, 1)$ density, and then using normal probability tables and the fact that

$$\int_a^b \theta e^{-\theta^2/2} \, d\theta = -e^{-\theta^2/2}\Big|_a^b = e^{-a^2/2} - e^{-b^2/2}.)$$

Thus a_3 is the Bayes decision.

4.4.4 Improper Priors and Generalized Bayes Rules

The role of improper priors in Bayesian inference was discussed in Section 4.3. They can play a similar role in Bayesian decision theory. Unfortunately, when the prior is improper the quantity $r(\pi, \delta) = E^\pi[R(\theta, \delta)]$ has no meaning (and is usually infinite), so that it cannot be used to define an optimal rule. Usually, however, the formal posterior, $\pi(\theta|x)$, will exist, and can in some sense be interpreted as the believed posterior distribution. It is thus reasonable to define the *optimal* rule, for a given x, as that action which minimizes the posterior expected loss. Since the normalizing factor $m(x)$ has no influence on the minimization problem, the following is a more formal statement of the decision method.

Definition 5. If π is an improper prior in a decision problem with loss L, a *generalized Bayes rule*, for given x, is an action which minimizes

$$\int_\Theta L(\theta, a) f(x|\theta) dF^\pi(\theta),$$

or, if $0 < m(x) < \infty$, which minimizes the posterior expected loss.

The above method of choosing a decision rule has no compelling rationality principle behind it, and may not always be good. (This will be seen in Section 4.5.) Nevertheless, generalized Bayes rules are useful for three reasons. The first is that, if no prior information is available, a generalized Bayes rule with respect to a noninformative prior will usually be a very reasonable decision procedure. In Example 7 of Subsection 4.3.1, for instance, the given estimator would be the generalized Bayes rule for squared-error loss. (For squared-error loss, the mean of the posterior minimizes the posterior expected loss.)

The second use of generalized Bayes rules is in the development of robust Bayes estimators when the prior information is rather vague. This will be seen in Section 4.6.

Finally, generalized Bayes rules are interesting from a theoretical viewpoint, due to the fact that in many important situations, it can be shown that *all* admissible rules must be generalized Bayes. Certain results of this nature will be discussed in Chapter 8.

4.4.5 Empirical Bayes Analysis and Compound Decision Problems

Empirical Bayes statistical analysis (introduced by Robbins (1955)) deals with the use of auxiliary data (past or current) to aid in the construction of Bayes rules. In Subsection 3.2.4 the use of past data in constructing the prior was discussed. The development of Bayes rules from such past data is the usual empirical Bayes problem, and will be discussed first. Following that will be a discussion of compound decision problems, in which the use of empirical Bayes methods in dealing simultaneously with several inference or decision problems is considered.

I. *Empirical Bayes Methods*

It is desired to make an inference or decision concerning an unknown parameter θ_0. Sample information, X_0, with density $f(x_0|\theta_0)$ will be available. As in Subsection 3.2.4, we also assume there are available past observations $x_1, \ldots, x_n$, from independent random variables X_i distributed according to densities $f(x_i|\theta_i)$, and that the θ_i (including θ_0) are from a common prior density $\pi(\theta)$.

The most natural empirical Bayes method is to use $x_0, x_1, \ldots, x_n$ in the determination of $\pi(\theta)$ (as in Subsection 3.2.4), and to use this prior in the calculation of the Bayes rule. The easiest way to use the x_i to develop $\pi(\theta)$ (as discussed in Subsection 3.2.4), is to assume a certain functional form for θ and to use the x_i to estimate the parameters of this form. For calculational simplicity, it is often convenient to choose the functional form to be that of a conjugate family of priors. *If x_0 along with the x_i is used to estimate the parameters of the prior, the resulting Bayes rule is often surprisingly good, and quite robust with respect to misspecification of the prior.*

EXAMPLE 11. Assume $X_0 \sim \mathcal{N}(\theta_0, \sigma_f^2)$ (σ_f^2 known) is observed, and that a decision concerning θ_0 must be made. Past data $x_1, \ldots, x_n$ are available, where the X_i are independently $\mathcal{N}(\theta_i, \sigma_f^2)$. The θ_i (including θ_0) are thought to independently occur according to the common density π. For convenience, it is assumed that π is a $\mathcal{N}(\mu_\pi, \sigma_\pi^2)$ density, where μ_π and σ_π^2 are to be estimated from the past (and present) data. As in Example 15 of Subsection 3.2.4, the relationships $\mu_\pi = \mu_m$ and $\sigma_\pi^2 = \sigma_m^2 - \sigma_f^2$ (μ_m and σ_m^2 being the mean and variance of the marginal distribution of the X_i) can be used to give the following estimates of μ_π and σ_π^2:

$$\hat{\mu}_\pi = \bar{x} = \frac{1}{n+1} \sum_{i=0}^{n} x_i,$$

$$\hat{\sigma}_\pi^2 = (s^2 - \sigma_f^2)^+,$$

where $s^2 = (1/n) \sum_{i=0}^{n} (x_i - \bar{x})^2$. (Note that the current observation x_0 is being used in these estimates.) The prior will thus be assumed to be $\mathcal{N}(\hat{\mu}_\pi, \hat{\sigma}_\pi^2)$, for which standard Bayesian analyses can be conducted. For example, if it is desired to estimate θ_0 under squared-error loss, the mean of the posterior distribution of θ_0 given x_0 is the Bayes estimate. This is given by (see Example 1)

$$
\begin{aligned}
\mu(x_0) &= \frac{\sigma_f^2}{(\sigma_f^2 + \hat{\sigma}_\pi^2)} \hat{\mu}_\pi + \frac{\hat{\sigma}_\pi^2}{(\sigma_f^2 + \hat{\sigma}_\pi^2)} x_0 \\
&= x_0 - \frac{\sigma_f^2}{(\sigma_f^2 + \hat{\sigma}_\pi^2)} (x_0 - \hat{\mu}_\pi) \\
&= x_0 - \frac{\sigma_f^2}{\sigma_f^2 + (s^2 - \sigma_f^2)^+} (x_0 - \bar{x}) \\
&= x_0 - \min\left\{1, \frac{\sigma_f^2}{s^2}\right\} (x_0 - \bar{x}).
\end{aligned}
$$

It can be shown that $\mu(x_0)$ is a very robust estimator of θ_0. This is partially indicated by the observation that if x_0 is "extreme" (see Example 2 (continued) of Section 3.3), then s^2 will be very large and $(x_0 - \bar{x})/s^2$ will be small. The estimate $\mu(x_0)$ will thus be very close to x_0 (the standard estimate) when the observation seems to indicate that θ_0 is an outlier (i.e., not really generated from $\pi(\theta)$). In general, empirical Bayes estimators developed in the above fashion exhibit this favorable type of robustness.

As a specific example of this situation, consider once again the child who scored $x_0 = 115$ on his intelligence test. Assume now, however, that intelligence test scores of the child are available for 6 previous years. IQ's of 105, 127, 115, 130, 110, and 135 were observed. Since the true IQ can change from year to year, and the current IQ, θ_0, is of interest, these x_i are not to be treated as a sample from a common distribution. On the other hand, it is very reasonable to assume that the true yearly IQ's, θ_i, are from a common prior distribution. (A little care should be taken here. If the past observations seem to be nonrandom, say are increasing, this may indicate a trend in the θ_i. The assumption that the θ_i are a sample from a common distribution is then inappropriate.)

It can be calculated that, for the data $x_0, x_1, \ldots, x_6$, the sample mean and variance are $\bar{x} = 121$ and $s^2 = 108.9$. Since $\sigma_f^2 = 100$ in this example, it follows that estimates of the mean and variance of the normal prior are $\hat{\mu}_\pi = 121$ and $\sigma_\pi^2 = (s^2 - \sigma_f^2)^+ = 8.9$. The empirical Bayes estimate of the current IQ (under squared-error loss) is then

$$
\mu(x_0) = 115 - \min\left\{1, \frac{100}{108.9}\right\}(115 - 121) = 120.6.
$$

Although the empirical Bayes approach discussed above usually works well, any of the other empirical Bayes techniques for estimating π that were discussed in Subsection 3.2.4 can also be used. A different kind of empirical Bayes technique was introduced by Robbins (1955). This method is based on the observation that a Bayes rule can sometimes be explicitly represented in terms of $m(x)$, the marginal or predictive distribution of x. The past data can then be used to aid in the estimation of the function $m(x)$, from which approximations to the Bayes rule can be obtained. The problem of estimating π is thus bypassed.

EXAMPLE 12. If $X_0 \sim \mathscr{P}(\theta_0)$ and L is squared-error loss, then the Bayes rule is

$$\delta^{\pi}(x_0) = E^{\pi(\theta|x_0)}[\theta] = \int \theta \pi(\theta|x_0)d\theta$$

$$= \frac{\int \theta f(x_0|\theta)\pi(\theta)d\theta}{m(x_0)}$$

$$= \frac{\int \theta^{x_0+1}e^{-\theta}[x_0!]^{-1}\pi(\theta)d\theta}{m(x_0)}$$

$$= \frac{(x_0 + 1) \int f(x_0 + 1|\theta)\pi(\theta)d\theta}{m(x_0)}$$

$$= \frac{(x_0 + 1)m(x_0 + 1)}{m(x_0)}.$$

Assume that the past data $X_1, \ldots, X_n$ are independently $\mathscr{P}(\theta_i)$, and that the θ_i are a sample from the prior density $\pi(\theta)$. Then $X_0, X_1, \ldots, X_n$ are unconditionally a sample from the distribution with density m, and $m(j)$ can be estimated by

$$\hat{m}(j) = \frac{\text{the number of } x_i \text{ equal to } j}{n + 1}.$$

The proposed estimator is then

$$\hat{\delta}^{\pi}(x_0) = \frac{(x_0 + 1)\hat{m}(x_0 + 1)}{\hat{m}(x_0)}.$$

Though quite easy to implement, there are unfortunately a number of difficulties with this empirical Bayes technique. First of all, the rule $\hat{\delta}^{\pi}(x_0)$ can be very unstable. In Example 12, for instance, if it so happens that $x_0 = 9$, while among $x_1, \ldots, x_n$ there are no x_i equal to 10, then $\hat{m}(10) = 0, \hat{m}(9) > 0$, and $\hat{\delta}^{\pi}(9) = 0$, an obviously absurd estimate. (One can "smooth" this estimator by a monotonization procedure that will be discussed in Chapter 8. Such a smoothing is necessary before the estimator is reasonable.)

A second (and more serious) difficulty with the above technique is that it works only for very special loss functions; loss functions for which δ^{π} can be represented in terms of m. This considerably limits the applicability of the method. The previously discussed empirical Bayes techniques do not suffer from either of these inadequacies, and are therefore recommended for use.

Thus far, only examples of empirical Bayes estimation have been considered. Clearly empirical Bayes methods can also be applied to other types of decision problems, such as hypothesis testing. The technique is the same. Simply use the past data to help derive the prior and hence the posterior, from which the posterior probabilities or expected losses of the hypotheses of interest can be determined. Unfortunately, empirical Bayes methods are not quite as attractive for use in hypothesis testing problems as in estimation. Indeed if the amount of past data is small, or the hypotheses have roughly equal prior probabilities, then the empirical Bayes tests can perform poorly. See Maritz (1970) for indications of this (and a good exposition of empirical Bayes methods in general). On the other hand, with large amounts of past data and a belief that the hypotheses have different prior probabilities, empirical Bayes tests can offer significant gains.

As a final comment, it should be noted that when the amount of past data is fairly small, the prior should be derived from both the past data and subjective beliefs. This was briefly discussed in Subsection 3.2.5.

II. *Compound Decision Problems*

There is another class of problems which are closely related to empirical Bayes problems. These are *compound decision problems*, in which $x_1, \ldots, x_p$ are observed, where independently the X_i have density $f(x|\theta_i)$, and it is desired to simultaneously make decisions involving the θ_i. (Note that $X_1, \ldots, X_p$ is not a sample from the same distribution, in that the θ_i can be different.) Often the θ_i can be considered to be a sample from a common prior distribution. Information about this prior can then be obtained from $x_1, \ldots, x_p$, using empirical Bayes methods. Indeed the analysis would be formally identical to the empirical Bayes analysis, except for the fact that the loss structure is different. (In the empirical Bayes problem, the loss is $L(\theta_0, a)$, where θ_0 is the current value of interest. In the compound decision problem the loss is $L(\theta_1, \ldots, \theta_p, a)$.)

EXAMPLE 13. As an example of a compound decision problem, assume it is desired to estimate the IQ's of 20 children who are in a special class for the gifted. As in Example 11, it is reasonable to assume that the true IQ's θ_i are a sample from a common prior distribution. It is again relatively safe, in this type of empirical Bayes setting, to assume that the prior is normal. An analysis as in Example 11 will then give the mean and variance of the prior.

If each θ_i were to be estimated by a multiple of squared-error loss (so the overall loss would be $\sum_{i=1}^{p} c_i(a_i - \theta_i)^2$), then the "empirical Bayes" estimator of θ_i would be the mean of the posterior or, as in Example 11,

$$\mu(x_i) = x_i - \min\left\{1, \frac{100}{s^2}\right\}(x_i - \bar{x}).$$

An interesting analysis of this empirical Bayes estimator can be found in Efron and Morris (1973), along with references to earlier works.

Empirical Bayes methods in compound decision problems usually work very well, even better than they work in true empirical Bayes problems. Empirical Bayes rules will generally be robust and improve upon the standard procedure, providing, of course, that the assumption that the θ_i are from a common prior distribution is appropriate.

In concluding this subsection, it should be mentioned that there is a more mathematical side to the study of empirical Bayes and compound decision problems. The basic mathematical question that can be asked is—as the amount of past data goes to infinity, does the Bayes risk (or average risk) of the decision rule used converge to the true minimal Bayes risk for the problem? When this is the case, the rule is said to be *asymptotically optimal*. For a discussion of this issue and lists of references, see Maritz (1970) and the review and analysis articles of Copas (1969) and Susarla (1979).

4.5 Admissibility of Bayes and Generalized Bayes Rules

Bayes rules (with proper priors) are virtually always admissible. The same cannot be said of generalized Bayes rules, however. The reasons for, and implications of, these statements will be discussed in this section.

4.5.1 Bayes Rules

The basic reason that a Bayes rule is virtually always admissible is that, if a rule with better risk $R(\theta, \delta)$ existed, that rule would also have better Bayes risk $r(\pi, \delta) = E^\pi[R(\theta, \delta)]$. (Recall that we are assuming in this chapter that the Bayes risk of the problem is finite, unless indicated otherwise.) Three specific theorems in this regard follow.

Theorem 1. *Assume that Θ is discrete (say $\Theta = \{\theta_1, \theta_2, \ldots\}$) and that the prior, π, gives positive probability to each $\theta_i \in \Theta$. A Bayes rule δ^π, with respect to π, is then admissible.*

PROOF. If δ^π is inadmissible, then there exists a rule δ with $R(\theta_i, \delta) \leq R(\theta_i, \delta^\pi)$ for all i, with strict inequality for, say, θ_k. Hence

$$r(\pi, \delta) = \sum_{i=1}^\infty R(\theta_i, \delta)\pi(\theta_i) < \sum_{i=1}^\infty R(\theta_i, \delta^\pi)\pi(\theta_i) = r(\pi, \delta^\pi),$$

the inequality being strict since $R(\theta_k, \delta) < R(\theta_k, \delta^\pi)$, $\pi(\theta_k) > 0$, and $r(\pi, \delta^\pi)$ $< \infty$. This contradicts the fact that δ^π is Bayes. Therefore, δ^π must be admissible. $\qquad\square$

The proofs of the next two theorems are similar proofs by contradiction, and will be left as exercises.

Theorem 2. *If a Bayes rule is unique, it is admissible.*

Theorem 3. *Assume that the risk functions $R(\theta, \delta)$ are continuous in θ for all decision rules δ. Assume also that the prior π gives positive probability to any subset of Θ. Then a Bayes rule with respect to π is admissible.* (Conditions under which risk functions are continuous are given in Chapter 8.)

In some situations (such as the case of finite Θ) even more can be said; namely that all admissible rules must be Bayes rules. Discussion of this will be delayed until Chapters 5 and 8.

Formal Bayes rules need not be admissible if their Bayes risks are infinite. The following example demonstrates this.

EXAMPLE 14. Assume $X \sim \mathcal{N}(\theta, 1)$, $\theta \sim \mathcal{N}(0, 1)$, and

$$L(\theta, a) = \exp\left\{\frac{3\theta^2}{4}\right\}(\theta - a)^2.$$

From Example 1, it is clear that $\pi(\theta|x)$ is a $\mathcal{N}(x/2, \frac{1}{2})$ density. Using Result 3, an easy calculation shows that the formal Bayes rule (i.e., the rule which minimizes the posterior expected loss) is given by $\delta^\pi(x) = 2x$. As in Example 4 of Section 1.3, a calculation then shows that

$$R(\theta, \delta^\pi) = \exp\left\{\frac{3\theta^2}{4}\right\}(4 + \theta^2) > \exp\left\{\frac{3\theta^2}{4}\right\}(1) = R(\theta, \delta_1),$$

where $\delta_1(x) = x$. Thus δ^π is seriously inadmissible. Note that $r(\pi, \delta^\pi) = E^\pi[R(\theta, \delta^\pi)] = \infty$, and indeed it can be shown that $r(\pi, \delta^*) = \infty$ for all $\delta^* \in \mathcal{D}^*$.

The possibility indicated in the above example is unsettling. The post-experimental Bayesian reasoning is unassailable. If the true prior and loss really are as given, and L was developed through utility theory, then one is forced (by utility analysis) to evaluate an action through posterior expected loss. But this results, from a pre-experimental basis, in a seriously inadmissible decision rule. If such a situation were to really occur, it would be best to trust the posterior analysis, reasoning that admissibility, being based on a measure of initial precision, is a suspect criterion. Of course, one can never determine π and L exactly, and, furthermore, standard utility axioms imply that a loss must be bounded. (See Chapter 2.) For a bounded loss the Bayes risk is clearly finite, and the above difficulty cannot arise.

4.5.2 Generalized Bayes Rules

As with formal Bayes rules, generalized Bayes rules need not be admissible. Unfortunately, the verification of admissibility (or inadmissibility) can be very difficult.

One situation in which a generalized Bayes rule, δ, can be easily shown to be admissible, is when the loss is positive and

$$r(\pi, \delta) = \int_{\Theta} R(\theta, \delta) dF^{\pi}(\theta) < \infty.$$

If π was proper, $r(\pi, \delta)$ would, of course, be the Bayes risk, but for improper π the meaning of $r(\pi, \delta)$ is unclear. Nevertheless, an argument identical to that leading to Result 1 of Subsection 4.4.1 then shows that the δ minimizing $r(\pi, \delta)$ is found by minimizing the posterior expected loss. Since this is exactly the way in which a generalized Bayes rule is defined, it follows that a generalized Bayes rule minimizes $r(\pi, \delta)$. Arguments, as in the previous subsection, can then be used to show that a generalized Bayes rule must be admissible.

It is unfortunately rather rare to have $r(\pi, \delta) < \infty$ for improper π. When $r(\pi, \delta) = \infty$, even "natural" generalized Bayes rules can be inadmissible, as the following examples show.

EXAMPLE 15. Assume $X \sim \mathcal{G}(\alpha, \beta)$ ($\alpha > 1$ known) is observed, and it is desired to estimate β under squared-error loss. Since β is a scale parameter, it is felt that the noninformative prior density $\pi(\beta) = \beta^{-1}$ should be used. The (formal) posterior density of β given x is then

$$\pi(\beta|x) = \frac{f(x|\beta)\pi(\beta)}{\int_0^{\infty} f(x|\beta)\pi(\beta)d\beta} = \frac{\beta^{-\alpha}e^{-x/\beta}\beta^{-1}}{\int_0^{\infty} \beta^{-\alpha}e^{-x/\beta}\beta^{-1}\,d\beta},$$

which is clearly recognizable as an $\mathcal{IG}(\alpha, x^{-1})$ density. (Recall that, here, x is a fixed constant and β is the random variable.) Since the loss is squared-error loss, the generalized Bayes estimator, δ^0, of β is the mean of the posterior. Using Appendix 1, this is $\delta^0(x) = x/(\alpha - 1)$.

Consider now the risk of the estimator $\delta_c(x) = cx$. Clearly (since X has mean $\alpha\beta$ and variance $\alpha\beta^2$)

$$
\begin{aligned}
R(\beta, \delta_c) &= E_\beta^X[cX - \beta]^2 \\
&= E^X[c(X - \alpha\beta) + (c\alpha - 1)\beta]^2 \\
&= c^2\alpha\beta^2 + (c\alpha - 1)^2\beta^2 \\
&= \beta^2[c^2\alpha + (c\alpha - 1)^2].
\end{aligned}
$$

Differentiating with respect to c and setting equal to zero shows that the value of c minimizing this expression is unique and is given by $c_0 = (\alpha + 1)^{-1}$. It follows that if $c \neq c_0$, then $R(\beta, \delta_{c_0}) < R(\beta, \delta_c)$ for all β, showing in particular that δ^0 (which is δ_c with $c = (\alpha - 1)^{-1}$) is inadmissible. Indeed the ratio of risks of δ^0 and δ_{c_0} is

$$
\frac{R(\beta, \delta^0)}{R(\beta, \delta_{c_0})} = \frac{\alpha(\alpha - 1)^{-2} + (\alpha/(\alpha - 1) - 1)^2}{\alpha(\alpha + 1)^{-2} + (\alpha/(\alpha + 1) - 1)^2} = \frac{(\alpha + 1)^2}{(\alpha - 1)^2}.
$$

For small α, δ^0 has significantly worse risk than δ_{c_0}.

EXAMPLE 16. Assume $\mathbf{X} = (X_1, X_2, \ldots, X_p)^t \sim \mathcal{N}_p(\boldsymbol{\theta}, \mathbf{I}_p)$, where $\boldsymbol{\theta} = (\theta_1, \ldots, \theta_p)^t$ and $\mathbf{I}_p$ is the $(p \times p)$ identity matrix. It is desired to estimate $\boldsymbol{\theta}$ under sum-of-squares error loss ($L(\boldsymbol{\theta}, \mathbf{a}) = \sum_{i=1}^{p} (\theta_i - a_i)^2$). (This could equivalently be stated as the problem of trying to simultaneously estimate p normal means from independent problems.) Since $\boldsymbol{\theta}$ is a location parameter, the noninformative prior density $\pi(\boldsymbol{\theta}) = 1$ is deemed appropriate. It is easy to see that the (formal) posterior density of $\boldsymbol{\theta}$ given $\mathbf{x}$ is then a $\mathcal{N}_p(\mathbf{x}, \mathbf{I}_p)$ density. The generalized Bayes estimator of $\boldsymbol{\theta}$ is the mean of the posterior (under sum-of-squares error loss, or indeed any quadratic loss), so $\delta^0(\mathbf{x}) = \mathbf{x} = (x_1, \ldots, x_p)^t$ is the generalized Bayes estimator. (If a sample of vectors $\mathbf{X}^1, \ldots, \mathbf{X}^n$ was taken, the generalized Bayes estimator would just be the vector of sample means.)

This most standard of estimators is admissible for $p = 1$ or 2 (see Chapter 8), but surprisingly is inadmissible for $p \geq 3$. Indeed James and Stein (1960) showed that

$$
\delta^{JS}(\mathbf{x}) = \left(1 - \frac{(p - 2)}{\sum_{i=1}^{p} x_i^2}\right)\mathbf{x}
$$

has $R(\boldsymbol{\theta}, \delta^{JS}) < R(\boldsymbol{\theta}, \delta^0)$ for all $\boldsymbol{\theta}$ (if $p \geq 3$). (The proof is outlined in the Exercises.) This result came as a great surprise to most statisticians, in that the rule $\delta^0(\mathbf{x}) = \mathbf{x}$ is so natural and satisfies so many "classical" optimality properties. Extensions of this result have since been obtained in many directions (see Berger et. al. (1977) and Berger (1980a) for recent references), establishing that, in several dimensions, "standard" estimators are often inadmissible for a wide range of densities and loss functions.

It should be mentioned that the inadmissibility in this example is in some sense less serious than that in Example 15. In fact, it so happens that the ratio of $R(\theta, \delta^{JS})$ to $R(\theta, \delta^0)$ is very close to one over most of the parameter space. Only in a small region (several standard deviations wide) near zero will the ratio of risks be significantly smaller than one. (This is in contrast to the situation of Example 15, in which the ratio of risks can be uniformly bad.) The estimator δ^{JS} can be modified so as to adjust the region of significant improvement to coincide with prior knowledge concerning θ. The point is that there must be, apriori, some reason to believe that θ is likely to lie in a certain fairly small region, before the use of δ^{JS} (or some modification) has a chance of being significantly beneficial. Indeed if there really is no prior information about θ, then δ^{JS} will turn out to be virtually equivalent to δ^0. The lesson to be learned from this example is thus not that δ^0 is particularly bad, but that one can *very safely* improve upon it (in terms of risk) when prior information is available. This idea will be explored more fully in the next section.

In the above examples, there again appears to be a conflict between the post-experimental analysis (minimizing the posterior expected loss) and the pre-experimental analysis (as embodied by admissibility). Here, however, the post-experimental analysis is not necessarily compelling. This is because the formal posterior distribution can not really be considered to be the post-experimental (subjective) probability distribution of θ, since it was developed from an improper prior.

To make further progress in understanding this situation, it is necessary to realize that an improper prior is generally just an approximation to reality, and that lurking in the background is some true (subjective) proper prior π_1. The question can then be raised of whether the generalized Bayes rule δ^0 (with respect to the approximate improper prior) is "better or worse" than an R-better rule δ^R (assuming δ^0 is inadmissible). Here, "better or worse" can be given a legitimate meaning in terms of posterior expected loss with respect to the true prior π_1. In the following, $\delta_1(x)$ will be said to be *P-better* than $\delta_2(x)$ (for a given x), if the posterior expected loss of $\delta_1(x)$ (with respect to π_1) is smaller than the posterior expected loss of $\delta_2(x)$.

It will, unfortunately, generally be true that $\delta^R(x)$ is P-better than $\delta^0(x)$ for some values of x, but worse for others. Since π_0 is unknown or unknowable (which is supposedly why the improper prior was used in the first place), we are left in a bit of a quandary as to whether δ^0 or δ^R should be used.

One point of interest is that δ^R will typically be P-better than δ^0 "on the average." "On the average" refers here to an average with respect to the true marginal distribution of X (with density $m(x) = E^{\pi_1}[f(x|\theta)]$). This can be made precise with the aid of the following lemma.

Lemma 2. *For any proper prior π and decision rule δ,*

$$r(\pi, \delta) = E^m[E^{\pi(\theta|X)}\{L(\theta, \delta(X))\}],$$

where m is the marginal distribution of X.

PROOF. Since π is proper and $L(\theta, a) \geq -K > -\infty$, orders of integration can be interchanged below, giving (in the continuous case for simplicity)

$$r(\pi, \delta) = \int_\Theta \int_{\mathscr{X}} L(\theta, \delta(x)) f(x|\theta) dx \pi(\theta) d\theta$$

$$= \int_{\mathscr{X}} \int_\Theta L(\theta, \delta(x)) f(x|\theta) \pi(\theta) d\theta \, dx$$

$$= \int_{\mathscr{X}} \int_\Theta L(\theta, \delta(x)) \pi(\theta|x) m(x) d\theta \, dx$$

$$= \int_{\mathscr{X}} E^{\pi(\theta|x)} \{ L(\theta, \delta(x)) \} m(x) dx$$

$$= E^m [E^{\pi(\theta|X)} \{ L(\theta, \delta(X)) \}]. \qquad \square$$

This lemma says simply that the Bayes risk is equal to the "average" posterior expected loss.

If now δ^R is R-better than δ^0, and furthermore $R(\theta, \delta^R) < R(\theta, \delta^0)$ for θ in a set with positive (π_1) probability (as certainly happens in Examples 15 and 16), then

$$r(\pi_1, \delta^R) = E^{\pi_1}[R(\theta, \delta^R)] < E^{\pi_1}[R(\theta, \delta^0)] = r(\pi_1, \delta^0).$$

Together with Lemma 2, this implies that

$$E^m[E^{\pi_1(\theta|X)}\{L(\theta, \delta^R(X))\}] < E^m[E^{\pi_1(\theta|X)}\{L(\theta, \delta^0(X))\}],$$

and hence that δ^R is "on the average" P-better than δ^0. This raises serious doubts about the use of δ^0, and incidently gives some sort of Bayesian justification for the concept of inadmissibility.

The above defence of admissibility as a criterion for evaluation of decision rules was presented in a slightly different manner by Hill (1974). He turned to the concept of *coherency*, a standard Bayesian term which generally refers to the desirability of acting in a manner such that betting situations involving a sure loss of money cannot be created. Indeed an interesting definition of coherency, in the decision-theoretic framework, would be the following.

Definition 6. Consider a game involving two players, the proponent of a decision rule δ_1 (call him player 1) and his opponent (player 2). Player 2 chooses a decision rule δ_2, communicating his choice to player 1. Player 1 then chooses a (countably-additive) proper prior distribution for the parameter θ of interest. The parameter θ is generated according to π, and a random variable X generated from the density $f(x|\theta)$. Player i pays the other player an amount $L(\theta, \delta_i(x))$. This game is to be played n times (with fixed $\pi, f, L, \delta_1,$ and δ_2). If, as $n \to \infty$, the probability that player 1 will lose money converges to one, no matter what π he chooses initially, then he is said to be *incoherent* in using δ_1.

The above concept of incoherency can be represented mathematically as follows. Assume that $(X_1, \theta_1), (X_2, \theta_2), \ldots, (X_n, \theta_n)$ is an independent sample from the joint density $h_\pi(x, \theta) = f(x|\theta)\pi(\theta)$. Then player 1 is incoherent in using δ_1 if there is a decision rule δ_2 such that, for any given proper prior π,

$$\lim_{n \to \infty} P\left(\sum_{i=1}^{n} [L(\theta_i, \delta_1(X_i)) - L(\theta_i, \delta_2(X_i))] > 0\right) = 1.$$

If $R(\theta, \delta_1)$ is bounded (so that the Bayes risk is finite for any π), it can be checked that it is incoherent to use δ_1 if and only if there exists another rule δ_2 with $R(\theta, \delta_2) < R(\theta, \delta_1)$ for all $\theta \in \Theta$. (The proof will be left as an exercise.) Thus incoherency is simply a slightly stronger form of inadmissibility.

In Example 16, the use of $\boldsymbol{\delta}^0(\mathbf{x}) = \mathbf{x}$ is incoherent (for $p \geq 3$) by the above result, since $R(\boldsymbol{\theta}, \boldsymbol{\delta}^0) = p$ is bounded. In Example 15, however, one cannot conclude that δ^0 is incoherent, since its risk is unbounded. (Player 1 could choose π to be $\mathscr{C}(0, 1)$, in which case $r(\pi, \delta_c)$ would be infinite for all c, making invalid any long run statement concerning loss or gain.) Example 15 can be modified, however, to yield an even stronger type of incoherency, namely one in which player 1 is allowed, at each repetition of the game, to choose β in any manner whatsoever (not necessarily according to some prior distribution π). This modification is also left for the Exercises.

The conclusion to be drawn from this subsection is that generalized Bayes rules need not always be good, and that the risk $R(\theta, \delta)$ can be useful in investigating their "goodness." Generalized Bayes rules are usually quite reasonable, however, and only rarely are seriously inadequate.

4.6 Robustness of Bayes Rules

4.6.1 Introduction

The problem of robustness has been alluded to several times. Recall that the robustness of a decision rule is simply the sensitivity of the rule to assumptions in the model about which there is uncertainty. Our model for decision problems contains three basic elements: f (the sample density), L (the loss function), and π (the prior density). This section is mainly concerned with discussing robustness with respect to the prior π, but a few comments about robustness with respect to f and L will be made first.

Robustness with respect to f has long been a subject of considerable statistical interest, being as almost all approaches to statistical analysis are based on modeling the sample information. In its beginnings (and still today), the subject was concerned with the detection and handling of "outliers" (sample observations that seem too extreme to be plausible). Much of the recent work on robustness has been concerned with the specification of a *class* of possible sample densities, with a statistical procedure being sought which behaves well (i.e., is robust) for all densities in the given class. See Huber (1972) for a survey of this approach.

We will not enter into a discussion of robustness with respect to the sample density for several reasons. First, it would simply take too much space to cover in an adequate fashion. Second, the results so far obtained are not directed explicitly towards decision analysis, and so it is not clear what the import of many of these findings is to decision theory. Finally, the specification of f is frequently less subjective than that of L and π, so concentration upon the robustness of losses and priors seems more natural for a book on decision theory. This is not to say that robustness considerations concerning f cannot have a significant influence upon the decision rule. Often they can. The best advice we can briefly offer (other than suggesting an extensive reading of the literature on this type of robustness) is to simply try different plausible models for f, in order to see how sensitive the conclusion is to the model. Indeed, this is often the best way of investigating other kinds of robustness as well. Simply vary all the elements of the problem, determining the effects of plausible changes in the model. With the interactive computer systems available these days, this approach is quite feasible.

One particular idea for dealing with the problem of robustness with respect to f deserves mention, because of its Bayesian spirit. If it is assumed that f belongs to some class, say $\mathscr{F}$, of possible distributions, a natural idea is to put a prior distribution on $\mathscr{F}$ and conduct a standard Bayesian analysis. As an example, it could be assumed that $\mathscr{F}$ is the class of all $\mathscr{T}(\alpha, \mu, \sigma^2)$ distributions, where μ and σ^2 are the unknown parameters of interest, but α is also considered unknown. The shape of the density is thus not fixed. (The standard assumption of normality, in contrast, assigns the density a perhaps too sharp-tailed shape.) One can now put a prior density on α (as well as μ and σ^2 if desired) and conduct a Bayesian analysis. See Box and Tiao (1973) for techniques for carrying out such an approach. The answers obtained using this approach appear to be reasonable, but more work needs to be done before the method can be definitely recommended.

The robustness of a decision rule with respect to the loss function has been discussed in several places. No theorems or specific results were given, but the following intuitive guidelines were suggested.

First, decision rules are usually robust with respect to the specification of "large" errors. In estimation, for example, if the loss is of the form $L(\theta - a)$, the decision rule is usually robust with respect to the form of L for large $(\theta - a)$. (This is simply because the probability of extremely large errors is small in most statistical investigations, and the tails of the sample density are usually "sharper" than the tails of L.) The exact form of L for small errors is usually quite important, but accurate specification of L for small errors is usually possible.

The feature of a loss which can cause the most serious robustness difficulties is a weighting factor $w(\theta)$. (The "error" is multiplied by the factor

$w(\theta)$, which indicates the importance of θ.) It was shown, however, that any such weighting factor has exactly the same effect on the decision rule as the prior density π. Robustness with respect to $w(\theta)$ will thus be subsumed in the discussion of the robustness with respect to π.

The rest of this section is devoted to the discussion of robustness with respect to specification of the prior. Study of this problem is crucial before we can apply Bayesian analysis with confidence. The main worry is that, in a Bayesian analysis, one could be led, by an inadequate description of prior beliefs, into making a bad decision. In Example 2 (continued) of Section 3.3, for instance, it was indicated that the tail of the prior density can have a considerable impact upon the decision reached, and yet it is very hard to accurately determine such a tail. It thus becomes important to determine the accuracy of prior specification needed for a good Bayesian analysis, and to determine the most suitable way of making use of vague prior information. For the most part, the discussion in this section will be phrased in terms of Bayesian decision analysis, but many of the ideas will apply as well to Bayesian inference.

In Subsection 4.6.2, we first look at the problem of *measuring* robustness with respect to the prior. In Subsection 4.6.3, general principles of robustness in estimation and hypothesis testing are discussed. Subsection 4.6.4 deals with robust Bayesian analysis for problems involving a normal mean, suggesting explicit robust procedures.

It should be emphasized at the outset that the study of the robustness of Bayes rules with respect to the prior is a relatively new and unexplored field. Many of the ideas stated here are merely plausible intuitive guidelines, rather than well-established principles. Hopefully, rapid further progress will be made in the field.

4.6.2 Measuring Robustness

The natural way to investigate robustness with respect to the prior is to specify a class Γ of plausible prior distributions, and see how the choice among the priors in Γ affects the analysis.

EXAMPLE 17. Assume Θ is a subset of R^1, and as usual let $F^\pi(y)$ denote the cumulative distribution function of the prior distribution π. Consider the following four choices of Γ:

$\Gamma_1 = \{\pi : |F^\pi(y) - F^{\pi_0}(y)| \leq \varepsilon \text{ for all } y\}$,

$\Gamma_2 = \{\pi : |z(\alpha_i) - z_0(\alpha_i)| \leq \varepsilon_i, i = 1, \ldots, k, \text{ where the } z(\alpha_i) \text{ and } z_0(\alpha_i) \text{ are the } \alpha_i\text{-fractiles of } \pi \text{ and } \pi_0 \text{ respectively}\}$,

$\Gamma_3 = \{\pi : |\mu_i - \mu_i^0| < \varepsilon_i, i = 1, \ldots, k, \text{ where } \mu_i = E^\pi[\theta^i] \text{ and } \mu_i^0 = E^{\pi_0}[\theta^i]\}$,

$\Gamma_4 = \{\pi : \pi \text{ has a density of a given functional form, } \pi(\theta | \gamma_1, \ldots, \gamma_k), \text{ where } \gamma_i \in A_i, i = 1, \ldots, k\}$.

The class Γ_1 is very natural, the idea being that π_0 is the subjectively chosen prior and all priors "close" to π_0 are considered plausible. The given definition of closeness (close CDFs) is reasonable, in that it essentially restricts the class of plausible priors to those which assign similar probabilities to subsets of Θ. (Again, it is probabilities of sets that can be most easily determined subjectively.)

The class Γ_2 is also very reasonable, in that one of the most useful methods of subjectively constructing a prior π_0 is through determination of several of its fractiles. It would be relatively easy to specify the accuracy ε_i with which it is felt that the fractiles have been determined. Of considerable interest would even be the class Γ_2', in which all ε_i are zero (i.e., the class of priors with a given set of fractiles).

The class Γ_3 is the class of priors whose first k moments are constrained to be close to the first k moments of a subjectively determined distribution π_0. One difficulty with this class is that, as discussed in Chapter 3, it is very hard to subjectively estimate prior moments (the possible exception being when Θ is a bounded set).

The class Γ_4 is the most restrictive class, consisting of prior densities of a given functional form whose parameters, γ_i, are constrained to lie in certain sets A_i. It is, unfortunately, very hard to justify a particular functional form for π.

Of these four classes of priors, Γ_1 and Γ_2 are by far the most attractive. They essentially fix certain subjective probabilities (which are relatively easy to determine), but allow variation in the other less easily specified features of the prior (such as the tail). The classes Γ_3 and Γ_4, on the other hand, fix aspects of the prior which are hard to determine subjectively, and do not allow enough variation in other aspects of the prior (such as the tail). Unfortunately, the good classes Γ_1 and Γ_2 tend to be much harder to deal with than the bad classes Γ_3 and Γ_4.

The robustness of a decision rule δ, with respect to a class Γ, can be measured in essentially two different ways. The first, and most attractive to a Bayesian, is through analysis of the effect on the posterior expected loss of changes in the prior. The second is through examination of $R(\theta, \delta)$ and $r(\pi, \delta)$. Both will be discussed.

I. *Posterior Robustness*

Suppose the estimate for the true prior is π_0, and that it is desired to investigate the robustness of the Bayes action a_0 (i.e., the action minimizing the posterior expected loss when π_0 is the prior), with respect to a class of plausible deviations from π_0. The action a_0 will be said to be *posterior robust* with respect to Γ, if, for all $\pi \in \Gamma$, the posterior expected loss of a_0 is close to the optimal posterior expected loss. (More formally, one could say that a_0 is *ε-posterior robust* if, for all $\pi \in \Gamma$, the posterior expected loss of a_0 is within ε of the optimal posterior expected loss.) This is the natural definition of robustness (at least to a Bayesian).

In many problems, insight can be gained concerning the posterior robustness of an action a_0 by simply investigating how close a_0 is to the Bayes action a_π (the action minimizing the posterior expected loss), for the various $\pi \in \Gamma$. In estimation under squared-error loss, for example, $a_\pi = E^{\pi(\theta|x)}[\theta]$, so that

$$
\begin{aligned}
E^{\pi(\theta|x)}[L(\theta, a_0)] - E^{\pi(\theta|x)}[L(\theta, a_\pi)] &= E^{\pi(\theta|x)}[(\theta - a_0)^2 - (\theta - a_\pi)^2] \\
&= E^{\pi(\theta|x)}[(a_\pi - a_0)(2\theta - a_\pi - a_0)] \\
&= (a_\pi - a_0)(2a_\pi - a_\pi - a_0) \\
&= (a_\pi - a_0)^2. \qquad (4.4)
\end{aligned}
$$

The posterior expected loss of a_0 is thus close to the optimal posterior expected loss if a_0 is close to the optimal Bayes action. In some of the following examples we will make use of this relationship, and merely investigate how close a proposed action is to the Bayes action.

EXAMPLE 18. When the sample size n is large, the likelihood function $f(x|\theta)$ will tend to be very peaked. For example, if $\mathbf{X} = (X_1, \ldots, X_n)$ is a sample from a $\mathcal{N}(\theta, 1)$ distribution, the likelihood function is a $\mathcal{N}(\bar{x}, n^{-1})$ density, which is very peaked about $\bar{x}$. For large enough n, the likelihood function will thus be much more concentrated than any reasonable prior π. To put this another way, $\pi(\theta)$ will tend to look flat in the area in which the likelihood function gives most of its weight. It can be shown that, in such a situation, the posterior density (which is proportional to the product of $f(\mathbf{x}|\theta)$ and $\pi(\theta)$) can be closely approximated by $f(\mathbf{x}|\theta)$ (properly normalized as a density for θ). Furthermore, this will be true for any prior in a reasonable class, Γ, of smooth priors. But if the posterior density is virtually the same for all $\pi \in \Gamma$, then certainly the Bayes action will be posterior robust with respect to Γ.

As a specific example, consider the normal situation mentioned above, and assume it is desired to estimate θ under squared-error loss. Since, for large enough n, the posterior is approximately $\mathcal{N}(\bar{x}, n^{-1})$, it is clear that the Bayes estimate of θ will be approximately $\bar{x}$. (It will be seen, however, that the n which is "large enough" may depend on $\bar{x}$, a somewhat unsettling possibility.) This phenomenon is known as the *principle of stable estimation* or *stable measurement* and is discussed in Edwards, Lindeman, and Savage (1963). (See also DeGroot (1970) and Dickey (1976) for related results.)

Unfortunately, this situation is really rather uninteresting from a decision-theoretic viewpoint. When the sample information is much greater than the prior information, it seems only natural that the prior information will have little effect on the Bayes action. Of much greater interest are those situations in which the prior information is significant, or at least not negligible.

EXAMPLE 19. Assume $X \sim \mathcal{N}(\theta, 1)$ is observed, and that it is desired to test $H_0: \theta \leq 0$ versus $H_1: \theta > 0$ under "0–1" loss. Let a_0 denote accepting H_0, and a_1 denote accepting H_1. It is thought that the prior distribution is a $\mathcal{N}(1, 4)$ density (denote this π_0), but it is believed possible for θ to be any prior in a class of the form Γ_1 (see Example 17). Since the loss is "0–1" loss, it is easy to see that the Bayes rule, for a given $\pi \in \Gamma_1$, is simply to choose a_0 if

$$P(\theta \leq 0 | x) > P(\theta > 0 | x),$$

and choose a_1 otherwise. (These probabilities are, of course, with respect to the posterior distribution of θ given x.) Now assume that $x = -10$ is observed. The sample information then heavily favors H_0, so much so that, for any π reasonably close to π_0, it will be true that

$$P(\theta \leq 0 | x = -10) > P(\theta > 0 | x = -10).$$

When $x = -10$ is observed, a_0 will thus be the Bayes action for all $\pi \in \Gamma_1$. The Bayes action is, therefore, extremely posterior robust when $x = -10$. Unfortunately, the exact verification of even the above simple inequality can be difficult for x closer to zero and any specific choice of ε in Γ_1.

EXAMPLE 20. Consider the situation of Example 2 (continued) in Section 3.3. Here, the median and the quartiles of the prior distribution are specified, so that a reasonable choice for Γ would be the class of priors with these fractiles. (This would be of the form Γ_2 in Example 17.) Working with this class is very hard. As a crude yet reasonable approximation, we could simply let Γ contain the $\mathcal{N}(0, 2.19)$ and $\mathscr{C}(0, 1)$ densities. The rationale is that these two densities, while having the same median and quartiles, are quite different, especially in their "tails." Hence they hopefully cover a reasonable amount of the variation in Γ.

For $x = 10$, the results from Example 2 (continued) show that the Bayes estimates are not posterior robust. The estimates resulting from the two priors are considerably different. For x near zero, however, the estimates are reasonably close. If $x = 1$, for example, the normal Bayes estimate is 0.69, while the Cauchy Bayes estimate (calculated numerically on a hand calculator) is 0.52. For $x = 2$, the two estimates are 1.37 and 1.27, respectively. Thus, for x near zero, we can tentatively conclude that the Bayes estimate is posterior robust.

The above examples point out several general features of posterior robustness that are of interest. First, the only situations in which posterior robustness is obvious are those in which the sample information is conclusive (as in Examples 18 and 19). While it is of interest to categorize such situations, the cases where the prior input is of significance are obviously more interesting. It should be noted in passing that when noninformative priors are used, the Bayes rules will usually be posterior robust with respect to, say, the choice of the noninformative prior. This is quite natural, in that the purpose of a noninformative prior is to ensure that the sample information dominates.

The second observation is that it is very hard to work with posterior robustness. In general, it may just be best (as in Example 20) to specify a reasonable class Γ, choose typical (different) members of Γ, and simply calculate the Bayes actions for these priors, observing how similar they are.

The final observation is that posterior robustness will often crucially depend on which x is observed. In Example 19, for instance, extreme x insured posterior robustness, while for x closer to zero no such claim could easily be made. In Example 20 the reverse seemed to hold. When x had large absolute value, the Bayes estimates were clearly not posterior robust, while, for smaller $|x|$, the Bayes estimates seemed to be posterior robust. Thus posterior robustness is something best investigated after the sample x is at hand.

II. *Risk Robustness*

If the Bayes action is posterior robust, there is no real need to investigate further. In the (frequent) situations where posterior robustness is found to be lacking, however, one must evaluate robustness in a different fashion. The most useful methods that have been developed depend on consideration of $R(\theta, \delta)$ and $r(\pi, \delta)$. The point is that, if posterior analysis does not lead to a definitive conclusion, consideration of overall average risk properties of a decision rule can be helpful. Again it will be desired to evaluate robustness with respect to a class Γ of possible priors; with the hope being to obtain a rule sensitive to the well-specified facets of the prior (supposedly common to the rules in Γ), and insensitive to the uncertainties in the prior specification. Several measures of risk robustness are possible, those discussed below being the most appealing.

The simplest (and in some ways the best) method of achieving robustness is through examination of the risk function, $R(\theta, \delta)$. The idea is simply to calculate and compare the risk functions of the various rules under consideration (often the Bayes rules δ^π for $\pi \in \Gamma$). It is frequently relatively easy to see which rules are sensitive to uncertainties in the prior specification, and which are not.

EXAMPLE 20 (continued). For the $\mathcal{N}(0, 2.19)$ prior density (π_N) and the $\mathscr{C}(0, 1)$ prior density (π_C), the risk functions $R(\theta, \delta_N)$ and $R(\theta, \delta_C)$ of the Bayes estimators δ_N and δ_C (with respect to π_N and π_C respectively) are given in Figure 4.1. Both rules will clearly do well when θ is near zero (i.e., the prior information appears correct). When θ is far from zero, however, δ_N does much worse than δ_C. Since there is uncertainty as to the true "tail" of the prior, with flat tails being a possibility (in which case "extreme" θ are quite possible), the rule δ_C seems intuitively more sensible. If one were very certain that

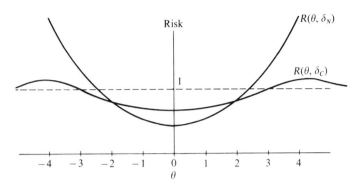

Figure 4.1

extreme θ could not occur, δ_N might be preferable, but such situations are relatively rare.

The above use of $R(\theta, \delta)$ is clearly not very rigorous. Nevertheless, it can be very helpful, even when a formal consideration of robustness is not being undertaken. Indeed it is almost always good practice, upon obtaining a Bayes rule δ^π, to look at $R(\theta, \delta^\pi)$ for any unappealing features. The examination of "classical" properties of a Bayes rule can also be helpful. The point is that one can, through such checks, sometimes gain insight into prior beliefs. In the above example, for instance, someone about to use δ_N might, after seeing $R(\theta, \delta_N)$, realize that "extreme" θ are entirely possible according to his prior beliefs, and hence conclude that using a normal prior is an error.

To perform a formal analysis of risk robustness, one is led to the use of the Bayes risk $r(\pi, \delta)$. Various features of the Bayes risk for $\pi \in \Gamma$ can be examined. The two most reasonable such robustness approaches are the Γ-minimax approach and the Γ-minimax regret approach. These will now be discussed.

A. The Γ-minimax Approach

Since we are uncertain as to which $\pi \in \Gamma$ is correct, it is natural to evaluate a rule δ in terms of the worst Bayes risk, $r(\pi, \delta)$, for $\pi \in \Gamma$. As in the similar minimax approach, it may be necessary to consider randomized rules δ^*. (See Sections 1.4 and 1.5.)

Definition 7. Define the Γ-*minimax risk* of a decision rule δ^* to be the quantity

$$r_\Gamma(\delta^*) = \sup_{\pi \in \Gamma} r(\pi, \delta^*).$$

Γ-minimax Principle. *A decision rule δ_1^* is preferred to a rule δ_2^* if*

$$r_\Gamma(\delta_1^*) < r_\Gamma(\delta_2^*).$$

Definition 8. The Γ-*minimax value* of the problem is defined to be

$$r_\Gamma = \inf_{\delta^* \in \mathscr{D}^*} r_\Gamma(\delta^*) = \inf_{\delta^* \in \mathscr{D}^*} \sup_{\pi \in \Gamma} r(\pi, \delta^*).$$

A rule δ^* is said to be Γ-*minimax* if $r_\Gamma(\delta^*) = r_\Gamma$.

The idea here is straightforward. The quantity $r_\Gamma(\delta^*)$ represents the "worst Bayes risk" that can happen if $\pi \in \Gamma$, and the goal is to seek a rule for which this worst Bayes risk is as small as possible. Noting that r_Γ is the lowest possible worst Bayes risk, it is clear that a Γ-minimax rule (if one exists) achieves the desired objective.

These ideas are very related to the minimax principle discussed in Section 1.5. Indeed if Γ is chosen to be the set of *all* priors, it can be shown that

$$\sup_{\pi \in \Gamma} r(\pi, \delta^*) = \sup_{\theta \in \Theta} R(\theta, \delta^*).$$

(The proof is left as an exercise.) In this situation, Γ-minimaxity clearly corresponds exactly with usual minimaxity. At the other extreme, if Γ is chosen to contain only one prior distribution π_0, then the Γ-minimax principle corresponds to the Bayes principle. Reasonable choices of Γ (as in Example 17) fall somewhere between these two extremes.

Measuring the robustness of a rule δ^* by $r_\Gamma(\delta^*)$ is reasonable. A rule with large Γ-minimax risk runs the chance of being very bad if the true prior from Γ is "unfavorable." On the other hand, a rule with $r_\Gamma(\delta^*)$ near r_Γ is quite safe no matter which $\pi \in \Gamma$ is correct. The concept of Γ-minimaxity was explicitly introduced by Robbins (1964), although ideas of a similar nature appeared earlier.

EXAMPLE 21. Assume $X \sim \mathcal{N}(\theta, 1)$, and that it is desired to estimate θ under squared-error loss, using the observation x. Since the loss is convex, it follows from Theorem 3 of Section 1.8 that only nonrandomized rules need be considered. Assume it is felt that the prior has mean μ and variance τ^2, but that otherwise nothing is known. It is then reasonable to let

$$\Gamma = \{\pi : E^\pi(\theta) = \mu \text{ and } E^\pi(\theta - \mu)^2 = \tau^2\}.$$

Consider the estimator

$$\delta_N(x) = \frac{\tau^2}{1 + \tau^2} x + \frac{1}{1 + \tau^2} \mu.$$

Clearly

$$R(\theta, \delta_N) = E_\theta^X \left(\frac{\tau^2}{1 + \tau^2} X + \frac{1}{1 + \tau^2} \mu - \theta \right)^2$$

$$= E_\theta^X \left(\frac{\tau^2}{1 + \tau^2} [X - \theta] + \frac{1}{1 + \tau^2} [\mu - \theta] \right)^2$$

$$= \frac{\tau^4}{(1 + \tau^2)^2} E_\theta^X [X - \theta]^2 + \frac{1}{(1 + \tau^2)^2} [\mu - \theta]^2$$

$$= \frac{\tau^4}{(1 + \tau^2)^2} + \frac{[\mu - \theta]^2}{(1 + \tau^2)^2}.$$

Hence, for any $\pi \in \Gamma$,

$$r(\pi, \delta_N) = E^\pi [R(\theta, \delta_N)] = \frac{\tau^4}{(1 + \tau^2)^2} + \frac{\tau^2}{(1 + \tau^2)^2} = \frac{\tau^2}{1 + \tau^2}. \qquad (4.5)$$

Note, however, that δ_N is the Bayes rule with respect to π_N, the $\mathcal{N}(\mu, \tau^2)$ prior. Hence for *any* rule δ,

$$r(\pi_N, \delta) \geq r(\pi_N, \delta_N) = \frac{\tau^2}{1 + \tau^2}.$$

This implies that

$$\sup_{\pi \in \Gamma} r(\pi, \delta) \geq r(\pi_N, \delta) \geq \frac{\tau^2}{1 + \tau^2}.$$

Combining this with (4.5), it can be concluded that, for all rules δ,

$$\sup_{\pi \in \Gamma} r(\pi, \delta) \geq \frac{\tau^2}{1 + \tau^2} = \sup_{\pi \in \Gamma} r(\pi, \delta_N).$$

Thus δ_N is Γ-minimax. (This result is a special case of a theorem in Jackson, Donovan, Zimmer, and Deely (1970).)

The above example has the unfortunate feature of dealing with a class, Γ, of priors that involves moment specifications. In Example 17 it was pointed out that such Γ are usually unreasonable, so that the result in Example 21 is of limited usefulness. Unfortunately, most of the literature on Γ-minimaxity is based on using Γ of this type, or of type Γ_4 in Example 17. Of greater interest would be Γ-minimax results for classes of the form Γ_1 or Γ_2 from Example 17. For these latter types of Γ, one can proceed (in the absence of good mathematical results) by again choosing typical (different) elements of Γ, and calculating $r(\pi, \delta)$ for the chosen priors and various possible decision rules.

EXAMPLE 20 (continued). Assume the $\mathcal{C}(0, 1)$ (π_C) and $\mathcal{N}(0, 2.19)$ (π_N) densities are selected as typical (but quite different) members of Γ. It is natural to consider δ_N, the Bayes rule with respect to the normal prior, and δ_C, the Bayes rule with respect to the Cauchy prior. A numerical calculation will show $r(\pi_N, \delta_C)$ to be significantly less than one, while (see Example 21)

$$r(\pi_C, \delta_N) = E^{\pi_C}\left[\frac{(2.19)^2}{(3.19)^2} + \frac{\theta^2}{(3.19)^2}\right] = \infty,$$

since the Cauchy distribution does not have a finite variance. While certainly not a very exhaustive investigation of Γ-minimaxity, this at least indicates that δ_N is very bad from a Γ-minimax viewpoint, while δ_C appears reasonable. Of course, the fact that $r(\pi_C, \delta_N) = \infty$ is due to the use of an unbounded loss function, but, even for bounded losses, δ_N will be a good deal worse than δ_C.

B. *The Γ-minimax Regret Approach*

A valid criticism of the Γ-minimax principle is that the quantity $r_\Gamma(\delta^*)$ is unduly responsive to unfavorable π. To be more precise, if there is a prior π_0 for which $r(\pi_0)$ (the Bayes risk of π_0) is exceptionally large, a Γ-minimax rule will tend to be Bayes (or nearly Bayes) with respect to π_0. (This will certainly happen, for example, if

$$r_\Gamma(\delta^*) = \sup_{\pi \in \Gamma} r(\pi, \delta^*) = r(\pi_0, \delta^*)$$

for all rules δ^*.) This is unreasonable in that, if π_0 is the true prior, one can *at best* suffer the risk $r(\pi_0)$. It is more sensible when looking at $r(\pi_0, \delta^*)$, therefore, to see how much worse it is than $r(\pi_0)$. In other words, a more natural quantity to consider is $r(\pi_0, \delta^*) - r(\pi_0)$. (An extensive discussion of the similar idea of regret loss is given in Chapter 5.)

Definition 9. Define the Γ-*minimax regret risk* of a decision rule δ^* to be

$$r_\Gamma^*(\delta^*) = \sup_{\pi \in \Gamma} [r(\pi, \delta^*) - r(\pi)].$$

Γ-minimax Regret Principle. *A decision rule δ_1^* is preferred to a rule δ_2^* if $r_\Gamma^*(\delta_1^*) < r_\Gamma^*(\delta_2^*)$.*

Definition 10. The Γ-*minimax regret value* of the problem is defined to be

$$r_\Gamma^* = \inf_{\delta^* \in \mathscr{D}^*} r_\Gamma^*(\delta^*) = \inf_{\delta^* \in \mathscr{D}^*} \sup_{\pi \in \Gamma} [r(\pi, \delta^*) - r(\pi)].$$

A rule δ^* is said to be a Γ-*minimax regret rule* if $r_\Gamma^*(\delta^*) = r_\Gamma^*$.

Working with Γ-minimax regret is similar to, though perhaps somewhat harder than, working with Γ-minimaxity. In many statistical situations, the two approaches tend to give similar results. In the situation of Example 20 (continued), for instance, δ_N has infinite Γ-minimax regret risk, while δ_C is reasonable.

Discussion

Pure Bayesians do not endorse the Γ-minimax or Γ-minimax regret principles, because they involve averages over the sample space $\mathscr{X}$ (in the calculation of $r(\pi, \delta^*)$). Several versions of Γ-minimaxity based on posterior expected loss have been introduced. These measures prove inadequate, however, for reasons indicated in the following example.

EXAMPLE 22. Assume that actions are to be compared on the basis of

$$h_\Gamma(a) = \sup_{\pi \in \Gamma} \{E^{\pi(\theta|x)}[L(\theta, a)] - \inf_{a \in \mathscr{A}} E^{\pi(\theta|x)}[L(\theta, a)]\},$$

which is similar to Γ-minimax regret, but uses posterior expected loss instead of Bayes risk. Assuming squared-error loss and letting $\mu(x) = E^{\pi(\theta|x)}[\theta]$, it is clear from (4.4) that

$$h_\Gamma(a) = \sup_{\pi \in \Gamma} [\mu(x) - a]^2.$$

Choosing an action to minimize $h_\Gamma(a)$ provides little discrimination among priors. For example, if Γ consists of two priors, π_1 and π_2, with corresponding posterior means $\mu_1(x)$ and $\mu_2(x)$ (which are the Bayes actions for squared-error loss), then clearly

$$h_\Gamma(\mu_1(x)) = [\mu_2(x) - \mu_1(x)]^2 = [\mu_1(x) - \mu_2(x)]^2 = h_\Gamma(\mu_2(x)).$$

Thus the Bayes actions of either of the two priors are considered equally as good. (Of course the "optimal" action would be $[\mu_1(x) + \mu_2(x)]/2$.) This seems unreasonable in light of the discussion in Example 20 (continued).

If disuaded from using $h_\Gamma(a)$, a pure Bayesian might then suggest that a prior distribution be placed on Γ itself, and the resulting Bayes action obtained. Alternatively, he might simply say that, if there is a lack of posterior robustness, one must more carefully decide upon the prior distribution, i.e., carefully choose (subjectively) among the priors in Γ. Though in a strict sense this is correct, in practice it would not be at all unusual to be in a situation where further specification of the prior is impossible, either because of a lack of time, or simply because the user feels he has exhausted his prior information.

This reply to the Bayesian criticism can be phrased another way. If the statistician is to be forced to deal with such uncertain situations repeatedly, he will be dealing with repetitive samples (albeit from possibly different sample spaces), so that long run averages over samples are reasonable in a "mega-problem" sense. Indeed theorems can be established which show that if one behaves in a nonrobust fashion (say with respect to Γ-minimax regret) for reasonable classes of Γ, then, in the long run, serious loss will be incurred. (The details would involve putting reasonable priors on Γ for different problems, etc.)

The unfortunately difficult problem remains of determining Γ-minimax or Γ-minimax regret rules for Γ of real interest, such as Γ_1 and Γ_2 of Example 17. The problem seems very difficult analytically. Indeed, even if attention is just limited to nonrandomized rules, a rigorous analysis seems almost impossible.

An adhoc way of dealing with the problem has already been discussed. Simply choose representative priors from Γ, and calculate $r(\pi, \delta^*)$ for these priors and various reasonable decision rules (usually the Bayes rules for the chosen priors). Denoting the set of chosen priors by Γ^*, choose the rule which minimizes

$$\max_{\pi \in \Gamma^*} \left[r(\pi, \delta^*) - r(\pi) \right].$$

(Again considering this "regret" risk is more appealing than just considering $r(\pi, \delta^*)$.) If the chosen priors accurately reflect the variation in Γ, the resulting rule will usually be reasonable.

Due to the difficulty in using the above ideas in specific problems, the idea of trying to develop "robust" priors suggests itself. In other words, it would be useful to know, for a given decision problem, which priors generally yield robust rules and which do not. The remainder of the section deals with this issue.

4.6.3 The Development of Robust Priors

In this subsection we discuss, mainly in an intuitive fashion, which kinds of priors tend to be robust. The word "robust" here is used rather loosely, and would perhaps be better replaced by "good." It often happens, however, that the "good" priors recommended here give rules which are quite robust according to the measures of the preceding subsection.

Almost by definition, the noninformative priors discussed in Chapter 3 are very robust. In the same vein, the maximum entropy priors introduced in that chapter will usually also be robust (providing the constraints used are not moment conditions involving second or higher moments).

For typical subjectively chosen priors, one must distinguish between the "central" portion of the prior and the "tail." By the central portion of the prior is meant that part which would be easily constructed (subjectively) using the techniques of Chapter 3. This would usually be the part constructed on, say, the apriori 90% credible region for θ. The tail, conversely, is the part of the prior constructed upon the remainder of the parameter space, i.e., the extreme regions of small probability.

Bayes procedures will usually be robust with respect to small changes in the central portion of the prior, but only rarely will be robust with respect to large changes. Indeed about the only situation, in which robustness with respect to large changes in the central portion occurs, is when the sample information overwhelms the prior information, as in Examples 18 and 19. When the prior information matters, one cannot expect to have robustness with respect to significant changes in it. Thus it is important to try to accurately specify the central portion of the prior.

The tail of the prior is hard to specify so robustness with respect to this tail is desirable. (Note that in some cases, such as when Θ is a small bounded set, there may be no tail to worry about, in that the prior can be determined accurately over all of Θ.) The tail of the prior will not have a serious impact if the observation x is such that the likelihood function, $l(\theta) = f(x|\theta)$, is predominantly concentrated in the central portion of the prior. (The posterior is then determined mainly by the likelihood function and the central portion of the prior.) When x is "extreme," however, in the sense that the likelihood function gives considerable weight to the tail of the prior, the posterior will be significantly affected by the type of prior tail chosen. This will cause a lack of robustness, except in situations such as Example 19. One must thus choose the kind of tail effect that is desired.

Two arguments suggest trying to choose a tail which has a minimal impact on the posterior. The first argument is that, when the likelihood function gives most of its weight to the tail of the prior, the indication is that the prior information may be wrong. Hence the influence of the prior (here the tail) should intuitively be minimized. The second argument for choosing a noninfluential tail is that risk robustness (discussed in the previous subsection) tends to be much worse for Bayes rules based on influential tails, than for Bayes rules based on noninfluential tails. Significant evidence of this is given in Rubin (1977).

To minimize the influence of the tail of the prior, a prior with a "flat" tail should be used. A prior density, $\pi(\theta)$, has a flat tail if $\pi(\theta)$ decreases (as $|\theta|$ increases) considerably *slower* than the likelihood function. This will ensure that the likelihood function dominates the tail of the prior. The following example demonstrates this idea.

EXAMPLE 23. Assume $f(x|\theta)$ is a $\mathcal{N}(\theta, \sigma^2)$ density (σ^2 known). If the prior is π_1, a $\mathcal{N}(\mu, \tau^2)$ density, the posterior density (see Example 1) is $\mathcal{N}(\mu(x), \rho^{-1})$, where $\rho = (\tau^2 + \sigma^2)/\tau^2\sigma^2$. If the prior is π_2, a $\mathcal{T}(\alpha, \mu, \tau^2)$ density, it can be shown by a Taylor expansion of $\pi_2(\theta)$ about x that, for $|x - \mu|$ moderately large (compared to $\alpha^{1/2}\tau$ and $\alpha\sigma$)

$$\pi_2(\theta|x) \cong f(x|\theta) + \frac{(\theta - x)f(x|\theta)\pi_2'(x)}{\pi_2(x)}$$

$$= f(x|\theta) - \frac{(\alpha + 1)(\theta - x)f(x|\theta)(x - \mu)}{\alpha\tau^2 + (x - \mu)^2}.$$

(For the details of this kind of calculation, see Berger and Srinivasan (1978).) The second term of this expression is essentially the effect on the posterior of the tail of π_2. (When $|x - \mu|$ is moderately large compared to σ and τ, then x is in the tail of the prior.) Note that the first term, $f(x|\theta)$, is the posterior that would result from the noninformative prior $\pi(\theta) = 1$. As $|x - \mu|$ becomes very large (i.e., x becomes more "extreme"), the second term becomes less and less important, as desired. (Note that $\theta - x$ will usually be of the order of σ.) Observe also that the size of the second term depends on α, the degrees of freedom of the t distribution. Hence the fewer the degrees of freedom assumed for the t prior, the smaller is the significance of the tail of the prior.

Contrast this situation with that of the normal prior π_1 (which can be considered a limiting case of the t prior as $\alpha \to \infty$). The posterior is seriously affected by the tail of π_1. Indeed the effect increases in severity as x becomes more extreme. For instance, the posterior mean of $\pi_1(\theta|x)$ is

$$\mu_1(x) = x - \frac{\sigma^2}{(\sigma^2 + \tau^2)}(x - \mu).$$

The effect of π_1 is again in the second term, which here is linearly increasing in $x - \mu$. The posterior mean of $\pi_2(\theta|x)$, on the other hand, is approximately

$$\mu_2(x) = \int \theta\pi(\theta|x)d\theta = \int \theta f(x|\theta)d\theta - \frac{(\alpha + 1)(x - \mu)}{\alpha\tau^2 + (x - \mu)^2}\int \theta(\theta - x)f(x|\theta)d\theta$$

$$= x - \frac{(\alpha + 1)(x - \mu)\sigma^2}{\alpha\tau^2 + (x - \mu)^2},$$

which converges to x as $|x - \mu| \to \infty$. The tail of the t prior thus seems much more desirable. Note that the "central" portion of a t prior can be made to match quite closely with the central portion of a normal prior. Hence the use of t priors (instead of conjugate normal priors) seems definitely in order if one uses the given functional form approach to develop the prior. (Of course, the Bayesian calculations then have to be carried out on a computer or a calculator, but this is not too great a hardship.)

The above observation has been made previously by a number of authors, among them Tiao and Zellner (1964), Anscombe (1963), Dawid (1973), Hill (1974), and Dickey (1974). Rubin (1977) has also shown that priors with tails decreasing as $\exp\{-c|\theta - \mu|\}$ give reasonably robust posteriors. The point is that all of these prior densities (except the normal) have tails which are flatter (decrease more slowly) than the likelihood function (which behaves as $\exp\{-c|\theta - x|^2\}$).

From the above example, one further interesting observation can be made, namely that an extremely accurate sample is no guarantee of prior robustness. Indeed, for the normal prior in the above example, the effect of the prior on the posterior mean is in the addition of the term

$-\sigma^2(x - \mu)/(\sigma^2 + \tau^2)$. If the sample is very accurate, then σ^2 will be small, yet if x is too extreme (i.e., $|x - \mu|$ too large), the prior will still have a huge effect. Thus caution must always be used in doing Bayesian analysis when x is extreme.

The goal of this discussion has been to instill a sense of caution in the choice of the tail or functional form of a prior. For example, the discussion indicates that the use of conjugate priors can be very dangerous if x is extreme. (Conjugate prior densities have tails of the same form as the likelihood function, not flatter as would be desired.) If uncertain in a given situation as to whether a particular tail is appropriate or not, an examination of the risk function, $R(\theta, \delta)$, of the Bayes rule should help resolve the issue.

4.6.4 Robust Bayesian Procedures for a Multivariate Normal Mean

If only very vague prior information is available, it is useful to have Bayesian procedures which can incorporate this prior information, and yet are extremely robust or safe when the prior information is wrong. Such procedures should ideally combine ease of use, with the features of offering significant gains if the vague prior information is correct and of being conservative when the prior information appears wrong. Procedures having these properties have been developed for certain situations involving a multivariate normal mean, and will be presented in this subsection. Similar results for various Poisson and binomial problems can be found in Albert (1979). It should be stressed that these "shortcut" Bayesian procedures are not as good as a thorough standard Bayesian analysis, in terms of accurately using all of the prior information. Indeed, in being conservative, they perhaps deemphasize the prior information. They are useful when (i) only vague prior information is available; (ii) a rigorous Bayesian analysis would be too time consuming or expensive; or (iii) one wants to be conservative in application of the Bayesian approach.

Inference and decision problems concerning a multivariate normal mean, $\boldsymbol{\theta} = (\theta_1, \ldots, \theta_p)^t$, occur frequently in statistics. (Of course, setting $p = 1$ will give the univariate situation.) Included in this area of study is not only standard normal inference, but also more complicated situations such as regression analysis. Relatively simple robust Bayesian procedures will be developed for inference and decision problems concerning $\boldsymbol{\theta}$.

In true multivariate settings, the robust Bayesian procedures that will be developed also have another interpretation. Recall from Example 16 that the usual estimator, $\boldsymbol{\delta}^0$, of $\boldsymbol{\theta}$ is inadmissible for $p \geq 3$. There has been a great deal of research into finding improved estimators for $\boldsymbol{\theta}$. Much of the Stein-estimation and ridge regression literature falls into this category. The robust Bayesian estimators developed here can likewise be viewed as improvements upon $\boldsymbol{\delta}^0$. In fact, a strong case can be made that only through a robust Bayesian approach can significant improvement upon δ^0 be made. (This is partially indicated in the discussion following Example 16. For a more extensive discussion see Berger (1980b).)

To get down to details, assume $\mathbf{X} = (X_1, X_2, \ldots, X_p)^t$ is observed, where $\mathbf{X} \sim \mathcal{N}_p(\boldsymbol{\theta}, \boldsymbol{\Sigma})$. (Usually, of course, a sample $\mathbf{X}^{(1)}, \ldots, \mathbf{X}^{(n)}$ of vector observations will be taken, in which case $\mathbf{X}$ will be the vector of sample means.) For simplicity, we start out by assuming that the covariance matrix $\boldsymbol{\Sigma}$ is known.

I. *Procedures When $\boldsymbol{\Sigma}$ Is Known*

The particular prior that will be used to construct the robust procedures is

$$g_n(\boldsymbol{\theta}) = (2\pi)^{-p/2} \int_0^1 [\det\{\mathbf{B}(\lambda)\}]^{-1/2}$$

$$\times \exp\{-\tfrac{1}{2}(\boldsymbol{\theta} - \boldsymbol{\mu})^t \mathbf{B}(\lambda)^{-1}(\boldsymbol{\theta} - \boldsymbol{\mu})\}\lambda^{n-1-p/2} \, d\lambda,$$

where $\boldsymbol{\mu} = (\mu_1, \mu_2, \ldots, \mu_p)^t$, $\mathbf{B}(\lambda) = \rho[\lambda^{-1}(\boldsymbol{\Sigma} + \mathbf{A}) - \boldsymbol{\Sigma}]$, $\rho = n/(n+1)$, $\mathbf{A}$ is a $(p \times p)$ positive definite matrix, $n = \max\{(p-2)/2, \tfrac{1}{2}\}$, and *det* stands for determinant. The vector $\boldsymbol{\mu}$ and matrix $\mathbf{A}$ will be the subjective prior inputs and will roughly represent a prior mean and a prior covariance matrix, respectively. More will be said about them later.

A useful way of thinking about g_n is to observe that given $\lambda, \boldsymbol{\theta} \sim \mathcal{N}(\boldsymbol{\mu}, \mathbf{B}(\lambda))$, while λ is given the density $\lambda^{n-1-p/2} I_{(0, 1)}(\lambda)$. Note that the density of λ, and hence g_n, is improper for the given choice of n. This is because extremely flat tails for the prior are sought, so as to lead to very robust procedures. (See Subsection 4.6.3.) Observe, finally, that $g_n(\boldsymbol{\theta})$ is unimodal (with mode $\boldsymbol{\mu}$) and symmetric about $\boldsymbol{\mu}$, in the sense that $g_n(\boldsymbol{\mu} + \mathbf{z}) = g_n(\boldsymbol{\mu} - \mathbf{z})$. Hence g_n is useful mainly for those situations in which the true prior is judged to be approximately unimodal and symmetric. For an explanation of why this particular prior was chosen, see Berger (1980b).

Unfortunately, $g_n(\boldsymbol{\theta})$ cannot usually be explicitly calculated. Of far more importance, however, is the fact that it has a posterior distribution $\pi_n(\boldsymbol{\theta}|\mathbf{x})$ whose mean, $\boldsymbol{\mu}_n(\mathbf{x})$, and covariance matrix, $\boldsymbol{\Sigma}_n(\mathbf{x})$, can be explicitly calculated. Indeed, a calculation in Berger (1980b) shows that

$$\boldsymbol{\mu}_n(\mathbf{x}) = E^{\pi_n(\boldsymbol{\theta}|\mathbf{x})}[\boldsymbol{\theta}] = \mathbf{x} - \frac{r_n(\|\mathbf{x}\|^2)\boldsymbol{\Sigma}(\boldsymbol{\Sigma} + \mathbf{A})^{-1}}{\rho\|\mathbf{x}\|^2}(\mathbf{x} - \boldsymbol{\mu}),$$

where $\|\mathbf{x}\|^2 = (\mathbf{x} - \boldsymbol{\mu})^t(\boldsymbol{\Sigma} + \mathbf{A})^{-1}(\mathbf{x} - \boldsymbol{\mu})/\rho$ and

$$r_n(v) = 2n\left(1 - \frac{1}{n\int_0^1 \lambda^{n-1} e^{-(\lambda-1)v/2} \, d\lambda}\right).$$

The function r_n can be evaluated as follows. First, a calculation shows that

$$r_1(v) = 2\left(1 - \frac{v}{2(e^{v/2} - 1)}\right)$$

and

$$r_{0.5}(v) = \left(1 - \frac{v^{1/2}}{(\pi/2)^{1/2} e^{v/2} \, \mathrm{erf}((v/2)^{1/2})}\right),$$

where

$$\mathrm{erf}\left(\left(\frac{v}{2}\right)^{1/2}\right) = \left(\frac{2}{\pi}\right)^{1/2} \int_0^{v^{1/2}} \exp\left\{\frac{-t^2}{2}\right\} dt.$$

The recurrence formula

$$r_{n+1}(v) = [2(n + 1) + v] - \frac{2nv}{r_n(v)}$$

can then be used to find r_n for higher values of n. A calculation also shows that the covariance matrix of the posterior (variance if $p = 1$) is

$$\Sigma_n(\mathbf{x}) = \Sigma - \frac{r_n(\|\mathbf{x}\|^2)}{\rho \|\mathbf{x}\|^2} \Sigma(\Sigma + A)^{-1}\Sigma + \frac{r_n(\|\mathbf{x}\|^2)[r_{n+1}(\|\mathbf{x}\|^2) - r_n(\|\mathbf{x}\|^2)]}{\rho^2 \|\mathbf{x}\|^4}$$

$$\times \Sigma(\Sigma + A)^{-1}(\mathbf{x} - \boldsymbol{\mu})(\mathbf{x} - \boldsymbol{\mu})^t(\Sigma + A)^{-1}\Sigma.$$

For some applications, it suffices to know the posterior mean and covariance matrix. For others, however, the entire posterior is needed, and explicit calculation again becomes a problem. In such situations, it turns out to work surprisingly well to approximate $\pi_n(\boldsymbol{\theta}|\mathbf{x})$ by a $\mathcal{N}_p(\boldsymbol{\mu}_n(\mathbf{x}), \Sigma_n(\mathbf{x}))$ density. Denote this approximation $\hat{\pi}_n(\boldsymbol{\theta}|\mathbf{x})$. (Such an approximation was used in a similar setting by Morris (1977).) All the standard Bayesian analyses can be easily done using $\hat{\pi}_n(\boldsymbol{\theta}|\mathbf{x})$. Some of the properties of the resultant procedures are discussed below.

Consider first the problem of estimating $\boldsymbol{\theta}$. The natural (generalized Bayes) estimator of $\boldsymbol{\theta}$ for a symmetric loss (i.e., a loss in which underestimation is as harmful as overestimation in each coordinate) is just the mean of $\hat{\pi}_n(\boldsymbol{\theta}|\mathbf{x})$. For such a loss (or for inference problems) the suggested estimator of $\boldsymbol{\theta}$ is thus

$$\delta^n(\mathbf{x}) = \boldsymbol{\mu}_n(\mathbf{x}).$$

In Berger (1980b) an extensive discussion of the robustness of this estimator is given, for the quadratic loss

$$L(\delta, \boldsymbol{\theta}) = (\delta - \boldsymbol{\theta})^t Q(\delta - \boldsymbol{\theta}),$$

Q a positive definite $(p \times p)$ matrix. The estimator is shown to be remarkably robust, especially when $p \geq 3$. (By robustness, here, is meant Bayes risk robustness with respect to various alternate priors.) Indeed, even if the prior inputs (μ and A) are drastically wrong, the Bayes risk (for any prior) of δ^n is seldom much worse than $tr(Q\Sigma)$ (the trace of $(Q\Sigma)$), which is the Bayes risk of the usual estimator $\delta^0(x) = x$. (An easy calculation shows that $R(\theta, \delta^0) = tr(Q\Sigma)$ for all θ, so that $r(\pi, \delta^0) = tr(Q\Sigma)$ for all proper π.) For $p \geq 3$ and the above quadratic loss, the following even more surprising result was obtained.

Theorem 4. $R(\theta, \delta^n) \leq R(\theta, \delta^0)$ *for all* θ *(and hence* $r(\pi, \delta^n) \leq r(\pi, \delta^0)$ *for all* π*)* *if*

$$(p + 2)ch_{max}\{\Sigma Q\Sigma(\Sigma + A)^{-1}\} \leq 2\{\Sigma Q\Sigma(\Sigma + A)^{-1}\}.$$

(ch_{max} stands for maximum characteristic root.) This is, in particular, true if Q, Σ, and A are multiples of the identity matrix and $p \geq 3$.

Another indication of the robustness of δ^n is that when $|x - \mu|$ is large, it can be shown that

$$\delta^n(x) \cong x - \frac{2n\Sigma(\Sigma + A)^{-1}(x - \mu)}{\rho\|x\|^2} \cong x.$$

Thus, as in Example 23 where t priors were considered, the prior information is essentially ignored when the observation casts doubt upon it.

EXAMPLE 24. In the IQ example, where $X \sim \mathcal{N}(\theta, 100)$ is observed, suppose it is felt that the true distribution of θ might have longer tails than the normal distribution. To guard against this, it is decided to use $\delta^n(x) = \mu_n(x)$ to estimate θ. The inputs μ and A are chosen to be 100 and 225, respectively, as these are felt to be the prior mean and variance. Noting that $p = 1$, $n = \frac{1}{2}$, and $\rho = \frac{1}{3}$, it follows that

$$\|x\|^2 = \frac{(x - \mu)^2}{(\frac{1}{3})(\sigma^2 + A)} = \frac{3(x - 100)^2}{325},$$

and (defining $\|x\| = (\|x\|^2)^{1/2}$),

$$\delta^n(x) = x - \left(1 - \frac{\|x\|}{(\pi/2)^{1/2} \exp\{\|x\|^2/2\}erf\{\|x\|/2^{1/2}\}}\right)\frac{100}{x - 100}.$$

For the child scoring $x = 115$ on the test, $\delta^n(x) = 115 - 3.476 = 111.523$ (compared to the estimate 110.39 when the normal prior is used). For $x = 150$, $\delta^n(x) = 150 - 2.000 = 148$ (compared to the estimate 134.62 for the normal prior). Clearly δ^n is more conservative than the Bayes estimator for a normal prior, especially when x is extreme.

Credible regions for θ are easily found (using $\hat{\pi}_n(\theta|x)$) by noting that a $\mathcal{N}_p(\mu_n(x), \Sigma_n(x))$ density is decreasing in

$$[\theta - \mu_n(x)]'\Sigma_n(x)^{-1}[\theta - \mu_n(x)],$$

a quantity which has a chi-square distribution with p degrees of freedom. It follows that the (approximate) $100(1 - \alpha)\%$ HPD credible region for θ is the ellipsoid (interval in one dimension)

$$C_n(\mathbf{x}) = \{\theta : [\theta - \mu_n(\mathbf{x})]^t \Sigma_n(\mathbf{x})^{-1} [\theta - \mu_n(\mathbf{x})] \leq \chi_p^2(1 - \alpha)\},$$

where $\chi_p^2(1 - \alpha)$ is the $(1 - \alpha)$-fractile of the chi-square distribution with p degrees of freedom.

In evaluating the robustness of $C_n(\mathbf{x})$, it is useful to compare the classical probability of coverage of $C_n(\mathbf{x})$ with that of the classical $100(1 - \alpha)\%$ confidence ellipsoid

$$C_0(\mathbf{x}) = \{\theta : (\theta - \mathbf{x})^t \Sigma^{-1} (\theta - \mathbf{x}) \leq \chi_p^2(1 - \alpha)\}.$$

(C_0 is, in some sense, a very robust confidence region, in that its expected probability of coverage is $1 - \alpha$ no matter what the prior.) The comparison is carried out in Berger (1980b) where, especially for $p \geq 3$, $C_n(\mathbf{x})$ is shown to have classical probability of coverage better than that of $C_0(\mathbf{x})$ over "most" of the parameter space. This indicates a high degree of robustness involving the confidence coefficient.

The other important property of a credible or confidence region is its size. A good measure of size for ellipsoids is volume. $C_n(\mathbf{x})$ again compares very favorably with $C_0(\mathbf{x})$ with respect to volume, being smaller for "most" $\mathbf{x}$. Indeed, the following theorem from Berger (1980b) gives an often satisfied condition (for $p \geq 2$) under which $C_n(\mathbf{x})$ is always smaller than $C_0(\mathbf{x})$.

Theorem 5. $C_n(\mathbf{x})$ *has smaller volume than* $C_0(\mathbf{x})$ *for all* $\mathbf{x}$, *if* $\mathrm{tr}[\Sigma(\Sigma + \mathbf{A})^{-1}] \geq 2\mathrm{ch}_{\max}[\Sigma(\Sigma + \mathbf{A})^{-1}]$.

In conclusion, therefore, $C_n(\mathbf{x})$ compares very favorably with $C_0(\mathbf{x})$ according to the classical properties of size and probability of coverage. This indicates a high degree of robustness with respect to misspecification of prior information. An example of the use of $C_n(\mathbf{x})$ follows.

EXAMPLE 24 (continued). Here, with $n = \frac{1}{2}$ and $\rho = \frac{1}{3}$,

$$\Sigma_n(x) = \sigma^2 - \frac{r_{0.5}(\|x\|^2)\sigma^4}{(\frac{1}{3})\|x\|^2(\sigma^2 + A)}$$

$$+ \frac{r_{0.5}(\|x\|^2)[r_{1.5}(\|x\|^2) - r_{0.5}(\|x\|^2)]\sigma^4(x - \mu)^2}{(\frac{1}{3})^2\|x\|^4(\sigma^2 + A)^2}$$

$$= \sigma^2 + \frac{3r_{0.5}(\|x\|^2)[r_{1.5}(\|x\|^2) - r_{0.5}(\|x\|^2) - 1]\sigma^4}{\|x\|^2(\sigma^2 + A)}.$$

With $\sigma^2 = 100$, $A = 225$, and $x = 115$, we get as before that $\|x\|^2 = 2.077$ and $r_{0.5}(2.077) = 0.521$. The recurrence formula gives

$$r_{1.5}(2.077) = \left[2\left(\frac{1}{2} + 1\right) + 2.077\right] - \frac{2(\frac{1}{2})(2.007)}{0.521} = 1.090.$$

Calculation then gives that

$$\Sigma_{0.5}(x) = 100 - 9.98 = 91.02.$$

(The posterior variance for a normal prior was calculated in Example 1 to be 69.23.) Hence a 95% credible region for θ is

$$C_{0.5}(115) = \{\theta : [\theta - \mu_{0.5}(115)]\Sigma_{0.5}(115)^{-1}[\theta - \mu_{0.5}(115)] \leq 3.84\}$$

$$= \left\{\theta : \frac{(\theta - 111.52)^2}{91.02} \leq 3.84\right\}$$

$$= (111.52 - 18.70, 111.52 + 18.70) = (92.82, 130.22).$$

(The usual 95% confidence interval is (95.4, 134.6), while the 95% Bayesian credible region for a normal prior is (94.08, 126.70).)

For $x = 150$, a similar calculation shows that $\Sigma_{0.5}(150) = 104$, and so the 95% credible region is

$$C_{0.5}(150) = (128.01, 167.99)$$

(compared to the usual interval (130.40, 169.60), and the normal prior credible interval (118.31, 150.93)). Note that $C_{0.5}(150)$ is slightly larger than $C_0(150)$. This will always happen for $p = 1$ and x far from μ, but the increase in length will never be more than about 7%.

Testing can also be done using $\hat{\pi}_n(\theta | x)$. Since the calculations are the same as for any normal posterior, no examples will be given.

II. *Development of* μ *and* A

As indicated earlier, μ and A are roughly meant to represent the prior mean and covariance matrix, respectively. There are a number of ways to develop them. At the crudest level, one can simply guess the mean μ_i and standard deviation τ_i of each θ_i, assume the θ_i are independent and set $\mu = (\mu_1, \ldots, \mu_p)^t$ and A equal to the diagonal matrix with diagonal elements τ_i^2. In making such estimates, it is often convenient to pretend that the θ_i are normally distributed. Then, for example, μ_i and τ_i could be found by determining a prior 50% credible region for θ_i, equating it with $(\mu_i - 0.675\tau_i, \mu_i + 0.675\tau_i)$, and solving for μ_i and τ_i. Alternatively, the prior density of each θ_i could be determined by standard methods, and the μ_i and τ_i estimated from these. (Of course, if the so-determined prior densities are very nonsymmetric or are not unimodal, then the use of the prior g_n may be inappropriate.)

More complicated situations can also be handled easily. One commonly occurring situation is when the θ_i are thought to have a common prior mean. For example, it is often assumed that the θ_i are a sample from a $\mathcal{N}(\theta_0, \tau^2)$ distribution, but that θ_0 is itself not completely known and has, say, a $\mathcal{N}(\mu_0, \gamma^2)$ distribution. This model is discussed by Lindley and Smith (1972), who show that it is equivalent to assuming that $\boldsymbol{\theta}$ has a p-variate normal distribution with mean $\boldsymbol{\mu} = \mu_0 \mathbf{1}$ ($\mathbf{1} = (1, 1, \ldots, 1)^t$) and covariance matrix $\mathbf{A} = (\tau^2 \mathbf{I}_p + \gamma^2 \langle \mathbf{1} \rangle)$ ($\langle \mathbf{1} \rangle$ being the $(p \times p)$ matrix of all ones). Thus it is only necessary to estimate τ^2 (the variance of the θ_i about their common mean), μ_0 (the guess for the common mean), and γ^2 (the variance for the guess μ_0) in order to specify $\boldsymbol{\mu}$ and $\mathbf{A}$ in this model. An example follows.

EXAMPLE 25. An IQ test is to be given to a class of p graduate statistics students. Presumably, the members of the class are considerably above average in intelligence, so it would be grossly inappropriate to use any prior distribution with mean 100. It is reasonable to feel that the true IQ's, θ_i, of the class members are a sample from a common prior distribution. Assume it is felt that the variance of this prior is about 100. (Thus the IQ's are assumed to vary about a common mean with standard deviation 10.) The best guess for the mean of the common prior (i.e., the "average" IQ) is 125. This guess is felt to have a prior variance of 36. Thus $\tau^2 = 100$, $\mu_0 = 125$, and $\gamma^2 = 36$. The appropriate choices of $\boldsymbol{\mu}$ and $\mathbf{A}$, for use in the robust Bayesian analysis, are thus $\boldsymbol{\mu} = (125, 125, \ldots, 125)^t$, and $\mathbf{A}$ equal to the $(p \times p)$ matrix with diagonal elements 136 and off-diagonal elements 36. The results of Part I can then be used to make Bayesian decisions and inferences concerning $\boldsymbol{\theta} = (\theta_1, \ldots, \theta_p)^t$.

Another situation of interest is when linear restrictions among the θ_i are thought to hold. Assume it is believed that the k linear restrictions ($k < p$)

$$\sum_{j=1}^{p} b_{ij} \theta_j = d_i, \qquad i = 1, \ldots, k,$$

hold. Letting $\mathbf{B}$ be the $(k \times p)$ matrix with elements b_{ij}, and $\mathbf{d} = (d_1, \ldots, d_k)^t$, this can be written as

$$\mathbf{B\theta} = \mathbf{d}.$$

It is natural to assume that $\mathbf{B}$ has rank k (i.e., no restriction is implied by other restrictions), and that the above equation is consistent (i.e., no sets of restrictions are contradictory).

Only rarely will these restrictions be certain to hold. Far more frequently, it will be felt that $\mathbf{B\theta}$ has a prior distribution with mean $\mathbf{d}$ and a covariance matrix $\mathbf{C}$ (again reflecting the believed accuracy of the restrictions). When $k = p$, one can simply define $\boldsymbol{\mu} = \mathbf{B}^{-1}\mathbf{d}$ and $\mathbf{A} = \mathbf{B}^{-1}\mathbf{C}(\mathbf{B}^{-1})^t$, corresponding to the transformation of the prior information about $\mathbf{B\theta}$ to prior information about $\boldsymbol{\theta}$. When $k < p$, it can be shown that the following analysis is appropriate.

1. For the posterior mean, use the formula

$$\boldsymbol{\mu}_n(\mathbf{x}) = \mathbf{x} - \frac{r_n(\|\mathbf{x}\|^2)\Sigma\mathbf{B}^t(\mathbf{B}\Sigma\mathbf{B}^t + \mathbf{C})^{-1}(\mathbf{B}\mathbf{x} - \mathbf{d})}{\rho\|\mathbf{x}\|^2}, \tag{4.6}$$

where $\|\mathbf{x}\|^2 = (\mathbf{B}\mathbf{x} - \mathbf{d})^t(\mathbf{B}\Sigma\mathbf{B}^t + \mathbf{C})^{-1}(\mathbf{B}\mathbf{x} - \mathbf{d})/\rho$, and $\rho = n/(n+1)$.
2. For $\Sigma_n(\mathbf{x})$, use the formula (defining $\mathbf{T} = (\mathbf{B}\Sigma\mathbf{B}^t + \mathbf{C})$)

$$\Sigma_n(\mathbf{x}) = \Sigma - \frac{r_n(\|\mathbf{x}\|^2)\Sigma\mathbf{B}^t\mathbf{T}^{-1}\mathbf{B}\Sigma}{\rho\|\mathbf{x}\|^2}$$

$$+ \frac{r_n[r_{n+1} - r_n]}{\rho^2\|\mathbf{x}\|^4}\Sigma\mathbf{B}^t\mathbf{T}^{-1}(\mathbf{B}\mathbf{x} - \mathbf{d})(\mathbf{B}\mathbf{x} - \mathbf{d})^t\mathbf{T}^{-1}\mathbf{B}\Sigma. \tag{4.7}$$

3. Replace p by k, so that

$$n = \max\left\{\frac{k-2}{2}, \frac{1}{2}\right\}. \tag{4.8}$$

The justification for this analysis is rather technical, and will merely be sketched here. The key idea is that for $\boldsymbol{\theta} \in \Lambda = \{\boldsymbol{\theta}: \mathbf{B}\boldsymbol{\theta} = \mathbf{0}\}$, the restrictions carry no apriori information. Thus by giving only k restrictions, it is being said that there are no prior beliefs about the $(p - k)$-dimensional set Λ. A reasonable way to model this is to construct a prior distribution on Λ but send the variances of the prior to infinity, reflecting a lack of prior information. The details of such an analysis are given in Appendix 2, the conclusions being as in (4.6) and (4.7). It is also shown in Appendix 2 that k, not p, is the proper effective dimension of the problem, in that the correction terms (to $\mathbf{x}$ and Σ in $\boldsymbol{\mu}_n(\mathbf{x})$ and $\Sigma_n(\mathbf{x})$) are really acting on a k-dimensional subspace.

III. *Procedures When Σ Is Partially Unknown*

The previously discussed situation of known Σ is, of course, somewhat uncommon. A more frequently encountered situation is that in which $\Sigma = \sigma^2\Sigma_0$, Σ_0 being a known matrix and σ^2 an unknown constant. The one-dimensional problem with unknown variance is automatically of this type. In higher dimensions, this situation generally occurs in problems such as regression analysis. The standard model for regression can be stated as $\mathbf{Y} = \mathbf{B}\boldsymbol{\theta} + \boldsymbol{\epsilon}$, where $\mathbf{Y} = (Y_1, \ldots, Y_n)^t$ is a vector of observations, $\boldsymbol{\theta} = (\theta_1, \ldots, \theta_p)^t (p < n)$ is a vector of unknown regression coefficients, $\mathbf{B}$ is an $n \times p$ known design matrix of rank p, and $\boldsymbol{\varepsilon} = (\varepsilon_1, \ldots, \varepsilon_n)^t$ is a random error which has an n-variate normal distribution with mean $\mathbf{0}$ and covariance matrix $\sigma^2 I_n$, σ^2 being an unknown constant. The usual least squares estimator of $\boldsymbol{\theta}$ is

$$\mathbf{X} = (\mathbf{B}^t\mathbf{B})^{-1}\mathbf{B}^t\mathbf{Y}.$$

It can be shown that $\mathbf{X} \sim \mathcal{N}_p(\boldsymbol{\theta}, \sigma^2(\mathbf{B}^t\mathbf{B})^{-1})$, so the problem of making decisions or inferences about $\boldsymbol{\theta}$ based on $\mathbf{X}$ reduces to the problem mentioned above with $\boldsymbol{\Sigma}_0 = (\mathbf{B}^t\mathbf{B})^{-1}$.

When σ^2 is unknown, there is virtually always an estimate of it obtainable from the data; for example, the sample variance if $p = 1$. Generally, this estimate will be based on a statistic S^2, with S^2/σ^2 having a chi-square distribution with m degrees of freedom. (Denote the corresponding density $h(s^2 | \sigma^2)$.) The best estimate of σ^2 for our purposes, namely robust Bayesian analysis concerning $\boldsymbol{\theta}$, is

$$\hat{\sigma}^2 = \frac{s^2}{m + 2}. \tag{4.9}$$

See Berger (1980b) for justification of this choice.

A true Bayesian analysis of this problem would consist of giving $\boldsymbol{\theta}$ and σ^2 a joint prior density and calculating the Bayes rule. This is virtually impossible (without resorting to the computer) for any prior except the unsuitable conjugate prior (see Exercise 12). We can try, however, to obtain a reasonable approximation to a posterior density which arises from a robust type of prior. A prior which suggests itself as suitable is

$$\pi_n(\boldsymbol{\theta}, \sigma^2) = g_n(\boldsymbol{\theta} | \sigma^2)\sigma^{-2},$$

where $g_n(\boldsymbol{\theta} | \sigma^2)$ is simply $g_n(\boldsymbol{\theta})$ with $\boldsymbol{\Sigma}$ replaced by $\sigma^2\boldsymbol{\Sigma}_0$. The "marginal" prior density of σ^2 is simply the noninformative prior $\pi(\sigma^2) = \sigma^{-2}$. This seems reasonable since we are concerned with decisions concerning $\boldsymbol{\theta}$. The parameter σ^2 is just a nuisance parameter, and giving it a noninformative prior should reduce its influence on decisions about $\boldsymbol{\theta}$. (Of course if specific prior information about σ^2 was available, it would be appropriate to use it here, as well as in defining an estimate $\hat{\sigma}^2$.)

An argument given in Appendix 2 suggests that a reasonable approximation to the posterior distribution of $\boldsymbol{\theta}$, given $\mathbf{x}$ and s^2, is

$$\hat{\pi}_n(\boldsymbol{\theta} | \mathbf{x}, s^2) = \tilde{k}(\mathbf{x}, s^2) \left\{ 1 + \frac{1}{m} [\boldsymbol{\theta} - \boldsymbol{\mu}_n(\mathbf{x}, \hat{\sigma}^2)]^t \left[\frac{m + 2}{m} \boldsymbol{\Sigma}_n(\mathbf{x}, \hat{\sigma}^2) \right]^{-1} \right.$$
$$\left. \times [\boldsymbol{\theta} - \boldsymbol{\mu}_n(\mathbf{x}, \hat{\sigma}^2)] \right\}^{-(m + p)/2}, \tag{4.10}$$

where $\boldsymbol{\mu}_n(\mathbf{x}, \hat{\sigma}^2)$ and $\boldsymbol{\Sigma}_n(\mathbf{x}, \hat{\sigma}^2)$ denote $\boldsymbol{\mu}_n(\mathbf{x})$ and $\boldsymbol{\Sigma}_n(\mathbf{x})$ with $\boldsymbol{\Sigma} = \sigma^2\boldsymbol{\Sigma}_0$ replaced by $\hat{\sigma}^2\boldsymbol{\Sigma}_0$, and $\tilde{k}(\mathbf{x}, s^2)$ is the appropriate normalizing constant. This is recognizable as a multivariate t distribution with m degrees of freedom, location vector $\boldsymbol{\mu}_n(\mathbf{x}, \hat{\sigma}^2)$, and scale matrix $(m + 2)\boldsymbol{\Sigma}_n(\mathbf{x}, \hat{\sigma}^2)/m$.

Working with a multivariate t posterior is relatively easy. The mean of the posterior is, of course, $\boldsymbol{\mu}_n(\mathbf{x}, \hat{\sigma}^2)$, and is suitable for use as the generalized Bayes estimator of $\boldsymbol{\theta}$ when the loss is symmetric. Indeed this estimator is evaluated in Berger (1980b), and is shown to be very robust.

HPD credible regions are also easily obtainable. Noting that, for the multivariate t distribution,

$$\frac{1}{p} [\boldsymbol{\theta} - \boldsymbol{\mu}_n]' \left[\frac{m + 2}{m} \boldsymbol{\Sigma}_n \right]^{-1} [\boldsymbol{\theta} - \boldsymbol{\mu}_n] \sim \mathscr{F}(p, m),$$

the $100(1 - \alpha)\%$ HPD credible region for $\boldsymbol{\theta}$ is clearly the ellipse

$$C_n(\mathbf{x}, s^2) = \{\boldsymbol{\theta} : [\boldsymbol{\theta} - \boldsymbol{\mu}_n(\mathbf{x}, \hat{\sigma}^2)]' \boldsymbol{\Sigma}_n(\mathbf{x}, \hat{\sigma}^2)^{-1} [\boldsymbol{\theta} - \boldsymbol{\mu}_n(\mathbf{x}, \hat{\sigma}^2)]$$
$$\leq p(1 + 2/m) F_{p, m}(1 - \alpha)\},$$

where $F_{p, m}(1 - \alpha)$ is the $(1 - \alpha)$-fractile of the $\mathscr{F}(p, m)$ distribution. In terms of probability of coverage and size, these regions are shown in Berger (1980b) to compare very favorably with the classical confidence ellipsoids.

EXAMPLE 26. An independent trucker wishes to determine the average gas mileage of his recently purchased truck. In 5 runs, he obtains mileages of 8.5, 10.1, 9.0, 8.0, and 8.9 miles per gallon. Each of these observations can be considered to have arisen (independently) from a $\mathcal{N}(\theta, \sigma^2)$ distribution, where θ is the true average gas mileage and σ^2 is also unknown. The trucker obtained information from the manufacturer that, among similar trucks made, the average gas mileage was distributed according to a distribution with mean 9.14 and standard deviation 0.3. A robust Bayesian analysis of θ is to be conducted.

The sufficient statistics for (θ, σ^2) are $\overline{X}$ and $S^2 = \Sigma(X_i - \overline{X})^2$. Letting $X = \overline{X}$, noting that X has variance $\sigma_X^2 = \sigma^2/5$, and observing that

$$\frac{S^2/5}{\sigma^2/5} = \frac{S^2}{\sigma^2} \sim \chi^2(4),$$

the estimate of σ_X^2 given by (4.9) is

$$\hat{\sigma}_X^2 = \frac{s^2/5}{4 + 2} = \frac{s^2}{30}.$$

Calculation shows that $x = \overline{x} = 8.9$ and $\hat{\sigma}_X^2 \cong 0.0807$.

The prior information indicates that $\mu = 9.14$ and $A = 0.09$ are appropriate for use in the robust Bayesian analysis. Also, since $p = 1$, it follows that $n = \frac{1}{2}$ and $\rho = \frac{1}{3}$ should be used. Calculation then gives that

$$\|x\|^2 = \frac{(x - \mu)^2}{\rho(\hat{\sigma}_X^2 + A)} \cong 1.00,$$

$$r_{0.5}(\|x\|^2) \cong 0.291,$$

$$\mu_{0.5}(x, \hat{\sigma}_X^2) \cong 9.0,$$

$$\Sigma_{0.5}(x, \hat{\sigma}_X^2) \cong 0.0867.$$

The robust estimator of θ is thus 9.0, and a 90% HPD credible region is

$$C_n(x, s^2) = \left\{ \theta : \frac{(\theta - 9.0)^2}{0.0867} < \left(1 + \frac{2}{4} \right) (4.54) \right\} = (8.4, 9.6).$$

Hypothesis testing can also be done in the standard Bayesian fashion using $\hat{\pi}_n(\theta \,|\, \mathbf{x}, s^2)$. Tables of the t distribution can prove helpful.

When Σ is more completely unknown, the question of how to proceed in a robust Bayesian fashion is very difficult. Answers are not yet known.

4.6.5 The Robustness of Noninformative Priors

When using a noninformative prior, the robustness concerns are usually somewhat different than the concerns when using a proper prior. Only rarely will it be necessary to choose from a class of "correct" noninformative priors which give rise to substantially different inferences or decision rules. The robustness concerns instead tend to center on the two questions: (i) Is a correct (i.e., properly objective) noninformative prior being used? (ii) Is the noninformative prior an appropriate reflection of true prior beliefs?

We have considered question (i) in several places, and found that there are rarely easy answers. In trying to decide whether or not a proposed non-informative prior is properly objective, a number of features such as in-variance under reformulation (see Subsection 3.2.2) and admissibility (see Subsection 4.5.2) must be considered. An interesting example of the care that must be taken in selecting a noninformative prior can be found in Stone (1971).

The second question above has not yet been specifically discussed, and so it is to this issue we now turn. At first sight, the concern of question (ii) seems illfounded, since we are supposedly using the noninformative prior because of a lack of prior information. It will rarely be the case that there is absolutely no prior information, however, so it is important to know when very weak or vague prior information can be ignored and a noninformative prior used. We have already encountered one situation in which even vague prior information should be employed in preference to a noninformative prior, namely the situation of estimating a multivariate normal mean. Here, the generalized Bayes estimator with respect to the noninformative prior $\pi(\boldsymbol{\theta}) = 1$ is inadmissible if $p \geq 3$ (see Subsection 4.5.2), and can be usefully and safely improved upon if vague prior information is available (see Subsection 4.6.4). It will indeed be generally true that, in high dimensions, one should be very concerned about the incorporation of even weak prior information into the analysis, partly because of admissibility problems similar to that indicated above, and partly because even weak prior information can be more reliable than certain facets of the sample information (such as when multicollinearity is encountered in regression studies).

Another indication of the need to keep the true prior in mind arises from the study of a clever example constructed by Stein (1962). This example also constitutes, at first sight, a devasting critique of the likelihood principle, providing us with further incentive for a detailed examination.

EXAMPLE 27. Suppose that we are investigating some unknown quantity $\theta > 0$, and can measure it in either of two ways. The first method of measurement (Experiment 1) results in an observation $X \sim \mathcal{N}(\theta, \sigma^2)$, while the second method of measurement (Experiment 2) results in an observation Y which has density

$$f(y|\theta) = cy^{-1} \exp\left\{ -\frac{d^2}{2}\left(1 - \frac{\theta}{y}\right)^2 \right\} I_{(0, b\theta)}(y),$$

where b and d are constants and c is the appropriate normalizing constant. Writing $f(y|\theta)$ as

$$f(y|\theta) = c\theta^{-1}\left(\frac{y}{\theta}\right)^{-1} \exp\left\{ -\frac{d^2}{2}\left(1 - \left[\frac{y}{\theta}\right]^{-1}\right)^2 \right\} I_{(0, b)}\left(\frac{y}{\theta}\right),$$

it is clear that θ is a scale parameter. Hence c is independent of θ, and indeed is given by

$$c = \left[\int_0^b y^{-1} \exp\left\{ -\frac{d^2}{2}(1 - y^{-1})^2 \right\} dy \right]^{-1}.$$

The likelihood functions, $l_x(\theta)$ and $l_y(\theta)$, for the observations X and Y, are (ignoring multiplicative constants and recalling that $\theta > 0$)

$$l_x(\theta) = \exp\left\{ -\frac{1}{2\sigma^2}(\theta - x)^2 \right\} I_{(0, \infty)}(\theta),$$

$$l_y(\theta) = \exp\left\{ -\frac{d^2}{2}\left(1 - \frac{\theta}{y}\right)^2 \right\} I_{(y/b, \infty)}(\theta)$$

$$= \exp\left\{ -\frac{d^2}{2y^2}(\theta - y)^2 \right\} I_{(y/b, \infty)}(\theta).$$

Suppose now that d is large (say 50), that b is enormous (say $10^{10^{1000}}$), and that the observations happen to be such that $x = y$ and $\sigma = y/d$. The likelihood functions $l_x(\theta)$ and $l_y(\theta)$ are then identical, except for the factors $I_{(0, \infty)}(\theta)$ and $I_{(y/b, \infty)}(\theta)$. The truncation points 0 and y/b are virtually equivalent, however. To see this, observe that y/b and y/d are much smaller than y, so that $l_y(\theta)$ is essentially a normal likelihood function with "mean" y and "standard deviation" y/d. (The truncation point is almost 50 standard deviations from the mean y.) The same conclusion holds for $l_x(\theta)$ ($x/\sigma = y/[y/d] = 50$), so that the two likelihood functions are essentially identical.

It follows from the likelihood principle that the same inferences or decisions concerning θ should be made in each situation.

Suppose that it is desired to find a confidence region for θ, or alternatively an "objective" credible region. This is easy to do in Experiment 1. Note, for instance, that θ is a location parameter, so that $\pi(\theta) = 1$ is the natural noninformative prior. Since $l_x(\theta)$ is almost exactly a normal likelihood function (for x as given earlier), it follows that an appropriate credible region would be $(x - K\sigma, x + K\sigma)$, where K depends on the desired degree of confidence. A classical statistician would arrive at the same conclusion (unless x/σ was moderately close to zero).

It then follows from the likelihood principle that the credible (or confidence) region for θ in Experiment 2 should be

$$\left(y - \frac{Ky}{d}, y + \frac{Ky}{d}\right), \tag{4.11}$$

assuming, of course, that $x = y$ and $\sigma = y/d$. Consider, however, the classical confidence level of this interval. If, say, $K < 25$, then

$$P_\theta\left(Y - \frac{KY}{d} < \theta < Y + \frac{KY}{d}\right) < P_\theta\left(Y - \frac{KY}{d} < \theta\right)$$

$$= P_\theta\left(Y < \left(1 - \frac{K}{d}\right)^{-1}\theta\right)$$

$$< P_\theta\left(\frac{Y}{\theta} < 2\right)$$

$$< 10^{-100}, \tag{4.12}$$

the last bound being obtained from calculations in Appendix 2. This seems to indicate that the credible region in (4.11) is actually terrible. One can object to (4.12) as being a measure of initial precision and hence unreliable. The coup de grace is delivered, however, when it is recalled that θ is a scale parameter in Experiment 2, so that an objective Bayesian analysis would use the noninformative prior $\pi(\theta) = \theta^{-1}$. It can then be calculated that the posterior probability of the interval in (4.11) is exactly the classical probability of coverage in (4.12). The conclusion appears to be that the likelihood principle has produced a disastrous inference.

The salvation of the likelihood principle lies in recognizing that the use of the noninformative prior in the analysis of Experiment 1 is not strictly correct, in that $\pi(\theta) = 1$ is being used as an approximation to the true prior. For instance, imagine that the true prior is $\mathcal{U}(0, \beta)$, where β is very large. It is then certainly reasonable to use $\pi(\theta) = 1$ (for $\theta > 0$) as an approximation to this true prior in Experiment 1, the error caused being insignificant. The use of $\pi(\theta) = 1$ in Experiment 2 turns out to be a horrible approximation, however. To see this, consider the posterior distributions of θ, given y, with respect to $\pi_1(\theta) = 1$ (for $\theta > 0$) and $\pi_2(\theta) = \beta^{-1} I_{(0, \beta)}(\theta)$. We have already argued that

$$\pi_1(\theta | y) = \frac{\pi_1(\theta) l_y(\theta)}{\int \pi_1(\theta) l_y(\theta) d\theta} \cong \frac{d}{(2\pi)^{1/2} y} \exp\left\{ - \frac{d^2}{2y^2} (\theta - y)^2 \right\}.$$

The true posterior, on the other hand, is

$$\pi_2(\theta | y) = \frac{\pi_2(\theta) l_y(\theta)}{\int \pi_2(\theta) l_y(\theta) d\theta} = \frac{\exp\left\{ - \dfrac{d^2}{2y^2} (\theta - y)^2 \right\} I_{(y/b, \beta)}(\theta)}{\displaystyle\int_{y/b}^{\beta} \exp\left\{ - \dfrac{d^2}{2y^2} (\theta - y)^2 \right\} d\theta},$$

which for $y > \beta$ is drastically different than $\pi_1(\theta | y)$. Now, letting m denote the marginal density of Y for the true prior π_2, it is clear that

$$P^m(Y > \beta) = E^{\pi_2}[P_\theta(Y > \beta)] = 1 - E^{\pi_2}[P_\theta(Y < \beta)],$$

which, by a calculation similar to that in (4.12), can be shown to be insignificantly different than 1. Hence, $\pi_1(\theta | Y)$ will differ from $\pi_2(\theta | Y)$ with enormously high probability (with respect to m), so that π_1 is a very bad approximation to the true prior.

Note that the difficulty above does not lie with the likelihood principle. The likelihood principle does not guarantee that a good approximation to the true prior in one problem need be a good approximation to the true prior in another problem with the same likelihood function. It only states that the correct decision (here the decision with respect to the true prior) should be the same in both problems.

The basic point of this example has been to indicate that a noninformative prior can be a very bad approximation to the true prior, even when the information is extremely vague. (A similar point is made in Dickey (1976).) This example has also pointed out the care needed in selecting a noninformative prior, and has reemphasized the limitations of the likelihood principle.

4.7 Conclusions

Philosophical and intuitive considerations tend to support the use of Bayesian analysis. Unfortunately, the difficulties and uncertainties involved in Bayesian analysis somewhat restrict its applicability. It is, therefore, worthwhile to reiterate those situations in which Bayesian analysis is particularly appropriate.

The greatest need for Bayesian analysis is in decision problems for which prior and loss information is an obviously crucial part of the problem. The most obvious such problems are two (or more) action decision problems (classically treated as hypothesis tests). For problems of this type, the use of prior and loss information seems necessary to make a decision (or, in classical terminology, to choose the size of the test).

Problems which have reasonable classical solutions, but in which significant prior information is available, also call for Bayesian analysis; but for very careful Bayesian analysis. In particular, it is important to ensure that the conclusion is robust with respect to misspecification of the prior. Posterior robustness, if present, is the most reassuring property, but when not attainable, the procedure used should at least be risk robust. In particular, it is necessary to be alert to the need for flat tails for the prior density, and to be very wary of the use of conjugate priors.

Even with vague (or no) prior information, certain Bayesian procedures are very useful. Vague prior information can be safely used in the conservative robust Bayesian procedures of Subsection 4.6.4. Vague prior information from past (or current) data can also be safely used in certain empirical Bayes rules. Finally, even if no prior information is present, the objective Bayesian techniques based on noninformative priors can be extremely useful in analyzing statistical problems (even inference problems), particularly those problems in which classical solutions are awkward and hard to find, or where final precision is suspected to differ from initial precision. (Recall that it is only through the Bayesian concepts of posterior probability and posterior expected loss that final precision can even be meaningfully defined.)

It was also indicated in Section 4.5 that Bayesian ideas play a crucial role in many of the theoretical developments of mathematical statistics, such as investigations of admissibility. Further evidence of this will be seen in Chapter 8.

A final reminder should be given that, if a Bayesian analysis is used, the sample information, prior input, and loss function should be clearly stated, along with the Bayes conclusion, enabling a person in disagreement with the prior or loss to use the data to arrive at his personal Bayes conclusion.

Exercises

Section 4.2

1. Prove Lemma 1.

2. There are three coins in a box. One is a two-headed coin, another is a two-tailed coin, and the third is a fair coin. When one of the three coins is selected at random and flipped, it shows heads. What is the probability that it is the two-headed coin?

3. (DeGroot (1970)) Suppose that, with probability $\frac{1}{10}$, a signal is present in a certain system at any given time, and that, with probability $\frac{9}{10}$, no signal is present. A measurement made on the system when a signal is present is normally distributed with mean 50 and variance 1, and a measurement made on the system when no signal is present is normally distributed with mean 52 and variance 1. Suppose that a measurement made on the system at a certain time has the value x. Show that the

posterior probability that a signal is present is greater than the posterior probability that no signal is present, if $x < 51 - \frac{1}{2} \log 9$.

4. A scientific journal, in an attempt to maintain experimental standards, insists that all reported statistical results have (classical) error probability of α_0 (or better). To consider a very simple model of this situation, assume that all statistical tests conducted are of the form $H_0 : \theta = \theta_0$ versus $H_1 : \theta = \theta_1$, where θ_0 represents the standard and θ_1 the new proposal. Experimental results are reported in the journal only if the new proposal is verified with an error probability of $\alpha \leq \alpha_0$. (Note that $\alpha = P_{\theta_0}$ (accepting H_1)).) Let β denote the power of the test (i.e., $\beta = P_{\theta_1}$ (accepting H_1)). Assume further that α and β are fixed for all experiments conducted, with α being the specified value α_0. Let π_0 denote the proportion of all experiments conducted in which θ_0 is correct, and π_1 denote the proportion of experiments in which θ_1 is correct.
    (a) Show that the proportion of articles published in the journal that have correct results (i.e., $P(\theta = \theta_1 |$ the test accepts H_1)) is $\pi_1 \beta / [\alpha_0 + \pi_1(\beta - \alpha_0)]$. (Note that many people naively believe that the journal is guaranteeing a proportion of $(1 - \alpha_0)$ of correct articles.)
    (b) Show that the proportion of correct published results is never less than π_1. (Note that $\beta \geq \alpha$ for reasonable tests.)

5. Suppose that X is $\mathscr{B}(n, \theta)$. Suppose also that θ has a $\mathscr{B}e(\alpha, \beta)$ prior distribution. Show that the posterior distribution of θ given x is $\mathscr{B}e(\alpha + x, \beta + n - x)$. What is a conjugate family for the binomial distribution?

6. Suppose that $\mathbf{X} = (X_1, \ldots, X_n)$ is a random sample from an exponential distribution. Thus $X_i \sim \mathscr{E}(\theta)$ (independently). Suppose also that the prior distribution of θ is $\mathscr{I}\mathscr{G}(\alpha, \beta)$. Show that the posterior distribution of θ given $\mathbf{x}$ is

$$\mathscr{I}\mathscr{G}\left(n + \alpha, \left[\left(\sum_{i=1}^{n} x_i\right) + \beta^{-1}\right]^{-1}\right).$$

7. Suppose that $\mathbf{X} = (X_1, \ldots, X_n)$ is a random sample from a $\mathscr{U}(0, \theta)$ distribution. Let θ have a $\mathscr{P}a(\theta_0, \alpha)$ distribution. Show that the posterior distribution of θ given $\mathbf{x}$ is $\mathscr{P}a(\max\{\theta_0, x_1, \ldots, x_n\}, \alpha + n)$.

8. Suppose that X is $\mathscr{G}(n/2, 2\theta)$ (so that X/θ is χ_n^2), while θ has an $\mathscr{I}\mathscr{G}(\alpha, \beta)$ distribution. Show that the posterior distribution of θ given x is $\mathscr{I}\mathscr{G}(n/2 + \alpha, [x/2 + \beta^{-1}]^{-1})$.

9. Suppose that $\mathbf{X} = (X_1, \ldots, X_k)^t \sim \mathscr{M}(n, \boldsymbol{\theta})$, and that $\boldsymbol{\theta} = (\theta_1, \ldots, \theta_k)^t$ has a $\mathscr{D}(\boldsymbol{\alpha})$ prior distribution $(\boldsymbol{\alpha} = (\alpha_1, \ldots, \alpha_k)^t)$. Show that the posterior distribution of $\boldsymbol{\theta}$ given $\mathbf{x}$ is $\mathscr{D}((\boldsymbol{\alpha} + \mathbf{x}))$.

10. Suppose that $\mathbf{X} = (X_1, \ldots, X_n)$ is a sample from a $\mathscr{N}\mathscr{B}(m, \theta)$ distribution, and that θ has a $\mathscr{B}e(\alpha, \beta)$ prior distribution. Show that the posterior distribution of θ given $\mathbf{x}$ is $\mathscr{B}e(\alpha + mn, (\sum_{i=1}^{n} x_i) + \beta)$.

11. Suppose that $\mathbf{X} = (X_1, \ldots, X_p)^t \sim \mathscr{N}_p(\boldsymbol{\theta}, \boldsymbol{\Sigma})$ and that $\boldsymbol{\theta}$ has a $\mathscr{N}_p(\boldsymbol{\mu}, \mathbf{A})$ prior distribution. (Here $\boldsymbol{\theta}$ and $\boldsymbol{\mu}$ are p-vectors, while $\boldsymbol{\Sigma}$ and $\mathbf{A}$ are $(p \times p)$ positive definite matrices.) Also, $\boldsymbol{\Sigma}, \boldsymbol{\mu}$, and $\mathbf{A}$ are assumed known. Show that the posterior distribution of $\boldsymbol{\theta}$ given $\mathbf{x}$ is a p-variate normal distribution with mean

$$\mathbf{x} - \boldsymbol{\Sigma}(\boldsymbol{\Sigma} + \mathbf{A})^{-1}(\mathbf{x} - \boldsymbol{\mu})$$

and covariance matrix

$$(\mathbf{A}^{-1} + \boldsymbol{\Sigma}^{-1})^{-1}.$$

(*Hint*: Unless familiar with matrix algebra, it is probably easiest to simultaneously diagonalize $\boldsymbol{\Sigma}$ and $\mathbf{A}$, do the calculation for the transformed distributions, and then transform back to the original coordinates.)

12. Suppose that $\mathbf{X} = (X_1, \ldots, X_n)$ is a sample from a $\mathcal{N}(\theta, \sigma^2)$ distribution, where both θ and σ^2 are unknown. The prior density of θ and σ^2 is

$$\pi(\theta, \sigma^2) = \pi_1(\theta|\sigma^2)\pi_2(\sigma^2),$$

where $\pi_1(\theta|\sigma^2)$ is a $\mathcal{N}(\mu, \tau\sigma^2)$ density and $\pi_2(\sigma^2)$ is an $\mathcal{IG}(\alpha, \beta)$ density.
   (a) Show that the joint posterior density of θ and σ^2 given $\mathbf{x}$ is

$$\pi(\theta, \sigma^2|\mathbf{x}) = \pi_1(\theta|\sigma^2, \mathbf{x})\pi_2(\sigma^2|\mathbf{x})$$

   where $\pi_1(\theta|\sigma^2, \mathbf{x})$ is a normal density with mean $\mu(\mathbf{x}) = (\mu + n\tau\bar{x})/(n\tau + 1)$ (here $\bar{x} = (1/n)\sum_{i=1}^{n} x_i$) and variance $(\tau^{-1} + n)^{-1}\sigma^2$, and $\pi_2(\sigma^2|\mathbf{x})$ is an inverted gamma density with parameters $\alpha + (n-1)/2$ and β', where

$$\beta' = \left[\beta^{-1} + \frac{1}{2}\sum_{i=1}^{n}(x_i - \bar{x})^2 + \frac{n(\bar{x} - \mu)^2}{2(1 + n\tau)}\right]^{-1}.$$

   (b) Show that the marginal posterior density of σ^2 given $\mathbf{x}$ is $\mathcal{IG}(\alpha + (n-1)/2, \beta')$. (To find the marginal posterior density of σ^2 given $\mathbf{x}$, just integrate out over θ in the joint posterior density.)
   (c) Show that the marginal posterior density of θ given $\mathbf{x}$ is a

$$\mathcal{T}(2\alpha + n - 1, \mu(\mathbf{x}), [(\tau^{-1} + n)(\alpha + (n-1)/2)\beta']^{-1})$$

   density.
   (d) State why the joint prior density in this problem is from a conjugate family for the distribution of $\mathbf{X}$. (Note that, for this prior, the conditional prior variance of θ given σ^2 is proportional to σ^2. This is unattractive, in that prior knowledge of θ should generally not depend on the sample variance. If, for example, the X_i are measurements of some real quantity θ, it seems silly to base prior beliefs about θ on the accuracy of the measuring instrument. It must be admitted that the robust prior used in Subsection 4.6.4 suffers from a similar intuitive inadequacy. The excellent results obtained from its use, however, indicate that the above intuitive objection is not necessarily damning.)

13. General Motors wants to forecast new car sales for the next year. The number of cars sold in a year is known to be a random variable with a $\mathcal{N}((10^8)\theta, (10^6)^2)$ distribution, where θ is the unemployment rate during the year. The prior density for θ next year is thought to be (approximately) $\mathcal{N}(0.06, (0.01)^2)$. What is the distribution of car sales for next year? (I.e., find the marginal or predictive distribution of car sales next year.)

14. Assume $\mathbf{X} = (X_1, \ldots, X_n)$ is a sample from a $\mathcal{P}(\theta)$ distribution. The improper noninformative prior $\pi(\theta) = \theta^{-1}I_{(0,\infty)}(\theta)$ is to be used. Find the (formal) posterior density of θ given $\mathbf{x}$, for $\mathbf{x} \neq (0, 0, \ldots, 0)$. (If $\mathbf{x} = (0, \ldots, 0)$, the (formal) posterior does not exist.)

15. Assume X is $\mathcal{B}(n, \theta)$.
   (a) If the improper prior density $\pi(\theta) = [\theta(1 - \theta)]^{-1}I_{(0, 1)}(\theta)$ is used, find the (formal) posterior density of θ given x, for $1 \le x \le n - 1$.
   (b) Find the posterior density of θ given x, when $\pi(\theta) = I_{(0, 1)}(\theta)$.

16. Assume $\mathbf{X} = (X_1, \ldots, X_n)$ is a sample from a $\mathcal{N}(\theta, \sigma^2)$ distribution, where θ and σ^2 are unknown. Let θ and σ^2 have the joint improper noninformative prior density

$$\pi(\theta, \sigma^2) = \sigma^{-2}I_{(0, \infty)}(\sigma^2).$$

(In Subsection 3.2.2, it was stated that a reasonable noninformative prior for (θ, σ) is $\pi(\theta, \sigma) = \sigma^{-1}I_{(0, \infty)}(\sigma)$. This transforms into the above prior for (θ, σ^2).)
   (a) Show that the (formal) posterior density of θ and σ^2 given $\mathbf{x}$ is

$$\pi(\theta, \sigma^2 | \mathbf{x}) = \pi_1(\theta | \sigma^2, \mathbf{x})\pi_2(\sigma^2 | \mathbf{x}),$$

where $\pi_1(\theta | \sigma^2, \mathbf{x})$ is a $\mathcal{N}(\bar{x}, \sigma^2/n)$ density and $\pi_2(\sigma^2 | \mathbf{x})$ is an $\mathcal{IG}((n - 1)/2,$ $[\frac{1}{2}\sum_{i=1}^{n}(x_i - \bar{x})^2]^{-1})$ density.
   (b) Show that the marginal posterior density of σ^2 given $\mathbf{x}$ is an $\mathcal{IG}((n - 1)/2,$ $[\frac{1}{2}\sum_{i=1}^{n}(x_i - \bar{x})^2]^{-1})$ density.
   (c) Show that the marginal posterior density of θ given $\mathbf{x}$ is a $\mathcal{T}(n - 1, \bar{x}, \sum_{i=1}^{n}$ $(x_i - \bar{x})^2/n(n - 1))$ density.

Section 4.3

17. Find the generalized maximum likelihood estimate of θ in Exercise
   (a) 5, (b) 6, (c) 7, (d) 8, (e) 9, (f) 10, (g) 11, (h) 12c, (i) 14,
   (j) 15, (k) 16c, and (1) in Example 5.

18. Find the posterior mean in Exercise
   (a) 5, (b) 6, (c) 7, (d) 8, (e) 9, (f) 10, (g) 11, (h) 12b, (i) 12c,
   (j) 14, (k) 15, (l) 16b, (m) 16c, and (n) in Example 5.

19. Find the median of the posterior distribution in Exercise (a) 5 (when $\alpha = \beta = n = x = 1$), (b) 6 (when $\alpha = n = 1$), (c) 7, (d) 12b (when $\alpha = 1, n = 2$), (e) 12c, (f) 14, (g) 16b (when $n = 2$), (h) 16c.

20. Find the $100(1 - \alpha)\%$ HPD credible region in Exercise (a) 7, (b) 11, (c) 12c, (d) 14 (when $\sum_{i=1}^{n} x_i = 1$), (e) 15a (when $n = 3, x = 1$), (f) 16b (when $n = 2$), (g) 16c.

21. A large shipment of parts is received, out of which 5 are tested for defects. The number of defective parts, X, is assumed to have a $\mathcal{B}(5, \theta)$ distribution. From past shipments, it is known that θ has a $\mathcal{B}e(1, 9)$ prior distribution. Find the 95% HPD credible region for θ, if $x = 0$ is observed.

22. A production lot of electronic components is to be tested to determine θ, the mean lifetime. A sample of 5 components is drawn, and the lifetimes $X_1, \ldots, X_5$ are observed. It is known that $X_i \sim \mathcal{E}(\theta)$. From past records it is known that, among production lots, θ is distributed according to an $\mathcal{IG}(10, 0.01)$ distribution. The 5 observations are 15, 12, 14, 10, 12. Find the generalized maximum likelihood estimate of θ, and the mean of the posterior of θ given the data.

23. The weekly number of fires, X, in a town has a $\mathscr{P}(\theta)$ distribution. It is desired to find a 90% HPD credible region for θ. Nothing is known apriori about θ, so the non-informative prior $\pi(\theta) = \theta^{-1}I_{(0, \infty)}(\theta)$ is deemed appropriate. The number of fires observed for five weekly periods was $0, 1, 1, 0, 0$. What is the desired credible region?

24. Consider the situation in Example 8 of Subsection 1.6.1.
    (a) Using the natural noninformative prior $\pi(\theta) = 1$, show that the posterior probability, given $\mathbf{x}$, that θ is in a region C is given by

    $$[1 + \min\{x_i\} - \max\{x_i\}]^{-1} \int_C I_A(\theta)d\theta,$$

    where $A = (\max\{x_i\} - \frac{1}{2}, \min\{x_i\} + \frac{1}{2})$.
    (b) Relate this result to the discussion of initial and final precision in the given example.

25. From path perturbations of a nearby sun, the mass θ of a neutron star is to be determined. Five observations 1.2, 1.6, 1.3, 1.4, and 1.4 are obtained. Each observation is (independently) normally distributed with mean θ and unknown variance σ^2. Apriori nothing is known about θ and σ^2, so the noninformative prior density $\pi(\theta, \sigma^2) = \sigma^{-2}$ is used. Find a 90% HPD credible region for θ.

26. The waiting time for a bus at a given corner at a certain time of day is known to have a $\mathscr{U}(0, \theta)$ distribution. It is desired to test $H_0 : 0 \le \theta \le 15$ versus $H_1 : \theta > 15$. From other similar routes, it is known that θ has a $\mathscr{P}a(5, 3)$ distribution. If waiting times of 10, 3, 2, 5, and 14 are observed at the given corner, calculate the posterior probability of each hypothesis and the posterior odds ratio.

27. In the situation of Exercise 21, it is desired to test $H_0 : \theta \le 0.1$ versus $H_1 : \theta > 0.1$. Find the posterior probabilities of the two hypotheses, and the posterior odds ratio.

28. In the situation of Exercise 25, it is desired to test $H_0 : \theta \le 1$ versus $H_1 : \theta > 1$. Find the posterior probabilities of the two hypotheses, and the posterior odds ratio.

29. (DeGroot (1970)) Consider two boxes A and B, each of which contains both red balls and green balls. It is known that, in one of the boxes, $\frac{1}{2}$ of the balls are red and $\frac{1}{2}$ are green, and that, in the other box, $\frac{1}{4}$ of the balls are red and $\frac{3}{4}$ are green. Let the box in which $\frac{1}{2}$ are red be denoted box W, and suppose $P(W = A) = \xi$ and $P(W = B) = 1 - \xi$. Suppose that the statistician may select one ball at random from either box A or box B and that, after observing its color, he must decide whether $W = A$ or $W = B$. Prove that if $\frac{1}{2} < \xi < \frac{2}{3}$, then in order to maximize the probability of making a correct decision, he should select the ball from box B. Prove also that if $\frac{2}{3} \le \xi \le 1$, then it does not matter from which box the ball is selected.

30. Theory predicts that θ, the melting point of a particular substance under a pressure of 10^6 atmospheres, is 4.01. The procedure for measuring this melting point is fairly inaccurate, due to the high pressure. Indeed it is known that an observation X has a $\mathscr{N}(\theta, 1)$ distribution. Five independent experiments give observations of 4.9, 4.3, 5.1, 4.6, and 2.9. The prior probability that $\theta = 4.01$ is 0.5. The remaining values of θ are given the density

$$\pi(\theta) = 0.5\left(\frac{2}{\pi}\right)^{1/2}e^{-2(\theta - 4.01)^2}.$$

Formulate and conduct a Bayesian test of the proposed theory.

31. Electronic components I and II have lifetimes X_1 and X_2 which have $\mathscr{E}(\theta_1)$ and $\mathscr{E}(\theta_2)$ densities, respectively. It is desired to estimate the mean lifetimes θ_1 and θ_2. Component I contains component II as a subcomponent, and will fail if the subcomponent does (or if something else goes wrong). Hence $\theta_1 < \theta_2$. Two independent observations, X_1^1 and X_1^2, of the lifetimes of component I are taken. Likewise, two observations X_2^1 and X_2^2 of the lifetimes of component II are taken. The X_2^i $(i = 1, 2)$ are independent of each other, and also of the X_1^i $(i = 1, 2)$. (The four observations are taken from different components.) It is decided that a reasonable noninformative prior for the situation is

$$\pi(\theta_1, \theta_2) = \theta_1^{-1}\theta_2^{-1}I_{(0,\,\theta_2)}(\theta_1)I_{(0,\,\infty)}(\theta_2).$$

Find reasonable Bayesian estimates of θ_1 and θ_2.

Section 4.4

32. Prove Result 1 of Subsection 4.4.1 for randomized rules. (You may assume that all interchanges in orders of integration are legal.)

33. Prove Result 3 of Subsection 4.4.2. (You may assume that all integrals exist.)

34. Show that, in estimation of a vector $\boldsymbol{\theta} = (\theta_1, \theta_2, \ldots, \theta_p)^t$ by $\mathbf{a} = (a_1, \ldots, a_p)^t$ under a quadratic loss

$$L(\boldsymbol{\theta}, \mathbf{a}) = (\boldsymbol{\theta} - \mathbf{a})^t\mathbf{Q}(\boldsymbol{\theta} - \mathbf{a}),$$

where $\mathbf{Q}$ is a $(p \times p)$ positive definite matrix, the Bayes estimator of $\boldsymbol{\theta}$ is

$$\delta^\pi(x) = E^{\pi(\boldsymbol{\theta}|x)}[\boldsymbol{\theta}].$$

(You may assume that $\pi(\theta|x)$ and all integrals involved exist.)

35. Prove Result 5 of Subsection 4.4.2. (You may assume that $\pi(\theta|x)$ exists and that there is an action with finite posterior expected loss.)

36. If $X \sim \mathscr{B}(n, \theta)$ and $\theta \sim \mathscr{B}e(\alpha, \beta)$, find the Bayes estimator of θ under loss

$$L(\theta, a) = \frac{(\theta - a)^2}{\theta(1 - \theta)}.$$

(Be careful about the treatment of $x = 0$ and $x = n$.)

37. If $X \sim \mathscr{G}(n/2, 2\theta)$ and $\theta \sim \mathscr{I}\mathscr{G}(\alpha, \beta)$, find the Bayes estimator of θ under loss

$$L(\theta, a) = \left(\frac{a}{\theta} - 1\right)^2 = \frac{1}{\theta^2}(a - \theta)^2.$$

38. Assume θ, x, and a are real, $\pi(\theta|x)$ is symmetric and unimodal, and L is an increasing function of $|\theta - a|$. Show that the Bayes rule is then the mode of $\pi(\theta|x)$. (You may assume that all risk integrals exist.)

39. In the situation of Exercise 21, find the Bayes estimate of θ under loss
    (a) $L(\theta, a) = (\theta - a)^2$,
    (b) $L(\theta, a) = |\theta - a|$,
    (c) $L(\theta, a) = (\theta - a)^2/\theta(1 - \theta)$,
    (d) $L(\theta, a) = (\theta - a)$ if $\theta > a$; $L(\theta, a) = 2(a - \theta)$ if $\theta \le a$.

40. In the IQ example, where $X \sim \mathcal{N}(\theta, 100)$ and $\theta \sim \mathcal{N}(100, 225)$, assume it is important to detect particularly high or low IQ's. Indeed the weighted loss

$$L(\theta, a) = (\theta - a)^2 e^{(\theta - 100)^2/900}$$

is deemed appropriate. (Note that this means that detecting an IQ of 145 (or 55) is about 9 times as important as detecting an IQ of 100.) Find the Bayes estimator of θ.

41. In the situation of Exercise 9, find the Bayes estimator of $\boldsymbol{\theta}$ under loss

$$L(\boldsymbol{\theta}, \mathbf{a}) = \sum_{i=1}^{k} (\theta_i - a_i)^2.$$

Show that the Bayes risk of the estimator is

$$\frac{\alpha_0^2 - \sum_{i=1}^{k} \alpha_i^2}{\alpha_0(\alpha_0 + 1)(\alpha_0 + n)},$$

where $\alpha_0 = \sum_{i=1}^{k} \alpha_i$.

42. In the situation of Exercise 21, let a_0 denote the action "decide $0 \leq \theta \leq 0.15$," and a_1 denote the action "decide $\theta > 0.15$." Conduct the Bayes test under the loss

(a) "0–1" loss,

(b) $L(\theta, a_0) = \begin{cases} 1 & \text{if } \theta > 0.15, \\ 0 & \text{if } \theta \leq 0.15, \end{cases}$

$L(\theta, a_1) = \begin{cases} 2 & \text{if } \theta \leq 0.15, \\ 0 & \text{if } \theta > 0.15, \end{cases}$

(c) $L(\theta, a_0) = \begin{cases} 1 & \text{if } \theta > 0.15, \\ 0 & \text{if } \theta \leq 0.15, \end{cases}$

$L(\theta, a_1) = \begin{cases} 0.15 - \theta & \text{if } \theta \leq 0.15, \\ 0 & \text{if } \theta > 0.15. \end{cases}$

43. A company periodically samples products coming off a production line, in order to make sure the production process is running smoothly. They choose a sample of size 5 and observe the number of defectives. Past records show that the proportion of defectives, θ, varies according to a $\mathcal{B}e(1, 9)$ distribution. The loss in letting the production process run is 10θ, while the loss in stopping the production line, recalibrating, and starting up again is 1. What is the Bayes decision if one defective is observed in a sample?

44. A missile can travel at either a high or a low trajectory. The missile's effectiveness decreases linearly with the distance by which it misses its target, up to a distance of 2 miles at which it is totally ineffective.

If a low trajectory is used, the missile is safe from antimissile fire. However, its accuracy is subject to the proportion of cloud cover (θ). Indeed the distance, d, by which it misses its target is uniformly distributed on $(0, \theta)$. For the target area, θ is known to have the probability density

$$\pi_1(\theta) = 6\theta(1 - \theta)I_{(0, 1)}(\theta).$$

If a high trajectory is used, the missile will hit the target exactly, unless it is first destroyed by antimissile fire. From previous experience, the probability, ξ, of the missile being destroyed is thought to have the prior density $\pi_2(\xi) = 2(1 - \xi)I_{(0, 1)}(\xi)$. An experiment is conducted to provide further information about ξ. Two missiles are launched using a high trajectory, out of which none are shot down.

(a) Give the loss incurred in having the missile miss by a distance d. (Let 0 stand for a perfect hit and 1 for a total miss.)

(b) What is the optimal Bayes trajectory?

45. A wildcat oilman must decide how to finance the drilling of a well. It costs $100,000 to drill the well. The oilman has available 3 options: a_1—finance the drilling himself (retaining all the profits); a_2—accept $70,000 from investors in return for paying them 50% of the oil profits; a_3—accept $120,000 from investors in return for paying them 90% of the oil profits. The oil profits will be 3θ, where θ is the number of barrels of oil in the well. From past data, it is believed that $\theta = 0$ with probability 0.9, while the $\theta > 0$ have density

$$\pi(\theta) = \frac{0.1}{300,000} e^{-\theta/300,000} I_{(0, \infty)}(\theta).$$

A seismic test is performed to determine the likelihood of oil in the given area. The test tells which type of geological structure, x_1, x_2, or x_3, is present. It is known that the probabilities of the x_i given θ are $f(x_1|\theta) = 0.8e^{-\theta/100,000}$, $f(x_2|\theta) = 0.2$, $f(x_3|\theta) = 0.8(1 - e^{-\theta/100,000})$.

(a) For monetary loss, what is the Bayes action if x_1 is observed?

(b) For monetary loss, what are the Bayes actions if x_2 and x_3 are observed?

(c) If the oilman has the utility function

$$U(z) = \begin{cases} 1 - e^{-(10^{-6})z} & \text{if } z \geq 0, \\ -(1 - e^{2(10^{-6})z}) & \text{if } z < 0, \end{cases}$$

where z is monetary gain or loss, what is the Bayes action if x_1 is observed?

46. A device has been created which can supposedly classify blood as type A, B, AB, or O. The device measures a quantity X, which has density

$$f(x|\theta) = e^{-(x-\theta)}I_{(\theta, \infty)}(x).$$

If $0 < \theta < 1$, the blood is of type AB; if $1 < \theta < 2$, the blood is of type A; if $2 < \theta < 3$, the blood is of type B; and if $\theta > 3$, the blood is of type O. In the population as a whole, θ is distributed according to the density

$$\pi(\theta) = e^{-\theta}I_{(0, \infty)}(\theta).$$

The loss in misclassifying the blood is given in the following table.

		Classified As			
		AB	A	B	O
	AB	0	1	1	2
True	A	1	0	2	2
Blood					
Type	B	1	2	0	2
	O	3	3	3	0

If $x = 4$ is observed, what is the Bayes action?

47. At a certain stage of an industrial process, the concentration, θ, of a chemical must be estimated. The loss in estimating θ is reasonably approximated by squared-error loss. The measurement, X, of θ has a $\mathcal{N}(\theta, (0.01)^2)$ distribution. Five measurements are available from determinations of the chemical concentration when the process was run in the past. These measurements are 3.29, 3.31, 3.35, 3.33, and 3.30. Each arose from (independent) $\mathcal{N}(\theta_i, (0.01)^2)$ distributions.
    (a) If $x = 3.34$ is the current measurement, what is the empirical Bayes estimator of θ? (Assume the θ_i are from a normal prior.)
    (b) For $x = 3.34$, what is the empirical Bayes 95% HPD credible region for θ?

48. In the situation of Exercise 47, assume the first three past measurements were $\mathcal{N}(\theta_i, (0.02)^2)$. (A less accurate measurement procedure was used.) Find an empirical Bayes estimate of θ. (*Hint*: If $X_i \sim \mathcal{N}(\mu, \tau_i^2)$, $i = 1, \ldots, n$, then

$$\tilde{X} = \left(\sum_{i=1}^{n} \tau_i^{-2} \right)^{-1} \sum_{i=1}^{n} \frac{X_i}{\tau_i^2}$$

is the usual unbiased estimator of μ, and

$$E\left[\sum_{i=1}^{n} \frac{(X_i - \tilde{X})^2}{\tau_i^2} \right] = (n - 1).$$

Assume that the prior distribution of the θ_i in this problem is normal, and use the above facts to derive estimates of the prior mean and variance.)

49. A steel mill casts p large steel beams. It is necessary to determine, for each beam, the average number of defects or impurities per cubic foot. (For the ith beam, denote this quantity θ_i.) On each beam, n sample cubic-foot regions are examined, and the number of defects in each region is determined. (For the ith beam, denote these $X_i^1, X_i^2, \ldots, X_i^n$.) The X_i^j have $\mathcal{P}(\theta_i)$ distributions. If the θ_i are to be estimated under squared-error loss, show that a reasonable empirical Bayes estimator of each θ_i is

$$\delta_i^{EB}(\mathbf{x}) = \begin{cases} \dfrac{\dfrac{\bar{x}^2}{(ns^2 - \bar{x})} + n\bar{x}_i}{\dfrac{\bar{x}}{(ns^2 - \bar{x})} + n} & \text{if } ns^2 > \bar{x}, \\[4ex] \bar{x} & \text{if } ns^2 \leq \bar{x}, \end{cases}$$

where $\bar{x}_i = (1/n) \sum_{j=1}^{n} x_i^j$, $\bar{x} = (1/p) \sum_{i=1}^{p} \bar{x}_i$, and $s^2 = (1/(p-1)) \sum_{i=1}^{p} (\bar{x}_i - \bar{x})^2$.
    (*Hint*: Assume the θ_i have a common $\mathcal{G}(\alpha, \beta)$ prior, as in Example 5. To find estimates of α and β based on the sufficient statistics $\bar{X}_i$, use Lemma 1 of Subsection 3.2.4. Assume that $ns^2 > \bar{x}$ initially. To determine the estimator for $ns^2 \leq \bar{x}$, take the limit of the above estimator as $ns^2 \to \bar{x}$.)

50. In the situation of Exercise 4, the journal editors decide to investigate the problem. They survey all of the recent contributors to the journal, and determine the total number of experiments, N, that were conducted by the contributors. Let x denote the number of such experiments that were reported in the journal (i.e., the experiments where H_1 was accepted by a size α_0 test). Again assume all experiments had fixed $\alpha \, (= \alpha_0)$ and $\beta \, (> \alpha_0)$.

(a) Show that a reasonable empirical Bayes estimator of π_1, is (defining $\hat{p} = x/N$)

$$\hat{\pi}_1 = \frac{\hat{p} - \alpha_0}{\beta - \alpha_0},$$

(truncated at zero and one to ensure it is a probability).

(b) If $\alpha_0 = 0.05$, $\beta = 0.8$, $N = 500$, and $x = 75$, what is the estimate of the proportion of correct articles in the journal?

Section 4.5

51. Prove Theorem 2.

52. Prove Theorem 3.

53. If $X \sim \mathcal{B}(n, \theta)$ and it is desired to estimate θ under squared-error loss, show that $\delta(x) = x/n$ is admissible. (*Hint*: Consider the improper prior density $\pi(\theta) = \theta^{-1}(1 - \theta)^{-1}$. You may assume that all risk functions $R(\theta, \delta)$ are continuous.)

54. Prove the result in Example 16.

Step 1. Write (defining $|\mathbf{x}|^2 = \sum_{i=1}^p x_i^2$)

$$\delta_i^{JS}(\mathbf{x}) - \theta_i = (x_i - \theta_i) - \frac{(p - 2)x_i}{|\mathbf{x}|^2},$$

and expand the loss.

Step 2. Use integration by parts to show that

$$\int_{-\infty}^{\infty} x_i(x_i - \theta_i)|\mathbf{x}|^{-2}e^{-(x_i - \theta_i)^2/2}\, dx_i = \int_{-\infty}^{\infty} [|\mathbf{x}|^{-2} - 2x_i^2|\mathbf{x}|^{-4}]e^{-(x_i - \theta_i)^2/2}\, dx_i.$$

Step 3. Collect all terms and show that $\{R(\boldsymbol{\theta}, \boldsymbol{\delta}^0) - R(\boldsymbol{\theta}, \boldsymbol{\delta}^{JS})\}$ is an integral whose integrand is positive.

55. Prove that a decision rule δ^1 (which has bounded risk) is "incoherent" if and only if there exists another rule δ^2 with $R(\theta, \delta^2) < R(\theta, \delta^1)$ for all $\theta \in \Theta$.

56. Assume $X \sim \mathcal{G}(\alpha, \beta)$ (α known) is observed, and that it is desired to estimate β under loss

$$L(\beta, a) = \left(1 - \frac{a}{\beta}\right)^2.$$

It is decided to use the improper prior density $\pi(\beta) = \beta^{-2}$.

(a) Show that the generalized Bayes estimator of β is

$$\delta^0(x) = \frac{x}{\alpha + 2}.$$

(b) Show that δ^0 is inadmissible.

(c) Show that δ^0 is incoherent, in the strong sense that, no matter how player 1 chooses β at each stage of the game, the probability that he will lose money converges to one as $n \to \infty$.

Section 4.6

57. Assume $X \sim \mathcal{N}(\theta, 1)$ is observed, and that it is desired to estimate θ under squared-error loss. It is felt that θ has a $\mathcal{N}(2, 3)$ prior distribution, but the estimated mean and variance could each be in error by 1 unit. Hence the class of plausible priors is

$$\Gamma = \{\pi : \pi \text{ is a } \mathcal{N}(\mu, \tau^2) \text{ density with } 1 \le \mu \le 3 \text{ and } 2 \le \tau^2 \le 4\}.$$

   (a) Is the Bayes action (with respect to the $\mathcal{N}(2, 3)$ prior) posterior robust when $x = 2$ is observed?
   (b) Is the Bayes action posterior robust when $x = 10$ is observed?

58. Consider the situation of Exercise 57, but assume it is desired to test $H_0 : \theta \le 0$ versus $H_1 : \theta > 0$ under "0–1" loss. Is the Bayes action (with respect to the $\mathcal{N}(2, 3)$ prior) posterior robust for the observation
   (a) $x = 0$?
   (b) $x = -1$?
   (c) $x = -2$?

59. Let $X \sim \mathcal{N}(\theta, 1)$ be observed, and assume it is desired to estimate θ under squared-error loss. The class of possible priors is considered to be

$$\Gamma = \{\pi : \pi \text{ is a } \mathcal{N}(0, \sigma^2) \text{ density, with } 0 < \sigma^2 < \infty\}.$$

   (a) Let δ be any Bayes rule from a prior in Γ. Is δ Bayes risk robust with respect to Γ? Explain.
   (b) Answer the questions in part (a) with Γ replaced by

$$\Gamma' = \{\pi : \pi \text{ is a } \mathcal{N}(\mu, 1) \text{ density, with } -\infty < \mu < \infty\}.$$

   (c) Find a decision rule which is Bayes risk robust for both Γ and Γ'.

60. Assume that $R(\theta, \delta^*)$ is continuous in θ.
   (a) Prove that, if $\Gamma = \{\text{all prior distributions}\}$, then

$$\sup_{\pi \in \Gamma} r(\pi, \delta^*) = \sup_{\theta \in \Theta} R(\theta, \delta^*).$$

   (b) Prove that, if $\Theta = (-\infty, \infty)$ and

$$\Gamma = \{\pi : \pi \text{ is a } \mathcal{N}(\mu, \sigma^2) \text{ density, with } -\infty < \mu < \infty \text{ and } 0 < \sigma^2 < \infty\},$$

   then

$$\sup_{\pi \in \Gamma} r(\pi, \delta^*) = \sup_{\theta \in \Theta} R(\theta, \delta^*).$$

61. Prove that, if a decision rule δ^* has constant risk $(R(\theta, \delta^*))$ and is Bayes with respect to some proper prior $\pi \in \Gamma$, then δ^* is Γ-minimax.

62. Assume $X \sim \mathcal{B}(n, \theta)$ is observed, and that it is desired to estimate θ under squared-error loss. Let Γ be the class of all symmetric proper prior distributions. Find a Γ-minimax estimator. (*Hint*: Use Exercise 61, considering Bayes rules for conjugate priors.)

63. Assume $X \sim \mathcal{B}(1, \theta)$ is observed, and that it is desired to estimate θ under squared-error loss. It is felt that the prior mean is $\mu = \frac{3}{4}$. Letting Γ be the class of prior distributions satisfying this constraint, find the Γ-minimax estimator of θ. (Show

first that only nonrandomized rules need be considered. Then show that $0 \leq E^{\pi}(\theta - \mu)^2 \leq \mu(1 - \mu)$.)

64. Assume $X \sim \mathscr{E}(\theta)$ is observed, where $\Theta = \{1, 2\}$. It is desired to test $H_0: \theta = 1$ versus $H_1: \theta = 2$ under "0–1" loss. It is known that $a \leq \pi_0 \leq b$, where π_0 is the prior probability of θ_0. You may assume that it is only necessary to consider the most powerful tests, which have rejection regions of the form $\{x: x > c\}$.
   (a) Find the Γ-minimax test when $a = 0, b = 1$.
   (b) Find the Γ-minimax regret test when $a = 0, b = 1$.
   (c) Find the Γ-minimax test for arbitrary a and b ($0 \leq a < b \leq 1$).

65. A baseball player, after 3 weeks of the season, is batting 0.430. This is, approximately, an observation of the random variable $X \sim \mathcal{N}(\theta, 0.0025)$, where θ is his true batting average for the year (i.e., his batting average at the end of the season). It is desired to test $H_0: \theta \leq 0.400$ versus $H_1: \theta > 0.009$. From previous yearly batting averages of the player, it is concluded that θ has a $\mathcal{T}(3, 0.260, 0.0009)$ prior density.
   (a) What is the classical significance level of the observation?
   (b) What is the posterior probability (given $x = 0.430$) of H_0? (*Hint:* Use the approximation to $\pi(\theta|x)$ given in Example 23. You may assume that $|x - \mu|$ is large enough.)

66. Assume $X \sim \mathscr{U}(0, \theta)$ is observed, and that it is desired to estimate θ under squared-error loss. Let $\Gamma = \{\pi_1, \pi_2\}$, where π_1 is a $\mathscr{G}(2, \beta)$ prior density and π_2 is the prior density

$$\pi_2(\theta) = 6\alpha^{-2}\theta\left(1 + \frac{\theta}{\alpha}\right)^{-4} I_{(0, \infty)}(\theta).$$

The median of the prior is felt to be 6.
   (a) Determine α and β.
   (b) Calculate the Bayes estimators of θ with respect to π_1 and π_2.
   (c) Calculate $R(\theta, \delta)$ for each of the Bayes estimators.
   (d) Which of the two rules is more appealing if large θ are thought possible?

67. Assume $\mathbf{X} = (X_1, X_2)^t \sim \mathcal{N}_2(\mathbf{\theta}, (\begin{smallmatrix} 1 & 0.5 \\ 0.5 & 1 \end{smallmatrix}))$. The prior mean of $\mathbf{\theta}$ is $(1, 2)^t$ and the prior covariance matrix is $(\begin{smallmatrix} 2 & 0 \\ 0 & 2 \end{smallmatrix})$. Assume $\mathbf{x} = (1.8, 2.2)^t$ is observed.
   (a) Find the robust Bayesian estimator of $\mathbf{\theta}$ (given in Subsection 4.6.4) under a quadratic loss.
   (b) Find the robust 95% credible ellipsoid for $\mathbf{\theta}$.

68. Archeological digs discovered Hominid remains at 3 different sites. The remains were clearly of the same species. The geological structures within which they were found were similar, coming from about the same 500,000 year period. Geologists estimate this period to be about 8 million years ago, plus or minus 1 million years. A radiocarbon dating technique, used on the 3 remains, gave ages of 8.5 million, 9 million, and 7.8 million years. The technique is known to give a result which is normally distributed, with mean $\theta = $ true age, and standard deviation 600,000 years. It is desired to estimate $\mathbf{\theta} = (\theta_1, \theta_2, \theta_3)^t$ (θ_i is the true age of the ith remains) under a quadratic loss. The radiocarbon dating technique is considered much more reliable than the geological information, so the geological information is to be considered vague prior information for which a robust prior should be used.

(a) Determine $\mathbf{\mu}$ and $\mathbf{A}$ for the robust Bayesian analysis of Subsection 4.6.4. (*Hint*: The belief that the geological structures existed in the same 500,000-year period can be modeled by saying that the θ_i have a common prior mean, θ_0, and prior standard deviation, 250,000, say.)

(b) Find the robust Bayesian estimator of $\mathbf{\theta}$.

(c) Find the robust 99% credible ellipsoid for $\mathbf{\theta}$.

69. The sufficient statistic from a regression study in econometrics is the least-squares estimator $\mathbf{x} = (1.1, 0.3, -0.4, 2.2)^t$, which can be considered to be an observation from a $\mathcal{N}_4(\mathbf{\theta}, 0.3\mathbf{I}_4)$ distribution. Economic theory suggests that $\theta_1 - \theta_2 = 1$, and $\theta_3 = -1$. These linear restrictions are felt to hold with accuracies of 0.3 and 0.5 respectively. (Consider these standard deviations.) Apriori, nothing is known about θ_4, and there is thought to be no relationship between $\theta_1 - \theta_2$ and θ_3.

(a) Find the robust estimator of $\mathbf{\theta}$ (given in Subsection 4.6.4) under a quadratic loss.

(b) Find the robust 90% credible region for $\mathbf{\theta}$.

70. In the situation of Exercise 25, assume that past records show that neutron stars average about 1.3 in mass, with a standard deviation of 0.2. This prior information is rather vague, so robust Bayesian analysis is to be used.

(a) Calculate the robust estimator of θ (given in Subsection 4.6.4) under squared-error loss.

(b) Find the robust 90% credible region for θ.

CHAPTER 5

Minimax Analysis

5.1 Introduction

This chapter is devoted to the implementation and evaluation of decision-theoretic analysis based on the minimax principle introduced in Section 1.5. We began Chapter 4 with a discussion of axioms of rational behavior, and observed that they lead to a justification of Bayesian analysis. It would be nice to be able to say something similar about minimax analysis, but the unfortunate fact is that minimax analysis is not consistent with such sets of axioms. We are left in the uncomfortable position of asking why this chapter is of any interest. (Indeed many Bayesians will deny that it is of any interest.) It thus behooves us to start with a discussion of when minimax analysis can be useful.

Recall from Section 1.5 that the essence of the minimax principle is to try and protect against the worst possible state of nature. The one situation in which this is clearly appropriate is when the state of nature is determined by an intelligent opponent who desires to maximize your loss (see Section 1.4). You can then expect the worst possible state of nature to occur, and should plan accordingly. The study of this situation is called game theory, and is the subject of Section 5.2. (It should be mentioned that the axioms of rational behavior, alluded to earlier, are not valid in situations involving intelligent opponents.)

Statistical problems, on the other hand, involve a "neutral" nature, and it is then not clear why the minimax principle is useful. The most frequently given justification for minimax analysis in such problems is a possible desire for conservative behavior. A very simple example of this is Example 3 of Chapter 1. In a choice between a risky bond and a safe bond, a conservative attitude may well lead to the choice of the safe bond, even if its expected yield is lower than that of the risky bond. This consideration gets somewhat obviated by the fact that a utility function (if constructed) will naturally incorporate the desired conservatism, leaving no further need for explicit conservative action. This will be discussed more fully in Section 5.4. It can at least be said that, if a decision is to be made without the use of a utility approach (say loss is expressed solely in monetary terms), then a conservative principle may be appealing to some.

Perhaps the greatest use of the minimax principle is in situations for which no prior information is available. There is then no natural decision principle by which to proceed, and the minimax principle is often suggested as a good choice. Frequently the minimax principle will prove reasonable in such problems, but two notes of caution should be sounded. First, the minimax principle can lead to bad decision rules. This will be indicated in Section 5.4. Second, the minimax principle can be devilishly hard to implement. The alternative approach, discussed in Chapter 4, of using noninformative priors and Bayesian methodology is far simpler and rarely gives worse results. Indeed, for problems in which the minimax approach is feasible, the two approaches will frequently give the same result. (Reasons for this will be indicated in Chapter 6, where a tie-in with the invariance principle will also be discussed.) It can definitely be argued, however, that, due to the possible inadequacies of rules based on noninformative priors, it is wise to investigate such problems from a minimax viewpoint also. This is especially true when "standard" statistical procedures are being recommended for nonspecialists to use. Such procedures should generally be objective (i.e., independent of prior information). Due to their importance, they should be examined from many directions; the Bayesian with noninformative prior and minimax approaches being two of the most appealing.

The final use of minimax rules, that should be mentioned, is that of providing a yardstick for Bayesian robustness investigations. In Subsection 4.6.2 the principle of Γ-minimaxity was introduced as an aid in the study of robustness with respect to specification of the prior. It was pointed out that, if Γ is the class of all priors, then Γ-minimaxity is simply minimaxity. In some sense, the implication is that a minimax rule is the most robust rule with respect to specification of the prior. (Essentially, it protects against the "prior" being concentrated at the "worst" state of nature.) The robustness of proposed Bayesian rules can thus be partially indicated by comparison of the rules with the minimax rule.

We feel that the above reasons provide adequate justification for studying the minimax approach. It is probably true, however, that the considerable theoretical popularity of the approach is not so much due to these justifications as to the fact that minimax theory is much richer mathematically than Bayesian theory. (Research involving difficult mathematics tends to be more prestigious.) This richness is partially indicated in this chapter, though only certain special cases can be considered.

Section 5.2 discusses game theory, and lays the mathematical foundation for the application of the minimax principle. Section 5.3 relates this theory to statistical problems. Section 5.4 gives a critical discussion of minimax analysis.

5.2 Game Theory

Game theory originated with work of Borel (1921) and von Neumann (1928), and was extensively developed in von Neumann and Morgenstern (1944). The goal of game theory is the development of optimal strategies for action in competitive situations involving two or more intelligent antagonists. Such problems can be encountered in business situations involving competitors, in military or political settings of conflict between groups, and of course in games.

   In Subsection 5.2.1 the basic elements of game theory will be discussed. Subsections 5.2.2 and 5.2.3 deal with explicit methods of solving games. Subsections 5.2.4, and especially 5.2.5 and 5.2.6, are more theoretically oriented, giving a fairly complete mathematical development for the case of finite Θ.

5.2.1 Basic Elements

We shall consider only games involving two opponents, henceforth to be called *players*. The statistician will be identified with player II (II for short), and his opponent will be called player I (or just I).

I. *Strategies*

In game theory, actions of players are usually called *strategies*, the terminology being designed to indicate that a strategy will involve a complete description of the "moves" that will be made in the game. In chess, for example, a strategy consists of a complete specification of all moves you will make throughout the game, including the response you will have to any given move of your opponent. To put this another way, a strategy can be thought of as a recipe (or computer program) which can be followed mechanically (say by a computer) to play the game. Clearly, good strategies can be very complicated, and in games such as chess seem almost unobtainable. (On the other hand, the computer programs that have recently been developed to play chess are nothing but strategies in the above sense, and indeed are very good strategies. Already, only extremely good chess players can beat the best computer strategies, and, in the near future, computers may become unbeatable.)

The set of strategies available to I will be denoted Θ, while $\mathscr{A}$ will stand for the set of possible strategies for II. (Hopefully this change in the interpretation of Θ will not cause confusion.)

II. *Two-Person Zero-Sum Games*

If player I chooses strategy $\theta \in \Theta$ and II chooses strategy $a \in \mathscr{A}$, it will be assumed that I *gains*, and II *loses*, an amount $L(\theta, a)$. We will continue to refer to L as the loss (to player II), though in game theory it is usually referred to as the *payoff function* (for I). For technical convenience, it will be assumed that $L(\theta, a) \geq -K$ for some finite constant K.

A game, such as defined above, is called a *two-person zero-sum game*. The reason for calling it a two-person game is obvious. The "zero sum" refers to the fact that the sum of the losses (or the sum of the gains) for the two players is zero, since a loss for one is a gain for the other. This introduces an enormous simplification of the theory, since the two players can then gain nothing by cooperation. Cooperation is senseless (feelings of altruism aside), since any extra gain to your opponent (through cooperation) comes directly from your own pocket. It can thus be assumed that each player is trying to maximize his gain *and* his opponents loss. This makes the mathematical analysis relatively easy.

Zero-sum games are, of course, rather rare. In business settings, for example, competing companies are rarely in zero-sum situations. Cooperation (such as price fixing) will often be mutually beneficial to both. Nevertheless, zero-sum games serve as a useful introduction to game theory. Several examples of zero-sum games follow.

EXAMPLE 1. Refer again to the game of matching pennies discussed in Section 1.4 of Chapter 1. Each player has two strategies, and the loss matrix is

Player II

		a_1	a_2
	θ_1	-1	1
Player I	θ_2	1	-1

This is clearly a zero-sum game, since one player's loss is the other's gain.

EXAMPLE 2. Two countries, I and II, are at war. II has two airfields, and can defend one but not both. Let a_1 and a_2 denote defending airfield 1 and airfield 2 respectively. Country I can attack only one of the airfields. Denote the two possible strategies θ_1 and θ_2. If I attacks a defended airfield, it will immediately withdraw with no loss to either side. If I attacks an undefended airfield, the airfield will be destroyed. Airfield 1 is twice as valuable as airfield 2 to II. Letting 1 denote the value (to II) of airfield 2, it follows that the loss matrix is

	a_1	a_2
θ_1	0	2
θ_2	1	0

This is a zero-sum game, providing the values to I of the destruction of the airfields are the same as the values of the airfields to II.

EXAMPLE 3. Each player simultaneously extends one or two fingers on each hand. The number of fingers extended on the right hand of each player is the player's "choice," while the number of fingers extended on the left hand is a guess of the opponent's choice. If only *one* player guesses his opponent's choice correctly, he receives a payoff (from the other player) consisting of the total number of extended fingers (for both players). Otherwise there is no payoff.

For each player, let (i, j) denote the strategy "extend i fingers on your left hand and j fingers on your right hand." The loss matrix is then

		Player II			
		(1, 1)	(1, 2)	(2, 1)	(2, 2)
	(1, 1)	0	−5	5	0
	(1, 2)	5	0	0	−7
Player I	(2, 1)	−5	0	0	7
	(2, 2)	0	7	−7	0

The game is clearly zero sum.

EXAMPLE 4. Player I chooses a number $\theta \in \Theta = [0, 1]$, and II chooses a number $a \in \mathscr{A} = [0, 1]$. The loss to II (and gain to I) is $L(\theta, a) = |\theta - a|$.

EXAMPLE 5. Two companies, I and II, are the sole producers of widgets. In two of the firms which purchase widgets, the employees who decide whether to buy from I or II take bribes. Label these two firms A and B. Firm A buys 2000 widgets per year, while firm B buys 3000 widgets. Companies I and II set aside $10,000 per year for bribery purposes. Each company must decide how much of the bribe money to allocate to A, and how much to allocate to B. Each company can expect an order from a bribed firm in proportion to the bribe ratio. In other words, if I and II bribe A with θ and a amounts of money respectively, I will obtain an order from A of 2000 $\times \theta/(\theta + a)$ widgets. Since the bribes for B will then be $10,000 - \theta$ and $10,000 - a$, I will receive an order from B of

$$\frac{3000(10,000 - \theta)}{20,000 - [a + \theta]}$$

widgets. (If both x and y are zero, define $x/(x + y)$ as $\frac{1}{2}$.) Letting the loss to II be represented by the total sales of I to A and B, the loss function is

$$L(\theta, a) = \frac{2000\,\theta}{\theta + a} + \frac{3000(10,000 - \theta)}{20,000 - [a + \theta]}.$$

This can be considered a zero-sum game, since any sale made by I is a sale lost by II. Having the $10,000 bribery cost go to someone outside the game may seem to violate the zero-sum condition. This is not the case, however, since the $10,000 will *always* be spent. The money, therefore, has no effect on the choice of strategy. If, instead, the companies were trying to decide how much total bribe money to spend, the game would not be zero sum for the above reason. Note how delicate the zero-sum property really is. Because of this, it is extremely difficult to find realistic zero-sum games in business settings.

One facet of the above example deserves further emphasis, namely the fact that adding a constant to the loss function of II (or gain function of I) does not change the problem in terms of which strategies are optimal. This has two useful consequences. First, in verifying the zero-sum property, one can separately calculate the loss function for II and the gain function for I, and check that their difference is constant. Either function will then serve for the purpose of determining optimal strategies. Secondly, it will sometimes be of use to add a constant to the loss function (say, to make it positive). Again, this will not affect the conclusions.

So far, we have ignored the role of utility theory in the formulation of a game. As discussed in Chapter 2, the "values" of outcomes of a game should generally be measured in terms of utilities. This, however, poses a serious problem for game theory, in that the utility of a loss of z by player II will usually not be the negative of the utility of a gain of z by I. (Even if the utility functions of the two players are the same, the utility of a loss is frequently not the negative of the utility of the corresponding gain.) The game will then not be zero sum. (An obvious example of this would be playing matching pennies with a $1000 payoff.) Of course, if the outcome, z, of a game is always a fairly small amount of money, then the utility functions $U_i(z)$ ($i = 1, 2$) of the two players will tend to be approximately equal to z. The game can then be considered to be approximately zero sum.

The reader may by now be quite discouraged as to the range of applicability of two-person zero-sum games. The reasons for studying them, however, transcend their limited usefulness. In the first place, there is a considerable theory on non-zero-sum games, for which zero-sum games can be considered an introduction. Secondly, the theory of two-person zero-sum games will be seen to apply directly to minimax analysis in strictly statistical settings. The reason the above problems are not encountered in such situations is that one just pretends that the statistician's loss is nature's gain and that nature is intelligent (i.e., out to maximize the loss). The theory of two-person zero-sum games then clearly applies. Of course serious questions can be raised concerning the desirability of so pretending. This issue will be discussed in Section 5.4.

In the remainder of the section it will be *assumed* that the loss is developed from utility considerations. (For problems that are stated in terms of money, this will entail assuming that the utility functions of the players are roughly the identity functions $U_i(z) = z$.) The reason for assuming this (besides the basic desire to accurately represent "value") is that, in game theory, it is of crucial importance to allow randomized strategies, and to evaluate random situations in terms of expected loss. As discussed in Chapter 2, it is precisely when losses are given in terms of utilities that this is justified.

In light of the above assumption, the loss function in a random situation will be *defined* as the expected loss to player II. In other words, if, for given strategies θ and a, the loss to player II is the random quantity Z, then $L(\theta, a) = E_{\theta, a}[Z]$.

EXAMPLE 6. Consider the game of matching pennies, but assume that, after I chooses θ_i, a spy reports the choice to II. Unfortunately, the reliability of the spy (i.e., the probability of his being correct) is only $p > \frac{1}{2}$. The possible strategies for II can be represented by $(1, 1)$, $(1, 2)$, $(2, 1)$, and $(2, 2)$, where (i, j) indicates that II chooses a_i if the spy announces θ_1, and a_j if the spy announces θ_2. (Recall that a strategy, by definition, consists of a complete description of the actions to be taken in light of all possible contingencies.) If, say, I chooses θ_1 and II chooses $(1, 2)$, the expected loss to II is clearly

$$(-1) P(\text{spy says } \theta_1) + (1) P(\text{spy says } \theta_2) = -p + (1 - p) = 1 - 2p.$$

Similarly, the entire loss matrix can be calculated to be

	$(1, 1)$	$(1, 2)$	$(2, 1)$	$(2, 2)$
θ_1	-1	$1 - 2p$	$2p - 1$	1
θ_2	1	$1 - 2p$	$2p - 1$	-1

.

EXAMPLE 7. Ann arrives home from work at a random time between 4 and 5. She always goes out to dinner at 5. Mark and Jim are dating Ann, and would each like to take her to dinner. They must call her at home, before she leaves, in order to arrange to meet her for dinner. Unfortunately, they each have only one coin for a phone call. Whoever calls first, while Ann is at home, will get the dinner date. The utility function for both Mark and Jim is

U(getting the date) $= 1,$
U(other man getting the date) $= -1,$
U(neither getting the date) $= 0.$

The game will clearly be zero sum, since one man's gain is the other's loss.

Let Mark be player I and Jim be player II, and let θ and a denote the times they choose to call. We can clearly assume that $\Theta = \mathcal{A} = [4, 5]$. Let T denote the time at which Ann arrives home from work. We know that $T \sim \mathcal{U}(4, 5)$. If $T = t$, the utility of (θ, a) to I is

$$U_t(\theta, a) = \begin{cases} 1 & \text{if } t < \theta < a \quad \text{or} \quad a < t < \theta, \\ -1 & \text{if } t < a < \theta \quad \text{or} \quad \theta < t < a, \\ 0 & \text{if } a < t \quad \text{and} \quad \theta < t. \end{cases}$$

The gain to I (or loss to II) is thus

$$L(\theta, a) = E^T[U_T(\theta, a)] = \begin{cases} (1)P(T < \theta) + (-1)P(\theta < T < a) & \text{if } \theta < a, \\ (1)P(a < T < \theta) + (-1)P(T < a) & \text{if } \theta > a, \end{cases}$$

$$= \begin{cases} 2\theta - 4 - a & \text{if } \theta < a, \\ \theta + 4 - 2a & \text{if } \theta > a. \end{cases}$$

III. *Randomized Strategies*

As indicated in Section 1.4, it will be crucial to allow the use of randomized strategies. By a *randomized strategy* will be meant a probability distribution on the strategy space. As in Section 1.4, δ^* will be used to represent a randomized strategy for player II. For player I, a randomized strategy is a probability distribution on Θ, which for consistency we will denote by π. (Note the change in emphasis, however. Player II does not necessarily think that θ is distributed according to π. Instead, π is chosen by, and perhaps known only to, I.)

The loss when randomized strategies are used will again just be expected loss. Thus if I chooses π and II chooses δ^*, define

$$L(\pi, \delta^*) = E^\pi E^{\delta^*} L(\theta, a) = \int_\Theta \int_{\mathcal{A}} L(\theta, a) dF^{\delta^*}(a) dF^\pi(\theta). \tag{5.1}$$

(By Fubini's theorem and the assumption that $L(\theta, a) \geq -K$, it does not matter in which order the expectation is taken.)

As in Section 1.4, a (or θ) are to be identified with $\langle a \rangle$ (or $\langle \theta \rangle$), which are defined to be the probability distributions which choose a (or θ) with probability one. Hence $L(\theta, \delta^*) = E^{\delta^*}[L(\theta, a)]$ and $L(\pi, a) = E^\pi[L(\theta, a)]$. Hopefully no confusion will result from this multiple use of L. Note that, in statistical problems, the quantity $L(\pi, \delta^*)$ has been called $r(\pi, \delta^*)$.

Only randomized strategies with finite loss will be considered. Let $\mathscr{A}^*$ denote the set of all δ^* for which $L(\theta, \delta^*) < \infty$ for all $\theta \in \Theta$, and let Θ^* denote the set of all π for which $L(\pi, a) < \infty$ for all $a \in \mathscr{A}$.

EXAMPLE 2 (continued). For randomized strategies π and δ^*, (5.1) becomes

$$L(\pi, \delta^*) = \sum_{i=1}^{2} \sum_{j=1}^{2} L(\theta_i, a_j)\pi(\theta_i)\delta^*(a_j)$$

$$= (0)\pi(\theta_1)\delta^*(a_1) + (2)\pi(\theta_1)\delta^*(a_2) + (1)\pi(\theta_2)\delta^*(a_1)$$

$$+ (0)\pi(\theta_2)\delta^*(a_2)$$

$$= 2\pi(\theta_1) + \delta^*(a_1) - 3\pi(\theta_1)\delta^*(a_1)$$

(using the facts that $\pi(\theta_2) = 1 - \pi(\theta_1)$ and $\delta^*(a_2) = 1 - \delta^*(a_1)$).

EXAMPLE 4 (continued). Randomized strategies are probability distributions on $[0, 1]$. If $\pi(\theta)$ and $\delta^*(a)$ are probability *densities* on $[0, 1]$, then

$$L(\pi, \delta^*) = \int_0^1 \int_0^1 |\theta - a| \pi(\theta)\delta^*(a)da\, d\theta.$$

IV. *Admissibility and Bayes Strategies*

The concepts of admissible strategies and Bayes strategies will prove useful. A strategy δ_1^* for II is *admissible* if there is no strategy $\delta_2^* \in \mathscr{A}^*$ for which $L(\theta, \delta_2^*) \leq L(\theta, \delta_1^*)$ for all $\theta \in \Theta$, with strict inequality for some θ. A strategy is *inadmissible* if such a δ_2^* exists. The definition of admissible and inadmissible strategies for I is analogous. A strategy δ_1^* for II is *Bayes with respect to* π, if $L(\pi, \delta_1^*) = \inf_{a \in \mathscr{A}} L(\pi, a)$. The quantity $L(\pi) = \inf_{a \in \mathscr{A}} L(\pi, a)$ is called the *Bayes loss* of π. These concepts are all, of course, merely translations into the game-theoretic setting of the corresponding statistical ideas.

EXAMPLE 6 (continued). Since $p > \frac{1}{2}$, the strategy $(2, 1)$ is inadmissible, being dominated by $(1, 2)$. If π is given by $\pi(\theta_1) = \pi(\theta_2) = \frac{1}{2}$, then $L(\pi, \delta^*)$ can be calculated to be

$$L(\pi, \delta^*) = (1 - 2p)\delta^*((1, 2)) + (2p - 1)\delta^*((2, 1)).$$

Furthermore,

$$\inf_{a \in \mathscr{A}} L(\pi, a) = \min\{0, (1 - 2p), (2p - 1), 0\} = 1 - 2p.$$

Since the Bayes strategies with respect to π are those for which $L(\pi, \delta^*)$ $= 1 - 2p$, it is clear that the only Bayes strategy is $\delta^*((1, 2)) = 1$ (i.e., choose $(1, 2)$ with probability one).

V. Optimal Strategies and Value

In choosing a strategy, it will be seen that, in some sense, player II should use the minimax principle. For clarity, we restate the definition of a minimax strategy, as it applies to this setting.

Definition 1. A *minimax strategy* for player II is a (randomized) strategy δ^{*M} which minimizes $\sup_{\theta \in \Theta} L(\theta, \delta^*)$, i.e., a strategy for which

$$\sup_{\theta \in \Theta} L(\theta, \delta^{*M}) = \inf_{\delta^* \in \mathscr{A}^*} \sup_{\theta \in \Theta} L(\theta, \delta^*).$$

The quantity on the right-hand side of the above equation is called the *minimax value* of the game (many call it the *upper value*), and will be denoted $\overline{V}$.

Player I may also desire to act according to the minimax principle. Since L is his gain, however, the goal should be phrased in terms of maximizing the minimum possible gain.

Definition 2. A *maximin strategy* for player I is a (randomized) strategy π^M which maximizes $\inf_{a \in \mathscr{A}} L(\pi, a)$, i.e., a strategy for which

$$\inf_{a \in \mathscr{A}} L(\pi^M, a) = \sup_{\pi \in \Theta^*} \inf_{a \in \mathscr{A}} L(\pi, a).$$

The quantity on the right-hand side of the above equation is called the *maximin value* of the game (many call it the *lower value*), and will be denoted $\underline{V}$.

The following lemma will be needed later, and shows that $\inf_{a \in \mathscr{A}}$ and $\sup_{\theta \in \Theta}$ can be replaced by $\inf_{\delta^* \in \mathscr{A}^*}$ and $\sup_{\pi \in \Theta^*}$ in the above definitions, proving that minimax and maximin strategies also protect against the worst possible randomized strategy of the opponent. The proof of the lemma is left as an exercise.

Lemma 1. For any strategies δ_0^* and π_0,

(a) $\sup_{\pi \in \Theta^*} L(\pi, \delta_0^*) = \sup_{\theta \in \Theta} L(\theta, \delta_0^*)$,
(b) $\inf_{\delta^* \in \mathscr{A}^*} L(\pi_0, \delta^*) = \inf_{a \in \mathscr{A}} L(\pi_0, a)$.

Of considerable interest is the relationship between $\overline{V}$ and $\underline{V}$. The following lemma gives one important fact. The proof is easy and is also left as an exercise.

Lemma 2. $\underline{V} \leq \overline{V}$.

In many games it so happens that $\underline{V} = \overline{V}$. This is so noteworthy that it deserves its own terminology.

Definition 3. If $\underline{V} = \overline{V}$, the game is said to have *value* $V = \underline{V} = \overline{V}$. If, in addition, the players have minimax and maximin strategies, the game is said to be *strictly determined*.

EXAMPLE 1 (continued). In Section 1.5, it was seen that a minimax strategy for the game of matching pennies is $\delta^*(a_1) = \delta^*(a_2) = \frac{1}{2}$, and that $\overline{V} = 0$. By symmetry, it is clear that a maximin strategy for I is $\pi(\theta_1) = \pi(\theta_2) = \frac{1}{2}$, and that $\underline{V} = 0$. The game thus has value $V = 0$ and is strictly determined.

In a strictly determined game, it is, in some sense, irrational for the players to use anything but their minimax (or maximin) strategies, providing they are playing against an intelligent opponent. Consider player II, for example. By using δ^{*M}, his loss will never be *more* than $V (= \overline{V})$. On the other hand, it seems plausible to believe that I will be using his maximin strategy, in which case II's loss can never be *less* than $V (= \underline{V})$. Using δ^{*M} to guarantee at most a loss of V thus seems natural. A nonminimax rule can never gain (and can incur considerable additional loss) if indeed I is using his maximin rule. Player I, by similar reasoning, should decide to use his maximin rule against an intelligent opponent. Note that in a strictly determined game there is no advantage in *knowing* that your opponent will be using a particular minimax or maximin strategy. This, in some sense, explains the phrase "strictly determined." Before the game even begins, the optimal strategies and (expected) outcome can be known.

It will be seen in Subsection 5.2.6 that a wide variety of two-person zero-sum games have values and are strictly determined. In particular, we will explicitly prove that if Θ is finite (and certain technical conditions hold), then the game has a value and is strictly determined. (This is the minimax theorem.)

5.2.2 General Techniques for Solving Games

By *solving* a game, we will mean finding the value and the minimax strategy. (The maximin strategy may also be of interest, though we tend to identify with player II.) Occasionally, it will be possible to explicitly solve a game by directly calculating the maximin and minimax strategies. Some situations in which this can be done are mentioned first.

I. *The Direct Method of Solving Games*

It is sometimes possible to find a minimax or maximin strategy directly from the definitions. To find a minimax strategy, for example, one can attempt to calculate the function $\overline{L}(\delta^*) = \sup_\theta L(\theta, \delta^*)$, and try to directly minimize it over all $\delta^* \in \mathscr{A}^*$. Usually this is a hopeless task, but in some interesting problems it can be done. The problems in which this approach will prove useful are certain statistical problems of Section 5.3 in which, by elimination of inadmissible strategies, the set $\mathscr{A}^*$ can be reduced to a low-dimensional space. If $\bar{L}(\delta^*)$ is not too complicated, the minimization can then be carried out.

Likewise, it will sometimes be possible to directly calculate $\underline{L}(\pi)$ (the Bayes loss of π), and maximize it over all $\pi \in \Theta^*$. Even if this can be done, however, one is still left with the problem of finding a minimax strategy. The following theorem can prove helpful in this regard. The proof of the theorem follows directly from the definitions, and is left as an exercise.

Theorem 1. *Assume that π^M is a maximin strategy for* I *and that the game has a value. Then any minimax strategy is a Bayes strategy with respect to π^M.*

In most games, the brute force approach described above will prove to be too difficult. Unfortunately, there is, in general, no other deterministic technique known for solving games. (Certain deterministic techniques are known for special cases, however, such as that discussed in the next subsection.)

The most useful general method for solving games is to try and guess a solution. This method will be discussed in the remainder of the subsection. The first problem which must be dealt with is that of determining whether a guessed optimal strategy really is minimax or maximin.

II. *Verification of Minimaxity*

The following theorem provides the basic tool for verifying minimaxity.

Theorem 2. *Let π_0 and δ_0^* be strategies for* I *and* II *respectively, and assume that for all $\theta \in \Theta$ and $a \in \mathscr{A}$,*

$$L(\theta, \delta_0^*) \leq L(\pi_0, a). \tag{5.2}$$

Then the game has value $V = L(\pi_0, \delta_0^*)$ and is strictly determined, with π_0 and δ_0^* being maximin and minimax strategies.

PROOF. It is clear that

$$\bar{V} = \inf_{\delta^*} \sup_{\theta} L(\theta, \delta^*) \leq \sup_{\theta} L(\theta, \delta_0^*),$$

and

$$\inf_a L(\pi_0, a) \leq \sup_{\pi} \inf_a L(\pi, a) = \underline{V}.$$

Together with (5.2), these inequalities show that

$$\bar{V} \leq \sup_{\theta} L(\theta, \delta_0^*) \leq \inf_a L(\pi_0, a) \leq \underline{V}.$$

By Lemma 2, $\underline{V} \leq \overline{V}$, implying that

$$\overline{V} = \sup_{\theta} L(\theta, \delta_0^*) = \inf_{a} L(\pi_0, a) = \underline{V}. \tag{5.3}$$

It follows, by definition, that the game has value $V = \underline{V} = \overline{V}$, and that δ_0^* and π_0 are minimax and maximin strategies.

To prove that $L(\pi_0, \delta_0^*) = V$, note that

$$\inf_{\delta^*} L(\pi_0, \delta^*) \leq L(\pi_0, \delta_0^*) \leq \sup_{\pi} L(\pi, \delta_0^*).$$

Together with Lemma 1 and (5.3), this gives the desired result.   □

EXAMPLE 8. Consider a game with the following loss matrix. Appended to the table are the row minima and column maxima.

	a_1	a_2	a_3	a_4	$\inf_a L(\theta_i, a)$
θ_1	7	2	5	1	1
θ_2	2	2	3	4	2
θ_3	5	3	4	4	3
θ_4	3	2	1	6	1
$\sup_\theta L(\theta, a_i)$	7	3	5	6	

It is clear that θ_3 and a_2 are best among nonrandomized strategies, according to the maximin and minimax principles respectively. Furthermore, since

$$L(\theta, a_2) \leq L(\theta_3, a)$$

for all θ and a, Theorem 2 implies that θ_3 and a_2 are maximin and minimax among all strategies, and that the game has value $V = L(\theta_3, a_2) = 3$. (It was rather lucky to find nonrandomized strategies that are minimax and maximin.)

The following theorem is a useful generalization of Theorem 2. Its proof is similar and will be left as an exercise.

Theorem 3

(a) *Let $\{\pi_n\}$ and δ_0^* be strategies such that*

$$\sup_{\theta} L(\theta, \delta_0^*) \leq \lim_{n \to \infty} \inf_{a} L(\pi_n, a).$$

Then the game has a value and δ_0^* is a minimax strategy for II.

(b) *Let π_0 and $\{\delta_n^*\}$ be strategies such that*

$$\limsup_{n \to \infty} \sup_\theta L(\theta, \delta_n^*) \le \inf_a L(\pi_0, a).$$

Then the game has a value and π_0 is a maximin strategy for I.

III. The Guess Method of Solving Games

The main methods of guessing solutions are based on the following theorem.

Theorem 4. *Assume the game has a value V, and that π^M and δ^{*M} are maximin and minimax strategies. Define*

$$\Theta_V = \{\theta \in \Theta : L(\theta, \delta^{*M}) = V\},$$

and

$$\mathscr{A}_V = \{a \in \mathscr{A} : L(\pi^M, a) = V\}.$$

Then $\pi^M(\Theta_V) = 1$ and $\delta^{*M}(\mathscr{A}_V) = 1$.

PROOF. We prove only that $\pi^M(\Theta_V) = 1$. The proof that $\delta^{*M}(\mathscr{A}_V) = 1$ is identical.

Since π^M and δ^{*M} are maximin and minimax strategies and the game has value V, it can be shown, as in Theorem 2, that $L(\pi^M, \delta^{*M}) = V$. Hence

$$0 = V - L(\pi^M, \delta^{*M}) = E^{\pi^M}[V - L(\theta, \delta^{*M})]$$

$$= \int_{\Theta_V^c} [V - L(\theta, \delta^{*M})] dF^{\pi^M}(\theta). \tag{5.4}$$

Since δ^{*M} is minimax, we know that $L(\theta, \delta^{*M}) \le V$ for all $\theta \in \Theta$. By the definition of Θ_V, it follows that $V - L(\theta, \delta^{*M}) > 0$ for $\theta \in \Theta_V^c$. Together with (5.4), this implies that $\pi^M(\Theta_V^c) = 0$, giving the desired conclusion. □

The implications of this theorem are twofold. First, it shows that, if either π^M or δ^{*M} can be guessed, then to find the other optimum strategy (needed for the verification of the solution through Theorem 1) it suffices to look at randomized strategies on Θ_V or $\mathscr{A}_V$. This is frequently a considerable simplification. (Note that any randomized strategy on $\mathscr{A}_V$ is Bayes with respect to π^M. Theorem 4 can thus be considered a more explicit version of Theorem 1.)

The second implication of Theorem 4 is that minimax or maximin strategies will often have constant loss, namely when $\Theta_V = \Theta$ or $\mathscr{A}_V = \mathscr{A}$. This concept is of enough importance to deserve its own name.

Definition 4. A strategy π_0 is an *equalizer strategy* for I if $L(\pi_0, a) = C$ (some constant) for all $a \in \mathscr{A}$. A strategy δ_0^* is an *equalizer strategy* for II if $L(\theta, \delta_0^*) = C'$ (some constant) for all $\theta \in \Theta$.

Theorem 4 thus suggests that an equalizer strategy might be a good guess for a minimax or maximin strategy. The guess method of solving games can now be stated as follows.

Step 1. Eliminate from the game as many inadmissible strategies as possible. (This is always the way to begin any method of solution.)

Step 2. Guess either π^M or δ^{*M}. If no obvious guess is available, look for an equalizer strategy.

Step 3. If δ^* is the guess from Step 2, calculate $\hat{V} = \sup_\theta L(\theta, \delta^*)$. If π is the guess, calculate $\hat{V} = \inf_a L(\pi, a)$.

Step 4. Determine $\Theta_{\hat{V}}$ or $\mathscr{A}_{\hat{V}}$ (depending on whether δ^* or π was guessed), and examine randomized strategies on this set to obtain a guess for the remaining optimum strategy. Again, looking for an equalizer strategy on the set may prove helpful.

Step 5. Use Theorem 2 to determine if the guesses for π^M and δ^{*M} are indeed maximin and minimax.

Sometimes Step 4 will fail because the reasonable guess for the other optimal strategy is not a proper strategy (i.e., is not a proper probability distribution). In such cases, however, a sequence of strategies can often be found which converge, in some sense, to the improper strategy. Theorem 3 can be used, in such situations, to draw the desired conclusions. Examples of this will be seen in Section 5.3. We now give some examples of application of the basic guess method.

EXAMPLE 4 (continued). The loss is $L(\theta, a) = |\theta - a|$. Note that, for $a \in [0, 1]$,

$$\sup_{\theta \in [0, 1]} |\theta - a| = \max\{a, 1 - a\}.$$

Since

$$\inf_{a \in [0, 1]} \sup_{\theta \in [0, 1]} |\theta - a| = \inf_{a \in [0, 1]} \max\{a, 1 - a\} = \tfrac{1}{2},$$

the minimum being attained at $a_0 = \tfrac{1}{2}$, reasonable guesses for the minimax strategy and the value are a_0 and $\tfrac{1}{2}$. (It is hard to see how a randomized strategy could help II.)

Observe next that

$$\Theta_{1/2} = \{\theta \in [0, 1]: L(\theta, a_0) = |\theta - \tfrac{1}{2}| = \tfrac{1}{2}\} = \{0, 1\}.$$

Thus the guess for π^M should give probability one to this set. The obvious choice is

$$\pi_0 = \tfrac{1}{2}\langle 0 \rangle + \tfrac{1}{2}\langle 1 \rangle$$

(i.e., the probability distribution which gives probability $\tfrac{1}{2}$ to each $\theta = 0$ and $\theta = 1$).

It remains only to verify, by Theorem 2, that a_0 and π_0 are indeed minimax and maximin. For all $a \in [0, 1]$,

$$L(\pi_0, a) = \tfrac{1}{2}L(0, a) + \tfrac{1}{2}L(1, a) = \tfrac{1}{2}a + \tfrac{1}{2}(1 - a) = \tfrac{1}{2}.$$

Since $L(0, a_0) \le \tfrac{1}{2}$, it follows that the condition of Theorem 2 is satisfied. Therefore, π_0 is maximin, a_0 is minimax, and the value is $V = \tfrac{1}{2}$.

EXAMPLE 6 (continued). It has already been observed that the strategy $(2, 1)$ for II is inadmissible. Eliminating this strategy gives the reduced game

	(1, 1)	(1, 2)	(2, 2)
θ_1	-1	$1 - 2p$	1
θ_2	1	$1 - 2p$	-1

Equalizer strategies could be calculated, but symmetry suggests that the maximin strategy for I might be

$$\pi_0 = \tfrac{1}{2}\langle\theta_1\rangle + \tfrac{1}{2}\langle\theta_2\rangle.$$

It was earlier calculated that $\inf_a L(\pi_0, a) = 1 - 2p$, and that $\Theta_{1-2p} = \{(1, 2)\}$. Since $L(\theta, (1, 2)) = 1 - 2p$ for both θ_1 and θ_2, we can conclude from Theorem 2 that π_0 is maximin, $(1, 2)$ is minimax, and $1 - 2p$ is the value.

EXAMPLE 7 (continued). There is no obvious maximin or minimax strategy. Hence, let us look for an equalizer strategy. It is clear that it will be necessary to consider randomized strategies. (The opponent could easily beat a non-randomized strategy.) Hence consider densities $\pi(\theta)$ and $\delta^*(a)$ on $\Theta = \mathscr{A} = [4, 5]$. By symmetry, both optimal strategies should be the same (and the value should be zero), so we confine our attention to finding an equalizer strategy π for I.

Note first that

$$L(\pi, a) = \int_4^5 L(\theta, a)\pi(\theta)d\theta$$

$$= \int_4^a [2\theta - 4 - a]\pi(\theta)d\theta + \int_a^5 [\theta + 4 - 2a]\pi(\theta)d\theta.$$

If this is to be an equalizer strategy, $L(\pi, a)$ must be constant for $a \in [4, 5]$, so that the derivative of L must be zero. Clearly

$$\frac{d}{da} L(\pi, a) = [2a - 4 - a]\pi(a) - \int_4^a \pi(\theta)d\theta$$

$$- [a + 4 - 2a]\pi(a) - 2\int_a^5 \pi(\theta)d\theta$$

$$= [2a - 8]\pi(a) - \int_4^a \pi(\theta)d\theta - 2\int_a^5 \pi(\theta)d\theta.$$

This is still rather complicated, so consider the second derivative, which must also be zero. Calculation gives (letting π' denote the derivative of π)

$$\frac{d^2}{da^2} L(\pi, a) = \pi(a) \left[3 + (2a - 8) \frac{\pi'(a)}{\pi(a)} \right]$$

$$= \pi(a) \left[3 + (2a - 8) \frac{d}{da} (\log \pi(a)) \right].$$

Setting equal to zero and solving gives that

$$\frac{d}{da} \log \pi(a) = \frac{-3}{2a - 8}.$$

Integrating gives

$$\log \pi(a) = c + -\tfrac{3}{2} \log(2a - 8),$$

or $\pi(a) = K(2a - 8)^{-3/2}$. Unfortunately, $\int_4^5 (2a - 8)^{-3/2} \, da = \infty$, so this can not be normalized to give a proper density. Rather than giving up, however, it seems reasonable to try and modify the density to eliminate the offending portion. This suggests considering (for $4 < \alpha < 5$)

$$\pi_\alpha(\theta) = \begin{cases} K_\alpha (2\theta - 8)^{-3/2} & \text{if } \alpha \le \theta \le 5, \\ 0 & \text{if } \theta < \alpha. \end{cases}$$

A calculation shows that the proper normalizing constant is $K_\alpha = \{(2\alpha - 8)^{-1/2} - 2^{-1/2}\}^{-1}$. Further calculation gives

$$L(\pi_\alpha, a) = \begin{cases} 8 + (\alpha - 4)^{1/2} - 2a & \text{if } a \le \alpha, \\ [(\alpha - 4)^{-1/2} - 1]^{-1}\{a[2 - (\alpha - 4)^{-1/2}] - 7 \\ \qquad + 4(\alpha - 4)^{-1/2} - 2(\alpha - 4)^{1/2}\} & \text{if } a \ge \alpha. \end{cases}$$

Choosing $\alpha = \tfrac{17}{4}$ gives

$$L(\pi_{17/4}, a) = \begin{cases} \tfrac{17}{2} - 2a & \text{if } a \le \tfrac{17}{4}, \\ 0 & \text{if } a \ge \tfrac{17}{4}. \end{cases}$$

Clearly $L(\pi_{17/4}, a) \ge 0$. (Note that $\pi_{17/4}$ is an equalizer strategy for $a \ge \tfrac{17}{4}$, with larger gain for $a < \tfrac{17}{4}$.)

By symmetry, we try, as our guess for δ^{*M},

$$\delta^*_{17/4}(a) = \begin{cases} K_{17/4}(2a - 8)^{-3/2} & \text{if } \tfrac{17}{4} \le a \le 5, \\ 0 & \text{if } a < \tfrac{17}{4}. \end{cases}$$

Also by symmetry, $L(\theta, \delta^*_{17/4}) \le 0$ for $4 \le \theta \le 5$. Hence we can conclude from Theorem 2 that $\pi_{17/4}$ and $\delta^*_{17/4}$ are maximin and minimax strategies, and that the value of the game is zero.

The methods of solving games that have been discussed in this subsection are by no means foolproof. If direct calculation fails, if δ^{*M} or π^M

cannot be guessed, or if equalizer strategies cannot be found or are not solutions, then we are out of luck. The next subsection discusses an important special case of game theory in which an explicit solution can always be obtained.

5.2.3 Finite Games

A *finite game* is a (two-person zero-sum) game in which the sets of (non-randomized) strategies, Θ and $\mathscr{A}$, are finite. Finite games are important in game theory, since, in many games, each player will have only a finite set of options available to him. They are less important in statistical games, however, since the set of strategies available to the statistician will be the set of all decision rules, which is rarely finite.

It will be shown in Subsection 5.2.6 that all finite games have values and are strictly determined. Of even greater interest is that explicit procedures exist for solving finite games. One such procedure will be presented in this subsection.

Assume $\Theta = \{\theta_1, \theta_2, \ldots, \theta_m\}$ and $\mathscr{A} = \{a_1, a_2, \ldots, a_n\}$. The loss function can then be represented by the $(m \times n)$ loss matrix $\mathbf{L}$, whose elements are $l_{ij} = L(\theta_i, a_j)$. We will identify randomized strategies π and δ^* with probability vectors

$$\pi = (\pi_1, \pi_2, \ldots, \pi_m)^t \quad \text{and} \quad \delta^* = (\delta_1^*, \delta_2^*, \ldots, \delta_n^*)^t,$$

where $\pi_i = \pi(\theta_i)$ and $\delta_i^* = \delta^*(a_i)$.

The following theorem provides a starting point for the investigation of finite games. It is valid for all games, but is mainly useful in solving finite games.

Theorem 5. *If both* I *and* II *have equalizer strategies, then the game has a value and the equalizer strategies are maximin and minimax strategies.*

PROOF. If π and δ^* are the equalizer strategies, then $L(\theta, \delta^*) = K_1$ for all $\theta \in \Theta$ and $L(\pi, a) = K_2$ for all $a \in \mathscr{A}$. But clearly

$$L(\pi, \delta^*) = E^\pi L(\theta, \delta^*) = E^\pi K_1 = K_1$$

and

$$L(\pi, \delta^*) = E^{\delta^*} L(\pi, a) = E^{\delta^*} K_2 = K_2.$$

Hence $K_1 = K_2$ and Theorem 2 gives the desired result. $\qquad\square$

Definition 5. If, in a finite game, π and δ^* are equalizer strategies for I and II, then the pair (π, δ^*) is called a *simple solution* of the game.

As a first step in solving finite games, the problem of finding simple solutions (for those games that have them) must be addressed.

I. *Finding a Simple Solution*

Assume that $m = n$, and that $\mathbf{L}$ is a nonsingular matrix. We search for strategies $\boldsymbol{\pi}$ and $\boldsymbol{\delta}^*$ such that $L(\boldsymbol{\pi}, a) = L(\theta, \boldsymbol{\delta}^*) = K$ for all $\theta \in \Theta$ and $a \in \mathscr{A}$. Note that

$$L(\boldsymbol{\pi}, a_j) = \sum_{i=1}^m \pi_i L(\theta_i, a_j) = \sum_{i=1}^m \pi_i l_{ij}.$$

Hence if $L(\boldsymbol{\pi}, a_j) = K$ for $j = 1, \ldots, m$, then

$$\boldsymbol{\pi}^t \mathbf{L} = K\mathbf{1},$$

where $\mathbf{1}$ is the row vector of all ones. Similarly, if $L(\theta_i, \boldsymbol{\delta}^*) = K$ for $i = 1, \ldots, m$, then

$$\mathbf{L}\boldsymbol{\delta}^* = K\mathbf{1}^t.$$

Since $\mathbf{L}$ is nonsingular, solutions to these equations must be of the form

$$\boldsymbol{\pi} = K(\mathbf{L}^{-1})^t\mathbf{1}^t \quad \text{and} \quad \boldsymbol{\delta}^* = K\mathbf{L}^{-1}\mathbf{1}^t. \tag{5.5}$$

Since $\boldsymbol{\pi}$ and $\boldsymbol{\delta}^*$ must be probability vectors, it is clear that the following condition must be satisfied.

Condition 1. *The components of* $(\mathbf{L}^{-1})^t\mathbf{1}^t$ *and* $\mathbf{L}^{-1}\mathbf{1}^t$ *(i.e., the row and column sums of* $\mathbf{L}^{-1}$*) must all have the same sign.*

If Condition 1 holds, the components of $\boldsymbol{\pi}$ (and also the components of $\boldsymbol{\delta}^*$) will sum to one if $K = 1/(\mathbf{1}\mathbf{L}^{-1}\mathbf{1}^t)$. This analysis is summarized as

Theorem 6. *If* $\mathbf{L}$ *is an* $(m \times m)$ *nonsingular matrix satisfying Condition 1, then a simple solution to the game is given by* $(\boldsymbol{\pi}, \boldsymbol{\delta}^*)$, *where*

$$\boldsymbol{\pi} = (\mathbf{L}^{-1})^t\mathbf{1}^t/(\mathbf{1}\mathbf{L}^{-1}\mathbf{1}^t) \quad \text{and} \quad \boldsymbol{\delta}^* = \mathbf{L}^{-1}\mathbf{1}^t/(\mathbf{1}\mathbf{L}^{-1}\mathbf{1}^t).$$

Furthermore, if Condition 1 is violated, there is no simple solution.

EXAMPLE 9. Assume $\mathbf{L}$ is

	a_1	a_2	a_3
θ_1	6	0	6
θ_2	8	-2	0
θ_3	4	6	5

A calculation shows that

$$\mathbf{L}^{-1} = \frac{1}{276} \begin{pmatrix} -10 & 36 & 12 \\ -40 & 6 & 48 \\ 56 & -36 & -12 \end{pmatrix}.$$

It is clear that the row and column sums of $\mathbf{L}^{-1}$ are all positive, so that Condition 1 is satisfied. A simple calculation using Theorem 6 then gives that a simple solution to the game is

$$\pi = \left(\frac{1}{10}, \frac{1}{10}, \frac{8}{10}\right)^t \quad \text{and} \quad \delta^* = \left(\frac{19}{30}, \frac{7}{30}, \frac{4}{30}\right)^t.$$

II. *Solving Finite Games*

A simple solution to a finite game may not exist. If such is the case, however, there will exist simple solutions of *subgames* that are solutions for the original game. Indeed the following procedure will locate all minimax and maximin solutions to the game.

Step 1. Ensure that the value of the game is nonzero. If by no other method, this can be achieved by adding a fixed constant to each element of $\mathbf{L}$ to make all elements positive. (Recall that adding a constant to the loss function does not affect the solutions.)

Step 2. Using Condition 1, find all nonsingular square submatrices of $\mathbf{L}$ which have simple solutions. Calculate these simple solutions, using Theorem 6.

Step 3. Write the simple solutions found in step 2 as vectors in the original game, by filling in zeroes in the coordinates corresponding to the strategies deleted to arrive at the subgames. Then check, using Theorem 2, whether or not these vectors are maximin and minimax in the original game.

Step 4. Form the convex hulls of the minimax vectors and maximin vectors found in step 3. These consist of all minimax and maximin strategies.

We will not prove here that the above procedure works. The interested reader can find such a proof in Blackwell and Girshick (1954) (see Theorem 2.7.3).

Several observations should be made about the above procedure. First, at all stages of the investigation inadmissible strategies should be eliminated. (A game or subgame having an inadmissible strategy can not have a simple solution.) Second, frequently only one minimax strategy is wanted. If this is the case, it is usually easiest to begin by checking for nonrandomized minimax and maximin strategies, as in Example 8. (This corresponds to looking at the (1×1) subgames, using the above procedure.) If this fails, it is probably best to next see if a simple solution exists for the entire game (or for one of the largest square subgames). If this also fails to yield a solution, it is necessary to just start checking all the square subgames. In one sense, it is best to start with the (2×2) subgames, and work your way up. The advantage of this is that the calculation of inverses, made at each stage, can be useful at the next stage. Let us look at some examples.

EXAMPLE 10. Assume **L** is

	a_1	a_2	a_3	a_4	a_5
θ_1	3	5	-2	2	1
θ_2	3	6	-1	2	4
θ_3	4	3	6	7	8

.

We first note that θ_1 is inadmissible, being dominated by θ_2. Hence we can eliminate θ_1, reducing the game to

	a_1	a_2	a_3	a_4	a_5
θ_2	3	6	-1	2	4
θ_3	4	3	6	7	8

.

In this reduced game, a_4 and a_5 are inadmissible, being dominated by a_3. (Aren't we lucky though?) This leaves us with

	a_1	a_2	a_3
θ_2	3	6	-1
θ_3	4	3	6

.

Next we check to see if a pair of nonrandomized strategies might happen to work. The row minima and column maxima are

3	6	-1	-1
4	3	6	3
4	6	6	

.

Thus, the best nonrandomized strategy for II is a_1, and $L(\theta, a_1) \leq 4$, but the best nonrandomized strategy for I is θ_2, and $L(\theta_2, a) \geq 3$. Alas, Theorem 2 does not apply, so we have to look at the (2×2) subgames.

The (2×2) subgame

	a_1	a_2
θ_2	3	6
θ_3	4	3

can be checked to have the simple solution

$$\pi = \left(\frac{1}{4}, \frac{3}{4}\right)^t \quad \text{and} \quad \delta^* = \left(\frac{3}{4}, \frac{1}{4}\right)^t.$$

This corresponds in the original (reduced) game to

$$\pi = \left(\frac{1}{4}, \frac{3}{4}\right)^t \quad \text{and} \quad \delta^* = \left(\frac{3}{4}, \frac{1}{4}, 0\right)^t.$$

To see if this is a solution, note that $L(\pi, a_1) = \frac{1}{4}(3) + \frac{3}{4}(4) = \frac{15}{4}$, $L(\pi, a_2) = \frac{15}{4}$, $L(\pi, a_3) = \frac{17}{4}$, $L(\theta_2, \delta^*) = \frac{15}{4}$, and $L(\theta_3, \delta^*) = \frac{15}{4}$. Since $L(\theta, \delta^*) \leq L(\pi, a)$, Theorem 2 gives that it is indeed a solution. The other two (2×2) subgames have solutions which are not solutions to the original (reduced) game. There is thus only one minimax and one maximin strategy. In the original (nonreduced) game, these strategies are

$$\pi = \left(0, \frac{1}{4}, \frac{3}{4}\right)^t \quad \text{and} \quad \delta^* = \left(\frac{3}{4}, \frac{1}{4}, 0, 0\right)^t.$$

In the above example, we did not worry about step 1 of the procedure, namely ensuring that the game had a nonzero value. It turned out, of course, to have value $\frac{15}{4}$, so that all was well. If, say, a computer program was to be used to implement the procedure, it would undoubtedly be beneficial to always incorporate step 1. When solving games by hand, however, there are often reasons to ignore the step. The following example demonstrates this.

EXAMPLE 3 (continued). From the symmetry of the game, it is clear that the value will be zero, so there is a temptation to add, say, 1 to each entry, and proceed with the calculation. Of course, we then have a (4×4) matrix, sixteen (3×3) matrices, thirty-four (2×2) matrices, and the nonrandomized strategies to check. Clearly some inspiration is needed instead, and looking at all those zeros in the original matrix (with zero being the value of the game) provides some. If we just concentrate on the nonzero entries, two (2×2) subgames stand out, namely

	(1, 1)	(2, 2)
(1, 2)	5	-7
(2, 1)	-5	7

and

	(1, 2)	(2, 1)
(1, 1)	-5	5
(2, 2)	7	-7

.

Let us solve the first of these. There is no nonrandomized solution, so we must find a simple solution. Since $|\mathbf{L}| = 35 - 35 = 0$, we must first add, say, 1 to each element of the matrix, before applying Theorem 6. The simple solution can then be calculated to be

$$\pi = \left(\frac{1}{2}, \frac{1}{2}\right)^t \quad \text{and} \quad \delta^* = \left(\frac{7}{12}, \frac{5}{12}\right)^t.$$

In the original problem, this corresponds to

$$\pi^1 = \left(0, \frac{1}{2}, \frac{1}{2}, 0\right)^t \quad \text{and} \quad \delta^{*1} = \left(\frac{7}{12}, 0, 0, \frac{5}{12}\right)^t,$$

which can easily be checked to be maximin and minimax.

The second subgame is really just the first subgame with the roles of I and II reversed. Hence it will give rise to the maximin and minimax solutions

$$\pi^2 = \left(\frac{7}{12}, 0, 0, \frac{5}{12}\right)^t \quad \text{and} \quad \delta^{*2} = \left(0, \frac{1}{2}, \frac{1}{2}, 0\right)^t$$

in the original game.

Finally, any convex combination of these two maximin or two minimax strategies will also be maximin or minimax. Hence any strategy of the form

$$\left(\frac{7}{12}(1 - \alpha), \frac{1}{2}\alpha, \frac{1}{2}\alpha, \frac{5}{12}(1 - \alpha)\right)^t$$

is minimax or maximin for $0 \le \alpha \le 1$. Of course, there may be other maximin or minimax strategies, but these should be enough.

There are other methods of solving finite games based on linear programming methods. Of particular note is the simplex method, which is actually a more commonly used method of solving large games than the method discussed here. Unfortunately, the simplex method requires considerably more mathematical development.

For further discussion and examples of finite games the reader is referred to the delightfully amusing book *The Compleat Strategyst* by Williams (1954).

5.2.4 Games with Finite Θ

Assume $\Theta = \{\theta_1, \theta_2, \ldots, \theta_m\}$. The game can then be reformulated geometrically, so that geometric techniques can be brought to bear in obtaining a solution. As a method of solving games, this geometric approach is generally less useful than the approaches discussed in the two previous subsections. Theoretically, however, the approach is of great interest, since minimax theorems (i.e., theorems which state that the game has a value and that minimax rules exist) can be easily developed through geometric arguments. This subsection discusses the reformulation rather informally, leaving the explicit minimax theorems for the next two subsections.

I. *Reformulation as an S-Game*

The key to the reformulation is to transform the (perhaps complicated) set of all possible randomized strategies for player II into a simple geometric set in R^m.

Definition 6. For each randomized strategy $\delta^* \in \mathscr{A}^*$, let

$$R_i(\delta^*) = L(\theta_i, \delta^*),$$

and define

$$\mathbf{R}(\delta^*) = (R_1(\delta^*), R_2(\delta^*), \ldots, R_m(\delta^*))^t.$$

The point $\mathbf{R}(\delta^*)$ in m-dimensional Euclidean space is called the *risk point* of δ^*. The set

$$S = \{\mathbf{R}(\delta^*): \delta^* \in \mathscr{A}^*\}$$

is called the *risk set* of the game. Also, define $S_\mathscr{A}$ as the set of all risk points $\mathbf{R}(a)$ corresponding to nonrandomized actions $a \in \mathscr{A}$.

The following lemma shows that the risk set is convex, and indicates how it can be determined.

Lemma 3. *The risk set S is the convex hull (see Section 1.8) of $S_\mathscr{A}$.*

PROOF. Consider a randomized strategy $\delta^* \in \mathscr{A}^*$. Since $L(\theta_i, \delta^*) = E^{\delta^*} L(\theta_i, a)$, it is clear that

$$\mathbf{R}(\delta^*) = (E^{\delta^*} L(\theta_1, a), \ldots, E^{\delta^*} L(\theta_m, a))^t = E^{\delta^*} \mathbf{R}(a),$$

the expectation being taken componentwise. Choosing δ^* to be a randomized strategy of the form

$$\delta^* = \sum_{i=1}^{\infty} p_i \langle a_i \rangle,$$

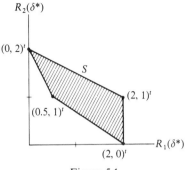

Figure 5.1

where $0 \le p_i \le 1$, $\sum_{i=1}^{\infty} p_i = 1$, and $a_i \in \mathcal{A}$, it follows that

$$\mathbf{R}(\delta^*) = \sum_{i=1}^{\infty} p_i \mathbf{R}(a_i).$$

From Definition 16 of Section 1.8, it follows that the convex hull of $S_{\mathcal{A}}$ is a subset of S.

Consider now any randomized strategy $\delta^* \in \mathcal{A}^*$, and let $\mathbf{X} = \mathbf{R}(a)$ be a random vector with the distribution induced by δ^*. Since δ^* has finite loss (by the definition of $\mathcal{A}^*$) and $\mathbf{X} = \mathbf{R}(a)$ is in the convex hull of $S_{\mathcal{A}}$, it follows from Lemma 2 of Section 1.8 that $E[\mathbf{X}] = E^{\delta^*}[\mathbf{R}(a)] = \mathbf{R}(\delta^*)$ is in the convex hull of $S_{\mathcal{A}}$. Thus S is a subset of the convex hull of $S_{\mathcal{A}}$. The conclusion follows.   □

EXAMPLE 11. Assume the loss matrix for a two-person zero-sum game is

	a_1	a_2	a_3	a_4
θ_1	2	2	0	0.5
θ_2	0	1	2	1

Since $\mathcal{A}$ consists of a_1, a_2, a_3, and a_4, the set $S_{\mathcal{A}}$ consists of the four points $(2, 0)^t$, $(2, 1)^t$, $(0, 2)^t$, and $(0.5, 1)^t$. Graphing these and forming their convex hull gives the risk set S shown in Figure 5.1.

To complete the geometric reformulation of the game, geometric meanings must be given to the strategies of I and to the loss. Nonrandomized strategies for I are easy. They correspond simply to the choice of a coordinate of the risk point. In other words, saying that I chooses strategy θ_i is equivalent (from the viewpoint of loss) to saying that I chooses the ith coordinate of any risk point. As in the previous subsection, a randomized strategy for I can be thought of as a probability vector

$$\pi = (\pi_1, \pi_2, \ldots, \pi_m)^t,$$

where π_i is the probability of choosing coordinate i (or the probability of choosing θ_i). The set of all such probability vectors will be denoted Ω_m, and is called the *simplex* in R^m.

The loss incurred if II chooses strategy δ^* and I chooses strategy π is clearly

$$L(\pi, \delta^*) = \sum_{i=1}^{m} \pi_i L(\theta_i, \delta^*) = \pi^t \mathbf{R}(\delta^*).$$

This completes the geometric description of the game. Instead of considering Θ^*, $\mathscr{A}^*$, and L, it suffices to deal with S, Ω_m, and $L^*(\pi, \mathbf{s}) = \pi^t \mathbf{s}$, with the interpretation that II chooses a point $\mathbf{s} = (s_1, \ldots, s_m)^t \in S$ (i.e., some $\mathbf{R}(\delta^*)$), I chooses $\pi \in \Omega_m$, and the loss (to II) is then $L^*(\pi, \mathbf{s}) = \pi^t \mathbf{s}$. (Note that $\pi^t \mathbf{s}$ is just the dot product of the vectors π and $\mathbf{s}$.)

Part of the simplicity of the above geometric formulation of the game is that only S need be specified to define the game. The other elements, Ω_m and $L^*(\pi, \mathbf{s}) = \pi^t \mathbf{s}$, are automatically associated with the game. Such a geometric game is, therefore, simply called an *S-game*.

It will be seen in the next subsection that S-games are usually strictly determined. The remainder of this subsection is devoted to geometric techniques of actually solving such games. The techniques discussed will also form the basis of the theoretical arguments of the next subsection.

II. *Finding Minimax Strategies in S-games*

From the definition of a minimax strategy (and Lemma 1), it is clear that a minimax strategy in an S-game is a point $\mathbf{s}^M \in S$ such that

$$\sup_{\pi \in \Omega_m} \pi^t \mathbf{s}^M = \max_i s_i^M = \inf_{\mathbf{s} \in S} \max_i s_i = \inf_{\mathbf{s} \in S} \sup_{\pi \in \Omega_m} \pi^t \mathbf{s}. \qquad (5.6)$$

In an S-game, we will call a minimax strategy a *minimax risk point*. In locating a minimax risk point, the concept of a lower quantant proves useful.

Definition 7. The α-*lower quantant in R^m*, to be denoted Q_α, is the set

$$Q_\alpha = \{\mathbf{z} = (z_1, \ldots, z_m)^t \in R^m : z_i \leq \alpha \quad \text{for } i = 1, \ldots, m\}.$$

The *corner* of Q_α is the point $(\alpha, \alpha, \ldots, \alpha)^t$. (The set Q_α is thus the set of points whose maximum coordinate is less than or equal to α.)

EXAMPLE 12. For $m = 2$ and $\alpha > 0$, Q_α is the shaded region in Figure 5.2.

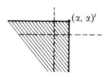

Figure 5.2

Definition 8. If S is the risk set of an S-game, define $S_\alpha = S \cap Q_\alpha$.

Note that S_α contains those points in S whose maximum coordinate is less than or equal to α. Therefore, if we can find a smallest α for which Q_α intersects S, line (5.6) implies that we will have found minimax risk points. The following theorem makes this precise. The proof is left as an exercise.

Theorem 7. *Let*

$$\alpha_M = \inf\{\alpha: S_\alpha \text{ is not empty}\}.$$

If $\alpha_M > -\infty$ and S_{α_M} is nonempty, then S_{α_M} consists of all minimax risk points in S.

EXAMPLE 11 (continued). The risk set is reproduced in Figure 5.3, along with Q_{α_M}. Clearly Q_{α_M} intersects S at the corner $(\alpha_M, \alpha_M)^t$ of Q_{α_M}. Hence S_{α_M} is the point on the line joining $(0.5, 1)^t$ and $(2, 0)^t$ which has equal coordinates. The line between $(0.5, 1)^t$ and $(2, 0)^t$ can be written

$$l = \{\tau(0.5, 1)^t + (1 - \tau)(2, 0)^t = (2 - 1.5\tau, \tau)^t: 0 \le \tau \le 1\}.$$

The point with equal coordinates is clearly the point for which $2 - 1.5\tau = \tau$, or $\tau = 0.8$. Thus S_{α_M} is the single point $(0.8, 0.8)^t$. This is, by Theorem 7, the sole minimax risk point.

Note that this game is a finite game, and could have been solved by the method of the preceding subsection. The advantage of the geometric approach is that it immediately indicates the proper subgame to consider (namely that involving a_1 and a_4).

At this point, it is worthwhile to pause and consider how Q_{α_M} can intersect S. The following possibilities exist:

(i) S_{α_M} is empty. This will happen, for example, if S is an open set. Usually, however, S is closed.

(ii) S_{α_M} consists of the single point $(\alpha_M, \alpha_M, \dots, \alpha_M)^t$. This was the situation in Example 11 (continued), and is the most frequently occurring case.

(iii) S_{α_M} is a set along the "side" of Q_{α_M}. It could be either a point or a convex subset of the side of Q_{α_M}, as the two parts of Figure 5.4 show.

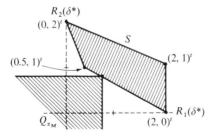

Figure 5.3

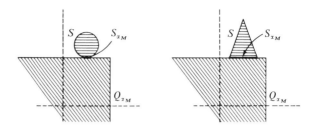

Figure 5.4

In obtaining the minimax risk point in complicated situations, the problem can be considerably simplified by noting that, roughly speaking, only the "lower left edge" of S need be considered. This idea is made precise in the following definitions and theorems. The symbol $\bar{S}$ will be used to denote the *closure* of S (i.e., the union of S and all its limit points, or alternatively the smallest closed set containing S).

Definition 9. A point $z \in R^m$ is a *lower boundary point* of S if $z \in \bar{S}$ and there is no other point $y \in \bar{S}$ such that $y_i \leq z_i$ for $i = 1, \ldots, m$. The set of all lower boundary points of S will be denoted $\lambda(S)$.

In R^2, $\lambda(S)$ consists of all lower left or southwest points of $\bar{S}$. In Figure 5.5, $\lambda(S)$ is indicated for several sets S.

Intuitively, risk points not in $\lambda(S)$ can be improved upon by points in $\lambda(S)$. In looking for a minimax strategy, therefore, it often suffices to confine the search to $\lambda(S)$. The conditions needed for this to be true are that $\lambda(S)$ must exist and must be a subset of S. The following concepts are needed in verifying these conditions.

Definition 10. A set $S \subset R^m$ is *bounded from below* if, for some finite number K and all $\mathbf{s} = (s_1, \ldots, s_m)^t \in S$, $s_i \geq -K$ for $i = 1, \ldots, m$.

It is necessary to have S bounded from below to ensure the existence of $\lambda(S)$. Recall that we are assuming in this chapter that $L(\theta, a) \geq -K > -\infty$. The following lemma shows that this implies that S is indeed bounded from below.

Lemma 4. *A risk set $S \subset R^m$ is bounded from below if $L(\theta_i, a) \geq -K > -\infty$ for all $a \in \mathcal{A}$ and $i = 1, \ldots, m$.*

PROOF. Clearly $s_i = L(\theta_i, \delta^*) = E^{\delta^*}L(\theta_i, a) \geq -K$. $\qquad\square$

If S is closed, then $\lambda(S)$ is a subset of S (since then $S = \bar{S}$). More generally, we define the concept of closed from below.

Definition 11. A convex set $S \subset R^m$ is *closed from below* if $\lambda(S) \subset S$.

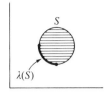 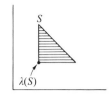 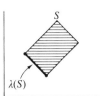

Figure 5.5

Usually, one just verifies that S is closed from below by showing that it is closed. The following lemma is an example. More interesting statistical examples will be seen in Section 5.3.

Lemma 5. *If $\mathscr{A}$ is finite, then the risk set S is closed.*

PROOF. Assume $\mathscr{A} = \{a_1, \ldots, a_n\}$. By Lemma 3, S is the convex hull of $\{\mathbf{R}(a_1), \ldots, \mathbf{R}(a_n)\}$. It is a straightforward exercise in limits and convexity to show that the convex hull of a finite set of points is closed. □

The following theorem, based on Lemma 7 of the next subsection, shows that frequently we need consider only points in $\lambda(S)$.

Theorem 8. *Assume that the risk set S is bounded from below and closed from below. Then any risk point $\mathbf{s} \notin \lambda(S)$ corresponds to an inadmissible strategy for* II. *Indeed, there exists a strategy corresponding to a point $\mathbf{s}' \in \lambda(S)$ for which $s_i' \leq s_i$ for $i = 1, \ldots, m$, with strict inequality for some i.*

PROOF. Lemma 7 of Subsection 5.2.5 shows that there exists a $\mathbf{y} \in \lambda(S)$ for which $y_i \leq s_i$, with strict inequality for some i. Since S is closed from below, $\mathbf{y} \in S$, giving the desired conclusion. □

Under the conditions of the above theorem, there is no reason to consider strategies other than those corresponding to points in $\lambda(S)$. In particular, the theorem shows that, if there is a minimax risk point not in $\lambda(S)$, then there is a better minimax risk point in $\lambda(S)$. It is, therefore, of interest to discuss how $\lambda(S)$ can be obtained. In simple situations such as Example 11 (continued), $\lambda(S)$ can be easily determined geometrically. In more complicated situations, however, an alternate approach is needed. The following theorems lead to such an approach.

Theorem 9. *Any strategy whose risk point is in $\lambda(S)$ is admissible.*

Theorem 10. *If a strategy in an S game is admissible, then it is Bayes with respect to some $\pi \in \Omega_m$.*

Theorem 11. *If the risk set S is closed from below and bounded from below,
then $\lambda(S)$ is a subset of the risk points arising from Bayes strategies.*

The proofs of Theorems 9 and 10 are left as exercises. (The proof of
Theorem 10 requires results from the next subsection.) Theorem 11 is an
immediate consequence of Theorems 9 and 10. Note that not all Bayes risk
points need be in $\lambda(S)$. [The second graph in Figure 5.5 is an example of this.
Any point on the left edge of S is Bayes with respect to $\pi^0 = (1, 0)^t$. ($L(\pi^0, \mathbf{s})$
$= s_1$, which is minimized at any point along this left edge.) The only point
which is in $\lambda(S)$, however, is the lower left corner of S.] When π has no zero
coordinates, however, Theorem 1 of Section 4.5 shows that any Bayes
strategy is admissible, implying (via Theorem 8) that the corresponding
risk point is in $\lambda(S)$.

Theorem 11 provides a useful tool for calculating $\lambda(S)$. Frequently it is
possible to explicitly determine all Bayes strategies for a game. Under the
conditions of Theorem 11, $\lambda(S)$ is then a subset of the set of risk points
corresponding to the Bayes strategies. Indeed, except possibly for risk points
corresponding to Bayes strategies arising from π having zero coordinates,
the two sets will be identical.

The important applications of this Bayesian technique for obtaining
$\lambda(S)$ are to statistical games, and will be illustrated in Section 5.3. Indeed,
it is generally unnecessary to even explicitly calculate $\lambda(S)$. The reduction
of the problem to consideration of only Bayes strategies is often a great
enough simplification to allow easy application of the techniques of Subsection 5.2.2.

When m is large, finding the minimax strategy can be difficult, even if $\lambda(S)$
has been obtained. In trying to solve such games, it is useful to recall the ways
in which Q_{α_M} can intersect $\lambda(S)$. First, it can intersect at the corner $(\alpha_M, \ldots,$
$\alpha_M)^t$. If this is the case, then the minimax risk point will be from an equalizer
strategy. It is often quite easy to find an equalizer strategy with risk point in
$\lambda(S)$, providing one exists. (An exercise will be to show that an admissible
equalizer strategy is minimax. Hence an equalizer strategy with risk point
in $\lambda(S)$ is always minimax by Theorem 9.)

Unfortunately, an equalizer strategy with risk point in $\lambda(S)$ will not always
exist. This happens when $\lambda(S)$ intersects Q_{α_M} in a side. Note that any surface
or edge of Q_{α_M} can be written as a set of the form

$$W = \{\mathbf{z} \in R^m : z_i = \alpha \quad \text{for} \quad i \in I, z_i \leq \alpha \quad \text{for} \quad i \notin I\},$$

where $I = \{i(1), \ldots, i(k)\}$ is some set of integers. The problem in finding an
equalizer strategy lies with the coordinates $i \notin I$. An obvious idea is to ignore
these coordinates and consider

$$\lambda_I(S) = \{(s_{i(1)}, s_{i(2)}, \ldots, s_{i(k)})^t : \mathbf{s} \in \lambda(S)\}.$$

(Essentially, this corresponds to projecting $\lambda(S)$ onto the k-dimensional
subspace determined by the coordinates $i \in I$.) This will determine a new and

smaller S game, one in which the minimax risk point will have equal co-ordinates. This suggests the following procedure for determining a minimax strategy in a complicated S game:

 (i) Determine $\lambda(S)$, and make sure that $\lambda(S) \subset S$.
 (ii) Look for an equalizer strategy with risk point in $\lambda(S)$. If there isn't one, try to use the techniques of Subsection 5.2.2.
(iii) If (ii) fails, consider subproblems formed by deleting coordinates from the points $\mathbf{s} \in \lambda(S)$. Find the equalizer strategies for all such subgames, and determine the corresponding strategies in the original game.
(iv) Find the best strategy in this set according to the minimax principle. This strategy will be minimax.

III. *Finding Maximin Strategies in S-Games*

We now address the problem of determining a maximin strategy in an S-game. From the definition of a maximin strategy, it follows that $\pi^M \in \Omega_m$ is maximin in an S-game if

$$\inf_{s \in S} (\pi^M)'\mathbf{s} = \sup_{\pi \in \Omega_m} \inf_{\mathbf{s} \in S} \pi'\mathbf{s}. \tag{5.7}$$

It will be seen that a maximin strategy has an interesting and useful interpreta-tion in terms of a "tangent plane" to S at a minimax risk point. The following definition presents the needed concept.

Definition 12. A *hyperplane* in R^m is a set of the form

$$H(\xi, k) = \left\{ \mathbf{z} \in R^m : \xi'\mathbf{z} = \sum_{i=1}^m \xi_i z_i = k \right\},$$

where k is some real number, $\xi \in R^m$, and $\xi \neq \mathbf{0}$ (the zero vector).

The following properties of a hyperplane are easy to check and aid in understanding its nature:

 (i) A hyperplane is an $(m - 1)$-dimensional plane (a line in R^2, a plane in R^3, etc.).
 (ii) The hyperplane $H(\xi, k)$ is perpendicular to the line $l = \{\lambda\xi: -\infty < \lambda < \infty\}$. To see this, observe that if $\mathbf{x} \in H(\xi, k)$, $\mathbf{y} \in H(\xi, k)$, and $\lambda\xi \in l$, then

$$(\lambda\xi)'(\mathbf{x} - \mathbf{y}) = \lambda(\xi'\mathbf{x} - \xi'\mathbf{y}) = \lambda(k - k) = 0.$$

(This is what "perpendicular" means mathematically.)
(iii) If l is a line in R^m and $\mathbf{z}^0 \in R^m$, the hyperplane passing through $\mathbf{z}^0$ and perpendicular to l is $H(\xi, k)$, where $\xi = \mathbf{y}^1 - \mathbf{y}^2$ and $k = (\mathbf{z}^0)'(\mathbf{y}^1 - \mathbf{y}^2)$, $\mathbf{y}^1$ and $\mathbf{y}^2$ being any distinct points of l.

(iv) Hyperplanes $H(\xi, k)$, for fixed ξ and varying k, are parallel.

(v) If $\pi \in \Omega_m$, then $H(\pi, k)$ passes through the point $(k, k, \ldots, k)^t$ (since $\sum_{i=1}^{m} k\pi_i = k$), and has "nonpositive slope." (In R^2, for example, the slope of the hyperplane (a line) is $-\pi_1/\pi_2$.)

The reason for introducing hyperplanes is that if $\pi \in \Omega_m$ is player I's strategy, then $H(\pi, k) \cap S$ is the set of risk points in S with loss k. (The loss in an S-game is π's, and $H(\pi, k)$ is defined as those points $\mathbf{z}$ for which $\pi^t \mathbf{z} = k$.) Hence the hyperplanes $H(\pi, k)$, for varying k, partition S into sets of constant loss. This will be seen in subsection 5.2.6 to lead to the following result, which will here be stated informally.

Result 1. *Assume that* $\mathbf{s}^M$ *is a minimax risk point for* II. *Let* $H(\pi^0, k)$ *be a hyperplane passing through* $\mathbf{s}^M$, *and "tangent" to* S, *where* $\pi^0 \in \Omega_m$. *Then* π^0 *is a maximin strategy for* I, *and the game has value* $(\pi^0)^t \mathbf{s}^M = k$.

EXAMPLE 11 (continued). The hyperplane tangent to S at $\mathbf{s}^M = (0.8, 0.8)^t$ is clearly the line passing through $(0.5, 1)^t$ and $(2, 0)^t$. This line can be written as

$$l = \{\mathbf{z} \in R^2 : (0.4, 0.6)\mathbf{z} = 0.8\},$$

which is the hyperplane $H((0.4, 0.6)^t, 0.8)$. By the above result, $(0.4, 0.6)^t$ is a maximin strategy for I and the game has value 0.8.

5.2.5 The Supporting and Separating Hyperplane Theorems

To make further theoretical progress towards establishing the existence of minimax strategies, it is necessary to develop two famous mathematical theorems: the supporting hyperplane theorem and the separating hyperplane theorem. We begin with some needed definitions.

Definition 13. A *boundary point* $\mathbf{s}^0$ of a set $S \subset R^m$ is a point such that every sphere about $\mathbf{s}^0$ contains points of both S and S^c.

Definition 14. A *supporting hyperplane* to a set $S \subset R^m$, at a boundary point $\mathbf{s}^0$ of S, is a hyperplane, $H(\xi, k)$ $(\xi \neq 0)$, which contains $\mathbf{s}^0$ (i.e., $\xi^t \mathbf{s}^0 = k$) and for which $\xi^t \mathbf{s} \geq k$ when $\mathbf{s} \in S$. A *separating hyperplane* for sets S_1 and S_2 is a hyperplane, $H(\xi, k)$ $(\xi \neq 0)$, such that $\xi^t \mathbf{s}^1 \geq k$ for $\mathbf{s}^1 \in S_1$ and $\xi^t \mathbf{s}^2 \leq k$ for $\mathbf{s}^2 \in S_2$.

The set of points $\{\mathbf{z} \in R^m : \xi^t \mathbf{z} \geq k\}$ is the half-space lying on one side of the hyperplane $H(\xi, k)$. Hence a supporting hyperplane to a set is a tangent hyperplane for which the set lies entirely on one side of the hyperplane. A separating hyperplane for two sets is a hyperplane for which one set lies on one side of the hyperplane, and the other set lies on the other side. Our goal will be to prove that a convex set has a supporting hyperplane at every boundary point, and that any two disjoint convex sets have a separating hyperplane. These results can be obtained from the following lemma.

Lemma 6. *If S is a closed convex set in R^m and $\mathbf{x}^0 \notin S$, then there is a hyperplane separating S and $\mathbf{x}^0$.*

PROOF. The proof will be geometric and involves several steps.

Step 1. We first show that there is a unique $\mathbf{s}^0 \in S$ nearest to $\mathbf{x}^0$, in the sense that $|\mathbf{s}^0 - \mathbf{x}^0| = \inf_{\mathbf{s} \in S} |\mathbf{s} - \mathbf{x}^0|$. To see this, choose $\mathbf{s}^n \in S$ so that $|\mathbf{s}^n - \mathbf{x}^0| \to \inf_{\mathbf{s} \in S} |\mathbf{s} - \mathbf{x}^0|$. It is easy to show that $\{\mathbf{s}^n\}$ can be chosen to be a bounded sequence, so that, by the Bolzano–Weierstrass theorem, $\{\mathbf{s}^n\}$ has a convergent subsequence $\{\mathbf{s}^{n(i)}\}$ with a limit point $\mathbf{s}^0$. Since S is closed, $\mathbf{s}^0 \in S$. Clearly

$$|\mathbf{s}^0 - \mathbf{x}^0| = \lim_{n \to \infty} |\mathbf{s}^{n(i)} - \mathbf{x}^0| = \inf_{\mathbf{s} \in S} |\mathbf{s} - \mathbf{x}^0|.$$

To see that $\mathbf{s}^0$ is unique, assume that there exists an $\mathbf{s}' \in S$ such that $\mathbf{s}' \neq \mathbf{s}^0$ and $|\mathbf{s}' - \mathbf{x}^0| = |\mathbf{s}^0 - \mathbf{x}^0|$. Then the points $\mathbf{x}^0$, $\mathbf{s}^0$, and $\mathbf{s}'$ form an isosceles triangle, and the midpoint of the line segment $\overline{\mathbf{s}'\mathbf{s}^0}$ joining $\mathbf{s}'$ and $\mathbf{s}^0$ is closer to $\mathbf{x}^0$ than are either $\mathbf{s}'$ or $\mathbf{s}^0$. But since S is convex, this midpoint is also in S, contradicting the assumption that $\mathbf{s}^0$ is closest to $\mathbf{x}^0$. Hence $\mathbf{s}^0$ must be unique.

Step 2. Define $\xi = (\mathbf{s}^0 - \mathbf{x}^0)$ and $k = (|\mathbf{s}^0|^2 - |\mathbf{x}^0|^2)/2$. From property (iii) of hyperplanes, discussed in the previous subsection, it is clear that $H(\xi, k)$ is the hyperplane perpendicular to the line segment $\overline{\mathbf{x}^0\mathbf{s}^0}$ and passing through the midpoint $(\mathbf{x}^0 + \mathbf{s}^0)/2$ of the line segment. Also, since

$$0 < \tfrac{1}{2}|\mathbf{s}^0 - \mathbf{x}^0|^2 = \tfrac{1}{2}(\xi'\mathbf{s}^0 - \xi'\mathbf{x}^0),$$

it follows that $\xi'\mathbf{x}^0 < \xi'\mathbf{s}^0$. We can conclude that

$$\xi'\mathbf{x}^0 < \tfrac{1}{2}(\xi'\mathbf{x}^0 + \xi'\mathbf{s}^0)(= k) < \xi'\mathbf{s}^0,$$

so that $H(\xi, k)$ separates $\mathbf{x}^0$ and $\mathbf{s}^0$.

Step 3. We next show that $H(\xi, k) \cap S$ is empty. To prove this, assume the contrary, namely that $\mathbf{s}^1 \in S$ and $\xi'\mathbf{s}^1 = k$. Because $H(\xi, k)$ is the perpendicular bisector of $\overline{\mathbf{x}^0\mathbf{s}^0}$, the triangle joining the points $\mathbf{x}^0$, $\mathbf{s}^0$, and $\mathbf{s}^1$ is isosceles, with $\overline{\mathbf{x}^0\mathbf{s}^0}$ as base. Let $\mathbf{s}^2$ be the point on $\overline{\mathbf{s}^0\mathbf{s}^1}$ for which $\overline{\mathbf{x}^0\mathbf{s}^2}$ is perpendicular to $\overline{\mathbf{s}^0\mathbf{s}^1}$ (see Figure 5.6). Then $|\mathbf{x}^0 - \mathbf{s}^2| < |\mathbf{x}^0 - \mathbf{s}^0|$, and since $\mathbf{s}^2 \in S$ (by convexity), Step 1 is again contradicted. It follows that $H(\xi, k) \cap S$ must be empty.

Step 4. We conclude the proof by showing that $\xi'\mathbf{s} > k$ for $\mathbf{s} \in S$, so that $H(\xi, k)$ separates $\mathbf{x}^0$ and S. To see this, assume that $\mathbf{s}^1 \in S$ and that

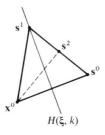

Figure 5.6

$\xi's^1 = \alpha_1 \le k$. From Step 2, we know that $\xi's^0 = \alpha_0 > k$. Let $\lambda = (k - \alpha_1)/(\alpha_0 - \alpha_1)$, and note that $0 \le \lambda < 1$. By convexity, $s^2 = (\lambda s^0 + (1 - \lambda)s^1) \in S$, but

$$\xi's^2 = \lambda\alpha_0 + (1 - \lambda)\alpha_1 = \alpha_1 + \lambda(\alpha_0 - \alpha_1) = k.$$

This contradicts the result of Step 3, yielding the desired conclusion. □

Theorem 12 (The Supporting Hyperplane Theorem). *If s^0 is a boundary point of a convex set S, then there is a supporting hyperplane to S at s^0.*

PROOF. It can be checked that S and $\bar{S}$ (the closure of S) have the same boundary points. From the definition of a boundary point, it follows that there are points $x^m \notin \bar{S}$ such that $x^m \to s^0$ (i.e., $\lim_{m \to \infty} |x^m - s^0| = 0$). By Lemma 6, there are hyperplanes $H(\xi^m, k_m)$ such that

$$(\xi^m)'s \ge k_m \quad \text{for } s \in \bar{S}, \quad \text{and} \quad (\xi^m)'x^m \le k_m. \tag{5.8}$$

The hyperplanes and inequalities in (5.8) are not affected if ξ^m and k_m are replaced by $\tau^m = \xi^m/|\xi^m|$ and $k'_m = k_m/|\xi^m|$. Thus for $H(\tau^m, k'_m)$,

$$(\tau^m)'s \ge k'_m \quad \text{for } s \in \bar{S}, \quad \text{and} \quad (\tau^m)'x^m \le k'_m. \tag{5.9}$$

Observe that since $|\tau^m| = 1$ for all m, the Bolzano–Weierstrass theorem implies that the sequence $\{\tau^m\}$ has a convergent subsequence $\{\tau^{m(i)}\}$. Let $\tau^0 = \lim_{i \to \infty} \tau^{m(i)}$. We must now show that the sequence $\{k'_{m(i)}\}$ has a convergent subsequence. Note first that for any fixed $s \in S$, a use of Schwarz's inequality in (5.9) gives

$$k'_m \le (\tau^m)'s \le |\tau^m||s| = |s|.$$

Similarly,

$$k'_m \ge (\tau^m)'x^m \ge -|\tau^m||x^m| = -|x^m|.$$

Since $x^m \to s^0$, these inequalities imply that $\{k'_{m(i)}\}$ is a bounded sequence. Another application of the Bolzano–Weierstrass theorem thus yields a convergent subsequence $\{k'_{m(i(j))}\}$, with say limit k_0.

Since (by (5.9)) $k'_{m(i(j))} \le (\tau^{m(i(j))})'s$ for all $s \in \bar{S}$, it follows that

$$k_0 \le (\tau^0)'s \quad \text{for all } s \in \bar{S}. \tag{5.10}$$

Likewise, since $k'_{m(i(j))} \geq (\tau^{m(i(j))})^t \mathbf{x}^{m(i(j))}$, it follows that $k_0 \geq (\tau^0)^t \mathbf{s}^0$. Together with (5.10), this shows that

$$(\tau^0)^t \mathbf{s}^0 = k_0. \tag{5.11}$$

From (5.10) and (5.11), we can conclude that $H(\tau^0, k_0)$ is a supporting hyperplane to S at $\mathbf{s}^0$. □

Theorem 13 (The Separating Hyperplane Theorem). *If S_1 and S_2 are disjoint convex subsets of R^m, then there exists a vector $\xi \in R^m$ ($\xi \neq \mathbf{0}$) such that*

$$\xi^t \mathbf{s}^1 \geq \xi^t \mathbf{s}^2$$

for all $\mathbf{s}^1 \in S_1$ and $\mathbf{s}^2 \in S_2$. Indeed defining

$$k = \sup_{\mathbf{s}^2 \in S_2} \xi^t \mathbf{s}^2,$$

the hyperplane $H(\xi, k)$ separates S_1 and S_2.

PROOF. Let

$$A = \{\mathbf{x} = \mathbf{s}^1 - \mathbf{s}^2 : \mathbf{s}^1 \in S_1 \quad \text{and} \quad \mathbf{s}^2 \in S_2\}.$$

It is straightforward to check that A is convex. Also, $\mathbf{0} \notin A$, since S_1 and S_2 are disjoint. Two cases must now be considered.

Case 1. Assume $\mathbf{0} \in \bar{A}$ (i.e., $\mathbf{0}$ is a boundary point of A). Then, by Theorem 12, there is a supporting hyperplane, $H(\xi, k)$, to A at $\mathbf{0}$. By the definition of a supporting hyperplane, it is clear that $k = \xi^t \mathbf{0} = 0$, and $\xi^t \mathbf{x} \geq k = 0$ for $\mathbf{x} \in A$. Hence, for $\mathbf{s}^1 \in S_1$ and $\mathbf{s}^2 \in S_2$, it follows that $\xi^t(\mathbf{s}^1 - \mathbf{s}^2) \geq 0$. This gives the first conclusion of the theorem. The final conclusion follows from the observation that

$$\xi^t \mathbf{s}^1 \geq \sup_{\mathbf{s}^2 \in S_2} \xi^t \mathbf{s}^2 \geq \xi^t \mathbf{s}^2.$$

Case 2. Assume $\mathbf{0} \notin \bar{A}$. Then, by Lemma 6, there exists a hyperplane separating $\mathbf{0}$ and $\bar{A}$. The remainder of the argument proceeds as in Case 1. □

The main application of the above theorems will be in proving the minimax theorem in the next subsection. First, however, we will use them to prove three other results: Lemma 2 of Chapter 1 and Jensen's inequality (both discussed in Section 1.8), and Lemma 7 (alluded to in the proof of Theorem 8 in the previous subsection).

Lemma 2 of Chapter 1. *Let $\mathbf{X}$ be an m-variate random vector such that $E[|\mathbf{X}|] < \infty$ and $P(\mathbf{X} \in S) = 1$, where S is a convex subset of R^m. Then $E[\mathbf{X}] \in S$.*

PROOF. Define $\mathbf{Y} = \mathbf{X} - E[\mathbf{X}]$, and let

$$S' = S - E[\mathbf{X}] = \{\mathbf{y} : \mathbf{y} = \mathbf{x} - E[\mathbf{X}] \quad \text{for some } \mathbf{x} \in S\}.$$

Note that S' is convex, $P(\mathbf{Y} \in S') = 1$, and $E[\mathbf{Y}] = \mathbf{0}$. Showing that $E[\mathbf{X}] \in S$ is clearly equivalent to showing that $\mathbf{0} \in S'$. We will establish this by induction on m.

When $m = 0$, $\mathbf{Y}$ is degenerate (a point), so that $E[\mathbf{Y}] = \mathbf{Y} \in S'$. Now suppose that the result holds for all dimensions up to and including $m - 1$. We must show that the result is then true for dimension m. This will be established by contradiction. Thus assume that $\mathbf{0} \notin S'$. Then, by Theorem 13, there exists a vector $\boldsymbol{\xi} \neq \mathbf{0}$ in R^m such that $\boldsymbol{\xi}^t \mathbf{y} \geq \boldsymbol{\xi}^t \mathbf{0} = 0$ for all $\mathbf{y} \in S'$. Defining $Z = \boldsymbol{\xi}^t \mathbf{Y}$, it follows that $P(Z \geq 0) = 1$. However, $E[Z] = \boldsymbol{\xi}^t E[\mathbf{Y}] = 0$, so that it must be true that $P(Z = 0) = 1$. Hence, with probability one, $\mathbf{Y}$ lies in the hyperplane defined by $\boldsymbol{\xi}^t \mathbf{y} = 0$. Now define $S'' = S' \cap \{\mathbf{y} : \boldsymbol{\xi}^t \mathbf{y} = 0\}$, and observe that S'' is a convex subset of an $(m - 1)$-dimensional Euclidean space, and that $P(\mathbf{Y} \in S'') = 1$ and $E[\mathbf{Y}] = \mathbf{0}$. By the induction hypothesis, $\mathbf{0} \in S''$. Since $S'' \subset S'$, this contradicts the supposition that $\mathbf{0} \notin S'$, completing the proof. $\qquad\square$

Theorem 14 (Jensen's inequality). *Let $g(\mathbf{x})$ be a convex real-valued function defined on a convex subset S of R^m, and let $\mathbf{X}$ be an m-variate random vector which has finite expectation $E[\mathbf{X}]$. Suppose, also, that $P(\mathbf{X} \in S) = 1$. Then*

$$g(E[\mathbf{X}]) \leq E[g(\mathbf{X})],$$

with strict inequality if g is strictly convex and $\mathbf{X}$ is not concentrated at a point.

PROOF. The proof will be done by induction on m. For $m = 0$ the theorem is trivially satisfied, since S is a single point. Assume next that the theorem holds for all dimensions up to and including $(m - 1)$. It must now be shown that the result holds for dimension m. To this end, define

$$B = \{(\mathbf{x}^t, y)^t \in R^{m+1} : \mathbf{x} \in S, y \in R^1, \text{ and } y \geq g(\mathbf{x})\}.$$

Step 1. We first show that B is convex in R^{m+1}. If $(\mathbf{x}^t, y_1)^t$ and $(\mathbf{z}^t, y_2)^t$ are two points in B, then

$$\lambda(\mathbf{x}^t, y_1) + (1 - \lambda)(\mathbf{z}^t, y_2) = ([\lambda \mathbf{x} + (1 - \lambda)\mathbf{z}]^t, \lambda y_1 + (1 - \lambda)y_2).$$

But, since S is convex, $[\lambda \mathbf{x} + (1 - \lambda)\mathbf{z}] \in S$ for $0 \leq \lambda \leq 1$. Also, since $y_1 \geq g(\mathbf{x})$, $y_2 \geq g(\mathbf{z})$, and g is convex,

$$\lambda y_1 + (1 - \lambda)y_2 \geq \lambda g(\mathbf{x}) + (1 - \lambda)g(\mathbf{z}) \geq g(\lambda \mathbf{x} + (1 - \lambda)\mathbf{z}).$$

Therefore, $[\lambda(\mathbf{x}^t, y_1) + (1 - \lambda)(\mathbf{z}^t, y_2)]^t \in B$ for $0 \leq \lambda \leq 1$.

Step 2. By Lemma 2 of Chapter 1, $E[\mathbf{X}] \in S$. It follows that $\mathbf{b}^0 = (E[\mathbf{X}]^t, g(E[\mathbf{X}]))^t$ is a boundary point of B.

Step 3. Let $H(\boldsymbol{\xi}, k)$ be the supporting hyperplane to B at $\mathbf{b}^0$. Writing $\boldsymbol{\xi} = (\boldsymbol{\tau}^t, \rho)^t$, where $\boldsymbol{\tau} \in R^m$ and $\rho \in R^1$, it follows that

$$\boldsymbol{\xi}^t \mathbf{b}^0 = \boldsymbol{\tau}^t E[\mathbf{X}] + \rho g(E[\mathbf{X}]) = k, \qquad (5.12)$$

and

$$\xi^t(\mathbf{x}^t, y)^t = \tau^t \mathbf{x} + \rho y \geq k \quad \text{for } \mathbf{x} \in S \text{ and } y \geq g(\mathbf{x}). \tag{5.13}$$

Letting $\mathbf{x} = \mathbf{X}$ and $y = g(\mathbf{X})$ in (5.12) and (5.13), it follows that, with probability one,

$$\tau^t \mathbf{X} + \rho g(\mathbf{X}) \geq \tau^t E[\mathbf{X}] + \rho g(E[\mathbf{X}]). \tag{5.14}$$

Step 4. Observe that $\rho \geq 0$. (If $\rho < 0$, line (5.13) will be contradicted by sending y to infinity). If $\rho > 0$, taking expectations in (5.14) and cancelling common terms gives the desired result. If $\rho = 0$, it follows from (5.14) that

$$h(\mathbf{X}) = \tau^t(\mathbf{X} - E[\mathbf{X}]) \geq 0.$$

On the other hand, clearly $E[h(\mathbf{X})] = 0$. It follows that $h(\mathbf{X}) = 0$ with probability one, or equivalently that

$$P(\tau^t \mathbf{X} = k) = 1.$$

This means that $\mathbf{X}$ is concentrated on the hyperplane $H(\tau, k)$ with probability one. Let $S_H = S \cap H(\tau, k)$. Since the intersection of convex sets is convex, S_H is convex. Also, $P(\mathbf{X} \in S_H) = 1$. Since S_H is an $(m-1)$-dimensional set, the induction hypothesis can be applied to give the desired conclusion. (The conclusion about strict inequality follows by noting that, for $\rho \neq 0$, the inequality in (5.14) is strict when g is strictly convex. Since $\mathbf{X}$ is not concentrated at a point, ρ must be nonzero for some nonzero dimension.) □

Lemma 7. *In an S-game, assume that the risk set S is bounded from below. If $\mathbf{s} \in S$ but $\mathbf{s} \notin \lambda(S)$ ($\lambda(S)$ is the lower boundary of S), then there exists a point $\mathbf{y} \in \lambda(S)$ such that $y_i \leq s_i$, the inequality being strict for some i.*

PROOF. The proof will proceed by induction on m. For $m = 0$, S contains only one point, and the result is trivially satisfied. Assume next that the result holds for all dimensions up to and including $m - 1$. It must now be shown that the lemma holds for m dimensions. To this end, define

$$T = \{\mathbf{x} \in \bar{S} : x_i \leq s_i \quad \text{for } i = 1, \ldots, m\}.$$

Step 1. It is easy to check that T is convex, bounded, and closed. As a consequence of T being bounded, note that $t_m = \inf_{\mathbf{x} \in T} x_m$ is finite.

Step 2. Define $T_m = \{\mathbf{x} \in T : x_m = t_m\}$. We must show that T_m is not empty. To this end, let $\{\mathbf{x}^n\}$ be a sequence of points in T such that $x_m^n \to t_m$. Since T is bounded, the Bolzano–Weierstrass theorem implies the existence of a subsequence $\{\mathbf{x}^{n(i)}\}$ converging to a point $\mathbf{x}^0$. Since T is closed, $\mathbf{x}^0 \in T$. But clearly $x_m^0 = t_m$, so that $\mathbf{x}^0 \in T_m$.

Step 3. Let $T_m' = \{(x_1, \ldots, x_{m-1})^t : \mathbf{x} \in T_m\}$. It is easy to verify that T_m' is bounded, closed, and convex. It thus satisfies the induction hypothesis, from which it can be concluded that there exists a point $\mathbf{z} = (z_1, \ldots, z_{m-1})^t \in \lambda(T_m')$ such that $z_i \leq x_i^0$ for $i = 1, \ldots, m - 1$.

Step 4. Define $\mathbf{y} = (z_1, \ldots, z_{m-1}, t_m)^t$. Since T'_m and T are closed, $\mathbf{y} \in T$. Hence $y_i \leq s_i$ for $i = 1, \ldots, m$. Also, $\mathbf{y} \in \lambda(S)$. If it were not, then for some $\mathbf{y}' \in \bar{S}$, it would follow that $y'_i \leq y_i$ with strict inequality for some i. But the inequality can't be strict for $i = m$ by the definition of t_m, while, for $i < m$, strict inequality would violate the fact that $\mathbf{z} \in \lambda(T'_m)$. (Clearly y' would also be in T_m, and $(y'_1, \ldots, y'_{m-1})$ would be in T'_m.)

Step 5. At least one of the inequalities $y_i \leq s_i$ must be strict, since $\mathbf{y}$ and $\mathbf{s}$ are different points. (One is in $\lambda(S)$, while the other is not.) $\qquad\square$

5.2.6 The Minimax Theorem

We are now ready to prove the fundamental theorem concerning the existence of minimax strategies. The theorem will be proven only for finite Θ. Generalizations to other situations will be discussed, however.

Theorem 15 (The Minimax Theorem). *Consider a (two-person zero-sum) game in which $\Theta = \{\theta_1, \theta_2, \ldots, \theta_m\}$. Assume that the risk set S is bounded from below. Then the game has value*

$$V = \inf_{\delta^* \in \mathscr{A}^*} \sup_{\pi \in \Theta^*} L(\pi, \delta^*) = \sup_{\pi \in \Theta^*} \inf_{\delta^* \in \mathscr{A}^*} L(\pi, \delta^*),$$

and a maximin strategy π^M exists. Moreover, if S is closed from below, then a minimax strategy δ^{*M} exists, and $L(\pi^M, \delta^{*M}) = V$.

PROOF. Consider the problem in terms of the S-game formulation, as discussed in Subsection 5.2.4. The strategy spaces are then S and Ω_m, and the loss is $\pi^t \mathbf{s}$. As in Theorem 7 of Subsection 5.2.4, consider $S_\alpha = Q_\alpha \cap S$ and $\alpha_M = \inf\{\alpha: S_\alpha \text{ is not empty}\}$. Note that α_M is finite, since S is bounded from below.

The basic idea of the proof will be to find a separating hyperplane between S and the interior of Q_{α_M}. This hyperplane will give rise to a maximin strategy. Also, it will follow that $V = \alpha_M$ and that S_{α_M} will consist of the minimax risk points.

Step 1. Construction of the hyperplane: Let

$$T = \{\mathbf{x} \in R^m: x_i < \alpha_M \quad \text{for } i = 1, \ldots, m\}.$$

(Thus T is the interior of Q_{α_M}.) It is easy to check that T is a convex set, and S and T are obviously disjoint. Since S is also convex, Theorem 13 can be used to conclude that there is a hyperplane $H(\xi, k)$ separating S and T, such that

$$\xi^t \mathbf{s} \geq k \quad \text{for } \mathbf{s} \in S, \qquad \xi^t \mathbf{x} \leq k \quad \text{for } \mathbf{x} \in T, \quad \text{and} \quad k = \sup_{\mathbf{x} \in T} \xi^t \mathbf{x}. \quad (5.15)$$

Step 2. The vector ξ has $\xi_i \geq 0$ for $i = 1, \ldots, m$. This follows from the observation that, if $\xi_j < 0$, letting $x_j \to -\infty$ in (5.15) reveals a contradiction. Note, as a consequence, that

$$k = \sup_{\mathbf{x} \in T} \xi'\mathbf{x} = \xi'(\alpha_M, \ldots, \alpha_M) = \alpha_M \sum_{i=1}^{m} \xi_i.$$

Step 3. Dividing ξ and k by $(\sum_{i=1}^{m} \xi_i)$ shows that the hyperplane $H(\xi, k)$ can be rewritten $H(\pi, \alpha_M)$, where $\pi \in \Omega_m$ is given by $\pi_i = \xi_i/(\sum_{j=1}^{m} \xi_j)$. Note also that (5.15) can be rewritten

$$\pi'\mathbf{s} \geq \alpha_M \quad \text{for } \mathbf{s} \in S, \quad \text{and} \quad \pi'\mathbf{x} \leq \alpha_M \quad \text{for } \mathbf{x} \in T. \tag{5.16}$$

Step 4. From (5.16), it is clear that $\inf_{\mathbf{s} \in S} \pi'\mathbf{s} \geq \alpha_M$.

Step 5. There exists a sequence $\{\mathbf{s}^n\}$ of risk points in S such that

$$\lim_{n \to \infty} \max_i \{s_i^n\} = \alpha_M.$$

This follows from the fact that S_α is nonempty for each $\alpha > \alpha_M$. In particular, choosing $\mathbf{s}^n \in S_{(\alpha_M + 1/n)}$ gives the desired result.

Step 6. By Steps 4 and 5, together with Lemma 1 in Subsection 5.2.1, the hypothesis of Theorem 3(b) (Subsection 5.2.2) is satisfied for the S-game. Hence the game has value α_M and π is a maximin strategy.

Step 7. Assume that S is closed from below. Consider the sequence $\{\mathbf{s}^n\}$ found in Step 5. This is clearly a bounded sequence, since S is bounded from below and the $Q_{(\alpha_M + 1/n)}$ all have a common bound from above. Hence, by the Bolzano–Weierstrass theorem, a subsequence $\{\mathbf{s}^{n(i)}\}$ exists which converges to a limit point $\mathbf{s}^0$. Clearly $\mathbf{s}^0 \in \bar{S}$ and $\max_i \{s_i^0\} = \alpha_M$.

If $\mathbf{s}^0 \in \lambda(S)$, then, since S is closed from below, $\mathbf{s}^0 \in S$. Since $\max_i \{s_i^0\} = \alpha_M$, which is the value of the game, it follows that $\mathbf{s}^0$ is a minimax risk point. If $\mathbf{s}^0 \notin \lambda(S)$, then by Lemma 7 there exists an $\mathbf{s}' \in \lambda(S)$ such that $s_i' \leq s_i^0 \leq \alpha_M$. By the previous argument, $\mathbf{s}' \in S$ and is a minimax risk point. This completes the proof. $\qquad \square$

Versions of the minimax theorem hold in settings other than that considered above. As an example, we state the following theorem, which can be found in Blackwell and Girshick (1954).

Theorem 16. *If $\mathscr{A}$ is a closed, bounded, and convex subset of R^n, and $L(\theta, a)$ is, for each θ, a continuous convex function of a, then the game has a value and player II has a minimax strategy which is nonrandomized. If, in addition, Θ is a closed bounded subset of R^m and $L(\theta, a)$ is continuous in θ for each a, then player I has a maximin strategy which randomizes among at most $n + 1$ nonrandomized strategies.*

There are quite general minimax theorems that hold in a wide variety of settings. Unfortunately, these theorems involve advanced topological and measure-theoretic concepts. Some simple versions of such theorems can be found in Ferguson (1967). For more powerful advanced theorems see Le Cam (1955) and Brown (1976). The latter work is particularly recommended because of its detailed development and explanations, including explanations of many of the advanced mathematical concepts needed.

It is, of course, not always true that minimax and maximin strategies exist, or that the game has a value. Indeed the basic assumptions in the minimax theorem, that the risk set be closed from below and bounded from below, are quite essential. For example, if the risk set is open, then there is no minimax strategy. (The concept of an ε-*minimax* strategy has been developed for such a situation. This is a strategy δ^* for which $\sup_\theta L(\theta, \delta^*) \leq \bar{V} + \varepsilon$; in other words, a stategy within ε of being optimal according to the minimax principle.)

For unbounded strategy spaces, even more serious difficulties can be encountered. The following is an example in which the game doesn't even have a value.

EXAMPLE 13. Consider the game in which each player chooses a positive integer, with the player who chooses the largest integer winning 1 from the other player. Here $\Theta = \mathscr{A} = \{1, 2, \ldots\}$, and

$$L(\theta, a) = \begin{cases} 1 & \text{if } \theta > a, \\ 0 & \text{if } \theta = a, \\ -1 & \text{if } \theta < a. \end{cases}$$

A randomized strategy for player I is a probability vector $\boldsymbol{\pi} = (\pi_1, \pi_2, \ldots)^t$, where π_i is the probability of selecting integer i. Clearly

$$L(\boldsymbol{\pi}, a) = \left(\sum_{\{i > a\}} \pi_i \right) - \left(\sum_{\{i < a\}} \pi_i \right).$$

For any fixed $\boldsymbol{\pi}$, it follows that

$$\inf_a L(\boldsymbol{\pi}, a) = \lim_{a \to \infty} L(\boldsymbol{\pi}, a) = -1.$$

Hence

$$\underline{V} = \sup_{\boldsymbol{\pi}} \inf_a L(\boldsymbol{\pi}, a) = -1.$$

It can similarly be calculated that $\bar{V} = 1$. Since $\underline{V} \neq \bar{V}$, the game does not have a value. There are clearly no optimum strategies in this game.

5.3 Statistical Games

5.3.1 Introduction

A statistical decision problem (with action space $\mathscr{A}$, state-of-nature space Θ, and loss L) can be viewed as a two-person zero-sum game in which the statistician is player II and nature is player I. The strategy space for the statistician will be assumed to be $\mathscr{D}^*$, the space of all randomized decision rules, while the strategy space for nature is Θ. The minimax approach views the problem as that of choosing among rules $\delta^* \in \mathscr{D}^*$, before experimentation. (Some criticisms of this viewpoint will be presented in the next section.) Since the loss to the statistician will be $L(\theta, \delta^*(X, \cdot))$, and X (the sample observation) is random, the proper measure of loss for this game is the risk function

$$R(\theta, \delta^*) = E^X L(\theta, \delta^*(X, \cdot)).$$

It is, of course, necessary to consider randomized strategies. A randomized strategy for the statistician is, by definition, a probability distribution on $\mathscr{D}^*$. Since $\mathscr{D}^*$ is the space of randomized decision rules, the obvious question arises as to whether another randomization is necessary. The answer is no, as the following lemma shows.

Lemma 8. *Let P be a probability distribution on $\mathscr{D}^*$. Define $\delta_P^*(x, A)$, for all $x \in \mathscr{X}$ and $A \subset \mathscr{A}$, by*

$$\delta_P^*(x, A) = E^P[\delta^*(x, A)].$$

Then δ_P^* is equivalent to P, in the sense that

$$R(\theta, \delta_P^*) = E^P[R(\theta, \delta^*)].$$

PROOF. By definition,

$$
\begin{aligned}
L(\theta, \delta_P^*(x, \cdot)) &= E^{\delta_P^*(x, \cdot)}[L(\theta, a)] \\
&= E^P E^{\delta^*(x, \cdot)}[L(\theta, a)].
\end{aligned}
$$

Hence

$$
\begin{aligned}
R(\theta, \delta_P^*) &= E^X L(\theta, \delta_P^*(X, \cdot)) \\
&= E^X E^P E^{\delta^*(X, \cdot)}[L(\theta, a)] \\
&= E^P E^X E^{\delta^*(X, \cdot)}[L(\theta, a)] \\
&= E^P[R(\theta, \delta^*)].
\end{aligned}
$$

The interchange in the order of integration above is justified by Fubini's theorem, since $L(\theta, a) \geq -K > -\infty$ by the original assumption on L. $\square$

The above lemma is not quite correct technically, the problem being that δ_P^* need not necessarily be measurable, and hence need not be in $\mathscr{D}^*$. This problem does not arise in reasonable statistical situations, however, and need not concern us.

The import of Lemma 8 is that it is unnecessary to consider randomized strategies on $\mathscr{D}^*$, since the risk function of any randomized strategy can be duplicated by that of a randomized decision rule in $\mathscr{D}^*$. Therefore, in applying to statistical games the game-theoretic results of Section 5.2, both $\mathscr{A}$ and $\mathscr{A}^*$ will be taken to be $\mathscr{D}^*$. Note, in particular, that the definition of a minimax strategy then coincides with that of a minimax decision rule as given in Section 1.5.

Randomized strategies for nature are again probability distributions $\pi \in \Theta^*$. The expected loss if nature uses $\pi \in \Theta^*$ and the statistician uses $\delta^* \in \mathscr{D}^*$ is clearly $r(\pi, \delta^*) = E^{\pi}[R(\theta, \delta^*)]$, the Bayes risk of δ^* with respect to π. In statistical games, a maximin strategy for nature is more commonly called a *least favorable prior distribution*. The reason is that nature is no longer an intelligent opponent, and the statistician is really just trying, through the minimax approach, to protect against the worst or least favorable possible values of θ.

In the remainder of the chapter, we will tend to use the statistical, as opposed to game-theoretic, terminology. Subsection 5.3.2 deals with general techniques for solving statistical games. Subsection 5.3.3 discusses the situation of finite Θ.

5.3.2 General Techniques for Solving Statistical Games

The game-theoretic techniques of Subsection 5.2.2 can be readily adapted to solve statistical games. We discuss three basic methods of solution here. A fourth method will be mentioned in Chapter 6, after invariance has been discussed.

I. *The Direct Method of Solving Statistical Games*

If the class $\mathscr{D}^*$ of decision rules is small enough, or can be reduced by admissibility considerations to a small enough set, the minimax rule can be calculated directly from the definition. Chapter 8 is devoted to the use of admissibility in reducing $\mathscr{D}^*$. Here we will content ourselves with an example in a standard situation.

EXAMPLE 14. Assume $X \sim \mathcal{N}(\theta, \sigma^2)$, σ^2 known, is observed, and that it is desired to test $H_0 : \theta \leq \theta_0$ versus $H_1 : \theta > \theta_0$, under "0–K_i" loss. A randomized decision rule in a testing situation is usually represented by a test function $\phi(x)$, where $\phi(x)$ is the probability of rejecting the null hypothesis when $X = x$ is observed. (Thus $\phi(x) = \delta^*(x, a_1) = 1 - \delta^*(x, a_0)$, where a_i denotes accepting H_i.)

It will be seen in Chapter 8 that only the "uniformly most powerful" tests $\phi_c(x) = I_{(c, \infty)}(x)$ need be considered. (Any other test can be improved upon by a test ϕ_c, for some c.) Clearly

$$R(\theta, \phi_c) = \begin{cases} K_1 P_\theta(X > c) & \text{if } \theta \leq \theta_0, \\ K_0 P_\theta(X < c) & \text{if } \theta > \theta_0. \end{cases}$$

Since $\beta(\theta) = P_\theta(X > c)$ is increasing in θ, it follows that

$$\sup_\theta R(\theta, \phi_c) = \max\left\{\sup_{\theta \le \theta_0} K_1\beta(\theta), \sup_{\theta > \theta_0} K_0[1 - \beta(\theta)]\right\}$$

$$= \max\{K_1\beta(\theta_0), K_0[1 - \beta(\theta_0)]\}.$$

Letting $z = \beta(\theta_0)$, and graphing the functions $K_1 z$ and $K_0(1 - z)$, it becomes clear that $\max\{K_1 z, K_0(1 - z)\}$ is minimized when $K_1 z = K_0(1 - z)$, or $z = K_0/(K_1 + K_0)$. But if

$$\beta(\theta_0) = P_{\theta_0}(X > c) = K_0/(K_1 + K_0),$$

it follows that c is the $1 - K_0/(K_1 + K_0) = K_1/(K_1 + K_0)$-fractile of the $\mathcal{N}(\theta_0, \sigma^2)$ distribution. Denoting this by $z(K_1/(K_1 + K_0))$, it can be concluded that

$$\inf_{\delta^* \in \mathscr{D}^*} \sup_\theta R(\theta, \delta^*) = \inf_c \sup_\theta R(\theta, \phi_c) = \sup_\theta R(\theta, \phi_{z(K_1/(K_1 + K_0))}).$$

Hence $\phi_{z(K_1/(K_1 + K_0))}$ is minimax.

II. *Guessing a Least Favorable Prior*

A very useful method of determining a minimax rule is to guess a least favorable prior distribution, determine the resulting Bayes rule, and check to see if this rule is minimax. In verifying minimaxity, the following consequence of Theorem 2 of Subsection 5.2.2 proves to be very useful. (Its proof will be left as an exercise.)

Theorem 17. *If $\delta_0^* \in \mathscr{D}^*$ is Bayes with respect to $\pi_0 \in \Theta^*$, and*

$$R(\theta, \delta_0^*) \le r(\pi_0, \delta_0^*)$$

for all $\theta \in \Theta$, then δ_0^* is minimax and π_0 is least favorable.

Often, the obvious guess for a least favorable prior is an improper prior π. The generalized Bayes rule, δ^π, is then a good guess for the minimax rule, but if $r(\pi, \delta^\pi)$ is infinite, Theorem 17 will not apply. Frequently, however, a sequence of proper priors $\{\pi_n\}$ can be found, such that $[c_n \pi_n(\theta)] \to \pi(\theta)$ for all θ, where the c_n are appropriate constants. The following immediate consequence of Theorem 3(a) can then be useful.

Theorem 18. *Assume that $\{\pi_n\}$ is a sequence of proper priors and δ_0^* is a decision rule such that*

$$R(\theta, \delta_0^*) \le \lim_{n \to \infty} r(\pi_n) < \infty,$$

for all $\theta \in \Theta$. Then δ_0^* is minimax.

The sequence $\{\pi_n\}$ can usually be chosen to be any convenient sequence such that constants c_n can be found for which $c_n \pi_n \to \pi$. Choosing an appropriate sequence of conjugate prior densities often succeeds, and is calculationally simple. See Brown (1976) for some general theorems for situations in which conjugate priors do not work.

EXAMPLE 15. Assume $X \sim \mathcal{N}(\theta, 1)$ is observed, and that it is desired to estimate θ under squared-error loss. The obvious guess for a least favorable prior is the noninformative prior density $\pi(\theta) = 1$. (It contains no helpful information about θ.) The generalized Bayes rule, with respect to π, was seen in Chapter 4 to be $\delta_0(x) = x$.

Since π is improper, we must look for an approximating sequence $\{\pi_n\}$ of proper priors. A reasonable choice for π_n is a $\mathcal{N}(0, n)$ density, since $(2\pi n)^{1/2} \pi_n(\theta) \to \pi(\theta) = 1$ for all θ. (Intuitively, the π_n are very flat for large n, and approximate a uniform density.)

From previous calculations, we know that the Bayes risk of π_n is $r(\pi_n) = n/(n + 1)$. Since

$$R(\theta, \delta_0) = E_\theta(X - \theta)^2 = 1 = \lim_{n \to \infty} r(\pi_n)$$

for all θ, Theorem 18 can be used to conclude that δ_0 is minimax.

EXAMPLE 16. Assume $X \sim \mathcal{E}(\theta)$ is observed. The parameter space is $\Theta = (0, 1] \cup [2, \infty)$, and it is desired to test $H_0 : 0 < \theta \le 1$ versus $H_1 : 2 \le \theta < \infty$. Let a_i denote accepting H_i. The loss function is given by

$$L(\theta, a_0) = \begin{cases} 0 & \text{if } 0 < \theta \le 1, \\ 4 & \text{if } \theta \ge 2, \end{cases}$$

$$L(\theta, a_1) = \begin{cases} 0 & \text{if } \theta \ge 2, \\ 5 - \theta & \text{if } 0 < \theta \le 1. \end{cases}$$

It seems plausible that the least favorable prior is one which makes H_0 and H_1 as hard to distinguish as possible, namely one which gives positive probability only to the points $\theta = 1$ and $\theta = 2$. Assume that π is such a prior, and let $\pi_1 = \pi(1) = 1 - \pi(2)$. We still must find the least favorable choice of π_1.

To find the Bayes rule with respect to π, note that the posterior expected losses of a_0 and a_1 are (letting $m(x)$ denote the marginal density of X)

$$E^{\pi(\theta|x)}L(\theta, a_0) = 4(1 - \pi_1)(\tfrac{1}{2}e^{-x/2})/m(x)$$

and

$$E^{\pi(\theta|x)}L(\theta, a_1) = 4\pi_1 e^{-x}/m(x).$$

Thus the Bayes rule is to choose a_0 if

$$(1 - \pi_1)(e^{-x/2})/m(x) < 2\pi_1 e^{-x}/m(x),$$

which can be rewritten as

$$x < 2 \log[2\pi_1/(1 - \pi_1)] = c.$$

We will, therefore, consider the class of rules defined by the test functions $\phi_c(x) = I_{(c, \infty)}(x)$. (This reduction could also have been established using results on uniformly most powerful tests from Chapter 8.)

To find the least favorable π_1, or alternatively the least favorable c, note that

$$R(\theta, \phi_c) = \begin{cases} \int_c^\infty (5 - \theta)\theta^{-1}e^{-x/\theta} \, dx & \text{if } 0 < \theta \leq 1, \\[2ex] \int_0^c 4\theta^{-1}e^{-x/\theta} \, dx & \text{if } \theta \geq 2, \end{cases}$$

$$= \begin{cases} (5 - \theta)e^{-c/\theta} & \text{if } 0 < \theta \leq 1, \\ 4(1 - e^{-c/\theta}) & \text{if } \theta \geq 2. \end{cases}$$

Define

$$h(c) = \sup_{0 < \theta \leq 1} (5 - \theta)e^{-c/\theta} \quad \text{and} \quad g(c) = \sup_{2 \leq \theta < \infty} 4(1 - e^{-c/\theta}).$$

Clearly

$$\bar{R}(c) = \sup_{\theta \in \Theta} R(\theta, \phi_c) = \max\{h(c), g(c)\}.$$

Note that $h(c)$ is strictly decreasing in c, with $h(0) = 5$ and $\lim_{c \to \infty} h(c) = 0$. Also, $g(c)$ is strictly increasing in c, with $g(0) = 0$ and $\lim_{c \to \infty} g(c) = 4$. Hence $h(c)$ and $g(c)$ are equal for just one value of c, call it c_0, and $\bar{R}(c_0) = \inf_c \bar{R}(c)$. The test ϕ_{c_0} is a good candidate for a minimax test.

To find c_0, note first that $4(1 - e^{-c/\theta})$ is decreasing in θ, so that $g(c) = 4(1 - e^{-c/2})$. Next observe that

$$\frac{d}{d\theta} [(5 - \theta)e^{-c/\theta}] = -e^{-c/\theta} + (5 - \theta)c\theta^{-2}e^{-c/\theta}$$

$$= \theta^{-2}e^{-c/\theta}(-\theta^2 - \theta c + 5c).$$

This derivative is positive for $0 < \theta \leq 1$, providing $\theta^2 + \theta c - 5c < 0$. The roots of the equation $\theta^2 + \theta c - 5c = 0$ are $\frac{1}{2}(-c \pm [c^2 + 20c]^{1/2})$, one of which is negative, while the other is larger than 1 for $c > \frac{1}{4}$. Hence if $c > \frac{1}{4}$ and $0 < \theta \leq 1$, it follows that $\theta^2 + \theta c - 5c < 0$, and $(5 - \theta)e^{-c/\theta}$ is maximized at $\theta = 1$. Thus $h(c) = 4e^{-c}$ for $c > \frac{1}{4}$.

Let's assume the solution to $h(c) = g(c)$ is some $c > \frac{1}{4}$. Then we want to solve the equation

$$4e^{-c} = 4(1 - e^{-c/2}).$$

Letting $z = e^{-c/2}$, this is equivalent to solving $4z^2 = 4(1 - z)$. The positive solution of this latter equation is $z \cong 0.618$, which corresponds to $c \cong 0.96$

in the original equation. Since $c > \frac{1}{4}$, this is indeed the unique solution. Note that $c = 0.96$ corresponds to $\pi_1 \cong 0.45$.

Observe finally that for $\pi_1 \cong 0.45$,

$$
\begin{aligned}
r(\pi) = r(\pi, \phi_{0.96}) &= \pi_1 R(1, \phi_{0.96}) + (1 - \pi_1) R(2, \phi_{0.96}) \\
&= \pi_1 h(0.96) + (1 - \pi_1) g(0.96) \\
&= h(0.96)
\end{aligned}
$$

(since $h(0.96) = g(0.96)$). Also, as shown earlier, $R(\theta, \phi_{0.96}) \leq h(0.96)$ for all $\theta \in \Theta$. Hence Theorem 17 can be used to conclude that $\phi_{0.96}$ is a minimax test, and π is least favorable.

III. *Equalizer Rules*

The third method of determining a minimax decision rule is to search for an equalizer rule δ_0^*, i.e., a rule for which $R(\theta, \delta_0^*) = C$ for all θ. If δ_0^* can be shown to be Bayes with respect to a prior π, then since $r(\pi, \delta_0^*) = E^\pi[C] = C$, Theorem 17 can be used to conclude that δ_0^* is minimax and π is least favorable.

EXAMPLE 17. Assume $X \sim \mathcal{B}(n, \theta)$ is observed, and that it is desired to estimate θ under squared-error loss. Let us try to find an equalizer rule of the form $\delta(x) = ax + b$. Clearly

$$
\begin{aligned}
R(\theta, \delta) = E_\theta[aX + b - \theta]^2 &= E_\theta[a(X - n\theta) + \{b + (an - 1)\theta\}]^2 \\
&= a^2 n\theta(1 - \theta) + \{b + (an - 1)\theta\}^2 \\
&= \theta^2[-a^2 n + (an - 1)^2] + \theta[a^2 n + 2b(an - 1)] + b^2.
\end{aligned}
$$

For the risk to be constant in θ, we must have $-a^2 n + (an - 1)^2 = 0$ and $a^2 n + 2b(an - 1) = 0$. Solving these equations for a and b gives $a = (n + \sqrt{n})^{-1}$ and $b = \sqrt{n}/[2(n + \sqrt{n})]$. Thus

$$
\delta_0(x) = ax + b = \frac{x + \sqrt{n}/2}{n + \sqrt{n}}
$$

is an equalizer rule.

To complete the argument, we must show that δ_0 is Bayes. From Chapter 4 (Exercise 5), we know that the mean of the posterior distribution arising from a $\mathcal{B}e(\alpha, \beta)$ prior is $(x + \alpha)/(\alpha + \beta + n)$. The equalizer rule δ_0 is clearly of this form with $\alpha = \beta = \sqrt{n}/2$. Hence δ_0 is Bayes, and must, by Theorem 17, be minimax.

Often an equalizer rule δ_0^* will not be Bayes itself, but will be Bayes in the limit, in the sense that there will exist a sequence of priors $\{\pi_n\}$ such that

$$
\lim_{n \to \infty} r(\pi_n, \delta_0^*) = \lim_{n \to \infty} r(\pi_n).
$$

Such a δ_0^* is called *extended Bayes*. If an extended Bayes equalizer rule can be found, it is minimax by Theorem 18. Example 15 illustrates such a situation.

When dealing with finite Θ, it frequently happens that a minimax rule can be found by looking for an equalizer rule corresponding to a point with equal coordinates on the lower boundary of the risk set. This was indicated in Subsection 5.2.4, and will be discussed further in the next subsection.

It should be emphasized that the three methods discussed above for finding a minimax rule are not really distinct in the sense that only one can apply. Frequently, two or all three of the techniques will be useful in the determination of a minimax rule. The methods can just be thought of as three helpful guidelines to employ in tackling a statistical game.

5.3.3 Statistical Games with Finite Θ

When $\Theta = \{\theta_1, \theta_2, \ldots, \theta_m\}$, the statistical problem can be converted to an S-game. The risk set will then be

$$S = \{\mathbf{R}(\delta^*) = (R(\theta_1, \delta^*), \ldots, R(\theta_m, \delta^*))^t : \delta^* \in \mathscr{D}^*\}.$$

When S can be explicitly constructed, the methods of Subsection 5.2.4 can be used to find a minimax rule. Unfortunately, the space $\mathscr{D}^*$ of decision rules is usually quite complicated, so that obtaining S in its entirety is difficult. Frequently, however, the lower boundary, $\lambda(S)$, can be obtained, and a minimax risk point found for this much reduced set. Theorem 11 can be very helpful in obtaining $\lambda(S)$, since it shows that $\lambda(S)$ is contained in the set of risk points corresponding to Bayes rules. In order to apply the theorem, however, it is necessary to verify that S is closed from below and bounded from below. These conditions are also needed to apply the minimax theorem, which ensures the existence of a minimax rule. We, therefore, give a brief discussion of the verification of these conditions in statistical games.

Under the assumption that $L(\theta, a) \geq -K > -\infty$ (which we are making), it is easy to check that $R(\theta, \delta^*) \geq -K$. Hence S will clearly be bounded from below.

It is considerably more difficult to determine if S is closed from below. Usually this is done by showing that S is closed. To show that S is closed, it is useful to consider

$$W = \{\mathbf{w}(a) = (w_1(a), \ldots, w_m(a))^t : w_i(a) = L(\theta_i, a) \quad \text{and} \quad a \in \mathscr{A}\}.$$

This is the set of "loss points" in R^m. The following lemma gives a simple condition, in terms of W, under which S is closed and bounded.

Lemma 9. *If $W \subset R^m$ is closed and bounded, then so is the risk set S.*

Unfortunately, the proof of the above lemma involves measure theory and so is beyond the scope of the book. A nonmeasure-theoretic proof for discrete distributions can be found in Blackwell and Girshick (1954).

The following lemma, in turn, states simple conditions under which W is closed and bounded. Its proof will also be omitted.

Lemma 10. *If* (i) $\mathscr{A}$ *is finite, or* (ii) $\mathscr{A}$ *is a bounded closed subset of* R^m *with* $L(\theta_i, a)$ *continuous in* a *for* $i = 1, \ldots, m$, *then* W *is closed and bounded, and hence* S *is closed and bounded.*

Of course, S will be closed under far more general conditions than those of Lemma 10. Indeed only very rarely will S not be closed in statistical problems. The theory is, therefore, mainly of academic interest.

We next discuss two typical situations in which Θ is finite: testing simple hypotheses and classification problems.

I. Testing Simple Hypotheses

Assume it is desired to test $H_0: \theta = \theta_0$ versus $H_1: \theta = \theta_1$, based on the sample observation X. Let a_i denote accepting H_i ($i = 0, 1$), and assume "0–K_i" loss is used. As usual, a rule $\delta^* \in \mathscr{D}^*$ will be represented by a test function $\phi(x)$, where $\phi(x) = \delta^*(x, a_1)$ is the probability of rejecting when x is observed. Define

$$\alpha_0(\phi) = E_{\theta_0}[\phi(X)] = \text{probability of type I error,}$$

$$\alpha_1(\phi) = E_{\theta_1}[1 - \phi(X)] = \text{probability of type II error.}$$

It is easy to check that $R(\theta_0, \phi) = K_1 \alpha_0(\phi)$ and $R(\theta_1, \phi) = K_0 \alpha_1(\phi)$. Thus the risk set is

$$S = \{(K_1 \alpha_0(\phi), K_0 \alpha_1(\phi))^t : \phi \in \mathscr{D}^*\}.$$

Since $\mathscr{A}$ is finite, Lemma 10 can be used to conclude that S is closed and bounded. We thus know that a minimax rule exists, and that $\lambda(S)$ is a subset of the Bayes risk points.

In this situation, we can actually say a good deal about the shape of S. Indeed S must have a form similar to that shown in Figure 5.7. This follows

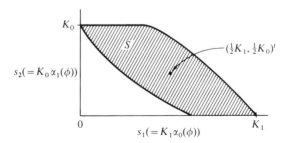

Figure 5.7

from noting that (i) $0 \le \alpha_i(\phi) \le 1$, (ii) $(0, K_0)^t$ and $(K_1, 0)^t$ are in S (arising from $\phi(x) \equiv 0$ and $\phi(x) \equiv 1$ respectively), and (iii) S is symmetric about $(\frac{1}{2}K_1, \frac{1}{2}K_0)^t$ (if $(s_1, s_2)^t$ arises from ϕ, then $(1 - s_1, 1 - s_2)^t$ arises from $(1 - \phi)$).

From Figure 5.7, it is clear that the minimax risk point is the point in $\lambda(S)$ with equal coordinates. Furthermore, this minimax point is the unique minimax point. (S can intersect Q_{α_M} solely at the corner $(\alpha_M, \alpha_M)^t$.) Since any point in $\lambda(S)$ is a Bayes risk point, it follows that the minimax rule is the Bayes rule which has constant risk. (Theorem 17 could have been used directly to show that such a rule is minimax, but we now know that the minimax risk point is unique, and more importantly that this approach will always succeed in finding a minimax rule.)

Bayes rules for this situation are very simple. Indeed, in Subsection 4.4.3 it was observed that they are of the form

$$\phi(x) = \begin{cases} 1 & \text{if } K_0 \pi(\theta_1 | x) > K_1 \pi(\theta_0 | x), \\ \gamma(x) & \text{if } K_0 \pi(\theta_1 | x) = K_1 \pi(\theta_0 | x), \\ 0 & \text{if } K_0 \pi(\theta_1 | x) < K_1 \pi(\theta_0 | x), \end{cases}$$

where $0 \le \gamma(x) \le 1$ is arbitrary and $\pi(\theta_i | x)$ is the posterior probability of θ_i given x. From the definition of posterior probability, it follows that ϕ can be rewritten

$$\phi(x) = \begin{cases} 1 & \text{if } K_0 \pi_1 f(x | \theta_1) > K_1 \pi_0 f(x | \theta_0), \\ \gamma(x) & \text{if } K_0 \pi_1 f(x | \theta_1) = K_1 \pi_0 f(x | \theta_0), \\ 0 & \text{if } K_0 \pi_1 f(x | \theta_1) < K_1 \pi_0 f(x | \theta_0), \end{cases}$$

where π_i is the prior probability of θ_i ($i = 0, 1$). These tests are simply the usual most powerful tests of H_0 versus H_1. The test of this form for which $K_1 \alpha_0(\phi) = K_0 \alpha_1(\phi)$ will be minimax.

EXAMPLE 18. Assume $X \sim \mathscr{B}(n, \theta)$ is observed, and that it is desired to test $H_0 : \theta = \theta_0$ versus $H_1 : \theta = \theta_1$, where $\theta_0 < \theta_1$. Note that $f(x | \theta)$ has monotone likelihood ratio (i.e., if $\theta < \theta'$, the likelihood ratio $f(x | \theta')/f(x | \theta)$ is a non-decreasing function of x). Hence the Bayes tests can be rewritten

$$\phi(x) = \begin{cases} 1 & \text{if } x > j, \\ \gamma & \text{if } x = j, \\ 0 & \text{if } x < j, \end{cases}$$

where j is some integer (depending on the K_i and π_i). For a test of this form,

$$\alpha_0(\phi) = P_{\theta_0}(X > j) + \gamma P_{\theta_0}(X = j),$$

and

$$\alpha_1(\phi) = P_{\theta_1}(X < j) + (1 - \gamma) P_{\theta_1}(X = j).$$

We seek j and γ for which $K_1 \alpha_0(\phi) = K_0 \alpha_1(\phi)$.

As an explicit example, assume that $n = 15$, $\theta_0 = \frac{1}{4}$, $\theta_1 = \frac{1}{2}$, $K_1 = 1$, and $K_0 = 2$. A table of binomial probabilities shows that only $j = 5$ can possibly work. For this value of j,

$$K_1 \alpha_0(\phi) = 0.1484 + \gamma(0.1651),$$
$$K_0 \alpha_1(\phi) = 2[0.0592 + (1 - \gamma)(0.0916)].$$

Setting these expressions equal to each other and solving for γ gives $\gamma \cong 0.44$. The minimax test is thus

$$\phi(x) = \begin{cases} 1 & \text{if } x > 5, \\ 0.44 & \text{if } x = 5, \\ 0 & \text{if } x < 5. \end{cases}$$

II. *Classification Problems*

It is desired to classify an observation X as belonging to one of m populations. If X belongs to the ith population, X occurs according to the density $f(x|\theta_i)$. Thus the problem is to decide among $\{\theta_1, \theta_2, \ldots, \theta_m\}$. Let a_i denote the decision that θ_i is the true state of nature, and assume that the loss for an incorrect decision is 1, while the loss for a correct decision is 0. Thus

$$L(\theta_i, a_j) = \begin{cases} 1 & \text{if } i \neq j, \\ 0 & \text{if } i = j. \end{cases} \tag{5.17}$$

For simplicity, let $\phi_i(x) = \delta^*(x, a_i)$ denote the probability of taking action a_i when x is observed, and let $\boldsymbol{\phi} = (\phi_1, \phi_2, \ldots, \phi_m)$. Clearly

$$R(\theta_i, \boldsymbol{\phi}) = \sum_{j=1}^{m} L(\theta_i, a_j) E_{\theta_i}[\phi_j(X)]$$

$$= 1 - E_{\theta_i}[\phi_i(X)]. \tag{5.18}$$

Since $\mathscr{A}$ and Θ are finite, it follows from Lemma 10 that the risk set is closed and bounded. This in turn implies that there exists a minimax rule among the class of all Bayes rules. It can even be shown, as in the situation of testing simple hypotheses, that this minimax rule is unique and has constant risk. Hence we again seek a constant risk Bayes rule.

The posterior expected loss of action a_i is simply

$$E^{\pi(\theta|x)}[L(\theta, a_i)] = \sum_{j \neq i} \pi(\theta_j|x) = 1 - \pi(\theta_i|x).$$

A Bayes action is an action that minimizes this posterior expected loss, or, equivalently, one that maximizes $\pi(\theta_i|x)$. Since $\pi(\theta_i|x) = \pi_i f(x|\theta_i)/m(x)$, where π_i is the prior probability of θ_i and $m(x)$ is the marginal density of X, it is clear that $\pi(\theta_i|x)$ is maximized for those i for which $\pi_i f(x|\theta_i)$ is maximized. A Bayes rule is thus a rule for which $\phi_i(x) > 0$ only if $\pi_i f(x|\theta_i) = \max_j \pi_j f(x|\theta_j)$. Any minimax rule will be a constant risk rule of this form.

EXAMPLE 19. Assume $X \sim \mathscr{E}(\theta)$ and $\Theta = \{\theta_1, \theta_2, \ldots, \theta_m\}$, where $\theta_1 < \theta_2 < \cdots < \theta_m$. It is desired to classify X as arising from the distribution indexed by $\theta_1, \theta_2, \ldots,$ or θ_m, with the loss as given in (5.17).

To find the minimax rule for this problem, we will seek a constant risk Bayes rule. In determining the form of a Bayes rule, note that for $i < j$,

$$\pi_i f(x|\theta_i) = \pi_i \theta_i^{-1} e^{-x/\theta_i} > \pi_j \theta_j^{-1} e^{-x/\theta_j} = \pi_j f(x|\theta_j) \qquad (5.19)$$

if and only if

$$x < c_{ij} = \frac{\theta_i \theta_j}{\theta_j - \theta_i} \left(\log \frac{\pi_i}{\pi_j} + \log \frac{\theta_j}{\theta_i} \right). \qquad (5.20)$$

On the other hand, for $j < i$,

$$\pi_i f(x|\theta_i) > \pi_j f(x|\theta_j) \quad \text{if and only if } x > c_{ji}. \qquad (5.21)$$

We will show that these relationships imply the existence of constants $0 = \alpha_0 \le \alpha_1 \le \cdots \le \alpha_m = \infty$, such that

$$\phi_i(x) = 1 \quad \text{for } \alpha_{i-1} < x < \alpha_i, \quad i = 1, \ldots, m. \qquad (5.22)$$

Note first that $\pi_i f(x|\theta_i) = \pi_j f(x|\theta_j)$ only if $x = c_{ij}$. Since $\{x: x = c_{ij}, 1 \le i \le m, 1 \le j \le m\}$ is finite, it follows that, with probability one, $\phi_i(X)$ is zero or one. But (5.19), (5.20), and (5.21) imply that $\phi_i(x) = 1$ if and only if

$$\max_{1 \le j < i} \{c_{ji}\} < x < \min_{i < j \le m} \{c_{ij}\}.$$

This shows that $\phi_i(x) = 1$ for x in some interval. The fact that the intervals must be ordered according to i follows directly from (5.19) and (5.20), noting that if $i < j$, $\phi_i(x_i) = 1$, and $\phi_j(x_j) = 1$ (so that $\pi_i f(x_i|\theta_i) > \pi_j f(x_i|\theta_j)$ and $\pi_i f(x_j|\theta_i) < \pi_j f(x_j|\theta_j)$), then $x_i < c_{ij} < x_j$.

For a decision rule of the form (5.22), it is clear from (5.18) that

$$R(\theta_i, \phi) = 1 - \int_{\alpha_{i-1}}^{\alpha_i} \theta_i^{-1} \exp\left\{ \frac{-x}{\theta_i} \right\} dx = 1 - \exp\left\{ \frac{-\alpha_{i-1}}{\theta_i} \right\} + \exp\left\{ \frac{-\alpha_i}{\theta_i} \right\}. \qquad (5.23)$$

To find a constant risk rule of this form, simply set the $R(\theta_i, \phi)$ equal to each other and solve for the α_i.

As an explicit example, assume that $m = 3$, $\theta_1 = 1$, $\theta_2 = 2$, and $\theta_3 = 4$. Setting the risks in (5.23) equal to each other, results in the equations

$$e^{-\alpha_1} = 1 - e^{-\alpha_1/2} + e^{-\alpha_2/2} = 1 - e^{-\alpha_2/4}.$$

Letting $z = e^{-\alpha_2/4}$ and $y = e^{-\alpha_1/2}$, these equations become

$$y^2 = 1 - y + z^2 = 1 - z.$$

Clearly $z = 1 - y^2$, so that the equation $y^2 = 1 - y + z^2$ can be rewritten $y^2 = 1 - y + (1 - y^2)^2$, or

$$y^4 - 3y^2 - y + 2 = 0.$$

The appropriate solution to this is $y \cong 0.74$, from which it can be calculated that $z \cong 1 - (0.74)^2 = 0.45$, $\alpha_1 \cong 0.60$, and $\alpha_2 \cong 1.60$. (These can be checked to correspond to the prior with $\pi_1 = 0.23$, $\pi_2 = 0.33$, and $\pi_3 = 0.44$.) The minimax rule is thus to decide a_1 (i.e., classify X as arising from $f(x|\theta_1)$) if $0 < X < 0.6$, decide a_2 if $0.6 < X < 1.6$, and decide a_3 if $X > 1.6$.

5.4 Evaluation of the Minimax Principle

In this section, we will evaluate the minimax principle from a statistical viewpoint. Thus we will be discussing the consequences of treating nature as an intelligent opponent. Since we are simply pretending to act as if this were true, the criticisms given in Section 5.2 concerning the applicability of game theory do not apply. Instead, the concern is whether or not the minimax principle gives good results.

We will begin with a discussion of admissibility of minimax rules. Subsection 5.4.2 then considers the minimax approach from the viewpoint of rationality. In Subsection 5.4.3, the minimax approach is compared with the Bayesian approach, and it is argued that the minimax approach is successful only if it corresponds to a reasonable Bayesian approach. Subsection 5.4.4 discusses the relationship between the minimax approach and a desire for conservative action. Subsection 5.4.5 introduces a criterion called *minimax regret*, which, if used, alleviates some of the problems of the minimax approach.

5.4.1 Admissibility of Minimax Rules

Minimax rules are usually, but not always, admissible. Many of the minimax rules encountered in this chapter were also proper Bayes rules with finite Bayes risks. The results of Subsection 4.5.1 can be used to prove admissibility for such rules.

Certain admissibility results have been implicitly derived for finite Θ. Indeed if the risk set S is closed from below and bounded from below, then, from the minimax theorem and Theorems 8 and 9 it follows that an admissible minimax rule exists. Note, however, that not all minimax rules are admissible. Indeed, all points in $Q_{\alpha_M} \cap S$ are minimax, yet only those in $Q_{\alpha_M} \cap \lambda(S)$ can be both minimax and admissible. (The second graph in Figure 5.4 is an example in which $Q_{\alpha_M} \cap S$ is not equal to $Q_{\alpha_M} \cap \lambda(S)$.)

A situation in which inadmissible minimax rules abound is when all risk functions are unbounded. Then, since $\sup_\theta R(\theta, \delta^*) = \infty$ for all $\delta^* \in \mathscr{D}^*$, all rules are minimax. Of course, no one would seriously propose using the minimax principle in such a situation.

When a minimax rule corresponds to a generalized Bayes rule, as in Example 15, admissibility becomes hard to verify. A useful technique does exist, however, for proving admissibility in such situations. The technique involves consideration of sequences of proper priors, as in Subsection 5.3.2, and will be discussed in Chapter 8.

As could be expected from Subsection 4.5.2, minimax estimators corresponding to improper priors can be inadmissible. The most important example of this is estimation of a p-variate normal mean under quadratic loss. The usual estimator $\delta^0(\mathbf{x}) = \mathbf{x}$ (where $\mathbf{x}$ is the sample mean) is minimax. (The proof will be left as an exercise.) Recall, however, from Example 16 of Subsection 4.5.2, that δ^0 is inadmissible when $p \geq 3$. Indeed wide classes of estimators have been found which have risks less than δ^0. Since δ^0 is minimax, any such better estimator is also minimax. An interesting problem is thus to find a "good" minimax estimator. In deciding what "good" means, the discussion in Example 16 of Section 4.5 should be kept in mind. There it was argued that if significant improvement upon δ^0 is to be obtained, prior information must be used. (Significant improvement can be obtained only for $\boldsymbol{\theta}$ in a relatively small, but selectable, region of the parameter space. Prior information should be employed to ensure that the minimax estimator used is significantly better than δ^0 for those $\boldsymbol{\theta}$ with high prior probability.) The pleasant fact is that one can easily incorporate prior information (in terms of a prior mean and a prior covariance matrix) into certain minimax estimators. Such estimators are developed in Berger (1979), to which the reader is referred for details. Note that the prior information will, understandably, have less of an effect in a minimax estimator than in the more purely Bayesian estimator of Subsection 4.6.4. Thus the Bayesian minimax estimator should be used only when the prior information is deemed very untrustworthy.

5.4.2 Rationality and the Minimax Principle

At the beginning of the chapter, it was stated that the minimax principle violates the axioms of rational behavior which were discussed in Chapters 2 and 4. The problem is caused not only by the use of the minimax principle, but also by the use of $R(\theta, \delta^*)$ as a measure of loss. We discuss the latter point first.

In Chapter 1 it was pointed out that the use of $R(\theta, \delta^*)$ violates the likelihood principle (and hence the axioms of rational behavior), since it involves an average over the sample space. The risk function was, to an extent, redeemed in Chapter 4, where it was seen to be important in robustness studies. The fact remains, however, that the risk function is not necessarily a good measure of loss for a statistical problem. In a statistical situation, the statistician will observe X before making a decision. Using, as the loss, an

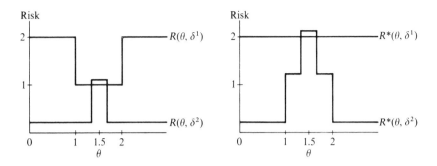

Figure 5.8

average over all X seems to contradict common sense, as well as the basic ideas of game theory. (In game theory, one averages over all unknown random quantities, but not over something known.) Of course, if faced with a sequence of experiments or a problem of experimental design, averages over $\mathscr{X}$ are certainly appropriate.

The above objection to the minimax principle is somewhat philosophical. A more significant objection is that the minimax principle, by considering $\sup_\theta R(\theta, \delta^*)$, can violate the rationality principles in serious ways. As an example of this, consider Figure 5.8. The first graph in this figure contains the risk functions of two rules, δ^1 and δ^2. The rule δ^2 is clearly preferred according to the minimax principle, and would probably be preferred by any principle (providing θ is not felt to be concentrated near 1.5). Now imagine we are told that for $1 < \theta < 2$, we must incur an additional fixed loss of 1. The new risk functions are then those in the second graph of Figure 5.8, and δ^1 is now preferred to δ^2 according to the minimax principle. This is a clear violation of the axioms of rational behavior (in particular Axiom 3 in Section 2.2 is violated), and seems rather silly. Why should we change our minds about the best rule just because of an additional unavoidable loss that will be incurred for both rules? (To avoid nitpicking, let's assume that the utility function for the problem is linear.) This example is still rather artificial, but similar problems will be seen for more realistic situations in the next subsection.

5.4.3 Comparison with the Bayesian Approach

When considered from a Bayesian viewpoint, it is clear that the minimax approach can be unreasonable. Consider the second graph in Figure 5.8 of the preceding subsection, for example. Unless the prior information is concentrated near 1.5, it would be absurd to prefer δ^1 to δ^2 (as suggested by the minimax principle). The following discrete example also illustrates this problem.

EXAMPLE 20. Assume $\Theta = \{\theta_1, \theta_2\}$, $\mathscr{A} = \{a_1, a_2\}$, and the loss matrix is

	a_1	a_2
θ_1	10	10.01
θ_2	8	-8

Since $\sup_\theta L(\theta, a_1) = 10$ and $\sup_\theta L(\theta, a_2) = 10.01$, the best nonrandomized action (according to the minimax principle) is a_1. Observe also that $L(\theta_1, a) \geq 10$ for all $a \in \mathscr{A}$. Hence $L(\theta_1, a_1) \leq L(\theta_1, a)$, and Theorem 2 implies that a_1 is a minimax rule. It can also be shown to be the unique minimax rule.

From a practical viewpoint, action a_1 is unappealing when compared to a_2. If θ_1 occurs, a_1 is only slightly better than a_2, while for θ_2 it is considerably worse. (Recall that θ is not being determined by an intelligent opponent, so there is no reason to think that θ_1 is certain to occur.) This point is emphasized by a Bayesian analysis, which shows that a_1 is preferred to a_2 only if the prior probability of θ_1 is greater than 0.9994. This probability seems unrealistically large, indicating that a_2 will generally be best.

The above two examples are, of course, extreme, but they indicate the problem. A minimax rule can be very bad if it does not correspond to reasonable prior beliefs. Let's look at further examples of a more realistic nature.

EXAMPLE 21. A physician diagnoses a disease as being one of three possibilities, θ_1, θ_2, or θ_3, and can prescribe medicine a_1, a_2, or a_3. Through consideration of the seriousness of each disease and the effectiveness of the various medicines, he arrives at the following loss matrix.

	a_1	a_2	a_3
θ_1	7	1	3
θ_2	0	1	6
θ_3	1	2	0

The minimax rule turns out to be

$$\delta^* = \frac{3}{49} \langle a_1 \rangle + \frac{39}{49} \langle a_2 \rangle + \frac{7}{49} \langle a_3 \rangle.$$

(The proof is left as an exercise.) This does not seem unreasonable, but neither does it appear to be obviously optimal. More insight can be obtained by observing that this rule is Bayes with respect to the prior $\pi = (\frac{7}{49}, \frac{10}{49}, \frac{32}{49})^t$

(which is least favorable). If this prior is in rough agreement with the physician's beliefs concerning the likelihood of each disease, then the minimax rule is fine. Otherwise, it may not be good.

Turning to true statistical problems, consider first the testing of simple hypotheses, as discussed in Subsection 5.3.3. It was seen there that a minimax test is always a Bayes rule with respect to certain prior probabilities of the hypotheses. If these prior probabilities correspond to true prior beliefs, or are at least close, use of the minimax rule is reasonable. Otherwise, however, use of the minimax rule seems ill advised. A similar observation can be made concerning many of the other examples in the chapter, such as Examples 16 and 19.

It can be argued that the above examples are decision problems, and that in inference problems where objectivity is desired the minimax approach will fare better. This is to an extent true, but the following examples indicate that caution should still be used.

EXAMPLE 22 (Due to Herman Rubin). Assume $X \sim \mathscr{B}(n, \theta)$ is observed, where $\Theta = (0, 1]$, $\mathscr{A} = [0, 1]$, and that it is desired to estimate θ under loss

$$L(\theta, a) = \min\left\{2, \left(1 - \frac{a}{\theta}\right)^2\right\}.$$

(The loss is truncated at 2, in order to allay suspicions concerning the unrealistic nature of an unbounded loss.)

It turns out that the rule $\delta_0(x) \equiv 0$ is the unique minimax rule. We will only show here that it is the unique minimax rule among the class of all nonrandomized rules, leaving the proof for randomized rules as an exercise.

Note first that $R(\theta, \delta_0) = 1$ for all $\theta \in \Theta$. Now consider a nonrandomized rule δ which is not identically zero. Then

$$B = \{x \in \mathscr{X} : \delta(x) > 0\}$$

is nonempty. Define $c = \min_{x \in B}\{\delta(x)\}$, and note that $L(\theta, \delta(x)) = 2$ for $\theta < c/(1 + \sqrt{2})$ and $x \in B$. Thus if $\theta < c/(1 + \sqrt{2})$, it follows that

$$R(\theta, \delta) = E^X L(\theta, \delta(X)) = \sum_{x \in B} (2) f(x | \theta) + \sum_{x \notin B} (1) f(x | \theta)$$

$$= 1 + \sum_{x \in B} f(x | \theta) > 1.$$

Hence no nonrandomized rule has maximum risk of 1 or less, and the conclusion follows.

The rule δ_0 does not seem particularly sensible or objective. The loss function is very reasonable, yet the minimax principle says to ignore the data and estimate θ to be zero. This would only be appropriate if there was a very strong prior belief that θ was near zero.

EXAMPLE 17 (continued). This is an example in which, at first sight, the minimax rule

$$\delta_0(x) = \frac{x + \sqrt{n}/2}{n + \sqrt{n}}$$

seems very reasonable. It is enlightening, however, to investigate the rule from a Bayesian viewpoint.

We saw that δ_0 corresponds to a Bayes rule from a $\mathscr{B}e(\sqrt{n}/2, \sqrt{n}/2)$ prior. The mean of this prior is $\frac{1}{2}$, and the variance is $1/[4(1 + \sqrt{n})]$. The prior mean seems natural (if one is trying to be objective), but the prior variance does not. Indeed if n is large, the use of δ_0 clearly corresponds to having strong prior beliefs that θ is concentrated near $\frac{1}{2}$. When n is small, the prior seems more reasonable. Indeed for $n = 1$, the prior is the Box–Tiao noninformative prior (see Example 8 of Chapter 3), while, for $n = 4$, the prior is the uniform prior on $(0, 1)$. Both seem very reasonable. The Bayesian viewpoint thus suggests that δ_0 is attractive for small n (at least when objectivity is desired), but unattractive for large n. This conclusion is strongly supported by a visual examination of the risk function of δ_0 for various n. A calculation shows that

$$R(\theta, \delta_0) = \frac{1}{[4(1 + \sqrt{n})^2]}.$$

For various n, the normalized risk functions $[nR(\theta, \delta_0)]$ are graphed in Figure 5.9. (These are, of course, the constant lines.) For purposes of comparison, the normalized risk of the usual estimator $\delta(x) = x/n$ is also graphed. This is given by

$$nR(\theta, \delta) = nE_\theta[\theta - X/n]^2 = \theta(1 - \theta).$$

The minimax rule compares very favorably with $\delta(x) = x/n$ for small n, but rather unfavorably for large n.

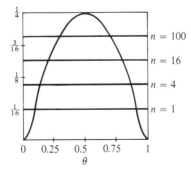

Figure 5.9

The purpose of this subsection has not just been to point out inadequacies of minimax rules, but also to indicate that, to properly evaluate decision rules, Bayesian reasoning is almost indispensable. When a decision rule is derived in a non-Bayesian fashion, one should check that it corresponds to a reasonable prior distribution. In Chapter 4, we argued that a Bayesian should not trust his analysis too completely. He should also look at classical properties of his decision rule, as an aid in investigating robustness. This argument, in the reverse direction, is even more compelling. A rule derived in a non-Bayesian fashion should be investigated from a Bayesian viewpoint to ensure that it is sensible.

5.4.4 The Desire to Act Conservatively

The last bastion of defense for the minimax principle is the argument that someone might really want to act conservatively, no matter how silly the result seems to be. The obvious counter-argument has already been mentioned, namely that conservatism will naturally be built into the utility function, and hence into the loss and risk function. Further attempts at conservatism would be overkill. The possible loophole in this argument is the need to develop the loss through a utility analysis. We saw in Chapter 2 that doing this is very hard, and a supporter of the minimax principle might argue that it is far simpler to assume, say, a linear utility (if money is involved) and to incorporate the desired conservatism through the minimax principle. We could, of course, argue against this on "rationality" grounds and give examples where it doesn't work, but instead we will hoist the minimax man by his own petard. If this is the way he desires to act, there can then be no justification in statistical problems for randomization. If several actions are available, the conservative action is obviously that with the smallest maximum loss. Randomizing among actions is taking a gamble; risking a larger than necessary loss. To put this another way, the justification for evaluating randomized rules through expected loss was utility theory. If one argues that utility theory doesn't apply, then randomized rules can no longer be evaluated through expected loss, and much of minimax theory is inapplicable. But if utility theory does apply, it is wrong to evaluate a rule by its worst possible loss or risk.

5.4.5 Minimax Regret

In many situations, the worst inadequacies of the minimax approach can be partially alleviated through use of what is called the minimax regret approach. The key idea can be seen by considering Example 20. Note that if θ_1 is the state of nature, the loss is bound to be at least 10. The minimax strategy ignores this, and tries to protect against 10.01. An obvious way to remedy the situation is to consider

$$L^*(\theta, a) = L(\theta, a) - \inf_{a \in \mathscr{A}} L(\theta, a).$$

For a given θ, this will result in evaluating actions on the basis of how they compare with the best possible action. In other words, it will be the *differences* in losses between the actions that matter, not the absolute magnitudes of the losses. The function $L^*(\theta, a)$ is called *regret loss* (since it gives the regret we have for not using the best action) and is reputed to have originated with J. Savage.

Regret loss can be dealt with exactly as is a usual loss. Indeed defining

$$R^*(\theta, \delta^*) = E_\theta L^*(\theta, \delta^*(X, \cdot)),$$

where for a randomized rule δ^*

$$L^*(\theta, \delta^*(x, \cdot)) = E^{\delta^*(x, \cdot)}[L^*(\theta, a)],$$

one can formally define the following decision principle.

Minimax Regret Principle. *A rule δ_1^* is preferred to δ_2^* if*

$$\sup_\theta R^*(\theta, \delta_1^*) < \sup_\theta R^*(\theta, \delta_2^*).$$

Definition 15. A *minimax regret* decision rule δ^{*MR} is a rule which is minimax for the loss L^*.

EXAMPLE 20 (continued). The regret loss matrix is easily calculated to be

	a_1	a_2
θ_1	0	0.01
θ_2	16	0

The minimax regret rule is simply the minimax rule for this loss. This can be calculated to be

$$\delta^{*MR} = \frac{1}{1601} \langle a_1 \rangle + \frac{1600}{1601} \langle a_2 \rangle.$$

Hence a_2 is selected with probability nearly equal to one, exactly as intuition would suggest. Contrast this with the opposite behavior of δ^{*M} for the original loss matrix.

In many of the statistical problems we have encountered, $\inf_{a \in \mathscr{A}} L(\theta, a) = 0$. The "standard" losses of Section 2.4 all satisfy this condition, for example. In such a situation it is clear that $L^*(\theta, a) = L(\theta, a)$ and $R^*(\theta, \delta^*) = R(\theta, \delta^*)$. The minimax and minimax regret approaches then coincide. This is probably why minimax rules in standard statistical situations are usually much more reasonable than the minimax rule in Example 20.

It is interesting to note that analysis according to the Bayesian principle is unaffected by the use of L^* instead of L. For example, defining $r(\theta) = \inf_a L(\theta, a)$, the Bayes risk of a rule δ under L^* is

$$
\begin{aligned}
r^*(\pi, \delta) &= E^\pi R^*(\theta, \delta) = E^\pi E_\theta^X L^*(\theta, \delta(X)) \\
&= E^\pi E_\theta^X [L(\theta, \delta(X)) - r(\theta)] \\
&= r(\pi, \delta) - E^\pi [r(\theta)].
\end{aligned}
$$

Providing $E^\pi[r(\theta)]$ is finite, minimizing $r^*(\pi, \delta)$ (over δ) is thus equivalent to minimizing $r(\pi, \delta)$. The same result can be demonstrated for minimizing the posterior expected loss. It is thus as rational to be basing a decision on L^* as on L, and the former seems definitely more attractive for the minimax approach (at least when L is developed through utility theory).

5.4.6 Conclusions

In actually making decisions, the use of the minimax principle is definitely suspect. It may be of some use when dealing with an intelligent opponent, but the conditions needed for a strict application of the principle are quite unrealistic and restrictive. In problems of statistical decision theory, the principle can lead to very bad results, and works well only when it happens to coincide with reasonable prior information. (The minimax regret principle works somewhat better in statistical situations.)

When dealing with problems of statistical inference, the minimax principle tends to be more successful, especially when used with standard losses. The reason for this success, however, is that it will frequently correspond to an objective Bayesian approach (in which, say, a noninformative prior is used). Indeed the best method of evaluating a minimax rule is to determine the prior distribution to which it corresponds, and to observe whether or not this prior information is reasonable. Being as the minimax approach tends to be much more difficult than a Bayesian approach (using, say, a noninformative prior), the Bayesian approach seems superior. Of course, we have seen that the Bayesian approach has problems of its own, particularly that of robustness. Because of this, it is often very useful to compare the risk of a Bayes rule with that of the minimax rule, in an attempt to detect unappealing features of the Bayes rule. The concern here is that, through misspecification of the prior information, a dangerously nonconservative rule could result. The minimax rule, being naturally conservative, can, in comparison, point out such a problem. What we are really saying is that, while the Bayesian approach is generally superior, a decision rule should be examined from as many angles as possible.

Exercises

Subsection 5.2.1

1. Prove Lemma 1.

2. Prove Lemma 2.

3. Prove that a unique minimax strategy is admissible.

4. For a two-person zero-sum game in which $\mathscr{A}$ is a closed bounded convex subset of R^m and L is convex in a for each $\theta \in \Theta$, prove that there exists an $a_0 \in \mathscr{A}$ such that

$$\sup_{\theta \in \Theta} L(\theta, a_0) = \overline{V}.$$

Subsection 5.2.2

5. Prove Theorem 1.

6. Prove Theorem 3.

7. In Example 2, find the minimax and maximin strategies and the value of the game.

8. Prove that, if an equalizer strategy is admissible, then it is minimax (or maximin).

9. Assume $\Theta = \mathscr{A} = [0, 1]$. Find minimax and maximin strategies and the value of the game for each of the following losses:
   (a) $\theta - 2\theta a + a/2$,
   (b) $(\theta - a)^2$,
   (c) $\theta^2 - \theta + a - a^2$,
   (d) $a - 2\theta a + 1$,
   (e) $|\theta - a| - (\theta - a)^2$.

10. (Blackwell and Girshick (1954)). Consider the following game: I chooses a number θ, where $0 \le \theta \le 1$. II consists of two partners II_1 and II_2. II_1 observes θ, then chooses a number z, where $0 \le z \le 1$. The number z is then told to II_2 who proceeds to choose a number a, $0 \le a \le 1$, and pays to I the amount $[z + |\theta - a|]$. II_2 and II_1 can agree, before the game, on the manner in which II_1 will choose z.
    (a) What is the strategy space for II?
    (b) Show that the game has value zero.
    (c) Find the class of all nonrandomized maximin strategies.
    (d) Show that no minimax strategy exists.

Subsection 5.2.3

In the following exercises, solving a game will mean finding a minimax strategy, a maximin strategy, and the value of the game.

11. Solve the game in Example 21 (Subsection 5.4.3).

12. Solve the game of *scissors-paper-stone*, in which each player can choose between the strategies scissors (s), paper (p), and stone (r), and the loss matrix is

	s	p	r
s	0	1	−1
p	−1	0	1
r	1	−1	0

13. Solve the game with loss matrix

	a_1	a_2	a_3
θ_1	l_1	0	0
θ_2	0	l_2	0
θ_3	0	0	l_3

14. Let $\Theta = \mathscr{A} = \{1, 2, \ldots, m\}$. Assume the loss matrix is given by

$$l_{ij} = \begin{cases} 1 & \text{if } |i - j| = 0 \quad \text{or } 1, \\ 0 & \text{otherwise.} \end{cases}$$

Solve the game.

15. (Blackwell and Girshick (1954)). Solve the following game of *hide and seek*. II can hide at location A, B, C, or D. Hiding at A is free, hiding at B or C costs 1 unit, and hiding at D costs 2 units. (The cost is to be payed to I at the end of the game). I can choose to look for II in only one of A, B, or C. If he finds II, he will be payed an additional 3 units by II.

16. The good guys (army G) are engaged in a war with the bad guys (army B). B (player I) must go through mountain pass 1 or pass 2. G (player II) has a choice of 3 strategies to defend the passes: a_1—use all available men to defend pass 1; a_2—use all available men to defend pass 2; a_3—use $\frac{1}{2}$ of the men at each pass. The loss to G is the difference between the number of G companies destroyed and the number of B companies destroyed. In defending pass 1 with all available men, G will lose 2 of their companies while destroying 10 of B's. In defending pass 2 with all available men, G will lose 2 compared with 12 for B. If G splits its force and B goes through pass 1, the losses will be 8 for B and 5 for G, while if B goes through pass 2, the losses will be 10 for B and 5 for G.
    (a) Solve the game.
    (b) A spy reports that the probability that B will choose pass 1 is 0.8. What strategy should G now use?

17. Tom and Burgess together inherit an antique pipe, valued at $400. They agree to decide ownership by the method of sealed bids. They each write down a bid and

put it in an envelope. They open the envelopes together, and the higher bidder receives the pipe, while paying the amount of his bid to the other player. If the two bids are equal, a coin flip decides who gets the pipe, the winner receiving the pipe and paying the other the amount of the bid.

(a) Solve the game, assuming any bid from $0 to $400 is allowed.

(b) Solve the game (finding at least two minimax and two maximin strategies) if only bids in $100 increments are allowed.

18. There is an interesting card game called *liar's poker* (also known by a number of less refined names). Consider the following very simplified version of the game. A large deck of cards contains only 2's, 3's, and 4's, in equal proportions. (The deck is so large that, at all stages of the game, the probability of drawing either a 2, 3, or 4 can be considered to be $\frac{1}{3}$.)

Player I draws a card. He claims that its denomination is i ($i = 2, 3,$ or 4). Player II can either believe I (call this action b) or call him a liar (action l). If II takes action l, and I's card is really an i, II loses 1. If II takes action l and I's card is not an i, II wins 1. If II takes action b, I gives him the drawn card. II can now either keep the card, or discard it and draw a new one from the deck. He must then claim that the card is a j, where j is an integer larger than i. I can then take action b or action l. If he says "l," he wins or loses according to whether or not II was lying. If he says "b," he then gets II's card, and can either keep it or take another, after which he must claim $k > j$. If the game has reached this stage, it is clear that $k = 4$ (and $i = 2$, $j = 3$). Whenever a claim of $k = 4$ is made, the other player can not improve the hand, since 4 is the largest possible hand. Hence the only sensible action, and the only one we will allow, is for a player to say l if his opponent claims 4.

Find the minimax and maximin strategies for the game, and show that the value of the game is 4/9.

19. Prove that, in a finite game, the sets of maximin and minimax strategies are bounded and convex.

Subsection 5.2.4

20. Prove Theorem 7.

21. Prove Theorem 9.

22. Consider the finite game with loss matrix

	a_1	a_2	a_3	a_4	a_5
θ_1	4	5	8	2	6
θ_2	1	8	5	6	6

(a) Graph the risk set S.

(b) Find the minimax strategy and the value of the game.

(c) Find the maximin strategy, and determine the tangent line to S at the minimax point.

23. For the following S games find (i) the value, (ii) the minimax risk point, (iii) the maximin strategy and the tangent line to S at the minimax point, and (iv) the Bayes risk point with respect to $\pi = (\frac{1}{3}, \frac{2}{3})^t$.
    (a) $S = \{\mathbf{x} \in R^2 : (x_1 - 8)^2 + (x_2 - 3)^2 \le 9\}$.
    (b) $S = \{\mathbf{x} \in R^2 : (x_1 - 10)^2 + (x_2 - 10)^2 \le 400\}$.
    (c) $S = \{\mathbf{x} \in R^2 : x_1 > 0 \text{ and } x_2 \ge 1/(2x_1)\}$.

24. Let $K = \{\mathbf{x} \in R^2 : (x_1 - 8)^2 + (x_2 - 8)^2 \le 100\}, Q = \{\mathbf{x} \in R^2 : x_1 \ge 0 \text{ and } x_2 \ge 0\}$, and $P = \{(0, 2)^t\}$. Consider the S-game in which $S = K \cap Q - P$.
    (a) Graph the set S, and describe the set
        (i) of admissible risk points,
        (ii) of Bayes risk points,
        (iii) of Bayes risk points against π which have no zero coordinates.
    (b) Show that the last conclusion in Theorem 8 is false for this situation.
    (c) Use S to demonstrate that a Bayes risk point need not always exist.
    (d) Which Bayes risk points are inadmissible?

25. (a) Prove that, if S is closed and bounded, a Bayes risk point always exists.
    (b) Give an example in which S is closed and bounded from below, and yet a Bayes risk point does not exist for at least one π.

26. Give an example of a finite game in which a nonrandomized strategy a_0 is a minimax strategy and is Bayes with respect to π, yet π is not maximin.

Subsections 5.2.5 and 5.2.6

27. Prove Theorem 10 of Subsection 5.2.4.

28. (a) Prove that if S_1 and S_2 are closed disjoint convex subsets of R^m, and at least one of them is bounded, then there exists a vector $\xi \in R^m$ such that

$$\sup_{\mathbf{s}^2 \in S_2} \xi^t \mathbf{s}^2 < \inf_{\mathbf{s}^1 \in S_1} \xi^t \mathbf{s}^1.$$

    (b) Find a counterexample to the above result if both sets are unbounded.

29. For the situation of Exercise 10, find ε-minimax strategies for II.

Subsection 5.3.2

30. Prove Theorem 17.

31. Prove Theorem 18.

32. An IQ test score $X \sim \mathcal{N}(\theta, 100)$ is to be observed, on the basis of which it is desired to test $H_0 : \theta \le 100$ versus $H_1 : \theta > 100$. The loss in incorrectly concluding that $\theta \le 100$ is 3, while the loss in incorrectly deciding that $\theta > 100$ is 1. A correct decision loses zero. What is the minimax decision if $x = 90$ is observed?

33. Assume that the waiting time, X, for a bus has a $\mathcal{U}(0, \theta)$ distribution. It is desired to test $H_0 : \theta \le 10$ versus $H_1 : \theta > 10$. The loss in incorrectly deciding that $\theta \le 10$ is $(\theta - 10)^2$, while the loss in incorrectly concluding that $\theta > 10$ is 10. The loss of a correct decision is zero.

(a) If n independent observations $X_1, \ldots, X_n$ are taken, determine the minimax test. (You may assume that, from admissibility considerations, only tests which reject when $z = \max\{x_i\} > c$ (where $c \leq 10$) need be considered, and furthermore, that any such test is admissible.)

(b) If five observations, 1, 5, 9, 3, and 4, are taken, what is the minimax decision.

34. Assume $\mathbf{X} \sim \mathcal{N}_p(\mathbf{\theta}, \mathbf{\Sigma})$, $\mathbf{\Sigma}$ known, and that it is desired to estimate $\mathbf{\theta}$ under a quadratic loss. Prove that $\delta^0(\mathbf{x}) = \mathbf{x}$ is minimax.

35. Let $\Theta = (0, \infty)$, $\mathscr{A} = [0, \infty)$, $X \sim \mathscr{P}(\theta)$, and $L(\theta, a) = (\theta - a)^2/\theta$.
(a) Show that $\delta_0(x) = x$ is an equalizer rule.
(b) Show that δ_0 is generalized Bayes with respect to $\pi(\theta) = 1$ on Θ.
(c) Show that δ_0 is minimax.

36. Let $\Theta = (0, 1)$, $\mathscr{A} = [0, 1]$, $X \sim \mathscr{B}(n, \theta)$, and $L(\theta, a) = (\theta - a)^2/[\theta(1 - \theta)]$. Show that $\delta(x) = x/n$ is a minimax estimator of θ, and find the least favorable prior distribution.

37. (Ferguson (1967)). Let $\Theta = [0, 1)$, $\mathscr{A} = [0, 1]$, $X \sim \mathscr{Ge}(1 - \theta)$, and $L(\theta, a) = (\theta - a)^2/(1 - \theta)$.
(a) Write the risk function, $R(\theta, \delta)$, of a nonrandomized estimator δ as a power series in θ.
(b) Show that the only nonrandomized equalizer rule is

$$\delta_0(i) = \begin{cases} \frac{1}{2} & \text{if } i = 0, \\ 1 & \text{if } i \geq 1. \end{cases}$$

(c) Show that a nonrandomized rule is Bayes with respect to a prior π if and only if $\delta(i) = \mu_{i+1}/\mu_i$ ($i = 0, 1, 2, \ldots$), where $\mu_i = E^\pi[\theta^i]$.
(d) Show that δ_0 is minimax. (*Hint*: Observe that the $\mu_i (i \geq 1)$ can be equal for a distribution π on $[0, 1]$ only if π is concentrated on $\theta = 0$ and $\theta = 1$. Note, however, that $\Theta = [0, 1)$ for this problem.)

38. (Ferguson (1967)). Let Θ be the set of all distributions over $[0, 1]$, let $\mathscr{A} = [0, 1]$, and let $L(\theta, a) = (\mu_1 - a)^2$, where μ_1 is the mean of the distribution θ. (Note that θ refers to the entire distribution, not just a parameter value.) Let $X_1, \ldots, X_n$ be a sample of size n from the distribution θ, and let $X = X_1 + X_2 + \cdots + X_n$.
(a) Show that $\delta_0(x) = [x + \sqrt{n}/2]/(n + \sqrt{n})$ has risk function

$$R(\theta, \delta_0) = \frac{n(\mu_2 - \mu_1 + \frac{1}{4})}{(n + \sqrt{n})^2},$$

where $\mu_2 = E^\theta[X^2]$.
(b) Show that $(\mu_2 - \mu_1)$ (and hence $R(\theta, \delta_0)$) is maximized if and only if θ is concentrated on zero and one.
(c) Prove that δ_0 is minimax.

39. Assume $X \sim \mathscr{B}(1, \theta)$, and that it is desired to estimate θ under loss $L(\theta, a) = |\theta - a|$. Find the minimax rule, the least favorable prior distribution, and the value of the game.

40. (Blackwell and Girshick (1954)). Let $X_1, \ldots, X_n$ be a sample from a $\mathcal{N}(\theta, \sigma^2)$ distribution. It is desired to test

$$H_0 : \sigma^2 = \sigma_0^2, \qquad -\infty < \theta < \infty,$$

versus

$$H_1 : \sigma^2 = \sigma_1^2, \qquad \theta = \theta_1 \quad (\text{where } \sigma_0^2 < \sigma_1^2).$$

The loss is "$0-K_i$" loss.
   (a) Show the following:
      (i) There exists a minimax rule of the form: accept H_0 when $\sum_{i=1}^{n} (x_i - \bar{x})^2 \leq k$ and accept H_1 when $\sum_{i=1}^{n} (x_i - \bar{x})^2 > k$.
      (ii) The following is a least favorable prior distribution: give the point (θ_1, σ_1^2) prior probability ξ; and give the set $\Omega_0 = \{(\theta, \sigma_0^2) : \theta \in R^1\}$ prior probability $1 - \xi$, where, furthermore, the density of θ in Ω_0 is chosen to be $\pi_1(\theta)$ $= [n/2\pi(\sigma_1^2 - \sigma_0^2)]^{1/2} \exp\{-n(\theta - \theta_1)^2/[2(\sigma_1^2 - \sigma_0^2)]\}$.
      (*Hint*: Show that, for any k, there exists a value of ξ for which the proposed decision rule is Bayes against the above prior, and that there exists a value of ξ, and hence a value of k, which makes the maximum risk under H_0 and H_1 equal. Note that, if nature employs the above prior, then the marginal distributions of $\bar{X}$ under H_0 and H_1 (i.e., with respect to the conditional priors on Ω_0 and (θ_1, σ_1^2) separately) are the same. This makes $\bar{X}$ useless for discriminating between H_0 and H_1.)
   (b) Given an equation from which k can be determined.

Subsection 5.3.3

41. Give an example, for finite Θ, in which the set of loss points W is closed but not bounded, and in which the risk set S is not closed. (*Hint*: Find a set W which is closed but unbounded, for which the convex hull of W is not closed.)

42. For the following situations involving the testing of simple hypotheses, sketch the risk set S, and find the minimax rule and the least favorable prior distribution. Assume the loss is "$0-1$" loss.
   (a) $H_0 : X \sim \mathcal{U}(0, 1)$ versus $H_1 : X \sim \mathcal{U}(\frac{1}{2}, \frac{3}{2})$.
   (b) $H_0 : X \sim \mathcal{B}(2, \frac{1}{2})$ versus $H_1 : X \sim \mathcal{B}(2, \frac{2}{3})$.
   (c) $H_0 : X \sim \mathcal{G}(1, 1)$ versus $H_1 : X \sim \mathcal{G}(1, 2)$.

43. Assume $X \sim \mathcal{B}(10, \theta)$ and that it is desired to test $H_0 : \theta = 0.4$ versus $H_1 : \theta = 0.6$ under "$0-1$" loss. Obtain the minimax procedure and compute the least favorable prior distribution.

44. Assume X has density

$$f(x|\theta) = 2^{-(x+\theta)}, \quad \text{for } x = 1 - \theta, 2 - \theta, \ldots \ .$$

It is desired to test $H_0 : \theta = 0$ versus $H_1 : \theta = 1$ under "$0-1$" loss.
   (a) Sketch the risk set S.
   (b) Find a minimax decision rule.
   (c) Find a least favorable prior distribution.
   (d) Find a nonrandomized minimax decision rule.

45. Let $(X_1, \ldots, X_{100})$ be a sample from a $\mathcal{N}(\theta, 25)$ distribution. It is desired to test $H_0: \theta = 0$ versus $H_1: \theta = 2$ under "$0-K_i$" loss, where $K_0 = 10$ and $K_1 = 25$. Obtain the minimax procedure and compute the least favorable prior distribution.

46. We are given two coins and are told that one of them is fair but that the other is biased, having a *known* probability $p > \frac{1}{2}$ of falling heads when flipped. The problem is to decide which coin is biased on the basis of n tosses of each coin. Assuming "$0-1$" loss, determine the minimax procedure.

47. In Exercise 46, assume that we are allowed a third possible action, namely deciding that the experiment is inconclusive. If the loss for this decision is l (where $l < \frac{1}{2}$), find a minimax procedure.

48. Let $X \sim \mathscr{P}(\theta)$, and assume that it is desired to test $H_0: \theta = 1$ versus $H_1: \theta = 2$ under "$0-1$" loss. Find the form of the Bayes tests for this problem. Using these Bayes tests, determine an adequate number of points in $\lambda(S)$ (the lower boundary of the risk set) and sketch this lower boundary. Find the minimax test and the least favorable prior distribution.

49. Let $X \sim \mathscr{P}(\theta)$, where $\Theta = \{1, 2\}$, $\mathscr{A} = \{a_1, a_2, a_3\}$, and the loss matrix is

		a_1	a_2	a_3
	1	0	20	10
θ	2	50	0	20

.

(a) Show that the Bayes rules are of the following form: decide a_1 if $x < k - (\log 3)/\log 2$, decide a_3 if $k - (\log 3)/(\log 2) < x < k - 1$, and decide a_2 if $x > k - 1$. (On the boundaries of these regions, randomization is, of course, allowed.)

(b) Sketch $\lambda(S)$ (the lower boundary of the risk set), by finding an adequate number of Bayes risk points. (It suffices to look at $k = \frac{1}{2}i + \frac{1}{3}$ for various integers i. This choice of k eliminates the need to worry about the boundaries of the acceptance regions.)

(c) Find the minimax rule and the least favorable prior distribution.

50. Assume that X is an observation from the density

$$f(x|\theta) = e^{-(x-\theta)}I_{(\theta, \infty)}(x),$$

and that the parameter space is $\Theta = \{1, 2, 3\}$. It is desired to classify X as arising from $f(x|1)$, $f(x|2)$, or $f(x|3)$, under a "$0-1$" loss (zero for the correct decision, one for an incorrect decision).

(a) Find the form of the Bayes rules for this problem.

(b) Find the minimax rule and the least favorable prior distribution.

Section 5.4

51. For the situation of Example 22, show that $\delta_0(x) \equiv 0$ is the unique minimax rule (among the class $\mathscr{D}^*$ of all randomized rules).

52. In Exercise 46 of Chapter 4, assume that no data, x, is available.
   (a) Using the given loss matrix, find the minimax rule for blood classification, and find the least favorable prior distribution.
      (*Hint*: Consider the subgame involving only the choices A, B, and O.)
   (b) Find the Bayes rule (for this no-data situation), and evaluate the performance of the minimax rule.

53. Discuss whether or not the minimax rule in the situation of Exercise 37 is reasonable from a Bayesian viewpoint.

54. Discuss whether or not the minimax rule in the situation of Exercise 39 is reasonable from a Bayesian viewpoint.

55. Assume that an S game has risk set

$$S = \{\mathbf{x} \in R^2 : (x_1 - 10)^2 + (x_2 - 1)^2 \leq 4\}.$$

   (a) Find the minimax strategy.
   (b) Convert S into S^*, the corresponding risk set if regret loss is used. Find the minimax regret strategy.

56. Prove that, if $\Theta = \{\theta_1, \theta_2\}$ and the risk set S is bounded from below and closed from below, then the minimax regret rule is an equalizer rule and is unique.

CHAPTER 6

Invariance

6.1 Introduction

The invariance principle is an intuitively appealing decision principle which is frequently used, even in classical statistics. It is interesting not only in its own right, but also because of its strong relationship with several other proposed approaches to statistics, including the *fiducial inference* of Fisher (1935), the *structural inference* of Fraser (1968), and the use of noninformative priors. Unfortunately, space precludes discussion of fiducial inference and structural inference. Many of the key ideas in these approaches will, however, be brought out in the discussion of invariance and its relationship to the use of noninformative priors. The basic idea of invariance is best conveyed through an example.

EXAMPLE 1. It is known that X, the decay time of a certain atomic particle, is exponentially distributed with density

$$f(x|\theta) = \theta^{-1} \exp\left\{\frac{-x}{\theta}\right\} I_{(0,\,\infty)}(x),$$

where $\theta > 0$ is unknown. It is desired to estimate θ on the basis of one observation X, under loss $L(\theta, a) = (1 - a/\theta)^2$. Imagine that X is measured in terms of seconds, and that a certain decision rule, $\delta_0(x)$, is proposed.

Consider now the decision problem that would result from measuring the decay time in minutes, instead of seconds. The observation would then be $Y = X/60$. Defining $\eta = \theta/60$, it is easy to check that the density of Y is

$$f(y|\eta) = \eta^{-1} \exp\left\{\frac{-y}{\eta}\right\} I_{(0,\,\infty)}(y),$$

where $\eta > 0$. If actions (to be denoted a^*) in this new problem are also expressed in terms of minutes, so that $a^* = a/60$, then it is clear that

$$L(\theta, a) = \left(1 - \frac{a}{\theta}\right)^2 = \left(1 - \frac{[a/60]}{[\theta/60]}\right)^2 = \left(1 - \frac{a^*}{\eta}\right)^2 = L(\eta, a^*).$$

It follows that the formal structure of the problem in terms of minutes (i.e., the class of densities, the parameter space, and the loss) is exactly the same as the structure of the problem in terms of seconds. It thus seems reasonable to use the same decision rule for the two formulations. Letting $\delta_0^*(y)$ denote the proposed decision rule for the transformed problem, this means that $\delta_0^*(y)$ should equal $\delta_0(y)$.

From another viewpoint, it seems reasonable to insist that the same decision be made no matter what unit of measurement is used. This implies that $\delta_0^*(y)$ should satisfy

$$\delta_0^*(y) = \frac{\delta_0(x)}{60}.$$

Combining this with the earlier conclusion results in the relationship

$$\delta_0(x) = 60\delta_0^*(y) = 60\delta_0(y) = 60\delta_0\left(\frac{x}{60}\right).$$

The above reasoning holds for any transformation of the form $Y = cX$, where $c > 0$. It follows that δ_0 should satisfy

$$\delta_0(x) = c^{-1}\delta_0(cx) \tag{6.1}$$

for all $c > 0$. The functional equation in (6.1) can be easily solved by setting $c = 1/x$, the result being

$$\delta_0(x) = x\delta_0(1).$$

The only decision rules consistent with the above intuitive reasoning are thus rules of the form $\delta_0(x) = Kx$, where K is a positive constant. Such rules are said to be *invariant* (for the given problem of course), and the invariance principle states that one should only use invariant rules. It will indeed be seen that there is a best invariant rule for this problem (i.e., a choice of K which minimizes the risk), so that the invariance principle completely determines the rule to be used.

In understanding the invariance principle, it is useful to consider the following variation of the above example.

EXAMPLE 2. Consider the situation of Example 1, but now assume that theoretical considerations imply that θ must be at least 120 seconds. The problem in terms of seconds then has the parameter space $\Theta = (120, \infty)$, while the corresponding problem in terms of minutes has the parameter space $(2, \infty)$. The structures of the original and transformed problems thus differ, and there is no reason to think that $\delta_0^*(y)$ should equal $\delta_0(y)$. It is still reasonable to expect that

$$\delta_0(x) = 60\delta_0^*(y) = 60\delta_0^*\left(\frac{x}{60}\right)$$

(the action taken should not depend on the unit of measurement), but, being unable to conclude that $\delta_0^*(y) = \delta_0(y)$, no further progress can be made.

Examples 1 and 2 clearly delineate the two intuitive arguments upon which the invariance approach is based. These two arguments can be paraphrased as follows:

Principle of Rational Invariance. *The action taken in a decision problem should not depend on the unit of measurement used, or other such arbitrarily chosen incidentals.*

Invariance Principle. *If two decision problems have the same formal structure (in terms of $\mathscr{X}$, Θ, $f(x|\theta)$, and L), then the same decision rule should be used in each problem.*

The relationship $\delta_0^*(y) = \delta_0(y)$, in Example 1, follows from the invariance principle. The principle of rational invariance, on the other hand, implies that, in both Examples 1 and 2, the relationship $\delta_0(x) = 60\delta_0^*(y)$ should hold.

The principle of rational invariance is so intuitively sensible that it merits little discussion. The invariance principle, on the other hand, though at first sight appealing, is in actuality rather unreasonable. This is because it ignores what we have seen to be the other crucial component of a decision problem, the prior information π. The invariance principle would be sensible if the prior, π, were included in the list of the formal structure of the problem, but it is not customary to do so. It should be kept in mind, therefore, that application of the invariance principle will only be sound for priors which are naturally "invariant." In Example 1, for instance, it is easy to see that a prior density, $\pi(\theta)$, in the original problem, transforms into

$$\pi^*(\eta) = c^{-1}\pi\left(\frac{\eta}{c}\right)$$

under the transformation $\eta = c\theta$. The original and transformed decision problems thus really have the same structure only if $\pi^*(\eta) = \pi(\eta)$, which, by the reasoning used for δ_0 in Example 1, implies that $\pi(\theta) = K/\theta$ for some positive constant K. Note that this prior density is the noninformative prior density discussed in Subsection 3.2.2 (since θ is a scale parameter). Hence the indication is that the invariance principle is suitable only when no prior information is available, and indeed that analysis by invariance will correspond to Bayesian analysis with a noninformative prior. Note that the inapplicability of the invariance principle in Example 2 can be reinterpreted in this light.

If invariance analysis is equivalent to the use of noninformative priors, a natural question is—why should we bother with a chapter on invariance? There are basically three reasons. First, people who don't like to talk about noninformative priors are welcome to do the same thing using invariance. Second, it is not strictly true that the two approaches always correspond, although when they don't, invariance is probably suspect. Third, and most importantly, it was seen in Subsection 3.2.2 that there are many possible choices for a noninformative prior. For example, the argument above, that an invariant prior in Example 1 should be $\pi(\theta) = K/\theta$, is not completely sound, since the resulting prior is improper. Indeed, as in Subsection 3.2.2, it seems that all one can logically conclude is that π, when improper, need only be "relatively invariant." (See Subsection 3.2.2 for the meaning of this.) It is unnecessary to examine this concept in detail, since it will be seen (in Section 6.6) that invariance suggests one particular noninformative prior for use, namely that which is called the right invariant Haar measure on the group of transformations.

A proper understanding of invariance can be obtained only through the study of groups of transformations of a problem. No knowledge of group theory will be assumed in this chapter, but the reader with no previous exposure to groups should be warned that the chapter will not be light reading.

6.2 Formulation

In this section, the notation and structure needed to apply invariance are discussed.

6.2.1 Groups of Transformations

As in Example 1, the important concept will be that of transformations of the problem. For the moment, let $\mathscr{X}$ denote an arbitrary space (assumed to be a subset of R^n), and consider transformations of $\mathscr{X}$ into itself. We will be concerned only with transformations that are one-to-one and onto. (A transformation g is *one-to-one* if $g(x_1) = g(x_2) \Rightarrow x_1 = x_2$, and it is *onto* if the range of g is all of $\mathscr{X}$.)

If g_1 and g_2 are two transformations, it will be important to consider the *composition* of g_2 and g_1, which is the transformation, to be denoted $g_2 g_1$, which is defined by

$$g_2 g_1(x) = g_2(g_1(x)).$$

We are now ready to define a group of transformations.

Definition 1. A *group of transformations* of $\mathscr{X}$, to be denoted $\mathscr{G}$, is a set of (measurable) one-to-one and onto transformations of $\mathscr{X}$ into itself, which satisfies the following conditions:

(i) If $g_1 \in \mathscr{G}$ and $g_2 \in \mathscr{G}$, then $g_2 g_1 \in \mathscr{G}$.
(ii) If $g \in \mathscr{G}$, then g^{-1}, the inverse transformation defined by the relation $g^{-1}(g(x)) = x$, is in $\mathscr{G}$.
(iii) The identity transformation e, defined by $e(x) = x$, is in $\mathscr{G}$. (This actually follows from (i) and (ii).)

EXAMPLE 3. Let $\mathscr{X} = R^1$ or $\mathscr{X} = (0, \infty)$, and consider the group of transformations $\mathscr{G} = \{g_c : c > 0\}$, where $g_c(x) = cx$. This will be called the *multiplicative group* or the group of *scale transformations*. Clearly the functions g_c are one-to-one and onto. Note that

$$g_{c_2} g_{c_1}(x) = g_{c_2}(g_{c_1}(x)) = g_{c_2}(c_1 x) = c_2 c_1 x = g_{c_2 c_1}(x),$$

so that

$$g_{c_2} g_{c_1} = g_{c_2 c_1} \in \mathscr{G}.$$

It can similarly be checked that $g_c^{-1} = g_{c^{-1}} \in \mathscr{G}$ and $e = g_1 \in \mathscr{G}$, so that $\mathscr{G}$ is indeed a group of transformations. Note that this was the group considered in Example 1.

EXAMPLE 4. Let $\mathscr{X} = R^1$, and consider the group of transformations $\mathscr{G} = \{g_c : c \in R^1\}$, where $g_c(x) = x + c$. Clearly the functions g_c are one-to-one and onto, $g_{c_2} g_{c_1} = g_{(c_2 + c_1)} \in \mathscr{G}$, $g_c^{-1} = g_{(-c)} \in \mathscr{G}$, and $e = g_0 \in \mathscr{G}$. This group will be called the *additive group* or *location group* (on R^1).

EXAMPLE 5. Let $\mathscr{X} = R^1$, and consider the group of transformations

$$\mathscr{G} = \{g_{b, c} : -\infty < b < \infty, 0 < c < \infty\},$$

where $g_{b, c}(x) = cx + b$. Clearly

$$g_{b_2, c_2} g_{b_1, c_1}(x) = g_{b_2, c_2}(c_1 x + b_1) = c_2(c_1 x + b_1) + b_2 = g_{(c_2 b_1 + b_2), c_2 c_1}(x),$$

so that $g_{b_2, c_2} g_{b_1, c_1} = g_{(c_2 b_1 + b_2), c_2 c_1} \in \mathscr{G}$. It can similarly be checked that $g_{b, c}^{-1} = g_{-b/c, 1/c} \in \mathscr{G}$, and that $e = g_{0, 1} \in \mathscr{G}$. This group will be called the *affine group* (on R^1).

EXAMPLE 6. Let $\mathbf{x} = (x_1, x_2, \ldots, x_n)$, where each $x_i \in \mathscr{X}_0 \subset R^1$. (Formally, $\mathscr{X} = \mathscr{X}_0 \times \mathscr{X}_0 \times \cdots \times \mathscr{X}_0$.) Consider the group of transformations $\mathscr{G} = \{g_{\mathbf{i}} : \mathbf{i} = (i_1, i_2, \ldots, i_n)$ is some ordering of the integers $(1, 2, \ldots, n)\}$, where $g_{\mathbf{i}}(\mathbf{x}) = (x_{i_1}, x_{i_2}, \ldots, x_{i_n})$. It will be left as an exercise to check that this is indeed a group of transformations. This group is called the *permutation group*.

6.2.2 Invariant Decision Problems

In this subsection, we formally define the concept that a group of transformations can result in transformed problems of equivalent structure. As usual, X will denote a random variable (or vector) with sample space $\mathscr{X}$ and density $f(x|\theta)$. Also, $\mathscr{F}$ will denote the class of all densities $f(x|\theta)$ for $\theta \in \Theta$. If $\mathscr{G}$ is a group of transformations of $\mathscr{X}$ (which we will also call a group of transformations of X), we want to consider the problems based on observation of the random variables $g(X)$.

Definition 2. The family of densities $\mathscr{F}$ is said to be *invariant under the group* $\mathscr{G}$ if, for every $g \in \mathscr{G}$ and $\theta \in \Theta$, there exists a unique $\theta^* \in \Theta$ such that $Y = g(X)$ has density $f(y|\theta^*)$. In such a situation, θ^* will be denoted $\bar{g}(\theta)$.

The following equations (for $A \subset \mathscr{X}$ and integrable function h) follow immediately from Definition 2, and will be frequently used:

$$P_\theta(g(X) \in A) = P_{\bar{g}(\theta)}(X \in A), \tag{6.2}$$

and

$$E_\theta[h(g(X))] = E_{\bar{g}(\theta)}[h(X)]. \tag{6.3}$$

For a given g, the transformation $\theta \to \bar{g}(\theta)$ is a transformation of Θ into itself. It will be left as an exercise to show that, if $\mathscr{F}$ is invariant under $\mathscr{G}$, then

$$\overline{\mathscr{G}} = \{\bar{g} : g \in \mathscr{G}\}$$

is a group of transformations of Θ. We will henceforth use this fact.

To be invariant, a decision problem must also have a loss function which is unchanged by the relevant transformations. To avoid complications, we will assume that no two actions have identical loss for all θ.

Definition 3. If $\mathscr{F}$ is invariant under the group $\mathscr{G}$, a loss function $L(\theta, a)$ is said to be *invariant under* $\mathscr{G}$ if, for every $g \in \mathscr{G}$ and $a \in \mathscr{A}$, there exists an $a^* \in \mathscr{A}$ such that $L(\theta, a) = L(\bar{g}(\theta), a^*)$ for all $\theta \in \Theta$. In such a situation, the action a^* will be denoted $\tilde{g}(a)$, and the decision problem will itself be said to be *invariant under* $\mathscr{G}$.

The action a^*, in the above definition, can be shown to be unique, because of the assumption that no two actions have identical loss and because of the fact that $\bar{g}$ is onto. It is also true that

$$\tilde{\mathscr{G}} = \{\tilde{g} : g \in \mathscr{G}\}$$

is a group of transformations of $\mathscr{A}$ into itself. The proof of this will be left as an exercise.

Instead of beginning with the group $\mathscr{G}$ of transformations on $\mathscr{X}$ and deriving from it the groups $\bar{\mathscr{G}}$ and $\tilde{\mathscr{G}}$, we could have just started with one big composite group with vector elements of the form (g_1, g_2, g_3), where g_1, g_2, and g_3 operate on $\mathscr{X}$, Θ, and $\mathscr{A}$ respectively. This has a certain theoretical advantage in manipulation and is slightly more general, but is also somewhat obscure at first sight. We, therefore, opted for the $\mathscr{G}, \bar{\mathscr{G}}, \tilde{\mathscr{G}}$ approach. One will encounter both sets of notations in the literature.

EXAMPLE 1 (continued). Consider the group of scale transformations defined in Example 3. Clearly $Y = g_c(X) = cX$ has density

$$c^{-1}f\left(\frac{y}{c}\Big|\theta\right) = (c\theta)^{-1}\exp\left\{\frac{-y}{c\theta}\right\}I_{(0,\infty)}(y) = f(y|c\theta).$$

Hence $\bar{g}_c(\theta) = c\theta$ is the induced transformation of Θ, and the class $\mathscr{F}$ of exponential densities is clearly invariant under $\mathscr{G}$. It is also easy to see that $\tilde{g}(a) = ca$, since

$$L(\theta, a) = \left(1 - \frac{a}{\theta}\right)^2 = \left(1 - \frac{\tilde{g}(a)}{\bar{g}(\theta)}\right)^2 = L(\bar{g}(\theta), \tilde{g}(a)).$$

Hence the loss and decision problem are invariant under $\mathscr{G}$. Note that $\mathscr{G}, \bar{\mathscr{G}}$, and $\tilde{\mathscr{G}}$ are the same group of transformations.

EXAMPLE 7. Assume that $X \sim \mathscr{N}(\theta, 1)$, and that it is desired to estimate θ under a loss of the form $L(\theta, a) = W(|\theta - a|)$. Let $\mathscr{G}$ be the group of additive transformations introduced in Example 4. Clearly $Y = g_c(X) = X + c$ has a $\mathscr{N}((\theta + c), 1)$ density. Hence $\bar{g}_c(\theta) = \theta + c$, and $\mathscr{F}$ is invariant under $\mathscr{G}$. Also, if $\tilde{g}_c(a) = a + c$, then

$$L(\theta, a) = W(|\theta - a|) = W(|\bar{g}_c(\theta) - \tilde{g}_c(a)|) = L(\bar{g}_c(\theta), \tilde{g}_c(a)),$$

so that the loss and problem are invariant under $\mathscr{G}$. Note that $\mathscr{G}, \bar{\mathscr{G}}$, and $\tilde{\mathscr{G}}$ are the same group.

EXAMPLE 8. Assume that $X \sim \mathscr{B}(n, \theta)$, and that it is desired to estimate θ under squared-error loss. Let $\mathscr{G} = \{e, g^*\}$, where e is the identity transformation and g^* is the transformation $g^*(x) = n - x$. Clearly $Y = g^*(X) = n - X$ has a $\mathscr{B}(n, 1 - \theta)$ density, so that $\mathscr{F}$ is invariant under $\mathscr{G}$, with $\bar{g}^*(\theta) = 1 - \theta$. The loss and decision problem are also invariant, as can be seen by defining $\tilde{g}^*(a) = 1 - a$.

EXAMPLE 9. Assume that $X \sim \mathscr{N}(\theta, \sigma^2)$, both θ and σ^2 unknown, and that it is desired to test $H_0: \theta \leq 0$ versus $H_1: \theta > 0$ under "0–1" loss. Here $\mathscr{A} = \{a_0, a_1\}$, where a_i denotes accepting H_i. Let $\mathscr{G}$ be the group of scale transformations given in Example 3. Clearly $Y = g_c(X) = cX$ has a $\mathscr{N}(c\theta, c^2\sigma^2)$ density, so that $\mathscr{F}$ is invariant under $\mathscr{G}$, with $\bar{g}_c((\theta, \sigma^2)) = (c\theta, c^2\sigma^2)$. (Note that $\bar{g}_c$ is a transformation on $\Theta = R^1 \times (0, \infty)$.) Note also that if $\theta < 0$, then $c\theta < 0$, while if $\theta > 0$, then $c\theta > 0$. Hence, defining $\tilde{g}_c(a) = \tilde{e}(a) = a$ (the identity transformation), it is clear that the loss is invariant under $\mathcal{G}$. Interestingly enough, $\tilde{\mathcal{G}}$ consists only of $\tilde{e}$.

As in the above example, it is frequently the case in hypothesis testing that $\tilde{\mathcal{G}}$ consists only of the identity transformation. (The group operation will usually not cause a change in the hypothesis accepted.) When this is the case, an invariant loss must satisfy

$$L(\theta, a_i) = L(\bar{g}(\theta), \tilde{g}(a_i)) = L(\bar{g}(\theta), a_i).$$

Of the various standard testing losses we have considered, only "0-K_i" loss will generally satisfy this condition, and then only if Θ_0 and Θ_1 (the parameter regions under the null and alternative hypotheses) are invariant subspaces, in the sense that, for all g, $\bar{g}(\theta) \in \Theta_i$ when $\theta \in \Theta_i$ (for $i = 0, 1$). (In other words, Θ_0 and Θ_1 must be mapped back into themselves.) Thus invariance in hypothesis testing has come to mean essentially that the loss is "0-K_i" loss, and that Θ_0 and Θ_1 are invariant subspaces. (It is possible for invariance in hypothesis testing to take other forms. In Example 9, for instance, one could enlarge $\mathcal{G}$ to include the transformations $g_c(x) = cx$ for $c < 0$. These transformations would have the effect of interchanging Θ_0 and Θ_1, so that $\tilde{\mathcal{G}}$ would also include the transformation that switches actions.)

6.2.3 Invariant Decision Rules

In an invariant decision problem, the formal structures of the problems involving X and $Y = g(X)$ are identical. Hence the invariance principle states that δ and δ^*, the decision rules used in the X and Y problems, respectively, should be identical. The principle of rational invariance, in addition, states that the actions taken in the two problems should correspond, or that

$$\tilde{g}(\delta(x)) = \delta^*(y).$$

Combining these principles, it follows that a decision rule should be invariant in the sense of the following definition.

Definition 4. If a decision problem is invariant under a group $\mathcal{G}$ of transformations, a (nonrandomized) decision rule, $\delta(x)$, is *invariant under $\mathcal{G}$* if, for all $x \in \mathcal{X}$ and $g \in \mathcal{G}$,

$$\delta(g(x)) = \tilde{g}(\delta(x)). \tag{6.4}$$

Let $\mathcal{D}_I$ denote the set of all (nonrandomized) invariant decision rules.

In Example 1, the invariant decision rules were explicitly found. We content ourselves with one further example here.

EXAMPLE 9 (continued). Using the results in Example 9, Equation (6.4) becomes

$$\delta(cx) = \delta(x). \tag{6.5}$$

Imagine now that $\delta(x_0) = a_i$ for some $x_0 > 0$. Then (6.5) implies that $\delta(x) = a_i$ for all $x > 0$. A similar result holds for $x < 0$. The conclusion is that the only invariant (nonrandomized) decision rules are $\delta_{0,0}$, $\delta_{0,1}$, $\delta_{1,0}$, and $\delta_{1,1}$, where

$$\delta_{i,j}(x) = \begin{cases} a_i & \text{if } x < 0, \\ a_j & \text{if } x > 0. \end{cases}$$

The crucial property of invariant decision rules is that their risk functions are constant on "orbits" of Θ.

Definition 5. Two points, θ_1 and θ_2, in Θ are said to be *equivalent* if $\theta_2 = \bar{g}(\theta_1)$ for some $\bar{g} \in \bar{\mathscr{G}}$. An *orbit* in Θ is an equivalence class of such points. Thus the θ_0-orbit in Θ, to be denoted $\Theta(\theta_0)$, is the set

$$\Theta(\theta_0) = \{\bar{g}(\theta_0): \bar{g} \in \bar{\mathscr{G}}\}.$$

Theorem 1. *The risk function of an invariant decision rule δ is constant on orbits of Θ, or, equivalently,*

$$R(\theta, \delta) = R(\bar{g}(\theta), \delta)$$

for all $\theta \in \Theta$ and $\bar{g} \in \bar{\mathscr{G}}$.

PROOF. Clearly

$$\begin{aligned} R(\theta, \delta) &= E_\theta L(\theta, \delta(X)) \\ &= E_\theta L(\bar{g}(\theta), \tilde{g}(\delta(X))) \quad \text{(invariance of loss)} \\ &= E_\theta L(\bar{g}(\theta), \delta(g(X))) \quad \text{(invariance of } \delta) \\ &= E_{\bar{g}(\theta)} L(\bar{g}(\theta), \delta(X)) \quad \text{(invariance of distributions and (6.3))} \\ &= R(\bar{g}(\theta), \delta(X)), \end{aligned}$$

completing the proof.   □

EXAMPLE 1 (continued). Recalling that $\bar{g}_c(\theta) = c\theta$, it is clear that all points in Θ are equivalent ($\theta_1 = c\theta_2$ for some c), so that Θ is itself an orbit. It follows from Theorem 1 that any invariant decision rule has constant risk for all θ. This can be verified by the direct calculation (letting $\delta_K(x) = Kx$)

$$\begin{aligned} R(\theta, \delta_K) &= E_\theta\left(1 - \frac{\delta_K(X)}{\theta}\right)^2 \\ &= \int_0^\infty \theta^{-1}\left(1 - \frac{Kx}{\theta}\right)^2 \exp\left\{\frac{-x}{\theta}\right\} dx \\ &= 1 - 2K + 2K^2. \end{aligned}$$

The special situation in which the risk function of an invariant rule is constant is of great importance and deserves further investigation.

Definition 6. A group $\bar{\mathscr{G}}$ of transformations of Θ is said to be *transitive* if Θ consists of a single orbit, or equivalently if, for any θ_1 and θ_2 in Θ, there exists some $\bar{g} \in \bar{\mathscr{G}}$ for which $\theta_2 = \bar{g}(\theta_1)$.

If $\bar{\mathscr{G}}$ is transitive, then from Theorem 1 it is clear that any invariant decision rule has a constant risk. An invariant decision rule which minimizes this constant risk will be called a *best invariant decision rule*.

EXAMPLE 1 (continued). All that remains to be done is to find the optimal value of K. Clearly

$$\frac{d}{dK} R(\theta, \delta_K) = -2 + 4K,$$

so that $K = \frac{1}{2}$ is the minimizing value of K. Hence $\delta_{1/2}(x) = x/2$ is the best invariant decision rule.

Even when $\bar{\mathscr{G}}$ is not transitive on Θ, the class $\mathscr{D}_I$ of invariant procedures is often small enough so that an "optimal" invariant rule can easily be selected according to some other principle. We will not actively pursue such situations here.

Invariant randomized decision rules can also be considered, but for simplicity we will not do so. Randomization is sometimes useful in testing problems, but is seldom needed in estimation problems. The justification for the latter statement is that $\bar{\mathscr{G}}$ will usually be transitive in estimation problems to which invariance is applied, so that a best invariant rule will typically exist. It can be shown for such a situation that, providing the group $\mathscr{G}$ is not too large (see Section 6.9), a nonrandomized best invariant rule will always exist. (The proof is related to the proof that a nonrandomized Bayes rule exists, and can be found in Kiefer (1957).) This will be true, in particular, when $\mathscr{G}$ can be identified with Θ, as will be the case in virtually all of our estimation examples.

As a final comment, it is important to note that, if possible, sufficiency should always be used to reduce the complexity of a problem before applying invariance. This, of course, is true for all decision principles.

6.3 Location Parameter Problems

One of the simplest and most natural applications of invariance is to location parameter problems. The concept of a location parameter was defined in Subsection 3.2.2. Recall that θ is a location parameter (or a location vector in higher-dimensional settings) if the density of X is of the form $f(x - \theta)$.

Consider first the one-dimensional estimation problem, in which $\mathcal{X} = \Theta = \mathcal{A} = R^1$, and θ is a location parameter. Assume also that the loss is a function of $a - \theta$, say $L(a - \theta)$. As in Example 7, it is easy to check that this problem is invariant under the group $\mathcal{G} = \{g_c : g_c(x) = x + c\}$, and that $\bar{\mathcal{G}} = \tilde{\mathcal{G}} = \mathcal{G}$. Hence (6.4), the determining equation for invariant rules, becomes

$$\delta(x + c) = \delta(x) + c.$$

Choosing $c = -x$, it follows that $\delta(0) = \delta(x) - x$, or

$$\delta(x) = x + K \tag{6.6}$$

(where $K = \delta(0)$). Any invariant rule must thus be of this form.

It is easy to check, in this situation, that $\bar{\mathcal{G}}$ is transitive on Θ, so that any rule of the form (6.6) has constant risk

$$R(\theta, \delta) = R(0, \delta) = E_0 L(X + K). \tag{6.7}$$

The best invariant decision rule (assuming one exists) is simply that rule of the form (6.6) for which K minimizes (6.7).

The minimization of (6.7) is a problem we encountered in Bayesian analysis with a noninformative prior. The analogy is of enough interest to recall that development. For a location parameter, the noninformative prior is the constant prior $\pi(\theta) = 1$. The posterior density for this prior is

$$\pi(\theta | x) = \frac{\pi(\theta) f(x - \theta)}{\int f(x - \theta) d\theta} = f(x - \theta).$$

Hence the posterior expected loss is

$$E^{\pi(\theta|x)}[L(a - \theta)] = \int_{-\infty}^{\infty} L(a - \theta) f(x - \theta) d\theta$$

$$= \int_{-\infty}^{\infty} L(y + a - x) f(y) dy \quad \text{(letting } y = x - \theta)$$

$$= E_0 L(X + K) \quad \text{(letting } a = x + K).$$

The generalized Bayes rule is thus also $\delta(x) = a = x + K$, where K minimizes (6.7). The results of Chapter 4 can thus be applied to the minimization of (6.7). If, for example, L is squared-error loss, then we know that the generalized Bayes rule is the posterior mean

$$\int_{-\infty}^{\infty} \theta f(x - \theta) d\theta = x - \int_{-\infty}^{\infty} y f(y) dy.$$

Equating this with $\delta(x) = x + K$, it is clear that the optimum choice of K is $-E_0[X]$. If L is absolute error loss, it can similarly be shown that the optimal choice of K is $-m$, where m is the median of X when $\theta = 0$. Two other useful results concerning the optimum value of K are given in Exercises 10 and 11.

The equivalence shown in the above situation between the best invariant estimator and the generalized Bayes rule will be seen in Section 6.6 to be part of a very general phenomenon.

EXAMPLE 10. Assume that $X_1, X_2, \ldots, X_n$ is a sample from a $\mathcal{N}(\theta, \sigma^2)$ distribution, σ^2 known. The sample mean, $\bar{X}$, is sufficient for θ, and has a $\mathcal{N}(\theta, \sigma^2/n)$ distribution. Clearly θ is a location parameter for this distribution. Hence, by the above results, the best invariant estimator of θ under squared-error loss is

$$\delta(\bar{x}) = \bar{x} - E_0[\bar{X}] = \bar{x}.$$

Since the median of $\bar{X}$ when $\theta = 0$ is $m = 0$, it also follows that the above estimator is best invariant under absolute error loss. Indeed, it can be shown, using Exercise 11, that this estimator is best invariant for any loss which is increasing in $|\theta - a|$.

For location vector problems (i.e., problems in which $\mathbf{X} = (X_1, \ldots, X_p)^t$ has density $f(\mathbf{x} - \boldsymbol{\theta})$, the location vector $\boldsymbol{\theta} = (\theta_1, \ldots, \theta_p)^t$ being unknown), exactly the same kinds of results can be obtained. The appropriate group of transformations is the additive group on R^p, defined by

$$\mathcal{G} = \{g_{\mathbf{c}} : \mathbf{c} = (c_1, \ldots, c_p)^t \in R^p\},$$

where $g_{\mathbf{c}}(\mathbf{x}) = \mathbf{x} + \mathbf{c}$. The analysis and conclusions in this situation are virtually identical to those in the 1-dimensional case.

Pitman's Estimator

A somewhat different problem arises when a sample $X_1, \ldots, X_n$ is taken from a 1-dimensional location density $f(x - \theta)$. This is a special case of the more general situation in which $\mathbf{X} = (X_1, \ldots, X_n)$ has density $f(x_1 - \theta, \ldots, x_n - \theta)$. The relevant group of transformations for this problem is

$$\mathcal{G} = \{g_c : g_c(\mathbf{x}) = (x_1 + c, \ldots, x_n + c), \text{ where } c \in R^1\}.$$

It is easy to check that $\bar{\mathcal{G}}$ is simply the additive group on $\Theta = R^1$, which is transitive. It follows that if the loss is of the form $L(a - \theta)$, then a best invariant rule can be sought. Unfortunately, the derivation of such a rule is considerably more difficult here than in the single observational case, and will be delayed until Section 6.5. It turns out, however (see Section 6.6), that the best invariant rule again corresponds to the generalized Bayes rule with respect to the noninformative prior $\pi(\theta) = 1$. It follows that the best invariant estimator is that action which minimizes

$$E^{\pi(\theta|\mathbf{x})}[L(a - \theta)] = \frac{\int_{-\infty}^{\infty} L(a - \theta) f(x_1 - \theta, \ldots, x_n - \theta) d\theta}{\int_{-\infty}^{\infty} f(x_1 - \theta, \ldots, x_n - \theta) d\theta}.$$

When L is squared-error loss, the minimizing action is the posterior mean, so that the best invariant estimator is

$$\delta(\mathbf{x}) = \frac{\int_{-\infty}^{\infty} \theta f(x_1 - \theta, \ldots, x_n - \theta) d\theta}{\int_{-\infty}^{\infty} f(x_1 - \theta, \ldots, x_n - \theta) d\theta}.$$

This estimator is called Pitman's estimator, and was derived in Pitman (1939).

6.4 Other Examples of Invariance

I. *Scale Parameter Problems*

In Subsection 3.2.2 it was stated that $\theta(>0)$ is a scale parameter if $X \in R^1$ or $X \in (0, \infty)$ has a density of the form $\theta^{-1} f(x/\theta)$. If the loss is of the form $L(a/\theta)$, it can be checked, as in Example 1, that the problem is invariant under the group of scale transformations.

Rather than carrying out a general analysis in this situation, we simply note that the problem can be transformed into an invariant location parameter problem. To see this, assume for simplicity that $X > 0$, and consider the transformation $Y = \log X$ and $\eta = \log \theta$. The density of Y given η is clearly $f(\exp\{y - \eta\})$, which is a location density with location parameter η. Defining $a^* = \log a$, the loss in estimating η by a^* is clearly

$$L\left(\frac{a}{\theta}\right) = L\left(\frac{\exp\{a^*\}}{\exp\{\eta\}}\right) = L(\exp\{a^* - \eta\}),$$

which is invariant in the location parameter problem. One can thus use the results of the previous section to obtain the best invariant rule, $\delta^*(y)$, for the transformed problem. Converting back to the original problem results in the decision rule

$$\delta(x) = \exp\{\delta^*(\log x)\}.$$

It can easily be checked that this is indeed a best invariant rule for the original scale parameter problem.

EXAMPLE 11. Assume that $X_1, X_2, \ldots, X_n$ is a sample from a $\mathcal{N}(0, \sigma^2)$ distribution, and that it is desired to estimate σ^2 under loss

$$L(\sigma^2, a) = (\log a - \log \sigma^2)^2 = \left(\log\left[\frac{a}{\sigma^2}\right]\right)^2.$$

It is easy to check that $Z = \sum_{i=1}^{n} X_i^2 \sim \mathcal{G}(n/2, 2\sigma^2)$ is sufficient for σ^2. For this density, σ^2 is a scale parameter, and the group of scale transformations leaves the problem invariant.

Transforming to a location parameter problem results in the consideration of $Y = \log Z$, $\eta = \log \sigma^2$, and $L^*(\eta, a^*) = (a^* - \eta)^2$. From Section 6.3, it follows that the best invariant estimator in the transformed problem is

$$\delta^*(y) = y - E_0[Y].$$

Noting that $E_{\eta=0}[Y] = E_{\sigma^2=1}[\log Z]$, it can be concluded that the best invariant estimator for the original scale parameter problem is

$$\delta(z) = \exp\{\delta^*(\log z)\} = \exp\{(\log z) - E_{\sigma^2=1}[\log Z]\}$$

$$= \frac{z}{\exp\{E_{\sigma^2=1}[\log Z]\}}.$$

The quantity $\exp\{E_{\sigma^2=1}[\log Z]\}$ can be numerically calculated, and is very close to $(n-1)$ for $n \geq 2$.

II. Location-Scale Parameter Problems

In Subsection 3.2.2, a location-scale density was defined to be a density of the form $\sigma^{-1}f([x - \theta]/\sigma)$, where $x \in R^1$ and both $\theta \in R^1$ and $\sigma > 0$ are unknown. The class of such densities is invariant under the group of affine transformations $g_{b,c}(x) = cx + b$ (see Example 5), since $Y = g_{b,c}(X) = cX + b$ has density $(c\sigma)^{-1}f([y - (b + c\theta)]/(c\sigma))$. The group, $\mathcal{G}$, of induced transformations of

$$\Theta = \{(\theta, \sigma): \theta \in R^1 \text{ and } \sigma > 0\}$$

thus consists of the transformations defined by

$$\bar{g}_{b,c}((\theta, \sigma)) = (c\theta + b, c\sigma).$$

Clearly $\bar{\mathcal{G}}$ is transitive, so that a best invariant rule can be sought when the loss is invariant. Some specific examples will be given in the Exercises and in Section 6.6.

III. A Non-transitive Example

Consider the binomial estimation problem of Example 8. The only restriction imposed by (6.4) is that

$$\delta(n - x) = 1 - \delta(x),$$

which is a symmetry restriction. Any rule satisfying this restriction is invariant. Note that there are a large number of such procedures. Also, $\bar{\mathcal{G}} = \{\bar{e}, \bar{g}^*\}$ is not transitive on $\Theta = (0, 1)$, and indeed the orbits in Θ are simply the pairs of points of the form $\{\theta, 1 - \theta\}$. There is no best invariant decision rule for this problem, and invariance is not of much help in choosing a procedure.

6.5 Maximal Invariants

In dealing with statistical problems in which a sample of size greater than one is taken, it can be fairly difficult to apply invariance arguments. The concept of a maximal invariant can be very useful in simplifying such problems.

Definition 7. Let $\mathcal{G}$ be a group of transformations on a space $\mathcal{X}$. A function $T(x)$ on $\mathcal{X}$ is said to be *invariant* with respect to $\mathcal{G}$ if $T(g(x)) = T(x)$ for all $x \in \mathcal{X}$ and $g \in \mathcal{G}$. A function $T(x)$ is said to be *maximal invariant* with respect to $\mathcal{G}$ if it is invariant and satisfies

$$T(x_1) = T(x_2) \quad \text{implies} \quad x_1 = g(x_2) \quad \text{for some } g \in \mathcal{G}. \qquad (6.8)$$

These concepts are best pictured by recalling that $\mathcal{X}$ can be divided up into orbits of points that are equivalent under $\mathcal{G}$. An invariant function is a function which is constant on orbits. A maximal invariant is a function which is constant on orbits, and which assigns different values to different orbits. Note that if $\mathcal{G}$ is transitive on $\mathcal{X}$, so that $\mathcal{X}$ itself is an orbit, then the only maximal invariants are constant functions.

EXAMPLE 12 (Location Invariance). Let $\mathcal{X} = R^n$ and let $\mathcal{G}$ consist of the transformations

$$g_c((x_1, \ldots, x_n)) = (x_1 + c, \ldots, x_n + c).$$

(This would arise in a statistical problem in which a sample of size n was taken from a location density.) The $(n - 1)$-vector

$$\mathbf{T}(\mathbf{x}) = (x_1 - x_n, \ldots, x_{n-1} - x_n)$$

is then a maximal invariant. To see this, note that $\mathbf{T}(g_c(\mathbf{x})) = \mathbf{T}(\mathbf{x})$ (since $(x_i + c) - (x_n + c) = (x_i - x_n)$), implying that $\mathbf{T}$ is invariant. To check (6.8), observe that, if $\mathbf{T}(\mathbf{x}) = \mathbf{T}(\mathbf{x}')$, then $(x_i - x_n) = (x_i' - x_n')$ for all i. Hence $g_c(\mathbf{x}') = \mathbf{x}$ for $c = (x_n - x_n')$.

EXAMPLE 13 (Scale Invariance). Let $\mathcal{X} = R^n$ and let $\mathcal{G}$ consist of the transformations

$$g_c((x_1, \ldots, x_n)) = (cx_1, \ldots, cx_n),$$

where $c > 0$. (This would arise in a statistical problem in which a sample of size n was taken from a scale density.) Defining

$$z^2 = \sum_{i=1}^{n} x_i^2,$$

the function

$$T(\mathbf{x}) = \begin{cases} \mathbf{0} & \text{if } z = 0, \\ \left(\dfrac{x_1}{z}, \ldots, \dfrac{x_n}{z}\right) & \text{if } z \neq 0, \end{cases}$$

is a maximal invariant. The proof will be left as an exercise.

EXAMPLE 14 (Location-Scale Invariance). Let $\mathscr{X} = R^n$ and let $\mathscr{G}$ consist of the transformations

$$g_{b, c}((x_1, \ldots, x_n)) = (cx_1 + b, \ldots, cx_n + b),$$

where $c > 0$. Defining

$$\bar{x} = \frac{1}{n} \sum_{i=1}^{n} x_i \quad \text{and} \quad s^2 = \frac{1}{n} \sum_{i=1}^{n} (x_i - \bar{x})^2,$$

the function

$$T(\mathbf{x}) = \begin{cases} \mathbf{0} & \text{if } s = 0, \\ \left(\dfrac{x_1 - \bar{x}}{s}, \ldots, \dfrac{x_n - \bar{x}}{s}\right) & \text{if } s \neq 0, \end{cases}$$

is a maximal invariant. The proof is left as an exercise.

The major uses of maximal invariants are based on the following theorems.

Theorem 2. *Let $\mathscr{G}$ be a group of transformations of a space $\mathscr{X}$, and assume that $T(x)$ is a maximal invariant. Then a function $h(x)$ is invariant with respect to $\mathscr{G}$ if and only if h is a function of $T(x)$.*

PROOF. If $h(x) = s(T(x))$, say, then

$$h(g(x)) = s(T(g(x))) = s(T(x)) = h(x).$$

Hence h is invariant if it is a function of T.

To establish the "only if" part of the theorem, assume that h is invariant and that $T(x_1) = T(x_2)$. Then $x_1 = g(x_2)$ for some $g \in \mathscr{G}$, so that

$$h(x_1) = h(g(x_2)) = h(x_2).$$

This implies that h is a function of T.   □

Theorem 3. *Consider a statistical decision problem that is invariant under a group $\mathscr{G}$, and let $v(\theta)$ be a maximal invariant on Θ, with respect to $\bar{\mathscr{G}}$. Then, if $h(x)$ is invariant under $\mathscr{G}$, the distribution of $h(X)$ depends only on $v(\theta)$.*

PROOF. Observe that, for any fixed set $A \subset \mathscr{X}$,

$$P_{\bar{g}(\theta)}(h(X) \in A) = P_{\theta}(h(g(X)) \in A) \quad \text{(invariance of distribution)}$$
$$= P_{\theta}(h(X) \in A) \quad \text{(invariance of h)},$$

so that $s(\theta) = P_\theta(h(X) \in A)$ is an invariant function on Θ. By Theorem 2 (with $\mathscr{X}$ and $\mathscr{G}$ replaced by Θ and $\bar{\mathscr{G}}$), it follows that $s(\theta)$ is a function of $v(\theta)$. Since this is true for all A, the theorem follows.   □

We now briefly describe the application of the above results to testing and estimation problems.

Hypothesis Testing

In Example 9 and the subsequent discussion it was indicated that, for invariant hypothesis testing problems, it will typically be the case that an invariant decision rule satisfies $\delta(g(x)) = \delta(x)$ for all $g \in \mathscr{G}$ (i.e., the hypothesis accepted remains the same under transformation of the problem by g). But this means that $\delta(x)$ is an invariant function, which, by Theorem 2, implies that $\delta(x)$ is a function of the maximal invariant $T(x)$. Hence, for invariant hypothesis testing problems, it is frequently the case that the only invariant decision rules are those which are a function of the maximal invariant. Noting from Theorem 3 that the distribution of $T(X)$ depends only on the maximal invariant $v(\theta)$ on Θ, it follows that the invariance approach reduces the original problem to a test concerning $v(\theta)$, based on the observation $T(X)$. This can be a great simplification, as indicated in the following example.

EXAMPLE 15. Let $\mathbf{X} = (X_1, \ldots, X_n)$ have a density of the form $f(x_1 - \theta, \ldots, x_n - \theta)$ on R^n, where $\theta \in R^1$ is unknown. It is desired to test $H_0 : f = f_0$ versus $H_1 : f = f_1$, where f_0 and f_1 are known (up to θ). The loss is "0–1" loss. This problem is invariant under the group of transformations in Example 12, so that

$$\mathbf{T}(\mathbf{x}) = (x_1 - x_n, \ldots, x_{n-1} - x_n)$$

is a maximal invariant. Since $\bar{\mathscr{G}}$ is transitive on Θ, it is clear that the only maximal invariants on Θ are constant functions, which by Theorem 3 implies that the distribution of $\mathbf{Y} = \mathbf{T}(\mathbf{X})$ is independent of θ. (This, of course, is directly obvious here.) It follows that any invariant test will depend only on $\mathbf{Y}$, and hence that the problem can be reformulated as a test of $H_0 : f^* = f_0^*$ versus $H_1 : f^* = f_1^*$, where $*$ denotes a marginal density of $\mathbf{Y}$. Note that the joint density of $(Y_1, \ldots, Y_{n-1}, X_n)$ at, say, $\theta = 0$ is

$$f(y_1 + x_n, \ldots, y_{n-1} + x_n, x_n),$$

so that

$$f^*(\mathbf{y}) = \int_{-\infty}^{\infty} f(y_1 + x_n, \ldots, y_{n-1} + x_n, x_n) dx_n.$$

This new problem is just a test of a simple hypothesis against a simple alternative, and it is well known that the optimal or most powerful tests in such a situation (see Chapter 8) are to reject H_0 if $f_1^*(\mathbf{y}) \geq K f_0^*(\mathbf{y})$, where the constant K depends on the desired error probabilities (i.e., the desired risks under H_0 and H_1). In terms of the original problem, these tests are called *uniformly most powerful invariant* tests.

Estimation

The following considerations apply mainly to invariant estimation problems, but are potentially useful for any invariant decision problem in which $\bar{\mathscr{G}}$ is transitive on Θ. The technique that is discussed gives a conceptually simple way of determining a best invariant decision rule.

Assume that $\bar{\mathscr{G}}$ is transitive on Θ, and that $T(x)$ is a maximal invariant on $\mathscr{X}$. By Theorem 1, any invariant rule δ will have constant risk, so we need only consider, say, $\theta = \bar{e}$. Defining $Y = T(X)$ and, as usual, letting $E^{X|y}$ denote expectation with respect to the conditional distribution of X given $Y = y$, it is clear that

$$R(\bar{e}, \delta(X)) = E_{\bar{e}}^X[L(\bar{e}, \delta(X))] = E_{\bar{e}}^Y E_{\bar{e}}^{X|Y}[L(\bar{e}, \delta(X))].$$

It follows that an invariant rule which, for each y, minimizes

$$E_{\bar{e}}^{X|y}[L(\bar{e}, \delta(X))],$$

will be best invariant (measurability concerns aside). This last conditional problem is quite easy to solve. Note first that $\mathscr{X}(y) = \{x \in \mathscr{X} : T(x) = y\}$ is an orbit of $\mathscr{X}$, and that any $x \in \mathscr{X}(y)$ can be written (uniquely) as $x = g(x_y)$, where x_y is some fixed point in $\mathscr{X}(y)$. Now an invariant decision rule must satisfy

$$\delta(x) = \delta(g(x_y)) = \bar{g}\delta(x_y),$$

and so is specified by the choice of the $\delta(x_y)$. In the conditional problem, therefore, the conditional risk of δ depends only on the choice of $\delta(x_y)$. Finding the best choice will usually be a straightforward minimization problem.

EXAMPLE 16 (Pitman's Estimator). We now present the derivation of Pitman's estimator, which was briefly discussed in Section 6.3. The setup, recall, is that of observing $\mathbf{X} = (X_1, \ldots, X_n)$ which has density $f(x_1 - \theta, \ldots, x_n - \theta)$, and desiring to estimate θ under loss $L(a - \theta)$. From Example 12, we know that $\mathbf{T}(\mathbf{x}) = (x_1 - x_n, \ldots, x_{n-1} - x_n)$ is a maximal invariant for this problem. Setting $\mathbf{y} = \mathbf{T}(\mathbf{x})$ and observing that, on the $\mathscr{X}(\mathbf{y})$ orbit of $\mathscr{X}$, a point $\mathbf{x}$ can be written

$$\mathbf{x} = (y_1 + x_n, \ldots, y_{n-1} + x_n, x_n) = g_{x_n}((y_1, \ldots, y_{n-1}, 0)),$$

it is clear that, instead of working with the conditional distribution of $\mathbf{X}$ given $\mathbf{Y} = \mathbf{y}$, it will be more convenient (and equivalent) to work with the conditional distribution of X_n given $\mathbf{Y} = \mathbf{y}$. Choosing $\theta = \bar{e} = 0$ ($\mathcal{G}$ is transitive so the risk is constant), it is easy to show (see Example 15) that the conditional density of X_n, given $\mathbf{Y} = \mathbf{y}$, is

$$\frac{f(y_1 + x_n, \ldots, y_{n-1} + x_n, x_n)}{\int_{-\infty}^{\infty} f(y_1 + x_n, \ldots, y_{n-1} + x_n, x_n)dx_n}.$$

Since an invariant rule must satisfy

$$\delta(\mathbf{x}) = \delta(g_{x_n}((y_1, \ldots, y_{n-1}, 0))) = \delta((y_1, \ldots, y_{n-1}, 0)) + x_n, \qquad (6.9)$$

it follows that $\delta((y_1, \ldots, y_{n-1}, 0))$ must be chosen to minimize the conditional risk

$E_0^{X_n|\mathbf{y}}[L(\delta(\mathbf{X}) - 0)]$

$$= \frac{\int_{-\infty}^{\infty} L(\delta((y_1, \ldots, y_{n-1}, 0)) + x_n)f(y_1 + x_n, \ldots, y_{n-1} + x_n, x_n)dx_n}{\int_{-\infty}^{\infty} f(y_1 + x_n, \ldots, y_{n-1} + x_n, x_n)dx_n}.$$

The variable x_n in the above integrals is just a dummy variable of integration. Replace it by (say) z, and then make the change of variables $z = x_n - \theta$, where θ is the new variable of integration and x_n is the true observed value of X_n. Using (6.9), the conditional risk then becomes

$$\frac{\int_{-\infty}^{\infty} L(\delta(\mathbf{x}) - \theta)f(x_1 - \theta, \ldots, x_n - \theta)d\theta}{\int_{-\infty}^{\infty} f(x_1 - \theta, \ldots, x_n - \theta)d\theta}. \qquad (6.10)$$

The best invariant estimator is thus that action, $\delta(\mathbf{x})$, which minimizes (6.10), as stated in Section 6.3.

6.6 Invariance and Noninformative Priors

In Section 6.3 it was seen that the best invariant estimator of a location parameter is also the generalized Bayes rule with respect to the noninformative prior $\pi(\theta) = 1$. A similar relationship is valid in many situations in which $\mathcal{G}$ is transitive on Θ. Indeed it is then usually the case that the best invariant rule is (generalized) Bayes with respect to what is called the right invariant Haar measure on the group $\mathcal{G}$. To obtain this result in a general setting requires measure theory and advanced group theory. We will, therefore, restrict ourselves to rather simple (yet frequently occurring) groups, which can be dealt with by calculus.

6.6.1 Right and Left Invariant Haar Densities

We assume, for the remainder of this section, that the group $\mathcal{G}$ is a subset of R^p with positive Lebesgue measure (i.e., is not a discrete set or a set of lower dimension), and that for each fixed $\bar{g}_0 \in \mathcal{G}$, the transformations

$$\bar{g} \to \bar{g}_0\bar{g} \quad \text{and} \quad \bar{g} \to \bar{g}\bar{g}_0$$

have differentials and hence Jacobians. (It would actually be sufficient to require only that the transformations have differentials almost everywhere (i.e., except on a set of lower dimension). This would allow treatment of such groups as the orthogonal group (see Exercise 5). For simplicity, however, we will restrict ourselves to the everywhere differentiable case.)

Definition 8. Let $H^r_{\bar{g}_0}(\bar{g})$ denote the differential (i.e., matrix of first partial derivatives) of the transformation $\bar{g} \to \bar{g}\bar{g}_0$, and let

$$J^r_{\bar{g}_0}(\bar{g}) = |\det(H^r_{\bar{g}_0}(\bar{g}))|$$

denote the Jacobian of the transformation. Similarly, define $H^l_{\bar{g}_0}(\bar{g})$ and $J^l_{\bar{g}_0}(\bar{g})$ as the differential and Jacobian of the transformation $\bar{g} \to \bar{g}_0\bar{g}$.

EXAMPLE 17. Let $\mathcal{G}$ be the affine group on R^1 (see Example 5). The transformation $\bar{g}_{b,c}$ can be considered to be the point $(b, c) \in R^2$, so that we can represent $\mathcal{G}$ as

$$\mathcal{G} = \{(b, c): -\infty < b < \infty \text{ and } 0 < c < \infty\}.$$

In this new notation, the group operation $\bar{g} \to \bar{g}\bar{g}_0$ can be written

$$(b, c) \to (b, c)(b_0, c_0) = ([cb_0 + b], cc_0).$$

The function

$$t((b, c)) = (t_1, t_2) = ([cb_0 + b], cc_0),$$

has differential

$$H^r_{\bar{g}_0}((b, c)) = \begin{vmatrix} \dfrac{\partial t_1((b, c))}{\partial b} & \dfrac{\partial t_1((b, c))}{\partial c} \\ \dfrac{\partial t_2((b, c))}{\partial b} & \dfrac{\partial t_2((b, c))}{\partial c} \end{vmatrix} = \begin{pmatrix} 1 & b_0 \\ 0 & c_0 \end{pmatrix}.$$

The Jacobian of the transformation $\bar{g} \to \bar{g}\bar{g}_0$ is thus

$$J^r_{\bar{g}_0} = |\det(H^r_{\bar{g}_0})| = c_0.$$

It will be left as an exercise to show that the group transformation $\bar{g} \to \bar{g}_0\bar{g}$ has Jacobian $J^l_{\bar{g}_0} = c_0^2$.

Definition 9. A *right invariant Haar density* on $\mathcal{G}$, to be denoted $h^r(\bar{g})$, is a density (with respect to Lebesgue measure) which, for $A \subset \mathcal{G}$ and all $g_0 \in \mathcal{G}$, satisfies

$$\int_{A\bar{g}_0} h^r(y)dy = \int_A h^r(x)dx, \tag{6.11}$$

where $A\bar{g}_0 = \{\bar{g}\bar{g}_0: \bar{g} \in A\}$ and y and x are just dummy variables of integration.

Similarly, a *left invariant Haar density* on $\mathcal{G}$, to be denoted $h^l(\bar{g})$, must satisfy

$$\int_{\bar{g}_0 A} h^l(y)dy = \int_A h^l(x)dx, \tag{6.12}$$

where $\bar{g}_0 A = \{\bar{g}_0 \bar{g} : \bar{g} \in A\}$.

The idea behind invariant Haar densities is very similar to the idea behind invariant noninformative priors discussed in Subsection 3.2.2. Indeed, if h^r and h^l are probability densities, then (6.11) and (6.12) can be written

$$P^{h^r}(A\bar{g}_0) = P^{h^r}(A) \quad \text{and} \quad P^{h^l}(\bar{g}_0 A) = P^{h^l}(A),$$

implying that probabilities of sets are invariant under transformation of the sets by $\bar{g}_0$ on the right and left respectively. (Actually, when h^r and h^l are probability densities, it turns out that they must be equal, so that one can speak of the *invariant Haar density*.)

Note from (6.11) and (6.12) that h^r and h^l are not unique, since multiplying each by a constant will not affect the validity of the equations. The following is true, however.

Important Property. *The right and left invariant Haar densities, h^r and h^l, exist and are unique up to a multiplicative constant.*

For a proof of this property see Halmos (1950). Nachbin (1965) is also a useful reference.

Calculation of h^r and h^l

To determine h^r, simply make the change of variables $y = x\bar{g}_0$ on the left-hand side of (6.11). This integral then becomes

$$\int_{A\bar{g}_0} h^r(y)dy = \int_A h^r(x\bar{g}_0)J^r_{\bar{g}_0}(x)dx. \tag{6.13}$$

Using this in (6.11) gives

$$\int_A h^r(x\bar{g}_0)J^r_{\bar{g}_0}(x)dx = \int_A h^r(x)dx.$$

Since this must hold for all A, it follows that

$$h^r(x\bar{g}_0)J^r_{\bar{g}_0}(x) = h^r(x)$$

for all $x \in \mathcal{G}$ and $\bar{g}_0 \in \mathcal{G}$. Choosing $x = \bar{e}$ (the identity element in $\mathcal{G}$), this implies that

$$h^r(\bar{g}_0) = \frac{h^r(\bar{e})}{J^r_{\bar{g}_0}(\bar{e})}.$$

Since $h^r(\bar{e})$ is just a multiplicative constant, it can be ignored, and the following result is established.

Result 1. *The right invariant Haar density on $\bar{\mathscr{G}}$ is*

$$h^r(\bar{g}) = \frac{1}{J_{\bar{g}}^r(\bar{e})},$$

where $J_{\bar{g}}^r(x)$ is the Jacobian of the transformation $x \to x\bar{g}$.

It can similarly be shown that

$$h^l(\bar{g}_0 x)J_{\bar{g}_0}^l(x) = h^l(x), \tag{6.14}$$

so that the following result holds.

Result 2. *The left invariant Haar density on $\bar{\mathscr{G}}$ is*

$$h^l(\bar{g}) = \frac{1}{J_{\bar{g}}^l(\bar{e})},$$

where $J_{\bar{g}}^l(x)$ is the Jacobian of the transformation $x \to \bar{g}x$.

EXAMPLE 17 (continued). From Results 1 and 2 and the calculation in Example 17, it is clear that $h^r(\bar{g}) = 1/c$ and $h^l(\bar{g}) = 1/c^2$, where $\bar{g} = (b, c)$.

Left and Right Invariant (Generalized) Prior Densities

To relate the results on Haar densities to prior densities, we will assume that $\bar{\mathscr{G}}$ is *isomorphic* to Θ. This means that a one-to-one linear mapping between points in Θ and points in $\bar{\mathscr{G}}$ exists. In the cases considered here this will be satisfied because Θ and $\bar{\mathscr{G}}$ will be the same space. In the location-scale problem of Section 6.4, for instance,

$$\Theta = \{(\theta, \sigma): \theta \in R^1 \text{ and } \sigma > 0\},$$

while the group $\bar{\mathscr{G}} = \{(b, c): b \in R^1 \text{ and } c > 0\}$ (see Example 17). Hence the two spaces are the same. In such a situation we will denote the left and right invariant Haar densities on Θ (considered as a group) by $\pi^l(\theta)$ and $\pi^r(\theta)$, respectively, and will call them the *left invariant* and *right invariant* (generalized) prior densities. (The term "generalized" is used to indicate that these may be improper densities.) In the location-scale problem, for instance, it follows from Example 17 (continued) that $\pi^l((\theta, \sigma)) = 1/\sigma^2$ and $\pi^r((\theta, \sigma)) = 1/\sigma$. Note that these correspond to the two choices for a noninformative prior discussed in Example 7 in Subsection 3.2.2. Indeed, the general method discussed in that subsection of determining a noninformative prior can now be recognized as being simply the calculation of the left invariant Haar density.

6.6.2 The Best Invariant Rule

In this subsection, we establish the major result concerning the relationship of the best invariant rule to the (generalized) Bayes rule with respect to the right invariant prior density, $\pi^r(\theta)$. For simplicity, we will only consider the case in which $\mathcal{X}$, $\mathcal{G}$, $\bar{\mathcal{G}}$, and Θ are all isomorphic, although some comments about more general situations will be made. A good example to keep in mind is the following.

EXAMPLE 18. Assume that $X_1, \ldots, X_n$ is a sample from a $\mathcal{N}(\theta, \sigma^2)$ density, with θ and σ^2 both unknown. A sufficient statistic for (θ, σ) is $\mathbf{X} = (\bar{X}, S)$, where $\bar{X}$ is the sample mean and $S = [(1/n) \sum_{i=1}^{n} (X_i - \bar{X})^2]^{1/2}$. It is well known that $\bar{X}$ and S are independent, and that their joint density (for the appropriate constant K) is

$$f(\mathbf{x}|(\theta, \sigma)) = f((\bar{x}, s)|(\theta, \sigma))$$

$$= K\sigma^{-n}s^{(n-2)} \exp\left\{-\frac{n}{2\sigma^2}(\bar{x} - \theta)^2\right\}\exp\left\{-\frac{ns^2}{(2\sigma^2)}\right\}$$

on $\mathcal{X} = \{(\bar{x}, s): \bar{x} \in R^1 \text{ and } s > 0\}$. This density can easily be seen to be invariant under the group

$$\mathcal{G} = \{g_{b, c} = (b, c): b \in R^1 \text{ and } c > 0\},$$

where

$$g_{b, c}(\mathbf{x}) = (b, c)((\bar{x}, s)) = (c\bar{x} + b, cs).$$

Hence $\mathcal{X}$ and $\mathcal{G}$ are clearly the same space. It is also easy to check that Θ and $\bar{\mathcal{G}}$ are the same group as $\mathcal{X}$ and $\mathcal{G}$.

When $\mathcal{X}$, $\mathcal{G}$, $\bar{\mathcal{G}}$, and Θ are the same group, it is convenient to think of x and θ as group elements also. For instance, we can then write an invariant rule, $\delta(x)$, as $\delta(x) = \tilde{x}(\delta(e))$.

Result 3. *Consider an invariant decision problem in which $\mathcal{X}$, $\mathcal{G}$, $\bar{\mathcal{G}}$, and Θ are all isomorphic, with the common group being as in Subsection 6.6.1. Then, for an invariant decision rule $\delta(x) = \tilde{x}(a)$,*

$$E^{\pi^r(\theta|x)}[L(\theta, \tilde{x}(a))] = \int_{\mathcal{X}} L(\bar{e}, \tilde{y}(a))f(y|\bar{e})dy = R(\theta, \delta), \qquad (6.15)$$

where $\pi^r(\theta|x)$ is the posterior distribution of θ given x with respect to the right invariant (generalized) prior density, $\pi^r(\theta)$. Also, the (generalized) Bayes rule, with respect to π^r, and the best invariant decision rule coincide (if they exist) and are equal to $\delta^*(x) = \tilde{x}(a^*)$, where a^* minimizes the middle expression in (6.15).

PROOF. The proof will be carried out in several steps. All integrals will be assumed to be over the common group, unless indicated otherwise.

Step 1. $f(x|\bar{g}) = f(g^{-1}(x)|\bar{e})J^l_{g^{-1}}(x)$. To show this, note from (6.2) that

$$\int_{g^{-1}A} f(x|\theta)dx = \int_A f(x|\bar{g}(\theta))dx.$$

Making the change of variables $x = g^{-1}(y)$ (the Jacobian of which is $J^l_{g^{-1}}(y)$) in the first integral above, results in the equality

$$\int_A f(g^{-1}(y)|\theta)J^l_{g^{-1}}(y)dy = \int_A f(x|\bar{g}(\theta))dx.$$

Since this must be true for all A, it follows that (replacing y by x)

$$f(g^{-1}(x)|\theta)J^l_{g^{-1}}(x) = f(x|\bar{g}(\theta))$$

for all x, θ, and g. Choosing $\theta = \bar{e}$ gives the desired result.

Step 2. There exists a constant K such that, for any integrable function t,

$$\int t(x^{-1})h^r(x)dx = K \int t(y)h^l(y)dy, \tag{6.16}$$

where x^{-1} is the group inverse of x.

To see this, recall that

$$\int_A h^r(x)dx = \int_{Ag} h^r(x)dx. \tag{6.17}$$

Making the change of variables $x = y^{-1}$ in each integral, and defining $q(y) = h^r(y^{-1})J(y)$, where $J(y)$ is the Jacobian of the transformation, (6.17) becomes

$$\int_{A^{-1}} q(y)dy = \int_{(Ag)^{-1}} q(y)dy = \int_{g^{-1}A^{-1}} q(y)dy.$$

This implies that $q(y)$ is a left invariant Haar measure on the group. Since left invariant Haar measure is unique up to a multiplicative constant, it follows that $q(y)$ must equal $Kh^l(y)$ for some positive constant K. Performing the same change of variables on the left-hand side of (6.16) then gives the desired result.

Step 3. There exists a function $v(g)$ such that, for any integrable function t,

$$\int t(yg)h^l(y)dy = v(g) \int t(y)h^l(y)dy. \tag{6.18}$$

To see this, define

$$\mu(A) = \int_A h^l(y)dy$$

and

$$\mu_g(A) = \int_{Ag} h^l(y)dy.$$

Note that, for $g' \in \mathcal{G}$,

$$\mu_g(g'A) = \int_{g'Ag} h^l(y)dy = \int_{Ag} h^l(y)dy = \mu_g(A),$$

the middle equality following from the left invariance of h^l. Thus μ_g is what is called a *left invariant measure* on $\mathcal{G}$, which again must be unique up to a multiplicative constant. It follows that $\mu_g(A) = v(g)\mu(A)$ for some constant $v(g)$, i.e.,

$$\int_{Ag} h^l(y)dy = v(g) \int_A h^l(y)dy. \qquad (6.19)$$

The change of variables $y = xg$, on the left-hand side of (6.19), results in the equivalent equation

$$\int_A h^l(xg)J_g^r(x)dx = v(g) \int_A h^l(y)dy.$$

Since this is true for all A, we have that

$$h^l(yg)J_g^r(y) = v(g)h^l(y).$$

Making the same change of variables, $y = xg$, on the left-hand side of (6.18) gives the desired result.

Step 4. Observe that

$$\int L(\theta, \tilde{x}(a))f(x|\theta)h^r(\theta)d\theta$$

$$= K \int L(\bar{y}^{-1}, \tilde{x}(a))f(x|\bar{y}^{-1})h^l(y)dy \quad \text{(step 2)}$$

$$= K \int L(\bar{e}, \tilde{y}(\tilde{x}(a)))f(x|\bar{y}^{-1})h^l(y)dy \quad \text{(invariance of loss)}$$

$$= K \int L(\bar{e}, \widetilde{y\tilde{x}}(a))f(yx|\bar{e})J_y^l(x)h^l(y)dy \quad \text{(step 1)}$$

$$= K \int L(\bar{e}, \widetilde{y\tilde{x}}(a))f(yx|\bar{e})\frac{h^l(x)}{h^l(yx)}h^l(y)dy \quad \text{(from (6.14))}$$

$$= Kh^l(x)v(x) \int L(\bar{e}, \tilde{y}(a))f(y|\bar{e})\frac{1}{h^l(y)}h^l(y)dy \quad \text{(step 3)}$$

$$= Kh^l(x)v(x) \int L(\bar{e}, \tilde{y}(a))f(y|\bar{e})dy. \qquad (6.20)$$

Choosing $L(\theta, a) \equiv 1$ in (6.20) establishes that

$$\int f(x|\theta)h^r(\theta)d\theta = Kh^l(x)v(x) \int f(y|\bar{e})dy = Kh^l(x)v(x).$$

Since $\pi^r(\theta) = h^r(\theta)$, this implies that

$$\pi^r(\theta|x) = \frac{f(x|\theta)h^r(\theta)}{\int f(x|\theta)h^r(\theta)d\theta} = \frac{f(x|\theta)h^r(\theta)}{Kh^l(x)v(x)}.$$

The first equality in Equation (6.15) follows immediately from this and (6.20). The second equality in (6.15) follows from the transitivity of $\mathcal{G}$ (automatic when $\mathcal{G}$ and Θ are the same group), which, by Theorem 1, implies that any invariant rule must have constant risk, say, $R(\bar{e}, \delta)$. The final conclusions of the result follow immediately from (6.15). $\square$

EXAMPLE 18 (continued). In the situation of Example 18, assume that it is desired to estimate $(\alpha\theta + \beta\sigma)$ under a loss of the form

$$L((\theta, \sigma), a) = W\left(\frac{[\alpha\theta + \beta\sigma - a]}{\sigma}\right).$$

It can be checked that this loss is invariant when $\tilde{g}_{b,c}(a) = ca + \alpha b$, and hence that the decision problem is invariant.

We saw earlier that, for the group $\mathcal{G}$,

$$\pi^r((\theta, \sigma)) = \frac{1}{\sigma}.$$

Result 3 thus implies that the best invariant estimator is given by

$$\delta(\mathbf{x}) = \tilde{x}(a^*) = \tilde{g}_{\bar{x}, s}(a^*) = sa^* + \alpha\bar{x},$$

where a^* is that a which minimizes

$$\int_{\mathscr{X}} L(\bar{e}, \tilde{y}(a))f(y|\bar{e})dy$$

$$= \int_0^\infty \int_{-\infty}^\infty W\left(\frac{[0 + \beta(1) - \tilde{g}_{y_1, y_2}(a)]}{1}\right)f((y_1, y_2)|(0, 1))dy_1\, dy_2$$

$$= K \int_0^\infty \int_{-\infty}^\infty W(\beta - y_2 a - \alpha y_1)y_2^{n-2} \exp\left\{-\frac{n}{2}y_1^2\right\}\exp\left\{-\frac{n}{2}y_2^2\right\}dy_1\, dy_2.$$

Some explicit examples of this are given in the Exercises.

Observe that Result 3 settles, at least for invariant problems, the question of what is the correct choice for a noninformative prior. The right invariant Haar density is the correct choice. This is somewhat surprising, in light of the fact that the "natural" prior invariance argument of Subsection 3.2.2 led to the left invariant Haar density. (In Examples 5 and 6 of Chapter 3 the left and right invariant Haar densities are equal, but they differ for Example 7.) Following Example 7 in Chapter 3, however, it was pointed out that this natural invariance argument is not logically sound, and that all that can be concluded is that a noninformative prior should be what is called *relatively left invariant*. The choice of the right invariant Haar measure can be viewed as a sensible choice (for invariant problems) among this class of possible noninformative priors.

Analogs of Result 3 hold in much greater generality than discussed here. (See Kudo (1955), Stein (1965), Hora and Buehler (1965), and Zidek (1967) for indications of this.) The most important generalization is that to essentially arbitrary $\mathscr{X}$. This can be carried out by conditioning on the maximal invariant T (see Section 6.5), and noting that, in the conditional problem, the orbit $\mathscr{X}(t)$ will usually be isomorphic to $\mathscr{G}$. Providing everything else is satisfactory, it will follow that the best invariant rule in this conditional problem is the (generalized) Bayes rule with respect to the right invariant Haar density on $\mathscr{G}$. Since this is true for all conditional problems, it can be concluded that the overall best invariant rule is simply this (generalized) Bayes rule. Finding the generalized Bayes rule can be much easier than finding the best invariant estimator directly, as is evidenced by the derivations of Pitman's estimator in Sections 6.3 and 6.5.

When $\overline{\mathscr{G}}$ is not isomorphic to Θ, results similar to Result 3 can still be obtained, but involve more detailed properties of groups and subgroups.

6.6.3 Confidence and Credible Regions

In Example 8 of Chapter 4, it was observed that the classical $100(1 - \alpha)\%$ confidence interval for a normal mean (with known variance) is identical to the $100(1 - \alpha)\%$ HPD credible region based on the noninformative prior $\pi(\theta) = 1$. This observation was of considerable interest, since it showed that the classical interval has good "final precision" in this situation. It would be nice to show that such a correspondence holds in many situations, and indeed this can be done, using Result 3 of the previous subsection.

It is first necessary to decide exactly what a "classical $100(1 - \alpha)\%$ confidence rule" is. A *confidence rule*, $C(\cdot)$, is a function from $\mathscr{X}$ into the collection of subsets of Θ, with the interpretation that $C(x)$ will be the suggested confidence region when x is observed. A *confidence level* of $100(1 - \alpha)\%$ means that $P_\theta(\theta \in C(X)) \geq 1 - \alpha$ for all θ. (Note that this is a probability over X, not θ.)

If now the family of densities of X is invariant under a group $\mathscr{G}$, then it seems reasonable to require C to be an invariant confidence rule. This has come to mean that C should satisfy

$$C(g(x)) = \bar{g}C(x), \qquad (6.21)$$

where, as usual, $\bar{g}C(x) = \{\bar{g}(\theta): \theta \in C(x)\}$. The classical justification for this definition of an invariant confidence rule is that the probability of coverage is then appropriately invariant. It can also be justified by a decision-theoretic invariance argument based on an appropriate invariant loss, such as

$$L(\theta, C(x)) = \alpha I_{C(x)}(\theta) + \beta S(C(x)),$$

where $S(C(x))$ is an invariant measure of the "size" of $C(x)$ (i.e., $S(\bar{g}C(x)) = S(C(x))$).

For simplicity, we will henceforth assume, as in the previous subsection, that $\mathcal{X}$, $\mathcal{G}$, $\bar{\mathcal{G}}$, and Θ are all isomorphic, and that the common group is as in Subsection 6.6.1. Note that only continuous densities are thus being considered.

The first results of interest are obtained by letting the decision loss (as a technical device) be

$$L(\theta, C(x)) = I_{C(x)}(\theta).$$

It is clear that this is an invariant loss, that

$$R(\theta, C) = E_\theta^X[L(\theta, C(X))] = P_\theta(\theta \in C(X)),$$

and that

$$E^{\pi^r(\theta|x)}[L(\theta, C(x))] = P^{\pi^r(\theta|x)}(\theta \in C(x)),$$

where, as before, $\pi^r(\theta|x)$ is the posterior distribution with respect to the right invariant (generalized) prior, π^r. Equation (6.15) becomes, for this loss,

$$P^{\pi^r(\theta|x)}(\theta \in C(x)) = P_{\bar{e}}(\bar{e} \in C(X)) = P_\theta(\theta \in C(X)). \tag{6.22}$$

The second equality states that an invariant confidence rule has a constant probability of coverage (which could, of course, have been obtained from Theorem 1). More importantly, (6.22) says that the probability of coverage of an invariant confidence rule is equal to the posterior probability that θ is in $C(x)$ for the right invariant prior, π^r. This basically means that the measures of initial and final precision for an invariant confidence rule coincide in such invariant situations, which is quite appealing.

It remains to find the optimal invariant confidence rule. This could, of course (and probably should), be approached from a proper decision-theoretic viewpoint, with specification of the loss, etc., but let us instead examine the problem classically and from a Bayesian inference viewpoint. Thus we specify a desired probability of coverage, $(1 - \alpha)$, and seek the optimal invariant confidence rule in the class, $\mathscr{C}$, of invariant confidence rules with probability of coverage at least $1 - \alpha$. (By (6.22), this class will be the same whether we adopt the classical or Bayesian (with respect to π^r) interpretation of probability of coverage.)

The natural way of choosing among confidence rules in $\mathscr{C}$ is according to size. For this purpose, we must first decide upon a natural measure of size.

Following Kiefer (1965), one very appealing choice for the measure of the size of $C(x)$ is

$$S^l(C(x)) = \int_{C(x)} \pi^l(\theta)d\theta \qquad (6.23)$$

(i.e., size with respect to the left invariant (generalized) prior density). For location parameter problems, this corresponds to the volume of $C(x)$. To see that this is natural in other situations, consider the following example.

EXAMPLE 19. Assume that S^2 is to be observed, where $S^2/\sigma^2 \sim \chi^2(n)$, and that it is desired to construct a confidence interval, $C(s^2) = (L(s^2), U(s^2))$, for the scale parameter σ^2. Since $\pi^l(\sigma^2) = 1/\sigma^2$ for a scale parameter, (6.23) gives that

$$S^l(C(s^2)) = \int_{L(s^2)}^{U(s^2)} \sigma^{-2}\, d\sigma^2 = \log\left[\frac{U(s^2)}{L(s^2)}\right].$$

A more obvious measure of the size of $C(s^2)$ is just the length $[U(s^2) - L(s^2)]$. The decision as to which measure is the most reasonable is a subjective decision which must be made for each individual problem. The ratio measure $S^l(C(s^2))$ is very appealing for a scale parameter, however, and indeed corresponds to common practice. To see this, note that the usual form considered for $C(s^2)$ is (for an appropriate statistic $t(s^2)$)

$$C(s^2) = \left\{\sigma^2 : a < \frac{t(s^2)}{\sigma^2} < b\right\} = \left(\frac{t(s^2)}{b}, \frac{t(s^2)}{a}\right).$$

This interval is frequently felt to have the same size for all s^2, which is true when $S^l(C(s^2))$, and not length, is used to measure size.

Another appealing facet of $S^l(C(x))$, as a measure of size, is that it is constant for all x when C is invariant. To see this, note that, by choosing $x = e$ in (6.21) (recall we are assuming that $\mathcal{X}$ and $\mathcal{G}$ are the same group), it is clear that

$$C(g) = \bar{g}C(e). \qquad (6.24)$$

Hence

$$S^l(C(x)) = \int_{C(x)} \pi^l(\theta)d\theta = \int_{\bar{x}C(e)} \pi^l(\theta)d\theta = \int_{C(e)} \pi^l(\theta)d\theta,$$

the last step following from the left invariance of π^l.

Since size (as measured by S^l) and probability of coverage (Bayesian and classical) are constant for an invariant confidence rule, we can define an optimal invariant rule as follows.

Definition 10. In the above situation, a π^l-*optimal* $100(1 - \alpha)\%$ *invariant confidence rule*, $C(\cdot)$, is an invariant confidence rule which minimizes

$$S^l(C(x)) = \int_{C(e)} \pi^l(\theta)d\theta,$$

subject to

$$P^{\pi^r(\theta|x)}(\theta \in C(x)) = P^{\pi^r(\theta|e)}(\theta \in C(e)) = P^X_{\bar{e}}(\bar{e} \in C(X))$$

$$= P^X_\theta(\theta \in C(X)) \geq 1 - \alpha.$$

Note that the π^l-optimal $100(1 - \alpha)\%$ invariant confidence rule is, from the Bayesian viewpoint (with prior π^r), the $100(1 - \alpha)\%$ credible region which minimizes $S^l(C(x))$. This follows easily from Definition 10 and the facts that $S^l(C(x))$ and $P^{\pi^r(\theta|x)}(\theta \in C(x))$ are constant for this rule.

Result 4. *In the above situation, the π^l-optimal $100(1 - \alpha)\%$ invariant confidence rule is*

$$C(x) = \bar{x}C(e),$$

where

$$C(e) = \{\theta : \pi^r(\theta|e) > K\pi^l(\theta)\}$$

$$= \left\{\theta : \frac{f(e|\theta)\pi^r(\theta)}{\pi^l(\theta)} > K'\right\}, \qquad (6.25)$$

the constants K or K' being chosen so that

$$P^X_{\bar{e}}(\bar{e} \in C(X)) = P^{\pi^r(\theta|e)}(\theta \in C(e)) = 1 - \alpha. \qquad (6.26)$$

PROOF. Since we are in the continuous case, it can be assumed that $C(x)$ attains the desired probability of coverage, $1 - \alpha$. (Having a probability of coverage larger than $1 - \alpha$ will obviously lead to a larger size.) Hence it is only necessary to choose $C(e)$ to minimize

$$S^l(C(x)) = \int_{C(e)} \pi^l(\theta)d\theta,$$

subject to (6.26). It is easy to see that $C(e)$ should consist of those θ for which $\pi^l(\theta)$ is small compared to $\pi^r(\theta|e)$, which, together with the fact that $\pi^r(\theta|e) = f(e|\theta)\pi^r(\theta)/m(e)$, gives (6.25). □

EXAMPLE 20. Assume that $S^2/\sigma^2 \sim \chi^2(2)$, and that it is desired to construct a π^l-optimal $100(1 - \alpha)\%$ invariant confidence rule for σ^2. Clearly the problem is invariant, with σ^2 being a scale parameter, so that

$$\pi^l(\sigma^2) = \pi^r(\sigma^2) = \frac{1}{\sigma^2}.$$

It follows from (6.25) that $C(e) = C(1)$ is of the form

$$C(1) = \{\sigma^2: f(1|\sigma^2) > K'\}$$

$$= \left\{\sigma^2: \sigma^{-2} \exp\left\{-\frac{1}{2\sigma^2}\right\} > K''\right\}$$

$$= (a, b),$$

where a and b satisfy

$$a^{-1} \exp\left\{-\frac{1}{2a}\right\} = b^{-1} \exp\left\{-\frac{1}{2b}\right\}. \tag{6.27}$$

An easy calculation shows that

$$\pi^r(\sigma^2|1) = \frac{1}{2}(\sigma^2)^{-2} \exp\left\{-\frac{1}{2\sigma^2}\right\},$$

so that (6.26) implies that a and b must also satisfy

$$1 - \alpha = \int_a^b \frac{1}{2}(\sigma^2)^{-2} \exp\left\{-\frac{1}{2\sigma^2}\right\}d\sigma^2$$

$$= \int_{1/b}^{1/a} \frac{1}{2} \exp\left\{-\frac{1}{2}y\right\}dy \quad \left(\text{letting } y = \frac{1}{\sigma^2}\right)$$

$$= \exp\left\{-\frac{1}{2b}\right\} - \exp\left\{-\frac{1}{2a}\right\}. \tag{6.28}$$

Equations (6.27) and (6.28) can be numerically solved for a and b, and the desired confidence rule is then

$$C(s^2) = s^2 C(1) = (s^2 a, s^2 b).$$

Note that the π^l-optimal $100(1 - \alpha)\%$ invariant confidence rule will not, in general, equal the $100(1 - \alpha)\%$ HPD credible region with respect to π^r. This is because the HPD credible region is chosen to minimize the volume of $C(x)$, which as discussed earlier, may be less suitable than minimizing $S^l(C(x))$.

The correspondence indicated in (6.22) holds in much greater generality than that considered here. See Stein (1965) for a more general result.

6.7 Invariance and Minimaxity

The class of invariant decision rules is often much smaller than the class of all decision rules. This being the case, finding a minimax rule within the class of invariant rules is usually much easier than finding a minimax rule within the class of all rules. For example, a best invariant rule (if one exists) is clearly minimax within the class of invariant rules. It would, therefore, be nice if such a minimax invariant rule turned out to be minimax in the overall problem. This is frequently the case, and the following theorem indicates why.

For simplicity, the theorem will be given only for a finite group of transformations, $\mathscr{G} = \{g_1, g_2, \ldots, g_m\}$, such as those in Examples 6 and 8. Also, to avoid having to worry about randomized rules, we will assume that the loss is convex and that the invariant problem is such that

$$\tilde{g}\left(\frac{1}{m} \sum_{i=1}^{m} a_i\right) = \frac{1}{m} \sum_{i=1}^{m} \tilde{g}(a_i) \tag{6.29}$$

for all $g \in \mathscr{G}$. Equation (6.29) will be satisfied by most of the groups we have encountered, providing the action space $\mathscr{A}$ is convex.

Theorem 4. *Consider a decision problem that is invariant under a finite group,* $\mathscr{G} = \{g_1, g_2, \ldots, g_m\}$, *for which* $\tilde{\mathscr{G}}$ *satisfies* (6.29). *Assume also that* $\mathscr{A}$ *is convex and that the loss,* $L(\theta, a)$, *is convex in* a. *Then, if there exists a minimax rule, there will exist a minimax rule which is also invariant. Conversely, if an invariant rule is minimax within the class of all invariant rules, then it is minimax.*

PROOF. Since the loss is convex, we can restrict consideration to nonrandomized rules. It will be shown that, for any decision rule δ, there exists an invariant rule δ^I such that

$$\sup_{\theta} R(\theta, \delta^I) \le \sup_{\theta} R(\theta, \delta). \tag{6.30}$$

The conclusions of the theorem then follow immediately.

Define, for a given decision rule δ, the new rule

$$\delta^I(x) = \frac{1}{m} \sum_{i=1}^{m} \tilde{g}_i^{-1} \delta(g_i(x)).$$

To see that δ^I is an invariant decision rule, observe that

$$\delta^I(g(x)) = \frac{1}{m} \sum_{i=1}^{m} \tilde{g}_i^{-1} \delta(g_i(g(x)))$$

$$= \frac{1}{m} \sum_{i=1}^{m} \tilde{g}\tilde{g}^{-1} \tilde{g}_i^{-1} \delta(g_i(g(x)))$$

$$= \tilde{g}\left(\frac{1}{m} \sum_{i=1}^{m} (\tilde{g}_i \tilde{g})^{-1} \delta((g_i g)(x))\right) \quad \text{(using (6.29))}$$

$$= \tilde{g}\left(\frac{1}{m} \sum_{i=1}^{m} (\widetilde{g_i g})^{-1} \delta((g_i g)(x))\right)$$

$$= \tilde{g}(\delta^I(x)),$$

the last step following from the fact that, for any $g \in \mathcal{G}$, $\{g_1 g, \ldots, g_m g\}$ will just be a reordering of $\{g_1, \ldots, g_m\}$.

To verify (6.30), let δ^i denote $\tilde{g}_i^{-1} \delta(g_i(\cdot))$, and observe that

$$\sup_\theta R(\theta, \delta^I) \leq \sup_\theta \frac{1}{m} \sum_{i=1}^m R(\theta, \delta^i) \quad \text{(convexity of } L)$$

$$= \sup_\theta \frac{1}{m} \sum_{i=1}^m E_\theta[L(\bar{g}_i(\theta), \delta(g_i(X)))] \quad \text{(invariance of loss)}$$

$$= \sup_\theta \frac{1}{m} \sum_{i=1}^m E_{\bar{g}_i(\theta)}[L(\bar{g}_i(\theta), \delta(X))] \quad \text{(by (6.3))}$$

$$\leq \frac{1}{m} \sum_{i=1}^m \sup_\theta R(\bar{g}_i(\theta), \delta)$$

$$= \frac{1}{m} \sum_{i=1}^m \sup_\theta R(\theta, \delta) = \sup_\theta R(\theta, \delta).$$

This completes the proof.   □

EXAMPLE 21. Consider the situation of Example 8, where $X \sim \mathcal{B}(n, \theta)$, $\mathscr{A} = \Theta = [0, 1]$, $L(\theta, a) = (\theta - a)^2$, $\mathcal{G} = \{e, g^*\}$ (g^* being the transformation $g^*(x) = n - x$), $\bar{\mathcal{G}} = \{\bar{e}, \bar{g}^*\}$ ($\bar{g}^*$ being the transformation $\bar{g}^*(\theta) = 1 - \theta$), and $\tilde{\mathcal{G}}$ is the same as $\bar{\mathcal{G}}$. Note that

$$\begin{aligned}
\tilde{g}^*(\tfrac{1}{2}(a_1 + a_2)) &= 1 - \tfrac{1}{2}(a_1 + a_2) \\
&= \tfrac{1}{2}[(1 - a_1) + (1 - a_2)] \\
&= \tfrac{1}{2}(\tilde{g}^*(a_1) + \tilde{g}^*(a_2)),
\end{aligned}$$

so that (6.29) is satisfied. The other conditions of Theorem 4 are also clearly satisfied. It can be concluded that one need only search for a minimax rule within the class of invariant rules, i.e., those which satisfy

$$\delta(n - x) = 1 - \delta(x).$$

This is a helpful reduction of the problem.

It is quite generally true that a minimax rule within the class of invariant rules is an overall minimax rule. By reasoning similar to that in Theorem 4, this result can be established for any finite group or, more generally, for any group for which the Haar density (or Haar measure) has finite mass. (The average $(1/m) \sum_{i=1}^m$ in Theorem 4 gets replaced, in a sense, by an average over the Haar density, normalized to be a probability measure.) Even for groups which have infinite Haar measure (such as the groups in Examples 3, 4, and 5), it can often be shown that a minimax rule within the class of invariant rules is overall minimax. This result, known as the Hunt–Stein theorem, is unfortunately too difficult to be presented here. The crucial condition needed for the validity of the Hunt–Stein theorem concerns the nature of the group

$\mathcal{G}$. For example, the condition is satisfied if the group is what is called *amenable*. (All groups considered so far have been amenable.) The interested reader is referred to Kiefer (1957) (a very general exposition), Lehmann (1959) (an exposition for certain testing situations), Kiefer (1965) (an heuristic discussion with other references), and Bondar and Milnes (1980).

It is not always true that a minimax rule must be invariant. The following example (due to Stein) demonstrates this.

EXAMPLE 22. Assume that $\mathbf{X} \sim \mathcal{N}_p(\mathbf{0}, \mathbf{\Sigma})$ and that $\mathbf{Y} \sim \mathcal{N}_p(\mathbf{0}, \Delta\mathbf{\Sigma})$, where $\mathbf{X}$ and $\mathbf{Y}$ are independent and $p \geq 2$. Thus

$$\Theta = \{(\Delta, \mathbf{\Sigma}): \Delta > 0 \text{ and } \mathbf{\Sigma} \text{ is a nonsingular covariance matrix}\}.$$

Let $\mathscr{A} = (0, \infty)$, and assume that it is desired to estimate Δ under loss

$$L((\Delta, \mathbf{\Sigma}), a) = \begin{cases} 0 & \text{if } \left| 1 - \dfrac{a}{\Delta} \right| \leq \dfrac{1}{2}, \\ 1 & \text{if } \left| 1 - \dfrac{a}{\Delta} \right| > \dfrac{1}{2}. \end{cases}$$

Consider the group $\mathscr{G}$ of transformations

$$g_{\mathbf{B}}(\mathbf{x}, \mathbf{y}) = (\mathbf{Bx}, \mathbf{By}),$$

where $\mathbf{B}$ is any nonsingular $(p \times p)$ matrix, and $g_{\mathbf{B}_1}g_{\mathbf{B}_2} = g_{\mathbf{B}_1\mathbf{B}_2}$. It can be checked that the decision problem is invariant under $\mathscr{G}$, and that $\bar{g}_{\mathbf{B}}((\Delta, \mathbf{\Sigma})) = (\Delta, \mathbf{B\Sigma B}^t)$ and $\tilde{g}_{\mathbf{B}}(a) = a$. It follows that an invariant decision rule must satisfy

$$\delta(\mathbf{Bx}, \mathbf{By}) = \delta(g_{\mathbf{B}}(\mathbf{x}, \mathbf{y})) = \tilde{g}_{\mathbf{B}}(\delta(\mathbf{x}, \mathbf{y})) = \delta(\mathbf{x}, \mathbf{y}), \tag{6.31}$$

for all $\mathbf{B}$, $\mathbf{x}$, and $\mathbf{y}$. Letting $\mathbf{x} = \mathbf{e}_1 \equiv (1, 0, \ldots, 0)^t$, $\mathbf{y} = \mathbf{e}_p \equiv (0, \ldots, 0, 1)^t$, $\mathbf{b}^1$ denote the first column of $\mathbf{B}$, and $\mathbf{b}^p$ denote the last column of $\mathbf{B}$, (6.31) becomes

$$\delta(\mathbf{b}^1, \mathbf{b}^p) = \delta(\mathbf{e}_1, \mathbf{e}_p).$$

The only restriction on $\mathbf{b}^1$ and $\mathbf{b}^p$ is that they not be multiples of each other ($\mathbf{B}$ is nonsingular). We can hence conclude that δ must be constant with probability one; say, $\delta(\mathbf{x}, \mathbf{y}) = K$. For any such δ,

$$R((\Delta, \mathbf{\Sigma}), \delta) = \begin{cases} 0 & \text{if } \left| 1 - \dfrac{K}{\Delta} \right| \leq \dfrac{1}{2}, \\ 1 & \text{if } \left| 1 - \dfrac{K}{\Delta} \right| > \dfrac{1}{2}, \end{cases}$$

so that

$$\sup_{(\Delta, \mathbf{\Sigma})} R((\Delta, \mathbf{\Sigma}), \delta) = 1.$$

Any invariant rule thus has a minimax risk of 1. (This can be shown to be true for any randomized invariant rule as well.)

Consider now the decision rule

$$\delta(\mathbf{x}, \mathbf{y}) = \left| \frac{y_1}{x_1} \right|.$$

For this rule,

$$
\begin{aligned}
R((\Delta, \Sigma), \delta) &= E_{\Delta, \Sigma} L((\Delta, \Sigma), \delta(\mathbf{X}, \mathbf{Y})) \\
&= P_{\Delta, \Sigma}\left(\left| 1 - \frac{\delta(\mathbf{X}, \mathbf{Y})}{\Delta} \right| > \frac{1}{2} \right) \\
&= P_{\Delta, \Sigma}\left(\left| 1 - \frac{|Y_1/(\Delta\sigma_{11})|}{|X_1/\sigma_{11}|} \right| > \frac{1}{2} \right) \\
&= P\left(\left| 1 - \left| \frac{Z}{Z'} \right| \right| > \frac{1}{2} \right),
\end{aligned}
$$

where σ_{11} is the standard deviation of X_1, and $Z = Y_1/\Delta\sigma_{11}$ and $Z' = X_1/\sigma_{11}$ are independently $\mathcal{N}(0, 1)$. Clearly this probability is a constant (independent of (Δ, Σ)) which is less than one. Hence this rule has smaller minimax risk than any invariant rule.

The Hunt–Stein theorem fails in the above example because the group $\mathscr{G}$, called the full linear group, is too large. Frequently, in such problems, there are subgroups of $\mathscr{G}$ (such as the group of $(p \times p)$ lower-triangular matrices) which do satisfy the hypotheses of the Hunt–Stein theorem, and can hence be used to find a minimax rule.

6.8 Admissibility of Invariant Rules

When a best invariant decision rule exists, it is natural to ask if it is admissible. When the best invariant rule is a proper Bayes rule (for example, when the Haar density is a probability density), the answer is, of course, "yes." Usually, however, the best invariant rule will only be generalized Bayes (with respect to the right invariant Haar measure), and hence need not be admissible. Some typical situations in which the best invariant estimator is inadmissible follow.

EXAMPLE 23. Assume that $\mathbf{X} \sim \mathcal{N}_p(\mathbf{\theta}, \mathbf{I}_p)$, and that it is desired to estimate $\mathbf{\theta}$ under loss $L(\mathbf{\theta}, \mathbf{a}) = \sum_{i=1}^{p} (\theta_i - a_i)^2$. This problem is invariant under the p-dimensional additive group, and it is easy to see that $\delta_0(\mathbf{x}) = \mathbf{x}$ is the best invariant estimator. When $p \geq 3$, however, it was seen in Example 16 of Section 4.5 that δ_0 is inadmissible.

EXAMPLE 24. Assume that $X \sim \mathscr{C}(\theta, 1)$, and that it is desired to estimate θ under squared-error loss. This is a location invariant problem, so that the invariant estimators are of the form $\delta_c(x) = x + c$. Now

$$R(\theta, \delta_c) = E_\theta[(\theta - (X + c))^2] = \infty$$

for all c, while the noninvariant estimator $\delta^*(x) = 0$ has risk

$$R(\theta, \delta^*) = \theta^2 < R(\theta, \delta_c).$$

Hence all invariant estimators are inadmissible.

EXAMPLE 25. In an invariant estimation problem for which the best invariant estimator is not unique, it will usually be the case that any invariant rule is inadmissible. A general proof of this for location densities can be found in Farrell (1964). The basic idea of this proof can be seen in the following specific example due to Blackwell (1951).

Assume that X is either $\theta + 1$ or $\theta - 1$, with probability $\frac{1}{2}$ each. The loss is

$$L(\theta, a) = \begin{cases} |\theta - a| & \text{if } |\theta - a| \leq 1, \\ 1 & \text{if } |\theta - a| > 1, \end{cases}$$

and $\Theta = \mathscr{A} = (-\infty, \infty)$. This is a location invariant problem, so that the invariant rules are of the form $\delta_c(x) = x + c$. The risk of an invariant rule in a location problem is constant, so we need only calculate $R(0, \delta_c)$. This can easily be seen to be

$$R(0, \delta_c) = E_0[L(0, \delta_c(X))] = \begin{cases} 1 - (\frac{1}{2})|c| & \text{if } |c| \leq 1, \\ (\frac{1}{2})|c| & \text{if } 1 \leq |c| \leq 2, \\ 1 & \text{if } |c| \geq 2. \end{cases}$$

This is minimized at $c = +1$ and $c = -1$. Hence $\delta_1(x) = x + 1$ and $\delta_{-1}(x) = x - 1$ are both best invariant estimators.

Consider now the estimator

$$\delta^*(x) = \begin{cases} \delta_1(x) = x + 1 & \text{if } x < 0, \\ \delta_{-1}(x) = x - 1 & \text{if } x \geq 0. \end{cases}$$

This is not invariant, but has a risk function which is easily calculated to be

$$R(\theta, \delta^*) = \begin{cases} 0 & \text{if } -1 \leq \theta < 1, \\ \frac{1}{2} & \text{otherwise.} \end{cases}$$

Hence δ^* is R-better than δ_1 or δ_{-1}.

General admissibility results for invariant rules are hard to obtain. Some of the most general results can be found in Brown (1966), Brown and Fox (1974a), and Brown and Fox (1974b). These articles show, under very weak conditions, that the best invariant decision rule in one or two-dimensional location parameter or scale parameter problems is admissible. (The conditions do require that the best invariant rule be unique, and that the density have certain moments, precluding the situations in Examples 24 and 25.)

6.9 Conclusions

In this concluding discussion it will be assumed that no prior information is available. The invariance approach is then appealing, both intuitively and practically. The intuitive appeal was discussed in Section 6.1. The practical appeal lies in the relative ease of application of invariance. The major problem with invariance concerns the amount of invariance that can be used.

The first difficulty is that there may be too little invariance in a problem to lead to a significant simplification. In Section 6.4, for example, it was indicated that invariance considerations are of limited usefulness for the binomial distribution. Even worse are problems involving the Poisson distribution. It can be shown that no group of transformations (other than the identity transformation) leaves the family of Poisson densities invariant. Hence invariance is totally useless for Poisson problems. Finally, the invariance approach is limited by the necessity of having an invariant loss function. In location parameter estimation problems, typical losses tend to be invariant, but this need not be the case for other types of problems. In scale or location-scale parameter estimation problems, for instance, there are many reasonable losses that are not invariant. Even worse is the situation for testing problems, in which the only loss that will typically be invariant is "$0-K_i$" loss (see Subsection 6.2.2). This is a very serious limitation.

The second difficulty with invariance is that too much invariance may be available, as in Example 22. Indeed a modification of this example will be given as an exercise in which an even larger group is used and there are *no* invariant procedures. A more natural example of the difficulty caused by too much invariance follows.

EXAMPLE 26. Consider a location parameter problem in which X has density $f(|x - \theta|)$ on R^1, and in which the loss is of the form $L(\theta, a) = W(|\theta - a|)$. This problem is not only invariant under the additive group, but is also invariant under the transformation $X \rightarrow -X$. Analysis of this new invariance problem will be left as an exercise, but it can be shown that the *only* non-randomized invariant rule is $\delta_0(x) = x$. An example will be given in the Exercises in which δ_0 is worse than other translation invariant estimators of the form $\delta_c(x) = x + c$. Hence use of the additional transformation in the invariance argument is bad. (Actually, there are reasonable randomized invariant estimators for this problem, namely those that estimate $x + c$ and

$x - c$ with probability $\frac{1}{2}$ each. Having to consider randomized rules can itself be considered to be an undesirable complication, however.)

The solution to the problem of having too much invariance is simply to not use it all. One should generally use only the smallest group of transformations, $\mathscr{G}_0$, for which $\bar{\mathscr{G}}_0$ is transitive on Θ. If $\bar{\mathscr{G}}_0$ is transitive on Θ, a best invariant rule will usually exist, which is why transitivity is desirable. The use of a group of transformations, $\mathscr{G}$, which is larger than $\mathscr{G}_0$, serves no real purpose, however, since it only reduces the class of invariant rules. Indeed the best invariant rule for $\mathscr{G}_0$ may not be invariant under $\mathscr{G}$, so that the use of $\mathscr{G}$ instead of $\mathscr{G}_0$ can cause a definite increase in the risk of the invariant rule chosen. In Example 26, for instance, the additive group

$$\mathscr{G}_0 = \{g_c : g_c(x) = x + c, c \in R^1\}$$

results in a $\bar{\mathscr{G}}_0$ which is transitive on Θ. The additional use of the transformation $X \to -X$ reduces the class of nonrandomized invariant rules to the single rule $\delta_0(x) = x$, which may be a harmful reduction.

As a concluding consideration, the relationship between the invariance approach and the Bayesian noninformative prior approach should be discussed. In Section 6.6 it was shown that the two approaches are often virtually equivalent (if the right invariant (generalized) prior density is used as the noninformative prior). To this author, it seems preferable to approach a problem from the noninformative prior viewpoint, rather than from the invariance viewpoint. The reasons are that (i) the noninformative prior viewpoint is more widely applicable than the invariance viewpoint; (ii) the noninformative prior viewpoint at least forces some consideration of relative likelihoods of the various θ; and (iii) the noninformative prior approach will rarely lead to the difficulties encountered by the invariance approach when too much invariance is present. (In Example 26, for instance, the noninformative prior is $\pi(\theta) = 1$, and the application of the Bayesian noninformative prior approach will lead directly to the best translation invariant rule. One need not be concerned with how much invariance should be used.) Of course, the study of invariance has been very useful in suggesting a reasonable choice for the noninformative prior, namely the right invariant Haar density. Also, as always, it is good to examine a statistical problem from as many viewpoints as possible, and the invariance viewpoint can definitely be instructive.

Exercises

Section 6.2

1. Verify that the permutation group, given in Example 6, is indeed a group of transformations.

2. Verify that $\bar{\mathscr{G}}$ and $\tilde{\mathscr{G}}$ are groups of transformations of Θ and $\mathscr{A}$, respectively.

3. Assume that $\mathbf{X} \sim \mathcal{N}_p(\theta_1 \mathbf{1}, \theta_2^2 I_p)$, where $\mathbf{1} = (1, 1, \ldots, 1)^t$. The parameter space is $\Theta = \{(\theta_1, \theta_2): \theta_1 \in R^1 \text{ and } \theta_2 > 0\}$. Let $\mathscr{A} = R^1$ and $L(\theta, a) = (\theta_1 - a)^2/\theta_2^2$. Finally, let

$$\mathscr{G} = \{g_{b,c}: g_{b,c}(\mathbf{x}) = b\mathbf{x} + c\mathbf{1}, \text{ where } c \in R^1 \text{ and } b \neq 0\}.$$

(a) Show that $\mathscr{G}$ is a group of transformations.
(b) Show that the decision problem is invariant under $\mathscr{G}$, and find $\bar{\mathscr{G}}$ and $\tilde{\mathscr{G}}$.
(c) Determine the relationship which must be satisfied by an invariant decision rule.
(d) Show that an invariant decision rule must have constant risk.

4. Assume that $\mathbf{X} \sim \mathcal{N}_p(\theta_1 \mathbf{1}, \theta_2^2 I_p)$, where $\mathbf{1} = (1, 1, \ldots, 1)^t$. The parameter space is $\Theta = \{(\theta_1, \theta_2): \theta_1 \in R^1 \text{ and } \theta_2 > 0\}$. It is desired to test $H_0: \theta_1 \leq 0$ versus $H_1: \theta_1 > 0$ under "0–1" loss. Let

$$\mathscr{G} = \{g_c: g_c(\mathbf{x}) = c\mathbf{x}, \text{ where } c > 0\}.$$

(a) Show that the decision problem is invariant under $\mathscr{G}$, and find $\bar{\mathscr{G}}$ and $\tilde{\mathscr{G}}$.
(b) Find the form of invariant decision rules.

5. Assume that $\mathbf{X} \sim \mathcal{N}_p(\theta, I_p)$, where $\Theta = R^p$. The loss function is of the form $L(\theta, a) = W(|\theta|, a)$, so that it depends on θ only through its length. Let $\mathscr{G}$ be the group of orthogonal transformations of R^p. (Thus

$$\mathscr{G} = \{g_{\mathcal{O}}: g_{\mathcal{O}}(\mathbf{x}) = \mathcal{O}\mathbf{x}, \text{ where } \mathcal{O} \text{ is an orthogonal } (p \times p) \text{ matrix}\}.)$$

(a) Verify that $\mathscr{G}$ is indeed a group of transformations.
(b) Show that the decision problem is invariant under $\mathscr{G}$, and find $\bar{\mathscr{G}}$ and $\tilde{\mathscr{G}}$.
(c) Show that the class of invariant decision rules is the class of rules based on $|\mathbf{x}|$.
(d) Show that the risk function of an invariant decision rule depends only on $|\theta|$.

Section 6.3

6. Assume that $X \sim \mathscr{C}(\theta, \beta)$, where β is known, and that it is desired to estimate θ under loss

$$L(\theta, a) = \begin{cases} 0 & \text{if } |\theta - a| \leq c, \\ 1 & \text{if } |\theta - a| > c. \end{cases}$$

Find the best invariant estimator of θ.

7. Assume that $X \sim \mathcal{N}(\theta + 2, 1)$, and that it is desired to estimate θ under squared-error loss. Find the best invariant estimator of θ.

8. Assume that $\mathbf{X} = (X_1, X_2)$ has a density (on R^2) of the form $f(x_1 - \theta_1, x_2 - \theta_2)$, and that it is desired to estimate $(\theta_1 + \theta_2)/2$ under loss

$$L((\theta_1, \theta_2), a) = (\tfrac{1}{2}(\theta_1 + \theta_2) - a)^2.$$

Here $\mathscr{A} = R^1$ and $\Theta = R^2$.
(a) Show that the problem is invariant under the group

$$\mathscr{G} = \{g_{\mathbf{c}}: g_{\mathbf{c}}(\mathbf{x}) = (x_1 + c_1, x_2 + c_2), \text{ where } \mathbf{c} = (c_1, c_2) \in R^2\},$$

and find $\bar{\mathscr{G}}$ and $\tilde{\mathscr{G}}$.
(b) Find the best invariant decision rule.

9. Assume that $X_1, \ldots, X_n$ is a sample of size n from the density

$$f(x|\theta) = \exp\{-(x - \theta)\}I_{(\theta, \infty)}(x).$$

Find the best invariant estimator of θ for the loss function
(a) $L(\theta, a) = (\theta - a)^2$.
(b) $L(\theta, a) = |\theta - a|$.
(c) $L(\theta, a) = 0$ if $|\theta - a| \leq c$; $L(\theta, a) = 1$ if $|\theta - a| > c$.

10. Assume that X has a density of the form $f(|x - \theta|)$ on R^1, and that it is desired to estimate θ under a loss of the form $L(\theta, a) = W(|\theta - a|)$, where $W(z)$ is a convex function of $z \geq 0$. Prove that $\delta(x) = x$ is a best invariant estimator.

11. Assume that X has a unimodal density of the form $f(|x - \theta|)$ on R^1 (so that $f(z)$ is nonincreasing for $z \geq 0$) and that it is desired to estimate θ under a loss of the form $L(\theta, a) = W(|\theta - a|)$, where $W(z)$ is nondecreasing for $z \geq 0$. Prove that $\delta(x) = x$ is a best invariant estimator.

12. Assume that $X_1, \ldots, X_n$ is a sample from a $\mathcal{N}(\theta, 1)$ distribution, and that it is desired to estimate θ. Find the best invariant estimator of θ for the loss
(a) $L(\theta, a) = |\theta - a|^r, r \geq 1$.
(b) $L(\theta, a) = |\theta - a|^r, r < 1$.
(c) $L(\theta, a) = 0$ if $|\theta - a| \leq c$; $L(\theta, a) = 1$ if $|\theta - a| > c$.

13. Assume that $X_1, \ldots, X_n$ is a sample from the $\mathcal{U}(\theta - \frac{1}{2}, \theta + \frac{1}{2})$ distribution. Find the best invariant estimator of θ for the loss
(a) $L(\theta, a) = (\theta - a)^2$.
(b) $L(\theta, a) = |\theta - a|$.
(c) $L(\theta, a) = 0$ if $|\theta - a| \leq c$; $L(\theta, a) = 1$ if $|\theta - a| > c$.

14. Assume that $X_1, \ldots, X_n$ is a sample from the half-normal distribution, which has density

$$f(x|\theta) = \left(\frac{2}{\pi}\right)^{1/2} \exp\left\{-\frac{1}{2}(x - \theta)^2\right\}I_{(\theta, \infty)}(x).$$

Show that the best invariant estimator of θ under squared-error loss is

$$\delta(x) = \bar{x} - \frac{\exp\{-n[(\min x_i) - \bar{x}]^2/2\}}{(2n\pi)^{1/2}P(Z < n^{1/2}[(\min x_i) - \bar{x}])},$$

where Z is $\mathcal{N}(0, 1)$.

Section 6.4

15. Assume that $X_1, \ldots, X_n$ is a sample from the $\mathcal{G}(\alpha, \beta)$ distribution, with α known and β unknown. Find the best invariant estimator of β for the loss
(a) $L(\beta, a) = (1 - a/\beta)^2$.
(b) $L(\beta, a) = (a/\beta) - 1 - \log(a/\beta)$.

16. Assume that $X_1, \ldots, X_n$ is a sample from the $\mathcal{P}a(\theta, 1)$ distribution, where $\theta > 0$. Find the best invariant estimator of θ for the loss
(a) $L(\theta, a) = (1 - a/\theta)^2$, when $n \geq 3$.
(b) $L(\theta, a) = |\log a - \log \theta|$.
(c) $L(\theta, a) = |1 - a/\theta|$, when $n \geq 2$.

17. Assume that $X_1, \ldots, X_n$ is a sample from the $\mathcal{U}(0, \theta)$ distribution, where $\theta > 0$. Find the best invariant estimator of θ for the loss
   (a) $L(\theta, a) = (1 - a/\theta)^2$.
   (b) $L(\theta, a) = |1 - a/\theta|$.
   (c) $L(\theta, a) = 0$ if $c^{-1} \le a/\theta \le c$; $L(\theta, a) = 1$ otherwise.

18. Assume that $X_1, \ldots, X_n$ is a sample from the $\mathcal{N}(0, \sigma^2)$ distribution, where $\sigma > 0$.
   (a) Find the best invariant estimator of σ^2 for the loss $L(\sigma^2, a) = (1 - a/\sigma^2)^2$.
   (b) Find the best invariant estimator of σ for the loss $L(\sigma, a) = (1 - a/\sigma)^2$.

19. Assume that $X_1, \ldots, X_n$ are positive random variables with a joint density of the form $\theta^{-n} f(x_1/\theta, \ldots, x_n/\theta)$, where $\theta > 0$ is an unknown scale parameter. It is desired to estimate θ under a loss of the form $L(\theta, a) = W(a/\theta)$.
   (a) Show that the best invariant estimator of θ is that action, a, which minimizes

   $$\frac{\int_0^\infty \theta^{-(n+1)} W(a/\theta) f(x_1/\theta, \ldots, x_n/\theta) d\theta}{\int_0^\infty \theta^{-(n+1)} f(x_1/\theta, \ldots, x_n/\theta) d\theta}.$$

   (You may use the corresponding result for the location parameter case.)
   (b) If $L(\theta, a) = (1 - a/\theta)^2$, show that the best invariant estimator of θ is

   $$\delta(\mathbf{x}) = \frac{\int_0^\infty \theta^{-(n+2)} f(x_1/\theta, \ldots, x_n/\theta) d\theta}{\int_0^\infty \theta^{-(n+3)} f(x_1/\theta, \ldots, x_n/\theta) d\theta}.$$

   (c) If $X_1, \ldots, X_n$ are a sample from the $\mathcal{U}(\theta, 2\theta)$ distribution, where $\theta > 0$, and it is desired to estimate θ under loss $L(\theta, a) = (1 - a/\theta)^2$, show that the best invariant estimator of θ is

   $$\delta(\mathbf{x}) = \frac{(n+2)[(V/2)^{-(n+1)} - U^{-(n+1)}]}{(n+1)[(V/2)^{-(n+2)} - U^{-(n+2)}]},$$

   where $U = \min x_i$ and $V = \max x_i$.

Section 6.5

20. Verify that $\mathbf{T}(\mathbf{x})$ in Example 13 is indeed a maximal invariant.

21. Verify that $\mathbf{T}(\mathbf{x})$ in Example 14 is indeed a maximal invariant.

22. Assume that $\mathcal{X} = R^p$, and let $\mathcal{G}$ be the group of orthogonal transformations of $\mathcal{X}$ (see Exercise 5). Show that $T(\mathbf{x}) = \sum_{i=1}^p x_i^2$ is a maximal invariant.

23. Assume that X_1 and X_2 are independent observations from a common density, f. It is desired to test $H_0: f$ is $\mathcal{N}(0, 1)$ versus $H_1: f$ is $\mathscr{C}(0, 1)$ under "0–1" loss. Show that the uniformly most powerful invariant tests reject H_0 if $|X_1 - X_2| > K$ and accept H_0 otherwise, where K is a constant which depends on the desired error probabilities.

24. Assume that $X_1 \sim \mathcal{N}(\theta_1, 1)$ and (independently) $X_2 \sim \mathcal{N}(\theta_2, 1)$. It is desired to test $H_0: \theta_1 = \theta_2$ versus $H_1: \theta_1 < \theta_2$ under "0–1" loss. Let $\mathcal{G}$ be the group of transformations

   $$\mathcal{G} = \{g_c: g_c((x_1, x_2)) = (x_1 + c, x_2 + c)\}.$$

   (a) Show that the problem is invariant under $\mathcal{G}$, and find $\bar{\mathcal{G}}$ and $\tilde{\mathcal{G}}$.
   (b) Show that $T((x_1, x_2)) = (x_2 - x_1)$ is a maximal invariant.

(c) Show that the uniformly most powerful invariant tests reject H_0 if $Y = X_2 - X_1 > K$ and accept H_0 otherwise, where K is a constant which depends on the desired error probabilities.

25. Assume that $X_1, \ldots, X_n$ are a sample from the $\mathcal{N}(\theta, \sigma^2)$ distribution, both θ and σ^2 unknown. It is desired to test $H_0: \sigma^2 \geq 1$ versus $H_1: \sigma^2 < 1$ under "0–1" loss.
   (a) After reducing to the sufficient statistics $\bar{X}$ (the sample mean) and S^2 (the sample variance), show that the problem is invariant under the location group

   $$\mathcal{G} = \{g_c: g_c((\bar{x}, s^2)) = (\bar{x} + c, s^2), \text{ where } c \in R^1\}.$$

   (b) Show that $T((\bar{x}, s^2)) = s^2$ is a maximal invariant.
   (c) Show that the uniformly most powerful invariant tests reject H_0 if $S^2 < K$ and accept H_0 otherwise, where K is a constant which depends on the desired error probabilities.

Section 6.6

26. Calculate J_g^l in Example 17.

27. Prove Result 2.

28. Let $\mathcal{G}$ be the group of one-dimensional scale transformations, and identify each g_c with the point $c \in (0, \infty)$. Show that the left and right invariant Haar densities for this group are $h^l(c) = h^r(c) = 1/c$.

29. Let $\mathcal{G}$ be the p-dimensional location (or additive) group, and identify each g_c with the point $\mathbf{c} \in R^p$. Show that the left and right invariant Haar densities for this group are $h^l(\mathbf{c}) = h^r(\mathbf{c}) = 1$.

The following three problems deal with groups, $\mathcal{G}$, of matrix transformations of R^p. We will identify a transformation with the relevant matrix, so that $\mathbf{g} \in \mathcal{G}$ is a $(p \times p)$ matrix (with (i, j) element $g_{i, j}$), and the transformation is simply $\mathbf{x} \to \mathbf{g}\mathbf{x}$. The composition of two transformations (or the group multiplication) corresponds simply to matrix multiplication. Thus to find Haar densities, we must be concerned with the transformations of $\mathcal{G}$ given by $\mathbf{g} \to \mathbf{g}^0\mathbf{g}$ and $\mathbf{g} \to \mathbf{g}\mathbf{g}^0$. To calculate the Jacobians of these transformations, write the matrices $\mathbf{g}$, $\mathbf{g}^0$, $\mathbf{g}^0\mathbf{g}$, and $\mathbf{g}\mathbf{g}^0$ as vectors, by stringing the rows of the matrices end to end. Thus a $(p \times p)$ matrix will be treated as a vector in R^{p^2}. Coordinates which are always zero can be ignored, however, possibly reducing the dimension of the vector. The densities calculated for the transformations are then densities with respect to Lebesgue measure on the Euclidean space spanned by the reduced vectors.

30. If $\mathcal{G}$ is the group of nonsingular $(p \times p)$ diagonal matrices, show that the left and right invariant Haar densities (w.r.t. $\prod_{i=1}^p dg_{ii}$) are

$$h^l(\mathbf{g}) = h^r(\mathbf{g}) = \frac{1}{|\det \mathbf{g}|} = \frac{1}{\prod_{i=1}^p |g_{ii}|}.$$

31. Let $\mathcal{G}$ be the group of all linear transformations of R^p or, equivalently, the group of all $(p \times p)$ nonsingular matrices. Show that the left and right invariant Haar densities (w.r.t. $\prod_{i=1}^{p} \prod_{j=1}^{p} dg_{ij}$) are $h^l(\mathbf{g}) = h^r(\mathbf{g}) = |\det \mathbf{g}|^{-p}$,
    (a) when $p = 2$,
    (b) for general p.

32. Let $\mathcal{G}$ be the group of all $(p \times p)$ nonsingular lower triangular matrices (i.e., $g_{ij} = 0$ for $j > i$). Show that the left and right invariant Haar densities (w.r.t. $\prod_{i=1}^{p} \prod_{j=1}^{i} dg_{ij}$) are

    $$h^l(\mathbf{g}) = \frac{1}{\prod_{i=1}^{p} |g_{ii}|^i} \quad \text{and} \quad h^r(\mathbf{g}) = \frac{1}{\prod_{i=1}^{p} |g_{ii}|^{p+1-i}},$$

    (a) when $p = 2$,
    (b) for general p.

33. In the situation of Example 18, find the best invariant estimator for the loss
    (a) $L((\theta, \sigma), a) = (\alpha\theta + \beta\sigma - a)^2/\sigma^2$.
    (b) $L((\theta, \sigma), a) = (1 - a/\sigma)^2$.
    (c) $L((\theta, \sigma), a) = (\theta - a)^2/\sigma^2$.

34. Assume that $X_1, \ldots, X_n$ is a sample from the $\mathcal{U}(\theta - \sqrt{3}\sigma, \theta + \sqrt{3}\sigma)$ distribution, and that it is desired to estimate $\alpha\theta + \beta\sigma$ under the loss $L((\theta, \sigma), a) = (\alpha\theta + \beta\sigma - a)^2/\sigma^2$, where α and β are given constants. Find the generalized Bayes estimator with respect to the generalized prior density $\pi(\theta, \sigma) = 1/\sigma$ (on $\Theta = \{(\theta, \sigma): \theta \in R^1$ and $\sigma > 0\}$), and show that this is also the best invariant estimator.

35. In the situation of Example 20, find the π^l-optimal 90% invariant confidence rule for σ^2, and compare it to the 90% HPD credible region with respect to the generalized prior $\pi(\sigma^2) = 1/\sigma^2$.

36. Assume that X has density (on $(0, \infty)$)

    $$f(x|\beta) = \frac{2\beta}{\pi(\beta^2 + x^2)},$$

    where $\beta > 0$. Find the π^l-optimal 90% invariant confidence rule for β.

37. For a 1-dimensional location parameter problem, prove that the π^l-optimal $100(1 - \alpha)\%$ invariant confidence rule coincides with the $100(1 - \alpha)\%$ HPD credible region with respect to the noninformative prior $\pi(\theta) = 1$.

38. Assume that $X_1, \ldots, X_n$ is a sample from the $\mathcal{U}(0, \theta)$ distribution. Find the π^l-optimal $100(1 - \alpha)\%$ invariant confidence rule, and show that it coincides with the $100(1 - \alpha)\%$ HPD credible region with respect to the noninformative prior $\pi(\theta) = 1/\theta$.

Section 6.7

39. Assume that $X \sim \mathcal{B}(1, \theta)$ is observed, on the basis of which it is desired to estimate θ under loss $L(\theta, a) = |\theta - a|$. Find a minimax estimator of θ.

40. Assume that $X \in R^1$ has density

    $$f(x|\theta) = \frac{2\theta}{\pi(e^{\theta x} + e^{-\theta x})},$$

where $\theta > 0$. It is desired to estimate θ under a convex loss. Show that, to determine a minimax estimator, one need only consider estimators which are a function of $|x|$.

Sections 6.8 and 6.9

41. In Example 25, show that, for any constant b, the estimator

$$\delta_b^*(x) = \begin{cases} \delta_1(x) = x + 1 & \text{if } x < b, \\ \delta_{-1}(x) = x - 1 & \text{if } x \geq b, \end{cases}$$

is R-better than the best invariant estimators.

42. Consider the situation of Example 22.
    (a) Show that the given decision problem is actually invariant under the larger group

    $$\mathscr{G} = \{g_{\mathbf{B}, c}: g_{\mathbf{B}, c}(\mathbf{x}, \mathbf{y}) = (\mathbf{Bx}, c\mathbf{By}), \text{ where } \mathbf{B} \text{ is nonsingular and } c > 0\},$$

    and find $\bar{\mathscr{G}}$ and $\tilde{\mathscr{G}}$.
    (b) Show that there are *no* invariant decision rules for this problem. (Clearly, too much invariance has been used.)

43. In Example 26, let $\mathscr{G}$ be the group consisting of the transformations $g_{1, c}(x) = x + c$ and $g_{-1, c'}(x) = -x + c'$, where c and c' vary over R^1.
    (a) Show that the decision problem is invariant under $\mathscr{G}$, and find $\bar{\mathscr{G}}$ and $\tilde{\mathscr{G}}$.
    (b) Show that $\delta_0(x) = x$ is the only nonrandomized decision rule which is invariant under $\mathscr{G}$.
    (c) (Kiefer) Suppose that $f(|x - \theta|) = \frac{1}{2}I_{(1, 2)}(|x - \theta|)$, and that $W(|\theta - a|) = |\theta - a|^{1/2}$. Consider the estimators $\delta_c(x) = x + c$, and show that, for $|c| < 1$, $R(\theta, \delta_c) = R(0, \delta_c)$ is a strictly concave and symmetric function of c. Use this to conclude that $\delta_0(x) = x$ is inadmissible. (Note that since the best invariant translation estimator cannot be unique, it too will be inadmissible, though not as seriously so as δ_0.)
    (d) Consider the randomized (invariant) estimators of the form

    $$\delta_c^*(x, a) = \begin{cases} \frac{1}{2} & \text{if } a = x + c, \\ \frac{1}{2} & \text{if } a = x - c, \end{cases}$$

    (i.e., δ_c^* estimates $x + c$ and $x - c$ with probability $\frac{1}{2}$ each). Show that there are c for which δ_c^* is R-better than δ_0.
    (e) Prove that δ_c^* is inadmissible for any c.

CHAPTER 7

Preposterior and Sequential Analysis

7.1 Introduction

Until now, we have dealt only with the making of decisions or inferences. Another very important aspect of statistics is that of the choice of experiment, commonly called experimental design. Being as this choice must (usually) be made before the data (and hence the posterior distribution) can be obtained, the subject is frequently called *preposterior analysis* by Bayesians.

The goal of preposterior analysis is to choose the experiment or experimental design which minimizes overall cost. This overall cost consists of the decision loss *and* the cost of conducting and analyzing the experiment. We will essentially ignore the cost of analyzing the results (after all, statisticians are so underpaid that the cost of their labors is usually negligible), and thus consider only the decision loss and the cost of experimentation. Note that these last quantities are in opposition to each other. To lower the decision loss it will generally be necessary to run a larger experiment, whereby the experimental cost will be increased. In this chapter, we will be concerned with the balancing of these two costs.

The general problem of experimental design is very complicated, concerning choices among quite different experiments (say, a choice between a completely randomized design and a randomized block design, or maybe a choice of the values of the independent variables in a regression study). Though of considerable interest, investigation of such general questions is beyond the scope of this book. We will content ourselves with a study of the simplest design problem, that of deciding when to stop sampling.

To get specific, assume random variables $X_1, X_2, \ldots$ are available for observation. Let $\mathscr{X}_i$ be the sample space of X_i, define $\mathbf{X}^j = (X_1, X_2, \ldots, X_j)$, and assume that $\mathbf{X}^j$ has density $f_j(\mathbf{x}^j | \theta)$ on $\mathscr{X}^j = \mathscr{X}_1 \times \cdots \times \mathscr{X}_j$. As usual,

$\theta \in \Theta$ is the unknown state of nature, concerning which some inference or decision is to be made. Most of the examples we will consider deal with situations in which the X_i are independent observations from a common density $f(x|\theta)$. In such a situation,

$$f_j(\mathbf{x}^j | \theta) = \prod_{i=1}^{j} f(x_i | \theta),$$

and we will say that X_1, X_2, ... is a *sequential sample* from the density $f(x|\theta)$. It will be assumed that the observations can be taken in stages, or *sequentially*. This means that after observing, say, $\mathbf{X}^j = (X_1, \ldots, X_j)$, the experimenter has the option of either making an immediate decision or taking further observations.

The experimental cost in this setup is simply the cost of taking observations. This cost can depend on many factors, two of the most crucial being the number of observations ultimately taken, and the way in which the observations are taken (i.e., one at a time, in groups, etc.). To quantify this, let n denote the number of observations ultimately taken, let s denote the manner in which the observations are taken, and, as usual, let $a \in \mathscr{A}$ denote the action taken. Then

$$L(\theta, a, n, s)$$

will denote the overall loss or cost when θ turns out to be the true state of nature.

Frequently, it will be the case that $L(\theta, a, n, s)$ can be considered to be the sum of the *decision loss*, $L(\theta, a)$, and the *cost of observation* (or *sampling cost*), $C(n, s)$. This will happen when the decision maker has a (nearly) linear utility function, so that the combined loss is just the sum of the individual losses. If the utility function U is nonlinear and the situation involves, say, monetary gain or loss, then it will generally happen, instead, that $L(\theta, a, n, s) = -U(G(\theta, a) - C(n, s))$, where $G(\theta, a)$ represents the monetary gain when the pair (θ, a) occurs and $C(n, s)$ is the sampling cost.

Unfortunately, even the sequential decision problem in this generality is too hard to handle. The difficulty occurs in trying to deal with all possible methods, s, of taking observations. We will, therefore, restrict ourselves to studying the two most common methods of taking observations. The first is the *fixed sample size* method, in which one preselects a sample size n, observes $\mathbf{X}^n = (X_1, \ldots, X_n)$, and makes a decision. The overall loss for this situation will be denoted $L^F(\theta, a, n)$. This problem will be considered in the next section.

The second common method of taking observations is that of *sequential analysis*, in which the observations are taken one at a time, with a decision being made, after each observation, to either cease sampling (and choose an action $a \in \mathscr{A}$) or take another observation. This is the situation that will be discussed in the bulk of the chapter (Sections 7.3 through 7.7), and so, for simplicity, the overall loss will just be written $L(\theta, a, n)$ in this case.

An important special case of the preceding situation is that in which the decision loss is $L(\theta, a)$, the ith observation costs c_i, and the utility function is approximately linear. Then $L(\theta, a, n)$ will be of the form

$$L(\theta, a, n) = L(\theta, a) + \sum_{i=1}^{n} c_i. \tag{7.1}$$

In such a situation, the phrases "loss," "risk," "Bayes risk," etc., will refer to the overall loss $L(\theta, a, n)$ and its derived risks, while "decision loss," "decision risk," etc., will refer to $L(\theta, a)$ and its derived risks.

When the fixed sample size loss, $L^F(\theta, a, n)$, is equal to the sequential loss, $L(\theta, a, n)$, (essentially a statement that it is no cheaper to take observations in a batch than one at a time) a sequential analysis of the problem will usually be considerably cheaper than a fixed sample size analysis. To intuitively see why, consider a lot inspection situation in which it is desired to test $H_0 : \theta = 0.05$ versus $H_1 : \theta = 0.15$, where θ is the proportion of defectives in the lot. The possible observations, $X_1, X_2, \ldots$, are a sequential sample (i.e., are independent) from the $\mathscr{B}(1, \theta)$ distribution.

Suppose that the optimal fixed sample size experiment requires a sample of size $n = 100$, and imagine that, instead, we decide to observe the X_i sequentially. Now if it so happens that the first 50 items tested from the lot are all good, then there is clearly overwhelming evidence that H_0 is true. Taking another 50 observations (as required by the fixed sample size approach) would almost certainly be a waste of money.

At the other extreme in this example, imagine that all 100 observations are taken, out of which 10 defectives are observed. There is then very little evidence as to whether H_0 or H_1 is true, and if it is important to determine which is true (and it is known that θ can only be 0.05 or 0.15), then more observations are needed.

The advantage of sequential analysis should be clear. It allows one to gather exactly the correct amount of data needed for a decision of the desired accuracy.

A word of warning should be given. Sequential analysis is not easy. Much of the chapter may seem somewhat abstract and technical, but it is abstraction that cannot be avoided. A considerable amount of theory must be brought to bear to obtain reasonable answers to sequential problems. It should be mentioned that a great deal of the early development of this theory was done by Abraham Wald. See Wald (1947) and Wald (1950).

7.2 Optimal Fixed Sample Size

In determining the optimal fixed sample size in a decision problem, the most sensible approach to use is the Bayesian approach. This is because, in balancing the decision loss and the sampling cost for any given sample size, the only reasonable pre-experimental measure of the expected decision loss is the Bayes decision risk. Formally, we define

Definition 1. Assume that $L^F(\theta, a, n)$ is the loss in observing $\mathbf{X}^n = (X_1, \ldots, X_n)$ and taking action a, and that θ has the prior density $\pi(\theta)$. Let δ_n^π denote a Bayes decision rule for this problem (if one exists), and let

$$r^n(\pi) = E^\pi E_\theta^{\mathbf{X}^n} [L^F(\theta, \delta_n^\pi(\mathbf{X}^n), n)]$$

denote the Bayes risk for the problem. (δ_0^π and $r^0(\pi)$ are the corresponding quantities for the no-observation problem.)

The optimal fixed sample size is clearly that n which minimizes $r^n(\pi)$. This can often be found by simply differentiating $r^n(\pi)$ with respect to n and setting equal to zero. Some examples follow. In all examples it is assumed that L^F is of the form

$$L^F(\theta, a, n) = L(\theta, a) + C(n). \qquad (7.2)$$

It is clear, in such a situation, that δ_n^π will be the Bayes decision rule (based on n observations) for the loss $L(\theta, a)$. We will, as usual, use $r(\pi, \delta_n^\pi)$ to denote the Bayes decision risk of this rule.

EXAMPLE 1. Assume that $X_1, X_2, \ldots$ is a sequential sample from a $\mathcal{N}(\theta, \sigma^2)$ density (σ^2 known), and that it is desired to estimate θ under a loss of the form (7.2) with $L(\theta, a) = (\theta - a)^2$. The parameter θ is thought to have a $\mathcal{N}(\mu, \tau^2)$ prior density.

If $\mathbf{X}^n = (X_1, \ldots, X_n)$ is to be observed, we know that a sufficient statistic for θ is

$$\bar{X}_n = \frac{1}{n} \sum_{i=1}^n X_i.$$

As in Chapter 4, it follows that the posterior distribution of θ given $\mathbf{x}^n$, to be denoted $\pi^n(\theta | \bar{x}_n)$, is $\mathcal{N}(\mu_n(\bar{x}_n), \rho_n)$, where

$$\mu_n(\bar{x}_n) = \frac{\sigma^2}{\sigma^2 + n\tau^2} \mu + \frac{n\tau^2}{\sigma^2 + n\tau^2} \bar{x}_n,$$

and $\qquad\qquad\qquad\qquad\qquad\qquad\qquad\qquad\qquad\qquad\qquad\qquad (7.3)$

$$\rho_n = \frac{\sigma^2 \tau^2}{\sigma^2 + n\tau^2}.$$

Since the decision loss is squared-error loss, it follows that $\delta_n^\pi(\mathbf{x}^n) = \mu_n(\bar{x}_n)$ is the Bayes decision rule, and that

$$r(\pi, \delta_n^\pi) = \rho_n = \frac{\sigma^2 \tau^2}{\sigma^2 + n\tau^2}.$$

Case 1. Assume that each observation costs c, so that $C(n) = nc$. Then

$$r''(\pi) = r(\pi, \delta_n^\pi) + C(n) = \frac{\sigma^2 \tau^2}{\sigma^2 + n\tau^2} + nc.$$

Pretending that n is a continuous variable and differentiating with respect to n gives

$$\frac{d}{dn} r''(\pi) = -\frac{\sigma^2 \tau^4}{(\sigma^2 + n\tau^2)^2} + c.$$

Setting equal to zero and solving gives

$$n^* = \sigma c^{-1/2} - \frac{\sigma^2}{\tau^2}$$

as the approximate minimizing value of n. Since the second derivative of $r''(\pi)$ is positive, $r''(\pi)$ is strictly convex in n. It follows that the n minimizing $r''(\pi)$ is one (or both) of the integers closest to n^*, unless $n^* < 0$, in which case $n = 0$ minimizes $r''(\pi)$. (Choosing $n = 0$ corresponds to making a decision without taking observations.) The smallest attainable Bayes risk is thus approximately

$$r^{n^*}(\pi) = 2\sigma c^{1/2} - \frac{c\sigma^2}{\tau^2}.$$

Case 2. Assume that $C(n) = \log(1 + n)$. (Thus it is more efficient, in terms of cost per observation, to take larger samples.) Then

$$r''(\pi) = \frac{\sigma^2 \tau^2}{\sigma^2 + n\tau^2} + \log(1 + n),$$

and it can be checked that this is (approximately) minimized at

$$n^* = \frac{\sigma^2}{2} - \frac{\sigma^2}{\tau^2} + \frac{\sigma}{2\tau} [4(\tau^2 - \sigma^2) + \sigma^2 \tau^2]^{1/2}.$$

EXAMPLE 2. Consider the situation of Example 1, Case 1, except assume that the decision loss is now $L(\theta, a) = |\theta - a|^k$ $(k > 0)$. From Exercise 38 of Chapter 4, it is clear that $\delta_n^\pi(x^n) = \mu_n(\bar{x}_n)$ (see (7.3)) is still the Bayes rule. It follows, using Lemma 2 of Section 4.5, that

$$r(\pi, \delta_n^\pi) = E^{m_n} E^{\pi^n(\theta|\bar{X}_n)} [|\theta - \mu_n(\bar{X}_n)|^k],$$

where m_n is the marginal density of $\bar{X}_n$. But clearly

$$E^{\pi^n(\theta|\bar{X}_n)} [|\theta - \mu_n(\bar{X}_n)|^k] = v(k)(\rho_n)^{k/2} = v(k) \left(\frac{\sigma^2 \tau^2}{\sigma^2 + n\tau^2} \right)^{k/2},$$

where $v(k)$ is the kth absolute moment of a $\mathcal{N}(0, 1)$ distribution. Hence

$$r(\pi, \delta_n^\pi) = v(k) \left(\frac{\sigma^2 \tau^2}{\sigma^2 + n\tau^2} \right)^{k/2},$$

and

$$r^n(\pi) = v(k)\left(\frac{\sigma^2\tau^2}{\sigma^2 + n\tau^2}\right)^{k/2} + nc.$$

Differentiating and setting equal to zero gives an optimal n of (approximately)

$$n^* = \sigma^2\left(\frac{v(k)k}{2\sigma^2 c}\right)^{2/(k+2)} - \frac{\sigma^2}{\tau^2}.$$

Note that

$$r(\pi, \delta_{n^*}^\pi) = v(k)\left(\frac{\sigma^2\tau^2}{\sigma^2 + n^*\tau^2}\right)^{k/2} = v(k)\left(\frac{2c\sigma^2}{kv(k)}\right)^{k/(k+2)}$$

and

$$cn^* = c\sigma^2\left(\frac{kv(k)}{2c\sigma^2}\right)^{2/(k+2)} - \frac{c\sigma^2}{\tau^2} = \frac{kv(k)}{2}\left(\frac{2c\sigma^2}{kv(k)}\right)^{k/(k+2)} - \frac{c\sigma^2}{\tau^2}.$$

Hence $r^{n^*}(\pi)$ can be easily calculated. For later reference, observe that when c is very small,

$$r(\pi, \delta_{n^*}^\pi) \cong \frac{2cn^*}{k}$$

(since c is then much smaller than $c^{k/(k+2)}$). It follows that, for small c, the decision risk and the sampling cost are roughly proportional functions of c.

EXAMPLE 3. Let $X_1, X_2, \ldots$ be a sequential sample from a $\mathcal{N}(\theta, \sigma^2)$ density, σ^2 known. It is desired to test $H_0 : \theta \in \Theta_0$ versus $H_1 : \theta \in \Theta_1$, where Θ_0 is "less than" Θ_1 in the sense that, if $\theta_0 \in \Theta_0$ and $\theta_1 \in \Theta_1$ then $\theta_0 < \theta_1$. Let a_i denote accepting H_i, and assume that the loss is of the form (7.2) with $L(\theta, a_i)$ being zero if a correct decision is made and positive otherwise. Let $\pi(\theta)$ denote the prior density for θ.

If $\mathbf{X}^n = (X_1, \ldots, X_n)$ is to be observed, $\bar{X}_n$ will again be sufficient for θ. Letting $\pi^n(\theta|\bar{x}_n)$ again denote the posterior distribution of θ given $\mathbf{x}^n$, the Bayes decision rule is to select a_0 if

$$\int_{\Theta_1} L(\theta, a_0)dF^{\pi^n(\theta|\bar{x}_n)}(\theta) < \int_{\Theta_0} L(\theta, a_1)dF^{\pi^n(\theta|\bar{x}_n)}(\theta) \tag{7.4}$$

(i.e., if the posterior expected decision loss of a_0 is smaller than that of a_1). Multiplying through by $(2\pi\sigma^2/n)^{1/2}m_n(\bar{x}_n)$ in (7.4) (m_n is the marginal density) gives the equivalent inequality

$$\int_{\Theta_1} L(\theta, a_0)\exp\left\{-\frac{n}{2\sigma^2}(\bar{x}_n - \theta)^2\right\}dF^\pi(\theta)$$

$$< \int_{\Theta_0} L(\theta, a_1)\exp\left\{-\frac{n}{2\sigma^2}(\bar{x}_n - \theta)^2\right\}dF^\pi(\theta). \tag{7.5}$$

It will be seen in Chapter 8 that the inequality in (7.5) holds for $\bar{x}_n < K(n)$, where $K(n)$ is some constant. (This must be true for any admissible test.) The reverse inequality holds for $\bar{x}_n > K(n)$, and

$$\int_{\Theta_1} L(\theta, a_0)\exp\left\{-\frac{n}{2\sigma^2}(K(n) - \theta)^2\right\}dF^\pi(\theta)$$

$$= \int_{\Theta_0} L(\theta, a_1)\exp\left\{-\frac{n}{2\sigma^2}(K(n) - \theta)^2\right\}dF^\pi(\theta). \quad (7.6)$$

Thus the Bayes rule, δ_n^π, is to decide a_0 if $\bar{x}_n < K(n)$, decide a_1 if $\bar{x}_n > K(n)$, and do anything if $\bar{x}_n = K(n)$.

The decision risk of δ_n^π is clearly

$$R(\theta, \delta_n^\pi) = \begin{cases} L(\theta, a_0)P_\theta(\bar{X}_n < K(n)) & \text{if } \theta \in \Theta_1, \\ L(\theta, a_1)[1 - P_\theta(\bar{X}_n < K(n))] & \text{if } \theta \in \Theta_0, \end{cases}$$

and the Bayes decision risk is

$$r(\pi, \delta_n^\pi) = \int_{\Theta_1} L(\theta, a_0)P_\theta(\bar{X}_n < K(n))dF^\pi(\theta)$$

$$+ \int_{\Theta_0} L(\theta, a_1)[1 - P_\theta(\bar{X}_n < K(n))]dF^\pi(\theta). \quad (7.7)$$

Pretending that n is a continuous variable, it is shown in Appendix 3 that

$$\frac{d}{dn}r(\pi, \delta_n^\pi) = (8\pi n\sigma^2)^{-1/2}\left[\int_{\Theta_0} L(\theta, a_1)(\theta - K^*)\right.$$

$$\times \exp\left\{-\frac{n}{2\sigma^2}(K(n) - \theta)^2\right\}dF^\pi(\theta)$$

$$\left. - \int_{\Theta_1} L(\theta, a_0)(\theta - K^*)\exp\left\{-\frac{n}{2\sigma^2}(K(n) - \theta)^2\right\}dF^\pi(\theta)\right],$$

$$(7.8)$$

where K^* is any constant. (The calculation is often simplified by a convenient choice of K^*.)

Using (7.6) and (7.8), it is often easy to calculate

$$\frac{d}{dn}r^\pi(\pi) = \frac{d}{dn}[r(\pi, \delta_n^\pi) + C(n)]$$

and approximate the optimal n. Some specific cases follow.

Case 1. Assume $\Theta_0 = \{\theta_0\}$ and $\Theta_1 = \{\theta_1\}$. The situation is thus that of testing a simple hypothesis against a simple alternative. Using (7.6), an easy calculation shows that

$$K(n) = \frac{1}{2}(\theta_0 + \theta_1) + \frac{\sigma^2}{n(\theta_1 - \theta_0)}\log\left[\frac{L(\theta_0, a_1)\pi(\theta_0)}{L(\theta_1, a_0)\pi(\theta_1)}\right].$$

Also, (7.8) gives (letting $K^* = 0$)

$$\frac{d}{dn} r(\pi, \delta_n^\pi) = (8\pi n\sigma^2)^{-1/2} \left[L(\theta_0, a_1)\theta_0 \exp\left\{ -\frac{n}{2\sigma^2} (K(n) - \theta_0)^2 \right\} \pi(\theta_0) \right.$$

$$\left. - L(\theta_1, a_0)\theta_1 \exp\left\{ -\frac{n}{2\sigma^2} (K(n) - \theta_1)^2 \right\} \pi(\theta_1) \right].$$

The above equations simplify further if it happens that $L(\theta_0, a_1)\pi(\theta_0) = L(\theta_1, a_0)\pi(\theta_1) = b$ (say). Then

$$K(n) = \frac{\theta_0 + \theta_1}{2}$$

and

$$\frac{d}{dn} r(\pi, \delta_n^\pi) = \frac{-b(\theta_1 - \theta_0)}{(8\pi n\sigma^2)^{1/2}} \exp\left\{ -\frac{n}{8\sigma^2} (\theta_1 - \theta_0)^2 \right\}.$$

If now $C(n) = nc$, then

$$\frac{d}{dn} r^n(\pi) = \frac{-b(\theta_1 - \theta_0)}{(8\pi n\sigma^2)^{1/2}} \exp\left\{ -\frac{n}{8\sigma^2} (\theta_1 - \theta_0)^2 \right\} + c. \qquad (7.9)$$

This can be set equal to zero and numerically solved for the (approximate) optimal n.

It is interesting for later comparisons to note that when b/c is large (basically a statement that the decision loss is much larger than the cost of an observation), then it can be shown that the optimal n, above, is approximately

$$n^* = \frac{8\sigma^2}{(\theta_1 - \theta_0)^2} \left[\log \frac{b}{c} - \frac{1}{2} \log \log \frac{b}{c} + \log \frac{(\theta_1 - \theta_0)^2}{8\pi^{1/2}\sigma^2} \right].$$

(This approximation is good when $\log(b/c)$ is much larger than $8\sigma^2/(\theta_1 - \theta_0)^2$ and $\log \log(b/c)$.) Hence the optimal n is of the order of $\log(b/c)$. It can also be checked, in this situation, that

$$r(\pi, \delta_{n^*}^\pi) \cong 8\sigma^2 c(\theta_1 - \theta_0)^{-2},$$

while the sampling cost is

$$n^*c \cong 8\sigma^2 c(\theta_1 - \theta_0)^{-2} \log\left(\frac{b}{c}\right).$$

Since $\log(b/c)$ is large, the sampling cost clearly dominates the overall Bayes risk, $r^{n^*}(\pi)$. Note that this is in sharp contrast to the situations of Examples 1 and 2.

Case 2. Let $\Theta_0 = (-\infty, \theta_0]$, $\Theta_1 = (\theta_0, \infty)$, $L(\theta, a_0) = W(|\theta - \theta_0|)$ for $\theta > \theta_0$, and $L(\theta, a_1) = W(|\theta - \theta_0|)$ for $\theta < \theta_0$. Assume also that π is a $\mathcal{N}(\mu, \tau^2)$ prior density.

An analysis, given in Appendix 3, shows that

$$\frac{d}{dn} r(\pi, \delta_n^\pi) = -\frac{\exp\{-\frac{1}{2}(1/\tau^2 + \sigma^2/n\tau^4)(\theta_0 - \mu)^2\}\sigma\tau}{2\pi(\sigma^2 + n\tau^2)n^{1/2}} \int_0^\infty W(\rho_n^{1/2} y) y e^{-y^2/2}\, dy.$$

$$(7.10)$$

If, for instance, $W(y) = y^k$ $(k > 0)$, then (7.10) becomes

$$\frac{d}{dn} r(\pi, \delta_n^\pi) = -\frac{\exp\{-\frac{1}{2}(1/\tau^2 + \sigma^2/n\tau^4)(\theta_0 - \mu)^2\}\sigma\tau}{2\pi(\sigma^2 + n\tau^2)n^{1/2}} \cdot \frac{(2\pi)^{1/2}\rho_n^{k/2}v(k+1)}{2}$$

$$= -\frac{\exp\{-\frac{1}{2}(1/\tau^2 + \sigma^2/n\tau^4)(\theta_0 - \mu)^2\}v(k+1)(\sigma\tau)^{(k+1)}}{2(2\pi)^{1/2}(\sigma^2 + n\tau^2)^{(k+2)/2}n^{1/2}},$$

$$(7.11)$$

where $v(k+1)$, as before, is the $(k+1)$st absolute moment of a $\mathcal{N}(0, 1)$ distribution. Using this, it is an easy numerical task to minimize $r^\pi(\pi)$.

If $C(n) = nc$ and c is small, then n will be large. For large n, (7.11) is approximately

$$\frac{d}{dn} r(\pi, \delta_n^\pi) \cong -\frac{v(k+1)\sigma^{(k+1)}\exp\{-(1/2\tau^2)(\theta_0 - \mu)^2\}}{2(2\pi)^{1/2}\tau n^{(k+3)/2}}.$$

In this case, the optimal n (approximately that for which $(d/dn)r^\pi(\pi) = (d/dn) r(\pi, \delta_n^\pi) + c = 0$) is clearly

$$n^* = \left[\frac{v(k+1)\sigma^{(k+1)}\exp\{-(1/2\tau^2)(\theta_0 - \mu)^2\}}{2(2\pi)^{1/2}\tau c}\right]^{2/(k+3)}.$$

This situation is considerably different than Case 1, in which n^* was of the order $\log(b/c)$. Also, the Bayes decision risk and the sampling cost will be of comparable magnitude here, rather than the sampling cost dominating as in Case 1. Note that this is very similar to the result obtained in Example 2 for estimation. Futher discussion of this behavior will be given in Subsection 7.4.10.

It should be noted that, at least in the above examples, the optimal sample size, n^*, will be fairly robust with respect to the tail of the prior distribution. This is because the Bayes decision risk, $r(\pi, \delta_n^\pi)$, is not changed very much by small changes in the tail of the prior (although, as seen in Chapter 4, δ_n^π can change considerably). Hence for purposes of determining the optimal sample size, it is frequently reasonable to use simple priors, such as conjugate priors. In actually determining $\delta_{n^*}^\pi$, however, more attention must be paid to robustness.

7.3 Sequential Analysis—Notation

In Section 7.1 it was stated that the distinguishing feature of sequential analysis is that the observations are taken one at a time, with the experimenter having the option of stopping the experiment and making a decision at any time. The observations, as mentioned earlier, will be denoted $X_1, X_2, \ldots$, where $\mathbf{X}^n = (X_1, X_2, \ldots, X_n)$ has density $f_n(\mathbf{x}^n|\theta)$ (and distribution function $F_n(\mathbf{x}^n|\theta)$) on $\mathcal{X}^n = \mathcal{X}_1 \times \mathcal{X}_2 \times \cdots \times \mathcal{X}_n$. Also, let $\mathbf{X} = (X_1, X_2, \ldots)$, $\mathcal{X} = \mathcal{X}_1 \times \mathcal{X}_2 \times \cdots$, and, for notational convenience, let X_0 and $\mathbf{X}^0$ stand for "no observation taken." As usual, $\theta \in \Theta$ is the unknown state of nature, and $\pi(\theta)$ will denote a prior density on Θ.

If n observations are taken sequentially, at which point action $a \in \mathscr{A}$ is taken, then the loss when θ is the true state of nature will be denoted $L(\theta, a, n)$. It will be assumed that this loss is increasing in n. Also, losses of the special form (7.1) will often be considered.

A (nonrandomized) *sequential decision procedure* will be denoted

$$\mathbf{d} = (\tau, \delta),$$

and, as indicated, consists of two components. The first component, τ, is called the *stopping rule*, and consists of functions τ_0, $\tau_1(\mathbf{x}^1)$, $\tau_2(\mathbf{x}^2)$, $\ldots$, where $\tau_i(\mathbf{x}^i)$ is the probability (zero or one for a nonrandomized procedure) of stopping sampling and making a decision after $\mathbf{x}^i$ is observed. (τ_0 is the probability of making an immediate decision without sampling.) The second component, δ, is called the *decision rule* and consists of a series of decision functions δ_0, $\delta_1(\mathbf{x}^1)$, $\delta_2(\mathbf{x}^2)$, $\ldots$, where $\delta_i(\mathbf{x}^i)$ is the action to be taken if sampling has stopped after observing $\mathbf{x}^i$. (The definition of a randomized sequential decision procedure should be obvious. As we will, for the most part, be considering the problem from a Bayesian viewpoint, randomized procedures will not be needed.)

It is frequently convenient to talk in terms of the *stopping time*, N, rather than the stopping rule. The stopping time is simply the final sample size, i.e., the sample size at which τ says to stop and make a decision. Formally, the stopping time is the random function of $\mathbf{X}$ given (for a nonrandomized sequential procedure) by

$$N(\mathbf{X}) = \min\{n \geq 0 : \tau_n(\mathbf{X}^n) = 1\}.$$

For $n \geq 1$, let $\{N = n\}$ denote the set of all $\mathbf{x}^n \in \mathcal{X}^n$ for which $\tau_n(\mathbf{x}^n) = 1$ and $\tau_j(\mathbf{x}^j) = 0$ ($j < n$). Clearly $\{N = n\}$ is the set of observations for which the sequential procedure stops at time n. Note that

$$P_\theta(N < \infty) = P(N = 0) + \sum_{n=1}^{\infty} P_\theta(N = n)$$

$$= P(N = 0) + \sum_{n=1}^{\infty} \int_{\{N=n\}} dF_n(\mathbf{x}^n|\theta).$$

A sequential procedure will be called *proper* if $P_\theta(N < \infty) = 1$ for all $\theta \in \Theta$. (In a Bayesian setting, this need only hold for all θ in a set of probability one under the prior π.) We will restrict consideration to such procedures.

The *risk function* of a sequential procedure **d** is the expected loss

$$R(\theta, \mathbf{d}) = E_\theta[L(\theta, \delta_N(\mathbf{X}^N), N)]$$

$$= P(N = 0)L(\theta, \delta_0, 0) + \sum_{n=1}^{\infty} \int_{\{N=n\}} L(\theta, \delta_n(\mathbf{x}^n), n) dF_n(\mathbf{x}^n | \theta). \quad (7.12)$$

When the loss is as in (7.1),

$$R(\theta, \mathbf{d}) = P(N = 0)L(\theta, \delta_0) + \sum_{n=1}^{\infty} \int_{\{N=n\}} L(\theta, \delta_n(\mathbf{x}^n)) dF_n(\mathbf{x}^n | \theta)$$

$$+ \sum_{n=1}^{\infty} \left(\sum_{i=1}^{n} c_i \right) P_\theta(N = n).$$

7.4 Bayesian Sequential Analysis

7.4.1 Introduction

While Bayesian analysis in fixed sample size problems is straightforward (robustness considerations aside), Bayesian sequential analysis is very difficult. A considerable amount of notation and machinery will be needed to deal with the problem, all of which tends to obscure the simple idea that is involved. This idea is that at every stage of the procedure (i.e., after every given observation) one should compare the (posterior) Bayes risk of making an immediate decision with the "expected" (posterior) Bayes risk that will be obtained if more observations are taken. If it is cheaper to stop and make a decision, that is what should be done. To clarify this idea, we begin with a very simple illustration.

EXAMPLE 4. A manufacturing firm is trying to decide whether to build a new plant in Ohio (action a_0) or in Alabama (action a_1). The plant would cost \$1,000,000 less to build at the site in Alabama, but there is perhaps a lack of skilled labor in the area. (The site in Ohio has an abundance of skilled labor.) A total of 700 skilled workers are needed, and the company feels that θ, the size of the available skilled labor force near the site in Alabama, has a $\mathcal{N}(350, (100)^2)$ prior density. (For convenience, we will treat θ as a continuous variable.) The company will have to train workers if skilled workers are not

available, at a cost of $3500 each. Assuming the company has an approxi-
mately linear utility function for money, the decision loss can be written as

$$L(\theta, a) = \begin{cases} 1,000,000 & \text{if } a = a_0, \\ 3500(700 - \theta) & \text{if } a = a_1 \text{ and } 0 \leq \theta \leq 700, \\ 0 & \text{if } a = a_1 \text{ and } \theta > 700. \end{cases}$$

Suppose now that the company either can make an immediate decision, or
can commission a survey to be conducted (at a cost of $20,000), the result of
which would be an estimate, X, of θ. It is known that the accuracy of the survey
would be such that X would be $\mathcal{N}(\theta, (30)^2)$. The problem is to decide whether
or not to commission the survey (i.e., to decide whether to make an immediate
decision, or to take the observation and then make a decision).

The Bayes risk of an immediate decision is the smaller of $r(\pi, a_0) = 1,000,000$ and

$$r(\pi, a_1) = 3500 \int_0^{700} (700 - \theta)\pi(\theta)d\theta$$

$$\cong 3500 \int_{-\infty}^{\infty} (700 - \theta)\pi(\theta)d\theta$$

$$= 3500(700 - 350) = 1,225,000.$$

(The error in replacing the exact limits of integration above by ∞ and $-\infty$
is negligible.) Hence the Bayes risk of an immediate decision is 1,000,000.

If the survey is commissioned and x observed, the posterior density,
$\pi(\theta|x)$, is $\mathcal{N}(\mu(x), \rho^{-1})$, where

$$\mu(x) = \frac{900}{900 + 10,000}(350) + \frac{10,000}{900 + 10,000}(x) \cong 28.90 + (0.9174)x,$$

$$\rho^{-1} = \frac{(900)(10,000)}{(900 + 10,000)} \cong 825.66.$$

Hence

$$r(\pi(\theta|x), a_1) = 3500 \int_0^{700} (700 - \theta)\pi(\theta|x)d\theta,$$

which, if $100 < x < 600$ (so that $\mu(x)$ is over 4 standard deviations from 0
or 700), is approximately

$$3500 \int_{-\infty}^{\infty} (700 - \theta)\pi(\theta|x)d\theta = 3500[700 - \mu(x)]$$
$$= 3500[671.1 - (0.9174)x].$$

Clearly $r(\pi(\theta|x), a_0) = 1,000,000$, so that the Bayes risk of taking the survey, observing x, and then making a decision is

$$
\begin{aligned}
r(x) &= \min\{r(\pi(\theta|x), a_0), r(\pi(\theta|x), a_1)\} + 20,000 \\
&\cong \min\{(1,020,000), 3500[676.8 - (0.9174)x]\} \quad \text{(for } 100 < x < 600) \\
&= \begin{cases} 1,020,000 & \text{if } 100 < x < 420.08, \\ 3500[676.8 - (0.9174)x] & \text{if } 420.08 < x < 600. \end{cases}
\end{aligned}
$$

Note, however, that we do not know which x will occur. Therefore we can only evaluate the Bayes risk, $r(x)$, through expected value over X. The relevant distribution for X is the "predictive" or marginal distribution, $m(x)$, which in this situation is $\mathcal{N}(350, (100)^2 + (30)^2)$. Since $P^m(100 < X < 600) \cong 0.983$, it is clear that (approximately)

$$
\begin{aligned}
E^m[r(X)] &\cong \int_{-\infty}^{420.08} (1,020,000)m(x)dx \\
&\quad + \int_{420.08}^{\infty} 3500[676.8 - (0.9174)x]m(x)dx \\
&= 763,980 + 205,745 = 969,725.
\end{aligned}
$$

This is less than the Bayes risk of an immediate decision, so the survey would be well worth the money. (Note that the calculations here were quite easy, partly because it just "happened" that replacing limits of integration by $-\infty$ and ∞ (when desired) gave reasonable approximations. May you always be so lucky.)

Often in decision problems, such as that above, there will be a number of possible stages of investigation, each stage corresponding to the commission of a more elaborate (and expensive) screening study. Of course, it is also typical to have a large number of possible stages (observations) in standard statistical settings. Unfortunately, determining the expected Bayes risk of continuing to sample becomes progressively harder as the number of possible stages increases. The remainder of this section is devoted to methods of dealing with this difficulty. Many of the basic methods discussed were first developed in Arrow, Blackwell, and Girshick (1949), and in Wald (1950).

7.4.2 Notation

The *Bayes risk* of a sequential procedure $\mathbf{d}$ is defined to be

$$
r(\pi, \mathbf{d}) = E^\pi[R(\theta, \mathbf{d})].
$$

A sequential procedure which minimizes $r(\pi, \mathbf{d})$ (over all proper procedures) is called a *Bayes sequential procedure*, and will be denoted

$$
\mathbf{d}^\pi = (\tau^\pi, \delta^\pi).
$$

The *Bayes risk* of the problem is defined to be

$$r(\pi) = \inf_{\mathbf{d}} r(\pi, \mathbf{d}).$$

It is useful to introduce special notation for the marginal (predictive) and posterior densities. Thus define (for $n = 1, 2, \ldots$) the marginal densities

$$m_n(\mathbf{x}^n) = E^\pi[f_n(\mathbf{x}^n | \theta)] = \int_\Theta f_n(\mathbf{x}^n | \theta) dF^\pi(\theta),$$

and (assuming $m_n(\mathbf{x}^n) > 0$) the posterior densities

$$\pi^n(\theta) = \pi(\theta | \mathbf{x}^n) = \frac{f_n(\mathbf{x}^n | \theta)\pi(\theta)}{m_n(\mathbf{x}^n)}.$$

(It will have to be remembered that π^n depends on $\mathbf{x}^n$. This dependence is suppressed to simplify notation.)

It is important to think in a sequential fashion. Indeed, after each new observation is taken, it is useful to consider the new sequential problem which starts at that point. To be precise, assume $\mathbf{x}^n$ has been observed, and consider the new sequential experiment, to be denoted $\mathscr{E}_n(\mathbf{x}^n)$, for which the possible observations are $X_{n+1}, X_{n+2}, \ldots$, the loss is $L(\theta, a, j)$, and the prior is $\pi^n(\theta)$. The distributions of the X_i must, naturally, be considered to be the relevant conditional distributions given $\mathbf{x}^n$ and θ. Since we will usually deal with independent X_i, explicit discussion of these conditional distributions is unnecessary.

Definition 2. Let $\mathscr{D}^n$ denote the class of all proper (nonrandomized) sequential procedures in the problem $\mathscr{E}_n(\mathbf{x}^n)$, which has loss $L(\theta, a, j)$, prior $\pi^n(\theta)$, and sequential observations $X_{n+1}, X_{n+2}, \ldots$. Denote the Bayes risk of a procedure $\mathbf{d} \in \mathscr{D}^n$ by $r(\pi^n, \mathbf{d}, n)$, and let

$$r(\pi^n, n) = \inf_{\mathbf{d} \in \mathscr{D}^n} r(\pi^n, \mathbf{d}, n).$$

We will be very concerned with the quantity $r(\pi^n, n)$. This represents the (conditional on $\mathbf{x}^n$) Bayes risk of proceeding in an optimal fashion at stage n. (It must be remembered that $r(\pi^n, n)$ can depend on $\mathbf{x}^n$, both through π^n and through the distributions of $X_{n+1}, X_{n+2}, \ldots$. When (as usual) the observations are independent, however, $r(\pi^n, n)$ will only depend on $\mathbf{x}^n$ through π^n. For this reason, $\mathbf{x}^n$ is suppressed.) It will be convenient to let π^0 correspond to the original prior π, so that $r(\pi^0, 0) = r(\pi)$, the Bayes risk for the original problem.

The quantity $r(\pi^n, n)$ represents the smallest Bayes risk that can be attained once $\mathbf{x}^n$ has been observed. To decide whether or not to make an immediate decision, therefore, it is intuitively obvious that one should compare $r(\pi^n, n)$ to the Bayes risk of an immediate decision, going on if $r(\pi^n, n)$ is smaller.

Clearly, notation for the Bayes risk of an immediate decision will be needed. Thus let

$$r_0(\pi^n, a, n) = E^{\pi^n}[L(\theta, a, n)]$$

denote the posterior expected loss of action a at time n, and define

$$r_0(\pi^n, n) = \inf_{a \in \mathscr{A}} r_0(\pi^n, a, n).$$

This last quantity will be called the *posterior Bayes risk* at time n.

One other notational device will be frequently used. In a situation in which θ has prior π, and X has (conditional on θ) density $f(x|\theta)$ and marginal density $m^*(x)$, define, for any function $g(x)$,

$$E^*[g(X)] = E^{m^*}[g(X)] = E^\pi E_\theta^X[g(X)].$$

Thus the symbol E^* will stand for expectation over X, with respect to the implied marginal density of X.

7.4.3 The Bayes Decision Rule

Assuming, as usual, that $L(\theta, a, n) \geq -K$, it follows from interchanging orders of integration, as in Chapter 4, that

$$r(\pi, \mathbf{d}) = E^\pi[R(\theta, \mathbf{d})]$$

$$= P(N = 0)E^\pi[L(\theta, \delta_0, 0)]$$

$$+ \sum_{n=1}^{\infty} \int_\Theta \int_{\{N=n\}} L(\theta, \delta_n(\mathbf{x}^n), n) dF_n(\mathbf{x}^n|\theta) dF^\pi(\theta)$$

$$= P(N = 0)E^\pi[L(\theta, \delta_0, 0)]$$

$$+ \sum_{n=1}^{\infty} \int_{\{N=n\}} \int_\Theta L(\theta, \delta_n(\mathbf{x}^n), n) dF^{\pi^n}(\theta) dF^{m_n}(\mathbf{x}^n)$$

$$= P(N = 0)r_0(\pi, \delta_0, 0) + \sum_{n=1}^{\infty} \int_{\{N=n\}} r_0(\pi^n, \delta_n(\mathbf{x}^n), n) dF^{m_n}(\mathbf{x}^n).$$

From this expression, it is clear that $r(\pi, \mathbf{d})$ will be minimized if δ_0 and the δ_n are chosen to minimize (for each $\mathbf{x}^n$) the posterior expected loss $r_0(\pi^n, \delta_n(\mathbf{x}^n), n)$. This, of course, is exactly what is done in the fixed sample size situation, and can be summarized as

Result 1. *For $n = 0, 1, 2, \ldots$, assume that $\delta_n^\pi(\mathbf{x}^n)$ is a Bayes decision rule for the fixed sample size decision problem with observations $X_1, \ldots, X_n$ and loss $L(\theta, a, n)$. Then $\boldsymbol{\delta}^\pi = \{\delta_0^\pi, \delta_1^\pi, \ldots\}$ is a Bayes sequential decision rule.*

Half of the problem of determining the Bayes sequential procedure, $\mathbf{d}^\pi$, has thus been solved. Regardless of the stopping rule used, the optimal action, once one has stopped, is simply the Bayes action for the given observations. This is, of course, automatically called for if one adopts the post-experimental Bayesian viewpoint discussed in Chapter 4. Further discussion of the implications of this will be given in Section 7.7.

Unfortunately, the determination of the optimal stopping time, τ^π, is usually much harder than the determination of δ^π. Much of the remainder of the chapter is devoted to an analysis of this problem. We begin with a discussion of the one case in which the optimal stopping rule is easy to find.

7.4.4 Constant Posterior Bayes Risk

For each n, it may happen that $r_0(\pi^n, n)$, the posterior Bayes risk at time n, is a constant independent of the actual observation $\mathbf{x}^n$. Since (see Subsection 7.2)

$$r^n(\pi) = E^\pi E_\theta[L(\theta, \delta_n^\pi(\mathbf{X}^n), n)] = E^{m_n}[r_0(\pi^n, n)],$$

it is clear that if $r_0(\pi^n, n)$ is a constant, this constant must be $r^n(\pi)$.

Assuming a Bayes decision rule, δ^π, exists, we may, by Result 1, restrict the search for a Bayes procedure to procedures of the form $\mathbf{d} = (\tau, \delta^\pi)$. For such a procedure,

$$r(\pi, \mathbf{d}) = P(N = 0)r_0(\pi, \delta_0^\pi, 0) + \sum_{n=1}^{\infty} \int_{\{N=n\}} r_0(\pi^n, \delta_n^\pi(\mathbf{x}^n), n)dF^{m_n}(\mathbf{x}^n)$$

$$= P(N = 0)r^0(\pi) + \sum_{n=1}^{\infty} r^n(\pi)P^{m_n}(N = n).$$

Letting $\lambda_0 = P(N = 0)$, $\lambda_n = P^{m_n}(N = n)$ $(n \geq 1)$, and observing that $0 \leq \lambda_n \leq 1$ and $\sum_{n=0}^{\infty} \lambda_n = 1$, it is clear that the Bayes risk,

$$r(\pi, \mathbf{d}) = \sum_{n=0}^{\infty} r^n(\pi)\lambda_n,$$

is minimized when λ_n is nonzero only for those n for which $r^n(\pi)$ is minimized. Hence the choice of an optimal stopping rule corresponds exactly to the choice, before experimentation, of an optimal fixed sample size n. This is summarized as

Result 2. *If, for each n, $r_0(\pi^n, n)$ is a constant $(r^n(\pi))$ for all $\mathbf{x}^n$, then a Bayes sequential stopping rule is to stop after observing n^* observations, where n^* is a value of n which minimizes $r^n(\pi)$ (assuming such a value exists).*

EXAMPLE 5. Assume that $X_1, X_2, \ldots$ is a sequential random sample from a $\mathcal{N}(\theta, \sigma^2)$ distribution (σ^2 known), that it is desired to estimate θ under loss

$L(\theta, a, n) = (\theta - a)^2 + \sum_{i=1}^{n} c_i$, and that θ has a $\mathcal{N}(\mu, \tau^2)$ prior distribution. As in Example 1, the posterior distribution of θ given $\mathbf{x}^n = (x_1, \ldots, x_n)$ is $\mathcal{N}(\mu_n(\bar{x}_n), \rho_n)$, where $\rho_n = \sigma^2\tau^2/(\sigma^2 + n\tau^2)$ does not depend on $\mathbf{x}^n$. Since, for squared-error decision loss, the posterior mean is the Bayes action and the posterior variance is its posterior expected decision loss, it is clear that

$$r_0(\pi^n, n) = \rho_n + \sum_{i=1}^{n} c_i,$$

which does not depend on $\mathbf{x}^n$. Hence Result 2 applies, and the optimal sequential stopping rule is simply to choose that n for which $\rho_n + \sum_{i=1}^{n} c_i$ is minimized.

Unfortunately, it is extremely rare for the posterior Bayes risk to be independent of the observations. When it is not, finding the Bayes stopping rule is very difficult. In principle, a technique does exist for at least approximating (arbitrarily closely) the optimal stopping rule. It is to this technique we now turn.

7.4.5 The Bayes Truncated Procedure

The difficulty in determining a Bayes sequential stopping rule is that there is an infinite possible future to consider. An obvious method of bypassing this problem is to restrict consideration to procedures for which the stopping time is bounded. As mentioned in the introduction, it is also important to consider the sequential problems starting at time $n + 1$. These concepts are tied together in the following definition.

Definition 3. In the sequential experiment $\mathcal{E}_n(\mathbf{x}^n)$ (observations X_{n+1}, $X_{n+2}, \ldots$, loss $L(\theta, a, j)$, and prior π^n) with procedures $\mathcal{D}^n$, let $\mathcal{D}_m^n$ denote the subset of procedures in $\mathcal{D}^n$ which take at most m observations. These procedures will be called m-*truncated procedures*. Also, define

$$r_m(\pi^n, n) = \inf_{\mathbf{d} \in \mathcal{D}_m^n} r(\pi^n, \mathbf{d}, n),$$

which will be called the m-*truncated Bayes risk* for the sequential experiment starting at stage n.

The important concept to understand is that $r_m(\pi^n, n)$ represents the (conditional on $\mathbf{x}^n$) Bayes risk of performing in an optimal sequential fashion, given that stage n has been reached, and assuming that at most m additional observations can be taken. In particular, $r_m(\pi, 0)$ represents the Bayes risk in the original problem of the optimal m-truncated procedure. Note that the definition of $r_0(\pi^n, n)$ given here is consistent with the definition in Subsection 7.4.2. Note also that, since $\mathcal{D}_m^n \subset \mathcal{D}_{m+1}^n$, the functions $r_m(\pi^n, n)$ are clearly nonincreasing in m. (We can do no worse by allowing the option of taking more observations.)

A natural goal in the original sequential problem is to seek the optimal m-truncated procedure, in the hope that it will be close to $\mathbf{d}^\pi$ for suitable m. Formally we define

Definition 4. If there exists an m-truncated procedure, $\mathbf{d}^m = (\tau^m, \delta^m) \in \mathcal{D}_m^0$, for which $r(\pi, \mathbf{d}^m) = r_m(\pi, 0)$, then $\mathbf{d}^m$ will be called a *Bayes m-truncated procedure*.

Due to the finite future of truncated procedures, a Bayes m-truncated procedure turns out to be theoretically calculable. Indeed, such a procedure is given in the following theorem.

Theorem 1. *Assume that Bayes decision rules, δ_n^π, exist for all n, and that the functions $r_j(\pi^n, n)$ are finite for all $j \leq m$ and $n \leq m - j$. Then a Bayes m-truncated procedure, $\mathbf{d}^m$, is given by $\mathbf{d}^m = (\tau^m, \delta^\pi)$, where τ^m is the stopping rule which says to stop sampling and make a decision for the first n $(n = 0, 1, 2, \ldots, m)$ for which*

$$r_0(\pi^n, n) = r_{m-n}(\pi^n, n).$$

PROOF. The fact that δ^m must be δ^π follows from Result 1 of Subsection 7.4.3. The conclusion that τ^m should be as given follows from induction on m and Theorem 2 (which follows this theorem). The induction argument will be left as an exercise. □

The intuition behind $\mathbf{d}^m$ should be clear. Initially (at stage 0) one compares $r_0(\pi, 0)$, the Bayes risk of an immediate Bayes decision, with $r_m(\pi, 0)$, the overall m-truncated Bayes risk. If the two are equal, the risk of immediately stopping is equal to the overall optimal Bayes risk, so one should stop. If $r_0(\pi, 0)$ is greater than $r_m(\pi, 0)$, one can expect to do better by not immediately stopping, i.e., by observing X_1. After x_1 has been observed, compare $r_0(\pi^1, 1)$, the posterior Bayes risk of an immediate decision, with $r_{m-1}(\pi^1, 1)$, the $(m - 1)$-truncated Bayes risk at stage 1. (After x_1 is observed, at most $m - 1$ additional observations can be taken.) Again one should stop if $r_0(\pi^1, 1)$ and $r_{m-1}(\pi^1, 1)$ are equal, and continue sampling otherwise. Proceeding in the obvious fashion results in the stopping rule τ^m.

To find $\mathbf{d}^m$, it is thus only necessary to calculate the functions $r_j(\pi^n, n)$. In principle, this can always be done inductively, as shown in the following theorem. The proof of this theorem should be carefully read.

Theorem 2. *Assuming the quantities $r_j(\pi^n, n)$ are finite, they can be calculated inductively from the relationship*

$$r_j(\pi^n, n) = \min\{r_0(\pi^n, n), E^*[r_{j-1}(\pi^n(\theta \,|\, X_{n+1}), n + 1)]\}.$$

Here $\pi''(\theta \mid X_{n+1})$ is the posterior after observing X_{n+1} (i.e., is $\pi^{n+1}(\theta)$), and E^* (as defined earlier) is expectation with respect to the predictive (or marginal) distribution of X_{n+1} given $\mathbf{x}^n$. This predictive distribution has density

$$m^*(x_{n+1}) = \frac{m_{n+1}(\mathbf{x}^{n+1})}{m_n(\mathbf{x}^n)},$$

providing $m_n(\mathbf{x}^n) > 0$.

PROOF. The proof is given somewhat informally for ease of understanding, but can easily be made rigorous using an induction argument along the lines indicated. Note that the sequential experiment $\mathscr{E}_n(\mathbf{x}^n)$ is being considered (i.e., we imagine that the first n observations have already been taken).

Assume $j = 1$ (i.e., at most one additional observation can be taken). The only two possible courses of action are to then make an immediate decision, incurring posterior Bayes risk $r_0(\pi^n, n)$, or to observe X_{n+1} and then make a decision. In the latter case, the posterior Bayes risk will be $r_0(\pi''(\theta \mid X_{n+1}), n + 1)$. Since X_{n+1} is random, the expected posterior Bayes risk

$$E^*[r_0(\pi''(\theta \mid X_{n+1}), n + 1)]$$

measures the Bayes risk of observing X_{n+1} and then making a decision. Clearly $r_1(\pi^n, n)$, the Bayes risk of the optimal way of acting when at most one observation is allowed, must be the smaller of $r_0(\pi^n, n)$ and $E^*[r_0(\pi''(\theta \mid X_{n+1}), n + 1)]$.

Exactly the same reasoning holds for any j. Either an immediate decision must be made, incurring posterior Bayes risk $r_0(\pi^n, n)$, or X_{n+1} must be observed, in which case at most $j - 1$ more observations can be taken. The expected Bayes risk of this latter course of action is $E^*[r_{j-1}(\pi''(\theta \mid X_{n+1}), n + 1)]$, and so the smaller of this and $r_0(\pi^n, n)$ must be $r_j(\pi^n, n)$.

The predictive distribution of X_{n+1} given $\mathbf{x}^n$, with respect to which E^* is taken, can be most easily determined by taking the predictive distribution of $\mathbf{X}^{n+1}$ (i.e., $m_{n+1}(\mathbf{x}^{n+1})$) and conditioning on $\mathbf{x}^n$. The resulting density is (in the continuous case for simplicity)

$$m^*(x_{n+1}) = \frac{m_{n+1}(\mathbf{x}^{n+1})}{\int_{\mathscr{X}_{n+1}} m_{n+1}(\mathbf{x}^{n+1}) dx_{n+1}}$$

$$= \frac{m_{n+1}(\mathbf{x}^{n+1})}{\int_{\mathscr{X}_{n+1}} E^\pi[f_{n+1}(\mathbf{x}^{n+1} \mid \theta)] dx_{n+1}}$$

$$= \frac{m_{n+1}(\mathbf{x}^{n+1})}{E^\pi[f_n(\mathbf{x}^n \mid \theta)]}$$

$$= \frac{m_{n+1}(\mathbf{x}^{n+1})}{m_n(\mathbf{x}^n)}.$$

The theorem is thus established.   □

Note that, for all m,

$$r_m(\pi, 0) \geq r(\pi). \tag{7.13}$$

(Minimizing the Bayes risk over the subclass of procedures $\mathscr{D}_m^0$ results in a quantity at least as large as the minimum over all procedures.) Hence the computable quantities $r_m(\pi, 0)$ provide upper bounds on the true Bayes risk of the problem. More will be said about this in Subsection 7.4.8.

An important special case to consider is that in which $X_1, X_2, \ldots$ is a sequential sample from a common density $f(x|\theta)$, and $L(\theta, a, n)$ is of the form (7.1) with $c_i = c$. It is then easy to see that

$$r_0(\pi^n, n) = \rho_0(\pi^n) + nc,$$

where the quantity

$$\rho_0(\pi^n) = E^{\pi^n}[L(\theta, \delta_n^\pi(\mathbf{x}^n))]$$

is the posterior Bayes decision risk. It follows that

$$r_1(\pi^n, n) = \min\{\rho_0(\pi^n), E^*[\rho_0(\pi^n(\theta | X_{n+1}))] + c\} + nc,$$

and suggests defining inductively

$$\rho_j(\pi^n) = \min\{\rho_0(\pi^n), E^*[\rho_{j-1}(\pi^n(\theta | X_{n+1}))] + c\}. \tag{7.14}$$

It can be easily checked that

$$r_j(\pi^n, n) = \rho_j(\pi^n) + nc,$$

so that Theorem 1 can be restated as

Corollary 1.1. *Assume that $X_1, X_2, \ldots$ is a sequential sample, and that $L(\theta, a, n)$ $= L(\theta, a) + nc$. Then the Bayes m-truncated stopping rule, τ^m, is to stop sampling and make a decision for the first n ($n = 0, 1, \ldots, m$) for which*

$$\rho_0(\pi^n) = \rho_{m-n}(\pi^n),$$

providing these quantities are finite.

The advantage of using Corollary 1.1 (if it applies) is that sometimes the functions ρ_j can be explicitly computed for all possible posteriors. This means that only m functions need be calculated, instead of all the $r_j(\pi^n, n)$ for the various j, n, and $\mathbf{x}^n$. Note also that, in calculating E^* in (7.14),

$$m^*(x_{n+1}) = \frac{m_{n+1}(\mathbf{x}^{n+1})}{m_n(\mathbf{x}^n)} = E^{\pi^n}[f(x_{n+1}|\theta)],$$

the last expression often being easier to work with than the middle expression.

EXAMPLE 6. Assume that $X_1, X_2, \ldots$ is a sequential sample from a $\mathscr{B}(1, \theta)$ density, and that it is desired to test $H_0: \theta = \frac{1}{3}$ versus $H_1: \theta = \frac{2}{3}$. Let a_i denote accepting H_i ($i = 0, 1$), and suppose that $L(\theta, a, n) = L(\theta, a) + nc$

with $c = 1$ and $L(\theta, a)$ being "0–20" loss (i.e., no decision loss for a correct decision, and a decision loss of 20 for an incorrect decision). Finally, let π_i^* ($i = 0, 1$) denote the prior probability that H_i is true. (The symbols π_i ($i = 0, 1$) will be reserved for use as arbitrary prior probabilities of H_i.)

Imagine that it is desired to find $\mathbf{d}^2$, the optimal procedure among all those taking at most two observations. To use Corollary 1.1, the functions ρ_0, ρ_1, and ρ_2 must be calculated. It is easiest to calculate ρ_0 and ρ_1 for arbitrary π, later specializing to the π_i^{*n}.

To calculate $\rho_0(\pi)$, note that the Bayes risks of immediately deciding a_0 and a_1 are $20(1 - \pi_0)$ and $20\pi_0$, respectively, so that the Bayes action is a_0 if $\pi_0 > \frac{1}{2}$ and a_1 if $\pi_0 \leq \frac{1}{2}$. Hence

$$\rho_0(\pi) = \begin{cases} 20\pi_0 & \text{if } \pi_0 \leq \frac{1}{2}, \\ 20(1 - \pi_0) & \text{if } \pi_0 > \frac{1}{2}. \end{cases}$$

To determine the function $\rho_1(\pi)$ using (7.14), it is first necessary to calculate $E^*[\rho_0(\pi(\theta \mid X))]$. This expectation is calculated with respect to

$$m^*(x) = E^\pi[f(x \mid \theta)] = f(x \mid \tfrac{1}{3})\pi_0 + f(x \mid \tfrac{2}{3})\pi_1$$

$$= \begin{cases} (1 - \tfrac{1}{3})\pi_0 + (1 - \tfrac{2}{3})\pi_1 & \text{if } x = 0, \\ \tfrac{1}{3}\pi_0 + \tfrac{2}{3}\pi_1 & \text{if } x = 1, \end{cases}$$

$$= \begin{cases} \tfrac{1}{3}(1 + \pi_0) & \text{if } x = 0, \\ \tfrac{1}{3}(2 - \pi_0) & \text{if } x = 1. \end{cases}$$

Clearly $\pi(\theta \mid X)$ is determined by

$$\pi(\tfrac{1}{3} \mid 0) = \frac{\pi(\tfrac{1}{3}) f(0 \mid \tfrac{1}{3})}{m(0)} = \frac{2\pi_0}{1 + \pi_0},$$

$$\pi(\tfrac{1}{3} \mid 1) = \frac{\pi(\tfrac{1}{3}) f(1 \mid \tfrac{1}{3})}{m(1)} = \frac{\pi_0}{2 - \pi_0}. \tag{7.15}$$

Hence

$$\rho_0(\pi(\theta \mid 0)) = \begin{cases} 20\pi(\tfrac{1}{3} \mid 0) & \text{if } \pi(\tfrac{1}{3} \mid 0) \leq \frac{1}{2}, \\ 20[1 - \pi(\tfrac{1}{3} \mid 0)] & \text{if } \pi(\tfrac{1}{3} \mid 0) > \frac{1}{2}, \end{cases}$$

$$= \begin{cases} \dfrac{40\pi_0}{1 + \pi_0} & \text{if } \pi_0 \leq \frac{1}{3}, \\[2mm] \dfrac{20(1 - \pi_0)}{1 + \pi_0} & \text{if } \pi_0 > \frac{1}{3}, \end{cases}$$

and similarly

$$\rho_0(\pi(\theta \mid 1)) = \begin{cases} \dfrac{20\pi_0}{2 - \pi_0} & \text{if } \pi_0 \leq \frac{2}{3}, \\[2mm] \dfrac{40(1 - \pi_0)}{2 - \pi_0} & \text{if } \pi_0 > \frac{2}{3}. \end{cases}$$

Considering separately the regions $\pi_0 \leq \frac{1}{3}, \frac{1}{3} < \pi_0 \leq \frac{2}{3}$, and $\pi_0 > \frac{2}{3}$, it follows that

$$E^*[\rho_0(\pi(\theta|X))] = \rho_0(\pi(\theta|0))m(0) + \rho_0(\pi(\theta|1))m(1)$$

$$= \begin{cases} \left(\dfrac{40\pi_0}{1 + \pi_0}\right)\left(\dfrac{1 + \pi_0}{3}\right) + \left(\dfrac{20\pi_0}{2 - \pi_0}\right)\left(\dfrac{2 - \pi_0}{3}\right) \\ \qquad\qquad\qquad\qquad\qquad\qquad \text{if } \pi_0 \leq \tfrac{1}{3}, \\[6pt] \left(\dfrac{20(1 - \pi_0)}{1 + \pi_0}\right)\left(\dfrac{1 + \pi_0}{3}\right) + \left(\dfrac{20\pi_0}{2 - \pi_0}\right)\left(\dfrac{2 - \pi_0}{3}\right) \\ \qquad\qquad\qquad\qquad\qquad\qquad \text{if } \tfrac{1}{3} < \pi_0 \leq \tfrac{2}{3}, \\[6pt] \left(\dfrac{20(1 - \pi_0)}{1 + \pi_0}\right)\left(\dfrac{1 + \pi_0}{3}\right) + \left(\dfrac{40(1 - \pi_0)}{2 - \pi_0}\right)\left(\dfrac{2 - \pi_0}{3}\right) \\ \qquad\qquad\qquad\qquad\qquad\qquad \text{if } \tfrac{2}{3} < \pi_0, \end{cases}$$

$$= \begin{cases} 20\pi_0 & \text{if } \pi_0 \leq \tfrac{1}{3}, \\ \tfrac{20}{3} & \text{if } \tfrac{1}{3} < \pi_0 \leq \tfrac{2}{3}, \\ 20(1 - \pi_0) & \text{if } \tfrac{2}{3} < \pi_0. \end{cases}$$

Thus

$$\rho_1(\pi) = \min\{\rho_0(\pi), E^*[\rho_0(\pi(\theta|X))] + 1\}$$

$$= \begin{cases} 20\pi_0 & \text{if } \pi_0 \leq \tfrac{13}{30}, \\ \tfrac{23}{3} & \text{if } \tfrac{13}{30} < \pi_0 \leq \tfrac{17}{30}, \\ 20(1 - \pi_0) & \text{if } \tfrac{17}{30} < \pi_0. \end{cases} \qquad (7.16)$$

The calculation of $\rho_2(\pi)$ is similar. Rather than going through it in gory detail for all π, we will make life simple and assume that the original prior has $\pi_0^* = \frac{2}{5}$. (Note that, to apply Corollary 1.1, it is only necessary to calculate $\rho_2(\pi^*)$.)

Note first, from (7.15), that $\pi^*(\frac{1}{3}|0) = \frac{4}{7}$ and $\pi^*(\frac{1}{3}|1) = \frac{1}{4}$. Hence (7.16) implies that

$$\rho_1(\pi^*(\theta|0)) = 20(1 - \tfrac{4}{7}) = \tfrac{60}{7} \quad (\text{since } \pi^*(\tfrac{1}{3}|0) = \tfrac{4}{7} > \tfrac{17}{30})$$

and

$$\rho_1(\pi^*(\theta|1)) = \tfrac{20}{4} = 5 \quad (\text{since } \pi^*(\tfrac{1}{3}|1) = \tfrac{1}{4} < \tfrac{13}{30}).$$

Also, $m(0) = \frac{1}{3}(1 + \frac{2}{5}) = \frac{7}{15}$ and $m(1) = 1 - m(0) = \frac{8}{15}$, so that

$$E^*[\rho_1(\pi^*(\theta|X))] = \rho_1(\pi^*(\theta|0))m(0) + \rho_1(\pi^*(\theta|1))m(1)$$
$$= (\tfrac{60}{7})(\tfrac{7}{15}) + 5(\tfrac{8}{15}) = 6\tfrac{2}{3}.$$

Therefore,

$$\rho_2(\pi^*) = \min\{\rho_0(\pi^*), E^*[\rho_1(\pi^*(\theta|X))] + 1\} = \min\{\tfrac{40}{5}, 6\tfrac{2}{3}\} = 6\tfrac{2}{3}.$$

The optimal procedure, $\mathbf{d}^2$, is now given immediately by Corollary 1.1. For $\pi_0^* = \frac{2}{5}$, note that

$$\rho_0(\pi^*) = 8 > 6\frac{2}{3} = \rho_2(\pi^*),$$

so that X_1 should be observed. After observing X_1, $\rho_0(\pi^{*1})$ and $\rho_1(\pi^{*1})$ must be compared. If $x_1 = 0$, then

$$\pi_0^{*1} = \pi^{*1}(\tfrac{1}{3}) = \pi^*(\tfrac{1}{3}|0) = \tfrac{4}{7},$$

so that $\rho_0(\pi^{*1}) = 20(1 - \pi_0^{*1}) = \frac{60}{7}$ and $\rho_1(\pi^{*1}) = 20(1 - \pi_0^{*1}) = \frac{60}{7}$. Since $\rho_0(\pi^{*1}) = \rho_1(\pi^{*1})$, it is optimal to stop and decide a_0 (since $\pi_0^{*1} > \frac{1}{2}$). If $x_1 = 1$, then $\pi_0^{*1} = \pi^*(\tfrac{1}{3}|1) = \tfrac{1}{4}$, so that $\rho_0(\pi^{*1}) = \frac{20}{4} = 5$ and $\rho_1(\pi^{*1}) = \frac{20}{4} = 5$. Hence it is again optimal to stop, but now action a_1 should be taken (since $\pi_0^{*1} < \frac{1}{2}$). Note that it never pays to take the second observation (although, of course, it might pay if more than two observations could be taken).

The above example indicates the difficulty of actually computing the $\rho_j(\pi^n)$ or, more generally, the $r_j(\pi^n, n)$. Indeed, except for special cases, the calculations generally become unmanageable for large j. Even with a computer, the calculations can generally only be done for conjugate priors (so that the π^n depend on $\mathbf{x}^n$ only through a few parameters), and even then can be very hard for large j. It is thus to be hoped that $\mathbf{d}^m$, the Bayes m-truncated procedure, will be close to $\mathbf{d}^\pi$ for small or moderate m. This issue will be discussed in Subsection 7.4.8, but for now it is worthwhile to note that it frequently happens that the Bayes sequential procedure is, in fact, a truncated procedure. The following theorem gives a condition under which this is so. For simplicity, we restrict attention to the special case in which $L(\theta, a, n)$ is of the form (7.1).

Theorem 3. *Assume that $L(\theta, a, n)$ is of the form (7.1), with $L(\theta, a)$ being non-negative, and that the posterior Bayes decision risk at stage m satisfies $\rho_0(\pi^m) < c_{m+1}$ for all $\mathbf{x}^m$. Then a Bayes sequential procedure must be truncated at m.*

The proof of this theorem is obvious, since at stage m it costs more to take another observation than to make a decision. Often it is the case that, as $m \to \infty$, $\rho_0(\pi^m) \to 0$ uniformly in $\mathbf{x}^m$, in which case the condition of the theorem is sure to be satisfied for large enough m. An example follows.

EXAMPLE 7. Assume that $X_1, X_2, \ldots$ is a sequential sample from a $\mathcal{B}(1, \theta)$ distribution, and that it is desired to estimate θ under the loss $L(\theta, a, n) = (\theta - a)^2 + nc$. Assume that θ has a $\mathcal{U}(0, 1)$ prior distribution.

Letting $S_n = \sum_{i=1}^{n} X_i$ denote the sufficient statistic for θ, and noting that $S_n \sim \mathscr{B}(n, \theta)$, an easy calculation shows that $\pi^n(\theta) = \pi(\theta \mid s_n)$ (where $s_n = \sum_{i=1}^{n} x_i$) is a $\mathscr{B}e(s_n + 1, n - s_n + 1)$ density. Since the decision loss is squared-error loss, the posterior Bayes decision risk at time n is the variance of the posterior. From Appendix 1, this is given by

$$\rho_0(\pi^n) = \frac{(s_n + 1)(n - s_n + 1)}{(n + 2)^2(n + 3)}.$$

It can be checked that $(s_n + 1)(n - s_n + 1) \le (n + 2)^2/4$, so that

$$\rho_0(\pi^n) \le \frac{1}{4(n + 3)}.$$

Thus, letting m denote the smallest integer n for which $1/4(n + 3) < c$, Theorem 3 implies that the Bayes sequential procedure must be truncated at m.

Conditions more delicate than that in Theorem 3 can be derived, under which a Bayes sequential procedure is truncated. See S. N. Ray (1965) for a discussion of this. We content ourselves with a theorem involving one quite strong, yet still fairly easy to use, condition. The proof of the theorem is left as an exercise.

Theorem 4. *Assume that* $r_m(\pi, 0) \to r(\pi)$ *as* $m \to \infty$, *and that for all* $j \ge M$ *and all* $\mathbf{x}^j$,

$$r_0(\pi^j, j) \le E^*[r_0(\pi^j(\theta \mid X_{j+1}), j + 1)].$$

Then the Bayes M*-truncated procedure,* $\mathbf{d}^M$, *is a Bayes sequential procedure with respect to* π.

7.4.6 Look Ahead Procedures

The Bayes m-truncated procedure, $\mathbf{d}^m$, has the obvious failing that m must be significantly larger than the expected stopping time of the true Bayes procedure, $\mathbf{d}^\pi$, before $\mathbf{d}^m$ can be a reasonable approximation to $\mathbf{d}^\pi$. The difficulty of calculating $\mathbf{d}^m$ for large m makes this a serious problem when the Bayes procedure will be likely to require a fairly large sample. One obvious method of circumventing this difficulty is to use what we will call the *m-step look ahead* procedure. The idea is to look m steps ahead at every stage, rather than only looking ahead up to stage m. Formally we define

Definition 5. Let τ_L^m be the stopping rule (assuming it is well defined and proper) which stops for the first n $(n = 0, 1, 2, \ldots)$ for which

$$r_0(\pi^n, n) = r_m(\pi^n, n).$$

The procedure $\mathbf{d}_L^m = (\tau_L^m, \delta^\pi)$ will be called the *m-step look ahead procedure*.

The m-step look ahead procedure is a very reasonable procedure. Since it looks ahead farther than $\mathbf{d}^m$, it will have a smaller Bayes risk than $\mathbf{d}^m$. It will also tend to be a good approximation to $\mathbf{d}^\pi$ for much smaller m than is needed for $\mathbf{d}^m$ to be a good approximation. Evidence of this will be given in Subsection 7.4.8. Finally, $\mathbf{d}^m_L$ is usually not much harder to calculate than $\mathbf{d}^m$, since the difficulty in the calculation of either procedure is determined by the difficulty in calculation of the $r_m(\pi^n, n)$.

In the special situation of Corollary 1.1 of the preceding subsection, it is easy to see that the m-step look ahead procedure stops for the first n for which

$$\rho_0(\pi^n) = \rho_m(\pi^n).$$

An example follows.

EXAMPLE 6 (continued). We will find the 1-step look ahead procedure for this situation. It was calculated that, for all π,

$$\rho_0(\pi) = \begin{cases} 20\pi_0 & \text{if } \pi_0 \leq \frac{1}{2}, \\ 20(1 - \pi_0) & \text{if } \pi_0 > \frac{1}{2}, \end{cases}$$

and

$$\rho_1(\pi) = \begin{cases} 20\pi_0 & \text{if } \pi_0 \leq \frac{13}{30}, \\ \frac{23}{3} & \text{if } \frac{13}{30} < \pi_0 \leq \frac{17}{30}, \\ 20(1 - \pi_0) & \text{if } \frac{17}{30} < \pi_0, \end{cases}$$

where π_0 is the prior probability that $\theta = \frac{1}{3}$. Hence the 1-step look ahead procedure, when the true prior is π^*, stops for the first n for which

$$\rho_0(\pi^{*n}) = \rho_1(\pi^{*n}),$$

or, equivalently, for the first n for which

$$\pi_0^{*n} \leq \tfrac{13}{30} \quad \text{or} \quad \pi_0^{*n} \geq \tfrac{17}{30}. \tag{7.17}$$

Letting $s_n = \sum_{i=1}^n x_i$, it is clear that

$$\pi_0^{*n} = \pi^*(\tfrac{1}{3} | x_1, \ldots, x_n) = \frac{\pi_0^*(\tfrac{1}{3})^{s_n}(\tfrac{2}{3})^{n-s_n}}{\pi_0^*(\tfrac{1}{3})^{s_n}(\tfrac{2}{3})^{n-s_n} + (1 - \pi_0^*)(\tfrac{2}{3})^{s_n}(\tfrac{1}{3})^{n-s_n}}$$

$$= \{1 + [(\pi_0^*)^{-1} - 1]2^{(2s_n - n)}\}^{-1}.$$

A calculation then shows that (7.17) is equivalent to

$$|s_n - K^*| \geq \frac{\log(\tfrac{17}{13})}{2 \log 2},$$

where

$$K^* = \frac{1}{2}\left\{n - \frac{\log[(\pi_0^*)^{-1} - 1]}{2 \log 2}\right\}.$$

The 1-step look ahead procedure thus has a very simple form in this example.

In determining the m-step look ahead procedure, it is calculationally easiest to look ahead as few steps as necessary. The idea is that it may not be necessary to calculate $r_m(\pi^n, n)$ at every stage, since it may be the case that $r_0(\pi^n, n) > r_j(\pi^n, n)$ for some $j < m$, in which case one should certainly continue sampling. (If it is desirable to continue sampling when looking ahead j steps, it will also be desirable when looking ahead $m > j$ steps.) Thus, typically, the simplest way to proceed at stage n is to compare $r_0(\pi^n, n)$ with $r_1(\pi^n, n)$, going on if $r_0(\pi^n, n) > r_1(\pi^n, n)$. If the two quantities are equal, calculate $r_2(\pi^n, n)$ and compare with $r_0(\pi^n, n)$. Continue in the obvious manner, stopping whenever $r_m(\pi^n, n)$ is calculated and found to be equal to $r_0(\pi^n, n)$. Note that this stopping rule is exactly equivalent to τ_L^m, the stopping rule for the m-step look ahead procedure. This principle, of never looking ahead farther than necessary, can also be used in the calculation of $\mathbf{d}^m$ or any other truncated rule, and will usually save considerably on computation.

Another useful look ahead procedure has been proposed by Amster (1963). This procedure does not look ahead sequentially, but looks ahead with a fixed sample size rule. Formally, we define

Definition 6. Let $r^m(\pi^n, n)$ denote the Bayes risk for the fixed sample size problem with observations $X_{n+1}, \ldots, X_{n+m}$, prior π^n, and loss $L^F(\theta, a, m) = L(\theta, a, n + m)$. The *fixed sample size look ahead procedure* will be denoted $\mathbf{d}_{FS} = (\tau_{FS}, \delta^\pi)$, and τ_{FS} is the stopping rule which stops for the first n ($n = 0, 1, 2, \ldots$) for which

$$r_0(\pi^n, n) \leq \inf_{m \geq 1} r^m(\pi^n, n).$$

The rationale for this rule is that if, at stage n, there is a fixed sample size way of continuing, which has smaller Bayes risk than does making an immediate decision, then certainly another observation should be taken. The attractiveness of $\mathbf{d}_{FS}$ is that it is usually relatively easy to compute the fixed sample size Bayes risk $r^m(\pi^n, n)$, and hence $\mathbf{d}_{FS}$. An example follows.

EXAMPLE 8. As in Example 7, assume that $X_1, X_2, \ldots$ is a sequential sample from a $\mathcal{B}(1, \theta)$ density, and that it is desired to estimate θ under loss $L(\theta, a, n) = (\theta - a)^2 + nc$. Assume now, however, that θ has a $\mathcal{B}e(\alpha_0, \beta_0)$ prior.

Note that $S_n = \sum_{i=1}^n X_i$ is a sufficient statistic for θ and has a $\mathcal{B}(n, \theta)$ distribution. An easy calculation then shows that $\pi^n(\theta) = \pi(\theta|s_n)$ is a $\mathcal{B}e(\alpha_0 + s_n, \beta_0 + n - s_n)$ density. Define, for simplicity, $\alpha_n = \alpha_0 + s_n$ and $\beta_n = \beta_0 + n - s_n$. Since the decision loss is squared-error loss, the variance of the posterior will be the posterior Bayes decision risk. Hence

$$r_0(\pi^n, n) = \frac{\alpha_n \beta_n}{(\alpha_n + \beta_n)^2(\alpha_n + \beta_n + 1)} + nc.$$

To compute $r^m(\pi^n, n)$, define $Y_m = \sum_{i=n+1}^{n+m} X_i$, note that $Y_m \sim \mathcal{B}(m, \theta)$, and conclude, as above, that the posterior at time $n + m$ will be

$\mathscr{B}e(\alpha_n + y_m, \beta_n + m - y_m)$. The Bayes decision rule will be the posterior mean, namely

$$\delta(y_m) = \frac{\alpha_n + y_m}{\alpha_n + \beta_n + m}.$$

The Bayes risk, for prior π^n and loss $L(\theta, a, n + m)$, will thus be

$$r^m(\pi^n, n) = E^{\pi^n} E_\theta^{Y_m}[L(\theta, \delta(Y_m), n + m)]$$

$$= E^{\pi^n} E_\theta^{Y_m}[(\delta(Y_m) - \theta)^2] + (n + m)c$$

$$= \frac{\alpha_n \beta_n}{(\alpha_n + \beta_n + m)(\alpha_n + \beta_n)(\alpha_n + \beta_n + 1)} + (n + m)c,$$

the last step following from a fairly laborious calculation.

Now $\mathbf{d}_{FS}$ stops when $r_0(\pi^n, n) \leq r^m(\pi^n, n)$ for all $m \geq 1$, i.e., when

$$\frac{\alpha_n \beta_n}{(\alpha_n + \beta_n)^2(\alpha_n + \beta_n + 1)} + nc$$

$$\leq \frac{\alpha_n \beta_n}{(\alpha_n + \beta_n + m)(\alpha_n + \beta_n)(\alpha_n + \beta_n + 1)} + (n + m)c.$$

This inequality is equivalent to the inequality

$$\frac{\alpha_n \beta_n[(\alpha_n + \beta_n + m) - (\alpha_n + \beta_n)]}{(\alpha_n + \beta_n)^2(\alpha_n + \beta_n + 1)(\alpha_n + \beta_n + m)} \leq mc,$$

or

$$\frac{\alpha_n \beta_n}{(\alpha_n + \beta_n)^2(\alpha_n + \beta_n + 1)(\alpha_n + \beta_n + m)} \leq c.$$

This will hold for all $m \geq 1$ if and only if it holds for $m = 1$. The procedure $\mathbf{d}_{FS}$ thus stops for the first n for which

$$\frac{(\alpha_0 + s_n)(\beta_0 + n - s_n)}{(\alpha_0 + \beta_0 + n)^2(\alpha_0 + \beta_0 + n + 1)^2} \leq c.$$

This stopping rule, by the way, must also be that of $\mathbf{d}_L^1$, the 1-step look ahead procedure. This is because the stopping condition depends only on what happens for $m = 1$. But when only one more observation is considered, there is no difference between looking ahead in a sequential manner and looking ahead in a fixed sample size manner.

7.4.7 Inner Truncation

It can sometimes happen that the functions $r_m(\pi^n, n)$ are infinite (so that $\mathbf{d}^m$, $\mathbf{d}_L^m$, and $\mathbf{d}_{FS}$ are not well defined), but yet there do exist sequential procedures with finite Bayes risk. An example follows.

EXAMPLE 9. Let $X_1, X_2, \ldots$ be a sequential sample from the distribution which gives probability $\frac{1}{2}$ to the point zero, and is $\mathcal{N}(\theta, 1)$ with probability $\frac{1}{2}$. (This can be interpreted as a situation in which there is only a 50% chance of an observation being valid, $X_i = 0$ corresponding, for instance, to nonresponse.) Assume that the prior π is $\mathcal{C}(0, 1)$, and that $L(\theta, a, n) = (\theta - a)^2 + nc$.

Consider now the point $\mathbf{x}^n = \mathbf{0}^n = (0, \ldots, 0)$. The probability that this point will occur is clearly 2^{-n}. Also, for this point,

$$\pi^n(\theta) = \pi(\theta | \mathbf{0}^n) = \frac{\pi(\theta)2^{-n}}{\int \pi(\theta)2^{-n}d\theta} = \pi(\theta),$$

and so

$$r_0(\pi^n, n) = \inf_a E^{\pi^n}[(\theta - a)^2 + nc] = \inf_a E^\pi[(\theta - a)^2 + nc] = \infty.$$

It follows, by a simple induction argument, that $r_j(\pi^n, n) = \infty$, for all j, when $\mathbf{x}^n = \mathbf{0}^n$. The procedures $\mathbf{d}^m$, $\mathbf{d}_L^m$, and $\mathbf{d}_{FS}$ are thus not well defined when $\mathbf{x}^n = \mathbf{0}^n$. It is, furthermore, clear that any m-truncated procedure must have infinite Bayes risk, since the probability of observing $\mathbf{0}^m$ (for which the posterior Bayes risk is infinite) is positive.

There are reasonable sequential procedures with finite Bayes risk for this situation. Consider, for instance, the stopping rule τ^*, which says to stop sampling the first time a nonzero observation is obtained. (The probability of eventually observing a nonzero observation is one, so that this is a proper stopping time.) Assume that upon stopping, the decision rule $\delta_n^*(\mathbf{x}^n) = x_n$ will be used. The risk of $\mathbf{d}^* = (\tau^*, \delta^*)$ is

$$R(\theta, \mathbf{d}^*) = \sum_{n=1}^\infty \int_{\{N=n\}} [(\theta - x_n)^2 + nc]dF_n(\mathbf{x}^n | \theta)$$

$$= \sum_{n=1}^\infty 2^{-n} \int_{-\infty}^\infty [(\theta - x_n)^2 + nc](2\pi)^{-1/2} \exp\{-\tfrac{1}{2}(x_n - \theta)^2\}dx_n$$

$$= \sum_{n=1}^\infty 2^{-n}(1 + nc) = 1 + 2c.$$

Hence

$$r(\pi, \mathbf{d}^*) = E^\pi[R(\theta, \mathbf{d}^*)] = 1 + 2c < \infty.$$

The point of the above example is that procedures based on truncation cannot always be counted upon to exist, or to be good approximations to the Bayes procedure, $\mathbf{d}^\pi$. There does exist, however, a modification of the truncation technique which circumvents the indicated difficulty. This modification is called *inner truncation* and was introduced by Herman Rubin. Besides providing useful approximations to the Bayes procedure, inner truncation leads to a relatively simple proof (given in Subsection 7.4.9) of the existence of a Bayes procedure.

Definition 7. For a given sequential problem with loss $L(\theta, a, n)$, the *m-inner truncated loss* is defined to be

$$L^m(\theta, a, n) = \begin{cases} L(\theta, a, n) & \text{if } n < m, \\ \inf_a L(\theta, a, m) & \text{if } n \geq m. \end{cases} \tag{7.18}$$

The sequential problem with L replaced by L^m is called the *m-inner truncated problem*. A Bayes procedure for this new problem (assuming one exists) will be denoted $\mathbf{d}_1^m$, and will be called a *Bayes m-inner truncated procedure*. The Bayes risk of any procedure $\mathbf{d}$, in this problem, will be denoted $r_1^m(\pi, \mathbf{d})$.

The important feature of $L^m(\theta, a, n)$ is that, when $n = m$, it is assumed that the optimal action will be taken. It is enlightening to consider a loss of the form (7.1) with $\inf_a L(\theta, a) = 0$. The m-inner truncated loss is then

$$L^m(\theta, a, n) = \begin{cases} L(\theta, a) + \sum_{i=1}^{n} c_i & \text{if } n < m, \\ \sum_{i=1}^{m} c_i & \text{if } n \geq m. \end{cases} \tag{7.19}$$

In this situation, inner truncation essentially means that the decision loss will be waived if the mth observation is taken.

To find a Bayes m-inner truncated procedure, $\mathbf{d}_1^m$, note first that $L^m(\theta, a, n)$ is a constant (depending possibly upon θ) for $n \geq m$. Hence there can be no gain in taking more than m observations, and the investigation can be restricted to consideration of m-truncated procedures. The results of Subsection 7.4.5 are then immediately applicable; Theorems 1 and 2 giving the Bayes m-inner truncated procedure.

In interpreting Theorems 1 and 2 for this situation, it is helpful to indicate the dependence of the functions $r_j(\pi^n, n)$ on the inner truncation point m. (For the m-inner truncated problem, the $r_0(\pi^n, n)$ and hence the $r_j(\pi^n, n)$ must, of course, be calculated with respect to $L^m(\theta, a, n)$.) Thus let $r_j^m(\pi^n, n)$ denote the relevant quantities for the loss $L^m(\theta, a, n)$. The symbols $r_j(\pi^n, n)$ will be reserved for the Bayes risks for the original loss, $L(\theta, a, n)$. Note that

$$r_j^m(\pi^n, n) = r_j(\pi^n, n) \quad \text{if } n + j < m. \tag{7.20}$$

This is because the mth stage cannot be reached if $n + j < m$ (the $r_j^m(\pi^n, n)$ and $r_j(\pi^n, n)$ are the Bayes risks of optimally proceeding at most j steps beyond n), and $L^m(\theta, a, i) = L(\theta, a, i)$ for $i < m$.

Of particular interest is the quantity $r_m^m(\pi, 0)$, which, being the optimal Bayes risk among all procedures truncated at m for the loss $L^m(\theta, a, n)$, must be the Bayes risk of the m-inner truncated problem. (When $\mathbf{d}_1^m$ exists, it follows that $r_1^m(\pi, \mathbf{d}_1^m) = r_m^m(\pi, 0)$.) Note that, since

$$L^m(\theta, a, n) \leq L(\theta, a, n) \tag{7.21}$$

(recall that $L(\theta, a, j)$ is nondecreasing in j), it must be true that

$$r_m^m(\pi, 0) \leq r(\pi), \tag{7.22}$$

where $r(\pi)$, as usual, stands for the Bayes risk for the loss $L(\theta, a, n)$. The constants $r_m^m(\pi, 0)$ thus provide lower bounds for $r(\pi)$, complementing the upper bounds given in (7.13) of Subsection 7.4.5. From (7.22), it is also apparent that the difficulties encountered in Example 9 for regular truncation cannot occur for inner truncation. If there is a sequential procedure with finite Bayes risk, one can always find a truncated procedure with finite inner truncated Bayes risk.

As in Subsection 7.4.6, it is possible to define a look ahead procedure for inner truncation. The definition is complicated, however, by the fact that the loss must be changed as one looks ahead. The idea is that in looking ahead (say) m steps, one should imagine that the decision loss will be waived if m more observations are actually taken. Formally, the procedure is defined as follows.

Definition 8. Let τ_{IL}^m be the stopping rule (assuming it is proper) which stops for the first n $(n = 0, 1, 2, \ldots)$ for which

$$r_0(\pi^n, n) = r_m^{m+n}(\pi^n, n),$$

and let $\mathbf{d}_{IL}^m = (\tau_{IL}^m, \delta^\pi)$. This will be called the *m-step inner look ahead procedure*.

When $L(\theta, a, n)$ is of the form (7.1) with $\inf_a L(\theta, a) = 0$, the 1-step inner look ahead procedure, $\mathbf{d}_{IL}^1$, is particularly interesting. Using (7.19), an easy calculation shows that

$$r_1^{n+1}(\pi^n, n) = \min\left\{ r_0(\pi^n, n), \sum_{i=1}^{n+1} c_i \right\}.$$

Hence the 1-step inner look ahead procedure stops for the first n for which

$$r_0(\pi^n, n) \leq \sum_{i=1}^{n+1} c_i,$$

or, since $r_0(\pi^n, n) = \rho_0(\pi^n) + \sum_{i=1}^{n} c_i$, for the first n for which

$$\rho_0(\pi^n) \leq c_{n+1}.$$

In other words, $\mathbf{d}_{IL}^1$ stops sampling when the posterior Bayes decision risk is smaller than the cost of another observation. It is, of course, obvious that one would then want to stop.

7.4.8 Approximating the Bayes Procedure and the Bayes Risk

In this subsection, the accuracy of the various truncated and look ahead procedures (and their Bayes risks) as approximations to $\mathbf{d}^\pi$ (and $r(\pi)$) will be discussed. Considering first the Bayes risks, the following relationships were pointed out in previous subsections:

$$r_1^m(\pi, \mathbf{d}_1^m) \leq r(\pi) \leq r(\pi, \mathbf{d}_L^m) \leq r(\pi, \mathbf{d}^m). \tag{7.23}$$

Recall that $\mathbf{d}^m$ is the Bayes m-truncated procedure, $\mathbf{d}_L^m$ is the m-step look ahead procedure, and $\mathbf{d}_I^m$ is the Bayes m-inner truncated procedure. The bounds $r_I^m(\pi, \mathbf{d}_I^m)$ $(= r_m^\pi(\pi, 0))$ and $r(\pi, \mathbf{d}^m)$ $(= r_m(\pi, 0))$ are explicitly calculable using Theorem 2 in Subsection 7.4.5. Unfortunately, the bound $r(\pi, \mathbf{d}_L^m)$ is often too difficult to calculate.

It has been shown that the $r(\pi, \mathbf{d}^m)$ are nonincreasing in m, and it can similarly be shown that the $r_I^m(\pi, \mathbf{d}_I^m)$ are nondecreasing in m. It will, in fact, be shown in the next subsection that these quantities converge to $r(\pi)$ as $m \to \infty$. We can thus (theoretically) calculate arbitrarily close approximations to $r(\pi)$, and find procedures arbitrarily close to optimal, in terms of Bayes risk.

Another method of investigating the accuracy of the various procedures, as approximations to $\mathbf{d}^\pi$, is to consider the stopping times. Letting N^m, N_L^m, N^π, N_{IL}^m and N_{FS} denote the stopping times of $\mathbf{d}^m$, $\mathbf{d}_L^m$, $\mathbf{d}^\pi$, $\mathbf{d}_{IL}^m$, and $\mathbf{d}_{FS}$, respectively, it can be shown that

$$N^m \leq N_L^m \leq N^\pi \leq N_{IL}^m \quad \text{and} \quad N_{FS} \leq N^\pi. \tag{7.24}$$

(The proof will be left as an exercise.) These inequalities are useful in that if, in a given situation, (say) N_L^m and N_{IL}^m are close, then either stopping time (or one in between) should be nearly optimal.

To aid in understanding the behavior of all these Bayes risks and stopping times, we turn to some examples. Unfortunately, the behavior is quite dependent on the type of problem being dealt with. In particular, it is important to distinguish between testing and estimation problems.

I. *Testing*

The following example gives some indication of the behavior of the procedures in testing problems.

EXAMPLE 10. Assume that $X_1, X_2, \ldots$ is a sequential sample from a $\mathscr{B}(1, \theta)$ distribution, and that it is desired to test $H_0 : \theta = 0.4$ versus $H_1 : \theta = 0.6$. The loss is of the form (7.1) with "0–K" decision loss (zero for a correct decision and K for an incorrect decision) and $c_i = 1$. The prior distribution is $\pi(0.4) = \pi(0.6) = \frac{1}{2}$.

It can be shown, for this problem, that the procedures $\mathbf{d}^\pi$, $\mathbf{d}_{IL}^m$, $\mathbf{d}_L^m$, and $\mathbf{d}_{FS}$ all have stopping rules of the form

$$\text{stop for the first } n \text{ for which } |2s_n - n| = k, \tag{7.25}$$

where $s_n = \sum_{i=1}^n x_i$ and k is some integer.

Case 1. $K = 10^6$. This is a situation in which observations are cheap (compared to the decision loss). The true Bayes procedure, $\mathbf{d}^\pi$, has a stopping rule of the form (7.25) with $k = 28$. The Bayes risk is approximately 151.73, and the expected number of observations for $\mathbf{d}^\pi$ is approximately 140. The

Table 7.1 Look Ahead Procedures and Bayes Risks ($K = 10^6$)

m	$\mathbf{d}_L^m$	$\mathbf{d}_{IL}^m$	$r(\pi, \mathbf{d}_L^m)$	$r(\pi, \mathbf{d}_{IL}^m)$	$r(\pi, \mathbf{d}^m)$	$r_I^m(\pi, \mathbf{d}_I^m)$
1	1	35	400,001	175.7	400,001	1
2	2	33	307,696	166.6	400,001	2
3	3	32	228,580	162.3	352,002	3
4	4	31	164,962	158.48	352,002	4
5	5	31	116,383	158.48	317,444	5
6	6	31	80,731	158.48	317,444	6
7	7	30	55,322	155.21	289,798	7
8	8	30	37,590	155.21	289,798	8
9	9	30	25,396	155.21	266,575	9
10	10	30	17,094	155.21	266,575	10
15	13	29	5176.3	152.82	213,116	15
20	16	29	1599.9	152.82	186,108	20
25	17	29	1098.8	152.82	153,789	25
30	18	28	766.1	151.73	136,237	30
40	20	28	400.6	151.73	102,091	40
60	23	28	204.1	151.73	59,601	59.97
80	24	28	179.39	151.73	35,874	79.49
100	26	28	156.39	151.73	22,007	97.33
150	27	28	152.60	151.73	6851.4	128.67
200	28	28	151.73	151.73	2282.9	143.10
300	28	28	151.73	151.73	378.74	150.68
400	28	28	151.73	151.73	176.61	151.61
500	28	28	151.73	151.73	154.48	151.72
600	28	28	151.73	151.73	152.04	151.73
700	28	28	151.73	151.73	151.76	151.73

values of k in (7.25) for the look ahead procedures $\mathbf{d}_L^m$ and $\mathbf{d}_{IL}^m$ depend on m, and are given in the second and third columns of Table 7.1. Finally, the Bayes risks of $\mathbf{d}_L^m$, $\mathbf{d}_{IL}^m$, $\mathbf{d}^m$, and $\mathbf{d}_I^m$ (the last for the m-inner truncated loss $L^m(\theta, a, n)$) are given in the remaining columns of Table 7.1.

As expected, all Bayes risks converge to $r(\pi) = 151.73$, and the relationships in (7.23) and (7.24) are satisfied. Note that the truncated procedures $\mathbf{d}^m$ and $\mathbf{d}_I^m$ have Bayes risks which converge very slowly to $r(\pi)$. The truncation point, m, must be several hundred before the approximation is reasonably accurate. (This is to be expected, since the expected stopping time of $\mathbf{d}^\pi$ is about 140, and, unless the truncation point is considerably larger than this, there is not much hope of doing well.) The look ahead procedures do not suffer from this difficulty, and perform well for much smaller m. Indeed the look ahead procedures are exactly the Bayes procedure (i.e., $k = 28$) when $m = 200$ (for $\mathbf{d}_L^m$) and when $m = 30$ (for $\mathbf{d}_{IL}^m$). The m-step inner look ahead procedure, $\mathbf{d}_{IL}^m$, is particularly attractive, having a Bayes risk close to optimal even for very small m.

Table 7.2 Look Ahead Procedures and Bayes Risks
($K = 100$)

m	$\mathbf{d}_L^m$	$\mathbf{d}_{IL}^m$	$r(\pi, \mathbf{d}_L^m)$	$r(\pi, \mathbf{d}_{IL}^m)$	$r(\pi, \mathbf{d}^m)$	$r_I^m(\pi, \mathbf{d}_I^m)$
1	1	12	41.00	59.85	41.00	1.00
2	2	10	34.62	50.00	41.00	2.00
3	3	9	31.00	45.25	37.68	3.00
4	3	9	31.00	45.25	37.68	4.00
5	3	8	31.00	40.75	35.81	5.00
6	3	8	31.00	40.75	35.81	6.00
7	3	7	31.00	36.66	34.46	7.00
8	3	7	31.00	36.66	34.46	8.00
9	3	7	31.00	36.66	33.49	9.00
10	4	7	29.90	36.66	33.49	10.00
15	4	6	29.90	33.23	31.84	14.89
20	4	5	29.90	30.82	31.20	19.16
28	4	5	29.90	30.82	30.48	24.09
36	4	4	29.90	29.90	30.16	26.99
50	4	4	29.90	29.90	29.96	29.17
70	4	4	29.90	29.90	29.91	29.80
100	4	4	29.90	29.90	29.90	29.89

The fixed sample size look ahead procedure, $\mathbf{d}_{FS}$, has a stopping rule of the form (7.25) with $k = 21$, and has Bayes risk 305.4. This is moderately accurate as an approximation to $\mathbf{d}^\pi$.

Case 2. $K = 100$. This is a situation in which observations are fairly expensive. The true Bayes rule is now of the form (7.25) with $k = 4$. The Bayes risk is $r(\pi) = 29.90$, and the expected number of observations is 13.4. Table 7.2 gives the values of k and Bayes risks for the various procedures, in this situation.

Since the expected number of observations needed in this situation is small, it is not surprising that the truncated procedures do well for much smaller m than were needed in Case 1. Also in contrast to Case 1, $\mathbf{d}_L^m$ performs better than $\mathbf{d}_{IL}^m$ for small m. Indeed for m as small as three, $\mathbf{d}_L^m$ has Bayes risk very close to optimal.

The stopping rule for $\mathbf{d}_{FS}$, in this case, is of the form (7.25) with $k = 2$. The corresponding Bayes risk of 34.62 is quite good.

The above example suggests that for expensive observations (relative to the decision loss) or equivalently for situations in which only a small number of observations are likely to be needed, the m-step look ahead procedure is likely to do well for moderate or small m. When, on the other hand, observations are cheap (or a large sample size will be needed), the m-step inner look ahead procedure seems to be best. (The reason for the success of $\mathbf{d}_{IL}^m$, in such a situation, will be explained in Subsection 7.4.10.) In both cases, the performance of $\mathbf{d}_{FS}$ seems fair.

In case 1 of Example 10, the relative failure of $\mathbf{d}_L^m$ compared to $\mathbf{d}_{IL}^m$ may be somewhat surprising. The reason for this failure is indicated in the following example.

EXAMPLE 11. In the general sequential setup, assume that it is desired to test $H_0: \theta \in \Theta_0$ versus $H_1: \theta \in \Theta_1$. Let a_i denote accepting H_i $(i = 0, 1)$.

Suppose now that $\mathbf{x}^n$ has been observed, and that (say) $\delta_n(\mathbf{x}^n) = a_0$ is the Bayes action. This means that

$$E^{\pi^n}[L(\theta, a_0, n)] < E^{\pi^n}[L(\theta, a_1, n)],$$

and that the posterior Bayes risk is

$$r_0(\pi^n, n) = E^{\pi^n}[L(\theta, a_0, n)].$$

Now imagine that up to m more observations can be taken, but that, for all $j \le m$ and all $x_{n+1}, \ldots, x_{n+j}$,

$$E^{\pi^{n+j}}[L(\theta, a_0, n + j)] < E^{\pi^{n+j}}[L(\theta, a_1, n + j)]. \tag{7.26}$$

This means that no matter what the observations turn out to be, a_0 will still be the Bayes action upon stopping. In other words, m additional observations cannot possibly counter the evidence already existing for H_0. In Example 10, for instance, the Bayes action (upon stopping) is a_0 if $2s_n - n \le 0$, and is a_1 otherwise. If, at a certain stage, $2s_n - n = -20$, then clearly even 20 more observations cannot cause a change in action.

It is intuitively clear that, since $L(\theta, a, n)$ is increasing in n, the taking of more observations is wasteful if these observations cannot cause a change in action. This can be easily established rigorously, and the conclusion is that the m step look ahead procedure, $\mathbf{d}_L^m$, will stop at stage n when (7.26) holds.

The intuition to be gained here is that in order to expect to lower the posterior Bayes risk it is necessary to allow the possibility of taking enough observations so that our mind could be changed concerning the action to be taken. In testing, as fairly conclusive evidence for one hypothesis accumulates, $\mathbf{d}_L^m$ must, therefore, look quite far ahead before it will recognize that another observation might be desirable. This difficulty will be most pronounced when observations are cheap, in that a large number of observations will then probably be taken, and very conclusive evidence for one hypothesis will tend to accumulate.

II. Estimation

Estimation problems tend to be easier to deal with than testing problems. Indeed, for most estimation problems, the m-step look ahead procedure, $\mathbf{d}_L^m$, will perform very well for quite small m. To see why, imagine that we knew the infinite sequence $\mathbf{x} = (x_1, x_2, \ldots)$ that would occur, and were allowed to stop at any time n, with the proviso that, upon stopping, the Bayes rule $\delta_n^\pi(\mathbf{x}^n)$ must be used. Writing the posterior Bayes risk at time n as

$$V(\mathbf{x}, n) = r_0(\pi^n, n),$$

it is clear that the optimal n would be that which minimized $V(\mathbf{x}, n)$. Now it happens that, in estimation problems, $V(\mathbf{x}, n)$ is usually a fairly smooth function of n, behaving as in Figure 7.1. In Example 7, for instance,

$$V(\mathbf{x}, n) = r_0(\pi^n, n) = \frac{(s_n + 1)(n - s_n + 1)}{(n + 2)^2(n + 3)} + nc.$$

Graphing this for various $\mathbf{x}$ will convince you that $V(\mathbf{x}, n)$ often behaves as in Figure 7.1. The minimum value of $V(\mathbf{x}, n)$ will thus tend to occur when the graph begins to swing upwards, or, equivalently, for the first n for which $V(\mathbf{x}, n) < V(\mathbf{x}, n + 1)$. Of course, in reality, $V(\mathbf{x}, n + 1)$ is not known at stage n, but an m-step look ahead procedure will usually detect when $V(\mathbf{x}, n)$ is likely to swing up, even when m is small. Indeed the 1-step look ahead procedure will often succeed very well.

The m-step inner look ahead procedure is generally not very good in estimation problems, because the posterior Bayes risk, based on the inner truncated loss $L^m(\theta, a, n)$, can be a poor approximation to the true posterior Bayes risk, and can hence result in poor estimates of upcoming values of $V(\mathbf{x}, n)$. Indeed, by pretending that the optimal action will be taken m steps ahead, $\mathbf{d}_{IL}^m$ will tend to considerably overshoot the true turning point of $V(\mathbf{x}, n)$.

The fixed sample size look ahead procedure, $\mathbf{d}_{FS}$, will usually be roughly equivalent to $\mathbf{d}_L^m$ for m equal to one or two. It will hence perform reasonably well, but is advantageous only if it is easier to calculate than is $\mathbf{d}_L^m$.

Testing problems do not behave as nicely as estimation problems because $V(\mathbf{x}, n)$ for a testing problem will tend to have many ups and downs. The long term trend of $V(\mathbf{x}, n)$ will be as in Figure 7.1, but local oscillations can be quite large. A fairly large m is thus needed if $\mathbf{d}_L^m$ is to "look past" these local oscillations. This does suggest, however, that the reason $\mathbf{d}_{FS}$ performs fairly well in testing problems is that it can look quite far ahead, past the local oscillations.

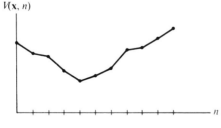

Figure 7.1

7.4.9 Theoretical Results

As mentioned in the previous subsection, $r_m(\pi, 0) = r(\pi, \mathbf{d}^m)$ and $r_1^m(\pi, 0) = r_1^m(\pi, \mathbf{d}_1^m)$ will usually converge to $r(\pi)$ as $m \to \infty$. Several theorems establishing this are given below. As a side benefit, one of the theorems gives conditions under which a Bayes procedure is guaranteed to exist.

For simplicity, it will be assumed throughout the subsection that Bayes decision rules, δ_n^π, exist for all n. The first two theorems will deal only with losses of the form (7.1). (Generalizations to arbitrary loss are given in the Exercises.) In these two theorems, the usual notation,

$$r(\pi, \delta_n^\pi) = E^\pi E_\theta [L(\theta, \delta_n^\pi(X^n))] = E^{m_n} E^{\pi^n} [L(\theta, \delta_n^\pi(X^n))],$$

will be used to denote the Bayes decision risk of δ_n^π. Hopefully, the simultaneous use of $r(\pi, \delta_n^\pi)$ and $r(\pi, \mathbf{d})$ will cause no confusion.

Theorem 5. *Assume that $L(\theta, a, n)$ is of the form (7.1) with $\inf_a L(\theta, a) = 0$, and that $\lim_{n \to \infty} r(\pi, \delta_n^\pi) = 0$. Then*

$$\lim_{m \to \infty} r_m(\pi, 0) = r(\pi)$$

(i.e., the Bayes risks of $\mathbf{d}^m$ converge to the true Bayes risk).

PROOF. Let τ^ε be a stopping rule for which the risk of $\mathbf{d}^\varepsilon = (\tau^\varepsilon, \delta^\pi)$ satisfies $r(\pi, \mathbf{d}^\varepsilon) < r(\pi) + \varepsilon$. (Such an "$\varepsilon$-Bayes" procedure must exist, even though a true Bayes procedure need not.) Define $\tau^{\varepsilon, m} = (\tau_0^{\varepsilon, m}, \tau_1^{\varepsilon, m}, \ldots)$ by

$$\tau_n^{\varepsilon, m} = \begin{cases} \tau_n^\varepsilon & \text{if } n < m, \\ 1 & \text{if } n = m. \end{cases}$$

The procedure $\mathbf{d}^{\varepsilon, m} = (\tau^{\varepsilon, m}, \delta^\pi)$ is thus the procedure $\mathbf{d}^\varepsilon$ truncated at m. Let N denote the stopping time of $\mathbf{d}^\varepsilon$, and define

$$\{N \geq m\} = \{\mathbf{x}^m \in \mathscr{X}^m : \tau_j^\varepsilon(\mathbf{x}^j) = 0 \text{ for all } j < m\}.$$

Clearly

$$r(\pi, \mathbf{d}^\varepsilon) - r(\pi, \mathbf{d}^{\varepsilon, m}) = \sum_{n=m}^\infty \int_{\{N=n\}} r_0(\pi^n, n) dF^{m_n}(\mathbf{x}^n) - \int_{\{N \geq m\}} r_0(\pi^m, m) dF^{m_m}(\mathbf{x}^m)$$

$$= \sum_{n=m}^\infty \int_{\{N=n\}} \left[E^{\pi^n}[L(\theta, \delta_n^\pi(\mathbf{x}^n))] + \sum_{i=1}^n c_i \right] dF^{m_n}(\mathbf{x}^n)$$

$$- \int_{\{N \geq m\}} \left[E^{\pi^m}[L(\theta, \delta_m^\pi(\mathbf{x}^m))] + \sum_{i=1}^m c_i \right] dF^{m_m}(\mathbf{x}^m)$$

$$\geq - \int_{\{N \geq m\}} E^{\pi^m}[L(\theta, \delta_m^\pi(\mathbf{x}^m))] dF^{m_m}(\mathbf{x}^m)$$

$$\text{(since the } c_i \text{ are positive)}$$

$$\geq - E^{m_m} E^{\pi^m}[L(\theta, \delta_m^\pi(X^m))] = -r(\pi, \delta_m^\pi).$$

By assumption, $r(\pi, \delta_m^\pi) < \varepsilon$ for large enough m, so that, for large enough m,

$$r(\pi, \mathbf{d}^{\varepsilon, m}) < r(\pi, \mathbf{d}^\varepsilon) + \varepsilon < r(\pi) + 2\varepsilon.$$

Since $r_m(\pi, 0) \leq r(\pi, \mathbf{d}^{\varepsilon, m})$ ($r_m(\pi, 0)$ is the minimum Bayes risk over *all* m-truncated procedures), it follows that, for large enough m,

$$r_m(\pi, 0) < r(\pi) + 2\varepsilon.$$

But $r(\pi) \leq r_m(\pi, 0)$, so it can be concluded that, for large enough m,

$$|r_m(\pi, 0) - r(\pi)| < 2\varepsilon.$$

Since ε was arbitrary, the conclusion follows. $\qquad\square$

Theorem 5 is actually true under conditions considerably weaker than $\lim_{n \to \infty} r(\pi, \delta_n^\pi) = 0$. This condition suffices for typical applications, however. Note that Theorem 5 and (7.23) (recall $r(\pi, \mathbf{d}^m) = r_m(\pi, 0)$) immediately imply that $\lim_{m \to \infty} r(\pi, \mathbf{d}_L^m) = r(\pi)$.

The following theorem establishes that the m-inner truncated Bayes risks, $r_m^m(\pi, 0)$ ($= r_1^m(\pi, \mathbf{d}_1^m)$), converge to $r(\pi)$ as $m \to \infty$, and also that the true Bayes risk of $\mathbf{d}_1^m$ converges to $r(\pi)$.

Theorem 6. *Assume that* $L(\theta, a, n)$ *is of the form* (7.1) *with* $\inf_a L(\theta, a) = 0$, *and that* $\lim_{n \to \infty} r(\pi, \delta_n^\pi) = 0$. *Then*

$$\lim_{m \to \infty} r_m^m(\pi, 0) = r(\pi) = \lim_{m \to \infty} r(\pi, \mathbf{d}_1^m).$$

PROOF. Let N denote the stopping time of $\mathbf{d}_1^m$. For any $\varepsilon > 0$,

$$r_m^m(\pi, 0) = r_1^m(\pi, \mathbf{d}_1^m)$$

$$= r(\pi, \mathbf{d}_1^m) - \int_{\{N = m\}} E^{\pi^m}[L(\theta, \delta_m^\pi(\mathbf{x}^m))] dF^{m m}(\mathbf{x}^m)$$

$$\geq r(\pi, \mathbf{d}_1^m) - r(\pi, \delta_m^\pi)$$

$$> r(\pi, \mathbf{d}_1^m) - \varepsilon$$

for large enough m (since $r(\pi, \delta_m^\pi) \to 0$). Hence

$$r(\pi) \leq r(\pi, \mathbf{d}_1^m) < r_m^m(\pi, 0) + \varepsilon$$

for large enough m. Combining this with (7.22) (in Subsection 7.4.7), it follows that, for large enough m,

$$|r(\pi) - r_m^m(\pi, 0)| < \varepsilon \quad \text{and} \quad |r(m, \mathbf{d}_1^m) - r(\pi)| < \varepsilon.$$

Since ε was arbitrary, the conclusion follows. $\qquad\square$

Versions of Theorems 5 and 6 appeared in Hoeffding (1960).

In a situation such as that of Example 9, $r(\pi, \delta_n^\pi)$ and $E^{m^n}[r_0(\pi^n, n)]$ are infinite for all n. Hence Theorems 5 and 6 do not apply. It can still be true, however, that $r_m^m(\pi, 0) \to r(\pi)$ as $m \to \infty$. The following theorem establishes this, and also proves the existence of a Bayes procedure, under certain conditions. This theorem is a special case of that in Magwire (1953).

Theorem 7. *Assume that*

(a) *there is a sequential procedure, $\mathbf{d}$, with finite Bayes risk, and*
(b) *with probability one (under π), $\inf_a L(\theta, a, m) \to \infty$ as $m \to \infty$ (i.e., the sampling cost goes to infinity as $m \to \infty$).*

Then

$$\lim_{m \to \infty} r_m^m(\pi, 0) = r(\pi).$$

Also, a Bayes sequential procedure, $\mathbf{d}^\pi$, exists, and $\mathbf{d}^\pi$ stops sampling for the first $n(n = 0, 1, \ldots)$ for which $r_0(\pi^n, n)$ is finite and

$$r_0(\pi^n, n) = r^\infty(\pi^n, n),$$

where r^∞ satisfies the equation

$$r^\infty(\pi^n, n) = \min\{r_0(\pi^n, n), E^*[r^\infty(\pi^n(\theta \mid X_{n+1}), n + 1)]\}.$$

PROOF. Consider again the m-inner truncated loss

$$L^m(\theta, a, n) = \begin{cases} L(\theta, a, n) & \text{if } n < m, \\ \inf_a L(\theta, a, m) & \text{if } n \geq m. \end{cases}$$

Observe that

$$L^m(\theta, a, n) \text{ is nondecreasing in } m, \text{ and } \lim_{m \to \infty} L^m(\theta, a, n) = L(\theta, a, n). \quad (7.27)$$

Consider the sequential problem with prior π^n, loss $L^m(\theta, a, j)$, and possible observations $X_{n+1}, X_{n+2}, \ldots$. Let $r^m(\pi^n, \mathbf{d}, n)$ denote the Bayes risk of a procedure $\mathbf{d}$ in this problem, and let $r^m(\pi^n, n)$ denote the Bayes risk for the problem. Observe that, if $n < m$, then

$$r^m(\pi^n, n) = \min\{r_0(\pi^n, n), E^*[r^m(\pi^n(\theta \mid X_{n+1}), n + 1)]\}. \quad (7.28)$$

This follows from applying Theorem 2 of Subsection 7.4.5 to the loss L^m, noting that $r^m(\pi^n, n) = r_{m-n}(\pi^n, n)$ in the notation of Theorem 2. (Recall from Subsection 7.4.7 that for the loss L^m one can restrict attention to m-truncated procedures.)

Since $L^m(\theta, a, n)$ and hence $r^m(\pi^n, n)$ are nondecreasing in m, it follows that

$$r^\infty(\pi^n, n) = \lim_{m \to \infty} r^m(\pi^n, n)$$

exists (though it could be infinite). The monotone convergence theorem hence implies that

$$\lim_{m \to \infty} E^*[r^m(\pi^n(\theta \mid X_{n+1}), n + 1)] = E^*[r^\infty(\pi^n(\theta \mid X_{n+1}), n + 1)].$$

Together with (7.28), these equalities imply that

$$r^\infty(\pi^n, n) = \min\{r_0(\pi^n, n), E^*[r^\infty(\pi^n(\theta \mid X_{n+1}), n + 1)]\}. \qquad (7.29)$$

Note also, from (7.27), that $r^m(\pi, 0) \leq r(\pi)$ for all m, so that

$$r^\infty(\pi, 0) = \lim_{m \to \infty} r^m(\pi, 0) \leq r(\pi). \qquad (7.30)$$

Consider now (for the original sequential problem) the stopping rule, to be denoted τ^*, which stops sampling for the first n for which $r_0(\pi^n, n) < \infty$ and $r_0(\pi^n, n) = r^\infty(\pi^n, n)$. The pseudoprocedure $\mathbf{d}^* = (\tau^*, \delta^\pi)$ will be shown to be a Bayes procedure for the original problem. (At this point we merely call $\mathbf{d}^*$ a pseudoprocedure because it has not yet been shown to stop sampling with probability one.)

As a first step, note that, since

$$L^m(\theta, a, n) = \inf_a L(\theta, a, m)$$

for $n \geq m$, it is immaterial what happens for $n \geq m$. Thus, even for a pseudo-procedure $\mathbf{d}$, $r^m(\pi^n, \mathbf{d}, n)$ is well defined, providing we conventionally assign a loss of $\inf_a L(\theta, a, m)$ to not stopping.

Now define $\mathbf{d}^n = (\tau^n, \delta^n)$, where $\tau^n = (\tau_n^*, \tau_{n+1}^*, \ldots)$ and $\delta^n = (\delta_n^\pi, \delta_{n+1}^\pi, \ldots)$. Clearly $\mathbf{d}^n$ is the procedure $\mathbf{d}^*$ restricted to the sequential problem continuing from stage n. The crucial step of the proof is to show that, for $n \leq m$,

$$r^m(\pi^n, \mathbf{d}^n, n) \leq r^\infty(\pi^n, n). \qquad (7.31)$$

This will be established by induction on $m - n$. Assume that $n \leq m$ in all of the following.

First, if $m - n = 0$, then

$$L^m(\theta, a, n) = \inf_a L(\theta, a, m).$$

Hence

$$r^m(\pi^n, \mathbf{d}^n, n) = E^{\pi^m}\left[\inf_a L(\theta, a, m)\right] = r^m(\pi^m, m) \leq r^\infty(\pi^m, m).$$

This establishes (7.31) for $m - n = 0$.

Assume now that (7.31) holds for $m - n = j$. We must show that it then hold for $m - n = j + 1$. Thus let $m - n = j + 1$, which in particular implies that $n < m$. Note first, from the definition of τ^*, that if

$$r_0(\pi^n, n) = r^\infty(\pi^n, n) < \infty, \qquad (7.32)$$

then $\mathbf{d}^n$ will make an immediate decision, incurring the posterior Bayes risk $r_0(\pi^n, n)$. Hence (7.31) is satisfied when (7.32) is true. If, instead, $r_0(\pi^n, n)$ is infinite or $r_0(\pi^n, n) > r^\infty(\pi^n, n)$, then the definition of τ^* ensures that another observation will be taken. In this case, therefore, familiar arguments show that

$$r^m(\pi^n, \mathbf{d}^n, n) = E^*[r^m(\pi^n(\theta \mid X_{n+1}), \mathbf{d}^{n+1}, n+1)]. \tag{7.33}$$

But

$$r^m(\pi^n(\theta \mid X_{n+1}), \mathbf{d}^{n+1}, n+1) = r^m(\pi^{n+1}, \mathbf{d}^{n+1}, n+1),$$

and $m - (n+1) = j$. Hence, by the induction hypothesis,

$$r^m(\pi^n(\theta \mid X_{n+1}), \mathbf{d}^{n+1}, n+1) \leq r^\infty(\pi^n(\theta \mid X_{n+1}), n+1).$$

Combining this with (7.33) shows that

$$r^m(\pi^n, \mathbf{d}^n, n) \leq E^*[r^\infty(\pi^n(\theta \mid X_{n+1}), n+1)]. \tag{7.34}$$

Since we are considering the case in which $r_0(\pi^n, n)$ is infinite or $r_0(\pi^n, n) > r^\infty(\pi^n, n)$, (7.34) and (7.29) imply (7.31). Thus (7.31) is established.

Taking the limit in (7.31) for $n = 0$ and using (7.30) shows that

$$\lim_{m \to \infty} r^m(\pi, \mathbf{d}^*, 0) \leq r^\infty(\pi, 0) \leq r(\pi). \tag{7.35}$$

Since $r(\pi) < \infty$ (by Condition (a) of the theorem), we can conclude that

$$\lim_{m \to \infty} r^m(\pi, \mathbf{d}^*, 0) < \infty. \tag{7.36}$$

Now, since $\inf_a L(\theta, a, m)$ was defined to be the loss if $\mathbf{d}^*$ does not stop sampling, it is clear that

$$r^m(\pi, \mathbf{d}^*, 0) \geq E^\pi\left[\left\{\inf_a L(\theta, a, m)\right\}\lambda(\theta)\right],$$

where $\lambda(\theta)$ is the probability (given θ) that $\mathbf{d}^*$ does not stop sampling. Hence (7.36) implies that

$$\lim_{m \to \infty} E^\pi\left[\left\{\inf_a L(\theta, a, m)\right\}\lambda(\theta)\right] < \infty.$$

A standard analysis argument shows that this is consistent with Condition (b) of the theorem only if $\lambda(\theta) = 0$ with probability one (with respect to π). Hence $\mathbf{d}^*$ is indeed a proper procedure.

Finally, (7.27) and another application of the monotone convergence theorem show that

$$\lim_{m \to \infty} r^m(\pi, \mathbf{d}^*, 0) = r(\pi, \mathbf{d}^*).$$

Together with (7.35), this implies that

$$r(\pi, \mathbf{d}^*) = r(\pi),$$

and hence that $\mathbf{d}^*$ is a Bayes procedure. It also follows from (7.35) that $r^\infty(\pi, 0) = r(\pi)$, so that

$$r_m^\infty(\pi, 0) = r^m(\pi, 0) \to r(\pi)$$

as $m \to \infty$. The remaining conclusions of the theorem are merely restatements of the definition of τ^* and (7.29). $\qquad\square$

The equation

$$r^\infty(\pi^n, n) = \min\{r_0(\pi^n, n), E^*[r^\infty(\pi^n(\theta | X_{n+1}), n + 1)]\} \qquad (7.37)$$

has a simple intuitive explanation. The quantity $r^\infty(\pi^n, n)$ can be seen to be the Bayes risk for the sequential problem continuing from stage n, so that

$$r^*(\pi^n, n) = E^*[r^\infty(\pi^n(\theta | X_{n+1}), n + 1)]$$

is the smallest Bayes risk among procedures which take at least one observation. Hence (7.37) merely states that the Bayes risk of the problem is the smaller of the posterior Bayes risk of an immediate decision and the minimum Bayes risk among procedures which take at least one observation. This, of course, seems intuitively obvious.

The following special case of Theorem 7 is of interest.

Corollary 7.1. *Suppose that*

(a) $X_1, X_2, \ldots$ *is a sequential sample,*
(b) $L(\theta, a, n) = L(\theta, a) + nc$, *where $c > 0$, and*
(c) *there is a sequential procedure, $\mathbf{d}$, with finite Bayes risk.*

Then a Bayes procedure, $\mathbf{d}^\pi$, exists, and $\mathbf{d}^\pi$ stops sampling for the first n for which $\rho_0(\pi^n)$ is finite and

$$\rho_0(\pi^n) = \rho^\infty(\pi^n),$$

where $\rho^\infty(\pi^n)$ satisfies the equation

$$\rho^\infty(\pi^n) = \min\{\rho_0(\pi^n), E^*[\rho^\infty(\pi^n(\theta | X))] + c\}.$$

PROOF. Recalling that $\rho_0(\pi^n) = \inf_a E^{\pi^n}[L(\theta, a)]$, it can easily be checked that

$$r_0(\pi^n, n) = \rho_0(\pi^n) + nc,$$

and that $r^\infty(\pi^n, n)$ can be written as

$$r^\infty(\pi^n, n) = \rho^\infty(\pi^n) + nc.$$

The result is immediate from Theorem 7, since (as always) we are assuming that $L(\theta, a) \geq K > -\infty$. $\qquad\square$

A sequential Bayes procedure need not always exist, as the following example shows.

EXAMPLE 12. Assume that $X_1, X_2, \ldots$ is a sequential sample from a $\mathcal{N}(\theta, 1)$ density, and that it is desired to estimate θ under loss

$$L(\theta, a, n) = (\theta - a)^2 + \sum_{i=1}^{n} c_i,$$

where $c_i = [2i(i + 1)]^{-1}$. It can easily be shown that

$$\sum_{i=1}^{n} c_i = \sum_{i=1}^{n} \frac{1}{2i(i + 1)} = \frac{1}{2}\left(1 - \frac{1}{n + 1}\right).$$

Hence

$$L(\theta, a, n) = (\theta - a)^2 + \frac{1}{2}\left(1 - \frac{1}{n + 1}\right).$$

If now the prior is $\mathcal{N}(0, 1)$, so that π^n is $\mathcal{N}(\mu_n, (n + 1)^{-1})$, then the posterior Bayes decision risk is

$$\rho_0(\pi^n) = E^{\pi^n}[(\theta - \mu_n)^2] = (n + 1)^{-1}.$$

Hence

$$r_0(\pi^n, n) = \frac{1}{n + 1} + \frac{1}{2}\left(1 - \frac{1}{n + 1}\right) = \frac{1}{2}\left(1 + \frac{1}{n + 1}\right).$$

This is decreasing in n, so that it never pays to stop sampling. Another observation always lowers the posterior Bayes risk. No proper Bayes procedure can, therefore, exist.

7.4.10 Other Techniques for Finding a Bayes Procedure

Although truncation methods are, in principle, capable of providing close approximations to the Bayes procedure, the considerable calculational difficulties often encountered with such methods suggest that consideration of other techniques is desirable. We briefly discuss some alternative techniques here.

I. Solution of the Functional Equation

One potentially useful method follows from Corollary 7.1 of the preceding subsection. This corollary shows (under the indicated conditions) that the Bayes procedure is determined by the function ρ^∞ which satisfies

$$\rho^\infty(\pi^n) = \min\{\rho_0(\pi^n), E^*[\rho^\infty(\pi^n(\theta \mid X))] + c\}. \qquad (7.38)$$

One can thus attempt to find the Bayes procedure by solving (7.38) for ρ^∞. (The solution to (7.38) is usually unique. This is so, for example, if $r(\pi, \delta_n^\pi) = E^{m^n}[\rho_0(\pi^n)] \to 0$ as $n \to \infty$. See DeGroot (1970) for a proof of this.)

Unfortunately, the calculational problems encountered in solving (7.38) are usually as difficult as those involved in finding truncated or look ahead procedures. Therefore, we will not discuss general techniques of solution. (See DeGroot (1970) for an introduction to the subject.)

In some special cases, (7.38) can be solved explicitly, or at least the solution can be reduced to a fairly simple numerical problem. The next section considers, in detail, one such very important special case. Here we content ourselves with a single example (due to Wald (1950)).

EXAMPLE 13. Assume that X_1, X_2, ... is a sequential sample from a $\mathcal{U}(\theta - \frac{1}{2}, \theta + \frac{1}{2})$ density, and that it is desired to estimate θ under loss

$$L(\theta, a, n) = 12(\theta - a)^2 + nc.$$

The prior distribution is $\mathcal{U}(a, b)$. A straightforward calculation shows that $\pi^n = \pi(\theta | x_1, \ldots, x_n)$ is $\mathcal{U}(a_n, b_n)$, where $a_n = \max\{a, (\max x_i) - \frac{1}{2}\}$, and $b_n = \min\{b, (\min x_i) + \frac{1}{2}\}$. The Bayes estimator at stage n is the posterior mean,

$$\delta_n^\pi(\mathbf{x}^n) = \frac{a_n + b_n}{2},$$

and the posterior decision risk is twelve times the posterior variance, i.e.,

$$\rho_0(\pi^n) = (b_n - a_n)^2.$$

Note that this is the square of the posterior range.

It is easy to check, in this situation, that the conditions of Corollary 7.1 are satisfied. Hence a Bayes procedure can be determined if the solution to (7.38) can be found. Note that all π^n are uniform distributions. Hence it suffices to find a solution to (7.38) for the class of uniform priors. By the reasoning in the previous paragraph, if π is any prior with range r, then the posterior Bayes decision risk will be

$$\rho_0(\pi) = r^2.$$

It thus seems reasonable to believe that $\rho^\infty(\pi)$ will also be a function of r, say

$$\rho^\infty(\pi) = h(r).$$

If this is true, then (7.38) becomes

$$h(r) = \min\{r^2, E^*[h(r(X))] + c\}, \tag{7.39}$$

where $r(X)$ is the posterior range of $\pi(\theta | X)$.

Intuition also suggests that the Bayes procedure will stop sampling when the posterior range gets small enough. But, from Corollary 7.1, we know that the Bayes procedure stops sampling when $\rho_0(\pi^n) = \rho^\infty(\pi^n)$. The conclusion is that $h(r)$ is likely to be of the form

$$h(r) = \begin{cases} r^2 & \text{if } r \le r_0, \\ g(r) & \text{if } r > r_0, \end{cases} \tag{7.40}$$

where $g(r) < r^2$ for $r > r_0$.

To proceed further, it is necessary to find a specific representation for $E^*[h(r(X))]$. A moments thought will make clear the fact that the exact interval specified by π is immaterial, as long as it has range r. It is convenient to choose π to be $\mathcal{U}(\frac{1}{2}, r + \frac{1}{2})$. An easy calculation then shows that the posterior range of $\pi(\theta|X)$ is

$$r(X) = \min\{r, X\} - \max\{0, X - 1\}, \tag{7.41}$$

and that the marginal density of X is

$$m(x) = r^{-1}r(x)I_{(0, r+1)}(x).$$

It is now necessary to distinguish between the two cases $r \le 1$ and $r > 1$. Consider first $r \le 1$. For such r, it follows from (7.41) that

$$r(x) = \begin{cases} x & \text{if } 0 < x < r, \\ r & \text{if } r \le x < 1, \\ r + 1 - x & \text{if } 1 \le x < r + 1. \end{cases}$$

Hence

$$
\begin{aligned}
E^*[h(r(X))] &= E^m[h(r(X))] \\
&= \frac{1}{r} \int_0^{r+1} r(x)h(r(x))dx \\
&= \frac{1}{r} \left[\int_0^r xh(x)dx + \int_r^1 rh(r)dx \right. \\
&\qquad \left. + \int_1^{r+1} (r + 1 - x)h(r + 1 - x)dx \right] \\
&= \frac{1}{r} \left[\int_0^r xh(x)dx + rh(r)(1 - r) + \int_0^r yh(y)dy \right] \\
&= \frac{2}{r} \int_0^r xh(x)dx + h(r)(1 - r).
\end{aligned}
$$

Using the form for h suggested in (7.40), this becomes (for $r > r_0$)

$$
\begin{aligned}
E^*[h(r(X))] &= \frac{2}{r} \int_0^{r_0} x^3\, dx + \frac{2}{r} \int_{r_0}^r xg(x)dx + g(r)(1 - r) \\
&= \frac{r_0^4}{2r} + \frac{2}{r} \int_{r_0}^r xg(x)dx + g(r)(1 - r).
\end{aligned}
$$

Inserting this in (7.39) and again using (7.40) gives (for $r > r_0$)

$$g(r) = \min\{r^2, E^*[h(r(X))] + c\}$$
$$= E^*[h(r(X))] + c$$
$$= \frac{r_0^4}{2r} + \frac{2}{r}\int_{r_0}^r xg(x)dx + g(r)(1 - r) + c.$$

Multiplying through by r and collecting terms results in the equation

$$0 = \frac{1}{2}r_0^4 + 2\int_{r_0}^r xg(x)dx - r^2g(r) + cr. \tag{7.42}$$

Differentiating both sides with respect to r gives (letting $g'(r) = dg(r)/dr$)

$$0 = 2rg(r) - 2rg(r) - r^2g'(r) + c$$
$$= -r^2g'(r) + c.$$

Hence $g'(r) = c/r^2$, which implies that

$$g(r) = K - \frac{c}{r}$$

for some constant K. Now it is reasonable to assume that $g(r_0) = r_0^2$ ($h(r)$ should be continuous), so that $K = r_0^2 + c/r_0$. Plugging

$$g(r) = r_0^2 + c(r_0^{-1} - r^{-1})$$

back into (7.42) and solving for r_0 gives $r_0 = (2c)^{1/3}$. The suggested function h is thus

$$h^*(r) = \begin{cases} r^2 & \text{if } r \le (2c)^{1/3}, \\ \frac{3}{2}(2c)^{2/3} - \frac{c}{r} & \text{if } (2c)^{1/3} < r \le 1, \end{cases}$$

and it can be checked that this is indeed a valid solution to (7.39).

Consider next the case $r > 1$. Note that it will still be the case that $r(X) \le 1$. A calculation (left as an exercise) shows that

$$E^*[h^*(r(X))] + c = \frac{3}{2}(2c)^{2/3} - \frac{c}{r}.$$

Hence, extending the definition of h^* to all $r > 0$ by

$$h^*(r) = \begin{cases} r^2 & \text{if } r \le (2c)^{1/3}, \\ \frac{3}{2}(2c)^{2/3} - \frac{c}{r} & \text{if } (2c)^{1/3} < r, \end{cases} \tag{7.43}$$

it follows that (7.39) is satisfied for all r.

It can also be shown that $r(\pi, \delta_n^\pi) \to 0$ as $n \to \infty$, so that the given solution to (7.38) is unique.

In conclusion, it has been shown that

$$\rho^\infty(\pi^n) = h^*(b_n - a_n).$$

Corollary 7.1 thus gives that the Bayes procedure is to stop sampling for the first n for which $\rho_0(\pi^n) = \rho^\infty(\pi^n)$, i.e., the first n for which

$$(b_n - a_n)^2 \le (2c)^{1/3},$$

and then use the Bayes estimate $(a_n + b_n)/2$.

Sometimes, one can infer that the Bayes procedure is of a particular form, depending on, say, a small number of unknown constants. If nothing else, this reduces the problem to a very tractable numerical problem (minimizing a Bayes risk over a small number of constants). A very important example of this will be given in the next section. See also Section 8.6 (Chapter 8).

Due to the difficulty in finding explicit Bayes procedures, a number of interesting theoretical studies have been performed, with the goal of finding "asymptotic" Bayes procedures. Virtually all such works assume that $c_j = c$ for all j, and are asymptotic in that they consider the problem as $c \to 0$. They are, hence, potentially relevant when the cost per observation is much smaller than the decision loss. (Unfortunately, this is usually not the case, in that sequential analysis is most often used with expensive observations. When observations are cheap, it is usually wasteful to analyze the situation after each observation, and taking batches of observations is often cheaper.)

The simplest asymptotic results to state are those of Bickel and Yahav (1967). Besides being of interest in the asymptotic sense, these results provide insight into the behavior of certain previously discussed sequential procedures.

The results of Bickel and Yahav pertain to quite general settings, but for this brief discussion we will assume that we have a sequential sample $X_1, X_2, \ldots$, that $L(\theta, a, n)$ is of the form (7.1), and that each observation costs $c_i = c$. The procedures that will be considered are called *asymptotically pointwise optimal*, which basically means that, as $c \to 0$, the posterior Bayes risks of the procedures, evaluated at the stopping point, converge to the corresponding posterior Bayes risk of the Bayes procedure, for almost all samples. See Bickel and Yahav (1967) and Kiefer and Sacks (1963) for a discussion of this and related concepts. It is again convenient to consider testing and estimation separately.

II. *Asymptotically Pointwise Optimal Procedures in Testing Problems*

It frequently happens, in testing problems, that (with probability one for each θ)

$$n^{-1} \log[\rho_0(\pi^n)] \to Y(\theta), \quad \text{where } P^\pi(-\infty < Y(\theta) < 0) = 1. \quad (7.44)$$

Consider, for instance, Example 3 in Section 7.2.

EXAMPLE 3 (revisited). The posterior Bayes decision risk is clearly the smaller of the posterior expected losses of a_0 and a_1, namely

$$\rho_0(\pi^n) = \min\left\{\int_{\Theta_1} L(\theta, a_0)dF^{\pi^n(\theta|\bar{X}_n)}(\theta), \int_{\Theta_0} L(\theta, a_1)dF^{\pi^n(\theta|\bar{X}_n)}(\theta)\right\}.$$

In Case 1, for which $\Theta_0 = \{\theta_0\}$ and $\Theta_1 = \{\theta_1\}$,

$$\rho_0(\pi^n) = \frac{n^{1/2}}{(2\pi)^{1/2}\sigma m_n(\bar{X}_n)} \min\left\{L(\theta_1, a_0)\pi(\theta_1)\exp\left[-\frac{n}{2\sigma^2}(\theta_1 - \bar{X}_n)^2\right],\right.$$

$$\left. L(\theta_0, a_1)\pi(\theta_0)\exp\left[-\frac{n}{2\sigma^2}(\theta_0 - \bar{X}_n)^2\right]\right\}. \quad (7.45)$$

Imagine now that θ_1 is true, so that $\bar{X}_n \to \theta_1$ with probability one. Then, for large enough n, the minimum in (7.45) will be (with probability approaching one)

$$L(\theta_0, a_1)\pi(\theta_0)\exp\left[-\frac{n}{2\sigma^2}(\theta_0 - \bar{X}_n)^2\right].$$

Hence, with probability one,

$$\lim_{n\to\infty} \frac{1}{n}\log[\rho_0(\pi^n)] = \lim_{n\to\infty} \frac{1}{n}\log\left[\frac{n^{1/2}L(\theta_0, a_1)\pi(\theta_0)}{(2\pi)^{1/2}\sigma}\right]$$

$$- \lim_{n\to\infty} \frac{1}{n}\log[m_n(\bar{X}_n)] - \lim_{n\to\infty} \frac{1}{2\sigma^2}(\theta_0 - \bar{X}_n)^2$$

$$= -\lim_{n\to\infty} \frac{1}{n}\log[m_n(\bar{X}_n)] - \frac{1}{2\sigma^2}(\theta_0 - \theta_1)^2.$$

Now

$$m_n(\bar{X}_n) = \frac{n^{1/2}}{(2\pi)^{1/2}\sigma}\left[\pi(\theta_0)\exp\left\{-\frac{n}{2\sigma^2}(\theta_0 - \bar{X}_n)^2\right\}\right.$$

$$\left. + \pi(\theta_1)\exp\left\{-\frac{n}{2\sigma^2}(\theta_1 - \bar{X}_n)^2\right\}\right],$$

for which it is easy to show that, with probability one,

$$\lim_{n\to\infty} \frac{1}{n}\log[m_n(\bar{X}_n)] = 0.$$

In conclusion, it is true that, with probability one,

$$\lim_{n\to\infty} \frac{1}{n}\log[\rho_0(\pi^n)] = -\frac{1}{2\sigma^2}(\theta_0 - \theta_1)^2.$$

The same result holds if θ_0 is the true state of nature. Thus (7.44) is clearly satisfied.

In Case 2 of Example 3 (where $\Theta_0 = (-\infty, \theta_0]$, $\Theta_1 = (\theta_0, \infty)$, and $W(y) = y^k$), it can be shown that, if θ^* is the true value of θ, then, with probability one,

$$\lim_{n \to \infty} \frac{1}{n} \log[\rho_0(\pi^n)] = -\frac{1}{2\sigma^2}(\theta_0 - \theta^*)^2.$$

Hence (7.44) is satisfied for the normal priors considered.

When (7.44) is satisfied, an asymptotically pointwise optimal procedure (see Bickel and Yahav (1967)) is to stop sampling for the first n for which

$$\rho_0(\pi^n) \leq c, \tag{7.46}$$

and then make the Bayes decision. As shown at the end of Subsection 7.4.7, this is exactly the 1-step inner look ahead procedure, $\mathbf{d}_{\mathrm{IL}}^1$. That this procedure turns out to be nearly optimal for very small c is somewhat surprising. It does explain, however, why, in Case 1 of Example 10 (Subsection 7.4.8), the procedure $\mathbf{d}_{\mathrm{IL}}^1$ performed so well.

Comparison of the stopping times of $\mathbf{d}_{\mathrm{IL}}^1$ and the optimal fixed sample size rule is instructive. Clearly (7.44) implies that, for large n,

$$\log[\rho_0(\pi^n)] \cong nY(\theta).$$

Since (7.46) is equivalent to

$$\log[\rho_0(\pi^n)] \leq \log c,$$

it follows that $\mathbf{d}_{\mathrm{IL}}^1$ will stop (approximately) for the first n for which

$$n \geq \frac{\log c}{Y(\theta)} = \frac{\log c^{-1}}{|Y(\theta)|}.$$

Hence the stopping time of $\mathbf{d}_{\mathrm{IL}}^1$ will be of the order of $\log c^{-1}$. This was also observed for the optimal fixed sample size rule in Case 1 of Example 3, which dealt with separated hypotheses. In Case 2 of Example 3, however, the hypotheses were connected, and it was then observed that the optimal fixed sample size was of the order $c^{-\lambda}$ (λ depending on the loss). Thus, for connected hypotheses, there appears to be a significant difference between the sample sizes needed for the fixed sample size approach and the sequential approach. The fixed sample size approach seems to take considerably more observations than are needed ($c^{-\lambda}$ compared with $\log c^{-1}$). The reason for this is that the fixed sample size approach gets very concerned about θ being near the joint boundary of the connected hypotheses, and chooses a very large sample size to protect against this possibility. The sequential procedure quickly realizes, however, when θ is away from the boundary, and can then make do with a fairly small sample size.

III. *Asymptotically Pointwise Optimal Procedures in Estimation Problems*

It frequently happens, in estimation problems, that (with probability one for each θ)

$$n^\beta \rho_0(\pi^n) \to Y(\theta), \quad \text{where } P^\pi(0 < Y(\theta) < \infty) = 1, \tag{7.47}$$

and β is some positive constant. For example, when $L(\theta, a) = |\theta - a|^k$, this condition is usually satisfied with $\beta = k/2$. See Example 2 (Section 7.2) and Example 7 (Subsection 7.4.5) for illustrations of this.

When (7.47) is satisfied, an asymptotically pointwise optimal procedure (see Bickel and Yahav (1967)) is to stop sampling for the first n for which

$$\rho_0(\pi^n) \le \frac{cn}{\beta}, \tag{7.48}$$

and then use the Bayes estimate. Note, from the discussion at the end of Example 2, that this is essentially the stopping rule for the optimal fixed sample size rule, except that $\rho_0(\pi^n)$ is used instead of

$$r(\pi, \delta_n^\pi) = E^{m^n}[\rho_0(\pi^n)].$$

Frequently, $\rho_0(\pi^n)$ and $r(\pi, \delta_n^\pi)$ will be similar functions. Indeed, (7.47) implies that, for large n and given θ,

$$\rho_0(\pi^n) \cong n^{-\beta} Y(\theta),$$

so that

$$r(\pi, \delta_n^\pi) = E^{m^n}[\rho_0(\pi^n)] = E^\pi E_\theta^{X^n}[\rho_0(\pi^n)] \cong n^{-\beta} E^\pi[Y(\theta)].$$

Hence the sample sizes for the asymptotically pointwise optimal procedure and optimal fixed sample size rule will tend to be comparable (in contrast to the testing situation with connected hypotheses).

It can also be shown that the asymptotically pointwise optimal procedure is (as $c \to 0$) usually equivalent to the 1-step look ahead procedure $\mathbf{d}_L^1$ (or, for that matter, any $\mathbf{d}_L^m$). All these procedures seek to minimize (see Subsection 7.4.8)

$$V(\mathbf{x}, n) = \rho_0(\pi^n) + nc \cong n^{-\beta} Y(\theta) + nc. \tag{7.49}$$

To see intuitively that the asymptotically pointwise optimal procedure minimizes this expression (asymptotically), differentiate with respect to n on the right-hand side of (7.49) and set equal to zero. The result is

$$0 = -\beta n^{-(\beta+1)} Y(\theta) + c \cong -\beta n^{-1} \rho_0(\pi^n) + c.$$

Clearly, the n which satisfies this equality will essentially be that determined by (7.48). Likewise, as discussed in Subsection 7.4.8, the look ahead procedures seek the minimum of $V(\mathbf{x}, n)$. They succeed, in an asymptotic sense, as $c \to 0$. A third class of procedures, based on this same idea, has been proposed by Alvo (1977) for certain special cases. They are better (i.e., less dependent on small c) than the asymptotically pointwise optimal procedure, and yet are quite easy to use. It is not clear, however, that they are superior to, say, $\mathbf{d}_L^1$.

IV. Asymptotically Optimal Procedures: Concluding Remarks

The major question concerning asymptotically optimal procedures is whether or not they are reasonable for moderately small c. The fact that they are based on the assumption that (7.44) or (7.47) give approximate expressions for $\log \rho_0(\pi^n)$ or $\rho_0(\pi^n)$, and that these expressions are independent of the prior, is cause for concern. It means that the procedures can be written in such a way that they do not depend on the prior. One wonders how successful they will then be, when c is such that the prior will matter. (When c is very small, enough observations will be taken to overwhelm the prior information.) The relevant look ahead procedures, as discussed in Subsection 7.4.8, seem much more attractive from this viewpoint.

Of course, to a classical statistician it may seem attractive to have a procedure which does not depend on the prior information. Thus work has been done on describing and evaluating, in a classical fashion, asymptotically optimal procedures such as those above. As an example, Schwarz (1962) has shown that, for testing $H_0 : \theta \leq -\lambda$ versus $H_1 : \theta \geq \lambda$ based on a sequential sample $X_1, X_2, \ldots$ from a $\mathcal{N}(\theta, 1)$ distribution, the asymptotically optimal test (for a quite general loss structure, with cost c per observation, and everywhere positive prior) is (approximately) to stop sampling for the first n for which

$$|s_n| = \left| \sum_{i=1}^n x_i \right| \geq [2n \log c^{-1}]^{1/2} - n\lambda,$$

deciding H_0 if s_n is negative and deciding H_1 if s_n in positive. This non-Bayesian procedure is evaluated classically in Woodroofe (1976), and is shown to have quite desirable properties. More general results of this nature can be found in Schwarz (1962), Schwarz (1968), and Woodroofe (1978). See also Kiefer and Sacks (1963) and Chernoff (1968) for other asymptotic results.

7.5 The Sequential Probability Ratio Test

The most commonly used sequential procedure is the sequential probability ratio test (SPRT), introduced by Wald in the 1940s. The SPRT is designed for testing a simple null hypothesis against a simple alternative hypothesis when a sequential sample $X_1, X_2, \ldots$ is available. The common density of the (independent) X_i will, as usual, be denoted $f(x|\theta)$, and the two hypotheses of interest will be denoted $H_0: \theta = \theta_0$ and $H_1: \theta = \theta_1$. The densities $f(x|\theta_0)$ and $f(x|\theta_1)$ need not actually be from the same parametric family. When they are not, the θ_i can just be considered to be indices.

When considering the problem from a sequential decision-theoretic viewpoint, it will be assumed that the loss is

$$L(\theta, a, n) = L(\theta, a) + nc,$$

where $L(\theta, a)$ is "$0 - K_i$" loss. Thus, letting a_i denote accepting H_i, the decision loss is $L(\theta_0, a_0) = L(\theta_1, a_1) = 0$, $L(\theta_0, a_1) = K_1$, and $L(\theta_1, a_0) = K_0$. The parameter space is formally $\Theta = \{\theta_0, \theta_1\}$, so that a prior π is specified by

$$\pi_0 \equiv \pi(\theta_0) = 1 - \pi(\theta_1) \equiv 1 - \pi_1.$$

We first derive the SPRT as a Bayes procedure, and in later sections discuss its classical properties.

7.5.1 The SPRT as a Bayes Procedure

The Bayes sequential problem, as described above, is of the type dealt with in Corollary 7.1 of Subsection 7.4.9. The conclusion of that corollary thus applies, namely that a Bayes procedure is given by $\mathbf{d}^\pi = (\tau^*, \delta^\pi)$, where δ^π is the Bayes decision rule and τ^* is the stopping rule which stops sampling for the first n ($n = 0, 1, 2, \ldots$) for which

$$\rho_0(\pi^n) = \rho^\infty(\pi^n). \tag{7.50}$$

Again $\rho_0(\pi^n)$ is the posterior Bayes decision risk at stage n, while $\rho^\infty(\pi^n)$ satisfies (for all n)

$$\rho^\infty(\pi^n) = \min\{\rho_0(\pi^n), \rho^*(\pi^n)\}, \tag{7.51}$$

where

$$\rho^*(\pi^n) = E^*[\rho^\infty(\pi^n(\theta|X))] + c, \tag{7.52}$$

the expectation being with respect to the predictive (or marginal) density of X induced by $\pi^n(\theta)$.

The posterior distributions, π^n, are determined by $\pi_0^n = \pi^n(\theta_0)$. Hence the functions ρ_0 and ρ^∞ can be considered to be functions of a single variable. For *any* prior π, clearly

$$\rho_0(\pi) = \inf_a E^\pi[L(\theta, a)] = \min\{\pi_1 K_0, \pi_0 K_1\} = \min\{(1 - \pi_0)K_0, \pi_0 K_1\}. \tag{7.53}$$

Also, note from the discussion at the end of Theorem 7 in Subsection 7.4.9 that

$$\rho^*(\pi) = \inf_{\mathbf{d}: N \geq 1} r(\pi, \mathbf{d}), \tag{7.54}$$

i.e., $\rho^*(\pi)$ is the minimum Bayes risk among procedures taking at least one observation. The following lemma describes the behavior of $\rho^*(\pi)$.

Lemma 1. *The function $\rho^*(\pi)$ is a concave continuous function of π_0, and is equal to c when $\pi_0 = 1$ or $\pi_0 = 0$.*

PROOF. For convenience, write $\rho^*(\pi_0)$, $r(\pi_0, \mathbf{d})$, etc., for the relevant Bayes risks. (Recall that π is determined by π_0.) It is easy to check, for $0 \leq \alpha \leq 1$, $0 \leq \pi_0 \leq 1$, and $0 \leq \pi_0' \leq 1$, that

$$r(\alpha\pi_0 + (1 - \alpha)\pi_0', \mathbf{d}) = \alpha r(\pi_0, \mathbf{d}) + (1 - \alpha)r(\pi_0', \mathbf{d}).$$

Hence

$$
\begin{aligned}
\rho^*(\alpha\pi_0 + (1 - \alpha)\pi_0') &= \inf_{\mathbf{d}:\, N \geq 1} r(\alpha\pi_0 + (1 - \alpha)\pi_0', \mathbf{d}) \\
&= \inf_{\mathbf{d}:\, N \geq 1} [\alpha r(\pi_0, \mathbf{d}) + (1 - \alpha)r(\pi_0', \mathbf{d})] \\
&\geq \inf_{\mathbf{d}:\, N \geq 1} [\alpha r(\pi_0, \mathbf{d})] + \inf_{\mathbf{d}:\, N \geq 1} [(1 - \alpha)r(\pi_0', \mathbf{d})] \\
&= \alpha\rho^*(\pi_0) + (1 - \alpha)\rho^*(\pi_0').
\end{aligned}
$$

This establishes that ρ^* is concave. The continuity of $\rho^*(\pi_0)$ for $0 < \pi_0 < 1$ follows from the well known fact that a convex or concave function on a convex subset, Ω, of R^1 is continuous on the interior of Ω.

To prove the remainder of the lemma, note, from (7.54) and the fact that the decision loss is nonnegative, that $\rho^*(\pi_0) \geq c$. Finally, let $\mathbf{d}_0$ be the procedure which stops after taking one observation and makes the Bayes decision. Clearly

$$\rho^*(\pi_0) \leq r(\pi_0, \mathbf{d}_0) = c + E^*[\rho_0(\pi(\theta|X))].$$

As $\pi_0 \to 0$ or $\pi_0 \to 1$, it is easy to check that $E^*[\rho_0(\pi(\theta|X))] \to 0$. Together with the fact that $\rho^*(\pi_0) \geq c$, this shows that $\rho^*(\pi_0)$ is continuous at $\pi_0 = 0$ and $\pi_0 = 1$, and is equal to c at these values.   □

Two cases must now be distinguished.

Case 1. $\rho_0(\pi) \leq \rho^*(\pi)$ for all π_0.

In this situation, the Bayes procedure is to immediately make the Bayes decision, taking no observations.

Case 2. $\rho_0(\pi) > \rho^*(\pi)$ for some π_0 $(0 < \pi_0 < 1)$.

In this situation, graphing $\rho_0(\pi)$ and $\rho^*(\pi)$ as functions of π_0 (using (7.53) and Lemma 1) results in Figure 7.2 below. From this figure it is clear that $\rho_0(\pi) > \rho^*(\pi)$ if $\pi_0' < \pi_0 < \pi_0''$. Together with (7.50), (7.51), and (7.53), this proves the following theorem. (From now on, π will again refer to the specific true prior for the problem.)

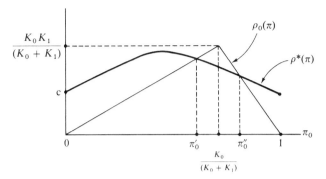

Figure 7.2

Theorem 8. *The Bayes sequential procedure,* $\mathbf{d}^\pi$, *stops sampling for the first* n $(n = 0, 1, 2, \ldots)$ *for which* $\pi_0^n \leq \pi_0'$ *or* $\pi_0^n \geq \pi_0''$, *deciding* a_0 *if* $\pi_0^n \geq \pi_0''$ *and* a_1 *if* $\pi_0^n \leq \pi_0'$. *The constants* π_0' *and* π_0'' *satisfy* $\pi_0' \leq K_0/(K_0 + K_1) \leq \pi_0''$.

Note that this theorem is also valid for Case 1, as can be seen by choosing $\pi_0' = \pi_0'' = K_0/(K_0 + K_1)$.

The Bayes sequential procedure can be written in a more enlightening form by defining the *likelihood ratio* of θ_1 to θ_0 at stage n as

$$L_n = \frac{\prod_{i=1}^n f(x_i|\theta_1)}{\prod_{i=1}^n f(x_i|\theta_0)},$$

and noting that

$$\pi_0^n = \pi(\theta_0|\mathbf{x}^n) = \frac{\pi(\theta_0) \prod_{i=1}^n f(x_i|\theta_0)}{\pi(\theta_0) \prod_{i=1}^n f(x_i|\theta_0) + \pi(\theta_1) \prod_{i=1}^n f(x_i|\theta_1)}$$

$$= \frac{1}{1 + (\pi_1/\pi_0) \prod_{i=1}^n (f(x_i|\theta_1)/f(x_i|\theta_0))}$$

$$= \frac{1}{1 + (\pi_1/\pi_0)L_n}.$$

(In this and subsequent expressions, define K/∞ as zero and $K/0$ as infinity.) Assuming $0 < \pi_0 < 1$ (which if not satisfied makes the problem trivial), it can easily be checked that $\pi_0^n \leq \pi_0'$ if and only if $L_n \geq \pi_0(1 - \pi_0')/(\pi_1\pi_0')$, while $\pi_0^n \geq \pi_0''$ if and only if $L_n \leq \pi_0(1 - \pi_0'')/(\pi_1\pi_0'')$. This establishes the following corollary to Theorem 8.

Corollary 8.1. *If* $0 < \pi_0 < 1$, *then the Bayes procedure,* $\mathbf{d}^\pi$, *is of the following form:*

$$\begin{aligned}
&\text{if } L_n \leq A, &&\text{stop sampling and decide } a_0; \\
&\text{if } L_n \geq B, &&\text{stop sampling and decide } a_1; &&(7.55) \\
&\text{if } A < L_n < B, &&\text{take another observation;}
\end{aligned}$$

where $A = \pi_0(1 - \pi_0'')/(\pi_1\pi_0'')$ *and* $B = \pi_0(1 - \pi_0')/(\pi_1\pi_0')$. *(Note that* $A \leq B$.)

From now on, we will assume that it is desirable to take at least one observation. This is, of course, equivalent to assuming that

$$\pi_0' < \pi_0 < \pi_0''. \tag{7.56}$$

The difficulty is that π_0' and π_0'' are not known, and the ensuing development, which is aimed at determining π_0' and π_0'', assumes (7.56). In applications, therefore, one must separately check whether or not the immediate Bayes decision has smaller Bayes risk than the optimal procedure derived by assuming (7.56). When (7.56) is satisfied, it is easy to check that $A < 1$ and $B > 1$.

Definition 8. The procedure defined by (7.55) with constants $A < 1$ and $B > 1$ is called the *sequential probability ratio test* (SPRT) with *stopping boundaries* A and B, and will be denoted $\mathbf{d}^{A, B}$.

The Bayesian problem can now be phrased as that of choosing A and B to minimize $r(\pi, \mathbf{d}^{A, B})$. To express the Bayes risk of $\mathbf{d}^{A, B}$ conveniently, let N denote the stopping time of $\mathbf{d}^{A, B}$, i.e.,

$$N = \min\{n: L_n \leq A \text{ or } L_n \geq B\},$$

and define the probabilities of Type I error and Type II error as

$$\alpha_0 = P_{\theta_0} \text{ (deciding } a_1) = P_{\theta_0}(L_N \geq B),$$

$$\alpha_1 = P_{\theta_1} \text{ (deciding } a_0) = P_{\theta_1}(L_N \leq A).$$

Also, let $E_{\theta_0} N$ and $E_{\theta_1} N$ denote the expected stopping times under θ_0 and θ_1 respectively. (It is being implicitly assumed that $P_{\theta_i}(N < \infty) = 1$ and $E_{\theta_i} N < \infty$. This will be verified later.) An easy calculation then gives

$$
\begin{aligned}
r(\pi, \mathbf{d}^{A, B}) &= \pi(\theta_0)R(\theta_0, \mathbf{d}^{A, B}) + \pi(\theta_1)R(\theta_1, \mathbf{d}^{A, B}) \\
&= \pi_0[\alpha_0 K_1 + c E_{\theta_0} N] + \pi_1[\alpha_1 K_0 + c E_{\theta_1} N]. \tag{7.57}
\end{aligned}
$$

The problem thus reduces to the calculation of α_0, α_1, $E_{\theta_0} N$, and $E_{\theta_1} N$, and the subsequent minimization of (7.57) over A and B. Unfortunately, only rarely can this program be analytically carried out. Two other options are available, however. First, numerical calculation and minimization of (7.57) is generally quite feasible, only two variables being involved. Second, reasonably accurate approximations to α_0, α_1, $E_{\theta_0} N$, and $E_{\theta_1} N$ exist, which simplify the calculation considerably. It is to these approximations that we now turn.

7.5.2 Approximating the Power Function and the Expected Sample Size

From a classical viewpoint, the relevant properties of an SPRT are the error probabilities, α_0 and α_1, and the expected sample sizes, $E_{\theta_0} N$ and $E_{\theta_1} N$. As these are also the quantities needed for a Bayesian analysis, it seems that nothing else need be considered. Unfortunately, this is too narrow a view in practice, in that it is unlikely that the simple versus simple hypothesis testing formulation of the problem is realistic. Far more common will be parametric situations in which, for example, it is desired to test $H_0 : \theta \leq \theta_0$ versus $H_1 : \theta \geq \theta_1$. Here θ_0 and θ_1 represent the boundaries of regions it is important to distinguish between, and the simple versus simple formulation would seem to be a reasonable approximation to this more complicated situation. Even if an SPRT is then used, however, it is clear that one must be concerned with all possible values of θ, and not just θ_0 and θ_1. Hence it is important to investigate the error probabilities and the expected sample sizes of an SPRT for all values of θ.

Because of the above reasoning, we will, in the following, deal with the more general situation in which the X_i are a sequential sample from the density $f(x|\theta)$, the parameter θ possibly assuming values other than θ_0 or θ_1. It is then important to consider

$$\beta(\theta) = P_\theta \text{ (deciding } a_1) = P_\theta(L_N \geq B),$$

$$\alpha(\theta) = P_\theta \text{ (deciding } a_0) = P_\theta(L_N \leq A),$$

and $E_\theta N$, for arbitrary values of θ. (The results obtained will, of course, also be valid for just θ_0 and θ_1. Note that $\alpha_0 = \beta(\theta_0)$ and $\alpha_1 = \alpha(\theta_1)$.) The function $\beta(\theta)$ is called the *power function*, $\alpha(\theta)$ is called the *operating character-istic* (OC) curve, and $E_\theta N$ is the *expected stopping time* (often called the average sample number (ASN)).

As mentioned earlier, it will be shown that $P_\theta(N < \infty) = 1$. Assuming this, it follows that

$$1 = P_\theta(N < \infty) = P_\theta(L_N \leq A) + P_\theta(L_N \geq B) = \alpha(\theta) + \beta(\theta). \quad (7.58)$$

Hence $\alpha(\theta) = 1 - \beta(\theta)$, and it is only necessary to determine, say, $\beta(\theta)$.

To obtain approximations to $\beta(\theta)$ and $E_\theta(N)$, it is helpful to consider the following reformulation of the SPRT. (This reformulation and much of the following development is due to Wald (1947).) Define

$$Z_i = \log\left[\frac{f(X_i|\theta_1)}{f(X_i|\theta_0)}\right],$$

where Z_i is allowed to take on the values $\pm \infty$. Note that the Z_i are i.i.d. (since the X_i are), and that

$$S_n = \sum_{i=1}^{n} Z_i = \log\left[\prod_{i=1}^{n} \frac{f(X_i|\theta_1)}{f(X_i|\theta_0)}\right] = \log L_n.$$

Because $\log y$ is monotone in y, it follows from Definition 8 and (7.55) that the SPRT $\mathbf{d}^{A, B}$ can be rewritten as follows:

$$\begin{aligned}
&\text{if } S_n \leq a = \log A, \quad \text{stop sampling and decide } a_0; \\
&\text{if } S_n \geq b = \log B, \quad \text{stop sampling and decide } a_1; \quad (7.59)\\
&\text{if } a < S_n < b, \qquad\quad \text{take another observation.}
\end{aligned}$$

In this formulation, we will denote the SPRT by $\mathbf{d}_{a,b}$. Note that $a < 0$ and $b > 0$, since $A < 1$ and $B > 1$.

The advantage of the above formulation of the problem is that S_n, being a sum of i.i.d. random variables, is much easier to deal with than is L_n. Indeed, $\mathbf{d}_{a,b}$ can be interpreted as a random walk, stopping when S_n reaches the "barriers" a and b. Though fruitful, this last interpretation is beyond the scope of the book.

EXAMPLE 14. Suppose $X_1, X_2, \ldots$ is a sequential sample from a $\mathcal{N}(\theta, \sigma^2)$ density, σ^2 known. It is desired to test $H_0 : \theta = \theta_0$ versus $H_1 : \theta = \theta_1 (\theta_0 < \theta_1)$. Clearly

$$Z_i = \log \frac{f(X_i | \theta_1)}{f(X_i | \theta_0)} = -\frac{1}{2\sigma^2} [(X_i - \theta_1)^2 - (X_i - \theta_0)^2]$$

$$= \frac{1}{\sigma^2} (\theta_1 - \theta_0) X_i + \frac{1}{2\sigma^2} (\theta_0^2 - \theta_1^2).$$

Hence

$$S_n = \sum_{i=1}^{n} Z_i = \frac{1}{\sigma^2} (\theta_1 - \theta_0) \sum_{i=1}^{n} X_i + \frac{n}{2\sigma^2} (\theta_0^2 - \theta_1^2)$$

$$= \frac{n}{\sigma^2} (\theta_1 - \theta_0) \bar{X}_n + \frac{n}{2\sigma^2} (\theta_0^2 - \theta_1^2).$$

The SPRT $\mathbf{d}_{a,b}$ can thus be written as follows:

if $\bar{X}_n < \dfrac{a\sigma^2}{n(\theta_1 - \theta_0)} + \dfrac{1}{2} (\theta_0 + \theta_1)$,   stop sampling and decide a_0;

if $\bar{X}_n > \dfrac{b\sigma^2}{n(\theta_1 - \theta_0)} + \dfrac{1}{2} (\theta_0 + \theta_1)$,   stop sampling and decide a_1;

and otherwise continue sampling.

In the remainder of the section, it will be assumed that we are considering an SPRT $\mathbf{d}_{a,b}$ with $a < 0$ and $b > 1$, and that N is the stopping time of the SPRT and $\beta(\theta)$ is its power function. We begin the development of the approximations to $\beta(\theta)$ and $E_\theta N$ by establishing, as promised, that $P_\theta(N < \infty) = 1$.

Theorem 9. *Let N be the stopping time of the SPRT $\mathbf{d}_{a,b}$. If $P_\theta(Z_i = 0) < 1$, then $P_\theta(N < \infty) = 1$ and all moments of N exist.*

PROOF. The proof follows Stein (1946). The index θ is immaterial to the proof, and so will be omitted.

Since $P(Z_i = 0) < 1$, either $P(Z_i > \varepsilon) > 0$ or $P(Z_i < -\varepsilon) > 0$ for some $\varepsilon > 0$. Assume that

$$P(Z_i > \varepsilon) = \lambda > 0,$$

the other case being handled similarly. Note that N is defined by ($N = \infty$ formally being allowed)

$$N = \min\{n: S_n \leq a \text{ or } S_n \geq b\}.$$

Letting m be an integer greater than $(b - a)/\varepsilon$, it follows from the independence of the Z_i that, for all j,

$$P(S_{j+m} - S_j > b - a) = P\left(\sum_{i=j+1}^{j+m} Z_i > b - a\right)$$

$$\geq P(Z_i > (b - a)/m, \text{ for } i = j + 1, \ldots, j + m)$$

$$\geq P(Z_i > \varepsilon, \text{ for } i = j + 1, \ldots, j + m) = \lambda^m.$$

Hence, again using the independence of the Z_i,

$$P(N \geq jm + 1) = P(a < S_i < b, \text{ for } i = 1, \ldots, jm)$$

$$\leq P(S_{im} - S_{(i-1)m} \leq (b - a), \text{ for } i = 1, \ldots, j)$$

$$= \prod_{i=1}^{j} P(S_{im} - S_{(i-1)m} \leq b - a) \leq (1 - \lambda^m)^j. \quad (7.60)$$

Define $\gamma = (1 - \lambda^m)^{-1}$ and $\rho = (1 - \lambda^m)^{1/m}$. For any given n, let j be that integer for which $jm < n \leq (j + 1)m$. It follows from (7.60) that

$$P(N \geq n) \leq P(N \geq jm + 1) \leq (1 - \lambda^m)^j = \gamma \rho^{(j+1)m} \leq \gamma \rho^n.$$

Hence

$$P(N < \infty) \geq 1 - P(N \geq n) \geq 1 - \gamma \rho^n.$$

Since this is true for all n, it is clear that $P(N < \infty) = 1$. Also,

$$E[N^k] = \sum_{n=0}^{\infty} n^k P(N = n) \leq \sum_{n=0}^{\infty} n^k P(N \geq n) \leq \sum_{n=0}^{\infty} n^k \gamma \rho^n < \infty,$$

so that all moments of N exist. The proof is complete. $\qquad \square$

The condition $P_\theta(Z_i = 0) < 1$, in the above lemma, is quite innocuous, since $Z_i = 0$ if and only if $f(X_i|\theta_1) = f(X_i|\theta_0)$. The condition thus ensures that $f(X_i|\theta_1)$ and $f(X_i|\theta_0)$ differ with positive probability, clearly a necessary condition to be able to distinguish between the two.

The basic tool that will be used in approximating $\beta(\theta)$ and $E_\theta N$ is the *fundamental identity of sequential analysis*, first established by Wald (1947). This identity involves consideration of

$$M_\theta(t) = E_\theta[e^{tZ_i}],$$

the moment generating function of the Z_i. It will be necessary to assume that $M_\theta(t)$ is finite (at least for t near zero), and also that the Z_i are finite valued.

Both of these conditions can be assumed, without loss of generality, by considering, in place of the Z_i,

$$Z_i^* = \begin{cases} (b-a) & \text{if } Z_i > (b-a), \\ Z_i & \text{if } |Z_i| \le (b-a), \\ -(b-a) & \text{if } Z_i < -(b-a). \end{cases} \tag{7.61}$$

The SPRT is unchanged if the Z_i are replaced by the Z_i^*. (Any Z_n, for which $|Z_n| > (b-a)$, would automatically cause S_n to jump outside the stopping boundaries. The same thing would happen, however, for $S_n^* = \sum_{i=1}^{n} Z_i^*$.) It is clear that the Z_i^* are finite valued, and that the moment generating function of the Z_i^* exists for all t. We will use the Z_i^* in place of the Z_i only if needed, however, since the Z_i are often calculationally easier to work with.

Theorem 10 (Fundamental Identity of Sequential Analysis). *If $P_\theta(Z_i = 0) < 1$ and $P_\theta(|Z_i| < \infty) = 1$, then*

$$E_\theta[\exp(tS_N)M_\theta(t)^{-N}] = 1, \tag{7.62}$$

for all t for which $M_\theta(t)$ is finite.

PROOF. (The proof that will be given (due to Bahadur (1958)) is rather unintuitive. Equation (7.62) is intuitively reasonable, however, as can be seen by verifying the equation for fixed n.)
    Define (assuming that $M_\theta(t) < \infty$)

$$g(z|t, \theta) = \frac{\exp(tz)f(z|\theta)}{M_\theta(t)}.$$

This is clearly a density in z, and does not give probability one to zero (since $\exp(tz)$ is positive, $M_\theta(t)$ is a constant, and $f(z|\theta)$ does not give probability one to zero). Pretending that the Z_i have density $g(z|t, \theta)$ and considering the SPRT based on the Z_i, it follows from Theorem 9 that

$$P_{t,\theta}(N_t < \infty) = 1,$$

where N_t is the stopping time for the SPRT in this new problem. Note, however, that in terms of the original Z_i (for simplicity only the continuous case is considered)

$$E_\theta[\exp(tS_N)M_\theta(t)^{-N}] = \sum_{n=1}^{\infty} \int_{\{N=n\}} \cdots \int \exp(tS_n)M_\theta(t)^{-n} \prod_{i=1}^{n} [f(z_i|\theta)dz_i]$$

$$= \sum_{n=1}^{\infty} \int_{\{N=n\}} \cdots \int \prod_{i=1}^{n} [\exp(tz_i)M_\theta(t)^{-1}f(z_i|\theta)dz_i]$$

$$= \sum_{n=1}^{\infty} \int_{\{N_t=n\}} \cdots \int \prod_{i=1}^{n} [g(z_i|t, \theta)dz_i] = P_{t,\theta}(N_t < \infty) = 1.$$

This completes the proof.   □

The next theorem is a direct consequence of the fundamental identity, and will itself be crucial in obtaining the approximations to $\beta(\theta)$ and $E_\theta N$.

Theorem 11. *Assume that* $P_\theta(Z_i = 0) < 1$, *that* $P_\theta(|Z_i| < \infty) = 1$, *and that* $M_\theta(t)$ *exists for* t *in a neighborhood of the origin. Then*

(i) $E_\theta[S_N] = \mu_\theta E_\theta N$, *and*
(ii) $E_\theta[S_N - N\mu_\theta]^2 = \sigma_\theta^2 E_\theta N$,

where $\mu_\theta = E_\theta[Z_i]$ *and* $\sigma_\theta^2 = E_\theta(Z_i - \mu_\theta)^2$.

PROOF. It can be shown that derivatives with respect to t can be taken inside the expectation sign of the fundamental identity. Hence (7.62) implies that

$$0 = \frac{d}{dt}1 = E_\theta\left[\frac{d}{dt}\{\exp(tS_N)M_\theta(t)^{-N}\}\right]$$

$$= E_\theta\left[S_N \exp(tS_N)M_\theta(t)^{-N} - N\exp(tS_N)M_\theta(t)^{-(N+1)}\left\{\frac{d}{dt}M_\theta(t)\right\}\right].$$

$$(7.63)$$

Notice that $M_\theta(0) = 1$, and that

$$\frac{d}{dt}M_\theta(t)\bigg|_{t=0} = E_\theta\left[\frac{d}{dt}\exp(tZ_i)\right]\bigg|_{t=0} = E_\theta[Z_i\exp(tZ_i)]\bigg|_{t=0}$$

$$= E_\theta[Z_i] = \mu_\theta. \qquad (7.64)$$

Hence, evaluating (7.63) at $t = 0$ gives

$$0 = E_\theta[S_N - N\mu_\theta],$$

which proves part (i).

The proof of part (ii) is similar (based on taking the second derivative) and is left as an exercise. $\qquad\square$

One final technical result is needed.

Lemma 2. *Assume that* $P_\theta(|Z_i| < \infty) = 1$, *that* $M_\theta(t)$ *exists for all* t, *that* $P_\theta(Z_i < 0) > 0$ *and* $P_\theta(Z_i > 0) > 0$, *and that* $\mu_\theta \neq 0$. *Then there exists a unique nonzero number* t_θ *for which* $M_\theta(t_\theta) = 1$.

PROOF. The proof is based on showing that, under the given conditions, $M_\theta(t)$ will be a function behaving as in Figure 7.3. To see that this is correct, note that

$$\frac{d^2}{dt^2}M_\theta(t) = E_\theta\left[\frac{d^2}{dt^2}\exp(tZ_i)\right] = E_\theta[Z_i^2\exp(tZ_i)] > 0,$$

the strict inequality following from the assumption that $P(Z_i = 0) < 1$. From Lemma 1 in Section 1.8, it follows that $M_\theta(t)$ is strictly convex.

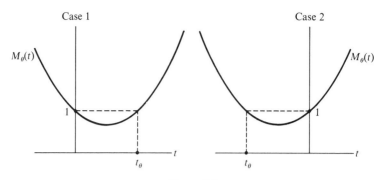

Figure 7.3

Note next that $M_\theta(0) = 1$ and, by (7.64), that

$$\frac{d}{dt} M_\theta(t) \bigg|_{t=0} = \mu_\theta \neq 0.$$

Finally, let $\varepsilon > 0$ and $\lambda > 0$ be such that $P_\theta(Z_i > \varepsilon) > \lambda$. Clearly, for $t > 0$,

$$M_\theta(t) = E_\theta[\exp(tZ_i)] \geq \lambda \exp(t\varepsilon).$$

Hence

$$\lim_{t \to \infty} M_\theta(t) \geq \lim_{t \to \infty} \lambda \exp(t\varepsilon) = \infty.$$

It can similarly be shown that

$$\lim_{t \to -\infty} M_\theta(t) = \infty.$$

These facts imply that $M_\theta(t)$ must behave as in Case 1 or Case 2 of Figure 7.3, giving the desired conclusion.   □

The conditions of this lemma are not particularly stringent. It has already been mentioned that, using (7.61) if necessary, $M_\theta(t)$ can be guaranteed to exist for all t. The conditions $P_\theta(Z_i < 0) > 0$ and $P_\theta(Z_i > 0) > 0$ merely ensure that trivialities are avoided. If, for instance, $P_\theta(Z_i < 0) = 0$, then S_n will be sure to exit through the b boundary. (Recall, we are assuming that $a < 0$ and $b > 0$.) In such a situation, it is obviously silly to take any observations, since the action that will be taken is already known. The calculation of t_θ will be seen to be relatively easy in many common situations.

The approximations to $\beta(\theta)$ and $E_\theta N$ are based on pretending that S_N hits the boundaries a and b *exactly*. In other words, we will pretend that S_N has the two-point distribution, P_θ^*, defined by

$$P_\theta^*(S_N = a) = P_\theta(S_N \leq a) \text{ and } P_\theta^*(S_N = b) = P_\theta(S_N \geq b). \quad (7.65)$$

The Wald Approximation to $\beta(\theta)$

Case 1. $\mu_\theta \neq 0$.
    Assume t_θ is such that $M_\theta(t_\theta) = 1$. The fundamental identity then implies that

$$1 = E_\theta[\exp(t_\theta S_N)M_\theta(t_\theta)^{-N}] = E_\theta[\exp(t_\theta S_N)].$$

Pretending that S_N has the distribution P_θ^* defined in (7.65), it follows that

$$1 \cong \exp(t_\theta a)P_\theta^*(S_N = a) + \exp(t_\theta b)P_\theta^*(S_N = b)$$

$$= \exp(t_\theta a)P_\theta(S_N \leq a) + \exp(t_\theta b)P_\theta(S_N \geq b). \qquad (7.66)$$

Now (7.58) implies that

$$P_\theta(S_N \leq a) + P_\theta(S_N \geq b) = 1, \qquad (7.67)$$

so that (7.66) gives

$$\beta(\theta) = P_\theta(S_N \geq b) \cong \frac{1 - \exp(t_\theta a)}{\exp(t_\theta b) - \exp(t_\theta a)} \stackrel{(\text{defn.})}{=} \tilde\beta(\theta). \qquad (7.68)$$

Case 2. $\mu_\theta = 0$.
    If $\mu_\theta = 0$, Theorem 11 (i) implies that $E_\theta[S_N] = 0$. Again pretending that S_N has the distribution P_θ^*, this becomes

$$aP_\theta(S_N \leq a) + bP_\theta(S_N \geq b) \cong 0.$$

Together with (7.67), this implies that

$$\beta(\theta) = P_\theta(S_N \geq b) \cong \frac{-a}{b-a} \stackrel{(\text{defn.})}{=} \tilde\beta(\theta). \qquad (7.69)$$

It can be shown that this agrees with (7.68) in the sense that as $\mu_\theta \to 0$ (so that $t_\theta \to 0$) the expression in (7.68) converges to that in (7.69).

The Wald Approximation to $E_\theta N$

Case 1. $\mu_\theta \neq 0$.
    Theorem 11 (i) implies that

$$E_\theta N = (\mu_\theta)^{-1} E_\theta[S_N]. \qquad (7.70)$$

Use of P_θ^* leads to the approximation

$$E_\theta S_N \cong aP_\theta(S_N \leq a) + bP_\theta(S_N \geq b) = a + (b-a)\beta(\theta).$$

Replacing $\beta(\theta)$ by its approximation $\tilde\beta(\theta)$ and inserting this expression into (7.70) gives

$$E_\theta N \cong (\mu_\theta)^{-1}[a + (b-a)\tilde\beta(\theta)] \stackrel{(\text{defn.})}{=} \tilde E_\theta N. \qquad (7.71)$$

Case 2. $\mu_\theta = 0$.

It is now necessary to use Theorem 11 (ii), which, for $\mu_\theta = 0$, states that

$$E_\theta N = (\sigma_\theta^2)^{-1} E_\theta(S_N^2).$$

Use of P_θ^* leads to the approximation

$$E_\theta[S_N^2] \cong a^2 P_\theta(S_N \leq a) + b^2 P_\theta(S_N \geq b)$$

$$\cong a^2 + (b^2 - a^2)\tilde{\beta}(\theta)$$

$$= a^2 + (b - a)(b + a)\left[\frac{-a}{b - a}\right] = -ab.$$

Hence

$$E_\theta N \cong \frac{-ab}{\sigma_\theta^2} \overset{\text{(defn.)}}{=} \tilde{E}_\theta^N. \tag{7.72}$$

This can be shown to be the limiting case of (7.71) as μ_θ (and hence t_θ) approach zero.

It is of particular interest to consider $\tilde{\alpha}_0 = \tilde{\beta}(\theta_0)$, $\tilde{\alpha}_1 = 1 - \tilde{\beta}(\theta_1)$, $\tilde{E}_{\theta_0} N$, and $\tilde{E}_{\theta_1} N$. To this end, note that if $P_{\theta_j}(|Z_i| < \infty) = 1$ for $j = 0, 1$, then

$$t_{\theta_0} = 1 \quad \text{and} \quad t_{\theta_1} = -1. \tag{7.73}$$

(The proof will be left as an exercise.) It is then easy to calculate, from (7.68) and (7.71), that

$$\tilde{\alpha}_0 = \frac{1 - \exp(a)}{\exp(b) - \exp(a)} = \frac{1 - A}{B - A},$$

$$\tilde{\alpha}_1 = 1 - \frac{1 - \exp(-a)}{\exp(-b) - \exp(-a)} = \frac{\exp(-b) - 1}{\exp(-b) - \exp(-a)}$$

$$= \frac{B^{-1} - 1}{B^{-1} - A^{-1}} = \frac{A(B - 1)}{B - A}, \tag{7.74}$$

$$\tilde{E}_{\theta_0} N = (\mu_{\theta_0})^{-1}[a + (b - a)\tilde{\alpha}_0],$$

and

$$\tilde{E}_{\theta_1} N = (\mu_{\theta_1})^{-1}[a + (b - a)(1 - \tilde{\alpha}_1)].$$

The approximations $\tilde{\alpha}_0$ and $\tilde{\alpha}_1$ are particularly interesting, in that they are distribution free, depending only on A and B. Note also that the equations for $\tilde{\alpha}_0$ and $\tilde{\alpha}_1$ can be solved for A and B, the result being $A = \tilde{\alpha}_1/(1 - \tilde{\alpha}_0)$ and $B = (1 - \tilde{\alpha}_1)/\tilde{\alpha}_0$. This suggests a way of determining approximate stopping boundaries for the SPRT, if it is desired to attain certain specified error probabilities. Indeed, if error probabilities α_0 and α_1 are desired (this is a classical approach, of course), the suggested SPRT is that with stopping boundaries

$$A^* = \frac{\alpha_1}{1 - \alpha_0} \quad \text{and} \quad B^* = \frac{1 - \alpha_1}{\alpha_0}. \tag{7.75}$$

EXAMPLE 14 (continued). To determine $\tilde{\beta}(\theta)$ and $\tilde{E}_\theta N$, note that

$$\mu_\theta = E_\theta[Z_i] = \frac{1}{\sigma^2}(\theta_1 - \theta_0)\theta + \frac{1}{2\sigma^2}(\theta_0^2 - \theta_1^2)$$

and

$$\sigma_\theta^2 = E_\theta(Z_i - \mu_\theta)^2 = E_\theta\left[\frac{1}{\sigma^2}(\theta_1 - \theta_0)(X_i - \theta)\right]^2 = \frac{1}{\sigma^2}(\theta_1 - \theta_0)^2.$$

A standard calculation also shows that

$$M_\theta(t) = E_\theta[\exp(tZ_i)]$$

$$= \exp\left\{-\frac{1}{2\sigma^2}t(\theta_1 - \theta_0)[\theta_1 + \theta_0 - 2\theta - t(\theta_1 - \theta_0)]\right\}.$$

Hence $M_\theta(t_\theta) = 1$ (for $t_\theta \neq 0$) if and only if

$$\theta_1 + \theta_0 - 2\theta - t_\theta(\theta_1 - \theta_0) = 0,$$

or, equivalently,

$$t_\theta = \frac{\theta_1 + \theta_0 - 2\theta}{\theta_1 - \theta_0}.$$

Using these formulas, it is easy to calculate the Wald approximations $\tilde{\beta}(\theta)$ and $\tilde{E}_\theta N$.

As a specific example, suppose $\sigma^2 = 1$, $\theta_0 = -\frac{1}{2}$, $\theta_1 = \frac{1}{2}$, and assume an SPRT with error probabilities $\alpha_0 = \alpha_1 = 0.1$ is desired. The approximations to the stopping boundaries of the desired SPRT are, from (7.75), $A^* = \frac{1}{9}$ and $B^* = 9$, or, equivalently, $a^* = -\log 9$ and $b^* = \log 9$ (for the Z_i formulation). To find $\tilde{\beta}(\theta)$ and $\tilde{E}_\theta N$ for $\mathbf{d}_{a^*, b^*}$, note first that $\mu_\theta = 0$, $\sigma_\theta^2 = 1$, and $t_\theta = -2\theta$.

Case 1. $\theta \neq 0$ (i.e., $\mu_\theta \neq 0$).

From (7.68) and (7.71) it is clear that

$$\tilde{\beta}(\theta) = \frac{1 - \exp(-2\theta a^*)}{\exp(-2\theta b^*) - \exp(-2\theta a^*)} = \frac{1 - 9^{2\theta}}{9^{-2\theta} - 9^{2\theta}}$$

and

$$\tilde{E}_\theta N = \theta^{-1}(\log 9)[-1 + 2\tilde{\beta}(\theta)].$$

In particular,

$$\tilde{E}_{\theta_1} N = \tilde{E}_{\theta_0} N = (-2)(\log 9)[-1 + 2(0.1)] \cong 3.52.$$

Case 2. $\theta = 0$ (i.e., $\mu_\theta = 0$).

For this case, (7.69) and (7.72) give that $\tilde{\beta}(0) = \frac{1}{2}$ and $\tilde{E}_0 N = (\log 9)^2 \cong 4.83$.

For purposes of comparison, it is interesting to note, in this example, that the optimal fixed sample size test with error probabilities $\alpha_0 = \alpha_1 = 0.1$ requires a sample of size $n \cong 6.55$. (Of course, n can't really be a fraction, but 6.55 corresponds, in some sense, to how much sample information is needed to achieve the desired error probabilities.) Thus the fixed sample size procedure requires, on the average, almost twice as many observations as does the SPRT. (Actually, as will be discussed in the next subsection, $\tilde{E}_{\theta_i} N$ is an underestimate of $E_{\theta_i} N$. The true value of $E_{\theta_i} N$ in this example is still, however, considerably smaller than 6.55.)

In certain situations the Wald approximations to $\beta(\theta)$ and $E_\theta N$ are exact. This is the case when S_N must hit a or b exactly, i.e., there is no "overshoot." Such a situation occurs when the Z_i can assume only the values $-v, 0,$ and v, for some constant v. If a and b are then chosen to be integral multiples of v, it is clear that S_N must hit a or b exactly. (There is no sense in choosing a or b to be other than integral multiples of v, since S_n can only move in steps of size $\pm v$.) An example follows.

EXAMPLE 15. Assume that $X_1, X_2, \ldots$ is a sequential sample from a $\mathscr{B}(1, \theta)$ distribution, and that it is desired to test $H_0 : \theta = \theta_0$ versus $H_1 : \theta = 1 - \theta_0$, where $0 < \theta_0 < \frac{1}{2}$. Clearly

$$Z_i = \log \frac{f(X_i | 1 - \theta_0)}{f(X_i | \theta_0)}$$

$$= \log \frac{(1 - \theta_0)^{X_i} (\theta_0)^{(1 - X_i)}}{(\theta_0)^{X_i} (1 - \theta_0)^{(1 - X_i)}} = (2X_i - 1) \log(\theta_0^{-1} - 1).$$

Setting $v = \log(\theta_0^{-1} - 1)$ and noting that X_i is zero or one, it follows that Z_i is either $-v$ or v. Hence, choosing $a = -jv$ and $b = kv$, where j and k are positive integers, the Wald approximations to $\beta(\theta)$ and $E_\theta N$ will be exact. The calculational details are left as an exercise.

It should be noted that exact SPRTs can sometimes be obtained by methods other than that above. See Ghosh (1970) for a discussion of this.

7.5.3 Accuracy of the Wald Approximations

The accuracy of the Wald approximations to $\beta(\theta)$ and $E_\theta N$ is, to a large extent, determined by the amount that S_N will tend to "overshoot" a or b. If this overshoot tends to be small, the approximations will be quite good. If the overshoot tends to be large, the approximations can be bad. (In such a situation, the approximations can sometimes be improved by using the

Table 7.3 Accuracy of the Wald Approximations

| θ | \multicolumn{4}{c}{$a = -2.5, b = 7.5$} | \multicolumn{4}{c}{$a = -5.0, b = 5.0$} |
	$\beta(\theta)$	$\tilde{\beta}(\theta)$	$E_\theta N$	$\tilde{E}_\theta N$	$\beta(\theta)$	$\tilde{\beta}(\theta)$	$E_\theta N$	$\tilde{E}_\theta N$
-1.000	0.0000	0.0000	3.37	2.50	0.0000	0.0000	5.87	5.00
-0.750	0.0000	0.0000	4.39	3.33	0.0003	0.0005	7.72	6.66
-0.500	0.0003	0.0005	6.43	4.99	0.0038	0.0067	11.35	9.87
-0.250	0.0139	0.0169	11.97	9.32	0.0579	0.0759	20.01	16.96
-0.125	0.0759	0.0776	18.14	13.79	0.1985	0.2227	27.18	22.18
0.000	0.2761	0.2500	25.17	18.75	0.5000	0.5000	31.42	25.00
0.125	0.5724	0.5063	26.71	20.50	0.8015	0.7773	27.18	22.18
0.250	0.7887	0.7183	23.16	18.73	0.9421	0.9241	20.01	16.96
0.500	0.9540	0.9180	15.41	13.36	0.9962	0.9933	11.35	9.87
0.750	0.9901	0.9765	10.91	9.69	0.9997	0.9995	7.72	6.66
1.000	0.9978	0.9933	8.35	7.43	1.0000	1.0000	5.87	5.00

Z_i^* (see (7.61)) in place of the Z_i, since the overshoot is then reduced when $|Z_i| > b - a$.) As a typical intermediate case, consider the situation of Example 14, in which the X_i are $\mathcal{N}(0, 1)$ and it is desired to test $H_0 : \theta = -\frac{1}{2}$ versus $H_1 : \theta = \frac{1}{2}$. In Table 7.3, the true values of $\beta(\theta)$ and $E_\theta N$ and the corresponding Wald approximations, $\tilde{\beta}(\theta)$ and $\tilde{E}_\theta N$, are given for two different SPRTs. (This table, in modified form, appeared in Ghosh (1970).)

An examination of the table shows that $\tilde{\beta}(\theta)$ and $\tilde{E}_\theta N$ are reasonably close to $\beta(\theta)$ and $E_\theta N$, and that $\tilde{E}_\theta N$ is consistently an underestimate of $E_\theta N$. Note also that $\tilde{\beta}(\theta) > \beta(\theta)$ for $\theta \leq -\frac{1}{2}$, while $\tilde{\alpha}(\theta) = 1 - \tilde{\beta}(\theta) < 1 - \beta(\theta) = \alpha(\theta)$ for $\theta \geq \frac{1}{2}$. This indicates that the Wald approximations tend to *overestimate* the true error probabilities. This is good from a conservative classical viewpoint, in that, if an SPRT is chosen using the Wald approximations so as to attain certain specified error probabilities, then the true error probabilities of the SPRT are probably smaller. The following theorem gives a theoretical justification for some of these comments.

Theorem 12. *Assume that the conditions of Lemma 2 are satisfied, and consider the SPRT $d^{A, B}$. The following inequalities then hold:*

$$A \geq A^* = \frac{\alpha_1}{1 - \alpha_0} \quad \text{and} \quad B \leq B^* = \frac{1 - \alpha_1}{\alpha_0}; \tag{7.76}$$

$$E_{\theta_0} N \geq (\mu_{\theta_0})^{-1}\left[(1 - \alpha_0)\log\left(\frac{\alpha_1}{1 - \alpha_0}\right) + \alpha_0 \log\left(\frac{1 - \alpha_1}{\alpha_0}\right)\right],$$

and   (7.77)

$$E_{\theta_1} N \geq (\mu_{\theta_1})^{-1}\left[\alpha_1 \log\left(\frac{\alpha_1}{1 - \alpha_0}\right) + (1 - \alpha_1)\log\left(\frac{1 - \alpha_1}{\alpha_0}\right)\right].$$

PROOF. For simplicity, we will deal only with the continuous case. Note that since $P_{\theta_j}(|Z_i| < \infty) = 1$ for $j = 0, 1$, the densities $f(x_i|\theta_0)$ and $f(x_i|\theta_1)$ must be mutually absolutely continuous. Clearly

$$\alpha_1 = P_{\theta_1}(L_N \leq A) = \sum_{n=1}^{\infty} \int \cdots \int_{B_n} \prod_{i=1}^{n} [f(x_i|\theta_1)dx_i], \qquad (7.78)$$

where $B_n = \{N = n\} \cap \{\mathbf{x}^n: L_n \leq A\}$. Now $L_n \leq A$ can be rewritten

$$\prod_{i=1}^{n} f(x_i|\theta_1) \leq A \prod_{i=1}^{n} f(x_i|\theta_0),$$

which, when used in (7.78), gives

$$\alpha_1 \leq \sum_{n=1}^{\infty} \int \cdots \int_{B_n} A \prod_{i=1}^{n} [f(x_i|\theta_0)dx_i] = AP_{\theta_0}(L_N \leq A).$$

Using (7.58), it follows that

$$\alpha_1 \leq A(1 - P_{\theta_0}(L_N \geq B)) = A(1 - \alpha_0),$$

proving the first inequality in (7.76). The second inequality follows similarly.

To prove the first inequality in (7.77), note that

$$E_{\theta_0}[S_N] = E_{\theta_0}[S_N|S_N \leq a]P_{\theta_0}(S_N \leq a) + E_{\theta_0}[S_N|S_N \geq b]P_{\theta_0}(S_N \geq b)$$

$$= E_{\theta_0}[S_N|S_N \leq a](1 - \alpha_0) + E_{\theta_0}[S_N|S_N \geq b]\alpha_0. \qquad (7.79)$$

Jensen's inequality (applied to $(-\log)$) gives

$$E_{\theta_0}[S_N|S_N \leq a] = E_{\theta_0}[\log L_N|S_N \leq a]$$

$$\leq \log E_{\theta_0}[L_N|S_N \leq a]$$

$$= \log\left[\{P_{\theta_0}(S_N \leq a)\}^{-1}\left\{\sum_{n=1}^{\infty} \int \cdots \int_{B_n} L_n \prod_{i=1}^{n} [f(x_i|\theta_0)dx_i]\right\}\right]$$

$$= \log\left[\{P_{\theta_0}(S_N \leq a)\}^{-1}\left\{\sum_{n=1}^{\infty} \int \cdots \int_{B_n} \prod_{i=1}^{n} [f(x_i|\theta_1)dx_i]\right\}\right]$$

$$= \log\left[\frac{P_{\theta_1}(S_N \leq a)}{P_{\theta_0}(S_N \leq a)}\right] = \log\left(\frac{\alpha_1}{1 - \alpha_0}\right). \qquad (7.80)$$

Similarly, it can be shown that

$$E_{\theta_0}[S_N|S_N \geq b] \leq \log\left(\frac{1 - \alpha_1}{\alpha_0}\right). \qquad (7.81)$$

Note also that

$$\mu_{\theta_0} = E_{\theta_0}[Z_i] = E_{\theta_0}\left[\log\left\{\frac{f(X_i|\theta_1)}{f(X_i|\theta_0)}\right\}\right]$$

$$< \log \int_{\mathscr{X}_i} \frac{f(x_i|\theta_1)}{f(x_i|\theta_0)} f(x_i|\theta_0)dx_i$$

$$= \log 1 = 0, \tag{7.82}$$

the strict inequality following from the strict convexity of $(-\log)$ and the fact that $P_{\theta_0}(Z_i = 0) < 1$. Finally, Theorem 11 (i) implies that

$$E_{\theta_0}[N] = \frac{E_{\theta_0}[S_N]}{\mu_{\theta_0}},$$

which together with (7.79), (7.80), (7.81), and (7.82) gives the desired result. The last inequality in (7.77) can be established by similar reasoning. $\square$

In interpreting this theorem, it is important to keep track of several different quantities. Imagine that we are in the standard situation (at least standard classically) of specifying desired α_0 and α_1. Let A and B denote the true stopping boundaries which give these error probabilities, let $A^* = \alpha_1/(1 - \alpha_0)$ and $B^* = (1 - \alpha_1)/\alpha_0$ be the Wald approximations to these stopping boundaries, and let α_0^* and α_1^* denote the error probabilities of $\mathbf{d}^{A^*, B^*}$. The inequalities in (7.76) show that $\mathbf{d}^{A^*, B^*}$ has more "distant" stopping boundaries than $\mathbf{d}^{A, B}$, and this will usually mean that α_0^* and α_1^* are smaller than α_0 and α_1. (This need not always be true, however. If it is absolutely necessary to guarantee error probabilities α_0 and α_1, one can use, as stopping boundaries, $A^{**} = \alpha_1$ and $B^{**} = 1/\alpha_0$. The proof that these stopping boundaries result in error probabilities $\alpha_0^{**} \le \alpha_0$ and $\alpha_1^{**} \le \alpha_1$ will be left as an exercise.)

Consider next the stopping times N and N^* of $\mathbf{d}^{A, B}$ and $\mathbf{d}^{A^*, B^*}$. Clearly $N \le N^*$. (It takes S_n at least as long to get to A^* or B^* as to A or B.) Hence the use of the approximations A^* and B^*, while usually lowering the error probabilities, will cause an increase in the stopping time. Studies in Wald (1947) indicate, however, that this increase is relatively modest.

Note that the question of how N^* differs from N is not the same as the question discussed earlier concerning how close the Wald approximation $\tilde{E}_\theta N$ is to $E_\theta N$. The inequalities in (7.77) are interesting in this regard, because the right-hand sides are $\tilde{E}_{\theta_i} N^*$ (the Wald approximations to the expected stopping times for the procedure $\mathbf{d}^{A^*, B^*}$). Combining these inequalities with the fact that $N \le N^*$, we have (for $i = 0, 1$)

$$\tilde{E}_{\theta_i} N^* \le E_{\theta_i} N \le E_{\theta_i} N^*.$$

This proves that the Wald approximations to $E_{\theta_i} N^*$ ($i = 0, 1$) are, indeed, underestimates.

7.5.4 Bayes Risk and Admissibility

Consider, once again, the Bayesian situation discussed in Subsection 7.5.1. The problem of finding a Bayes procedure was reduced to that of finding the SPRT which minimizes (7.57). An appealing simplification is to replace $\alpha_0, \alpha_1, E_{\theta_0} N$, and $E_{\theta_1} N$ in (7.57) by their Wald approximations. The approximate Bayes risk of $\mathbf{d}^{A, B}$ is then (using (7.74))

$$r(\pi, \mathbf{d}^{A, B}) \cong \pi_0 \left\{ \frac{(1 - A)}{(B - A)} K_1 + c(\mu_{\theta_0})^{-1} \left[(\log A) + \left(\log \frac{B}{A} \right) \frac{(1 - A)}{(B - A)} \right] \right\}$$
$$+ \pi_1 \left\{ \frac{A(B - 1)}{(B - A)} K_0 + c(\mu_{\theta_1})^{-1} \left[(\log A) + \left(\log \frac{B}{A} \right) \frac{B(1 - A)}{(B - A)} \right] \right\}.$$
$$(7.83)$$

This is numerically easy to minimize over A and B.

An even simpler approximation can be found when c is very small. For small c, it is likely that a large number of observations will be desired, which in turn implies that the optimal A must be small and the optimal B large. Assuming this in (7.83) gives

$$r(\pi, \mathbf{d}^{A, B}) \cong \pi_0 \left[\frac{1}{B} K_1 + c(\mu_{\theta_0})^{-1} \log A \right] + \pi_1 [A K_0 + c(\mu_{\theta_1})^{-1} \log B].$$

Differentiating with respect to A and B and setting equal to zero gives "optimal" A and B of

$$A = \frac{-c\pi_0}{\mu_{\theta_0} K_0 \pi_1} \quad \text{and} \quad B = \frac{\pi_0 K_1 \mu_{\theta_1}}{c\pi_1}. \qquad (7.84)$$

Of course, these solutions are subject to the inaccuracies of the Wald approximations.

Being as Bayes procedures are generally admissible, one would expect SPRTs to be admissible. This is true in the rather strong sense that, among all sequential procedures with fixed error probabilities α_0 and α_1, the SPRT with these error probabilities simultaneously minimizes both $E_{\theta_0} N$ and $E_{\theta_1} N$. This result was established by Wald and Wolfowitz (1948). We formally state the theorem below and indicate the idea of the proof. For convenience, let $\alpha_i(\mathbf{d})$ and $N(\mathbf{d})$ denote the error probabilities and stopping time of a procedure $\mathbf{d}$.

Theorem 13. Let $\mathbf{d}^{A, B}$ be an SPRT, and assume that $\mathbf{d}$ is any other sequential procedure for which

$$\alpha_0(\mathbf{d}) \leq \alpha_0(\mathbf{d}^{A, B}) \quad \text{and} \quad \alpha_1(\mathbf{d}) \leq \alpha_1(\mathbf{d}^{A, B}).$$

Then

$$E_{\theta_0}[N(\mathbf{d}^{A, B})] \leq E_{\theta_0}[N(\mathbf{d})] \quad \text{and} \quad E_{\theta_1}[N(\mathbf{d}^{A, B})] \leq E_{\theta_1}[N(\mathbf{d})].$$

PROOF. The proof is based on the fact that, for any $0 < \pi_0 < 1$, there exist positive constants c, K_0, and K_1 such that the given $\mathbf{d}^{A, B}$ is a Bayes procedure for the sequential problem with these constants. (See Ferguson (1967) for a proof of this.) It follows that $r(\pi, \mathbf{d}^{A, B}) \leq r(\pi, \mathbf{d})$ for any sequential procedure $\mathbf{d}$, or, equivalently,

$$\pi_0 K_1[\alpha_0(\mathbf{d}^{A, B}) - \alpha_0(\mathbf{d})] + (1 - \pi_0)K_0[\alpha_1(\mathbf{d}^{A, B}) - \alpha_1(\mathbf{d})]$$
$$\leq \pi_0 c\{E_{\theta_0}[N(\mathbf{d})] - E_{\theta_0}[N(\mathbf{d}^{A, B})]\}$$
$$+ (1 - \pi_0)c\{E_{\theta_1}[N(\mathbf{d})] - E_{\theta_1}[N(\mathbf{d}^{A, B})]\}.$$

By assumption, the left-hand side of this inequality is nonnegative, and so the right-hand side must be nonnegative. Dividing by c and letting $\pi_0 \to 0$ and $\pi_0 \to 1$ gives the desired result. $\qquad\square$

7.5.5 Other Uses of the SPRT

As mentioned at the beginning of Subsection 7.5.2, SPRTs are frequently used for testing problems which are more complicated than just testing simple against simple hypotheses. The most common such use is in testing $H_0: \theta \leq \theta_0$ versus $H_1: \theta \geq \theta_1(\theta_0 < \theta_1)$, where one is supposedly indifferent when $\theta_0 < \theta < \theta_1$. It is fairly natural, in this situation, to pretend that the problem is that of testing $H_0: \theta = \theta_0$ versus $H_1: \theta = \theta_1$, and to use the relevant SPRT. It can indeed be shown that, if the X_i have a density with monotone likelihood ratio in θ (see Section 8.3), then the SPRT with error probabilities α_0 and α_1 gives error probabilities $\alpha_0(\theta) \leq \alpha_0$ for $\theta < \theta_0$ and $\alpha_1(\theta) \leq \alpha_1$ for $\theta > \theta_1$. In a classical sense, therefore, an SPRT is very reasonable in this situation (though probably not optimal).

In the above situation, one could attempt to find the optimal SPRT from a Bayesian viewpoint. More generally, in any testing situation for which the true Bayes procedure is too hard to calculate, it may be reasonable to simply find the best SPRT (if the form of the SPRT seems natural for the problem). Thus, if it is desired to test $H_0: \theta \in \Theta_0$ versus $H_1: \theta \in \Theta_1$ (where $\theta_0 < \theta_1$ for $\theta_0 \in \Theta_0$ and $\theta_1 \in \Theta_1$) under decision loss $L(\theta, a_i)(i = 0, 1)$ for a wrong decision and zero loss for a correct decision, then the Bayes risk of the SPRT $\mathbf{d}^{A, B}$ will be

$$r(\pi, \mathbf{d}^{A, B}) = \int_{\Theta_0} L(\theta, a_1)\beta(\theta)dF^\pi(\theta)$$

$$+ \int_{\Theta_1} L(\theta, a_0)[1 - \beta(\theta)]dF^\pi(\theta) + cE^\pi[E_\theta N].$$

This can be numerically minimized over A and B (perhaps using the Wald approximations to $\beta(\theta)$ and $E_\theta N$), giving the optimal SPRT. Note that one must choose parameter values $\theta_0 \in \Theta_0$ and $\theta_1 \in \Theta_1$ from which to develop the SPRT. Sometimes there is a natural choice, as when testing $H_0: \theta \leq \theta_0$

versus $H_1 : \theta \geq \theta_1$. In some situations, the choice does not affect the form of the SPRT. In Example 14, for instance, if it were desired to test $H_0 : \theta \leq 0$ versus $H_1 : \theta > 0$, any symmetric choice of θ_0 and θ_1 (i.e., $\theta_0 = -\theta_1$) would result in an SPRT of the same form. It may also be possible, in some situations, to actually minimize $r(\pi, \mathbf{d}^{A, B})$ over the choice of θ_0 and θ_1, as well as over A and B.

There is another quite interesting Bayesian adaption of the SPRT for complicated testing situations such as discussed above. The idea is to use an SPRT with L_n replaced by the posterior odds ratio of Θ_1 to Θ_0, which (see Subsection 4.3.3) can be written

$$O_n = \frac{\int_{\Theta_1} [\prod_{i=1}^n f(x_i | \theta)] dF^\pi(\theta)}{\int_{\Theta_0} [\prod_{i=1}^n f(x_i | \theta)] dF^\pi(\theta)}.$$

(Note that if $\Theta_1 = \{\theta_1\}$ and $\Theta_0 = \{\theta_0\}$, then $O_n = (\pi_1/\pi_0) L_n$.) The resulting procedure can be written as follows:

if $O_n \leq A$,   stop sampling and decide a_0;

if $O_n \geq B$,   stop sampling and decide a_1;   (7.85)

if $A < O_n < B$,   take another observation.

(Such a procedure could be called a sequential posterior odds test, or a SPOT.) Unfortunately, working with such a procedure is considerably harder than working with an SPRT, since log O_n is not a sum of i.i.d. random variables. Nevertheless, the numerical minimization of the Bayes risk of such a test over A and B is feasible.

As one final flight of fancy, we mention that it may work well to replace O_n above by the ratio of the posterior expected loss of a_0 to the posterior expected loss of a_1 (resulting in a SPELT). Such a procedure incorporates the loss in an intuitively reasonable fashion. It should be noted that both the SPOT and the SPELT are related to modifications of the SPRT (using "weight functions") suggested by Wald (1947).

7.6 Minimax Sequential Procedures

A *minimax sequential procedure*, as one would expect, is a procedure which minimizes $\sup_\theta R(\theta, \mathbf{d})$ among all proper sequential procedures. (As in the nonsequential situation, it may be necessary to consider randomized procedures. We will avoid this issue, however.) The same techniques used in Chapter 5 to find minimax rules, particularly those based on Theorems 17 and 18 of that chapter, are valid and useful in the sequential setting also.

EXAMPLE 16. Assume that $X_1, X_2, \ldots$ is a sequential sample from a $\mathcal{N}(\theta, \sigma^2)$ distribution, σ^2 known, and that it is desired to estimate θ under loss $L(\theta, a, n) = (\theta - a)^2 + cn$. It was shown in Example 5 that the Bayes procedure for

π_m, the $\mathcal{N}(0, m)$ prior, is to take a sample of size n_m, where n_m is the integer n which minimizes $\sigma^2 m/(\sigma^2 + nm) + nc$, and then use the Bayes estimator. The Bayes risk of the procedure was shown to be

$$r(\pi_m) = \frac{\sigma^2 m}{\sigma^2 + mn_m} + n_m c. \tag{7.86}$$

Consider now the procedure $\mathbf{d}^*$, which takes a sample of size n^*, where n^* is the integer n which minimizes $\sigma^2/n + nc$, and then estimates θ by $\bar{x}_{n^*}$. Clearly

$$R(\theta, \mathbf{d}^*) = E_\theta[(\theta - \bar{X}_{n^*})^2 + n^*c] = \frac{\sigma^2}{n^*} + n^*c.$$

Now it is easy to see that, for large enough m, n_m cannot be zero. Hence (7.86) implies that

$$\lim_{m \to \infty} r(\pi_m) = \frac{\sigma^2}{\lim_{m \to \infty} n_m} + c \lim_{m \to \infty} n_m \geq \frac{\sigma^2}{n^*} + n^*c = R(\theta, \mathbf{d}^*).$$

It thus follows from the analog of Theorem 18 of Chapter 5 that $\mathbf{d}^*$ is minimax.

In estimation problems for which there is an equalizer (constant risk) decision rule, it frequently happens (as above) that the minimax sequential procedure is simply the optimal fixed sample size minimax decision rule. (This is demonstrated in considerable generality in Kiefer (1957), through invariance arguments.) Other than in such problems, however, finding minimax sequential procedures is quite hard. For example, to find the minimax sequential test of a simple null hypothesis versus a simple alternative, the Bayes SPRT which is an equalizer procedure must be found. In other words, one must find $0 \leq \pi_0 \leq 1$ ($\pi_0 = \pi(\theta_0)$) for which the resulting Bayes SPRT, $\mathbf{d}^{A, B}$, satisfies $R(\theta_0, \mathbf{d}^{A, B}) = R(\theta_1, \mathbf{d}^{A, B})$. This is usually fairly difficult. One of the few situations in which a minimax procedure that is actually sequential (i.e., not fixed sample size) can be explicitly calculated is given in Exercise 58.

7.7 Discussion of Sequential Analysis

By now it should be clear that sequential analysis is hard. Although general methods of solving sequential problems are known, only in a few simple situations are the methods easily manageable. Hopefully enough insight has been gained, however, to enable the reader to find reasonable approximate solutions for other, more complicated, situations. We conclude the chapter with a discussion of several issues involving Bayesian philosophy and the loss function.

7.7.1 Bayesian Philosophy

It is possible to construct natural frameworks involving sequential analysis in which only the Bayesian approach is rational. The argument is essentially the same as that sketched in Chapter 4, and will not be repeated.

In the same vein, it was argued earlier in the book that one should adopt a post-experimental (or posterior), rather than a pre-experimental, viewpoint. For Bayesian sequential analysis, however, we have seen that the two viewpoints can't really be separated. One must always compare the posterior Bayes risk of an immediate decision (a post-experimental quantity) with the expected Bayes risk of continuing sampling (a pre-experimental quantity) in order to decide when to stop sampling. This approach is post-experimental in spirit, however, since at each stage one uses the current posterior as the basis for comparing the present with the future. The presentation of the sequential probability ratio test tended to be classically (pre-experimentally) oriented, but the SPRT was shown to correspond to a true Bayes procedure. As usual, we would recommend actually choosing an SPRT according to Bayesian criteria.

A more philosophical issue of interest is that of the applicability of the likelihood principle. Several seemingly potent criticisms of the likelihood principle have been raised through consideration of sequential problems. The first criticism is that the likelihood function does not always suffice for determining the stopping rule. This is illustrated in the following example.

EXAMPLE 17. Imagine that each observation is of the form $X_i = (Z_i, Y_i)$. Here Y_i is 1 or 0, where $P(Y_{i+1} = 1 \mid Y_i = 1) = 1 - P(Y_{i+1} = 0 \mid Y_i = 1) = \frac{1}{2}$ and $P(Y_{i+1} = 0 \mid Y_i = 0) = 1$. (Define $Y_0 = 1$.) When $Y_i = 1$, Z_{i+1} will be independent of the previous Z_i and will have a $\mathcal{N}(\theta, 1)$ distribution. When $Y_i = 0$, on the other hand, Z_{i+1} will be zero. (This could correspond to a situation in which a piece of equipment is used to obtain the important observations Z_i, and Y_i tells whether the equipment will work the next time ($Y_i = 1$) or has irreparably broken ($Y_i = 0$).)

Imagine now that $x_1, \ldots, x_n$ have been observed, and that $y_i = 1$ for $i \leq n - 1$. The likelihood function for θ is then $\mathcal{N}(\bar{z}_n, 1/n)$ (since all the z_i are valid observations). The likelihood principle thus says that all decisions or inferences concerning θ should involve the data only through this likelihood function. It is obvious, however, that knowledge of y_n may be crucial in deciding what to do. If $y_n = 1$, it may be desirable to take another observation. If $y_n = 0$, on the other hand, taking another observation would be a waste of time (the equipment is broken), so an immediate decision should be made.

The reasoning in the above example is absolutely correct. The likelihood function may not always suffice for determining the stopping rule. This, however, is not a violation of the likelihood principle, but merely another example of a limitation that has already been discussed. It was pointed out in Chapter 1 that the likelihood principle applies only to the making of decisions or inferences *after* the data has been collected. When planning the experiment (here, deciding whether or not to take another observation), other sample information may be relevant. Indeed for Bayesian sequential analysis it will virtually always be necessary to at least consider the sample space $\mathscr{X}$ since in computing the expected Bayes risk of continuing sampling it is necessary to average over all possible future values of x.

The above limitation of the likelihood principle is also, incidentally, a limitation of the classical idea of sufficiency. In Example 17, a "sufficient sequence" of statistics for θ is the sequence of sample means of the valid (i.e., nonzero) observations z_i, and yet this sufficient sequence does not suffice for determining the stopping rule. Conditions can be given, however, under which only sequential procedures which are functions of such a sufficient sequence need be considered. (See Bahadur (1954) for a general development of these conditions.) The conditions are satisfied, in particular, by independent observations from a distribution in the exponential family.

A second frequently voiced criticism of the likelihood principle is based on the widespread belief that the final decision should depend on the stopping rule. A believer in the likelihood principle would say, of course, that the decision or inference made should be the same regardless of why sampling was stopped. The intuitive objection to this is that an experimenter, by stopping at a favorable time, could bias the results. Consider the following example.

EXAMPLE 18. Assume that $X_1, X_2, \ldots$ is a sequential sample from a $\mathscr{B}(1, \theta)$ distribution, and that it is desired to estimate θ under loss $L(\theta, a, n) = (\theta - a)^2 + nc$. Imagine that a believer in the likelihood principle decides to use a Bayesian approach with the noninformative prior $\pi(\theta) = \theta^{-1}(1 - \theta)^{-1}$. After observing $x_1, \ldots, x_n$, it follows that he will estimate θ by $\bar{x}_n$, regardless of the stopping rule used.

A classical statistician might disagree with this analysis, arguing that, among other things, a very biased stopping rule could have been used. For example, the stopping rule could have been

τ: stop sampling if $X_1 = 1$, and otherwise after observing X_2.

For this stopping rule,

$$E_{\theta, \tau}[\bar{X}_N] = \theta(1) + (1 - \theta)[\tfrac{1}{2}\theta + 0(1 - \theta)] = \theta + \tfrac{1}{2}\theta(1 - \theta).$$

The Bayes decision rule would thus be biased, in a classical sense, by the amount $\tfrac{1}{2}\theta(1 - \theta)$. The point here is that the experimenter might have wanted θ to appear large, and so purposely used a stopping rule, such as τ, for which $\bar{X}_N$ would tend to overestimate θ.

The classical position in the above example is correct, in the sense that classical criteria (such as bias and error probabilities) are very dependent on the stopping rule. We have seen, however, that classical criteria are suspect, especially in those situations in which they seem to contradict the likelihood principle or Bayesian analysis. The discussion in Subsection 1.6.2, particularly that concerning Example 12, is very relevant here, and could perhaps profitably be reread.

It is possible to turn the above criticism around, and argue that it is actually the classical statistician who is susceptible to fraudulent manipulation of the stopping rule. Consider Example 10 in Subsection 4.3.3, for instance. This example concerned the testing of a point null hypothesis $H_0: \theta = \theta_0$. It was pointed out that, for any $\alpha > 0$, the test statistic would be in the rejection region of a classical size α fixed sample size test, for some large sample size n, *even if H_0 were true*. Thus an experimenter who wanted to reject H_0 could choose any very small α and continue sampling until the test statistic rejects at that level. This would look very convincing classically, unless the experimenter was very carefully queried about his stopping rule. To a Bayesian, of course, the analysis in this problem is straightforward and does not depend on the stopping rule. The Bayesian simply looks at the available evidence, not caring how it was obtained, and makes a decision on the basis of that evidence. As the discussion of this example in Chapter 4 makes clear, the Bayesian will not be overly swayed by the test statistic being in the classical rejection region for a very large n, and hence will not be done in by the chicanery of the experimenter.

In a very strict sense, one ·often wonders how the classical statistician can do any analysis whatsover. The problem is that the point at which sampling or experimentation is stopped is often chosen subjectively, depending upon how the data looks so far and possibly upon such things as how late the experimenter is for dinner. A classical statistician cannot write down measures of initial precision for results so obtained. He must know the exact stopping rule to do so. In the same vein, consider the following example.

EXAMPLE 19. A poll is to be conducted to determine the attitude of voters towards a new tax proposal. It is desired to determine whether the majority of voters favor or oppose the proposal. An interviewer is sent out into the streets to ask the opinion of 1000 people (not a particularly good sampling plan, but brilliant compared to the next decision). Unfortunately, after asking only 200 people, all of whom are opposed to the tax proposal, it begins to rain and the interviewer is forced to return. Well, being run by classical statisticians, the polling organization sends the interviewer out the next day to obtain the other 800 opinions, the reasoning being that a valid classical analysis can not be performed unless the originally planned stopping rule is used. This is obviously silly. Of course, in reality, even the most adamant classicist would violate his principles and stop after the 200 "oppose" responses. To provide a classical evaluation of the situation, however, he would have to lie and pretend that some other stopping rule had been used.

7.7.2 The Loss Function

Loss functions more general than that considered in this chapter are some-times needed. In particular, it is sometimes important to allow the loss to depend on the observations. (An extreme example of this occurred in early tests of rocket propellant, in which a very bad batch of fuel would cause the testing equipment to blow up. Hence the observation (fuel quality) could have a significant effect on the experimental cost.) It can be checked, however, that most of the methods developed in this chapter, particularly the Bayesian techniques of Section 7.4, adapt, with obvious modifications, to this situation.

A more serious and difficult concern is the problem of observational cost. In Section 7.1 we introduced the general loss $L(\theta, a, n, s)$, where s denotes some prescribed method of sampling. Subsequently, however, only fixed sample size and one-at-a-time sequential sampling were considered. It may well be optimal to instead use a *sequential batch* plan, in which, say, an initial group of n_1 observations is taken, based on which a second group of size n_2 is taken, etc.. This will often be cheaper than a straight sequential sampling plan, because it is often more efficient to take a number of observations at the same time than to take them separately. This will especially be true if a fairly difficult analysis is needed at each stage to decide if sampling should be continued (and if the cost of the statistician is not negligible). Because of this difficulty, one-observation-at-a-time sequential analysis can only be said to be nearly optimal when the observations are very expen-sive (so that minimizing the total number of observations taken is para-mount), or when observations present themselves one at a time (say, products coming off a production line) with sufficient time between observations to conduct whatever analysis is needed.

Actually, even for the general loss $L(\theta, a, n, s)$, one could theoretically use the techniques of Section 7.4 to calculate the optimal procedure. In cal-culating the j-step look ahead Bayes risks, $r_j(\pi^n, n)$, however, one is now forced to consider all possible ways of selecting batches (of observations) of various sizes out of j additional observations. The calculational complexity quickly becomes ludicrous.

One attractive sequential batch sampling plan (which can often be mathematically handled) is to choose, at each stage, a batch of a fixed size m. (When $m = 1$, this corresponds to the usual sequential sampling.) The batches can then be considered to themselves be observations in a new sequential problem, and the techniques of this chapter can be brought to bear to find the best procedure, $\mathbf{d}_m$, in this new problem. By minimizing, in some sense, over m, the best fixed-batch-size sequential sampling plan can be found. An example follows.

EXAMPLE 20. Assume that a sequential sample $X_1, X_2, \ldots$ of $\mathcal{N}(\theta, 1)$ random variables is available, and that it is desired to test $H_0: \theta = -\frac{1}{2}$ versus

$H_1: \theta = \frac{1}{2}$ under "0–1" decision loss. The cost of taking a batch of observations of size m is C_m.

Note that

$$\overline{X}_i^m = \frac{1}{m} \sum_{j=(i-1)m+1}^{im} X_j$$

is a sufficient statistic for θ, based on $X_{(i-1)m+1}, \ldots, X_{im}$. It can also be shown that any stopping rule need only depend on $X_{(i-1)m+1}, \ldots, X_{im}$ through $\overline{X}_i^m$. It follows that if batches of size m are to be taken sequentially, one need only consider $\overline{X}_1^m, \overline{X}_2^m, \ldots$, which are i.i.d. $\mathcal{N}(\theta, 1/m)$. The problem thus reduces to an ordinary sequential problem with observations $\overline{X}_1^m, \overline{X}_2^m, \ldots$, decision loss $(\theta - a)^2$, and observational cost C_m. This can be dealt with as in Section 7.5. Suppose, for example, that a Bayesian approach is taken, and that $\mathbf{d}_m$ is the Bayes SPRT, with Bayes risk $r(\pi, \mathbf{d}_m)$. This Bayes risk can then be minimized over m, to obtain the optimal batch size.

Exercises

In all of the exercises, assume that the utility function is linear, so that the overall loss is the sum of the decision loss and the sampling cost. In problems involving a test between two hypotheses H_0 and H_1, let a_i denote accepting H_i ($i = 0, 1$).

Section 7.2

1. Assume that $X_1, X_2, \ldots$ is a sequential sample from a $\mathcal{N}(\theta, 1)$ density, that it is desired to estimate θ under squared-error decision loss, and that the cost of a fixed sample of size n is $C(n) = n(0.01)$. If θ has a $\mathcal{N}(1, 4)$ prior distribution, find the optimal fixed sample size rule and its Bayes risk.

2. Do the preceding exercise for
   (a) $C(n) = [\log(1 + n)](0.01)$.
   (b) $C(n) = n^{1/2}(0.01)$.

3. Consider the situation of Exercise 1, but assume that the decision loss is $L(\theta, a) = |\theta - a|$. Find the optimal fixed sample size rule and its Bayes risk.

4. Assume that $X_1, X_2, \ldots$ is a sequential sample from a $\mathcal{B}(1, \theta)$ density, that it is desired to estimate θ under decision loss $L(\theta, a) = (\theta - a)^2/\theta(1 - \theta)$, and that the cost of a fixed sample of size n is $C(n) = nc$. If θ has a $\mathcal{U}(0, 1)$ prior density, approximate the optimal fixed sample size.

5. Assume that $X_1, X_2, \ldots$ is a sequential sample from a $\mathcal{P}(\theta)$ density, that it is desired to estimate θ under decision loss $L(\theta, a) = (\theta - a)^2/\theta$, and that the cost of a fixed sample of size n is $C(n) = nc$. If θ has a $\mathcal{G}(\alpha, \beta)$ prior density, approximate the optimal fixed sample size.

6. Assume that $X_1, X_2, \ldots$ is a sequential sample from a $\mathcal{G}(1, \theta)$ density, that it is desired to estimate θ under decision loss $L(\theta, a) = (\theta - a)^2/\theta^2$, and that the cost of a fixed sample of size n is $C(n) = nc$. If θ has an $\mathcal{IG}(\alpha, \beta)$ prior density, approximate the optimal fixed sample size.

7. Assume that $X_1, X_2, \ldots$ is a sequential sample from a $\mathcal{G}e((1 + \theta)^{-1})$ density, that it is desired to estimate θ under decision loss $L(\theta, a) = (\theta - a)^2/\theta(1 - \theta)$, and that the cost of a fixed sample of size n is $C(n) = nc$. If θ has the prior density

$$\pi(\theta | \alpha, \beta) = \frac{\Gamma(\alpha + \beta)}{\Gamma(\alpha)\Gamma(\beta)} \theta^{\alpha - 1}(\theta + 1)^{-(\alpha + \beta)} I_{(0, \infty)}(\theta),$$

approximate the optimal fixed sample size.

8. Assume that $X_1, X_2, \ldots$ is a sequential sample from a $\mathcal{N}(\theta, 1)$ density, and that it is desired to test $H_0 : \theta = 0$ versus $H_1 : \theta = 1$. The decision loss is $L(\theta_0, a_0) = L(\theta_1, a_1) = 0$, $L(\theta_0, a_1) = 1$, and $L(\theta_1, a_0) = 2$. The cost of a fixed sample of size n is $C(n) = n(0.1)$. If the prior probabilities of θ_0 and θ_1 are $\frac{2}{3}$ and $\frac{1}{3}$, respectively, approximate the optimal fixed sample size.

9. Assume that $X_1, X_2, \ldots$ is a sequential sample from a $\mathcal{N}(\theta, 1)$ density, and that it is desired to test $H_0 : \theta \leq 0$ versus $H_1 : \theta \geq 0$. The decision loss is zero for a correct decision and $|\theta|$ for an incorrect decision. The cost of a fixed sample of size n is $C(n) = n(0.1)$. If the prior density of θ is $\mathcal{N}(0, 4)$, approximate the optimal fixed sample size.

10. Assume that $X_1, X_2, \ldots$ is a sequential sample from a $\mathcal{N}(\theta, \sigma^2)$ density (σ^2 known), and that it is desired to test $H_0 : \theta \leq \theta_0$ versus $H_1 : \theta \geq \theta_1$ ($\theta_0 < \theta_1$) under "0–1" decision loss. It is possible for θ to be between θ_0 and θ_1, but no decision loss will then be incurred, regardless of the action taken. Assume that θ has a $\mathcal{N}(\mu, \tau^2)$ prior density, and let δ_n^π denote the Bayes rule for a fixed sample of size n. Show (pretending n is a continuous variable) that

$$\frac{d}{dn} r(\pi, \delta_n^\pi) = \frac{-\sigma\tau}{2\pi(\sigma^2 + n\tau^2)n^{1/2}} \exp\left\{ -\frac{1}{2\tau^2} \left[\left(\frac{\theta_0 + \theta_1}{2} - \mu \right)^2 + \frac{(\theta_1 - \theta_0)^2}{4} \right] \right\}$$

$$\times \exp\left\{ -\frac{1}{2} \left[\frac{\sigma^2}{n\tau^4} \left(\frac{\theta_0 + \theta_1}{2} - \mu \right)^2 + \frac{n}{4\sigma^2} (\theta_1 - \theta_0)^2 \right] \right\}.$$

Section 7.4

11. In the situation of Exercise 4 of Chapter 1, assume that a computer consultant can be hired to help in the prediction of the team's winning proportion θ. The consultant will report $X \sim \mathcal{B}(1, \theta)$. (This is a rather silly report, but you will appreciate the ease in calculation.) How much money would you expect the consultant's report to be worth to you?

12. Find a Bayes sequential decision procedure for the situation in Exercise (a) 4, (b) 5, (c) 6, (d) 7.

13. Assume that $X_1, X_2, \ldots$ is a sequential sample from a $\mathcal{B}(1, \theta)$ density, and that it is desired to test $H_0 : \theta = \frac{1}{4}$ versus $H_1 : \theta = \frac{1}{2}$. The decision loss is $L(\theta_0, a_0) = L(\theta_1, a_1) = 0$, $L(\theta_0, a_1) = 10$, and $L(\theta_1, a_0) = 20$, while the cost of each observation is $c_i = 1$.
    (a) Letting π_0 denote the prior probability of θ_0, find $\mathbf{d}^1$, the Bayes 1-truncated procedure.
    (b) If $\pi_0 = \frac{2}{3}$, find $\mathbf{d}^2$.

14. In the situation of Example 7, find the Bayes 3-truncated procedure, $\mathbf{d}^3$, when $c = 0.01$.

15. Assume that $X_1, X_2, \ldots$ is a sequential sample from a $\mathscr{P}(\theta)$ density, that $L(\theta, a, n) = (\theta - a)^2 + n(\frac{1}{12})$, and that θ has a $\mathscr{G}(1, 1)$ prior density. Find the Bayes 3-truncated procedure, $\mathbf{d}^3$.

16. Assume that $X_1, X_2, \ldots$ is a sequential sample from a $\mathscr{B}(1, \theta)$ density, and that a decision between two possible actions, a_0 and a_1, must be made. The decision loss is $L(\theta, a_0) = \theta$ and $L(\theta, a_1) = 1 - \theta$, while each observation costs $c_i = \frac{1}{12}$. Find the Bayes 2-truncated procedure, $\mathbf{d}^2$.

17. Prove Theorem 1.

18. Assume that $X_1, X_2, \ldots$ is a sequential sample from a $\mathscr{B}(1, \theta)$ density, that $L(\theta, a, n) = (\theta - a)^2 + \sum_{i=1}^{n} [0.01(1 + 5/i)]$, and that θ has a $\mathscr{U}(0, 1)$ prior density. Use Theorem 3 to show that the Bayes sequential procedure must be truncated at $m = 17$.

19. Prove Theorem 4.

20. Use Theorem 4 to show that the procedure found in Exercise 14 is actually the sequential Bayes procedure, $\mathbf{d}^\pi$.

21. Use Theorem 4 to show that the procedure found in Exercise 16 is actually the sequential Bayes procedure, $\mathbf{d}^\pi$.

22. Find the 1-step look ahead procedure, $\mathbf{d}_L^1$, for the situation of (a) Example 7, (b) Exercise 13 (with $\pi_0 = \frac{2}{3}$), (c) Exercise 15, (d) Exercise 16.

23. Find the 2-step look ahead procedure, $\mathbf{d}_L^2$, for the situation of (a) Example 6, (b) Exercise 15, (c) Exercise 16.

24. For the situation of Exercise 9, describe how the fixed sample size look ahead procedure, $\mathbf{d}_{FS}$, would be implemented. (Note the relevance of (7.11).) Carry out the procedure for the sequential sample 0.5, 2, 1, 1.5, 0, 2.5, 2, 1, ...

25. Show that in Example 10, Case 2, the fixed sample size look ahead procedure, $\mathbf{d}_{FS}$, is as indicated.

26. Assume that $X_1, X_2, \ldots$ is a sequential sample from a $\mathscr{P}(\theta)$ density, that $L(\theta, a, n) = (\theta - a)^2 + nc$, and that θ has a $\mathscr{G}(\alpha, \beta)$ prior density. Show that the fixed sample size look ahead procedure, $\mathbf{d}_{FS}$, is the same as the 1-step look ahead procedure, $\mathbf{d}_L^1$.

27. Assume that $X_1, X_2, \ldots$ is a sequential sample from a $\mathscr{P}(\theta)$ density, that $L(\theta, a, n) = (\theta - a)^2 + \frac{1}{4}n$, and that θ has a $\mathscr{G}(1, 1)$ prior density. Find the Bayes 3-inner truncated procedure, $\mathbf{d}_I^3$.

28. Find the 1-step inner look ahead procedure, $\mathbf{d}_{IL}^1$, for the situation of (a) Example 6, (b) Example 7, (c) Exercise 15, (d) Exercise 16.

29. Find the 2-step inner look ahead procedure, $\mathbf{d}_{IL}^2$, for the situation of (a) Example 6, (b) Exercise 15.

30. Prove that the inequalities in (7.24) of Subsection 7.4.8 are valid.

31. Prove that Theorem 5 is true for a general loss, $L(\theta, a, n)$, providing the following condition is satisfied:

$$\lim_{n \to \infty} E^{\pi} E_{\theta}^{X}[L(\theta, \delta_n^{\pi}(X), n) - \inf_a L(\theta, a, n)] = 0.$$

32. Prove that Theorem 6 is true for a general loss, $L(\theta, a, n)$, providing the condition in Exercise 31 is satisfied.

33. Complete the analysis in Example 13, showing that $h^*(r)$ (defined by (7.43)) is a solution to (7.39) for $r > 1$.

34. Assume that $X_1, X_2, \ldots$ is a sequential sample from a $\mathcal{B}(1, \theta)$ density, that it is desired to test $H_0: \theta = \frac{1}{3}$ versus $H_1: \theta = \frac{2}{3}$ under "0-1" loss, that each observation costs c, and that $0 < \pi_0 < 1$ is the prior probability that $\theta = \frac{1}{3}$. Show that (7.44) is satisfied, and find an asymptotically pointwise optimal procedure.

35. Verify that (7.47) is satisfied and find an asymptotically pointwise optimal procedure for the situation of (a) Example 7, (b) Exercise 26.

36. In the situation of Example 2, verify that (7.47) is satisfied for $\beta = k/2$.

Section 7.5

37. It is desired to test the null hypothesis that a sequential sample has a $\mathcal{U}(0, 2)$ common density versus the alternative hypothesis that the common density is $\mathcal{U}(1, 3)$. The cost of each observation is c, and the decision loss is "$0-K_i$" loss. Let π_i denote the prior probability of H_i.
   (a) Show that the Bayes sequential procedure is either $\mathbf{d}_1$ or $\mathbf{d}_2$, where $\mathbf{d}_1$ is the procedure which makes an immediate Bayes decision, and $\mathbf{d}_2$ is the procedure which starts sampling and, at stage n, is given by the following:

   if $x_n \leq 1$,   stop sampling and accept H_0;
   if $x_n \geq 2$,   stop sampling and accept H_1;
   if $1 < x_n < 2$,   continue sampling.

   (b) Calculate the Bayes risks of $\mathbf{d}_1$ and $\mathbf{d}_2$.

38. It is desired to test the null hypothesis that a sequential sample has a $\mathcal{U}(0, 2)$ common density versus the alternative hypothesis that the common density is $\mathcal{U}(0, 1)$. The cost of each observation is c, and the decision loss is "$0-K_i$" loss. Let π_i denote the prior probability of H_i.
   (a) Show that the Bayes sequential procedure is one of the procedures $\mathbf{d}_J$ (J a nonnegative integer) defined as follows. The procedure $\mathbf{d}_0$ is simply the immediate Bayes decision. For $J \geq 1$, $\mathbf{d}_J$ starts sampling; stops sampling when stage $n = J$ is reached, deciding H_0 if $x_J \geq 1$ and deciding H_1 otherwise; and at stage $n < J$ is given by the following:

   if $x_n \geq 1$,   stop sampling and decide H_0;
   if $x_n < 1$,   continue sampling.

   (b) For $\mathbf{d}_J$ (with $J \geq 1$), show that $\alpha_0 = 2^{-J}$, $\alpha_1 = 0$, $E[N|H_0] = 2(1 - 2^{-J})$, and $E[N|H_1] = J$.
   (c) Find the Bayes sequential procedure if $K_0 = 2$, $K_1 = 1$, $c = \frac{1}{15}$, and $\pi_0 = \frac{1}{3}$.
   (d) Find the Bayes sequential procedure if $K_0 = 2$, $K_1 = 1$, $c = \frac{1}{15}$, and $\pi_0 = \frac{1}{8}$.

39. Assume that $X_1, X_2, \ldots$ is a sequential sample from the density

$$f(x|\theta) = e^{-(x-\theta)}I_{(\theta, \infty)}(x),$$

and that it is desired to test $H_0 : \theta = \theta_0$ versus $H_1 : \theta = \theta_1$ $(\theta_0 < \theta_1)$. The cost of each observation is c, and the decision loss is "$0-K_i$" loss. Let π_i denote the prior probability of H_i.

(a) Show that the Bayes sequential procedure is one of the procedures $\mathbf{d}_J$ (J a nonnegative integer) defined as follows. The procedure $\mathbf{d}_0$ is simply the immediate Bayes decision. For $J \geq 1$, $\mathbf{d}_J$ is the procedure which starts sampling; stops sampling when stage $n = J$ is reached, deciding H_0 if $x_J \leq \theta_1$ and deciding H_1 otherwise; and at stage $n < J$ is given by the following:

$$\text{if } x_n \leq \theta_1, \quad \text{stop sampling and decide } H_0;$$
$$\text{if } x_n > \theta_1, \quad \text{continue sampling.}$$

(b) For $\mathbf{d}_J$ (with $J \geq 1$), show that

$$\beta(\theta) = P_\theta(\text{deciding } H_1) = \begin{cases} 1 & \text{if } \theta \geq \theta_1, \\ e^{J(\theta - \theta_1)} & \text{if } \theta < \theta_1, \end{cases}$$

and that

$$E_\theta N = \begin{cases} J & \text{if } \theta \geq \theta_1, \\ \dfrac{1 - \exp\{J(\theta - \theta_1)\}}{1 - \exp\{(\theta - \theta_1)\}} & \text{if } \theta < \theta_1. \end{cases}$$

(c) If $0 < \pi_0 < 1$, show that, for small enough c, the Bayes sequential procedure is $\mathbf{d}_{J^*}$, where

$$J^* \cong (\theta_1 - \theta_0)^{-1} \log\left\{\frac{(\theta_1 - \theta_0)\pi_0}{\pi_1}\left[\frac{K_1}{c} - \frac{1}{1 - \exp(\theta_0 - \theta_1)}\right]\right\}.$$

40. Assume that $X_1, X_2, \ldots$ is a sequential sample from the $\mathscr{E}(\theta)$ density, and that it is desired to test $H_0 : \theta = \frac{1}{2}$ versus $H_1 : \theta = 1$.
(a) Using the Wald approximations, find the SPRT for which $\alpha_0 = \alpha_1 = 0.05$.
(b) Determine $\tilde{\beta}(\frac{2}{3})$ and $\tilde{\beta}(\log 2)$ for the SPRT in (a).
(c) Calculate $\tilde{E}_{1/2}N$, $\tilde{E}_1 N$, $\tilde{E}_{\log 2} N$, and $\tilde{E}_{2/3} N$ for the SPRT in (a).

41. Assume that $X_1, X_2, \ldots$ is a sequential sample from the $\mathscr{P}(\theta)$ density, and that it is desired to test $H_0 : \theta = 1$ versus $H_1 : \theta = 2$.
(a) Using the Wald approximations, find the SPRT for which $\alpha_0 = 0.05$ and $\alpha_1 = 0.1$.
(b) Calculate $\tilde{\beta}(\theta)$ and $\tilde{E}_\theta N$ at $\theta = 1$, $\theta = 2$, and $\theta = 1/\log 2$, for the SPRT in (a).

42. Assume that $X_1, X_2, \ldots$ is a sequential sample from the $\mathscr{G}e(\theta)$ density, and that it is desired to test $H_0 : \theta = \frac{1}{3}$ versus $H_1 : \theta = \frac{2}{3}$.
(a) Using the Wald approximations, find the SPRT for which $\alpha_0 = \alpha_1 = 0.1$.
(b) Show that $t_\theta = \log([1 - \theta]^{-1} - 1)/\log 2$, and give formulas for $\tilde{\beta}(\theta)$ and $\tilde{E}_\theta N$.

43. Assume that $X_1, X_2, \ldots$ is a sequential sample from the $\mathscr{N}(0, \sigma^2)$ density, and that it is desired to test $H_0 : \sigma^2 = 1$ versus $H_1 : \sigma^2 = 2$.
(a) Using the Wald approximations, find the SPRT for which $\alpha_0 = \alpha_1 = 0.01$.

(b) Calculate $\tilde{\beta}(\sigma^2)$ and $\tilde{E}_{\sigma^2}N$ at $\sigma^2 = 1$, $\sigma^2 = 2$, and $\sigma^2 = 2\log 2$, for the SPRT in (a).

44. Consider the situation of Example 15.
   (a) Show that, for the SPRT with $a = -jv$ and $b = kv$, $\beta(\theta)$ and $E_\theta N$ are given *exactly* by

$$\beta(\theta) = \begin{cases} \dfrac{1 - [\theta/(1-\theta)]^j}{[(1-\theta)/\theta]^k - [\theta/(1-\theta)]^j} & \text{if } \theta \neq \tfrac{1}{2}, \\[3mm] \dfrac{j}{k+j} & \text{if } \theta = \tfrac{1}{2}, \end{cases}$$

$$E_\theta N = \begin{cases} \dfrac{1}{(2\theta - 1)} \dfrac{k\{1 - [\theta/(1-\theta)]^j\} - j\{[(1-\theta)/\theta]^k - 1\}}{[(1-\theta)/\theta]^k - [\theta/(1-\theta)]^j} & \text{if } \theta \neq \tfrac{1}{2}, \\[3mm] jk & \text{if } \theta = \tfrac{1}{2}. \end{cases}$$

   (b) If $\theta_0 = \tfrac{1}{3}$, each observation costs $c = 1$, the decision loss is "0–20" loss, and the prior probability of θ_0 is $\tfrac{1}{2}$, find the Bayes sequential procedure.

45. It is known that one of two given coins is fair, and that the other coin has probability $\tfrac{2}{3}$ of coming up heads when flipped. It is desired to determine which of the coins is the fair coin. The coins, tossed simultaneously and independently, produce a sequential sample $(X_1, Y_1), (X_2, Y_2), \dots$, where X_i and Y_i are each 0 or 1, according as to whether the respective coin is a tail or a head. Determine the form of an SPRT for this problem, and calculate (exactly) the corresponding α_0, α_1, $E_{\theta_0}N$, and $E_{\theta_1}N$.

46. Prove part (ii) of Theorem 11.

47. Prove that (7.73) is true under the condition that $P_{\theta_j}(|Z_i| < \infty) = 1$ for $j = 0, 1$.

48. For $0 < \alpha_0 < 1$ and $0 < \alpha_1 < 1$, define $A^{**} = \alpha_1$, $B^{**} = 1/\alpha_0$, and let α_0^{**} and α_1^{**} denote the true error probabilities of the SPRT with stopping boundaries A^{**} and B^{**}. Using Theorem 12, show that $\alpha_0^{**} < \alpha_0$ and $\alpha_1^{**} < \alpha_1$.

49. Consider the situation of Exercise 39.
   (a) For any $a < 0$ and $b = J(\theta_1 - \theta_0)$ (J a positive integer), determine the SPRT $d_{a,b}$ and calculate the Wald approximations $\tilde{\alpha}_0$, $\tilde{\alpha}_1$, $\tilde{E}_{\theta_0}N$, and $\tilde{E}_{\theta_1}N$. (Note that the Z_i^* in (7.61) should be used.)
   (b) Show that as $a \to -\infty$, the Wald approximations to α_i and $E_{\theta_i}N$ ($i = 0, 1$) converge to the correct values.

50. For the situation considered in Section 7.5, namely testing a simple null hypothesis versus a simple alternative hypothesis, show that the asymptotically pointwise optimal procedure defined in Subsection 7.4.10 (you may assume (7.44) is satisfied) is an SPRT. Find the stopping boundaries of this SPRT, and compare with the small c approximations in (7.84).

51. Assume that $X_1, X_2, \dots$ is a sequential sample from a $\mathcal{N}(\theta, 1)$ density, and that it is desired to test $H_0: \theta = 0$ versus $H_1: \theta = 1$. The loss in incorrectly deciding H_0 is 30, in incorrectly deciding H_1 is 15, and is 0 otherwise. The cost of each observation is $c = 0.001$, and the prior probability that θ equals 0 is $\tfrac{2}{3}$. Find the Bayes sequential procedure. (You may use the small c approximations to the stopping boundaries, given in (7.84).)

52. In the situation of Exercise 42, assume that the decision loss is "0–20" loss, that each observation costs $c = 0.001$, and that the prior probability that θ equals $\frac{1}{3}$ is $\frac{1}{3}$. Find the Bayes sequential procedure. (You may use the small c approximations to the stopping boundaries, given in (7.84).)

53. Assume that $X_1, X_2, \ldots$ is a sequential sample from the $\mathscr{U}(0, \theta)$ density, and that it is desired to test $H_0 : \theta \geq 1$ versus $H_1 : \theta < 1$ under "0–1" loss. Each observation costs c, and θ has a $\mathscr{P}a(\frac{1}{2}, 1)$ prior density.
    (a) Show that any SPOT (as defined in (7.85)) is equivalent to a procedure, $\mathbf{d}_J$ (J a positive integer), which stops sampling when stage $n = J$ is reached, deciding H_0 if $x_J \geq 1$ and deciding H_1 otherwise; and which at stage $n < J$ is given by the following:

    $$\text{if } x_n \geq 1, \quad \text{stop sampling and decide } H_0;$$
    $$\text{if } x_n < 1, \quad \text{continue sampling.}$$

    (b) Show, for $\mathbf{d}_J$, that

    $$\beta(\theta) = \begin{cases} 1 & \text{if } \theta \leq 1, \\ \theta^{-J} & \text{if } \theta > 1, \end{cases}$$

    and

    $$E_\theta N = \begin{cases} J & \text{if } \theta \leq 1, \\ \dfrac{\theta(1 - \theta^{-J})}{\theta - 1} & \text{if } \theta > 1. \end{cases}$$

    (c) Calculate $r(\pi, \mathbf{d}_J)$, and show that the optimal J is approximately $c^{-1/2} - 2$.

Section 7.6

54. In the situation of Exercise 4, show that a minimax sequential procedure is to choose the integer n which minimizes $n^{-1} + nc$, take a sample of size n, and estimate θ by $n^{-1} \sum_{i=1}^{n} x_i$.

55. In the situation of Exercise 5, show that a minimax sequential procedure is to choose the integer n which minimizes $n^{-1} + nc$, take a sample of size n, and estimate θ by $n^{-1} \sum_{i=1}^{n} x_i$.

56. In the situation of Exercise 6, show that a minimax sequential procedure is to choose the integer n which minimizes $(n + 1)^{-1} + nc$, take a sample of size n, and estimate θ by $(n + 1)^{-1} \sum_{i=1}^{n} x_i$.

57. In the situation of Exercise 7, show that a minimax sequential procedure is to choose the integer n which minimizes $(n + 1)^{-1} + nc$, take a sample of size n, and estimate θ by $(n + 1)^{-1} \sum_{i=1}^{n} x_i$.

58. In the situation of Example 13, show that the following procedure is minimax: stop sampling for the first n for which $(b_n^* - a_n^*)^2 \leq (2c)^{1/3}$, and estimate θ by $(a_n^* + b_n^*)/2$, where $a_n^* = \max_{1 \leq i \leq n} \{x_i\} - \frac{1}{2}$ and $b_n^* = \min_{1 \leq i \leq n} \{x_i\} + \frac{1}{2}$.

Section 7.7

59. Assume that $X_1, X_2, \ldots$ is a sequential sample from a $\mathcal{N}(\theta, \sigma^2)$ density (σ^2 known), and that it is desired to estimate θ under squared-error decision loss. It is possible, at any stage, to take observations in batches of any size. A batch of m observations costs $c \log(m + 1)$. If the parameter θ has a $\mathcal{N}(\mu, \tau^2)$ prior density, find the optimal sampling procedure.

60. It is desired to test the null hypothesis that a sequential sample has a $\mathcal{U}(0, 2)$ common density versus the alternative hypothesis that the common density is $\mathcal{U}(1, 3)$. The decision loss is 0 for a correct decision and 20 for an incorrect decision. It is possible, at any stage, to take observations in batches. A batch of m observations costs $m^{1/2}$. The prior probability of each hypothesis is $\frac{1}{2}$.

    Let $\mathbf{d}_0$ denote the procedure which makes an immediate Bayes decision. Let $\mathbf{d}_m$ denote the procedure which takes successive samples (batches) of size m, stopping and deciding H_0 (deciding H_1) if any observation in the batch is less than one (greater than two), and taking another batch otherwise.

    (a) Why can attention be restricted to consideration of $\mathbf{d}_0$ and the $\mathbf{d}_m$?

    (b) Show that the Bayes risk of $\mathbf{d}_m$ is

    $$r(\pi, \mathbf{d}_m) = \frac{m^{1/2}}{1 - 2^{-m}}.$$

    (c) Show that $\mathbf{d}_2$ is the optimal procedure.

CHAPTER 8

Complete and Essentially Complete Classes

We have previously observed that it is unwise to use inadmissible decision rules. (The possible exception is when an inadmissible rule is very simple and easy to use, and is only slightly inadmissible.) It is, therefore, of interest to find, for a given problem, the class of acceptable (usually admissible) decision rules. Such a class is often much easier to work with, say in finding a minimax or a Γ-minimax decision rule, than is the class of all decision rules. In this chapter, we discuss several of the most important situations in which simple reduced classes of decision rules have been obtained. Unfortunately, the subject tends to be quite difficult mathematically, and so we will be able to give only a cursory introduction to some of the more profound results.

8.1 Preliminaries

We begin with definitions of the needed concepts.

Definition 1. A class $\mathscr{C}$ of decision rules is said to be *essentially complete* if, for any decision rule δ not in $\mathscr{C}$, there is a decision rule $\delta' \in \mathscr{C}$ which is R-better than or R-equivalent to δ.

Definition 2. A class $\mathscr{C}$ of decision rules is said to be *complete* if, for any decision rule δ not in $\mathscr{C}$, there is a decision rule $\delta' \in \mathscr{C}$ which is R-better than δ.

Definition 3. A class $\mathscr{C}$ of decision rules is said to be *minimal complete* if $\mathscr{C}$ is complete and if no proper subset of $\mathscr{C}$ is complete.

The following lemmas are instructive in the assimilation of the above concepts. The proofs of the first two are left as exercises.

Lemma 1. *A complete class must contain all admissible decision rules.*

Lemma 2. *If an admissible decision rule δ is not in an essentially complete class $\mathscr{C}$, then there must exist a decision rule δ' in $\mathscr{C}$ which is R-equivalent to δ.*

Lemma 3. *If a minimal complete class $\mathscr{C}$ exists, it is exactly the class of admissible decision rules.*

PROOF. Lemma 1 implies that the class of admissible rules is a subset of $\mathscr{C}$. It remains only to show that if $\delta \in \mathscr{C}$, then δ is admissible. This will be established by contradiction. Thus assume that $\delta \in \mathscr{C}$ and that δ is inadmissible. Note first that there then exists a $\delta' \in \mathscr{C}$ which is R-better than δ. This is because there exists a rule δ'' which is R-better than δ (inadmissibility of δ), and also a rule $\delta' \in \mathscr{C}$ which is R-better than δ'' if $\delta'' \notin \mathscr{C}$ (completeness of $\mathscr{C}$). Hence let $\mathscr{C}'$ be the set of all rules in $\mathscr{C}$, except δ. Clearly $\mathscr{C}'$ is a complete class, since if δ was used to improve upon a rule not in $\mathscr{C}$, then δ' could just as well have been used. But $\mathscr{C}'$ is a proper subset of $\mathscr{C}$, contradicting the assumption that $\mathscr{C}$ is minimal complete. Hence δ must be admissible.   □

The above definitions and results apply to sequential problems as well as to fixed sample size problems. We will, for the most part, consider only fixed sample size situations, however, since sequential problems tend to be more complex. Indeed only in Subsection 8.6.3 will the sequential situation be explicitly considered.

8.2 Complete and Essentially Complete Classes from Earlier Chapters

8.2.1 Decision Rules Based on a Sufficient Statistic

Theorem 1 in Section 1.7 established that the class of randomized decision rules based on a sufficient statistic is an essentially complete class. This class will usually not be a complete class. The widespread acceptance of the principle of sufficiency indicates, however, that in practice it is quite acceptable to reduce to an essentially complete class, rather than to a complete class. Indeed, an essentially complete class will typically be smaller than a complete class, and hence may be preferable.

8.2.2 Nonrandomized Decision Rules

In certain situations, the class of nonrandomized decision rules is a complete (or essentially complete) class. One such situation is that of convex loss, as was indicated by Theorem 3 in Section 1.8. Another common situation in which this is the case is that of finite action problems in which the densities $f(x|\theta)$ are all continuous. Certain results of this nature can be found in Dvoretsky, Wald, and Wolfowitz (1951).

8.2.3 Finite Θ

Several complete class theorems for situations involving finite Θ were given in Chapter 5. The most basic such result was Theorem 8 in Subsection 5.2.4, which can be restated as follows.

Theorem 1. *If Θ is finite and the risk set S is bounded from below and closed from below, then the set $\mathscr{C}$ of all decision rules which have risk points on $\lambda(S)$, the lower boundary of S, is a minimal complete class.*

PROOF. The fact that $\mathscr{C}$ is complete is an immediate consequence of Theorem 8 of Chapter 5. That $\mathscr{C}$ is minimal complete follows from Theorem 9 of Chapter 5 and Lemma 1 of this chapter.   □

The following theorem is an immediate consequence of Theorem 1 above and Theorem 11 of Chapter 5.

Theorem 2. *If Θ is finite and the risk set S is bounded from below and closed from below, then the set of Bayes decision rules is a complete class, and the set of admissible Bayes decision rules is a minimal complete class.*

Theorem 2 is typically the more useful of the above complete class theorems. This is because Bayes rules are usually quite easy to characterize in problems which involve finite Θ. To apply the above theorems it is, of course, necessary to verify that S is closed from below and bounded from below. Several general conditions which imply this were given in Subsection 5.5.3.

8.2.4 The Neyman–Pearson Lemma

The famous Neyman–Pearson lemma (Neyman and Pearson (1933)) was, to a large extent, responsible for establishing the school of thought that led to decision theory. The Neyman–Pearson lemma can indeed be considered to have been the first complete class theorem. It is concerned with testing a simple null hypothesis $H_0: \theta = \theta_0$, versus a simple alternative hypothesis, $H_1: \theta = \theta_1$. For convenience, we will assume that the relevant densities, $f(x|\theta_0)$ and $f(x|\theta_1)$, of the observation X are either both continuous or both discrete. The loss is taken to be "$0-K_i$" loss (i.e., incorrectly deciding a_i costs K_i, while a correct decision costs 0). As usual in testing, a decision rule will be represented by a test function, $\phi(x)$, which denotes the probability of rejecting the null hypothesis when x is observed. (Note that randomized decision rules are thus being considered.) Also, $\alpha_0(\phi)$ and $\alpha_1(\phi)$ will denote the probabilities of type I and type II error respectively. This problem was discussed in Subsection 5.3.3, which the reader might profitably reread at this point. Indeed the Neyman–Pearson lemma is basically a rigorous statement of the ideas discussed in that subsection.

Theorem 3 (Neyman–Pearson Lemma). *The tests of the form*

$$\phi(x) = \begin{cases} 1 & \text{if } f(x|\theta_1) > Kf(x|\theta_0), \\ \gamma(x) & \text{if } f(x|\theta_1) = Kf(x|\theta_0), \\ 0 & \text{if } f(x|\theta_1) < Kf(x|\theta_0), \end{cases} \tag{8.1}$$

where $0 \le \gamma(x) \le 1$ if $0 < K < \infty$ and $\gamma(x) = 0$ if $K = 0$, together with the test

$$\phi(x) = \begin{cases} 1 & \text{if } f(x|\theta_0) = 0, \\ 0 & \text{if } f(x|\theta_0) > 0, \end{cases} \tag{8.2}$$

(corresponding to $K = \infty$ above), form a minimal complete class of decision rules. The subclass of such tests with $\gamma(x) \equiv \gamma$ (a constant) is an essentially complete class.

For any α ($0 \le \alpha \le 1$), there exists a test ϕ of the form (8.1) or (8.2) with $\alpha_0(\phi) = \alpha$, and any such test is a most powerful test of size α (i.e., among all tests ϕ with $\alpha_0(\phi) \le \alpha$, such a test minimizes $\alpha_1(\phi)$).

PROOF. From Lemma 10 of Subsection 5.3.3 and Theorem 2 of this chapter, we know that the admissible Bayes rules form a minimal complete class. As in Subsection 5.3.3, it is easy to check that if π_0, the prior probability of θ_0, satisfies $0 < \pi_0 < 1$, then the Bayes rules are precisely the tests of the form (8.1) with $0 < K < \infty$. When $\pi_0 = 0$, any test which satisfies $\phi(x) = 1$ if $f(x|\theta_1) > 0$ is a Bayes test, since then $r(\pi, \phi) = \alpha_1(\phi) = 0$. Only the test of the form (8.1) with $K = 0$ and $\gamma(x) = 0$ is admissible, however, since it minimizes $\alpha_0(\phi)$ among all tests with $\alpha_1(\phi) = 0$. When $\pi_0 = 1$, it can similarly be shown that the test in (8.2) is the admissible Bayes test. Thus the tests in (8.1) and (8.2) are precisely the admissible Bayes tests, and hence form a minimal complete class.

To establish the essential completeness of the class of tests of the form (8.1) and (8.2) with $\gamma(x)$ constant, it suffices to show that for any test of the form (8.1), there is an R-equivalent test of the same form with $\gamma(x)$ constant. Thus let ϕ be of the form (8.1), with given K and $\gamma(x)$, and define $A_0 = \{x: f(x|\theta_1) < Kf(x|\theta_0)\}$, $A_1 = \{x: f(x|\theta_1) > Kf(x|\theta_0)\}$, and $A_2 = \{x: f(x|\theta_1) = Kf(x|\theta_0)\}$. Note that

$$\alpha_0(\phi) = E_{\theta_0}[\phi(X)] = P_{\theta_0}(A_1) + \int_{A_2} \gamma(x)dF(x|\theta_0) \tag{8.3}$$

and

$$\alpha_1(\phi) = E_{\theta_1}[1 - \phi(X)] = P_{\theta_1}(A_0) + \int_{A_2} (1 - \gamma(x))dF(x|\theta_1)$$

$$= P_{\theta_1}(A_0 \cup A_2) - \int_{A_2} \gamma(x)dF(x|\theta_1)$$

$$= P_{\theta_1}(A_0 \cup A_2) - K \int_{A_2} \gamma(x)dF(x|\theta_0). \tag{8.4}$$

Assume now that $\beta = \int_{A_2} dF(x|\theta_0) > 0$, since if $\beta = 0$ the result is vacuously correct. Consider the new test, ϕ', which is of the form (8.1) with the given K and

$$\gamma'(x) \equiv \beta^{-1} \int_{A_2} \gamma(x)dF(x|\theta_0).$$

It is easy to check, using (8.3) and (8.4), that $\alpha_0(\phi) = \alpha_0(\phi')$ and $\alpha_1(\phi) = \alpha_1(\phi')$. Hence $R(\theta_0, \phi) = K_1\alpha_0(\phi) = R(\theta_0, \phi')$ and $R(\theta_1, \phi) = K_0\alpha_1(\phi) = R(\theta_1, \phi')$, establishing the R-equivalence of ϕ and ϕ'.

The conclusion that the tests in (8.1) and (8.2) are most powerful of their size follows immediately from the fact that they are admissible tests. The existence of most powerful size α tests of the form (8.1) and (8.2) follows directly from the fact that the risk set is closed, bounded, convex, and contains (when $K_0 = K_1 = 1$) the risk points $(0, 1)^t$ and $(1, 0)^t$. (See Figure 5.7 of Subsection 5.3.3.) This completes the proof. $\square$

Example 18 in Subsection 5.3.3 demonstrates an application of the Neyman–Pearson lemma.

8.3 One-Sided Testing

From the Neyman–Pearson lemma it is possible to derive complete class theorems for certain testing situations that concern what are called one-sided tests. Such tests involve testing hypotheses of the form $H_0: \theta \in \Theta_0$ versus $H_1: \theta \in \Theta_1$, where Θ_0 and Θ_1 are subsets of the real line and Θ_0 is to the left (or right) of Θ_1. We begin the development by considering "0–1" loss, so that the risk function of a test ϕ is determined by the error probabilities of the test, or equivalently the power function

$$\beta_\phi(\theta) = E_\theta[\phi(X)] = P_\theta \text{ (rejecting } H_0).$$

The crucial concept needed is that of a uniformly most powerful test of size α.

Definition 4. A test ϕ of $H_0 : \theta \in \Theta_0$ versus $H_1 : \theta \in \Theta_1$ is said to have *size* α if

$$\sup_{\theta \in \Theta_0} E_\theta[\phi(X)] = \alpha.$$

A test ϕ_0 is said to be *uniformly most powerful* (UMP) of size α if it is of size α, and if, for any other test ϕ of size at most α,

$$E_\theta[\phi_0(X)] \geq E_\theta[\phi(X)]$$

for all $\theta \in \Theta_1$.

The concept of a uniformly most powerful test is a fairly natural extension to composite hypotheses of the idea of a most powerful test for simple hypotheses. Whereas most powerful tests virtually always exist, however, there is no reason to expect that UMP tests need exist, and indeed they only exist for certain special distributions and hypotheses. The most important class of distributions for which they sometimes exist is the class of distributions with monotone likelihood ratio. In the discussion and applications of monotone likelihood ratio, we will assume that the distributions have densities (either continuous or discrete) on R^1, and that Θ is a subset of R^1.

Definition 5. The distribution of X is said to have *monotone likelihood ratio* if, whenever $\theta_1 < \theta_2$, the likelihood ratio

$$\frac{f(x|\theta_2)}{f(x|\theta_1)}$$

is a nondecreasing function of x on the set for which at least one of the densities is nonzero. (As usual, a nonzero constant divided by zero is defined to be infinity.)

The distribution in the above definition would perhaps more logically be called a distribution with *nondecreasing likelihood ratio*. If faced with a distribution for which the likelihood ratio is nonincreasing, one need only make the change of variables $Y = -X$ or the reparameterization $\eta = -\theta$ to arrive at a distribution with nondecreasing likelihood ratio.

EXAMPLE 1. The most common distributions with monotone likelihood ratio are those from the *one-parameter exponential family*, i.e., those with densities of the form

$$f(x|\theta) = c(\theta)h(x)\exp\{Q(\theta)T(x)\},$$

where θ and x are in R^1 and c, h, Q, and T are real-valued functions. Clearly

$$\frac{f(x|\theta_2)}{f(x|\theta_1)} = \frac{c(\theta_2)}{c(\theta_1)} \exp\{[Q(\theta_2) - Q(\theta_1)]T(x)\}.$$

For $\theta_1 < \theta_2$, this is nondecreasing in x (on the set where $h(x)$ is nonzero) providing both $Q(\theta)$ and $T(x)$ are nondecreasing or nonincreasing. Note that if one defines $Y = T(X)$ and $\eta = Q(\theta)$, then the distribution of Y given η will always have monotone likelihood ratio.

The one-parameter exponential family includes such standard distributions as the normal (with either mean or variance fixed), the Poisson, the binomial, and the gamma (either parameter fixed). Also, a random sample from a distribution in the one-parameter exponential family will admit a sufficient statistic which itself has a distribution in the one-parameter exponential family. This ensures a wide range of applicability for this class of distributions.

EXAMPLE 2. The $\mathcal{U}(0, \theta + 1)$ distribution has monotone likelihood ratio. To see this, note that if $\theta_1 < \theta_2$, then

$$\frac{f(x|\theta_2)}{f(x|\theta_1)} = \begin{cases} \infty & \text{if } \theta_1 + 1 \leq x \text{ and } \theta_2 < x < \theta_2 + 1, \\ 1 & \text{if } \theta_1 < x < \theta_1 + 1 \text{ and } \theta_2 < x < \theta_2 + 1, \\ 0 & \text{if } \theta_1 < x < \theta_1 + 1 \text{ and } x \leq \theta_2. \end{cases}$$

This is clearly nondecreasing in x.

EXAMPLE 3. The $\mathcal{C}(\theta, 1)$ distribution does *not* have monotone likelihood ratio, as can be seen by noting that

$$\frac{f(x|\theta_2)}{f(x|\theta_1)} = \frac{1 + (x - \theta_1)^2}{1 + (x - \theta_2)^2}$$

converges to one as $x \to +\infty$ or as $x \to -\infty$.

The following theorem presents the key result concerning UMP tests.

Theorem 4. *Assume that the distribution of X has monotone likelihood ratio, and that it is desired to test $H_0: \theta \leq \theta_0$ versus $H_1: \theta > \theta_0$. Consider tests of the form*

$$\phi(x) = \begin{cases} 1 & \text{if } x > x_0, \\ \gamma & \text{if } x = x_0, \\ 0 & \text{if } x < x_0, \end{cases} \tag{8.5}$$

where $-\infty \leq x_0 \leq \infty$ and $0 \leq \gamma \leq 1$. The following facts are true:

(i) *The power function, $\beta_\phi(\theta) = E_\theta[\phi(X)]$, is nondecreasing in θ.*
(ii) *Any such test is UMP of its size, providing its size is not zero.*
(iii) *For any $0 \leq \alpha \leq 1$, there exists a test of the form (8.5) which is UMP of size α.*

PROOF. Let θ_1 and θ_2 be any points such that $\theta_1 < \theta_2$. The Neyman–Pearson lemma states that any test of the form

$$\phi(x) = \begin{cases} 1 & \text{if } f(x|\theta_2) > Kf(x|\theta_1), \\ \gamma(x) & \text{if } f(x|\theta_2) = Kf(x|\theta_1), \\ 0 & \text{if } f(x|\theta_2) < Kf(x|\theta_1), \end{cases} \tag{8.6}$$

for $0 \le K < \infty$, is most powerful of its size for testing $H_0: \theta = \theta_1$ versus $H_1: \theta = \theta_2$. We must first show that, since the distribution of X has monotone likelihood ratio, any test of the form (8.5) can be written as in (8.6), providing its size is nonzero. To see this when $x_0 = -\infty$, simply set $K = 0$ and $\gamma(x) = 1$ in (8.6). To verify this correspondence when $x_0 > -\infty$, note that the assumptions of monotone likelihood ratio and nonzero size imply that $x_0 < \infty$ and that $f(x_0|\theta_1) > 0$. Hence, simply define $K = f(x_0|\theta_2)/f(x_0|\theta_1)$ and

$$\gamma(x) = \begin{cases} 1 & \text{if } x > x_0 \text{ and } f(x|\theta_2) = Kf(x|\theta_1), \\ \gamma & \text{if } x = x_0, \\ 0 & \text{if } x < x_0 \text{ and } f(x|\theta_2) = Kf(x|\theta_1). \end{cases}$$

From the assumption of monotone likelihood ratio it follows that the test in (8.6), with this choice of K and $\gamma(x)$, is the same as the test in (8.5).

If now $\phi(x)$ is a most powerful size α ($\alpha > 0$) test of θ_1 versus θ_2, then since $\phi_0(x) \equiv \alpha$ is also a size α test, it follows that

$$E_{\theta_2}[\phi(X)] \ge E_{\theta_2}[\phi_0(X)] = \alpha = E_{\theta_1}[\phi(X)].$$

Of course, when $E_{\theta_1}[\phi(X)] = \alpha = 0$, it is trivially true that $E_{\theta_2}[\phi(X)] \ge E_{\theta_1}[\phi(X)]$. Hence in all cases, a test ϕ of the form (8.5) satisfies $E_{\theta_2}[\phi(X)] \ge E_{\theta_1}[\phi(X)]$, when $\theta_1 < \theta_2$. This establishes the first conclusion of the theorem.

To prove the second part of the theorem, consider the problem of testing $H_0: \theta = \theta_0$ versus $H_1: \theta = \theta_1$, where $\theta_1 > \theta_0$. By the above argument and the Neyman–Pearson lemma, a test ϕ of the form (8.5) is most powerful of its size, α, providing $\alpha > 0$. Since $\alpha = E_{\theta_0}[\phi(X)]$, this is true no matter what θ_1 is. Hence the tests in (8.5) are UMP size α tests of $H_0: \theta = \theta_0$ versus $H_1: \theta > \theta_0$, providing $\alpha > 0$. Finally, since $\beta_\phi(\theta)$ is nondecreasing, $E_\theta[\phi(X)] \le \alpha$ for all $\theta < \theta_0$. Thus ϕ is a size α test of $H_0: \theta \le \theta_0$ versus $H_1: \theta > \theta_0$, and Part (ii) of the theorem follows directly.

Part (iii) of the theorem is established, for $\alpha > 0$, by finding a most powerful size α test of $H_0: \theta = \theta_0$ versus $H_1: \theta = \theta_1$ (which exists by the Neyman–Pearson lemma), writing the test in the form (8.5), and applying Part (ii). For $\alpha = 0$, the Neyman–Pearson lemma gives that a most powerful test of $H_0: \theta = \theta_0$ versus $H_1: \theta = \theta_1$ ($\theta_1 > \theta_0$) is

$$\phi(x) = \begin{cases} 1 & \text{if } f(x|\theta_0) = 0, \\ 0 & \text{if } f(x|\theta_0) > 0. \end{cases} \tag{8.7}$$

Now $\{x: f(x|\theta_0) > 0\} = \{x: f(x|\theta_1)/f(x|\theta_0) < \infty\}$, and this latter set, by the definition of monotone likelihood ratio, is either $\{x: x < x_0\}$ or $\{x: x \le x_0\}$, where $-\infty < x_0 \le \infty$ is some constant. It follows that the test in (8.7) can be written as in (8.5). The proof that this test is uniformly most powerful proceeds exactly along the lines of the proof of Part (ii). $\square$

EXAMPLE 4. Assume that $X_1, X_2, \ldots, X_n$ is a sample from the $\mathcal{N}(\theta, 1)$ distribution, and that it is desired to test $H_0: \theta \le \theta_0$ versus $H_1: \theta > \theta_0$. Clearly $\bar{X} \sim \mathcal{N}(\theta, 1/n)$ is sufficient for θ, and its distribution has monotone likelihood ratio. Using Theorem 4 and the continuity of the density, it follows that a UMP size α test is to reject H_0 when $\bar{x} > x_0 = \theta_0 + n^{-1/2}z(1 - \alpha)$, where $z(1 - \alpha)$ is the $(1 - \alpha)$-fractile of the $\mathcal{N}(0, 1)$ distribution.

Note that, by symmetry, Theorem 4 also applies to testing $H_0: \theta \ge \theta_0$ versus $H_1: \theta < \theta_0$, with, of course, the form of the tests in (8.5) being changed to

$$\phi(x) = \begin{cases} 1 & \text{if } x < x_0, \\ \gamma & \text{if } x = x_0, \\ 0 & \text{if } x > x_0. \end{cases}$$

The following corollary to Theorem 4 will lead directly to the desired complete class theorem for one-sided testing.

Corollary 4.1. *Assume that the distribution of X has monotone likelihood ratio. For every test ϕ and every $\theta_0 \in \Theta$, there then exists a test ϕ' of the form (8.5) for which*

$$\begin{aligned} E_\theta[\phi'(X)] &\le E_\theta[\phi(X)] \quad \text{for } \theta \le \theta_0, \\ E_\theta[\phi'(X)] &\ge E_\theta[\phi(X)] \quad \text{for } \theta > \theta_0. \end{aligned} \tag{8.8}$$

PROOF. Define $\alpha = E_{\theta_0}[\phi(X)]$, and choose ϕ' to be a size α test of the form (8.3). Since ϕ' is UMP for testing $H_0: \theta \le \theta_0$ versus $H_1: \theta > \theta_0$, it is true that $E_\theta[\phi'(X)] \ge E_\theta[\phi(X)]$ for $\theta > \theta_0$. Since, by symmetry, $1 - \phi'$ is UMP of size $1 - \alpha$ for testing $H_0: \theta \ge \theta_0$ versus $H_1: \theta < \theta_0$, it similarly follows that $E_\theta[1 - \phi'(X)] \ge E_\theta[1 - \phi(X)]$ for $\theta < \theta_0$, completing the proof. $\square$

We finally come to the complete class theorem. It will be given for a fairly general loss function that embodies the spirit of one-sided testing. Assume that $\mathcal{A} = \{a_0, a_1\}$, and that $L(\theta, a_i)$ $(i = 0, 1)$ satisfies

$$\begin{aligned} L(\theta, a_1) - L(\theta, a_0) &\ge 0 \quad \text{if } \theta < \theta_0, \\ L(\theta, a_1) - L(\theta, a_0) &\le 0 \quad \text{if } \theta > \theta_0. \end{aligned} \tag{8.9}$$

Clearly action a_0 is preferred for $\theta < \theta_0$, while a_1 is preferred for $\theta > \theta_0$. Action a_0 thus corresponds to accepting $H_0: \theta < \theta_0$, while action a_1 corresponds to accepting $H_1: \theta > \theta_0$. Because of this correspondence, we will continue to write a decision rule as a test, $\phi(x)$, which should now, however, be interpreted as the probability of taking action a_1 after observing x. Note that, for $\theta = \theta_0$, (8.9) places no restriction on the loss. The complete class theorem follows, and is due to Karlin and Rubin (1956).

Theorem 5. *If the distribution of X has monotone likelihood ratio and the loss function is as in (8.9), then*

(i) *the class of tests in (8.5) is an essentially complete class; and*
(ii) *any test of the form (8.5) is admissible, providing $\{x: f(x|\theta) > 0\}$ is independent of θ and there exist numbers θ_1 and θ_2 in Θ, with $\theta_1 \leq \theta_0 \leq \theta_2$, such that $L(\theta_1, a_1) - L(\theta_1, a_0) > 0$ and $L(\theta_2, a_1) - L(\theta_2, a_0) < 0$.*

PROOF. Observe first that the risk function of a test ϕ^* can be written as

$$R(\theta, \phi^*) = L(\theta, a_0)(1 - E_\theta[\phi(X)]) + L(\theta, a_1)E_\theta[\phi(X)]$$
$$= L(\theta, a_0) + [L(\theta, a_1) - L(\theta, a_0)]E_\theta[\phi(X)]. \qquad (8.10)$$

For any test ϕ, let ϕ' be the test of the form (8.5) which satisfies (8.8). By (8.10),

$$R(\theta, \phi) - R(\theta, \phi') = [L(\theta, a_1) - L(\theta, a_0)](E_\theta[\phi(X)] - E_\theta[\phi'(X)]). \quad (8.11)$$

For $\theta > \theta_0$, (8.8) and (8.9) imply that both terms on the right-hand side of (8.11) are nonpositive; for $\theta < \theta_0$, both terms are nonnegative; and for $\theta = \theta_0$, $E_\theta[\phi(X)] = E_\theta[\phi'(X)]$. Hence $R(\theta, \phi) \geq R(\theta, \phi')$, implying that ϕ' is R-better than or R-equivalent to ϕ. The class of tests of the form (8.5) is thus essentially complete. The proof of Part (ii) of the theorem will be left as an exercise. $\qquad \square$

For an application of the above complete class theorem, see Example 14 in Subsection 5.3.2.

8.4 Monotone Decision Problems

The key features of the decision problem discussed in the preceding section were that the distribution of X had monotone likelihood ratio and that the actions and corresponding losses had a particular order. In this section, we consider more general problems with these same basic properties, and again obtain simple and useful essentially complete classes of decision rules. The case in which the action space is finite is considered first.

8.4.1 Monotone Multiple Decision Problems

A multiple decision problem is a problem in which only a finite set of actions, $\mathscr{A} = \{a_1, a_2, \ldots, a_k\}$ ($k \geq 2$) is available. It will be convenient, in such problems, to continue the use of testing notation, so that a randomized decision rule will be represented by

$$\boldsymbol{\phi} = (\phi_1(x), \ldots, \phi_k(x)),$$

where $\phi_i(x)$ is the probability that action a_i is chosen when $X = x$ is observed. Note that $\sum_{i=1}^{k} \phi_i(x) = 1$ for all x, and that

$$R(\theta, \boldsymbol{\phi}) = \sum_{i=1}^{k} L(\theta, a_i) E_\theta[\phi_i(X)]. \tag{8.12}$$

A monotone multiple decision problem can be loosely thought of as a problem in which the parameter space is a subset of the real line and is divided into ordered intervals, with action a_i corresponding to the decision that θ is in the ith interval. When $k = 2$, this is simply the one-sided testing situation discussed in Section 8.3. A typical example of a monotone problem in which $k = 3$ is a one-sided testing problem in which a third action—indecision—is allowed. Imagine, for example, that θ represents the true difference in performance between two drugs being tested. It is quite standard in such a situation to decide either that drug 1 is better (a_1), that there is no conclusive evidence supporting either drug (a_2), or that drug 2 is better (a_3). These actions can be thought of as corresponding to three regions of the parameter space, say $(-\infty, \theta_1]$, (θ_1, θ_2), and $[\theta_2, \infty)$, although this interpretation is not strictly necessary. What is necessary, for the problem to be monotone, is that the loss must be larger the more "incorrect" the action is. In the above example, for instance, if drug 1 is indeed significantly better than drug 2, then a_2 should incur less loss than a_3, since it is closer to being correct. This notion is made precise in the following definition.

Definition 6. A multiple decision problem in which Θ is a subset of R^1 is said to be *monotone* if, for some ordering of $\mathscr{A}$, say $\mathscr{A} = \{a_1, \ldots, a_k\}$, there exist numbers $\theta_1 \leq \theta_2 \leq \cdots \leq \theta_{k-1}$ (all in Θ) such that the loss function satisfies (for $i = 1, \ldots, k - 1$)

$$\begin{aligned} L(\theta, a_i) - L(\theta, a_{i+1}) &\leq 0 \quad \text{for } \theta < \theta_i, \\ L(\theta, a_i) - L(\theta, a_{i+1}) &\geq 0 \quad \text{for } \theta > \theta_i. \end{aligned} \tag{8.13}$$

When $k = 2$, the relationship in (8.13) is exactly that specified by (8.9). This does, therefore, appear to be a natural extension of the one-sided testing situation. Note also, as a direct consequence of the inequalities in (8.13), that action a_i is preferred if $\theta_{i-1} < \theta < \theta_i$.

The intuitively natural decision rules, for a monotone multiple decision problem in which the observation X is in R^1 and has a distribution with monotone likelihood ratio, are those rules which divide $\mathscr{X}$ into k ordered intervals, and choose action a_i if x is in the ith interval. For simplicity, we only consider the situation in which $\mathscr{X} = R^1$.

Definition 7. For a monotone multiple decision problem with $\mathscr{X} = R^1$, a decision rule $\boldsymbol{\phi} = (\phi_1, \ldots, \phi_k)$ is said to be *monotone* if

$$
\phi_i(x) = \begin{cases}
0 & \text{if } x < x_{i-1}, \\
\gamma'_{i-1} & \text{if } x = x_{i-1}, \\
1 & \text{if } x_{i-1} < x < x_i, \\
\gamma_i & \text{if } x = x_i, \\
0 & \text{if } x > x_i,
\end{cases}
$$

where $x_0, x_1, \ldots, x_k$ satisfy $-\infty = x_0 \le x_1 \le x_2 \le \cdots \le x_k = +\infty$, and $0 \le \gamma_i \le 1$ and $0 \le \gamma'_i \le 1$ for $i = 1, \ldots, k-1$.

The essentially complete class theorem for monotone multiple decision problems is due to Karlin and Rubin (1956), and can be considered to be a generalization of Theorem 5 (i).

Theorem 6. *For a monotone multiple decision problem in which the distribution of X has monotone likelihood ratio and $\mathscr{X} = R^1$, the class of monotone decision rules is essentially complete.*

PROOF. The theorem will be established by constructing, for any decision rule $\boldsymbol{\psi} = (\psi_1(x), \ldots, \psi_k(x))$, a monotone decision rule, $\boldsymbol{\phi}$, which is R-better than or R-equivalent to $\boldsymbol{\psi}$. To begin the construction, define

$$
\begin{aligned}
\psi^k(x) &= 0, \\
\psi^j(x) &= \sum_{i=j+1}^{k} \psi_i(x) \quad \text{for } j = 0, \ldots, k-1.
\end{aligned}
\tag{8.14}
$$

Clearly $0 \le \psi^j(x) \le 1$, so that ψ^j can be considered to be a test of $H_0: \theta \le \theta_j$ versus $H_1: \theta > \theta_j$. Using Corollary 4.1 in Section 8.3, it follows that for $j = 1, \ldots, k-1$ there exists a one-sided test, ϕ^j, of the form

$$
\phi^j(x) = \begin{cases}
1 & \text{if } x > x_j, \\
\gamma''_j & \text{if } x = x_j, \\
0 & \text{if } x < x_j,
\end{cases}
\tag{8.15}
$$

such that

$$
E_\theta[\phi^j(X)] - E_\theta[\psi^j(X)] \begin{cases}
\le 0 & \text{for } \theta < \theta_j, \\
= 0 & \text{for } \theta = \theta_j, \\
\ge 0 & \text{for } \theta > \theta_j.
\end{cases}
\tag{8.16}
$$

(Expression (8.16) will also hold for $j = 0$ and $j = k$ if we choose $\phi^0(x) \equiv 1$ and $\phi^k(x) \equiv 0$.) Since the ψ^j are nonincreasing in j, it can be shown that the

ϕ^j can be chosen to be nonincreasing in j. Noting the form of the ϕ^j, it follows that we can assume that $x_1 \leq x_2 \leq \cdots \leq x_{k-1}$ and $\gamma''_{j-1} \geq \gamma''_j$ if $x_{j-1} = x_j$. Hence the test $\boldsymbol{\phi} = (\phi_1, \ldots, \phi_k)$, defined by

$$\phi_i(x) = \phi^{i-1}(x) - \phi^i(x), \qquad i = 1, \ldots, k, \tag{8.17}$$

is a monotone decision rule. To complete the proof, we show that $R(\theta, \boldsymbol{\psi}) \geq R(\theta, \boldsymbol{\phi})$.

Observe, using (8.12), (8.14), and (8.17), that

$$
\begin{aligned}
R(\theta, \boldsymbol{\psi}) - R(\theta, \boldsymbol{\phi}) &= \sum_{i=1}^{k} L(\theta, a_i)\{E_\theta[\psi_i(X)] - E_\theta[\phi_i(X)]\} \\
&= \sum_{i=1}^{k} L(\theta, a_i)\{(E_\theta[\phi^i(X)] - E_\theta[\psi^i(X)]) \\
&\qquad - (E_\theta[\phi^{i-1}(X)] - E_\theta[\psi^{i-1}(X)])\} \\
&= \sum_{i=1}^{k-1} [L(\theta, a_i) - L(\theta, a_{i+1})](E_\theta[\phi^i(X)] - E_\theta[\psi^i(X)]).
\end{aligned}
$$

Using (8.13) and (8.16) it is easy to see that in each term of the above sum, the expressions $L(\theta, a_i) - L(\theta, a_{i+1})$ and $E_\theta[\phi^i(X)] - E_\theta[\psi^i(X)]$ are either the same sign or the last expression is zero. Hence $R(\theta, \boldsymbol{\psi}) \geq R(\theta, \boldsymbol{\phi})$ for all $\theta \in \Theta$, completing the proof. $\square$

Theorem 5 (ii) showed that a monotone decision rule is virtually always admissible when $k = 2$. This need not be the case when $k \geq 3$, however, as is shown in the Exercises. Conditions under which monotone rules are admissible can be found in Karlin and Rubin (1956), Karlin (1956), Karlin (1957a), and Karlin (1957b).

The above theorem is particularly useful, in that the proof provides an explicit method of improving upon a nonmonotone decision rule. The construction of an improvement is quite simple since it depends on the loss function only through the "cut points" $\theta_1, \ldots, \theta_{k-1}$.

EXAMPLE 5. Based on the observation $X \sim \mathcal{N}(\theta, 1)$, it is desired to decide whether $\theta < -1$ (action a_1), $|\theta| \leq 1$ (action a_2), or $\theta > 1$ (action a_3). The loss function is

$$L(\theta, a_1) = \begin{cases} 0 & \text{if } \theta < -1, \\ \theta + 1 & \text{if } |\theta| \leq 1, \\ 2(\theta + 1) & \text{if } \theta > 1, \end{cases}$$

$$L(\theta, a_2) = \begin{cases} 0 & \text{if } |\theta| \leq 1, \\ |\theta| - 1 & \text{if } |\theta| > 1, \end{cases}$$

$$L(\theta, a_3) = \begin{cases} 0 & \text{if } \theta > 1, \\ 1 - \theta & \text{if } |\theta| \leq 1, \\ 2(1 - \theta) & \text{if } \theta < -1. \end{cases}$$

Consider the decision rule ψ, defined by

$$\psi_1(x) = I_{(-3, -1)}(x), \qquad \psi_2(x) = I_A(x), \qquad \psi_3(x) = I_{(1, 3)}(x), \quad (8.18)$$

where $A = (-\infty, -3] \cup [-1, 1] \cup [3, \infty)$.

It is easy to check that (8.13) is satisfied for the above loss, with $\theta_1 = -1$ and $\theta_2 = 1$, so that the decision problem is monotone. The decision rule ψ is not monotone, however, and so can be improved upon using the construction in the proof of Theorem 6. We begin by defining, as in (8.14),

$$\psi^0(x) = 1, \qquad \psi^1(x) = I_{(-\infty, -3] \cup [-1, \infty)}(x),$$

$$\psi^2(x) = I_{(1, 3)}(x), \qquad \psi^3(x) = 0.$$

The next step is to find one-sided UMP tests, ϕ^j, of the same size as ψ^j, for testing $H_0 : \theta \le \theta_j$ versus $H_1 : \theta > \theta_j$, $j = 1, 2$. The desired UMP tests are clearly of the form

$$\phi^j(x) = \begin{cases} 1 & \text{if } x > x_j, \\ 0 & \text{if } x < x_j, \end{cases}$$

and to attain equality in size between ϕ^j and ψ^j it must be true that

$$P_{-1}(X > x_1) = P_{-1}(X < -3) + P_{-1}(X > -1) = 0.5227$$

and

$$P_1(X > x_2) = P_1(1 < X < 3) = 0.4773.$$

From a table of normal probabilities it is easy to calculate that $x_1 = -1.057$ and $x_2 = 1.057$.

To complete the construction, one merely calculates the improved rule ϕ, using (8.17). In this case, ϕ is given by

$$\phi_1(x) = I_{(-\infty, -1.057)}(x), \qquad \phi_2(x) = I_{[-1.057, 1.057]}(x),$$

$$\phi_3(x) = I_{(1.057, \infty)}(x).$$

8.4.2 Monotone Estimation Problems

In this subsection, we consider the situation in which $\mathscr{A}$ is a closed subset of R^1, Θ is an interval in R^1, and the distribution of X has monotone likelihood ratio.

Definition 8. In the above situation, a decision problem is said to be *monotone* if the loss function $L(\theta, a)$ is such that, for each θ,

(a) $L(\theta, a)$ attains its minimum as a function of a at a point $a = q(\theta)$, where q is an increasing function of θ;

(b) $L(\theta, a)$, considered as a function of a, increases as a moves away from $q(\theta)$.

The usual examples of monotone decision problems of the above type are estimation problems. If, for example, it is desired to estimate θ under loss $L(\theta, a) = W(|\theta - a|)$, where W is increasing, it is easy to check that the conditions in Definition 8 are satisfied with $q(\theta) = \theta$.

Definition 9. A *randomized monotone decision rule* $\delta^*(x, \cdot)$ is a randomized rule with the following property: if $x_1 > x_2$ and A_1 and A_2 are open sets in $\mathscr{A}$ with A_1 lying to the left of A_2, then either $\delta^*(x_1, A_1) = 0$ or $\delta^*(x_2, A_2) = 0$.

A *nonrandomized monotone decision rule* $\delta(x)$ is simply a rule which is nondecreasing in x.

The definition of a randomized monotone decision rule can be seen to imply, as a special case, that of a nonrandomized monotone decision rule, and is also consistent with the definition of a monotone rule for the finite action case.

Theorem 7. *For a monotone decision problem, as defined in Definition 8, the class of (randomized) monotone decision rules is an essentially complete class.*

The above theorem was developed in Karlin and Rubin (1956), to which the reader is referred for a detailed proof. As in the finite action case, the proof proceeds by actually constructing, for any given nonmonotone (randomized) decision rule δ_0^*, a monotone (randomized) decision rule δ_M^* which is R-better than or R-equivalent to δ_0^*. This improved monotone rule can be shown (under suitable conditions) to be that monotone rule which satisfies, for each fixed $a \in \mathscr{A}$, the equality

$$\int \delta_M^*(x, (-\infty, a]) dF^X(x | q^{-1}(a)) = \int \delta_0^*(x, (-\infty, a]) dF^X(x | q^{-1}(a)), \quad (8.19)$$

where q^{-1} is the inverse function of q, defined by $q^{-1}(q(a)) = a$. The expressions in (8.19) are simply the overall probabilities that the respective rules will select an action in $(-\infty, a]$ when $\theta = q^{-1}(a)$ (the point at which $L(\theta, a)$, considered as a function of θ, is minimized).

When X has a continuous density, (8.19) can be considerably simplified. This is because δ_M^* will then be a nonrandomized rule, say $\delta_M(x)$, so that (8.19) will become

$$P_{q^{-1}(a)}(\delta_M(X) \le a) = V(\delta_0^*, a) \equiv \int \delta_0^*(x, (-\infty, a]) dF^X(x | q^{-1}(a)).$$

$$(8.20)$$

Even greater simplification is possible when $\delta_M(x)$ is strictly increasing. (Since δ_M is monotone, recall that it must at least be nondecreasing.) Indeed, it is then clear that

$$P_{q^{-1}(a)}(\delta_M(X) \le a) = P_{q^{-1}(a)}(X \le \delta_M^{-1}(a)) = F(\delta_M^{-1}(a) | q^{-1}(a)),$$

where δ_M^{-1} is the inverse function of δ_M, and F, as usual, is the cumulative distribution function of X. In this situation, (8.20) thus becomes

$$F(\delta_M^{-1}(a)|q^{-1}(a)) = V(\delta_0^*, a). \tag{8.21}$$

Now this relationship must hold for any $a \in \mathscr{A}$, so that, in particular, it must hold for $a = \delta_M(x)$, the action to be taken when x is observed. Plugging this into (8.21), we arrive at the conclusion that $\delta_M(x)$ is the action a for which

$$F(x|q^{-1}(a)) = V(\delta_0^*, a). \tag{8.22}$$

EXAMPLE 6. Assume that $X \sim \mathcal{N}(\theta, 1)$, and that it is desired to estimate θ under a loss $W(|\theta - a|)$, where W is an increasing function. It is easy to check that this is a monotone decision problem in the sense of Definition 8, and that q (and hence q^{-1}) is the identity function (i.e., $q(\theta) = \theta$).

Consider the decision rule $\delta_0(x) = -cx$, where $c > 0$. This is clearly nonmonotone, since it is decreasing in x. Hence we can find an improved monotone rule via the preceding construction.

Letting F_0 denote the cumulative distribution function of the $\mathcal{N}(0, 1)$ distribution, note first that

$$
\begin{aligned}
V(\delta_0^*, a) = P_{q^{-1}(a)}(\delta_0(X) \le a) &= P_a(-cX \le a) \\
&= P_a(X \ge -a/c) \\
&= 1 - F_0(-a(1 + c^{-1})) \\
&= F_0(a(1 + c^{-1})).
\end{aligned}
$$

Also,

$$F(x|q^{-1}(a)) = F(x|a) = F_0(x - a),$$

so that (8.22) becomes

$$F_0(x - a) = F_0(a(1 + c^{-1})).$$

It follows that $x - a = a(1 + c^{-1})$, or equivalently that $a = x/(2 + c^{-1})$. The monotone rule which is better than δ_0 is thus $\delta_M(x) = x/(2 + c^{-1})$.

An important and natural application of the above "monotonization" technique is to empirical Bayes estimation, since many natural empirical Bayes estimators are not necessarily monotone. (See, for instance, Example 12 in Subsection 4.4.5.) The solution to (8.22), or more generally (8.19), will rarely be obtainable in closed form for such problems, but numerical calculation is quite feasible.

8.5 Limits of Bayes Rules

In Theorem 2 of Subsection 8.2.3 it was seen that the Bayes procedures form a complete class. Such a result holds in a number of other circumstances, including certain of the situations discussed in Sections 8.3 and 8.4 and many situations in which Θ is closed and bounded. (See Theorem 10 in Section 8.7 for one such result.) Unfortunately, it is not in general true that the Bayes rules form a complete class. If, for instance, $X \sim \mathcal{N}(\theta, 1)$ is observed and it is desired to estimate θ under squared-error loss, it will be seen that $\delta(x) = x$ is an admissible estimator. This decision rule is not a Bayes rule (though it is a generalized Bayes rule with respect to $\pi(\theta) \equiv 1$) and, since it is admissible, the Bayes rules cannot form a complete class.

It is true, in very great generality, that limits (in various senses) of Bayes rules form a complete class. Such results are, unfortunately, too advanced mathematically to be presented here. The interested reader can consult Wald (1950), Le Cam (1955), Stein (1955), Farrell (1968a), and Brown (1976) for several such results and related applications. Brown (1976) gives a particularly thorough discussion.

Another reason that we will not extensively discuss complete class theorems concerning limits of Bayes rules is that they are of limited direct usefulness. Such theorems are of great importance theoretically, however, in that it is sometimes possible to explicitly describe limits of Bayes rules, which can lead to useful complete class results. In the estimation problem mentioned earlier, for instance, it can be shown that the admissible limits of Bayes rules are a subset of the class of generalized Bayes rules. (By an abuse of notation, we will, in the remainder of the chapter, consider the term *generalized Bayes rule* to stand for either a generalized Bayes (improper prior) or a Bayes (proper prior) rule.) This example will be discussed further in Section 8.8. Certain other situations, in which the limits of Bayes rules have a particularly simple form, will be discussed in the next section.

8.6 Other Complete and Essentially Complete Classes of Tests

In this section we briefly discuss, without detailed proofs, several other interesting complete and essentially complete class results concerning testing.

8.6.1 Two-Sided Testing

It is frequently of interest to test hypotheses of the form $H_0: \theta = \theta_0$ versus $H_1: \theta \neq \theta_0$, or $H_0: \theta_1 \leq \theta \leq \theta_2$ versus $H_1: \theta < \theta_1$ or $\theta > \theta_2$. As in Section 8.3, an essentially complete class of tests can be obtained for this situation, providing the distribution of X is of a certain type. The relevant type here is called *Polya type 3*, and includes the distributions in the one-parameter exponential family.

The essentially complete class theorem can be stated in terms of a general two-action decision problem which corresponds to the above testing situation. Indeed, the needed conditions on the structure of the problem are that $\mathscr{A} = \{a_0, a_1\}$ and that the loss function satisfies

$$
\begin{aligned}
L(\theta, a_1) - L(\theta, a_0) &\geq 0 && \text{if } \theta_1 < \theta < \theta_2, \\
L(\theta, a_1) - L(\theta, a_0) &\leq 0 && \text{if } \theta < \theta_1 \text{ or } \theta > \theta_2.
\end{aligned}
\tag{8.23}
$$

It is then true that an essentially complete class of decision rules is the class of *two-sided tests* of the form

$$
\phi(x) = \begin{cases}
1 & \text{if } x < x_1 \text{ or } x > x_2, \\
\gamma_i & \text{if } x = x_i, \, i = 1, 2, \\
0 & \text{if } x_1 < x < x_2.
\end{cases}
$$

For a development of this theory, and generalizations to other two-action problems, see Karlin (1956).

8.6.2 Higher Dimensional Results

In the situation of the previous subsection, if X has a continuous density, then the class of two-sided tests is simply the class of tests whose acceptance region (for H_0) is an interval. (The boundary points of the acceptance region are immaterial for a continuous density.) The natural generalization of an interval to higher dimensions is a convex set, and indeed complete class results concerning such a generalization have been obtained. We state here only the simplest meaningful version of such a complete class result, one due to Birnbaum (1955).

Assume that $\mathbf{X}$ is a random vector in R^p with a continuous density from the p-dimensional exponential family, i.e.,

$$
f(\mathbf{x}|\boldsymbol{\theta}) = c(\boldsymbol{\theta})h(\mathbf{x})\exp\{\boldsymbol{\theta}'\mathbf{x}\},
$$

where $\boldsymbol{\theta} \in R^p$. (The multivariate normal distribution with known covariance matrix can be transformed so as to have a density of this form.) It is desired to test $H_0: \boldsymbol{\theta} = \boldsymbol{\theta}_0$ versus $H_1: \boldsymbol{\theta} \neq \boldsymbol{\theta}_0$, under, say, "0–1" loss. As shown in Birnbaum (1955), it is then true, under quite weak conditions, that the tests with convex acceptance regions (for H_0) form a minimal complete class. A rough outline of the proof is as follows.

First, it can be shown that all Bayes rules have convex acceptance regions, from which it follows easily that all limits of Bayes rules have convex acceptance regions. Since the limits of Bayes rules form a complete class, as alluded to in the previous section, it can be concluded that the tests with convex acceptance regions form a complete class. To prove that this complete class is minimal complete, it suffices to show that any test ϕ with a convex acceptance region A is admissible. This last fact is established by showing that for any other test ϕ' with a convex acceptance region A' whose size is no larger than that of ϕ (i.e., $E_{\theta_0}[\phi'(\mathbf{X})] \leq E_{\theta_0}[\phi(\mathbf{X})]$), there exists a sequence of points $\{\boldsymbol{\theta}_i\}$ with $|\boldsymbol{\theta}_i| \to \infty$ such that $E_{\boldsymbol{\theta}_i}[\phi'(\mathbf{X})] < E_{\boldsymbol{\theta}_i}[\phi(\mathbf{X})]$ for large enough i. In terms of risk functions, this means that if $R(\boldsymbol{\theta}_0, \phi') \leq R(\boldsymbol{\theta}_0, \phi)$, then

$$R(\boldsymbol{\theta}_i, \phi') = E_{\boldsymbol{\theta}_i}[1 - \phi'(\mathbf{X})] > E_{\boldsymbol{\theta}_i}[1 - \phi(\mathbf{X})] = R(\boldsymbol{\theta}_i, \phi)$$

for large enough i, proving the admissibility of ϕ. The sequence $\{\boldsymbol{\theta}_i\}$ is chosen as follows. First, it can be shown that there exists a convex set $B \subset A$ such that B is disjoint from A'. Let H be a supporting hyperplane to B, at say $\mathbf{x}_0 \in B$, which separates B and A'. Finally, let l_0 be the half line perpendicular to H at $\mathbf{x}_0$, and going from $\mathbf{x}_0$ to infinity through B. Choose the $\boldsymbol{\theta}_i$ to be points along l_0. The reason this works is that, as $|\boldsymbol{\theta}| \to \infty$ along this half line, the distribution of $\mathbf{X}$ gives much more mass to B (and hence A) than to A'.

The above result has been generalized in several directions. See, for example, Farrell (1968a) and Brown (1976).

8.6.3 Sequential Testing

Complete and essentially complete class results are of great potential usefulness in sequential analysis, due to the difficulties in finding optimal stopping rules. If the class of possible stopping rules can be substantially reduced, many otherwise intractable calculations may become feasible.

One quite useful sequential result was obtained by Sobel (1953) for the situation of testing $H_0: \theta \leq \theta_0$ versus $H_1: \theta > \theta_0$, based on a sequential sample from the density (on R^1)

$$f(x|\theta) = c(\theta)h(x)\exp\{\theta x\} \tag{8.24}$$

in the one-parameter exponential family. The loss was assumed to be of the form

$$L(\theta, a, n) = L(\theta, a) + C(n),$$

i.e., the sum of a decision loss and a sampling cost. Sobel (1953) assumed that (i) $C(n) \to \infty$, (ii) the loss specifies a region about θ_0 in which one is indifferent between H_0 and H_1, and (iii) the loss is zero for a correct decision and is nondecreasing in $\theta - \theta_0$ and $\theta_0 - \theta$ for incorrectly deciding H_0 and H_1, respectively. Brown, Cohen, and Strawderman (1980a and 1980b) show, however, that only Condition (iii) is actually needed for the essentially complete class result.

The basic result for the above situation is that the procedures of the following form constitute an essentially complete class of sequential procedures. Define $s_n = \sum_{i=1}^{n} x_i$, and let $\{a_1, a_2, \ldots\}$ and $\{b_1, b_2, \ldots\}$ be sequences of constants such that $a_i \leq b_i$ ($i = 1, 2, \ldots$). The procedure based on these constants is to

$$\begin{array}{ll}
\text{decide } H_0 & \text{if } s_n < a_n, \\
\text{decide } H_1 & \text{if } s_n > b_n, \\
\text{continue sampling} & \text{if } a_n < s_n < b_n,
\end{array} \qquad (8.25)$$

where randomization between deciding H_0 and continuing sampling is allowed if $s_n = a_n$, and randomization between deciding H_1 and continuing sampling is allowed if $s_n = b_n$.

Note that tests of the form (8.25) are a natural generalization of the sequential probability ratio test discussed in Section 7.5; indeed the SPRT of $H_0: \theta = \theta_0$ versus $H_1: \theta = \theta_1$, for the density (8.24), is of the form (8.25) with

$$a_n = (\theta_1 - \theta_0)^{-1}\left[a - n \log\left\{\frac{c(\theta_1)}{c(\theta_0)}\right\}\right],$$

$$b_n = (\theta_1 - \theta_0)^{-1}\left[b - n \log\left\{\frac{c(\theta_1)}{c(\theta_0)}\right\}\right].$$

For this reason, sequential tests of the form (8.25) are often called *generalized sequential probability ratio tests*. The term *monotone sequential tests* is also common and natural.

The proof of the above essentially complete class result is based on showing that Bayes procedures and limits of Bayes procedures are of the form (8.25), or are at least R-equivalent to procedures of the form (8.25). Since, again, the limits of Bayes procedures form a complete class, the result follows. For details, see Brown, Cohen, and Strawderman (1980a).

Several other interesting complete and essentially complete class results for sequential problems have been obtained by Brown, Cohen, and Strawderman (1980b). These results again apply to the situation in which the overall loss is the sum of a decision loss and the cost of observation. It is first shown that for a wide variety of sequential problems in which the closure of the null hypothesis is closed and bounded, the Bayes or generalized Bayes procedures form a complete or essentially complete class, the exact result depending on various features of the problem. One minor, but useful, consequence of such a result is that when dealing with a situation in which the Bayes or generalized Bayes procedures are known to be nonrandomized, the nonrandomized sequential procedures will form a complete or essentially complete class.

Another result obtained in Brown, Cohen, and Strawderman (1980b) is that the generalized Bayes tests form an essentially complete class for the one-sided testing problem considered by Sobel. Since the generalized Bayes tests are a subset of the class of rules of the form (8.25), this result provides a smaller essentially complete class than that obtained by Sobel. Unfortunately, it can be difficult to decide which procedures of the form (8.25) are, or are not, generalized Bayes.

8.7 Continuous Risk Functions

For a number of decision-theoretic results, it is important to know when decision rules have continuous risk functions. Theorem 3 in Section 4.5, Theorem 10 of this section, and Theorem 11 in the next section are typical examples of results for which this knowledge is needed. There are a variety of results establishing the continuity of risk functions; some proving that all decision rules have continuous risk functions and some showing that the decision rules with continuous risk functions form a complete class (and hence that any admissible decision rule has a continuous risk function). Unfortunately, these results and their proofs generally involve measure-theoretic notions. We will, therefore, merely state two quite useful theorems of this nature, and give another complete class result as an application.

Theorem 8. Suppose $\Theta \subset R^m$ and that $L(\theta, a)$ is a bounded function which is continuous in θ for each $a \in \mathscr{A}$. Suppose also that X has a density $f(x|\theta)$ which is continuous in θ for each $x \in \mathscr{X}$. Then all decision rules have continuous risk functions.

The most restrictive condition in the above theorem is the condition that the loss function be bounded. When Θ is unbounded, many standard losses, such as squared-error loss, will not satisfy this condition. The boundedness condition can be relaxed, as shown in the following theorem, at the expense of requiring more of the density.

Theorem 9. Suppose that $\mathscr{X}$, Θ, and $\mathscr{A}$ are subsets of R^1, with $\mathscr{A}$ being closed, and that the distribution of X has monotone likelihood ratio. Suppose also that $f(x|\theta)$ is continuous in θ for each $x \in \mathscr{X}$, and that the loss function $L(\theta, a)$ is such that

(a) $L(\theta, a)$ is continuous in θ for each $a \in \mathscr{A}$;
(b) $L(\theta, a)$ is nonincreasing in a for $a \leq \theta$ and is nondecreasing in a for $a \geq \theta$;
(c) there exist functions $K_1(\theta_1, \theta_2)$ and $K_2(\theta_1, \theta_2)$ on $\Theta \times \Theta$ which are bounded on all bounded subsets of $\Theta \times \Theta$, and such that

$$L(\theta_2, a) \leq K_1(\theta_1, \theta_2)L(\theta_1, a) + K_2(\theta_1, \theta_2)$$

for all $a \in \mathscr{A}$.

Then the decision rules with continuous, finite-valued risk functions form a complete class.

For proofs of the above theorems, and other such results, see Brown (1976). Ferguson (1967) also gives similar theorems.

EXAMPLE 7. Let $X \sim \mathcal{N}(\theta, 1)$ and assume that it is desired to estimate θ under squared-error loss. The only condition in Theorem 9 which is not obviously satisfied is Condition (c). To check this condition, note that

$$(\theta_2 - a)^2 = ([\theta_2 - \theta_1] + [\theta_1 - a])^2$$
$$\leq 2(\theta_2 - \theta_1)^2 + 2(\theta_1 - a)^2.$$

Hence Condition (c) is satisfied with $K_1(\theta_1, \theta_2) = 2$ and $K_2(\theta_1, \theta_2) = 2(\theta_2 - \theta_1)^2$. It can be concluded that the decision rules with continuous risk functions form a complete class.

As an example of a complete class result which requires continuity of the risk functions, we state the following theorem. This theorem can be found, in considerably greater generality and with a proof, in Brown (1976).

Theorem 10. *Assume that $\mathcal{A}$ and Θ are closed and bounded subsets of Euclidean space and, as usual, that X has a continuous or a discrete density. Assume also that $L(\theta, a)$ is a continuous function of a for each $\theta \in \Theta$, and that all decision rules have continuous risk functions. Then the Bayes rules form a complete class.*

8.8 Stein's Necessary and Sufficient Condition for Admissibility

8.8.1 Heuristic Statement of the Condition

Inasmuch as the class of admissible decision rules frequently forms a minimal complete class (see Blackwell and Girshick (1954) and Brown (1976) for certain theorems of this nature), conditions characterizing the admissible decision rules will frequently provide a characterization of a complete class. One of the most fruitful characterizations of admissible rules is what has come to be called *Stein's necessary and sufficient condition for admissibility*, developed in Stein (1955b). The basic result, as generalized by LeCam, is reported in Farrell (1968a). (See also Farrell (1968b).) Unfortunately, the result in its full generality involves mathematics beyond the level of this text. In Farrell (1968a), however, a more concrete version of the general result was developed, one which is more amenable to discussion at our level. This result can be roughly stated as follows.

Result 1. *Under suitable conditions, a decision rule δ is admissible if and only if there exists a sequence $\{\pi_n\}$ of (generalized) prior distributions such that*

(a) *each π_n gives mass only to a closed and bounded set (possibly different for each n), and hence has finite total mass;*

(b) *there is a closed and bounded set $C \subset \Theta$ to which each π_n gives mass one;*
(c) $\lim_{n \to \infty} [r(\pi_n, \delta) - r(\pi_n, \delta^n)] = 0$, *where δ^n is the Bayes decision rule with respect to π_n. (Note that since π_n has finite mass, there is usually no difficulty in talking about Bayes rules and Bayes risks.)*

For precise theorems of the above nature, and proofs, see Farrell (1968a) and Farrell (1968b). In the remainder of the section we explore the meaning and consequences of Result 1.

8.8.2 Proving Admissibility

Being a sufficient condition for admissibility, Result 1 obviously provides a tool for verifying the admissibility of a decision rule. The use of this sufficient condition actually predates Stein (1955b), first appearing in Blyth (1951). Although it is the "necessary" part of Result 1 that leads to complete class theorems, discussion and an example of the use of the sufficient condition are helpful in understanding the result. The rationale for the sufficient condition is quite elementary, and is given in the proof of the following easier to use version of the sufficient condition. This version can essentially be found in Farrell (1964) and Brown (1971).

Theorem 11. *Consider a decision problem in which Θ is a nondegenerate convex subset of Euclidean space (i.e., Θ has positive Lebesgue measure), and in which the decision rules with continuous risk functions form a complete class. Then an estimator δ_0 (with a continuous risk function) is admissible if there exists a sequence $\{\pi_n\}$ of (generalized) priors such that*

(a) *the Bayes risks $r(\pi_n, \delta_0)$ and $r(\pi_n, \delta^n)$ are finite for all n, where δ^n is the Bayes rule with respect to π_n;*
(b) *for any nondegenerate convex set $C \subset \Theta$, there exists a $K > 0$ and an integer N such that, for $n \geq N$,*

$$\int_C dF^{\pi_n}(\theta) \geq K;$$

(c) $\lim_{n \to \infty} [r(\pi_n, \delta_0) - r(\pi_n, \delta^n)] = 0$.

PROOF. Suppose δ_0 is not admissible. Then there exists a decision rule δ' such that $R(\theta, \delta') \leq R(\theta, \delta_0)$, with strict inequality for some θ, say θ_0. Since the rules with continuous risk functions form a complete class, it can be assumed that δ' has a continuous risk function. Since $R(\theta, \delta_0)$ is also continuous, it follows that there exist constants $\varepsilon_1 > 0$ and $\varepsilon_2 > 0$ such that $R(\theta, \delta') < R(\theta, \delta_0) - \varepsilon_1$ for $\theta \in C = \{\theta \in \Theta : |\theta - \theta_0| < \varepsilon_2\}$. Using this, Conditions (a) and (b), and the fact that $r(\pi_n, \delta'') \le r(\pi_n, \delta')$, it can be concluded that for $n \ge N$,

$$
\begin{aligned}
r(\pi_n, \delta_0) - r(\pi_n, \delta'') &\ge r(\pi_n, \delta_0) - r(\pi_n, \delta') \\
&= E^{\pi_n}[R(\theta, \delta_0) - R(\theta, \delta')] \\
&\ge \int_C [R(\theta, \delta_0) - R(\theta, \delta')] dF^{\pi_n}(\theta) \\
&\ge \varepsilon_1 \int_C dF^{\pi_n}(\theta) \ge \varepsilon_1 K.
\end{aligned}
$$

This contradicts Condition (c) of the theorem. Hence δ_0 must be admissible. $\square$

EXAMPLE 8 (Blyth (1951)). Suppose that $X \sim \mathcal{N}(\theta, 1)$ and that it is desired to estimate θ under squared-error loss. We seek to prove that the usual estimator, $\delta_0(x) = x$, is admissible.

The conditions of Theorem 11 will clearly be satisfied for this situation (see Example 7), once a suitable sequence $\{\pi_n\}$ is found. A convenient choice for π_n is the unnormalized normal density

$$
\pi_n(\theta) = (2\pi)^{-1/2} \exp\left\{\frac{-\theta^2}{2n}\right\}.
$$

If C is a nondegenerate convex subset of Θ, then clearly

$$
\int_C \pi_n(\theta) d\theta \ge \int_C \pi_1(\theta) d\theta = K > 0,
$$

so that Condition (b) of Theorem 11 is satisfied for this choice of the π_n. (Note that standard $\mathcal{N}(0, 1/n)$ prior densities would not satisfy this condition.) A straightforward Bayesian calculation, similar to that with normal priors, shows that $r(\pi_n, \delta_0) = \sqrt{n}$ and $r(\pi_n, \delta'') = \sqrt{n}n/(1 + n)$, verifying Condition (a). Finally,

$$
\begin{aligned}
\lim_{n \to \infty} [r(\pi_n, \delta_0) - r(\pi_n, \delta'')] &= \lim_{n \to \infty} \left[\sqrt{n}\left(1 - \frac{n}{n+1}\right)\right] \\
&= \lim_{n \to \infty} \left[\frac{\sqrt{n}}{1 + n}\right] = 0.
\end{aligned}
$$

Condition (c) of Theorem 11 is thus satisfied, and it can be concluded that δ_0 is admissible.

The above technique for proving admissibility is very similar to the technique presented in Theorem 18 of Subsection 5.3.2 for proving that a decision rule is minimax. The admissibility technique is more difficult, however, in that the necessity for the π_n to satisfy both Conditions (b) and (c) of Theorem

11 tends to be very restrictive. Indeed, in general, very elaborate (and difficult to work with) choices of the π_n are needed. See Stein (1959), James and Stein (1960), Farrell (1964), and Berger (1976) for indications of this.

8.8.3 Generalized Bayes Rules

We have already encountered testing situations in which the generalized Bayes rules form a complete class. In this subsection, we will discuss an estimation problem for which this is the case. The basic theorem (Theorem 12 below) is developed through the use of Result 1, by showing that if δ is admissible, so that a sequence $\{\pi_n\}$ as described in Result 1 exists, then the π_n converge (in a certain sense) to a generalized prior π, with respect to which δ is generalized Bayes. The detailed proof is again too difficult to be included here. The reader is referred to Berger and Srinivasan (1978) or Brown (1971) for such a proof. See also Sacks (1963).

Theorem 12. *Suppose that it is desired to estimate, under a quadratic loss, the (natural) parameter vector from a continuous distribution in the p-dimensional exponential family (see Subsection 8.6.2), and that the parameter space is closed. Then any admissible estimator is a generalized Bayes rule.*

The above theorem is useful for two reasons. First, in situations such as that of Theorem 12, it is known how to determine whether or not a rule δ is generalized Bayes. Second, in some such situations results are available concerning which generalized Bayes rules are admissible. It follows that the minimal complete class (or something close to it) can be stated in terms of verifiable conditions on the estimator, completing the task of the theoretical decision theorist.

The main situation in which the above program has been carried out is that of estimating a multivariate normal mean (known covariance matrix) under a quadratic loss. Theorem 12 clearly implies, for this situation, that any admissible estimator must be generalized Bayes. The following theorem (which can be found in Berger and Srinivasan (1978), a special case of which was given in Strawderman and Cohen (1971)) gives the conditions under which an estimator is generalized Bayes.

Theorem 13. *Suppose that $\mathbf{X} \sim \mathcal{N}_p(\boldsymbol{\theta}, \Sigma)$, Σ known, and that it is desired to estimate $\boldsymbol{\theta}$ under a quadratic loss. Then an estimator $\boldsymbol{\delta}(\mathbf{x})$ is generalized Bayes (and hence potentially admissible) if and only if*

(a) *the vector function $\mathbf{g}(\mathbf{x}) = \Sigma^{-1}\boldsymbol{\delta}(\mathbf{x})$ is continuously differentiable, and the $p \times p$ matrix of first partial derivatives of $\mathbf{g}$ is symmetric;*

(b) *$\exp\{h(\mathbf{x})\}$ is a Laplace transform (of some generalized prior), where $h(\mathbf{x})$ is the real-valued function which has $\mathbf{g}(\mathbf{x})$ as a gradient. (When Condition (a) holds, $h(\mathbf{x})$ is known to exist.)*

The function $h(\mathbf{x})$ can be found by calculating the line integral of $\mathbf{g}(\mathbf{x})$ along any path from a fixed point $\mathbf{x}_0$ to $\mathbf{x}$. The verification that $\exp\{h(\mathbf{x})\}$ is a Laplace transform can usually be carried out using techniques from Widder (1946) and Hirschmann and Widder (1955). Condition (a) is the easiest and in some sense the most important (see Berger and Srinivasan (1978)) condition to verify. As a simple example, consider the estimator $\delta(\mathbf{x}) = \mathbf{A}\mathbf{x}$, where $\mathbf{A}$ is a $p \times p$ matrix. Clearly $\mathbf{g}(\mathbf{x}) = \boldsymbol{\Sigma}^{-1}\mathbf{A}\mathbf{x}$ is continuously differentiable, and its matrix of first partial derivatives is $\boldsymbol{\Sigma}^{-1}\mathbf{A}$. Hence, for Condition (a) of Theorem 13 to be satisfied, it must be true that $\mathbf{A}$ is of the form $\boldsymbol{\Sigma}\mathbf{B}$, where $\mathbf{B}$ is a symmetric $p \times p$ matrix. Condition (b) is also relatively easy to check in this situation. Indeed $h(\mathbf{x})$ can be seen to be $h(\mathbf{x}) = \mathbf{x}'\mathbf{B}\mathbf{x}/2$, and $\exp\{h(\mathbf{x})\}$ is a Laplace transform of a generalized prior if and only if $\mathbf{B}$ is positive semi-definite.

To complete the analysis of the normal mean estimation problem, it is necessary to know when a generalized Bayes estimator is admissible. In a tour-de-force, Brown (1971) derived often quite simple conditions for determining whether or not a generalized Bayes estimator is admissible. These conditions are based on the behavior of $\delta(\mathbf{x})$ for large $|\mathbf{x}|$, or, alternatively, on the behavior of the generalized prior for large $|\boldsymbol{\theta}|$. (A very interesting relationship between the admissibility of the estimator and the recurrence of an associated diffusion process was also discovered in Brown (1971).) As a simple example of these conditions, we state the following theorem.

Theorem 14. *Suppose that* $\mathbf{X} \sim \mathcal{N}_p(\boldsymbol{\theta}, \mathbf{I}_p)$ *and that it is desired to estimate* $\boldsymbol{\theta}$ *under sum-of-squares error loss. Then a generalized Bayes estimator of the form*

$$\delta(\mathbf{x}) = (1 - h(|\mathbf{x}|))\mathbf{x}$$

is

(i) *inadmissible if there exist* $\varepsilon > 0$ *and* $K < \infty$ *such that*

$$h(|\mathbf{x}|) \leq -\frac{(2 - p + \varepsilon)}{|\mathbf{x}|^2}$$

for $|\mathbf{x}| > K$;
(ii) *admissible if there exist* $K_1 < \infty$ *and* $K_2 < \infty$ *such that* $|\mathbf{x}|h(|\mathbf{x}|) \leq K_1$ *for all* $\mathbf{x}$ *and*

$$h(|\mathbf{x}|) \geq -\frac{(2 - p)}{|\mathbf{x}|^2}$$

for $|\mathbf{x}| > K_2$.

As a simple application of Theorem 14, note that the usual estimator $\delta(\mathbf{x}) = \mathbf{x}$ (i.e., $h(\mathbf{x}) = 0$) is inadmissible if $p \geq 3$ and admissible if $p = 1$ or $p = 2$, facts that have been previously noted.

Exercises

Section 8.1

1. Prove Lemma 1.

2. Prove Lemma 2.

3. Prove that if $\mathscr{C}$ is a complete class and contains no proper essentially complete subclass, then $\mathscr{C}$ is a minimal complete class.

4. Prove that if the class of admissible rules is complete, it is minimal complete.

Section 8.2

5. Give an example, in terms of the risk set S, in which the conclusion of Theorem 1 is violated if S is not
   (a) closed from below,
   (b) bounded from below.

6. Use a modification of Exercise 24 of Chapter 5 (namely, a different choice of P) to show that the conclusion of Theorem 1 can be true even when S is not closed from below.

7. Find the minimal complete class of decision rules when $n = 2$ for the situation of
   (a) Exercise 46 of Chapter 5,
   (b) Exercise 47 of Chapter 5.

8. If $X \sim \mathscr{C}(\theta, 1)$, show that the test

$$\phi(x) = \begin{cases} 1 & \text{if } 1 < x < 3, \\ 0 & \text{otherwise,} \end{cases}$$

   is most powerful of its size for testing $H_0: \theta = 0$ versus $H_1: \theta = 1$.

9. Let ϕ be a most powerful test of size $0 < \alpha < 1$ for testing $H_0: \theta = \theta_0$ versus $H_1: \theta = \theta_1$. Show that $E_{\theta_1}[\phi(X)] > \alpha$, providing the distributions of X under θ_0 and θ_1 differ.

Section 8.3

10. Verify that the following distributions have monotone likelihood ratio:
    (a) $\mathscr{B}e(\alpha, \beta)$, β fixed,
    (b) $\mathscr{B}e(\alpha, \beta)$, α fixed (MLR in $-X$),
    (c) $\mathscr{U}(0, \theta)$,
    (d) $f(x|\alpha, \beta) = (2\beta)^{-1} \exp\{-|x - \alpha|/\beta\}$, β fixed,
    (e) $f(x|\theta) = \exp\{-(x - \theta)\}I_{(\theta, \infty)}(x)$.

11. Find a counterexample to Part (ii) of Theorem 4 if the size of the test is allowed to be zero.

12. If $X \sim \mathscr{C}(0, \theta)$, show that the sufficient statistic $|X|$ has monotone likelihood ratio.

13. Assume that $X_1, \ldots, X_n$ is a sample from the $\mathcal{U}(\theta, \theta + 1)$ distribution, and that it is desired to test $H_0: \theta \leq 0$ versus $H_1: \theta > 0$. Defining $t_1 = \min\{x_i\}$ and $t_2 = \max\{x_i\}$, show that

$$\phi(t_1, t_2) = \begin{cases} 0 & \text{if } t_1 < 1 - \alpha^{1/n} \text{ and } t_2 < 1, \\ 1 & \text{otherwise}, \end{cases}$$

is a UMP test of size α.

14. Prove Part (ii) of Theorem 5.

Section 8.4

15. Assume that $X \sim \mathcal{N}(\theta, 1)$, that $\Theta = [-1, 1]$, that $\mathscr{A} = \{a_1, a_2, a_3\}$, and that $L(\theta, a_1) = (\theta + 1)^2$, $L(\theta, a_2) = \theta^2$, and $L(\theta, a_3) = (\theta - 1)^2$. Show that this is a monotone multiple decision problem.

16. Assume that $X \sim \mathscr{B}(5, \theta)$, that $\Theta = [0, 1]$, that $\mathscr{A} = \{a_1, a_2, a_3\}$, and that the loss function satisfies (8.13) with $\theta_1 = \frac{1}{3}$ and $\theta_2 = \frac{2}{3}$. Find a monotone decision rule which is R-better than or R-equivalent to the decision rule ψ, defined by

$$\psi_1(x) = I_{\{0, 3\}}(x), \qquad \psi_2(x) = I_{\{1, 4\}}(x), \qquad \psi_3(x) = I_{\{2, 5\}}(x).$$

17. In the situation of Exercise 15, show that the monotone decision rule ϕ, defined by

$$\phi_1(x) = I_{(-\infty, -0.1)}(x), \qquad \phi_2(x) = I_{[-0.1, 0.1]}(x), \qquad \phi_3(x) = I_{(0.1, \infty)}(x)$$

is inadmissible.

18. In Definition 9, show that the definition of a nonrandomized monotone decision rule is consistent with the definition of a randomized monotone decision rule.

19. Assume that $X \sim \mathcal{N}(\theta, 1)$, that $\Theta = \mathscr{A} = (-\infty, \infty)$, and that $L(\theta, a) = (\theta - a)^2$. Someone proposes the estimator $\delta_0(x) = -cx + b$, where $c > 0$. Find an R-better monotone estimator.

20. Assume that $X \sim \mathcal{N}(\theta, 1)$, that $\Theta = \mathscr{A} = (-\infty, \infty)$, and that $L(\theta, a) = (\theta - a)^2$. Someone proposes the estimator

$$\delta_0(x) = \begin{cases} 0 & \text{if } x < -1, \\ x & \text{if } x \geq -1. \end{cases}$$

Show that an R-better monotone estimator, δ_M, can be described as follows. Let F_0 denote the cumulative distribution function of the $\mathcal{N}(0, 1)$ distribution, let F_0^{-1} denote the functional inverse of F_0, and define $\tau = F_0^{-1}(\frac{1}{2} - F_0(-1))$. If $-\infty < x < \tau$, then $\delta_M(x)$ is that action $a (-1 < a < 0)$ which satisfies

$$F_0(x - a) = \frac{1}{2} - F_0(-(1 + a));$$

if $\tau \leq x < 0$, then $\delta_M(x) = 0$; and if $x \geq 0$, then $\delta_M(x) = x$.

Section 8.6

21. Assume that $X \sim \mathscr{B}e(\theta, 1)$, that $\mathscr{A} = \{a_0, a_1\}$, and that the loss function is of the form (8.23). A test ϕ is proposed for which $E_{\theta_1}[\phi(X)] = 0.5$ and $E_{\theta_2}[\phi(X)] = 0.3$. Find a test that is R-better than or R-equivalent to ϕ.

Section 8.7

22. Verify that the following loss functions satisfy Condition (c) of Theorem 9:
    (a) $L(\theta, a) = |\theta - a|^k, k > 0, \Theta = \mathscr{A} = R^1$,
    (b) $L(\theta, a) = \exp\{|\theta - a|\}, \Theta = \mathscr{A} = R^1$,
    (c) $L(\theta, a) = (\log[a/\theta])^2, \Theta = \mathscr{A} = [1, \infty)$.

23. If $L(\theta, a) = \exp\{(\theta - a)^2\}$, where $\Theta = \mathscr{A} = R^1$, show that Condition (c) of Theorem 9 is violated.

24. Assume that $X \sim \mathscr{B}(1, \theta)$ is observed, and that it is desired to estimate $\theta \in [0, 1]$ under squared-error loss. Since the loss is convex, attention can be restricted to nonrandomized decision rules. A nonrandomized rule can be written as a vector (y, z), where $0 \leq y \leq 1$ and $0 \leq z \leq 1$ are the estimates of θ if $x = 0$ and $x = 1$ are observed, respectively.
    (a) Find a Bayes rule with respect to a given prior distribution π, and show that any prior distribution, π', with the same first two moments as π has the same Bayes rule.
    (b) Plot the set of all nonrandomized Bayes rules.
    (c) Show that the set of rules found in Part (b) is a complete class.
    (d) Show that the set of rules found in Part (b) is a minimal complete class. (*Hint*: Unless π gives mass one to $\theta = 0$ or to $\theta = 1$, show that the Bayes rule is unique. When π gives mass one to $\theta = 0$ or to $\theta = 1$, show directly that any Bayes rule is admissible.)

Section 8.8

25. Assume that $X \sim \mathscr{N}(\theta, 1)$, and that it is desired to estimate θ under loss $L(\theta, a) = |\theta - a|$. Show that $\delta_0(x) = x$ is an admissible estimator.

26. Assume that $\mathbf{X} \sim \mathscr{N}_p(\mathbf{0}, \mathbf{\Sigma})(p \geq 2)$, where $\mathbf{\Sigma}$ is known, and that it is desired to estimate $\mathbf{0}$ under a quadratic loss. Consider the estimator

$$\delta(\mathbf{x}) = (\mathbf{\Sigma}^{-1} + (\mathbf{x}'\mathbf{C}\mathbf{x})^{-1}\mathbf{A})^{-1}\mathbf{\Sigma}^{-1}\mathbf{x}, \qquad (8.26)$$

where $\mathbf{C}$ is positive definite. Show that unless $\mathbf{A}$ is a constant multiple of $\mathbf{C}$, such an estimator cannot be generalized Bayes, and hence cannot be admissible. (The estimators of the form (8.26) are called *adaptive ridge regression* estimators, and have been proposed for use as estimators of regression coefficients in standard linear regression.)

APPENDIX 1

Common Statistical Densities

For convenience, we list here several common statistical densities that are used in examples and exercises throughout the book. The listings are brief, giving only the name of the density, the abbreviation that will be used for the density, the sample space $\mathscr{X}$, the range of the parameter values, the density itself, useful moments of the density, important special cases, and a brief explanation if needed for clarification.

In the listings, det $\mathbf{B}$ will stand for the determinant of the matrix $\mathbf{B}$; the symbol $I_A(z)$ is defined by

$$I_A(z) = \begin{cases} 1 & \text{if } z \in A, \\ 0 & \text{if } z \notin A, \end{cases}$$

and is called the *indicator function* on the set A; and $\Gamma(\alpha)$ is the usual gamma function, defined by

$$\Gamma(\alpha) = \int_0^\infty e^{-x} x^{\alpha-1}\, dx.$$

We first list the continuous densities, followed by the discrete densities.

I. Continuous

1. Univariate Normal ($\mathscr{N}(\mu, \sigma^2)$): $\mathscr{X} = R^1$, $-\infty < \mu < \infty$, $\sigma^2 > 0$, and

$$f(x|\mu, \sigma^2) = \frac{1}{(2\pi)^{1/2}\sigma} e^{-(x-\mu)^2/2\sigma^2}.$$

Mean $= \mu$, Variance $= \sigma^2$.

2. p-Variate Normal ($\mathcal{N}_p(\boldsymbol{\mu}, \boldsymbol{\Sigma})$): $\mathscr{X} = R^p$, $\boldsymbol{\mu} = (\mu_1, \ldots, \mu_p)^t \in R^p$, $\boldsymbol{\Sigma}$ is a $(p \times p)$ positive definite matrix, and

$$f(\mathbf{x}|\boldsymbol{\mu}, \boldsymbol{\Sigma}) = \frac{1}{(2\pi)^{p/2}(\det \boldsymbol{\Sigma})^{1/2}} e^{-(\mathbf{x}-\boldsymbol{\mu})^t \boldsymbol{\Sigma}^{-1}(\mathbf{x}-\boldsymbol{\mu})/2}.$$

Mean $= \boldsymbol{\mu}$, Covariance matrix $= \boldsymbol{\Sigma}$.

3. Uniform ($\mathscr{U}(\alpha, \beta)$): $\mathscr{X} = (\alpha, \beta)$, $-\infty < \alpha < \infty$, $\alpha < \beta < \infty$, and

$$f(x|\alpha, \beta) = \frac{1}{\beta - \alpha} I_{(\alpha, \beta)}(x).$$

Mean $= \frac{1}{2}(\alpha + \beta)$, Variance $= (\beta - \alpha)^2/12$.

4. Gamma ($\mathscr{G}(\alpha, \beta)$): $\mathscr{X} = (0, \infty)$, $\alpha > 0$, $\beta > 0$, and

$$f(x|\alpha, \beta) = \frac{1}{\Gamma(\alpha)\beta^\alpha} x^{\alpha-1} e^{-x/\beta} I_{(0, \infty)}(x).$$

Mean $= \alpha\beta$, Variance $= \alpha\beta^2$.

Special Cases:

(a) Exponential ($\mathscr{E}(\beta)$): the $\mathscr{G}(1, \beta)$ density.
(b) Chi-square with n degrees of freedom ($\chi^2(n)$): the $\mathscr{G}(n/2, 2)$ density.

5. Beta ($\mathscr{B}e(\alpha, \beta)$): $\mathscr{X} = [0, 1]$, $\alpha > 0$, $\beta > 0$, and

$$f(x|\alpha, \beta) = \frac{\Gamma(\alpha + \beta)}{\Gamma(\alpha)\Gamma(\beta)} x^{\alpha-1}(1 - x)^{\beta-1} I_{[0, 1]}(x).$$

Mean $= \alpha/(\alpha + \beta)$, Variance $= \alpha\beta/(\alpha + \beta)^2(\alpha + \beta + 1)$.

6. Cauchy ($\mathscr{C}(\alpha, \beta)$): $\mathscr{X} = R^1$, $-\infty < \alpha < \infty$, $\beta > 0$, and

$$f(x|\alpha, \beta) = \frac{\beta}{\pi[\beta^2 + (x - \alpha)^2]}.$$

Mean and Variance do not exist.

7. F distribution with α and β degrees of freedom ($\mathscr{F}(\alpha, \beta)$): $\mathscr{X} = (0, \infty)$, $a > 0$, $\beta > 0$, and

$$f(x|\alpha, \beta) = \frac{\Gamma[(\alpha + \beta)/2]\alpha^{\alpha/2}\beta^{\beta/2}}{\Gamma(\alpha/2)\Gamma(\beta/2)} \cdot \frac{x^{\alpha/2-1}}{(\beta + \alpha x)^{(\alpha+\beta)/2}} I_{(0, \infty)}(x).$$

Mean $= \beta/(\beta - 2)$, Variance $= 2\beta^2(\alpha + \beta - 2)/\alpha(\beta - 4)(\beta - 2)^2$.

8. t distribution with α degrees of freedom, location parameter μ, and scale parameter σ^2 ($\mathscr{T}(\alpha, \mu, \sigma^2)$): $\mathscr{X} = R^1$, $\alpha > 0$, $-\infty < \mu < \infty$, $\sigma^2 > 0$, and

$$f(x|\alpha, \mu, \sigma^2) = \frac{\Gamma[(\alpha + 1)/2]}{\sigma(\alpha\pi)^{1/2}\Gamma(\alpha/2)} \left(1 + \frac{(x - \mu)^2}{\alpha\sigma^2}\right)^{-(\alpha+1)/2}$$

Mean $= \mu$, Variance $= \alpha\sigma^2/(\alpha - 2)$.
Note: $(X - \mu)^2/\sigma^2 \sim \mathscr{F}(1, \alpha)$.

9. p-Variate t distribution with α degrees of freedom, location vector $\boldsymbol{\mu}$, and scale matrix $\Sigma(\mathcal{T}_p(\alpha, \boldsymbol{\mu}, \Sigma))$: $\mathcal{X} = R^p$, $\alpha > 0$, $\boldsymbol{\mu} \in R^p$, Σ is a $(p \times p)$ positive definite matrix, and

$$f(\mathbf{x}|\alpha, \boldsymbol{\mu}, \Sigma) = \frac{\Gamma[(\alpha + p)/2]}{(\det \Sigma)^{1/2}(\alpha\pi)^{p/2}\Gamma(\alpha/2)} \left[1 + \frac{1}{\alpha}(\mathbf{x} - \boldsymbol{\mu})'\Sigma^{-1}(\mathbf{x} - \boldsymbol{\mu})\right]^{-(\alpha+p)/2}$$

Mean $= \boldsymbol{\mu}$, Covariance matrix $= \alpha\Sigma/(\alpha - 2)$.
Note: $(1/p)(\mathbf{X} - \boldsymbol{\mu})'\Sigma^{-1}(\mathbf{X} - \boldsymbol{\mu}) \sim \mathcal{F}(p, \alpha)$.

10. Inverse Gamma $(\mathcal{IG}(\alpha, \beta))$: $\mathcal{X} = (0, \infty)$, $\alpha > 0$, $\beta > 0$, and

$$f(x|\alpha, \beta) = \frac{1}{\Gamma(\alpha)\beta^\alpha x^{(\alpha+1)}} e^{-1/x\beta} I_{(0, \infty)}(x).$$

Mean $= 1/\beta(\alpha - 1)$, Variance $= 1/\beta^2(\alpha - 1)^2(\alpha - 2)$.
Note: $1/X \sim \mathcal{G}(\alpha, \beta)$.

11. Dirichlet $(\mathcal{D}(\boldsymbol{\alpha}))$: $\mathbf{x} = (x_1, \ldots, x_k)'$ where $\sum_{i=1}^k x_i = 1$ and $0 \le x_i \le 1$ for all i, $\boldsymbol{\alpha} = (\alpha_1, \ldots, \alpha_k)'$ where $\alpha_i > 0$ for all i, and (defining $\alpha_0 = \sum_{i=1}^k \alpha_i$),

$$f(\mathbf{x}|\boldsymbol{\alpha}) = \frac{\Gamma(\alpha_0)}{\prod_{i=1}^k \Gamma(\alpha_i)} \prod_{i=1}^k x_i^{(\alpha_i - 1)}.$$

Mean $(X_i) = \alpha_i/\alpha_0$, Variance $(X_i) = (\alpha_0 - \alpha_i)\alpha_i/\alpha_0^2(\alpha_0 + 1)$, Covariance $(X_i, X_j) = -\alpha_i\alpha_j/\alpha_0^2(\alpha_0 + 1)$.
Note: This is really only a $(k - 1)$-dimensional distribution because of the restriction on the x_i. In taking expectations with respect to this density, therefore, replace x_k by $1 - \sum_{i=1}^{k-1} x_i$ and integrate over $x_1, \ldots, x_{k-1}$.

12. Pareto $(\mathcal{Pa}(x_0, \alpha))$: $\mathcal{X} = (x_0, \infty)$, $0 < x_0 < \infty$, $\alpha > 0$, and

$$f(x|x_0, \alpha) = \frac{\alpha}{x_0}\left(\frac{x_0}{x}\right)^{\alpha+1} I_{(x_0, \infty)}(x).$$

Mean $= \alpha x_0/(\alpha - 1)$.

II. Discrete

1. Binomial $(\mathcal{B}(n, p))$: $\mathcal{X} = \{0, 1, 2, \ldots, n\}$, $0 \le p \le 1$, $n = 1, 2, \ldots$, and

$$f(x|n, p) = \binom{n}{x} p^x(1 - p)^{(n-x)},$$

where

$$\binom{n}{x} = \frac{n!}{(x!)(n - x)!}.$$

Mean $= np$, Variance $= np(1 - p)$.

Here, X is the number of successes in n independent trials when p is the probability of a success at each individual trial.

2. Poisson $(\mathscr{P}(\lambda))$: $\mathscr{X} = \{0, 1, 2, \ldots\}$, $\lambda > 0$, and

$$f(x|\lambda) = \frac{e^{-\lambda}\lambda^x}{x!}.$$

Mean $= \lambda$, Variance $= \lambda$.

3. Negative Binomial $(\mathscr{N}\mathscr{B}(\alpha, p))$: $\mathscr{X} = \{0, 1, \ldots\}$, $0 < p \leq 1$, $\alpha > 0$, and

$$f(x|\alpha, p) = \frac{\Gamma(\alpha + x)}{\Gamma(x + 1)\Gamma(\alpha)} p^\alpha (1 - p)^x.$$

Mean $= \alpha(1 - p)/p$, Variance $= \alpha(1 - p)/p^2$.

When α is an integer, X is the number of failures in a sequence of independent trials performed until α successes are observed, where p is the probability of a success at each individual trial.

Special Case: Geometric $(\mathscr{G}e(p))$: the $\mathscr{N}\mathscr{B}(1, p)$ density.

4. Multinomial $(\mathscr{M}(n, \mathbf{p}))$: $\mathbf{x} = (x_1, x_2, \ldots, x_k)^t$ where $\sum_{i=1}^k x_i = n$ and each x_i is an integer between 0 and n, $\mathbf{p} = (p_1, \ldots, p_k)^t$ where $\sum_{i=1}^k p_i = 1$ and $0 \leq p_i \leq 1$ for all i, and

$$f(\mathbf{x}|\mathbf{p}) = \frac{n!}{\prod_{i=1}^k (x_i!)} \prod_{i=1}^k p_i^{x_i}.$$

Mean $(X_i) = np_i$, Variance $(X_i) = np_i(1 - p_i)$, Covariance $(X_i, X_j) = -np_i p_j$.

If an independent sample of size n is drawn from a population of k types, where p_i is the probability that a single observation is of the ith type, then X_i is the number of individuals of the ith type in the sample.

Note: $k = 2$ gives the $\mathscr{B}(n, p)$ distribution, with $p = p_1 = 1 - p_2$.

APPENDIX 2

Technical Arguments from Chapter 4

I. Verification of Formulas (4.6) through (4.8)

Choose any $((p - k) \times p)$ matrix $\mathbf{G}$ such that

$$\mathbf{H} = \begin{pmatrix} \mathbf{B} \\ \mathbf{G} \end{pmatrix}$$

is nonsingular, and assume that $\mathbf{H}\theta$ has a prior distribution with mean $(\mathbf{d}, \xi)^t$ (ξ being any $(p - k)$-vector) and covariance matrix

$$\mathbf{C}_\tau = \begin{pmatrix} \mathbf{C} & \mathbf{0} \\ \mathbf{0} & \tau \mathbf{I}_{p-k} \end{pmatrix},$$

where $\mathbf{0}$ stands for a zero matrix of the appropriate dimension and τ is a positive constant. Letting $\tau \to \infty$ will appropriately model the apriori beliefs.

Since $\mathbf{H}$ is nonsingular, the prior information that $\mathbf{H}\theta$ has mean $(\mathbf{d}, \xi)^t$ and covariance matrix $\mathbf{C}_\tau$ implies (through a transformation) that θ has mean $\mu = \mathbf{H}^{-1}(\mathbf{d}, \xi)^t$ and covariance matrix $\mathbf{A}_\tau = \mathbf{H}^{-1}\mathbf{C}_\tau(\mathbf{H}^{-1})^t$. Note that

$$(\Sigma + \mathbf{A}_\tau)^{-1} = \mathbf{H}^t(\mathbf{H}\Sigma\mathbf{H}^t + \mathbf{H}\mathbf{A}_\tau\mathbf{H}^t)^{-1}\mathbf{H}$$
$$= \mathbf{H}^t(\mathbf{H}\Sigma\mathbf{H}^t + \mathbf{C}_\tau)^{-1}\mathbf{H}.$$

Writing

$$(\mathbf{H}\Sigma\mathbf{H}^t + \mathbf{C}_\tau)^{-1} = \begin{pmatrix} \mathbf{B}\Sigma\mathbf{B}^t + \mathbf{C} & \mathbf{B}\Sigma\mathbf{G}^t \\ \mathbf{G}\Sigma\mathbf{B}^t & \mathbf{G}\Sigma\mathbf{G}^t + \tau\mathbf{I}_{p-k} \end{pmatrix}^{-1},$$

and using the standard formula for the inverse of a partitioned matrix, it can be shown that

$$\lim_{\tau \to \infty} (\mathbf{H}\boldsymbol{\Sigma}\mathbf{H}^t + \mathbf{C}_\tau)^{-1} = \begin{pmatrix} (\mathbf{B}\boldsymbol{\Sigma}\mathbf{B}^t + \mathbf{C})^{-1} & \mathbf{0} \\ \mathbf{0} & \mathbf{0} \end{pmatrix}.$$

Hence

$$\lim_{\tau \to \infty} (\boldsymbol{\Sigma} + \mathbf{A}_\tau)^{-1} = \mathbf{H}^t \begin{pmatrix} (\mathbf{B}\boldsymbol{\Sigma}\mathbf{B}^t + \mathbf{C})^{-1} & \mathbf{0} \\ \mathbf{0} & \mathbf{0} \end{pmatrix} \mathbf{H}$$

$$= \mathbf{B}^t (\mathbf{B}\boldsymbol{\Sigma}\mathbf{B}^t + \mathbf{C})^{-1}\mathbf{B}.$$

Using this last quantity in place of $(\boldsymbol{\Sigma} + \mathbf{A})^{-1}$ in $\boldsymbol{\mu}_n(\mathbf{x})$ and $\boldsymbol{\Sigma}_n(\mathbf{x})$, and noting that

$$\mathbf{B}(\mathbf{x} - \boldsymbol{\mu}) = \mathbf{B}\mathbf{x} - \mathbf{B}\boldsymbol{\mu} = \mathbf{B}\mathbf{x} - \mathbf{d},$$

results in the formulas (4.6) and (4.7).

The replacement of p with k in (4.8) follows from the following observation. Let

$$\mathbf{D} = \boldsymbol{\Sigma}\mathbf{B}^t (\mathbf{B}\boldsymbol{\Sigma}\mathbf{B}^t)^{-1}\mathbf{B},$$

and define, for any p-vector $\mathbf{z}$, the decomposition

$$\mathbf{z} = \mathbf{z}^0 + \mathbf{z}^1,$$

where $\mathbf{z}^0 = (\mathbf{I} - \mathbf{D})\mathbf{z}$ and $\mathbf{z}^1 = \mathbf{D}\mathbf{z}$. Note that $\mathbf{B}\mathbf{D} = \mathbf{B}$, $\mathbf{D}\boldsymbol{\Sigma}\mathbf{B}^t = \boldsymbol{\Sigma}\mathbf{B}^t$,

$$\mathbf{B}(\mathbf{I} - \mathbf{D}) = \mathbf{B} - \mathbf{B}\mathbf{D} = \mathbf{B} - \mathbf{B} = \mathbf{0},$$

and

$$\mathbf{B}\mathbf{x} = \mathbf{B}(\mathbf{x}^0 + \mathbf{x}^1) = \mathbf{B}(\mathbf{I} - \mathbf{D})\mathbf{x} + \mathbf{B}\mathbf{x}^1 = \mathbf{B}\mathbf{x}^1.$$

It follows that $\boldsymbol{\theta}^1 = \mathbf{D}\boldsymbol{\theta}$ has posterior mean

$$\mathbf{D}\boldsymbol{\mu}_n(\mathbf{x}) = \mathbf{D}\mathbf{x} - \frac{r_n \mathbf{D}\boldsymbol{\Sigma}\mathbf{B}^t \mathbf{T}^{-1}(\mathbf{B}\mathbf{x} - \mathbf{d})}{\rho \|\mathbf{x}\|^2}$$

$$= \mathbf{x}^1 - \frac{r_n \boldsymbol{\Sigma}\mathbf{B}^t \mathbf{T}^{-1}(\mathbf{B}\mathbf{x}^1 - \mathbf{d})}{\rho \|\mathbf{x}^1\|^2},$$

and posterior covariance matrix

$$\mathbf{D}\boldsymbol{\Sigma}_n(\mathbf{x})\mathbf{D}^t = \mathbf{D}\boldsymbol{\Sigma}\mathbf{D}^t - \frac{r_n \boldsymbol{\Sigma}\mathbf{B}^t \mathbf{T}^{-1}\mathbf{B}\boldsymbol{\Sigma}}{\rho \|\mathbf{x}^1\|^2} + \frac{r_n[r_{n+1} - r_n]}{\rho^2 \|\mathbf{x}^1\|^4}$$

$$\times \boldsymbol{\Sigma}\mathbf{B}^t \mathbf{T}^{-1}(\mathbf{B}\mathbf{x}^1 - \mathbf{d})(\mathbf{B}\mathbf{x}^1 - \mathbf{d})^t \mathbf{T}^{-1}\mathbf{B}\boldsymbol{\Sigma}.$$

Noting also that

$$(\mathbf{I} - \mathbf{D})\boldsymbol{\Sigma}\mathbf{B}^t = \boldsymbol{\Sigma}\mathbf{B}^t - \mathbf{D}\boldsymbol{\Sigma}\mathbf{B}^t = \boldsymbol{\Sigma}\mathbf{B}^t - \boldsymbol{\Sigma}\mathbf{B}^t = \mathbf{0},$$

calculation shows that $\boldsymbol{\theta}^0$ has posterior mean $\mathbf{x}^0$ and posterior covariance matrix $(\mathbf{I} - \mathbf{D})\boldsymbol{\Sigma}(\mathbf{I} - \mathbf{D})^t$. These are the posterior mean and covariance matrix resulting from the noninformative prior. The above results thus indicate that the prior information can be considered to be concentrated on the subspace of Θ containing $\boldsymbol{\theta}^1$, which is a k-dimensional subspace since $\mathbf{B}$

and hence **D** have rank k. (This can be rigorously established by a limiting argument, similar to that above, involving g_n.) The conclusion is that p should be replaced by k in determining n.

II. Verification of Formula (4.10)

By definition, the posterior distribution of $\boldsymbol{\theta}$ and σ^2, given $\mathbf{x}$ and s^2, is

$$\pi_n(\boldsymbol{\theta}, \sigma^2 \mid \mathbf{x}, s^2) = \frac{g_n(\boldsymbol{\theta} \mid \sigma^2)\sigma^{-2}f(\mathbf{x} \mid \boldsymbol{\theta}, \sigma^2)h(s^2 \mid \sigma^2)}{m(\mathbf{x}, s^2)}, \qquad (A2.1)$$

where $m(\mathbf{x}, s^2)$ is the joint marginal density of $\mathbf{x}$ and s^2. Note that

$$g_n(\boldsymbol{\theta} \mid \sigma^2)f(\mathbf{x} \mid \boldsymbol{\theta}, \sigma^2) = \pi_n(\boldsymbol{\theta} \mid \mathbf{x}, \sigma^2)m(\mathbf{x} \mid \sigma^2), \qquad (A2.2)$$

where $\pi_n(\boldsymbol{\theta} \mid \mathbf{x}, \sigma^2)$ is the posterior distribution of $\boldsymbol{\theta}$ given $\mathbf{x}$ and σ^2, while $m(\mathbf{x} \mid \sigma^2)$ is the marginal density of $\mathbf{x}$ given σ^2.

The approximation that will be made consists of (i) replacing $m(\mathbf{x} \mid \sigma^2)$ by $m(\mathbf{x} \mid \hat{\sigma}^2)$, and (ii) replacing $\pi_n(\boldsymbol{\theta} \mid \mathbf{x}, \sigma^2)$ by a normal distribution (to be denoted $f_n(\boldsymbol{\theta})$) with mean $\boldsymbol{\mu}_n(\mathbf{x}, \hat{\sigma}^2)$ and covariance matrix $(\sigma^2/\hat{\sigma}^2)\boldsymbol{\Sigma}_n(\mathbf{x}, \hat{\sigma}^2)$. These approximations will be discussed after the derivation is complete. Using these approximations in (A2.2) and hence (A2.1), and defining

$$k(\mathbf{x}, s^2) = \frac{m(\mathbf{x} \mid \hat{\sigma}^2)}{m(\mathbf{x}, s^2)},$$

results in the following approximation to $\pi_n(\boldsymbol{\theta}, \sigma^2 \mid \mathbf{x}, s^2)$:

$$\hat{\pi}_n(\boldsymbol{\theta}, \sigma^2 \mid \mathbf{x}, s^2) = k(\mathbf{x}, s^2)f_n(\boldsymbol{\theta})\sigma^{-2}h(s^2 \mid \sigma^2).$$

To make decisions and inferences about $\boldsymbol{\theta}$, the marginal posterior distribution of $\boldsymbol{\theta}$ given $\mathbf{x}$ and s^2 is needed. This will be given by

$$\hat{\pi}_n(\boldsymbol{\theta} \mid \mathbf{x}, s^2) = k(\mathbf{x}, s^2) \int_0^\infty f_n(\boldsymbol{\theta})\sigma^{-2}h(s^2 \mid \sigma^2)d\sigma^2.$$

For notational convenience in evaluating this integral, let

$$Q(\boldsymbol{\theta}, \mathbf{x}, \hat{\sigma}^2) = [\boldsymbol{\theta} - \boldsymbol{\mu}_n(\mathbf{x}, \hat{\sigma}^2)]'\boldsymbol{\Sigma}_n^{-1}(\mathbf{x}, \hat{\sigma}^2)[\boldsymbol{\theta} - \boldsymbol{\mu}_n(\mathbf{x}, \hat{\sigma}^2)],$$

and define $k^*(\mathbf{x}, s^2)$ as $k(\mathbf{x}, s^2)$ multiplied by all multiplicative constants and factors (not involving $\boldsymbol{\theta}$ or σ^2) from the densities f_n and h. Then

$$\hat{\pi}_n(\boldsymbol{\theta} \mid \mathbf{x}, s^2) = k^*(\mathbf{x}, s^2) \int_0^\infty \sigma^{-p} \exp\left\{-\frac{\hat{\sigma}^2}{2\sigma^2} Q(\boldsymbol{\theta}, \mathbf{x}, \hat{\sigma}^2)\right\}\sigma^{-m}$$

$$\times \exp\left\{-\frac{s^2}{2\sigma^2}\right\}\sigma^{-2} d\sigma^2$$

$$= k^*(\mathbf{x}, s^2) \int_0^\infty \sigma^{-(m+p+2)} \exp\left\{-\frac{s^2}{2\sigma^2}\left[1 + \frac{Q(\boldsymbol{\theta}, \mathbf{x}, \hat{\sigma}^2)}{m+2}\right]\right\}d\sigma^2.$$

Making the change of variables

$$z = \frac{s^2}{2\sigma^2}\left[1 + \frac{Q(\theta, \mathbf{x}, \hat{\sigma}^2)}{m + 2}\right]$$

results in the expression

$$\hat{\pi}_n(\theta|\mathbf{x}, s^2) = k^*(\mathbf{x}, s^2) \int_0^\infty \frac{[2^{(m+p)/2}][z^{(m+p-2)/2}]e^{-z}}{s^{(m+p)}[1 + Q(\theta, \mathbf{x}, \hat{\sigma}^2)/(m + 2)]^{(m+p)/2}}\, dz.$$

Noting that $\int_0^\infty z^{(m+p-2)/2}e^{-z}\, dz = \Gamma([m + p]/2)$, and defining $\tilde{k}(\mathbf{x}, s^2)$ as $k^*(\mathbf{x}, s^2)$ multiplied by all new factors not involving θ above, we finally have

$$\hat{\pi}_n(\theta|\mathbf{x}, s^2) = \frac{\tilde{k}(\mathbf{x}, s^2)}{[1 + Q(\theta, \mathbf{x}, \hat{\sigma}^2)/(m + 2)]^{(m+p)/2}},$$

which is the expression in (4.10).

The rationale behind the approximations (i) and (ii) is that in the expression

$$\Sigma^{1/2}(\Sigma + \mathbf{A})^{-1}\Sigma^{1/2} = (\mathbf{I}_p + \Sigma^{-1/2}\mathbf{A}\Sigma^{-1/2})^{-1}$$
$$= (\mathbf{I}_p + \Sigma_0^{-1/2}\mathbf{A}\Sigma_0^{-1/2}/\sigma^2)^{-1},$$

replacing σ^2 by $\hat{\sigma}^2$ is a reasonable approximation, in that any resultant error is like an error in specifying $\mathbf{A}$. Results mentioned in Subsection 4.6.4 indicate that the procedures are robust against this type of error. The same type of argument holds for expressions like $\Sigma(\Sigma + \mathbf{A})^{-1}$ and $(\mathbf{X} - \mathbf{\mu})'(\Sigma + \mathbf{A})^{-1}$ $\times (\mathbf{X} - \mathbf{\mu})$. It can be seen that all terms in $m(\mathbf{x}|\sigma^2)$, $\mathbf{\mu}_n(\mathbf{x}, \sigma^2)$, and $\Sigma_n(\mathbf{x}, \sigma^2)$ are of this type, except for a multiple, Σ, of $\Sigma_n(\mathbf{x}, \sigma^2)$. This multiple cannot be approximated without significantly altering the distribution, so it is left as is, introducing the factor σ^2 in the approximation to the covariance matrix. The replacing of $\pi_n(\theta|\mathbf{x}, \sigma^2)$ by a normal distribution with the same approximate mean and covariance matrix is the same type of approximation used to good effect in Subsection 4.6.4.

III. Verification of Formula (4.12)

Note that

$$P_\theta\left(\frac{Y}{\theta} < 2\right) = \frac{\int_0^2 y^{-1}\exp\{-(d^2/2)(1 - y^{-1})^2\}dy}{\int_0^b y^{-1}\exp\{-(d^2/2)(1 - y^{-1})^2\}dy}$$

$$= \left[1 + \frac{\int_2^b y^{-1}\exp\{-(d^2/2)(1 - y^{-1})^2\}dy}{\int_0^2 y^{-1}\exp\{-(d^2/2)(1 - y^{-1})^2\}dy}\right]^{-1}.$$

Making the change of variables $z = y^{-1}$ gives

$$\int_0^2 y^{-1} \exp\left\{ -\frac{d^2}{2}(1 - y^{-1})^2 \right\} dy = \int_{1/2}^{\infty} z^{-1} \exp\left\{ -\frac{d^2}{2}(1 - z)^2 \right\} dz$$

$$< 2 \int_{-\infty}^{\infty} \exp\left\{ -\frac{d^2}{2}(1 - z)^2 \right\} dz$$

$$= \frac{2(2\pi)^{1/2}}{d} = \frac{2(2\pi)^{1/2}}{50}.$$

Also

$$\int_2^b y^{-1} \exp\left\{ -\frac{d^2}{2}(1 - y^{-1})^2 \right\} dy > \int_2^b y^{-1} \exp\left\{ -\frac{d^2}{2} \right\} dy$$

$$= \exp\left\{ -\frac{d^2}{2} \right\} \log\left(\frac{b}{2} \right)$$

$$= \exp\{-1250\} [10^{1000} \log 10 - \log 2]$$

$$> 10^{100}.$$

Hence

$$P_\theta\left(Y - \frac{KY}{d} < \theta < Y + \frac{KY}{d} \right) < \left[1 + \frac{10^{100}}{\{2(2\pi)^{1/2}/50\}} \right]^{-1}$$

$$< 10^{-100}.$$

APPENDIX 3

Technical Arguments from Chapter 7

I. Verification of Formula (7.8)

Letting $K'(n)$ denote the derivative of $K(n)$ (assuming it exists) it is clear that

$$\frac{d}{dn} P_\theta(\overline{X}_n < K(n)) = \frac{d}{dn} \int_{-\infty}^{K(n)} \left(\frac{n}{2\pi\sigma^2}\right)^{1/2} \exp\left\{-\frac{n}{2\sigma^2}(y-\theta)^2\right\} dy$$

$$= \left(\frac{n}{2\pi\sigma^2}\right)^{1/2} \exp\left\{-\frac{n}{2\sigma^2}(K(n)-\theta)^2\right\} K'(n)$$

$$+ \int_{-\infty}^{K(n)} \frac{1}{2\sigma(2\pi n)^{1/2}} \exp\left\{-\frac{n}{2\sigma^2}(y-\theta)^2\right\} dy$$

$$- \int_{-\infty}^{K(n)} \left(\frac{n}{2\pi\sigma^2}\right)^{1/2} \left(\frac{(y-\theta)^2}{2\sigma^2}\right) \exp\left\{-\frac{n}{2\sigma^2}(y-\theta)^2\right\} dy.$$

Integrating by parts shows that

$$\int_{-\infty}^{K(n)} (y-\theta)\left(\frac{-n(y-\theta)}{\sigma^2}\right) \exp\left\{-\frac{n}{2\sigma^2}(y-\theta)^2\right\} dy$$

$$= (y-\theta)\exp\left\{-\frac{n}{2\sigma^2}(y-\theta)^2\right\}\Big|_{-\infty}^{K(n)} - \int_{-\infty}^{K(n)} \exp\left\{-\frac{n}{2\sigma^2}(y-\theta)^2\right\} dy$$

$$= (K(n)-\theta)\exp\left\{-\frac{n}{2\sigma^2}(K(n)-\theta)^2\right\} - \int_{-\infty}^{K(n)} \exp\left\{-\frac{n}{2\sigma^2}(y-\theta)^2\right\} dy.$$

Hence

$$\frac{d}{dn} P_\theta(\bar{X}_n < K(n)) = \left(\frac{n}{2\pi\sigma^2}\right)^{1/2} \exp\left\{-\frac{n}{2\sigma^2}(K(n) - \theta)^2\right\} K'(n)$$

$$+ \int_{-\infty}^{K(n)} \frac{1}{2\sigma(2\pi n)^{1/2}} \exp\left\{-\frac{n}{2\sigma^2}(y - \theta)^2\right\} dy$$

$$+ \frac{1}{2\sigma(2\pi n)^{1/2}} \left[(K(n) - \theta)\exp\left\{-\frac{n}{2\sigma^2}(K(n) - \theta)^2\right\}\right.$$

$$\left. - \int_{-\infty}^{K(n)} \exp\left\{-\frac{n}{2\sigma^2}(y - \theta)^2\right\} dy\right]$$

$$= (2\pi n\sigma^2)^{-1/2} \exp\left\{-\frac{n}{2\sigma^2}(K(n) - \theta)^2\right\}$$

$$\times \left[nK'(n) + \frac{1}{2}(K(n) - \theta)\right].$$

Assuming that differentiation under the integral sign is valid in (7.7), it follows from the above result that

$$\frac{d}{dn} r(\pi, \delta_n^\pi) = \int_{\Theta_1} L(\theta, a_0)(2\pi n\sigma^2)^{-1/2} \exp\left\{-\frac{n}{2\sigma^2}(K(n) - \theta)^2\right\}$$

$$\times \left[nK'(n) + \frac{1}{2}(K(n) - \theta)\right] dF^\pi(\theta)$$

$$- \int_{\Theta_0} L(\theta, a_1)(2\pi n\sigma^2)^{-1/2} \exp\left\{-\frac{n}{2\sigma^2}(K(n) - \theta)^2\right\}$$

$$\times \left[nK'(n) + \frac{1}{2}(K(n) - \theta)\right] dF^\pi(\theta).$$

Formula (7.8) follows from this and (7.6).

II. Verification of Formula (7.10)

It is first necessary to determine $K(n)$. Recall that $\pi''(\theta|\bar{x}_n)$ is a $\mathcal{N}(\mu_n(\bar{x}_n), \rho_n)$ density (see (7.3)). Note also, from the definitions of the posterior density and the marginal density, that

$$\left(\frac{2\pi\sigma^2}{n}\right)^{-1/2} \exp\left\{-\frac{n}{2\sigma^2}(K(n) - \theta)^2\right\} \pi(\theta) = f(K(n)|\theta)\pi(\theta)$$

$$= m_n(K(n))\pi''(\theta|K(n)). \quad \text{(A3.1)}$$

Using this in (7.6) and eliminating common constants gives

$$\int_{\theta_0}^{\infty} W(|\theta - \theta_0|)\exp\left\{-\frac{1}{2\rho_n}[\theta - \mu_n(K(n))]^2\right\}d\theta$$

$$= \int_{-\infty}^{\theta_0} W(|\theta - \theta_0|)\exp\left\{-\frac{1}{2\rho_n}[\theta - \mu_n(K(n))]^2\right\}d\theta. \quad (A3.2)$$

From the symmetry of the situation, it is clear that equality is achieved in (A3.2) when

$$\mu_n(K(n)) = \theta_0, \quad (A3.3)$$

or (using (7.3)) when

$$K(n) = \left(1 + \frac{\sigma^2}{n\tau^2}\right)\theta_0 - \frac{\sigma^2}{n\tau^2}\mu. \quad (A3.4)$$

Using (A3.1) and (A3.3) in (7.8), and choosing $K^* = \theta_0$, gives

$$\frac{d}{dn}r(\pi, \delta_n^\pi) = \frac{m_n(K(n))}{2n}\left[\int_{-\infty}^{\theta_0} W(|\theta - \theta_0|)(\theta - \theta_0)\pi''(\theta|K(n))d\theta\right.$$

$$\left. - \int_{\theta_0}^{\infty} W(|\theta - \theta_0|)(\theta - \theta_0)\pi''(\theta|K(n))d\theta\right]$$

$$= \frac{m_n(K(n))}{2n}\left[\int_{-\infty}^{\theta_0} W(|\theta - \theta_0|)(\theta - \theta_0)(2\pi\rho_n)^{-1/2}\right.$$

$$\times \exp\left\{-\frac{1}{2\rho_n}(\theta - \theta_0)^2\right\}d\theta$$

$$- \int_{\theta_0}^{\infty} W(|\theta - \theta_0|)(\theta - \theta_0)(2\pi\rho_n)^{-1/2}$$

$$\left. \times \exp\left\{-\frac{1}{2\rho_n}(\theta - \theta_0)^2\right\}d\theta\right].$$

A change of variables ($y = (\theta - \theta_0)\rho_n^{-1/2}$) establishes that

$$\frac{d}{dn}r(\pi, \delta_n^\pi) = -n^{-1}m_n(K(n))\int_0^{\infty} W(\rho_n^{1/2}y)\rho_n^{1/2}y(2\pi)^{-1/2}e^{-y^2/2}\,dy. \quad (A3.5)$$

Recalling that

$$m_n(K(n)) = \left[2\pi\left(\tau^2 + \frac{\sigma^2}{n}\right)\right]^{-1/2}\exp\left\{-\frac{1}{2(\tau^2 + \sigma^2/n)}(K(n) - \mu)^2\right\},$$

and noting from (A3.4) that

$$[K(n) - \mu]^2 = \left[\left(1 + \frac{\sigma^2}{n\tau^2}\right)\theta_0 - \frac{\sigma^2}{n\tau^2}\mu - \mu\right]^2 = \left(1 + \frac{\sigma^2}{n\tau^2}\right)^2(\theta_0 - \mu)^2,$$

a little algebra shows that (A3.5) is equivalent to (7.10).

Bibliography

Albert, J. H., 1979. Robust Bayes estimation. Technical Report, Department of Statistics, Purdue University, West Lafayette.

Alvo, Mayer, 1977. Bayesian sequential estimates. *Ann. Statist.* **5**, 955–968.

Amster, S. J., 1963. A modified Bayes stopping rule. *Ann. Math. Statist.* **34**, 1404–1413.

Anscombe, F. J., 1963. Bayesian inference concerning many parameters with reference to supersaturated designs. *Bull. Int. Statist. Inst.* **40**, 721–733.

Antoniak, C. E., 1974. Mixtures of Dirichlet processes with applications to Bayesian nonparametric problems. *Ann. Statist.* **2**, 1152–1174.

Arrow, K. J., Blackwell, D., and Girshick, M. A., 1949. Bayes and minimax solutions of sequential decision problems. *Econometrika* **17**, 213–244.

Atchison, T. A., and Martz, H. F. (Eds.), 1969. *Proceedings of the Symposium on Empirical Bayes Estimation and Computing in Statistics.* Mathematics Series No. 6, Texas Tech. University, Lubbock.

Bahadur, R. R., 1954. Sufficiency and statistical decision functions. *Ann. Math. Statist.* **25**, 423–462.

Bahadur, R. R., 1958. A note on the fundamental identity of sequential analysis. *Ann. Math. Statist.* **29**, 534–543.

Barnard, G. A., 1962. Comments on Stein's "A remark on the likelihood principle." *J. Roy. Statist. Soc.* (Ser. A) **125**, 569–573.

Barnard, G. A., 1967. The use of the likelihood function in statistical practice. In *Proc. Fifth Berkeley Symp. Math. Statist. Probability* 1, 27–40. Univ. of California Press, Berkeley.

Barnett, V., 1973. *Comparative Statistical Inference.* Wiley, London.

Bayes, T., 1763. An essay towards solving a problem in the doctrine of chances. *Phil. Trans. Roy. Soc.* **53**, 370–418.

Becker, G. M., DeGroot, M. H., and Marschak, J., 1964. Measuring utility by a single-response sequential method. *Behavioral Sci.* **9**, 226–232.

Berger, J., 1976. Admissibility results for generalized Bayes estimators of coordinates of a location vector. *Ann. Statist.* **4**, 334–356.

Berger, J., 1979. Multivariate estimation with nonsymmetric loss functions. In *Optimizing Methods in Statistics,* J. S. Rustagi (Ed.). Academic Press, New York.

Berger, J., 1980a. Improving on inadmissible estimators in continuous exponential families with applications to simultaneous estimation of gamma scale parameters. *Ann. Statist.* **8**, No. 3.

Berger, J., 1980b. A robust generalized Bayes estimator and confidence region for a multivariate normal mean. *Ann. Statist.* **8**, No. 4.

Berger, J., Bock, M. E., Brown, L. D., Casella, G., and Gleser, L., 1977. Minimax estimation of a normal mean vector for arbitrary quadratic loss and unknown covariance matrix. *Ann. Statist.* **5**, 763–771.

Berger, J., and Srinivasan, C., 1978. Generalized Bayes estimators in multivariate problems. *Ann. Statist.* **6**, 783–801.

Bickel, P. J., and Yahav, J. A., 1967. Asymptotically pointwise optimal procedures in sequential analysis. In *Proc. 5th Berkeley Symp. Math. Statist. Prob.* 1, 401–413. Univ. of California Press, Berkeley.

Birnbaum, A., 1955. Characterizations of complete classes of tests of some multi-parametric hypotheses, with applications to likelihood ratio tests. *Ann. Math. Statist.* **26**, 21–36.

Birnbaum, A., 1962. On the foundations of statistical inference (with discussion). *J. Amer. Statist. Assoc.* **57**, 269–326.

Blackwell, D., 1951. On the translation parameter problem for discrete variables. *Ann. Math. Statist.* **18**, 105–110.

Blackwell, D., and Girshick, M. A., 1954. *Theory of Games and Statistical Decisions.* Wiley, New York.

Blyth, C. R., 1951. On minimax statistical decision procedures and their admissibility. *Ann. Math. Statist.* **22**, 22–42.

Bondar, V., and Milnes, P., 1980. A survey of Hunt–Stein and related conditions on groups. To appear in *Z. Wahrscheinlichkeitstheorie verw. Gebiete.*

Borel, E., 1921. La théorie du jeu et les équations intégrales à noyau symétrique. *C.R. Acad. Sci. Paris* **173**, 1304–1308.

Box, G. E. P., and Tiao, G. C., 1973. *Bayesian Inference in Statistical Analysis.* Addison-Wesley, Reading.

Brown, L. D., 1966. On the admissibility of invariant estimators of one or more location parameters. *Ann. Math. Statist.* **37**, 1087–1136.

Brown, L. D., 1971. Admissible estimators, recurrent diffusions, and insoluble boundary-value problems. *Ann. Math. Statist.* **42**, 855–903.

Brown, L. D. 1976. *Notes on Statistical Decision Theory.* (Unpublished lecture notes, Ithaca.)

Brown, L. D., Cohen, A., and Strawderman, W. E., 1980a. Monotonicity of Bayes sequential tests. *Ann. Statist.* **7**, 1222–1230.

Brown, L. D., Cohen, A., and Strawderman, W. E., 1980b. Complete classes for sequential tests of hypotheses. *Ann. Statist.* **8**, No. 2.

Brown, L. D., and Fox, M., 1974a. Admissibility of procedures in two-dimensional location parameter problems. *Ann. Statist.* **2**, 248–266.

Brown, L. D., and Fox, M., 1974b. Admissibility in statistical problems involving a location or scale parameter. *Ann. Statist.* **4**, 807–814.

Chernoff, H., 1968. Optimal stochastic control. *Sankhyā* (Ser. A) **30**, 221–252.

Chernoff, H., and Moses, L. E., 1959. *Elementary Decision Theory.* Wiely, New York.

Copas, J. B., 1969. Compound decisions and empirical Bayes (with discussion). *J. Roy. Statist. Soc.* (Ser. B) **31**, 397–425.

Cornfield, J., 1969. The Bayesian outlook and its applications. *Biometrics* **25**, 617–657.

Cox, D. R., 1958. Some problems connected with statistical inference. *Ann. Math. Statist.* **29**, 357–372.

Dawid, A. P., 1973. Posterior expectations for large observations. *Biometrika* **60**, 664–666.

Dawid, A. P., Stone, M., and Zidek, J. V., 1973. Marginalization paradoxes in Bayesian and structural inference (with Discussion). *J. Roy. Statist. Soc. (Ser. B)* **35**, 189–233.

de Finetti, B., 1937. Foresight: Its logical laws, its subjective sources. Translated and reprinted in *Studies in Subjective Probability*, Kyburg and Smokler (Eds.), 1964, 93–158. Wiley, New York.

DeGroot, M. H., 1970. *Optimal Statistical Decisions*. McGraw-Hill, New York.

Dickey, J. M., 1974. Bayesian alternatives to the F-test and least-squares estimate in the normal linear model. In *Studies in Bayesian Econometrics and Statistics*, S. E. Fienberg and A. Zellner (Eds.). North Holland, Amsterdam.

Dickey, J. M., 1976. Approximate posterior distributions. *J. Amer. Statist. Assoc.* **71**, 680–689.

Dvoretsky, A., Wald, A., and Wolfowitz, J., 1951. Elimination of randomization in certain statistical decision procedures and zero-sum two-person games. *Ann. Math. Statist.* **22**, 1–21.

Edwards, W., Lindeman, H., and Savage, L. J., 1963. Bayesian statistical inference for psychological research. *Psychol. Rev.* **70**, 193–242.

Efron, B., and Morris, C., 1973. Stein's estimation rule and its competitors—an empirical Bayes approach. *J. Amer. Statist. Assoc.* **68**, 117–130.

Ewing, G. M. 1969. *Calculus of Variations with Applications*. Norton, New York.

Farrell, R. H., 1964. Estimators of a location parameter in the absolutely continuous case. *Ann. Math. Statist.* **35**, 949–998.

Farrell, R. H., 1968a. Towards a theory of generalized Bayes tests. *Ann. Math. Statist.* **38**, 1–22.

Farrell, R. H., 1968b. On a necessary and sufficient condition for admissibility of estimators when strictly convex loss is used. *Ann. Math. Statist.* **38**, 23–28.

Ferguson, T. S., 1967. *Mathematical Statistics: A Decision-Theoretic Approach*. Academic Press, New York.

Ferguson, T. S., 1973. A Bayesian analysis of some nonparametric problems. *Ann. Statist.* **1**, 209–230.

Fishburn, P. C., 1964. *Decision and Value Theory*. Wiley, New York.

Fisher, R. A., 1935. The fiducial argument in statistical inference. *Annals of Eugenics* **6**, 391–398.

Fisher, R. A., 1959. *Statistical Methods and Scientific Inference* (2nd Ed.). Oliver and Boyd, Edinburgh.

Fraser, D. A. S., 1968. *The Structure of Inference*. Wiley, New York.

Ghosh, B. K., 1970. *Sequential Tests of Statistical Hypotheses*. Addison-Wesley, Reading.

Good, I. J., 1950. *Probability and the Weighing of Evidence*. Charles Griffin, London.

Good, I. J., 1965. *The Estimation of Probabilities: An Essay on Modern Bayesian Methods*. M.I.T. Press, Cambridge.

Good, I. J., 1973a. The Bayesian influence, or how to sweep subjectivism under the carpet. In *Foundations of Probability Theory, Statistical Inference, and Statistical Theories of Science*, Vol. II, W. L. Harper and C. A. Hooker (Eds.). Reidel, Boston.

Good, I. J., 1973b. The probabilistic explication of evidence, surprise, causality, explanation, and utility. In *Foundations of Statistical Inference*, V. P. Godambe and D. A. Sprott (Eds.). Holt, Rinehart, and Winston, Toronto.

Gupta, S. S., and Panchapakesan, S., 1979. *Multiple Decision Procedures: Theory and Methodology of Selecting and Ranking Populations*. Wiley, New York.

Halmos, P. R., 1950. *Measure Theory*. D. van Nostrand, New York. Second edition 1974. Springer-Verlag, New York.

Hartigan, J., 1964. Invariant prior distributions. *Ann. Math. Statist.* **35**, 836–845.

Hill, B., 1974. On coherence, inadmissibility, and inference about many parameters in the theory of least squares. In *Studies in Bayesian Econometrics and Statistics*, S. Fienberg and A. Zellner (Eds.). North Holland, Amsterdam.

Hirschmann, I. I., and Widder, D. V., 1955. *The Convolution Transform*. Princeton Univ. Press, Princeton.

Hodges, J. L., and Lehmann, E. L., 1952. The use of previous experience in reaching statistical decisions. *Ann. Math. Statist.* **23**, 396–407.

Hoeffding, W., 1960. Lower bounds for the expected sample size and the average risk of a sequential procedure. *Ann. Math. Statist.* **31**, 352–368.

Hogarth, R. M., 1975. Cognitive processes and the assessment of subjective probability distributions. *J. Amer. Statist. Assoc.* **70**, 271–294.

Hora, R. B., and Buehler, R. J., 1966. Fiducial theory and invariant estimation. *Ann. Math. Statist.* **37**, 643–656.

Huber, P. J., 1972. Robust statistics: a review. *Ann. Math. Statist.* **43**, 1041–1067.

Jackson, D. A., Donovan, T. M., Zimmer, W. J., and Deely, J. J., 1970. Γ_2-minimax estimators in the exponential family. *Biometrika* **57**, 439–443.

James, W., and Stein, C., 1960. Estimation with quadratic loss. In *Proc. Fourth Berkeley Symp. Math. Statist. Prob.* 1, 361–380. University of California Press, Berkeley.

Jaynes, E. T., 1968. Prior probabilities. *IEEE Transactions on Systems Science and Cybernetics*, **SSC-4**, 227–241.

Jeffreys, H., 1957. *Scientific Inference*. Cambridge University Press, London.

Jeffreys, H., 1961. *Theory of Probability* (3rd Ed.). Oxford University Press, London.

Judge, G., and Bock, M. E., 1977. *Implications of Pre-Test and Stein Rule Estimators in Econometrics*. North Holland, Amsterdam.

Karlin, S., 1956. Decision theory of Pólya type distributions; case of two actions, I. In *Proc. Third Berkeley Symp. on Prob. and Statist.* 1, 115–129. University of California Press, Berkeley.

Karlin, S., 1957a. Pólya type distributions, II. *Ann. Math. Statist.* **28**, 281–308.

Karlin, S., 1957b. Pólya type distributions, III: admissibility for multi-action problems. *Ann. Math. Statist.* **28**, 839–860.

Karlin, S., and Rubin, H., 1956. The theory of decision procedures for distributions with monotone likelihood ratio. *Ann. Math. Statist.* **27**, 272–299.

Keeney, R. L., and Raiffa, H., 1976. *Decisions with Multiple Objectives*. Wiley, New York.

Kiefer, J., 1957. Invariance, minimax sequential estimation, and continuous time processes. *Ann. Math. Statist.* **28**, 573–601.

Kiefer, J., 1966. Multivariate optimality results. In *Multivariate Analysis*, P. R. Krishnaiah (Ed.). Academic Press, New York.

Kiefer, J., 1977. Conditional confidence statements and confidence estimators (theory and methods). *J. Amer. Statist. Assoc.* **72**, 789–827.

Kiefer, J., and Sacks, J., 1963. Asymptotically optimum sequential inference and design. *Ann. Math. Statist.* **34**, 705–750.

Kudo, H., 1955. On minimax invariant estimates of the transformation parameter. Natural Science Report 6, 31–73, Ochanomizu University, Japan.

Le Cam, L., 1955. An extension of Wald's theory of statistical decision functions. *Ann. Math. Statist.* **26**, 69–81.

Lehmann, E. L., 1947. On families of admissible tests. *Ann. Math. Statist.* **18**, 97–104.

Lehmann, E. L., 1959. *Testing Statistical Hypotheses*. Wiley, New York.

Lindley, D. V., 1957. A statistical paradox. *Biometrika* **44**, 187–192.

Lindley, D. V., 1971. *Bayesian Statistics, A Review*. S.I.A.M., Philadelphia.

Lindley, D. V., 1976. Inference for a Bernoulli process (a Bayesian view). *The American Statistician* **30**, 112–118.

Lindley, D. V., 1977. A problem in forensic science. *Biometrika* **64**, 207–213.

Lindley, D. V., and Smith, A. F. M., 1972. Bayes estimates for the linear model. *J. Roy. Statist. Soc.* (Ser. B) **34**, 1–41.

Lord, F. M., 1969. Estimating true-score distributions in psychological testing (an empirical Bayes estimation problem). *Psychometrika* **34**, 259–299.

Lord, F. M., and Cressie, N., 1975. An empirical Bayes procedure for finding an interval estimate. *Sankhya* (Ser. B) **37**, 1–9.

Luce, R. D., and Raiffa, H., 1957. *Games and Decisions*. Wiley, New York.

Magwire, C. A., 1953. Sequential decisions involving the choice of experiments. Ph.D. Thesis, Stanford University.

Maritz, J. S., 1970. *Empirical Bayes Methods*. Methuen, London.

McKinsey, J. C. C., 1952. *Introduction to the Theory of Games*. McGraw-Hill, New York.

Morris, C., 1977. Interval estimation for empirical Bayes generalizations of Stein's estimator. The Rand Paper Series, Rand Corp., Santa Monica.

Nachbin, L., 1965. *The Haar Integral*. D. van Nostrand, New York.

Neyman, J., and Pearson, E. S., 1933. On the problem of the most efficient tests of statistical hypotheses. *Philos. Trans. Roy. Soc.* (Ser. A) **231**, 289–337.

Pitman, E. J. G., 1939. The estimation of location and scale parameters of a continuous population of any given form. *Biometrika* **30**, 391–421.

Pratt, J. W., 1962. Discussion of A. Birnbaum's "On the foundations of statistical inference." *J. Amer. Statist. Assoc.* **57**, 269–326.

Pratt, J. W., Raiffa, H., and Schlaifer, R., 1965. *Introduction to Statistical Decision Theory* (prelim. ed.). McGraw-Hill, New York.

Raiffa, H., 1968. *Decision Analysis: Introductory Lectures on Choices under Uncertainty*. Addison-Wesley, Reading.

Raiffa, H., and Schlaifer, R., 1961. *Applied Statistical Decision Theory*. Division of Research, Graduate School of Business Administration, Harvard University, Boston.

Ray, S. N., 1965. Bounds on the maximum sample size of a Bayes sequential procedure. *Ann. Math. Statist.* **36**, 859–878.

Robbins, H. E., 1955. An empirical Bayes approach to statistics. In *Proc. Third Berkeley Symp. Math. Statist. Prob.* 1, 157–164. University of California Press, Berkeley.

Robbins, H. E., 1964. The empirical Bayes approach to statistical decision problems. *Ann. Math. Statist.* **35**, 1–20.

Rosenkrantz, R. D., 1977. *Inference, Method, and Decision: Towards a Bayesian Philosophy of Science*. Reidel, Boston.

Rubin, H., 1974. Decision-theoretic approach to some multivariate problems. In *Multivariate Analysis* II, P. R. Krishnaiah (Ed.). Academic Press, New York.

Rubin, H., 1974. Axiomatic development of rational behavior. Technical Report, Department of Statistics, Purdue University, West Lafayette.

Rubin, H., 1977. Robust Bayesian estimation. In *Statistical Decision Theory and Related Topics* II, S. S. Gupta and D. S. Moore (Eds.). Academic Press, New York.

Sacks, J., 1963. Generalized Bayes solutions in estimation problems. *Ann. Math. Statist.* **34**, 751–768.

Savage, L. J., 1954. *The Foundations of Statistics*, Wiley, New York.

Savage, L. J., 1961. The subjective basis of statistical practice. Technical Report, Department of Statistics, University of Michigan, Ann Arbor.

Savage, L. J. (et al.), 1962. *The Foundations of Statistical Inference*. Methuen, London.

Savage, L. J., 1971. Elicitation of personal probabilities and expectations. *J. Amer. Statist. Assoc.* **66**, 783–801.

Schwarz, G., 1962. Asymptotic shapes of Bayes sequential testing regions. *Ann. Math. Statist.* **33**, 224–236.

Schwarz, G., 1968. Asymptotic shapes for sequential testing of truncation parameters. *Ann. Math. Statist.* **39**, 2038–2043.

Shafer, G., 1979. Lindley's paradox. Technical Report No. 125, Department of Statistics, Stanford University, Stanford.

Sobel, M., 1953. An essentially complete class of decision functions for certain standard sequential problems. *Ann. Math. Statist.* **24**, 319–337.

Stein, C., 1946. A note on cumulative sums. *Ann. Math. Statist.* **17**, 498–499.

Stein, C., 1955a. Inadmissibility of the usual estimator for the mean of a multivariate normal distribution. In *Proc. Third Berkeley Symp. Math. Statist. Prob.* 1, 197–206. University of California Press, Berkeley.

Stein, C., 1955b. A necessary and sufficient condition for admissibility. *Ann. Math. Statist.* **26**, 518–522.

Stein, C., 1959. The admissibility of Pitman's estimator of a single location parameter. *Ann. Math. Statist.* **30**, 970–979.

Stein, C., 1962. A remark on the likelihood principle. *J. Roy. Statist. Soc.* (Ser. A) **125**, 565–568.

Stein, C., 1965. Approximation of improper prior measures by prior probability measures. In *Bernouilli–Bayes–Laplace Festschr.*, 217–240. Springer-Verlag, New York.

Stone, M., 1963. Robustness of non-ideal decision procedures. *J. Amer. Statist. Assoc.* **58**, 480–486.

Stone, M., 1971. Strong inconsistency from uniform priors—with comments. *J. Amer. Statist. Assoc.* **71**, 114–125.

Strawderman, W. E., 1971. Proper Bayes minimax estimators of the multivariate normal mean. *Ann. Math. Statist.* **42**, 385–388.

Strawderman, W. E., and Cohen, A., 1971. Admissibility of estimators of the mean vector of a multivariate normal distribution with quadratic loss. *Ann. Math. Statist.* **42**, 270–296.

Susarla, V., 1979. Empirical Bayes theory. To appear in the *Encyclopedia of Statistical Sciences*. Wiley, New York.

Tiao, G. C., and Zellner, A., 1964. On the Bayesian estimation of multivariate regression. *J. Roy. Statist. Soc.* (Ser. B) **26**, 277–285.

Tjur, Tue, 1978. Statistical inference under the likelihood principle. Preprint 1, Institute of Mathematical Statistics, University of Copenhagen, Copenhagen.

Villegas, C., 1977. On the representation of ignorance. *J. Amer. Statist. Assoc.* **72**, 651–654.

Von Neumann, J., 1928. Zur theorie der gesellschaftspiele. *Math. Annalen* **100**, 295–320.

Von Neumann, J., and Morgenstern, O., 1944. *Theory of Games and Economic Behavior* (3rd Ed. 1953). Princeton University Press, Princeton.

Wald, A., 1947. *Sequential Analysis*. Wiley, New York.

Wald, A., 1950. *Statistical Decision Functions*. Wiley, New York.

Wald, A., and Wolfowitz, J., 1948. Optimum character of the sequential probability ratio test. *Ann. Math. Statist.* **19**, 326–339.

Weiss, L., 1961. *Statistical Decision Theory*. McGraw-Hill, New York.

Widder, D. V., 1946. *The Laplace Transform*. Princeton University Press, Princeton.

Williams, J. D., 1954. *The Compleat Strategyst*. McGraw-Hill, New York.

Winkler, R. L., 1967a. The quantification of judgement: some methodological suggestions. *J. Amer. Statist. Assoc.* **62**, 1105–1120.

Winkler, R. L., 1967b. The assessment of prior distributions in Bayesian analysis. *J. Amer. Statist. Assoc.* **62**, 776–800.

Winkler, R. L., 1972. *Introduction to Bayesian Inference and Decision*. Holt, Rinehart, and Winston, New York.

Woodroofe, M., 1976. Frequentist properties of Bayesian sequential tests. *Biometrika* **63**, 101–110.

Woodroofe, M., 1978. Large deviations of likelihood ratio statistics with applications to sequential testing. *Ann. Statist.* **6**, 72–84.

Zidek, J. V., 1967. On the admissibility of formal Bayes estimators. Technical Report No. 58, Department of Statistics, Stanford University, Stanford.

Notation and Abbreviations

The symbols listed here are those used throughout the book. Symbols specific to a given chapter are, for the most part, not listed. This glossary is for reference only, in that virtually all symbols are also explained when first used in the book. A page number after an entry indicates where in the book a more extensive explanation can be found.

Mathematical Notation

R^1, R^2, R^p: the line, the plane, p-dimensional Euclidean space.

y, **A**: bold-faced letters are column vectors or matrices. The (i, j)th element of a matrix **A** will be denoted A_{ij}.

$\mathbf{y}^t$, $\mathbf{A}^t$: the "t" denotes transpose.

$\mathbf{A}^{-1}$, det **A**, tr **A**: the inverse, determinant, and trace of a matrix **A**.

$\mathbf{I}_p$: the $(p \times p)$ identity matrix.

1, **0**: the vectors of all ones and zeroes, respectively.

$|\mathbf{y}|$: the Euclidean norm of $\mathbf{y} \in R^p$ (absolute value if $y \in R^1$). Thus $|\mathbf{y}| = (\sum_{i=1}^p y_i^2)^{1/2}$.

(a, b), $[a, b]$, $(a, b]$, $[a, b)$: the open interval from a to b, the closed interval, and half-open intervals.

$\{a, b\}$: the set consisting of the elements a and b.

B^c, $\bar{B}$: the complement and closure of the set B.

$I_B(y)$: the indicator function on the set B (equals one if $y \in B$ and zero otherwise).

$g'(y)$, $g''(y)$: the first and second derivatives of the function g.

$\log y$: the logarithm of y to the base e.

min, max, inf, sup, lim: minimum, maximum, infimum, supremum, and limit.

$\cap, \cup$: intersection, union.

$\cong$: approximately equal to.

$\overline{\mathbf{xy}}$: the line segment (in R^p) joining the points $\mathbf{x}$ and $\mathbf{y}$.

$\mathbf{x}_n \to \mathbf{x}_0$: the sequence of points $\{\mathbf{x}_n\}$ converges to $\mathbf{x}_0$, i.e.,

$$\lim_{n \to \infty} |\mathbf{x}_n - \mathbf{x}_0| = 0.$$

$\#$: the number of.

$\Gamma(\alpha)$: the gamma function.

$\binom{n}{x}$: defined as $n!/[x!(n-x)!]$.

Probabilistic Notation

X, $\mathcal{X}$, x: the random variable X, the sample space, a realization of X (p. 3).

θ, Θ: a parameter (or "state of nature"), the parameter space (p. 3).

$f(x|\theta)$, $F(x|\theta)$: the density of X given θ, the cumulative distribution function of X given θ (pp. 3, 4).

$\int h(x)dF(x|\theta)$: see page 4.

$P(A)$ or $P(X \in A)$: the probability of the set A (p. 3).

$E[h(X)]$: the expectation of $h(x)$ (p. 4).

Subscript on P or E (such as E_θ): a parameter value under which the probability or expectation is to be taken (p. 4).

Superscript on P, E, or F (such as E^X): clarifies the relevant random variable or distribution (p. 4).

$z(\alpha)$: the α-fractile of the distribution of the random variable X (p. 111).

Statistical Notation

H_0, H_1: null hypothesis, alternative hypothesis.

$\phi(x)$: a test function; i.e., $\phi(x)$ is the probability of rejecting the null hypothesis (zero or one for a nonrandomized text) when x is observed.

$\beta_\phi(\theta)$ or $\beta(\theta)$: the power function of a test; i.e., the probability of rejecting the null hypothesis when θ is the parameter value.

$\alpha_0(\phi)$ or α_0, $\alpha_1(\phi)$ or α_1: the probabilities of type I and type II errors, respectively, for testing $H_0: \theta = \theta_0$ versus $H_1: \theta = \theta_1$. Thus $\alpha_0 = \beta(\theta_0)$ and $\alpha_1 = 1 - \beta(\theta_1)$.

$\bar{x}$: the sample mean; i.e., $\bar{x} = 1/n \sum_{i=1}^n x_i$.

Decision Theoretic Notation

a, $\mathscr{A}$: action, action space (p. 3).

$L(\theta, a)$: the loss function (p. 3).

$\pi(\theta)$: the prior density for θ (p. 4).

δ, δ^*: nonrandomized decision rule (p. 7), randomized decision rule (p. 11).

$L(\theta, \delta^*)$: the loss function for a randomized decision rule (p. 11).

$R(\theta, \delta)$ and $R(\theta, \delta^*)$: the risk function (expected loss) of a decision rule (pp. 7 and 11).

$\mathscr{D}$: the class of nonrandomized decision rules with $R(\theta, \delta) < \infty$ for all θ (p. 10).

$\mathscr{D}^*$: the class of randomized decision rules with $R(\theta, \delta^*) < \infty$ for all θ (p. 12).

$\langle a \rangle, \langle \delta \rangle$ (x, A): "$\langle \ \rangle$" is a notational device used to denote the probability distribution which selects the enclosed quantity with probability one. Thus $\langle \delta \rangle(x, A) = I_A(\delta(x))$.

$r(\pi, \delta)$ and $r(\pi, \delta^*)$: the Bayes risk of a decision rule (p. 14).

δ^π: a Bayes decision rule (p. 15).

$r(\pi)$: the Bayes risk of π (i.e., $r(\pi) = r(\pi, \delta^\pi)$) (p. 15).

$l(\theta)$: the likelihood function (i.e., $l(\theta) = f(x|\theta)$) (p. 25).

$m(x)$: the marginal density of X (i.e., $m(x) = \int_\Theta f(x|\theta)dF^\pi(\theta)$) (p. 79).

$\pi(\theta|x)$: the posterior distribution of θ given x (i.e.,

$$\pi(\theta|x) = f(x|\theta)\pi(\theta)/m(x)$$

(p. 92).

C or $C(x)$: a confidence or credible region for θ (pp. 102 and 263).

$\mathscr{R}$: reward space (p. 41).

$U(r)$ or $U(\theta, a)$: utility function (p. 41).

Author Index

Subject Index

Springer Lecture Notes in Statistics

Editors: S. Fienberg, J. Gani, J. Keifer, K. Krickeberg

Applications of statistical methods in the life sciences, physics, engineering, political science, psychology, and other areas are the central topics of this new series. Relevant examples and the practicality of methods discussed are emphasized.

Volume 1

R. A. Fisher: An Appreciation

Edited by **S.E. Fienberg** and **D.V. Hinkley**, University of Minnesota—St. Paul.
Sir Ronald A. Fisher was one of the most productive and original statisticians of the 20th Century. This collection of 18 papers surveys the fundamental contributions he has made to modern statistical methods.
ISBN 0-387-90476-X

Volume 2

Mathematical Statistics and Probability Theory

Edited by **W. Klonecki, A. Kozek**, and **J. Rosinski.**
Eminent statisticians and probabilists cover current developments in their fields in this collection of 29 articles. Topics include central limit theorems, random fields, convexity and expectations, mathematical statistics, and statistical inference from stochastic processes. Three articles in honor of J. Neyman and his work are also presented.
ISBN 0-387-90493-X

Volume 3

Benefit-Cost Analysis of Data Used to Allocate Funds:
General Revenue Sharing

Bruce D. Spencer, Northwestern University.
This volume focuses on the cost of collecting and analyzing public data. The benefits and costs of alternative data programs are estimated and compared. Particular emphasis is given to funding in the General Revenue Sharing program, one of the largest allocation programs in the United States.
Contents: Loss Function and Benefit Measurement. The Delta Method. Data Used in General Revenue Sharing. Interstate Allocation in GRS. Intrastate Allocations in GRS. Computations and Analyses. Policy Perspectives and Recommendations. Appendix A: Tables of Biases in Data. Appendix B: Determination of General Revenue Sharing Allocations. Technical Appendix.
ISBN (not available)

Springer Series in Statistics

Advisors: **D. Brillinger,** University of California—Berkeley; **S. Fienberg,** University of Minnesota—St. Paul; **J. Gani,** CSIRO, Canberra; **J. Hartigan,** Yale University; **J. Kiefer,** University of California—Berkeley; **K. Krickeberg,** Université René Descartes, Paris.

Books in this new series are method- and field-oriented, covering statistical aspects of the physical, social, behavioral, and medical sciences, and other areas.

Measures of Association for Cross Classifications
Leo A. Goodman and **William H. Kruskal,** University of Chicago.

Four landmark papers on the selection of measures of association for data summary are presented in this volume. Stressing the necessity of one or more measure of association for each unique research problem, these papers provide an outstanding, comprehensive catalogue of existing measures. They also provide useful models for the development of new measures.

Topics covered include criteria for judging measures; large-sample errors for analogues of population measures; a novel approach to asymptotics; improved derivation of large-sample variances of measures; and historical and bibliographic material. Many examples accompany the text.

ISBN 0-387-90443-3